GPU Computing Gems
Jade Edition

Morgan Kaufmann's *Applications of GPU Computing* Series

Computing is quickly becoming the third pillar of scientific research, due in large part to the performance gains achieved through graphics processing units (GPUs), which have become ubiquitous in handhelds, laptops, desktops, and supercomputer clusters. Morgan Kaufmann's *Applications of GPU Computing* series offers training, examples, and inspiration for researchers, engineers, students, and supercomputing professionals who want to leverage the power of GPUs incorporated into their simulations or experiments. Each high-quality, peer-reviewed book is written by leading experts uniquely qualified to provide parallel computing insights and guidance.

Each *GPU Computing Gems* volume offers a snapshot of the state of parallel computing across a carefully selected subset of industry domains, giving you a window into the lead-edge research occurring across the breadth of science, and the opportunity to observe others' algorithm work that might apply to your own projects. Find out more at `http://mkp.com/gpu-computing-gems`.

Recommended Parallel Computing Titles

Programming Massively Parallel Processors
A Hands-on Approach
By David B. Kirk and Wen-mei W. Hwu
ISBN: 9780123814722

GPU Computing Gems: Emerald Edition
Editor-in-Chief: Wen-mei W. Hwu
ISBN: 9780123849885

The Art of Multiprocessor Programming
By Maurice Herlihy and Nir Shavit
ISBN: 9780123705914

An Introduction to Parallel Programming
By Peter Pacheco
ISBN: 9780123742605

Heterogeneous Computing with OpenCL
By Benedict R. Gaster, Lee Howes, David R. Kaeli, Perhaad Mistry, Dana Schaa
ISBN: 9780123877666

CUDA Application Design and Development
By Rob Farber
ISBN: 9780123884268
Coming Winter 2011

Distributed and Cloud Computing
By Kai Hwang, Geoffrey Fox, and Jack Dongarra
ISBN: 9780123858801
Coming Fall 2011

GPU Computing Gems
Jade Edition

Wen-mei W. Hwu

ELSEVIER

AMSTERDAM • BOSTON • HEIDELBERG • LONDON
NEW YORK • OXFORD • PARIS • SAN DIEGO
SAN FRANCISCO • SINGAPORE • SYDNEY • TOKYO

Morgan Kaufmann Publishers is an imprint of Elsevier

Acquiring Editor: Todd Green
Development Editor: Robyn Day
Project Manager: Paul Gottehrer
Designer: Dennis Schaefer

Morgan Kaufmann is an imprint of Elsevier
225 Wyman Street, Waltham, MA 02451, USA

Library of Congress Cataloging-in-Publication Data
Application submitted

British Library Cataloguing-in-Publication Data
A catalogue record for this book is available from the British Library.

ISBN: 978-0-12-385963-1

For information on all MK publications visit our website at *www.mkp.com*

Printed and bound by CPI Group (UK) Ltd, Croydon, CR0 4YY

Contents

SECTION 1   PARALLEL ALGORITHMS AND DATA STRUCTURES

SECTION 4 INTERACTIVE PHYSICS AND AI FOR GAMES AND ENGINEERING SIMULATION

Richard Tonge (NVIDIA)

SECTION 5 COMPUTATIONAL FINANCE

Thomas Bradley (NVIDIA)

SECTION 6 PROGRAMMING TOOLS AND TECHNIQUES

Cliff Woolley (NVIDIA)

Editors, Reviewers, and Authors

Editor-In-Chief
Wen-Mei W. Hwu, University of Illinois at Urbana-Champaign

Managing Editor
Andrew Schuh, University of Illinois at Urbana-Champaign

NVIDIA Editor
Nadeem Mohammad, NVIDIA Corporation

Area Editors
Thomas Bradley, NVIDIA Corporation (Section 5)

Frank Jargstorff, NVIDIA Corporation (Section 2)

Paulius Micikevicius, NVIDIA Corporation (Section 1)

Richard Tonge, NVIDIA Corporation (Section 4)

Peng Wang, NVIDIA Corporation (Section 3)

Cliff Wooley, NVIDIA Corporation (Section 6)

Reviewers
John Ashley, NVIDIA Corporation

Nathan Bell, NVIDIA Corporation

Avi Bleiweiss, NVIDIA Corporation

Jonathan Cohen, NVIDIA Corporation

Andrew Corrigan, Naval Research Lab

Mike Giles, Oxford University

Dilip Sequeira, NVIDIA Corporation

David Sullins, NVIDIA Corporation

Stanimire Tomov, University of Tennessee, Knoxville

Cliff Wooley, NVIDIA Corporation

Gernot Ziegler, NVIDIA Corporation

ix

Authors

Emmanuel Agullo, INRIA (Chapter 34)

Dan A. Alcantara, UC Davis (Chapter 4)

Jérémie Allard, INRIA Lille & Lille University (Chapter 21)

Nina Amenta, UC Davis (Chapter 4)

Mihai Anitescu, Argonne National Laboratory (Chapter 20)

V.G. Asouti, National Technical University of Athens (Chapter 17)

Cédric Augonnet, INRIA (Chapter 34)

James Balasalle, University of Denver (Chapter 6)

Nathan Bell, NVIDIA Corporation (Chapter 26)

Thomas Bradley, NVIDIA Corporation (Chapter 25)

Tobias Brandvik, University of Cambridge (Chapter 14)

Giuseppe Caggianese, Università degli Studi della Basilicata (Chapter 22)

Bryan Catanzaro, UC Berkeley (Chapter 27)

Cris Cecka, Stanford University (Chapter 16)

Daniel Cederman, Sweden Chalmers University of Technology (Chapter 35)

Ruinan Chang, UC San Diego (Chapter 19)

Jike Chong, Parasians LLC & UC Berkeley (Chapter 25)

Jonathan Cohen, NVIDIA Corporation (Chapters 11, 32)

Sylvain Collange, École normale supérieure de Lyon (Chapter 9)

Hadrien Courtecuisse, INRIA Lille & Lille University (Chapter 21)

David D. Cox, Harvard University (Chapter 33)

Eric Darve, Stanford University (Chapter 16)

Marc Daumas, Université de Perpignan (Chapter 9)

Andrew A. Davidson, UC Davis (Chapter 11)

David Defour, Université de Perpignan (Chapter 9)

Gregory Diamos, Georgia Institute of Technology (Chapter 30)

Andrea Di Blas, Oracle Corporation (Chapter 1)

Matthew F. Dixon, UC Davis (Chapter 25)

Jack Dongarra, University of Tennessee, Knoxville (Chapter 34)

Peter Eastman, Stanford University (Chapter 29)

Daniel Egloff, QuantAlea GmbH (Chapter 23)

Ugo Erra, Università degli Studi della Basilicata (Chapter 22)

Ahmed Fasih, Ohio State University (Chapter 27)

François Faure, INRIA Rhóne-Alpes & Grenoble University (Chapter 21)

Aldo Frezzotti, Politecnico di Milano (Chapter 15)

Michael Garland, NVIDIA Corporation (Chapters 2 and 3)

Gian Pietro Ghiroldi, Politecnico di Milano (Chapter 15)

K.C. Giannakoglou, National Technical University of Athens (Chapter 17)

Livio Gibelli, Politecnico di Milano (Chapter 15)

Mike Giles, Oxford University (Chapter 10)

Pawan Harish, International Institute of Information Technology, Hyderabad (Chapter 7)

Mark Harris, NVIDIA Corporation (Chapter 3)

John C. Hart, University of Illinois at Urbana-Champaign (Chapter 2)

Zhengyu He, Georgia Institute of Technology (Chapter 5)

Jan S. Hesthaven, Brown University (Chapter 18)

Toby Heyn, Univeristy of Wisconsin, Madison (Chapter 20)

Jared Hoberock, NVIDIA Corporation (Chapters 2 and 26)

Bo Hong, Georgia Institute of Technology (Chapter 5)

John Humphrey, EM Photonics, Inc. (Chapter 12)

Paul Ivanov, UC Berkeley (Chapter 27)

Yuntao Jia, University of Illinois at Urbana-Champaign (Chapter 2)

Tim Kaldewey, IBM (Chapter 1)

I.C. Kampolis, National Technical University of Athens (Chapter 17)

Eric Kelmelis, EM Photonics, Inc. (Chapter 12)

Andrew Kerr, Georgia Institute of Technology (Chapter 30)

Kurt Keutzer, UC Berkeley (Chapter 25)

Andreas Klöckner, New York University (Chapters 18 and 27)

Torben Larsen, Aalborg University (Chapter 28)

Yunsup Lee, UC Berkeley (Chapter 27)

Adrian Lew, Stanford University (Chapter 16)

Shaojing Li, UC San Diego (Chapter 19)

Vitaliy Lomakin, UC San Diego (Chapter 19)

Mario A. Lopez, University of Denver (Chapter 6)

Hatem Ltaief, University of Tennessee, Knoxville (Chapter 34)

Victor Lu, University of Illinois at Urbana-Champaign (Chapter 2)

James Malcolm, AccelerEyes (Chapter 28)

Hammad Mazhar, University of Wisconsin, Madison (Chapter 20)

Michael Mitzenmacher, Harvard University (Chapter 4)

Raymond Namyst, INRIA (Chapter 34)

P.J. Narayanan, International Institute of Information Technology, Hyderabad (Chapter 7)

Dan Negrut, University of Wisconsin, Madison (Chapter 20)

John D. Owens, UC Davis (Chapters 4, 11, 36)

Vijay Pande, Stanford University (Chapter 29)

Suryakant Patidar, NVIDIA Corporation (Chapter 7)

Arman Pazouki, Univeristy of Wisconsin, Madison (Chapter 20)

Hagen Peters, Christian-Albrechts-University of Kiel (Chapter 8)

Nicolas Pinto, Massachusetts Institute of Technology (Chapters 27 and 33)

Daniel Price, EM Photonics, Inc. (Chapter 12)

Gallagher Pryor, AccelerEyes (Chapter 28)

Graham Pullan, University of Cambridge (Chapter 14)

Simon J. Rees, Barclays Capital (Chapter 24)

Matthew J. Rutherford, University of Denver (Chapter 6)

Ole Schulz-Hildebrandt, Christian-Albrechts-University of Kiel (Chapter 8)

Assaf Schuster, Technion (Chapter 36)

Shubhabrata Sengupta, UC Davis (Chapter 4)

Eric Shaffer, University of Illinois at Urbana-Champaign (Chapter 13)

Mark Silberstein, Technion (Chapter 36)

Kyle Spagnoli, EM Photonics, Inc. (Chapter 12)

Robert Strzodka, Max Planck Institut Informatik (Chapter 31)

Alessandro Tasora, University of Parma (Chapter 20)

Samuel Thibault, INRIA (Chapter 34)

Stanimire Tomov, University of Tennessee, Knoxville (Chapter 34)

X.S. Trompoukis, National Technical University of Athens (Chapter 17)

Philippas Tsigas, Sweden Chalmers University of Technology (Chapter 35)

Vibhav Vineet, International Institute of Information Technology, Hyderabad (Chapter 7)

Vasily Volkov, UC Berkeley (Chapter 4)

Joseph Walkenhorst, Barclays Capital (Chapter 24)

Timothy Warburton, Rice University (Chapter 18)

Jiadong Wu, Georgia Institute of Technology (Chapter 5)

Sudhakar Yalamanchili, Georgia Institute of Technology (Chapter 30)

George Zagaris, Illinois Rocstar LLC (Chapter 13)

Yao Zhang, UC Davis (Chapter 11)

Introduction

Wen-mei W. Hwu

STATE OF GPU COMPUTING

We are in the golden age of the GPU computing. Since the introduction of CUDA in 2007, more than 100 million computers with CUDA capable GPUs have been shipped to end users. GPU computing application developers can now expect their application to have a mass market. With the introduction of OpenCL in 2010, researchers can now expect to develop GPU applications that can run on hardware from multiple vendors. Furthermore, from my own experience in teaching CUDA and OpenCL programming, C programmers can begin to write basic programs after only attending one lecture and reading one textbook chapter. With such a low barrier of entry, researchers all over the world have been engaged in developing new algorithms and applications to take advantage of the extreme floating point execution throughput of these GPUs.

Today, there is a large community of GPU computing practitioners. Many of them have reported 10 to 100 times speedup of their applications with GPU computing. To put this into perspective, with the historical $2\times$ performance growth every two years, these researchers are experiencing the equivalent of time travel of 8 to 12 years. That is, they are getting today the performance they would have to wait for 8 to 12 years if they went for the "free-ride" advancement of performance in microprocessors. Interestingly, such a free ride is no longer available. Furthermore, once they developed their application in CUDA, they will likely see continued performance growth of $2\times$ for every two years from this day forward.

After discussing with numerous researchers, I reached the conclusion that many of them are solving similar algorithm problems in their programming efforts. Although they are working on diverse applications, they often end up developing similar algorithmic strategies. The idea of *GPU Computing Gems* is to provide a convenient means for application developers in diverse application areas to benefit from each other's experience. When we issued the call for proposals for the first *GPU Computing Gems*, we received more than 280 submissions, an overwhelming response. In the end, we accepted 86 final chapters. Many high-quality proposals were not accepted because of concerns that they may not be accessible to a large audience. With so many chapters, we were forced to divide these gems into two volumes. In the first volume (Emerald Edition), we published 50 Gems from 10 diverse application areas. In this volume, we have collected 36 Gem articles written by researchers in 5 diverse application areas as well as programming tools and techniques. Each gem is first edited by an area editor who is a GPU computing expert in that area. This is followed by my own editing of these articles.

For applications, each Gems article reports a successful application experience in GPU computing. These articles describe the techniques or "secret sauce" that contributed to the success. The authors highlight the potential applicability of their techniques to other application areas. In our editorial process, we have emphasized the accessibility of these gems to researchers in other areas. For programming tools and techniques, the authors emphasize how an application developer can best benefit from their work.

I would like to thank several people who have worked tirelessly on this project. Nadeem Mohammad at NVIDIA and Andrew Schuh at UIUC have done so much heavy lifting for this project. Without them, it would have been impossible for me to coordinate so many authors and area editors. My area editors, whose names are in front of each section of this volume, have volunteered their valuable time and energy to improve the quality of the gems. They worked closely with the authors to make sure that the gems indeed meet high technical standard while remain accessible by a wide audience. I would like to thank all the authors who have shared their innovative work with the GPU computing community. All authors have worked hard to respond to our requests for improvements. It has been a true privilege to work with all these great people.

Online Resources

Visit `http://mkp.com/gpu-computing-gems` and click the Online Resources tab to connect to `http://gpucomputing.net`, the vibrant official community site for GPU computing, where you can download source code examples for most chapters and join discussions with other readers and GPU developers. You'll also find links to additional material including chapter walk-through videos and full-color versions of many figures from the book.

Parallel Algorithms and Data Structures

1

Paulius Micikevicius (NVIDIA)

IN THIS SECTION

It is well known that the best parallel approach to solving a problem is often different from the best sequential implementation. Thus, many commonly used algorithms and data structures need to be redesigned for scalable parallel computing. This section includes chapters that illustrate algorithm implementation techniques and approaches to data structure layout in order to achieve efficient GPU execution. There are three general requirements: high level of parallelism, coherent memory access by threads within warps, and coherent control flow within warps. Practical techniques for satisfying these requirements are illustrated with a diverse set of fundamental data structures and algorithms, including tree, hash tables, cellular automata, sorting, searching, graph algorithms, and others.

Chapter 1 by Kaldewey and Di Blas focuses on accelerating database searches. The authors introduce P-ary search approach and experimentally evaluate throughput and response time. The chapter illustrates how algorithm design was driven by GPU architectural features, including micro-benchmarks.

Chapter 2 by Jia et al. compares two approaches to parallelize graph centrality computation on GPUs — across edges and across nodes. While the edge-parallel approach involves more operations, it outperforms node-parallelization by offering better load balancing, a quality important to any parallel architecture. This approach can be adopted for breadth-first-traversal, and other graph algorithms.

Chapter 3 by Harris and Garland details how to leverage the Fermi GPU architecture to further accelerate prefix operations. It covers optimizations enabled by new hardware capabilities, such as intra-warp primitives (instructions that return a value based on the input of all threads in a warp) and bit-counting instructions.

Chapter 4 by Alcantara et al. describes GPU implementation of one of the fundamental data structures, hash tables. Since the textbook description of hashing is serial in nature, the authors choose cuckoo hashing, an approach more amenable to parallelization. Performance is measured for table creation and queries.

Chapter 5 by Wu et al. presents GPU implementations for the maximum network flow problem. A number of maximum network flow algorithms exhibit a high level of data dependency, creating a challenge for parallelization on any architecture. The authors show how algorithm design can be used to overcome this challenge for GPUs.

Chapter 6 by Balasalle et al. systematically walks the reader through the fundamental optimization steps when implementing a bandwidth-limited algorithm. Techniques include both data layout, as well as threadblock and computation configuration. While a cellular automaton is used for illustration, findings readily apply to other areas (for example, finite differences on regular grids).

Chapter 7 by Harish et al. describes a GPU implementation for Boruvka's minimum spanning tree algorithm, building it from three fundamental parallel operations — scan, segmented scan, and split. By relying on efficient GPU implementations of these operations, the authors improve load-balancing and performance for what usually is an irregular problem.

Chapter 8 by Peters and Schulz-Hildebrandt describe a GPU implementation of bitonic sort. This work is different from many GPU-sorting publications in that it focuses on an algorithm that is both comparison-based and is in-place. Thus, it provides a GPU option when these requirements cannot be met by radix sorts.

Large-Scale GPU Search

Tim Kaldewey and Andrea Di Blas

With P-ary search we developed a novel scalable parallel search algorithm that optimally leverages Single Instruction Multiple Data (SIMD) architectures like graphical processing unit (GPUs). It outperforms conventional search algorithms like binary search in terms of throughput and response time by up to two orders of magnitude. Moreover, P-ary search scales with the number of threads/cores used to collaboratively answer an individual search query. While response time for conventional search algorithms tends to increase with workload size, P-ary search provides nearly constant query response time, independent of workload. Finally, P-ary search is particularly suited for data structures like B-trees, which are widely used for database indexes.

1.1 INTRODUCTION

As search engines like Google and Yahoo! demonstrate every day, efficiently searching for information in large data collections has become an indispensable operation of the information age. Although disciplines like information retrieval have developed highly efficient algorithms to manage large quantities of data, at the system level searching large data sets is I/O bound. Rapidly growing main memory sizes eliminate disk I/O as a bottleneck, even for traditionally data-intensive applications like search. While the front lines may have shifted from disk to main memory I/O, the basic problem remains: processors are significantly faster than storage. On today's systems accessing main memory takes hundreds of compute cycles.

While memory bandwidth has been increasing continuously, we hit the "memory wall" for latency more than a decade ago [1, 2]. Moreover, the increases in memory bandwidth over the past decade are a result of the multi/many-core era, with GPUs being a poster child, offering memory bandwidth well in excess of 100 GB/s. However, achieving peak bandwidth requires concurrent (parallel) memory access from all cores. The obvious use of increasingly parallel architectures for large-scale search applications is to execute multiple search queries simultaneously, which often results in significant increases in throughput. Query response time, on the other hand, remains memory-latency bound, unless we abandon conventional serial algorithms and go back to the drawing board.

To grasp the implications of porting a memory-bound application like search to the GPU, we first conducted a brief memory performance analysis (see Section 1.2). Conventional threading models and the memory access pattern produced by concurrent search queries do not map well to the GPU's memory subsystem (see Section 1.3.2). With P-ary search we demonstrate how parallel memory access combined with the superior synchronization capabilities of SIMD architectures like GPUs can be leveraged to compensate for memory latency (see the section titled "P-ary Search: Parallel Search from Scratch"). P-ary search outperforms conventional search algorithms not only in terms of throughput but also response time (see Section 1.4). Implemented on a GPU it can outperform a similarly priced CPU by up to three times, and is compatible with existing index data structures like inverted lists and B-trees. We expect the underlying concepts of P-ary search — parallel memory access and exploiting efficient SIMD thread synchronization — to be applicable to an entire class of memory-bound applications (see Section 1.5).

1.2 MEMORY PERFORMANCE

With more than six times the memory bandwidth of contemporary CPUs, GPUs are leading the trend toward throughput computing. On the other hand, traditional search algorithms besides linear scan are latency bound since their iterations are data dependent. However, as large database systems usually serve many queries concurrently both metrics — latency and bandwidth — are relevant.

Memory latency is mainly a function of where the requested piece of data is located in the memory hierarchy. Comparing CPU and GPU memory latency in terms of elapsed clock cycles shows that global memory accesses on the GPU take approximately 1.5 times as long as main memory accesses on the CPU, and more than twice as long in terms of absolute time (Table 1.1). Although shared memory does not operate the same way as the L1 cache on the CPU, its latency is comparable.

Memory bandwidth, on the other hand, depends on multiple factors, such as sequential or random access pattern, read/write ratio, word size, and concurrency [3]. The effects of word size and read/write behavior on memory bandwidth are similar to the ones on the CPU — larger word sizes achieve better performance than small ones, and reads are faster than writes. On the other hand, the impact of concurrency and data access pattern require additional consideration when porting memory-bound applications to the GPU.

Little's Law, a general principle for queuing systems, can be used to derive how many concurrent memory operations are required to fully utilize memory bandwidth. It states that in a system that processes units of work at a certain average rate W, the average amount of time L that a unit spends inside the system is the product of W and λ, where λ is the average unit's arrival rate: $L = \lambda W$ [4]. Applying Little's Law to memory, the number of outstanding requests must match the product of latency and bandwidth. For our GTX 285 GPU the latency is 500 clock cycles, and the peak bandwidth

Table 1.1 Cache and Memory Latency Across the Memory Hierarchy for the Processors in Our Test System

Processor	L1/Shared Memory		L2		L3		Memory	
	[cc]	[ns]	[cc]	[ns]	[cc]	[ns]	[cc]	[ns]
Intel Core i7 2.6 GHz	4	1.54	10	3.84	40	15.4	350	134.6
NVIDIA GTX285 1.5 GHz	4	2.66	n/a	n/a	n/a	n/a	500	333.3

is 128 bytes per clock cycle — the physical bus width is 512 bits, or a 64-byte memory block, and two of these blocks are transferred per clock cycle — so:

$$\text{outstanding reads} = \text{latency} \times \text{bandwidth/request size} =$$
$$= 500\text{cc} \times 128\,\text{B/cc}/(4B/\text{request}) = 16\,\text{K requests}$$

assuming 4-byte reads as in the code in Section 1.4. This can be achieved using different combinations of number of threads and outstanding requests per thread. In our example, we could make full use of the global memory by having 1 K threads issue 16 independent reads each, or 2 K threads issue eight reads each, and so on.

The plots in Figure 1.1 show the case in which each thread has only one outstanding memory request. This serves as a baseline example, mimicking the behavior of conventional search algorithms that at any given time have at most one outstanding memory request per search (thread), due to data dependencies. Obviously, if there are no constraints issuing more than one read per thread it is much more efficient to issue multiple reads per thread to maximize memory utilization [5, 6]. In our case, to saturate memory bandwidth we need at least 16,000 threads, for instance as 64 blocks of 256 threads each, where we observe a local peak. The maximum bandwidth of 150 GB/s is not reached here because the number of threads cannot compensate for some overhead required to manage threads and blocks. Increasing the number of threads, the bandwidth takes a small hit before reaching its peak (Figure 1.1a). Although there are many options to launch 16,000 or more threads, only certain configurations can achieve memory bandwidth close to the maximum. Using fewer than 30 blocks is guaranteed to leave some of the 30 streaming multiprocessors (SMs) idle, and using more blocks that can actively fit the SMs will leave some blocks waiting until others finish and might create some load imbalance. Having mutliple threads per block is always desirable to improve efficiency, but a block cannot have more than 512 threads. Considering 4-byte reads as in our experiments, fewer than 16 threads per block cannot fully use memory coalescing as described below.

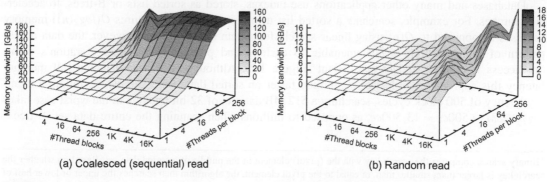

(a) Coalesced (sequential) read   (b) Random read

FIGURE 1.1

Memory bandwidth as a function of both access pattern and number of threads measured on an NVIDIA GTX285. All experiments have one outstanding read per thread, and access a total of 32 GB in units of 32-bit words.

Returning to Little's Law, we notice that it assumes that the full bandwidth be utilized, meaning, that all 64 bytes transferred with each memory block are useful bytes actually requested by an application, and not bytes that are transferred just because they belong to the same memory block. When any amount of data is accessed, with a minimum of one single byte, the entire 64-byte block that the data belongs to is actually transferred. To make sure that all bytes transferred are useful, it is necessary that accesses are *coalesced*, i.e. requests from different threads are presented to the memory management unit (MMU) in such a way that they can be packed into accesses that will use an entire 64-byte block. If, for example, the MMU can only find 10 threads that read 10 4-byte words from the same block, 40 bytes will actually be used and 24 will be discarded. It is clear that coalescing is extremely important to achieve high memory utilization, and that it is much easier when the access pattern is regular and contiguous. The experimental results in Figure 1.1b confirm that random-access memory bandwidth is significantly lower than in the coalesced case. A more comprehensive explanation of memory architecture, coalescing, and optimization techniques can be found in Nvidia's CUDA Programming Guide [7].

1.3 SEARCHING LARGE DATA SETS

The problem of searching is not theoretically difficult in itself, but quickly searching a large data set offers an exquisite example of how finding the right combination of algorithms and data structures for a specific architecture can dramatically improve performance.

1.3.1 Data Structures

Searching for specific values in unsorted data leaves no other choice than scanning the entire data set. The time to search an unsorted data set in memory is determined by sequential memory bandwidth, because the access pattern is nothing else but sequential reads. Performance is identical to that of coalesced reads (Figure 1.1a), which peak at about 150 GB/s on the GPU when using many thread blocks and many threads per block. On the other hand, searching sorted data or indexes can be implemented much more efficiently.

Databases and many other applications use indexes, stored as sorted lists or B-trees, to accelerate searches. For example, searching a sorted list using binary search[1] requires $O(log_2(n))$ memory accesses as opposed to $O(n)$ using linear search, for a data set of size n. However, the data access pattern of binary search is not amenable to caching and prefetching, as each iteration's memory access is data dependent and distant (Figure 1.2). Although each access incurs full memory latency this approach is orders of magnitude faster on sorted data. For example, assuming a memory latency of 500 clock cycles, searching a 512 MB data set of 32-bit integers in the worst case takes $log_2(128M) * 500cc = 13,500cc$, as opposed to millions when scanning the entire data set. B-trees[2]

---

[1] Binary search compares the search key with the (pivot) element in the middle of a sorted data set. Based on whether the search key is larger than, smaller than, or equal to the pivot element, the algorithm then searches the upper or lower half of the data set, or returns the current location if the search key was found.

[2] Searching a B-tree can be implemented comparing the search key with the elements in a node in ascending order, starting at the root. When an element larger than the search key is found, it takes the corresponding branch to the child node, which only contains elements in the same range as the search key, smaller than the current element and larger than the previous one. When an element equals the search key its position is returned.

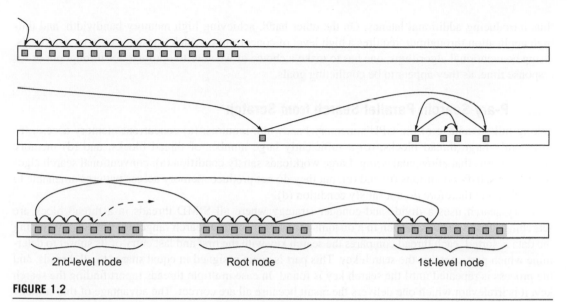

FIGURE 1.2

Memory access patterns of linear search (top), binary search (middle), and B-tree search (bottom).

group pivot elements as nodes and store them linearly, which makes them more amenable to caching (Figure 1.2). However, using the same threading model as one would on the CPU — assigning one thread to one search query — inevitably results in threads diverging quickly such that memory accesses across threads cannot be coalesced.

1.3.2 Limitations of Conventional Search Algorithms

Implementing a search function in CUDA can be done by simply addding a __global__ function qualifier to a *textbook* implementation of binary search. Obviously, the performance of such a naive implementation cannot even keep up with a basic CPU implementation [8]. Although optimizations like manual caching, using vector data types, and inlining functions can significantly improve response time and throughput [9], the basic problem remains: algorithms like binary search were designed for serial machines and not for massively parallel architectures like the GPU [10]. For instance, each iteration of binary search depends on the outcome of a single load and compare, and response time becomes simply a matter of memory latency (Table 1.1) multiplied by the number of iterations required to find the search key, $log_2(n)$. As the GPU has higher memory latency than the CPU, we cannot expect any improvements in response time.

Adopting the CPU threading model, simply running multiple searches concurrently — mapping one search query to one thread — makes matters worse, for two reasons. First, given the GPU's SIMD architecture, all threads within a thread block have to "wait" until all of them complete their searches. With increasing block size the likelihood for one of the threads to require worst-case runtime increases. Second, while all threads start with the same pivot element(s), they quickly diverge as each thread is assigned a different search key. The resulting memory access patterns are not amenable to caching or coalescing. Moreover, the large amount of small memory accesses is likely to lead to contention, thus introducing additional latency. On the other hand, achieving high memory bandwidth, and thus high application throughput, requires a high level of concurrency, which translates to large workloads. Using conventional algorithms, one has to make a choice of whether to optimize for throughput or for response time, as they appear to be conflicting goals.

1.3.3 P-ary Search: Parallel Search from Scratch

Taking full advantage of the GPU's memory bandwidth requires: (a) concurrent memory access, (b) sufficiently large thread blocks, (c) a sufficiently large number of thread blocks, and (d) memory access patterns that allow coalescing. Large workloads satisfy condition (a); conventional search algorithms can satisfy conditions (b) and (c), but they do not produce memory access patterns amenable to coalescing and therefore do not satisfy condition (d).

P-ary search uses a divide-and-conquer strategy where all SIMD threads in a thread block are searching for the same key, each in a disjoint subset of the initial search range (Figure 1.3). Assuming the data is sorted, each thread compares the search key with the first and last entry of its subset to determine which part contains the search key. This part is again assigned in equal shares to all threads, and the process is repeated until the search key is found. In case multiple threads report finding the search key, it is irrelevant which one delivers the result because all are correct. The advantage of this strategy is that memory accesses from multiple threads can leverage the GPU's memory gather capabilities, or — in case the data is stored in a B-tree — they can be coalesced. In both cases, if boundary keys are shared by neighboring threads, they can be loaded into shared memory, eliminating additional global memory accesses. The synchronization process at the end of each iteration to determine which thread holds the relevant part containing the search key also uses shared memory. In theory and in practice P-ary search scales with increasing numbers of threads and has a time complexity of $log_p(n)$, where p denotes the number of parallel threads.

P-ary Search on Sorted Lists

As opposed to conventional algorithms, P-ary search uses all threads within a thread block collaboratively, taking advantage of parallel memory accesses to accelerate a single search query. The parallel

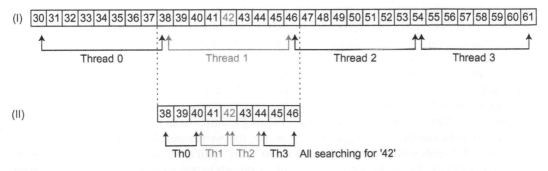

FIGURE 1.3

P-ary search implemented with four threads on a sorted list. Note that if the data is stored as a B-tree, the boundary keys are already adjacent, resulting in linear, faster memory access (Figure 1.4).

memory access pattern of P-ary search takes advantage of memory gather. We observe improvements in response time of up to an order of magnitude over binary search for large workloads.

The implementation closely follows the algorithm described above with a few optimizations (Listing 1.1). We keep a data structure, `cache`, that contains the search key and all pivot elements (boundary keys) of the subset for the current iteration in shared memory, to avoid repeated loads from global memory for the same elements. Each thread loads the search key from shared memory into its own private registers and keeps it there for all iterations. At the beginning of each iteration all threads cache their lower boundary key in shared memory, which at the same time marks the upper bound of the preceeding thread. As far as the last thread is concerned, we can either issue an additional load or, better, assume $+\infty$ as the upper bound. The location of the upper and lower boundary key of each thread is computed based on the thread ID. For example, in the first iteration thread 0 will load the key stored at `data[0*n/p]`, thread 1 will load the key stored at `data[1*n/p]`, and so on.[3] The next subset to search is determined by comparing the search key with the boundary keys. They are identified by an offset, `range_offset`, to the key range of the thread that found the search key and by dividing the length of the subset, `range_length`, by the number of threads per block, `BLOCKSIZE`. If a thread finds the search key within its boundaries, it updates the offset `range_offset` stored in shared memory so that all other threads can access it in the next iteration. The algorithm continues until the search range is smaller or equal to the number of threads, which means that we do not have to check anymore if a search key is located between two pivot elements. We only need to search number of `threads` consecutive keys in the data set from the current subset's offset to the search key and store the result if there is a match.

P-ary Search on B-trees

When we run P-ary search on a sorted list, only the last load can be coalesced as pivot elements are now stored sequentially. On the other hand, a B-tree groups pivot elements as nodes and stores them sequentially, allowing coalesced loads of all nodes (Figure 1.4). Although loading B-tree nodes is efficient due to memory coalescing, using shared memory as a cache still provides a performance advantage because pivot elements are read by multiple threads. In order to avoid multiple loads per node, we chose a node size equal to the block size. When each thread compares the search key to its boundary keys we also check for matches with the search key as the terminal condition. This becomes necessary if we store keys in all B-tree nodes including the inner ones. The location of the next node to be searched is calculated based on the position of the current node, the thread that finds the search key within its boundaries, and the number of child nodes.

1.4 EXPERIMENTAL EVALUATION

We evaluated P-ary search on the GPU both for throughput and for query response time. Compared with conventional search algorithms, we measured a twofold increase in throughput and observed that its response time is independent of workload. For large workloads, this corresponds to an improvement

---

[3]n denotes the number of keys and p the number of threads.

```
// cache for boundary keys indexed by threadId
__shared__ int cache[BLOCKSIZE+2] ;
// index to subset for current iteration
__shared__ int range_offset;

__global__ void parySearchGPU(int* data, int range_length, int*search_keys,
                              int* results)
{
    int sk,old_range_length=range_length,range_start;
    // initialize search range using a single thread
    if (threadIdx.x==0) {
        range_offset=0;
        // cache search key and upper bound in shared memory
        cache[BLOCKSIZE]= 0x7FFFFFFF;
        cache[BLOCKSIZE+1]= search_keys[blockIdx.x];
    }
    // require a sync, since each thread is going to read the above now
    __syncthreads();
    sk = cache[BLOCKSIZE+1];

    while (range_length>BLOCKSIZE){
        range_length = range_length/BLOCKSIZE;
        // check for division underflow
        if (range_length * BLOCKSIZE < old_range_length)
            range_length+=1;
        old_range_length=range_length;
        // cache the boundary keys
        range_start = range_offset + threadIdx.x * range_length;
        cache[threadIdx.x]=data[range_start];
        __syncthreads();

        // if the seached key is within this thread's subset,
        // make it the one for the next iteration
        if (sk>=cache[threadIdx.x] && sk<cache[threadIdx.x+1])
            range_offset = range_start;
        // all threads need to start next iteration with the new subset
        __syncthreads();
    }
    // store search result
    range_start = range_offset + threadIdx.x;
    if (sk==data[range_start])
        results[blockIdx.x]=range_start;
}
```

Listing 1.1. Complete code for P-ary search on sorted lists.

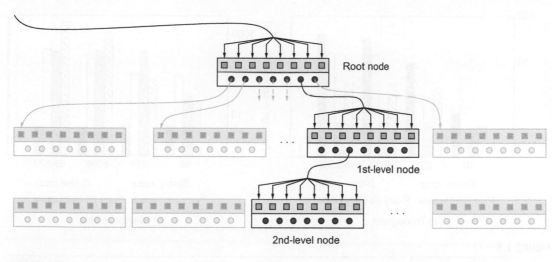

FIGURE 1.4

B-trees are particularly suited to P-ary search: loading an entire node can be achieved with one coalesced memory access. The keys in each node are then processed in parallel as shown in Figure 1.3.

of two orders of magnitude in response time over conventional algorithms. Comparing these results to a CPU implementation we observe an increase in throughput on our test system of up to 3×.

Experimental Setup

Experiments were conducted on an NVIDIA GTX285 1.5 GHz with 1 GB of GDDR3 RAM installed in a PC equipped with a Core i7 920 quad-core 2.6 GHz CPU with 12 GB of DDR3-1600 RAM. The machine was running CentOS Linux 5.4 64-bit edition with Kernel 2.6.28, NVIDIA graphics drivers version 190.53 and CUDA 2.3. The system was dedicated to the experiments with no other applications or users active and the GTX285 was installed as a secondary card, with graphical output disabled. GPU timing measurements use the `clock()` function and the measurements on the CPU use the `rdtsc` instruction, both providing cycle granularity. Frequency scaling was turned off in the system BIOS, so cycle counts directly translate into elapsed time. The CUDA C code for the GPU, as well as the C and inline assembly code for the CPU, were highly optimized and aggressive compiler optimizations (`-04`) were turned on.

Throughput

Figure 1.5a compares throughput of P-ary search to conventional search algorithms for different workloads. Although P-ary search outperforms conventional B-tree search for all workloads by at least 2 times, it lags behind binary search on list-based data structures. The reason for the wins and losses of the particular search algorithms are a direct result of their memory access pattern. Using sorted list data structures, binary search and P-ary search both generate mostly random-memory accesses when loading the pivot/boundary elements, which cannot be coalesced. The search path for multiple threads of binary search quickly diverge, and P-ary search requires memory gathers from distant locations. However, P-ary search stresses the memory throughput more than binary search because on average it

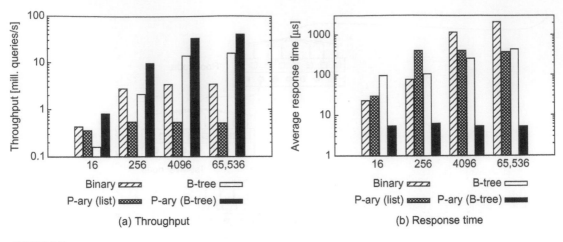

FIGURE 1.5

Performance of search algorithms with increasing workload size, searching 32-bit integer keys in a 512 MB data set comprising 128 M entries.

requires more memory accesses. Even sharing boundary keys and using $-\infty$ for the lower and $+\infty$ as an upper bound, at each of its $log_p(n)$ iterations P-ary search produces $p-1$ memory requests, while binary search requires only $log_2(n)$ total.

Storing data as a B-tree allows P-ary search's memory accesses to be always coalesced because pivot elements are located at consecutive memory locations and accessed by consecutive threads. On the other hand, multiple threads searching the B-tree for distinct keys have diverging search paths, which results in nonlinear memory accesses that cannot be coalesced. As a result we observe more than a twofold increase in application throughput, independent of workload. Given the GPU's massively parallel architecture, achieving peak throughput requires large workloads, at least 1000 concurrent queries. However, handling large amounts of queries simultaneously is not unusual for large database servers.

Response Time

Measuring query response or execution time demonstrates the strengths in the design of P-ary search. On B-tree data structures it provides constant response time independent of workload, but also improves response time for large-scale search operations on serial data structures (Figure 1.5b). The reason for the explosion in response time under heavy load conditions for conventional algorithms is the random memory access pattern produced by many concurrent threads with diverging search path. P-ary search produces a memory access pattern amenable to coalescing, which drastically reduces the number of memory requests, avoiding congestion.

Scalability

Obviously, increasing the number of threads for a single query increases the convergence rate of P-ary search. As one would expect, response time of P-ary search scales with increasing number of threads and the same applies to throughput (Figure 1.6). However, increasing the number of threads per block beyond the size of a warp (32 threads) has negligible impact on performance.

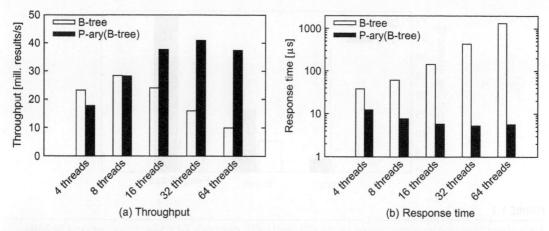

FIGURE 1.6

Scalability of P-ary search with increasing p, the number of threads per thread block. The figure refers to searching 64 K 32-bit integer keys in a 512 MB data set comprising 128 M entries organized as a number of threads wide B-tree.

On the other hand, for conventional search algorithms increasing the number of threads, and thus the number of concurrent queries, has a negative impact on performance. The reason is twofold. First, mapping one query to one thread of execution results in diverging memory access patterns that are not amenable to memory coalescing. Second, queries not only diverge but also complete at different times. Because GPU threads operate in an SIMD fashion, all threads have to wait until the last query finishes before they can start a new search. With increasing block size the likelihood that one query requires worst-case execution time increases, which renders an even larger amount of threads idle. All other experiments were conducted with the optimum block size maximizing throughput and response time of each algorithm.

GPU vs CPU

P-ary search has been ported to the CPU leveraging the CPU's vector unit [11] and it also outperforms conventional algorithms in terms of throughput by a factor of two (Figure 1.7). However, a similarly priced GPU like the one in our test system achieves approximately three times the throughput and similar response times. The reason is that GPUs offer a significantly higher degree of parallelism, which allows for a larger p than CPU vector size, 128 bits on x86. Furthermore, memory coalescing on the GPU is not limited by vector size, unlike vector registers on the CPU. This becomes crucial when operating on larger character strings, which are of growing importance for many applications, including databases.

1.5 CONCLUSION

Although in a "serial" world conventional algorithms like binary search might be optimal, the game changes when unleashing parallelism. Traditional multithreading approaches already indicate that

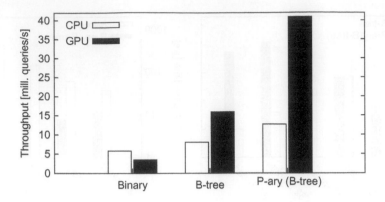

FIGURE 1.7

Throughput of search implementations on the CPU and GPU, executing 64 K search queries on a 512 MB data set comprising 128 M 32-bit integer keys.

parallel memory accesses increase memory and thus application throughput. Given the fast thread synchronization within a GPU thread block, we can put this increased throughput to work for a single search query to effectively reduce response time. From a broader perspective, we hope to have shown how going back to the drawing board and redesigning fundamental algorithms for new parallel architectures affords order-of-magnitude performance improvements now, but that it is the only choice we have to continue the evolution of the Information Age.

References

[1] W.A. Wulf, S.A. McKee, Hitting the memory wall: implications of the obvious, SIGARCH Comput. Archit. News 23 (1) (1995) 20–24.

[2] S.A. McKee, Reflections on the memory wall, CF'04: Proceedings of the 1st Conference on Computing Frontiers, Stamatis Vassiliadis, ACM, Ischia, Italy, 2004, p. 162.

[3] T. Kaldewey, A. Di Blas, J. Hagen, E. Sedlar, S.A. Brandt, Memory matters, in: I. Puaut (Ed.), RTSS'08: Work in Progress Proceedings of the 29th IEEE Real-Time Systems Symposium, IEEE, Barcelona, Spain, 2008, pp. 45–48.

[4] J.D.C. Little, A proof of the queueing formula $L = \lambda\,W$, Oper. Res. 9 (1961) 383–387.

[5] P. Micikevicius, Advanced CUDA C, GPU Technology Conference, San Jose, CA, 2009.

[6] V. Volkov, Use registers and multiple outputs per thread on GPU, PMAA'10: 6th International Workshop on Parallel Matrix Algorithms and Applications, Basel, Switzerland, 2010.

[7] Nvidia Corp, NVIDIA GPU Programming Guide. Version 2.3.1, 8/26/2009.

[8] T. Kaldewey, J. Hagen, A. Di Blas, E. Sedlar, Parallel search on video cards, HOTPAR'09: First USENIX Workshop on Hot Topics in Parallelism, Berkeley, CA, 2009.

[9] T. Kaldewey, Programming video cards for database applications, USENIX; login 34 (4) (2009) 21–34.

[10] A. Di Blas, T. Kaldewey, Data monster, IEEE Spectr. 46 (9) (2009) 46–51.

[11] B. Schlegel, R. Gemulla, W. Lehner, K-ary search on modern processors, in: P.A. Boncz, K.A. Ross (Eds.), DaMoN'09: Proceedings of the 5th International Workshop on Data Management on New Hardware, ACM, Providence, RI, 2009, pp. 52–60.

Edge v. Node Parallelism for Graph Centrality Metrics

Yuntao Jia, Victor Lu, Jared Hoberock, Michael Garland, and John C. Hart

Graphs help us model and understand various structures, but understanding large graphs, such as those now generated by instruments, simulations and the Internet, increasingly depend on statistics and characterizations. Centrality metrics indicate which nodes and edges are important, to better analyze, simplify, categorize and visualize large graphs, but are expensive to compute, especially on large graphs, and their parallel implementation on the most common "scale-free" graphs can suffer severe load imbalance [1]. This chapter proposes an improved edge-parallel approach for computing centrality metrics that can also accelerate breadth-first search and all-pairs shortest path.

2.1 INTRODUCTION

Centrality metrics help us analyze large graphs, but their computation can be quite time-consuming and is often the main bottleneck for graph processing. For example, computing betweenness centrality (BC) using the state-of-the-art sequential algorithm [2] on a flickr user network of 6.6 million relationships between 800,000 users takes about two days on a single thread of a 3.33 GHz Intel Core i7-975 central processing unit (CPU). Approximate BC computes faster [3], but the error can severely degrade some applications [4, 5].

Several have proposed parallel algorithms to accelerate the computation of centrality metrics. Bader and Madduri [6] implemented BC on the Cray MTA-2 shared memory multiprocessor, and Madduri et al. [7] refined the approach by reducing its need for atomic operations. Tu and Tan [8] implemented BC on Intel Clovertown and Sun Niagara1 multicore processors. To our knowledge, Sriram et al. [1] is the first and only effort to compute BC on the GPU, though similar parallel approaches have been used for GPU implementations of other graph algorithms [9]. Overall, these approaches have been shown to perform well on general graphs, but suboptimally on scale-free networks [1, 9].

Scale-free networks are graphs whose node degree distribution follows a power law [10]. They commonly result from real-world data ranging from natural, such as the protein interactions shown in Figure 2.1, to social, such as online friend networks like the aforementioned flickr example, prompting the development of several recent tools specialized for their analysis [4, 5, 11, 12]. This degree distribution, with many low-degree nodes and few high-degree nodes can severely degrade performance of parallel graph algorithms, including centrality metrics, breadth-first search (BFS) and all-pairs

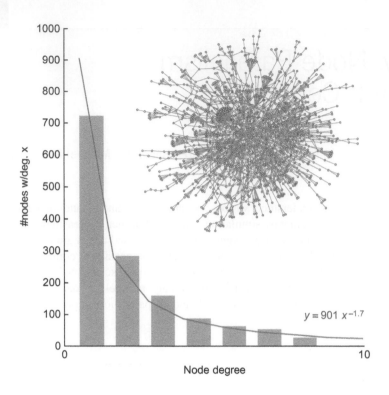

$$y = 901\ x^{-1.7}$$

FIGURE 2.1

Node degree distribution of the scale-free network "bo".

shortest path (APSP), that operate per-node with work proportional to node degree, because the degree (workload) variance creates a load imbalance and control flow divergence.

We propose instead a per-edge-parallel approach to computing centrality metrics and other graph operations that balances computation regardless of node degree variance. This new approach comes at the expense of an increase in the number of memory reads/writes (about four to seven times more in our tests), but enables more opportunities for coalesced accesses. Overall its benefits from load balancing outweigh the increase in memory accesses.

The presented solution and discussions assume unweighted and undirected input graphs.

2.2 BACKGROUND

Centrality metrics measure the importance of a node for various definitions of important. Central nodes are close to all nodes, so closeness centrality (1) sums the distance from a node to every other node, and graph centrality (2) uses the distance from a node to its most remote counterpart. Alternatively, crucial nodes might lie on more shortest paths than others. Stress centrality (3) measures the absolute number of shortest paths passing through a node, whereas betweenness centrality (4) measures the fraction of shortest paths passing through a vertex. Each of these can likewise measure the importance of an edge. Please note that $d_v(t)$ denotes the shortest-path distance from v to t, and $\sigma_{st}(v)$ represents the number of shortest paths from s to t through v.

$$CC(v) = 1/\sum_{t\in V} d_v(t) \qquad (1)$$

$$GC(v) = 1/\max_{t\in V} d_v(t) \qquad (2)$$

$$SC(v) = \sum_{s,t\in V} \sigma_{st}(v) \qquad (3)$$

$$BC(v) = \sum_{s,t\in V} \frac{\sigma_{st}(v)}{\sigma_{st}} \qquad (4)$$

FIGURE 2.2

Closeness, Graph, Stress and Betweenness Centrality.

Among the four centrality metrics, BC is the most complicated and most popular. Because the BC algorithm can be easily modified to compute the other three centrality metrics, we focus on BC.

The state-of-art sequential algorithm for computing BC [2] runs in time $O(mn)$, where m and n are the number of edges and nodes, respectively. As outlined in Algorithm 1, it computes BC (4) as a sum of *dependencies*

$$BC(v) = \sum_{s\in V} \delta_{s.}(v), \qquad (5)$$

$$\delta_{s.}(v) = \sum_{t\in V} \frac{\sigma_{st}(v)}{\sigma_{st}}, \qquad (6)$$

where $\delta_{s.}(v)$ is the dependency of s on v. Each outer loop iteration (lines 2–37) maps to a term in the summation of (5). Each iteration computes, for the corresponding node s, the dependencies $\{\delta_{s.}(v): \forall v \in V\}$, which accumulate into $\{BC(v): \forall v \in V\}$. Each iteration first performs a *forward propagation* phase (lines 3–23, a modified breath-first search) that computes the shortest-path (SP) distances $\{d_s(v) : v \in V\}$ and SP counts $\{\sigma_s(v) : \forall v \in V\}$. $N(v)$ denotes the nodes adjacent to v. Next, a *backward propagation* phase (lines 24–36) computes $\delta_{s.}(v)$ using the recursive relation (line 31) [2]

$$\delta_{s.}(v) = \sum_{w:v\in P_s(w)} \frac{\sigma_s(v)}{\sigma_s(w)}(\delta_{s.}(w)+1), \qquad (7)$$

and accumulates it into $BC(v)$. Here $P_s(w)$ represents the predecessors of w given the source node s.

Closeness centrality is similarly computed by a forward propagation without path counting from each node s and backward propagation replaced by (1), specifically $CC(s) \leftarrow 1/\sum_{v\in V} d_s(v)$. Graph centrality likewise propagates forward without path counting, replacing backward propagation with $GC(s) \leftarrow 1/\max_{v\in V} d_s(v)$. Stress centrality performs forward propagation with path counting, and back propagation, replacing lines 31 and 34 with

$$\delta_{s.}(v) \leftarrow \delta_{s.}(v) + \delta_{s.}(w) + 1, \qquad (8)$$

$$SC(v) \leftarrow SC(v) + \sigma_s(v)\delta_{s.}(v), \qquad (9)$$

where $\delta_s(v)$ denotes instead the number of "shortest-path suffixes" starting at s passing through v.

Algorithm 1: Sequential BC Computation

Require: Graph $G = (V, E)$
Ensure: BC(v) at every $v \in V$

1: Initialize BC(v) to 0, for all $v \in V$
2: **for** $s \in V$ **do**
3:     ▼ **Forward Propagation**
4:     Initialize $d_s(v)$ to ∞, for all $v \in V$
5:     Initialize $\sigma_s(v)$ to 0, for all $v \in V$
6:     $d_s(s) \leftarrow 0, \sigma_s(s) \leftarrow 1$
7:     $d \leftarrow 0$
8:     **while** not done **do**
9:         done $\leftarrow$ true
10:         **for** $v \in V$ where $d_s(v) = d$ **do**
11:             **for** $w \in N(v)$ **do**
12:                 **if** $d_s(w) = \infty$ **then**
13:                     $d_s(w) \leftarrow d + 1$
14:                     done $\leftarrow$ false
15:                 **end if**
16:                 ▼ Path Counting
17:                 **if** $d_s(w) = d + 1$ **then**
18:                     $\sigma_s(w) \leftarrow \sigma_s(w) + \sigma_s(v)$
19:                 **end if**
20:             **end for**
21:         **end for**
22:         $d \leftarrow d + 1$
23:     **end while**

24:     ▼ **Backward Propagation**
25:     Initialize $\delta_{s.}(v)$ to 0 for all $v \in V$
26:     **while** $d > 1$ **do**
27:         $d \leftarrow d - 1$
28:         **for** $v \in V$ where $d_s(v) = d$ **do**
29:             **for** $w \in N(v)$ **do**
30:                 **if** $d_s(w) = d + 1$ **then**
31:                     $\delta_{s.}(v) \leftarrow \delta_{s.}(v) + \frac{\sigma_s(v)}{\sigma_s(w)}(\delta_{s.}(w) + 1)$
32:                 **end if**
33:             **end for**
34:             BC(v) $\leftarrow$ BC(v) $+ \delta_{s.}(v)$
35:         **end for**
36:     **end while**
37: **end for**

Algorithm 2: Node-Parallel Forward Propagation Step

1: **for** $v \in V$ on wavefront **in parallel do**
2:    **for** $w \in N(v)$ **do**
3:       **if** $d_s(w) = \infty$ **then** $d_s(w) \leftarrow d + 1$
4:       **if** $d_s(w) = d + 1$ **then** $\sigma_s(w) \leftarrow \sigma_s(w) + \sigma_s(v)$
5:    **end for**
6: **end for**

Algorithm 3: Edge-Parallel Forward Propagation Step

1: **for** edge (v, w) incident to wavefront **in parallel do**
2:    **if** $d_s(w) = \infty$ **then** $d_s(w) \leftarrow d + 1$
3:    **if** $d_s(w) = d + 1$ **then** $\sigma_s(w) \leftarrow \sigma_s(w) + \sigma_s(v)$
4: **end for**

2.3 NODE V. EDGE PARALLELISM

To convert Algorithm 1 into a parallel GPU version, we first map the outer loop iterations (lines 2–37) to coarse-grain parallel thread blocks, then seek finer grain SIMD parallelism opportunities within each iteration. There are dependencies between iterations in both forward and backward propagation, so we look within a propagation step (lines 10–21 and 28–35).

Existing methods [1, 9] map wavefront nodes (the set of nodes with $d_s(v) = d$) to threads. We call this the *node-parallel* approach. As Algorithm 2 indicates, the inner for-loop over the node neighbors $N(v)$ of node v will vary depending on the degree of v, so threads corresponding to low-degree nodes must wait for the few higher-degree node threads in the same SIMD unit to complete, in both the forward and backward propagation steps.

These forward and backward propagation steps iterate across edges incident to nodes in the current front. Unfortunately, this configuration produces load imbalance owing to the varying work required by nodes along the front. For this reason, it is unsuited to parallelism. If we instead parallelize over the edges incident to the front directly, then each edge represents constant complexity: either an update of distance and shortest-path count or a no-op. Hence, such an *edge-parallel* approach, as shown in Algorithm 3, better balances load.

2.4 DATA STRUCTURE

We represent the graph as an edge list to better assign edges to threads. Each edge (v, w) appears twice in this list, as (v, w) and (w, v), to ensure that both "directions of computation" (forward and backward propagation) associated with each edge are properly processed. This edge list is sorted by the first node in each ordered pair, such that adjacent threads are assigned edges that likely emanate from the same node, leading to more opportunities for coalesced access of node attributes. Likewise, this ordering also encourages edge attribute coalescing.

Graphs are commonly specified by an adjacency list, an array of lists where each array element (corresponding to a node) contains a list of array indices corresponding to neighboring nodes. This structure is often linearized for graphical processing unit (GPU) processing as an indexed neighbor list, consisting of the concatenated neighbor lists nhbrs indexed by an offsets array, such that the neighbors of a node i are found at nhbrs[offsets[i]:offsets[i+1]-1]. Each thread of a node-parallel approach would then process a varying length list of neighbors, as shown in Figure 2.3a, resulting in load imbalance and less opportunity for coalescing.

We can convert the indexed neighbor "node" list into an edge list by replacing the node-indexed offset array with an edge-indexed "from" array that aligns with the original nhbrs[] array, which records at froms[j] the node that nhbrs[j] is a neighbor of as shown in Figure 2.3b. Hence (froms[j],nhbrs[j]) becomes the aforementioned edge list, and under this construction each edge would appear twice, and the edges are sorted by their first node.

There are a few additional arrays to maintain the propagation status and centrality value, including distances, numSPs, dependencies, nodeBCs, and predecessor. The first four correspond to the per-node quantities of Algorithm 1. The predecessor array records for a given node pair (v,w) whether w is a predecessor of v; predecessor[i] is true if nhbrs[i] is a predecessor of froms[i].

Listing 2.1 shows the CUDA implementation of these data structures. The cuGraph structure is read-only and shared by all thread blocks, whereas the cuBCData structure is duplicated across multiple thread blocks so that each thread block can propagate independently. If gridDim is the number of thread blocks, then the estimated global memory usage is

$$\text{Memory usage} = 16m + \text{gridDim}(16n + 2m) \text{ bytes.} \tag{10}$$

The optimal number of thread blocks gridDim would maximize GPU parallelism without exceeding GPU memory space. We set gridDim to the number of SMs (30). A larger number of thread blocks would better hide latency, but we found that for BC computation, larger numbers of thread blocks saturated the memory interface. To help hide memory latency, we set the number of threads in a block, blockDim, as large as possible (512).

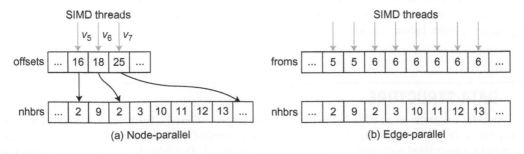

(a) Node-parallel   (b) Edge-parallel

FIGURE 2.3

Illustration of data structure design.

```
1   struct cuBCData {
2       int * distances;        // size n
3       int * numSPs;           // size n
4       bool * predecessor;     // size 2m
5       float * dependencies;   // size n
6       float * nodeBCs;        // size n
7   };
8   struct cuGraph {
9       int * froms;            // size 2m
10      int * nhbrs;            // size 2m
11  };
```

Listing 2.1. Data structures as defined for CUDA implementation of BC computation.

```
1   __shared__ bool done = false;
2   while (!done) {
3       __syncthreads();
4       done = true;
5       d++;
6       __syncthreads();
7
8       for (int eid = threadIdx; eid < 2 * nedge; eid += blockDim) {
9           int from = froms[eid];
10          if (distance[from] == d) {
11              int nhbr = nhbrs[eid];
12              int nhbr_dist = distance[nhbr];
13              if (nhbr_dist == -1) {
14                  distance[nhbr] = nhbr_dist = d + 1;
15                  done = false;
16              } else if (nhbr_dist < d) {
17                  predecessor[eid] = true;
18              }
19              if (nhbr_dist == d + 1) {
20                  atomicAdd(&numSPs[nhbr], numSPs[from]);
21              }
22          }
23      }
24      __syncthreads();
25  }
```

Listing 2.2. CUDA kernel for edge-parallel forward propagation phase.

2.5 IMPLEMENTATION

CUDA algorithms for forward and backward propagation are shown in Listings 2.2 and 2.3, less array and variable initiation shown earlier in Algorithm 1. For each thread `threadIdx`, we map the set of

```
1   while (d > 1) {
2     for (int eid = threadIdx; eid < 2 * nedge; eid += blockDim) {
3       int from = froms[eid];
4       if (distance[from] == d) {
5         if (predecessor[from]) {
6           int nhbr = nhbrs[eid];
7           float delta = (1.0f + dependency[from]) *
8                             numSPs[nhbr] / numSPs[from];
9           atomicAdd(&dependency[nhbr], delta);
10        }
11      }
12    }
13    d--;
14    __syncthreads();
15  }
16  for (int nid = threadIdx; nid < nnode; nid += blockDim) {
17.   nodeBC[nid] += dependency[nid];
18  }
```

Listing 2.3. CUDA kernel for edge-parallel backward propagation phase.

edges indexed by threadIdx+ k * blockDim, for some $k \geq 0$ given by Line 8 in Listing 2.2 and Line 2 in Listing 2.3, which promotes coalesced accesses to edge attributes.

The forward phase propagates the wavefront until all nodes are visited, indicated by the shared boolean done, initialized true at the start of each step (line 4), but is set false when a wavefront node finds a successor. Lines 8–23 implement Algorithm 3.

The backward phase visits nodes in the opposite wavefront propagation order as recorded by the forward phase. Each step identifies wavefront edges whose first-node distance equals the current wavefront distance d. These wavefront-edge first nodes accumulate dependency to their predecessor neighbor. The distance d is decremented, and the phase concludes when it reaches 1. When the backward phase completes, dependency is accumulated into node BC (Lines 16–18).

The accumulations on Line 20 of Listing 2.2 and Line 9 of Listing 2.3 must occur atomically since two threads could process edges with a common second node. These accumulations always occur from the first node into the second node, either accumulating SP count (from wavefront node to successor) or dependency (from wavefront node to predecessor). This choice specifically avoids contention between concurrent threads that likely share the same first node.

The dependency accumulation of the backward phase (line 9 of Listing 2.3) requires floating-point atomic operations introduced with the Fermi architecture. For earlier GPUs such as the GTX 280, we simply perform a node-parallel backward phase. Most of the results in this chapter were obtained on a GTX 480 using an edge-parallel backward phase.

In the forward phase, the second-node distance computation requires an extra level of indirection: distance indexed by the result of nhbrs. The backward phase avoids indirection by directly checking the predecessor array, which unlike distance, is coalesced.

2.6 ANALYSIS

The edge-parallel approach is better load balanced, but it also requires more memory accesses. We analyze this trade-off using a simplified BC kernel consisting only of a forward phase that simply performs distance updates. This step reduces it to a breadth-first traversal.

The number of reads performed by the node-parallel approach is $(In + 2n + 4m)n$, where I is the average number of propagation steps from any of the start nodes, and each propagation step reads the entire n-length `distance` array. The number of reads to `offset` is $2n$, and to `nhbrs` is $2m$. Each neighbor index then reads `distance` another $2m$ times.

The edge-parallel approach reads $(4Im + 4m)n$ times. The difference is the edge-parallel approach must perform $4m$ reads in order to identify wavefront nodes ($2m$ from `froms` and $2m$ from `distance`). Because the number of edges usually exceeds the number of nodes, the edge-parallel approach incurs significantly more memory bandwidth pressure, as measured in Table 2.1.

The number of *writes* by both approaches is similar, bounded from above by $(m - \chi)n$, where χ is the average number of edges lying on any wavefront emanating from a start node. This upper bound assumes each node's distance is set (redundantly) by all of its predecessors, which is not necessarily the case. In particular, predecessors that fetch v's distance after being set by another predecessor will not write to it.

Figure 2.4 shows memory throughput from an application point of view, which is computed by dividing the estimates in Table 2.1 by GPU running time. On the GTX 480, the linear increase in throughput with `gridDim`, modulo the drops[1] at 31 and 46, suggests the memory interface is not being saturated and that the additional memory requests incurred by the edge-parallel approach are being adequately absorbed by cache. This is in contrast to the Tesla S1070, where edge-parallel's additional requests quickly saturate the memory interface as `gridDim` increases.

Table 2.2 reports memory throughput computed using hardware performance counters. This provides further evidence that bandwidth is indeed being saturated on the Tesla S1070 and not on the GTX 480.

Table 2.1 Estimated Global Memory Reads and Writes in GB

	Node-Parallel	Edge-Parallel
sp500-038	0.026	0.117
bo	0.174	0.615
cg_web	0.523	2.362
as-rel.20071008	67.470	320.598
hep-th	213.603	1636.577

---

[1] The drop at 31 is probably due to an unbalanced assignment of thread blocks to SMs (i.e., among the 15 SMs one will have three thread blocks, whereas the others will have two), and the drop at 46 is probably due to a limited number of thread blocks that can run concurrently.

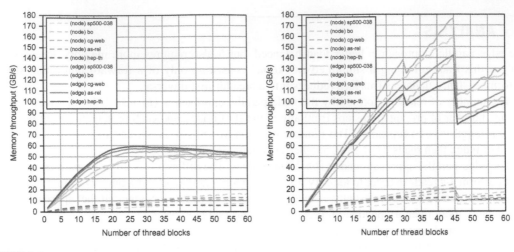

FIGURE 2.4

Memory throughput from application point of view as a function of the number of thread blocks, as measured on the Tesla S1070 (left) and the GTX 480 (right).

Table 2.2 Memory Throughput (GB/s) Measured Using Visual Profiler 3.2. Peak Throughput for the Tesla S1070 and GTX 480 are 102.5 GB/s and 177.4 GB/s, Respectively. Measurements were Performed with `gridDim` Set to 60 and 45 on the Tesla S1070 and GTX 480, Respectively

	Tesla S1070		GTX 480	
	Node-Par.	Edge-Par.	Node-Par.	Edge-Par.
sp500-038	45.4	63.7	2.0	5.0
bo	57.3	74.0	10.9	13.6
cg-web	58.8	69.1	6.5	9.3
as-rel	44.2	65.9	35.5	68.0
hep-th	34.8	61.4	1.6	2.2

The node-parallel approach has a lower memory throughput on both the Tesla S1070 and GTX 480. This can be attributed to SIMD underutilization and uncoalesced memory access. In particular, adjacent threads mapped to nodes with different node degree results in an idle SIMD lane that would otherwise perform useful memory operations. Unlike the edge-parallel approach, adjacent threads in general access nonadjacent items in `nhbrs`, resulting in fewer coalesced loads.

In summary, although the edge-parallel approach must pay the cost of more memory requests, the benefits of less SIMD divergence and more memory coalescing and the support of recent cache-based GPU architectures enable the edge-parallel approach to win over the node-parallel approach in the end.

2.7 RESULTS

We implemented all four centrality metrics using CUDA on the GPU and single-threaded C++ on the CPU for comparison. Except when otherwise specified, all experiments were performed on the UIUC IACAT accelerator cluster [13] of 8GB 3.33GHz Intel i7-975 CPUs and GTX 480 GPUs with 1.5GB memory. We tested these implementations on six real-world graphs of varying complexity, averaging five runtimes each shown in Table 2.3. (Practical BC computation for massive graphs like "flickr" use a random subset of nodes as wavefront start nodes. For "flickr" we used 4,096 start nodes.)

Table 2.3 shows that serial CPU computation of centrality metrics can become cumbersome on large graphs over 10,000 nodes. Figure 2.5 shows how parallelism on CPU and GPU accelerates these computations. Using OpenMP enabled a parallel BC implementation on a CPU with eight threads to be 1.6 times to 4.9 times faster except on the smallest network. Whereas our BC implementation on GTX 480 can be 6.9 times to 10.2 times faster, using 30 blocks of 512 threads. The same algorithm

Table 2.3 Test Dataset Complexity, Average Propagation Steps (*I*), and Centrality Metric Performance on a Single CPU Thread, in Seconds

Graph	Nodes	Edges	*I*	CC	GC	SC	BC
sp500-038	365	3206	5.49	0.006	0.006	0.22	0.22
bo	1458	1948	13.28	0.047	0.049	0.119	0.117
cg-web	2269	8131	7.34	0.160	0.160	0.506	0.503
as-rel	26242	53174	14.17	20	20	52	52
hep-th	27400	352021	10.14	76	75	251	225
flickr	820878	6625280	-	341	343	824	854

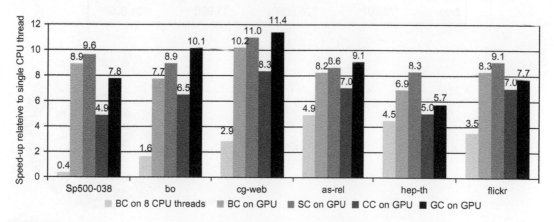

FIGURE 2.5

Speed-ups for computing centrality metrics on select data sets using mutithreaded CPU and GTX 480 GPU, relative to the running time of single CPU thread.

also accelerates SC, CC, and GC, from 4.9 times to 11.4 times, all relative to a single-threaded CPU implementation.

Our edge-parallel centrality algorithm can be modified to compute breadth-first search (BFS). Because BFS propagates a single wavefront, we parallelize a single propagation step using all threads in the grid and synchronize them by relaunching the kernel. Table 2.4 shows "Edge ||" outperforms a single-threaded "CPU" by 1.8 times to 6.1 times (except on the first small graph) and "Node ||" by 2.2 times to 7.5 times. To illustrate the relative importance of coalesced access pattern vs. little thread divergence in our edge-parallel approach, we randomly permute the thread-edge mapping in an implementation called "Edge ||-U." Here, threads still enjoy little divergence, but memory access is totally uncoalesced. As shown in Table 2.4, it performs worse than "Edge ||," illustrating the impact of *disabling* coalesced accesses. The performance degrades beyond "Node ||," which has thread divergence because of the larger number of accesses owing to edge parallelism and uncoalesced loads. However, the fact that "Edge ||-U" is faster than "Node ||" on "as-rel" clearly illustrates the importance of having less thread divergence.

We have used edge-parallel BC to accelerate two graph processing tools for social network visualization: simplification [4] and clustering [5], as demonstrated on a stock price affinity network in Figure 2.6. Graph simplification removes low-BC edges, retaining the highest-BC edges that likely represent communication pathways in a network. Graph clustering removes high-BC edges to discover low-BC communities, then merges them to discover inter-community affinities. Results in Figure 2.7

Table 2.4 BFS Runtime Performance on a GTX 480, in Milliseconds

	CPU	Node ||	Edge ||	Edge ||-U
cg-web	0.099	0.531	0.225	0.854
as-rel	0.891	3.670	0.489	1.644
hep-th	2.923	3.763	0.753	4.519
flickr	72.397	26.659	11.926	134.809

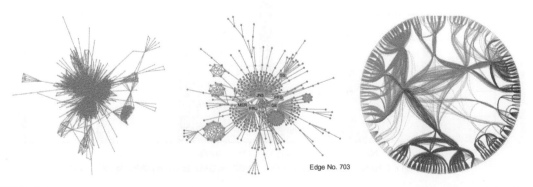

Edge No. 703

FIGURE 2.6

Input graph S&P 500-038 (left), simplified (center) and hierarchically clustered as edge bundles (right) using fast GPU centrality (see color insert).

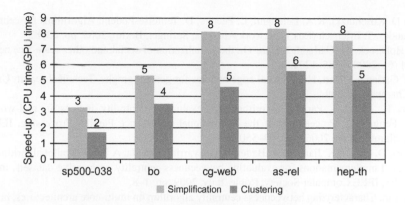

FIGURE 2.7

Speed-up (edge-parallel GPU v. serial CPU) of applications on a GTX 480.

indicates 2 to 8 times performance improvement for both tools by using edge-parallel BC, when compared to a serial CPU implementation.

2.8 CONCLUSIONS

For some graph algorithms such as computing centrality, breadth-first search, and even all-pairs short-est path, an edge-parallel approach improves GPU throughput with better load balancing and less thread divergence on scale-free networks. The edge-parallel approach is less appropriate for grids, meshes, and other graphs with low-degree variance, and it performs less well on dense graphs with many edges. The edge-parallel approach requires more GPU memory than node-parallel, which could limit its application to larger graphs than the ones we considered, for which one could investigate efficient inter-block synchronization techniques [14].

We believe the edge-parallel approach would benefit most scale-free network applications and should be investigated on further graph algorithms such as max flow. We did not consider directed or weighted graphs, which might use Dijkstra's algorithm for non-negative weights and the Bellman-Ford algorithm to handle negative weights.

This chapter is the result of several projects supported in part by the National Science Foundation under grant IIS-0534485, Intel, and the Universal Parallel Computing Research Center at the University of Illinois, sponsored by Intel and Microsoft.

References

[1] A. Sriram, K. Gautham, K. Kothapalli, P.J. Narayan, R. Govindarajulu, Evaluating centrality metrics in real-world networks on GPU, in: Proceedings of the International Conference High Performance Computing, Student Research Symposium, Kochi, India, 2009.
[2] U. Brandes, A faster algorithm for betweenness centrality, J. Math. Sociol. 25 (2001) 163–177.

[3] R. Jacob, D. Koschutzki, K.A. Lehmann, L. Peeters, D. Tenfelse-Podehl, Algorithms for centrality indices, in: U. Brandes, T. Erlebach (Eds.), Network Analysis, Springer, Berlin, 2005, pp. 62–82.

[4] Y. Jia, J. Hoberock, M. Garland, J. Hart, On the visualization of social and other scale-free networks, IEEE TVCG 14 (6) (2008) 1285–1292.

[5] Y. Jia, M. Garland, J. Hart, Hierarchical edge bundles for general graphs, Technical report, Univ. of Illinois Urbana Champaign, 2009.

[6] D. Bader, K. Madduri, Parallel algorithms for evaluating centrality indices in real-world networks, in: W.-C. Feng (Ed.), Proceedings of the International Conference Parallel Processing, IEEE Computer Society, Columbus, OH, 2006, pp. 539–550.

[7] K. Madduri, D. Ediger, K. Jiang, D.A. Bader, D. Chavarria-Miranda, A faster parallel algorithm and efficient multithreaded implementations for evaluating betweenness centrality on massive datasets, in: Proceedings of the IPDPS, IEEE Computer Society, Rome, Italy, 2009, pp. 1–8.

[8] D. Tu, G. Tan, Characterizing betweenness centrality algorithm on multi-core architectures, in: International Symposium on Parallel and Distributed Processing with Applications, IEEE Computer Society, Chengdu, Sichuan, China, 2009, pp. 182–189.

[9] P. Harish, V. Vineet, P.J. Narayanan, Large graph algorithms for massively multithreaded architectures, Technical report, Indian Institutes of Information Technology, 2009.

[10] A.-L. Barabasi, R. Albert, Emergence of scaling in random networks, Science 286 (5439) (1999) 509–512.

[11] D.H. Kim, J.D. Noh, H. Jeong, Scale-free trees: the skeletons of complex networks, Phys. Rev. E 70 (4) (2004) 046126+.

[12] A.Y. Wu, M. Garland, J. Han, Mining scale-free networks using geodesic clustering, in: W. Kim, R. Kohavi, J. Gehrke, W. DuMouchel (Eds.), Proceedings of the KDD, ACM, Seattle, WA, 2004, pp. 719–724.

[13] V. Kindratenko, J. Enos, G. Shi, M. Showerman, G. Arnold, J. Stone, J. Phillips, W. Hwu, GPU clusters for high-performance computing, in: Proc. Workshop on Parallel Programming on Accelerator Clusters, IEEE International Conference on Cluster Computing, 2009, pp. 1–8.

[14] S. Xiao, W.-C. Feng, Inter-Block GPU communication via fast barrier synchronization, in: Proceedings of the IPDPS, 24th IEEE International Symposium on Parallel and Distributed Processing, Atlanta, GA, 2010, pp. 1–12.

Optimizing Parallel Prefix Operations for the Fermi Architecture

Mark Harris and Michael Garland

The NVIDIA Fermi GPU architecture introduces new instructions designed to facilitate basic, but important, parallel primitives on per-thread predicates, as well as instructions for manipulating and querying bits within a word. This chapter demonstrates the application of these instructions in the construction of efficient parallel algorithm primitives such as reductions, scans, and segmented scans of binary or Boolean data.

3.1 INTRODUCTION TO PARALLEL PREFIX OPERATIONS

Scan (also known as parallel prefix sums), is a fundamental parallel building block that can form the basis of many efficient parallel algorithms, including sorting, computational geometry algorithms such as quickhull, and graph algorithms such as minimum spanning tree, to name just a few [1]. Given an input sequence of values

$$A = [a_0, a_1, a_2, \ldots, a_n]$$

and an arbitrary binary associative operator that we denote $\oplus$, the scan operation produces the output sequence

$$S = scan(\oplus, A) = [a_0, a_0 \oplus a_1, a_0 \oplus a_1 \oplus a_2, \ldots, a_0 \oplus \cdots \oplus a_n].$$

This scan is *inclusive* because each element s_i has accumulated values from all elements a_j where $j \leq i$. A related operation is the *exclusive* scan, where only elements with $j < i$ are accumulated:

$$X = exclusive\_scan(\oplus, p, A) = [p, p \oplus a_0, p \oplus a_0 \oplus a_1, \ldots, p \oplus \cdots \oplus a_{n-1}].$$

The exclusive scan operator requires an additional prefix value p, which is often assumed to be the identity value for the operator $\oplus$.

As a concrete example, applying inclusive scan with the $+$ operator to the input sequence [3 1 7 0 4 1 6 3] produces the result [3 4 11 11 15 16 22 25]; applying exclusive scan with prefix $p = 0$ to the same input produces the result [0 3 4 11 11 15 16 22].

In this chapter we focus on developing efficient intra-thread-block scan implementations, which are valuable in applications in which scan is used as an operator on local data. When the data are already in registers or on-chip memory, scan is generally instruction limited. A number of recent papers have explored the efficient implementation of global parallel prefix operations in CUDA [2–8]. In most cases, the operators used are simple arithmetic operations, such as integer or floating-point addition. These operators generally map to a single hardware instruction, and therefore the amount of work performed per element of the array is minimal. If the input and output arrays reside in external memory, the cost of transporting the data from external memory to on-chip registers and back dwarfs the cost of computation, and therefore the goal of most efficient GPU scan implementations has been to saturate the available memory bandwidth.

In a number of applications, the input elements are single bits with a value of zero or one. Alternatively, we can consider them to be Boolean predicates. There are two common operations on sequences of elements with corresponding Boolean true/false predicates: *stream compaction* (also known as *filter*), and *split*. Stream compaction removes all elements in the input stream that have false flags [6]. Stream compaction can be used, for example, to take a sequence of object collision test results and generate a sequence of pairs of colliding objects for computing collision response in a physics simulation. The split operation moves all elements with true flags to the beginning of the sequence, and all elements with false flags to the end. We can construct a radix sort for keys of arbitrary length by using the split operation on the sequence of keys by each of their bits in sequence from least to most significant bit [9, 10].

Because of the importance of binary scans, the architects of the NVIDIA Fermi GPU added some new operations for improving their efficiency. These operations allow the threads of a CUDA warp to compute cooperatively. The first is a new __ballot() intrinsic function for collecting "votes" from a warp of threads, and the second is a new scalar intrinsic called __popc() (short for "population count"). Using these new instructions we can construct efficient binary scans that execute fewer instructions and require much less shared memory than equivalent code that uses full 32-bit operations.

3.1.1 Intra-Warp Scan

Efficient scan implementations on NVIDIA GPUs frequently take advantage of the fact that the graphical processing unit (GPU) executes parallel threads in groups of 32 called warps. The threads of a warp execute in an Single Instruction, Multiple Data (SIMD) fashion, under which they collectively execute each instruction. The CUDA C code in Listing 3.1 shows how one might implement a parallel intra-warp scan primitive.

This function is tailored to operate within a warp in three ways. First, it assumes that the number of threads in a warp is 32, which limits the number of parallel steps to five. Second, because it assumes that the threads of a warp execute synchronously, it omits __syncthreads() that would otherwise be necessary when using shared memory. Finally, by padding the intermediate storage for each warp with zeros, it ensures legal indexing of the shared memory array without conditionals (note that this requires extra shared memory). The s_data variable is assumed to be a pointer to shared memory, and it must be declared volatile as shown to ensure that the stores to shared memory are executed; otherwise, in the absence of barrier synchronization, the compiler may incorrectly choose to keep intermediate values in registers. Because s_data is declared as volatile, it must be reread from shared memory on

```
__device__ int warp_scan(int val, volatile int *s_data)
{
    // pad each warp with zeros
    int idx = 2 * threadIdx.x -
        (threadIdx.x & (warpSize-1));
    s_data[idx] = 0;
    idx += warpSize;
    int t = s_data[idx] = val;

    s_data[idx] = t = t + s_data[idx - 1];
    s_data[idx] = t = t + s_data[idx - 2];
    s_data[idx] = t = t + s_data[idx - 4];
    s_data[idx] = t = t + s_data[idx - 8];
    s_data[idx] = t = t + s_data[idx -16];
    return s_data[idx-1];
}
```

Listing 3.1. CUDA implementation of an intra-warp exclusive plus-scan. Each calling thread passes a single input value to be scanned in val, and gets the resulting prefix element in the return value. The pointer s_data must point to __shared__ memory allocated large enough for two int values per calling thread.

every reference; therefore, a separate local variable t is required to keep the running sum in a register throughout the scan.

3.2 EFFICIENT BINARY PREFIX OPERATIONS ON FERMI

A central goal of CUDA is to enable cooperation among the threads in a block; this cooperation is very powerful because it enables collective parallel operations that are not bottlenecked by off-chip memory accesses. GPUs with Compute Capability 1.0 implemented the simple __syncthreads() barrier synchronization to allow threads within a block to cooperate via shared memory. Compute Capability 1.2 added a warp "vote" instruction that enabled two new intrinsics, __any() and __all(). Each of these functions takes a predicate[1] as input from each thread that calls it. __any() returns true to the calling thread if any thread in the same warp passes a true predicate, and __all() returns true only if all threads in the warp pass a true predicate. These intrinsics allow programs to make simple collective decisions within each warp.

Compute Capability 2.0, implemented by the Fermi GPU architecture, provides new instructions that enable more efficient implementation of reduction and scan operations on binary or Boolean inputs. We focus on the case where the operator in question is addition and the values held by each thread are predicates.

---

[1] We use the term *predicate* interchangeably for values which are (a) a single bit, (b) Boolean true/false values, or (c) integers that are either zero or non-zero.

3.2.1 Primitives Provided by Compute Capability 2.0

The CUDA C compiler provides a number of useful integer arithmetic functions that are supported on all CUDA devices (Appendix C.2.3, [11]). We use the following intrinsic functions to optimize parallel prefix operations.

`int __popc(int x)`   Population Count: Returns the number of bits that are set to 1 in the 32-bit integer x.

`int __clz(int x)`   Count Leading Zeros: Returns the number of consecutive zero bits beginning at the most significant bit of the 32-bit integer x.

On previous generations of NVIDIA processors, these intrinsic functions mapped to instruction sequences that are tens of instructions long. However, NVIDIA GPUs based on the Fermi architecture (Compute Capability 2.0) provide much more efficient support. In particular, the __popc() and __clz() intrinsics compile to a single machine instruction.

In addition to providing more efficient support for these integer arithmetic operations, Compute Capability 2.0 GPUs also introduce the capability to efficiently collect predicate values across parallel threads. The first such primitive that we use operates at the warp level.

`int __ballot(int p)`   Returns a 32-bit integer in which bit k is set if and only if the predicate p provided by the thread in lane k of the warp is non-zero.

This primitive is similar in spirit to the existing __any() and __all() warp vote functions. However, rather than computing a cumulative result, it returns the "ballot" of predicates provided by each thread in the warp. __ballot() provides a mechanism for quickly broadcasting one bit per thread among all the threads of a warp without using shared memory.

Finally, the Fermi architecture provides a new class of barrier intrinsics that simultaneously synchronize all the threads of a thread block and perform a reduction across a per-thread predicate. The three barrier intrinsics are:

`int __syncthreads_count(int p)`   Executes a barrier equivalent to __syncthreads() and returns the count of non-zero predicates p.

`int __syncthreads_and(int p)`   Executes a barrier equivalent to __syncthreads() and returns a non-zero value when all predicates p are non-zero.

`int __syncthreads_or(int p)`   Executes a barrier equivalent to __syncthreads() and returns a non-zero value when at least one predicate p is non-zero.

Every thread of the block provides a predicate value as it arrives at the barrier. When the barrier returns, the prescribed value is returned to every thread.

3.2.2 Implementing Binary Prefix Sums with Fermi Intrinsics

In this section we demonstrate the implementation and performance of efficient binary scans and segmented scans using the Compute Capability 2.0 intrinsics described in Section 3.2.1.

3.2.2.1 *Intra-Warp Binary Prefix Sums*

Consider the case in which every thread of a warp holds a single predicate. By combining the __ballot() and __popc() intrinsics, we can easily count the number of true values within the warp using the code shown in Listing 3.2.

We call this a binary reduction because the value held by each thread can be represented with a single bit. When the threads of a warp call this function, they each pass a single bool flag as an argument to the function. The __ballot() intrinsic packs the predicates from all threads in a warp into a single 32-bit integer and returns this integer to every thread. Each thread then individually counts the number of bits that are set in the 32-bit ballot using __popc(). This accomplishes a parallel reduction across all threads of the warp.

To compute the prefix sums of predicates across a warp requires only a small modification. Every thread receives the same 32-bit ballot containing the predicate bits from all threads in its warp, but it only counts the predicates from threads that have a lower index. The key is to construct a separate bit mask for each lane of the warp, as illustrated by the code in Listing 3.3.

For each lane k, lanemask_lt computes a 32-bit mask whose bits are 1 in positions less than k and 0 everywhere else. To compute the prefix sums, each thread applies its mask to the 32-bit ballot, and then counts the remaining bits using __popc(). By modifying the construction of the mask, we can construct the four fundamental prefix sums operations:

1. Forward inclusive scan: set all bits less than or equal to the current lane. (lanemask_le)
2. Forward exclusive scan: set all bits less than the current lane. (lanemask_lt)

```
__device__ unsigned int warp_count(bool p)
{
    unsigned int b = __ballot(p);
    return __popc(b);
}
```

Listing 3.2. Counting predicates within each warp.

```
__device__ unsigned int lanemask_lt()
{
    const unsigned int lane = threadIdx.x & (warpSize-1);
    return (1 << (lane)) - 1;
}

__device__ unsigned int warp_prefix_sums(bool p)
{
    const unsigned int mask = lanemask_lt();
    unsigned int b = __ballot(p);
    return __popc(b & mask);
}
```

Listing 3.3. Implementation of binary exclusive prefix sums within each warp.

3. Reverse inclusive scan: set all bits greater than or equal to the current lane. (`lanemask_ge`)
4. Reverse exclusive scan: set all bits greater than the current lane. (`lanemask_gt`)

Fermi hardware computes these lane masks internally and provides instructions for reading them, but doing so requires the use of inline PTX assembly. The `lanemask_lt` function in Listing 3.4 produces a lane mask in a single instruction, compared with four for the function in Listing 3.3. The PTX version is also more robust, because it is guaranteed to work correctly for multidimensional thread blocks. The source code accompanying this book includes a header that defines all four versions of `lanemask`.

We can extend the basic binary intra-warp scan (or reduction) technique to scans of multibit integer sequences by performing prefix sums one bit at a time and adding the individual results scaled by the appropriate power of two. For full 32-bit integers, the generic intra-warp scan shown in Listing 3.1 will outperform this approach. The bitwise scan requires one step per bit, but computes 32 results per step, whereas the generic intra-warp scan uses 32-bit arithmetic, but requires five steps to generate 32 results. The cost of one step of bitwise scan is four instructions, and for the generic scan it is three instructions. Clearly the generic scan will be faster for integers with more than about 4 bits, and our experiments confirm this.

3.2.2.2 *Intra-Warp Segmented Binary Prefix Sums*

Segmented scan generalizes scan by simultaneously performing separate parallel scans on arbitrary contiguous segments of the input sequence. For example, applying inclusive scan with the + operator to a sequence of integer sequences gives the following result:

```
         A = [ [3 1] [7 0  4] [1 6] [3] ]
segscan(A, +) = [ [3 4] [7 7 11] [1 7] [3] ]
```

Segmented scans are useful in mapping irregular computations such as quicksort and sparse matrix-vector multiplication onto regular parallel execution.

Segmented sequences augment the sequence of input values with a *segment descriptor* that encodes how the sequence is partitioned. A common segment descriptor representation is a *head flags* array that stores 1 for each element that begins a segment and 0 for all others. The head flags representation for the preceding example sequence is:

```
a.values = [ 3 1 7 0 4 1 6 3 ],
 a.flags = [ 1 0 1 0 0 1 0 1 ].
```

The intra-warp binary scan technique of Section 3.2.2 can be extended to binary segmented scan as demonstrated by the code in Listing 3.5. In addition to the predicate p, each thread passes a 32-bit hd

```
__device__ unsigned int lanemask_lt()
{
    unsigned int mask;
    asm("mov.u32 %0, %lanemask_lt;" : "=r"(mask));
    return mask;
}
```

Listing 3.4. Efficient lane mask computation using inline PTX assembly.

```
__device__ unsigned int warp_segscan(bool p,
                                     unsigned int hd)
{
    const unsigned int idx = threadIdx.x;
    const unsigned int mask = lanemask_lt();

    // Mask off head flags for lanes above this one.
    // We OR in the 1 because there's an implicit
    // segment boundary at the beginning of the warp.
    hd = (hd | 1) & mask;

    // Count # lanes >= first lane of the current segment
    unsigned int above = __clz(hd) + 1;

    // Mask that is 1 for every lane >= first lane
    // of current segment
    unsigned int segmask = ~((~0U) >> above);

    // Perform the scan
    unsigned int b = __ballot(p);
    return __popc(b & mask & segmask);
}
```

Listing 3.5. Implementation of intra-warp binary segmented prefix sums.

value that contains head flags for its entire warp.[2] __clz() is used to count the number of thread lanes greater than or equal to the thread's segment, and the count is used to compute a segment mask that is applied to the ballot along with the lane mask.

3.2.2.3 *Intra-Block Binary Reductions and Prefix Sums*

In CUDA programs, we often need to perform reductions and parallel prefix sums across entire thread blocks. Counting true predicates (a binary reduction) across an entire block simply requires a single call to __syncthreads_count(). We compared binary count using __syncthreads_count() to an efficient 32-bit parallel reduction [12]. We ran the test on an NVIDIA GeForce GTX 480 GPU using CUDA 3.1 on 32-bit Windows XP, with 512-thread blocks and a wide range of grid sizes. The __syncthreads_count() version is on average two times faster, as shown in Figure 3.1, and requires only a single line of code, compared with about 20 lines of code for the 32-bit parallel reduction.[3] __syncthreads_count() also uses no shared memory, whereas a 32-bit reduction uses 128 bytes per warp. As in the warp-level case, we can also use __syncthreads_count() to sum multibit integers by performing one reduction for each bit of the values, then scaling and adding the results together appropriately.

---

[2]Note hd can be computed from per-thread head flags using __ballot().
[3]Example code is included on the accompanying CD.

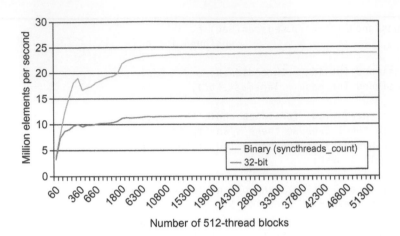

FIGURE 3.1

A performance comparison of intra-block binary counts (reductions) implemented with and without the Fermi __syncthreads_count() intrinsic.

```
__device__ int block_binary_prefix_sums(int x)
{
    extern __shared__ int sdata[];
    // A. Compute exclusive prefix sums within each warp
    int warpPrefix = warp_prefix_sums(x);

    int idx = threadIdx.x;
    int warpIdx = idx / warpSize;
    int laneIdx = idx & (warpSize - 1);

    // B. The last thread of each warp stores inclusive
    // prefix sum to the warp's index in shared memory
    if (laneIdx == warpSize - 1)
        sdata[warpIdx] = warpPrefix + x;
    __syncthreads();

    // C. One warp scans the warp partial sums
    if (idx < warpSize)
        sdata[idx] = warp_scan(sdata[idx], sdata);
    __syncthreads();

    // D. Each thread adds prefix sums of warp partial
    // sums to its own intra-warp prefix sums
    return warpPrefix + sdata[warpIdx];
}
```

Listing 3.6. Implementation of intra-block binary exclusive prefix sums.

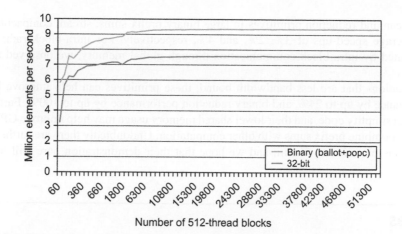

FIGURE 3.2

A performance comparison of intra-block binary prefix sums implemented with and without Fermi __ballot() and __popc() intrinsics.

In order to compute binary prefix sums across an entire thread block, we use warp-level prefix sums procedures as fundamental building blocks. We perform binary prefix sums within each warp independently, collecting the cumulative sums from each into shared memory. These partial sums are 5-bit integers, which we can combine with a single warp using either 5-bit binary prefix sums or generic 32-bit scan. As discussed in Section 3.2.2, for 5-bit integers, the generic 32-bit scan is slightly faster, so this is what we use in the code in Listing 3.6.

The main optimization that Fermi enables over previous architectures is the use of __ballot() and __popc() in the warp_prefix_sums() function. To measure the benefit of this optimization, we compared the code in Listing 3.6 to the same function modified to call warp_scan() rather than warp_prefix_sums() in step A. The relative performance of these two versions is shown in Figure 3.2 (The test configuration was the same as used for the binary reduction test of Figure 3.1.) The binary intra-block scan using hardware intrinsics is on average 24% faster than the 32-bit scan version, and the CUDA Visual Profiler shows that it executes about 31% fewer instructions. The binary scan with intrinsics also uses much less shared memory; only the single-warp call to warp_scan() in step C of Listing 3.6 requires shared memory, so at most 256 bytes of shared memory are needed per block, compared with 256 bytes *per warp* for a full 32-bit scan.

3.3 CONCLUSION

We have presented binary scan and reduction primitives that exploit new features of the Fermi architecture to accelerate important parallel algorithm building blocks. Often in applications that apply prefix sums to large sequences, bandwidth is the primary bottleneck because data must be shared between thread blocks, requiring global memory traffic and separate kernel launches. We experimented with binary scan and reduction primitives in large binary prefix sums, stream compaction, and radix sort, with average speed-ups of 3%, 2%, and 4%, respectively. For intra-block radix sort, which is not dominated by intra-block communication through global memory, we observed speed-ups as high as 12%.

For applications that are less bandwidth bound, these primitives can help improve binary prefix sums performance by up to 24%, and binary reduction performance by up to 100%. Furthermore, the intrinsics often simplify code, and their lower shared memory usage may help improve GPU occupancy in kernels that combine prefix sums with other computation. Undoubtedly there are further uses for the new instructions provided by Fermi, and we hope that their demonstration here will help others to experiment.

References

[1] G.E. Blelloch, Vector Models for Data-Parallel Computing, MIT Press, Cambridge, MA, 1990.

[2] M. Harris, S. Sengupta, J.D. Owens, Parallel prefix sum (scan) with CUDA, in: H. Nguyen (Ed.), GPU Gems 3 (Chapter 39), Addison Wesley, New York, 2007, pp. 851–876.

[3] S. Sengupta, M. Harris, Y. Zhang, J.D. Owens, Scan primitives for GPU computing, in: Graphics Hardware 2007, 2007, pp. 97–106.

[4] Y. Dotsenko, N.K. Govindaraju, P.-P. Sloan, C. Boyd, J. Manferdelli, Fast scan algorithms on graphics processors, in: Proceedings of the 22nd Annual International Conference on Supercomputing, ACM, 2008, pp. 205–213. http://portal.acm.org/citation.cfm?id=1375527&picked=prox.

[5] S. Sengupta, M. Harris, M. Garland, Efficient Parallel scan algorithms for GPUs, Technical Report NVR-2008-003, NVIDIA Corporation, 2008.

[6] M. Billeter, O. Olsson, U. Assarsson, Efficient stream compaction on wide SIMD many-core architectures, in: HPG '09: Proceedings of the Conference on High Performance Graphics 2009, ACM, New York, 2009, pp. 159–166.

[7] D. Merrill, A. Grimshaw, Parallel Scan for Stream Architectures, Technical Report CS2009-14, Department of Computer Science, University of Virginia, 2009.

[8] S. Sengupta, M. Harris, M. Garland, J.D. Owens, Efficient parallel scan algorithms for many-core GPUs, in: J. Dongarra, D.A. Bader, J. Kurzak (Eds.), Scientific Computing with Multicore and Accelerators, Chapman & Hall/CRC Computational Science (Chapter 19), Taylor & Francis, Boca Raton, FL, 2011, pp. 413–442.

[9] N. Satish, M. Harris, M. Garland, Designing efficient sorting algorithms for manycore GPUs, in: Proceedings of the 23rd IEEE International Parallel and Distributed Processing Symposium, IEEE Computer Society, 2009, pp. 1–10.

[10] D. Merrill, A. Grimshaw, Revisiting Sorting for GPGPU Stream Architectures, Technical Report CS2010-03, Department of Computer Science, University of Virginia, 2010.

[11] NVIDIA Corporation, NVIDIA CUDA Programming Guide, version 4.0. http://developer.download.nvidia.com/compute/cuda/4_0/toolkit/docs/CUDA_C_Programming_Guide.pdf, 2010 (accessed 27.07.11).

[12] M. Harris, Optimizing Parallel Reduction in CUDA. http://developer.download.nvidia.com/compute/DevZone/C/html/C/src/reduction/doc/reduction.pdf, 2007 (accessed 27.07.11).

Building an Efficient Hash Table on the GPU

4

Dan A. Alcantara, Vasily Volkov, Shubhabrata Sengupta,
Michael Mitzenmacher, John D. Owens, and Nina Amenta

Hash tables provide fast random access to compactly stored data. In this chapter, we describe a fast parallel method for building hash tables. It is both simpler and faster than previous methods: on a GTX 470, our implementation can achieve hash insertion rates of around 250 million pairs per second; a table containing 32 million items can be built in 130 ms and have all items retrieved in parallel in 66.8 ms. The key to this performance is minimizing the total number of uncoalesced memory accesses. We also discuss how to specialize the hash table for different situations and analyze our performance with respect to the hardware bottlenecks for uncoalesced memory access.

4.1 INTRODUCTION

Hash tables are one of the most basic data structures used to provide fast access and compact storage for sparse data. Data can typically be retrieved from a hash table using $O(1)$ memory accesses per item, on average. But this performance is achieved by using randomness to distribute the items in memory, which poses a problem on the GPU: uncoalesced memory accesses are an order of magnitude slower than sequential memory accesses. This forms a bottleneck for both hash table construction and retrieval.

In this chapter, we describe a fairly straightforward algorithm for parallel hash table construction on the GPU. We construct the table in global memory and use atomic operations to detect and resolve collisions. Construction and retrieval performance are limited almost entirely by the time required for these uncoalesced memory accesses, which are linear in the total number of accesses; so the design goal is to minimize the average number of accesses per insertion or lookup. In fact, we guarantee a constant *worst-case* bound on the number of accesses per lookup. Although this was thought to be essential in earlier work (such as our previous construction [1], or in Perfect Spatial Hashing [2]), it turns out to be important only in that it helps keep the average down, especially when many lookups are misses. Our previous construction also factors the work into independent thread blocks, makes use of shared memory, and reduces thread divergence during construction, but as this required more total uncoalesced memory accesses, it was not as effective a design.

One alternative to using a hash table is to store the data in a sorted array and access it via binary search. Sorted arrays can be built very quickly using radix sort because the memory access pattern of radix sort is very localized, allowing the GPU to coalesce many memory accesses and reduce their cost

39

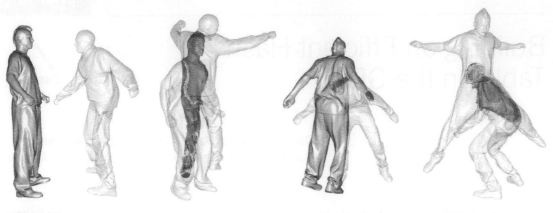

FIGURE 4.1

GPU hash tables are useful for dynamic spatial data. Shown here are four frames from an application performing Boolean intersections between two animated point clouds at interactive rates. Hash tables are built for both models' voxels every frame, then queried with the voxels of the other model to find surface intersections. A floodfill then determines which portions of each model are inside the other (see color insert).

significantly. However, binary search, which incurs as many as $\lg(N)$ probes in the worst case, is much less efficient than hash table lookup.

GPU hash tables are useful for interactive graphics applications, where they are used to store sparse spatial data — usually 3D models that are voxelized on a uniform grid. Rather than store the entire voxel grid, which is mostly empty, a hash table is built to hold just the occupied voxels. Querying the table with a voxel location then returns a positive result only when the voxel is occupied. This method is much more space-efficient and still allows all the lookups to be performed quickly. Example applications include volumetric painting [2] and collision detection between deforming models [1] (Figure 4.1). Hash tables are also useful in a GPGPU context for time-consuming matching algorithms. Many applications use hash tables as databases to find potential matches between different objects; two examples include image recognition and DNA alignment.

We provide an overview of our algorithm in Section 4.2, then go into the details of the construction of a basic hash table that stores a single value for each key in Section 4.3. We briefly describe how to extend our construction algorithm for more specialized hash tables in Section 4.4, then analyze the hash table's performance in Section 4.5. We conclude with future directions in Section 4.6.

4.2 OVERVIEW

We aim for a hash table that provides both fast construction and lookup of millions of key-value pairs on the GPU. Our previous work on GPU hash tables [1] had the same goals, but the method we present in this chapter is more flexible and efficient for modern GPUs, with superior construction time, lookup time, and memory requirements. Our solution is based on *cuckoo hashing* [3], which assigns each item a small, random set of slot choices for insertion (see Figure 4.2); each choice is determined by a different hash function. Items are moved between their choices to accommodate other items, but will

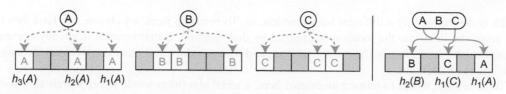

FIGURE 4.2

Cuckoo hashing uses multiple hash functions $h_i(k)$ to give keys a restricted set of insertion locations; in this case, each key may be placed in one of three locations indicated by the arrows (left). The algorithm finds a conflict-free configuration where each key is assigned its own slot (right), guaranteeing that any query can be answered within a constant number of probes.

always be located in exactly one location. The number of choices available for each item (typically three or four) is fixed for all items, guaranteeing that any item can be found after checking a constant number of slots.

This guarantee is one reason cuckoo hashing is a good fit for the GPU: when many threads each request an item from our hash table, we know that all of those requests will complete in constant time, keeping the average number of memory accesses per retrieval low. Another reason is that cuckoo hash table construction is efficient, allowing simultaneous insertion of many keys at the same time without the need for serialization. Moreover, it can be tailored for different situations: its parameters can be changed to balance between faster construction rates, higher retrieval efficiency, or tighter memory usage.

Although it is a probabilistic algorithm, cuckoo hashing has a high success rate for finding conflict-free placements; this counterintuitive result comes from its use of multiple hash functions. Essentially, moving the items during an insertion allows items to flow toward less contested slots of the table. Although these chains can be long once there are fewer slots available, we found that the median number of iterations required to insert any item was only one or two for our test cases.

Our hash table implementation inserts all items into the hash table in parallel. With our base configuration, the hash table uses $1.25N$ space for N items and allows each item four choices, guaranteeing that any item can be found after at most four probes.

4.3 BUILDING AND QUERYING A BASIC HASH TABLE

We begin by discussing the implementation of a basic hash table, which stores a single value for each unique key. The input consists of N pairs of 32-bit keys and values, where none of the keys are repeated. The value could represent indices into another structure, allowing a key to reference more than just 32 bits of data; we briefly discuss this in Section 4.5. In this section we describe an implementation that has an equal emphasis on construction time, lookup time, and memory usage, but Section 4.3.1 discusses trade-offs in our parameters that would allow more refined optimizations.

4.3.1 Construction

The construction process for a cuckoo hash table finds a configuration where each input item is inserted into a unique slot in the hash table. Each item is assigned a set of possible insertion locations, each of which is determined by a different hash function, h_i. To insert an item, we choose one hash function and insert the item into the location determined by that function. If that location is already occupied, we replace the item already there with our item, and then use the same process to reinsert the evicted item into the hash table.

To determine where to reinsert an evicted item, a serial algorithm would either search all possibilities until it finds an empty slot, or randomly select one of the hash functions. We choose a simpler approach, deterministically using each item's hash functions in round-robin order. An item evicted from slot $h_i(k)$ is reinserted into slot $h_{i+1}(k)$. When moved from its last slot, or when being inserted for the first time, the item uses $h_1(k)$.

This can result in chains of evictions, which terminate either when an empty slot is found (Figure 4.3) or when we determine it is too unlikely that one will be found. We allow several attempts to build the table in case of a failure. Three main parameters affect how often this occurs and how the table performs: the hash functions chosen, the size of the hash table, and the maximum number of evictions a single thread will allow. The failure rate can be driven arbitrarily low by tweaking these parameters, giving different tradeoffs in construction and access times.

4.3.1.1 *Parameters*

The hash functions $h_i(k)$ should ideally be tailored for the application so that they distribute all of the items as evenly as possible throughout the table. However, it is difficult to guarantee this for every given input. To achieve fast construction times, we instead rely on randomly generated hash functions of the form:

$$h_i(k) = (a_i \cdot k + b_i) \bmod p \bmod \textit{tableSize}$$

Here, $p = 334214459$ is a prime number, and *tableSize* is the number of slots in the table. Each h_i uses its own randomly generated constants a_i and b_i. These constants produce a set of weak hash functions, but they limit the number of slots under heavy contention and allow the table to be built successfully in most of our trials. We found that using an XOR operation worked better than multiplication

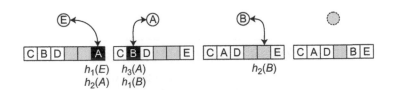

FIGURE 4.3

Insertion into a cuckoo hash table is a recursive process, where the table's contents are moved around to accommodate items being inserted. In this example, E needs to be inserted into slot $h_1(E)$ of the hash table (left), but the slot is already occupied by A. Cuckoo hashing swaps A and E and moves A to its next slot; in this case, A was evicted from slot $h_2(A)$, so it will move into slot $h_3(A)$. This process repeats until either an empty slot is found, or the algorithm determines that it is unlikely to find one (right).

at distributing the items for some datasets; the question of what implementable hash functions to use for cuckoo hashing for provable performance guarantees is a current research topic in theoretical computer science.[1]

Using four hash functions yields a good balance between all three metrics, though the hash table can be constructed with other numbers of hash functions. Using more functions allows each key more choices for insertion, making it easier to build the table and decreasing the construction time. However, this increases the average number of probes required to find an item in the table, increasing retrieval times. This is more obvious when querying for items not in the structure.

The size of the table affects how easily the construction algorithm can find a conflict-free configuration of the items. Given a fixed input dataset, bigger tables have less contention for each slot, reducing both the average length of an eviction chain and the average number of probes required to retrieve an item. Our experiments show that the fastest construction time is achieved using around $4N$ space, but this can be impractical for space-critical applications.

When memory usage is important, using more hash functions makes it easier to pack more items into a smaller table. Theoretical bounds on the minimum table size for differing numbers of hash functions were calculated by Dietzfelbinger et al. [5], but we found the smallest practical table sizes with our hash functions were slightly larger at $\sim 2.1N$, $1.1N$, $1.03N$, and $1.02N$ for two through five hash functions, respectively; our hash table uses $1.25N$ space, which limited the number of restarts and balanced construction and retrieval times.

The maximum number of iterations tells the algorithm when the insertion process is unlikely to terminate. Threads usually finish well before reaching a chain of this length, but the limit must be set carefully as it is the only way for the algorithm to terminate with a bad set of hash functions. Setting this number too high results in very expensive restarts, but setting it too low will cause the algorithm to declare failure too early.

There is no theoretical value for the limit, but it depends on both the table size and the number of items being inserted: cramming a large number of items into a small hash table greatly increases slot contention, resulting in longer eviction chains. For four hash functions and $1.25N$ space, we let threads follow chains of at most $7 \lg(N)$ evictions; for 32 million items, we saw an empirical restart rate of 0.56%.

4.3.1.2 *Building the Table*

Our hash table stores keys and their values interleaved, allowing key-value pairs to be retrieved with a single memory access. Each slot of the cuckoo hash table stores a 64-bit entry, with the key and its value stored in the upper and lower 32 bits, respectively.

Construction may require several attempts if the algorithm cannot find a conflict-free configuration of the items. Each attempt to build the table first initializes *cuckoo*[] with a special entry $\varnothing$, which signifies that the slot is empty; we used an item with a key of `0xffffffff` and value of zero. Random constants are then generated for all of the hash functions being used.

---

[1]See the original paper [3] for more on the theory and practice of the choice of hash function for cuckoo hashing, and subsequent work [4] for an analysis of why weak hash functions generally perform well in practice.

```
#define get_key(entry)            ((unsigned)((entry) >> 32))
#define make_entry(key,value) ((((unsigned long long)key) << 32) + (value))

// Load up the key—value pair into a 64—bit entry.
unsigned key              = keys[thread_index];
unsigned value            = values[thread_index];
unsigned long long entry = make_entry(key, value)

// New items are always inserted using their first hash function.
unsigned location         = hash_function_1(key);

// Repeat the insertion process while the thread still has an item.
for (int its = 0; its < max_iterations; its++) {
  // Insert the new item and check for an eviction.
  entry = atomicExch(&table[location], entry);
  key = get_key(entry);
  if (key == KEY_EMPTY) return true;

  // If an item was evicted, figure out where to reinsert the entry.
  unsigned location_1 = hash_function_1(key);
  unsigned location_2 = hash_function_2(key);
  unsigned location_3 = hash_function_3(key);
  unsigned location_4 = hash_function_4(key);
      if (location == location_1) location = location_2;
  else if (location == location_2) location = location_3;
  else if (location == location_3) location = location_4;
  else                             location = location_1;
};

// The eviction chain was too long; report the failure.
return false;
```

Listing 4.1. Inserting a new item into the hash table using four hash functions.

The cuckoo hashing algorithm is performed by a single kernel (Listing 4.1). The kernel is launched with N threads, each managing one item at a time from the input. Recall that threads complete their work when they successfully place their item (or the item(s) displaced by their item), but a thread block will not complete until all of its threads are done. Thus we choose a relatively small thread block size — 64 threads — that minimizes the number of threads within a block kept alive by a single thread's long eviction chain.

We treat key-value pairs as a single 64-bit entity, which keeps each value with its key throughout the entire process. An alternative would be to build the table using only the keys, but this would require a second pass to insert values into their proper locations. Using atomicExch() operations, each thread repeatedly swaps its current item with the contents of the slot determined by the current hash function. The atomic operations guarantee that no items are lost when threads simultaneously write into the same slot.

If the swap returned an $\varnothing$ item, the thread declares success and stops. Otherwise, the thread must reinsert the item it evicted. Because hash functions are used in round-robin order, the thread must figure out which hash function was previously used to insert it. It calculates the value of $h_i(k)$ for all of the hash functions, then checks which of those functions points to the slot it was evicted from. The evicted item is then reinserted using the next hash function in the series.

Our code snippet short-circuits after finding the earliest match, preventing the item from utilizing its full set of assigned slots when multiple hash functions return the same value. In practice, the rate of failure is unaffected, but it is an issue for tables containing only a few hundred items. This issue can be addressed either by advancing to the next function that doesn't point to the same location or by randomly picking a hash function to use.

We designate a failure by setting a flag when we reach the maximum eviction chain length, indicating that the table must be rebuilt from scratch. Once successfully built, we store the contents of the table, the number of slots in the table, and the hash function constants.

4.3.2 Retrieval

Retrieval of a query key can be performed by checking all of the locations identified by the hash functions (Listing 4.2). Each of the locations is then checked in order, either immediately returning the key's value as soon as it is found, or returning a "not found" value after all possible locations have been checked.

```
#define get_value(entry)  ((unsigned)((entry) & 0xffffffff))

// Compute all possible locations for the key.
unsigned location_1 = hash_function_1(key);
unsigned location_2 = hash_function_2(key);
unsigned location_3 = hash_function_3(key);
unsigned location_4 = hash_function_4(key);

// Keep checking locations until the key is found or all are checked.
unsigned long long entry;
if (get_key(entry = table[location_1]) != key)
  if (get_key(entry = table[location_2]) != key)
    if (get_key(entry = table[location_3]) != key)
      if (get_key(entry = table[location_4]) != key)
        entry = make_entry( 0, NOT_FOUND );

return get_value(entry);
```

Listing 4.2. Retrieving an item from the table using four hash functions.

4.4 SPECIALIZING THE HASH TABLE

The basic hash table can be specialized for different applications. In this section, we briefly describe some variations on the structure.

Sets are basic data structures for storing lists of nonrepeated elements; a typical operation is to check if some element is a member of the set. A hash table can be used to implement this because querying it with a key will indicate whether it was part of the original input. Construction of the hash table is modified slightly to work with just 32-bit keys so that each slot of the table contains only a key.

The input consists of 32-bit keys, which may or may not be unique. Similarly to the basic hash table construction, each thread manages a single key and uses 32-bit `atomicExch()` operations to swap their key with the contents of the table. The thread now stops if the slot was empty, or if the thread exchanged two copies of the same key. Once all threads have stopped, multiple copies of the same key may still be inserted in the table, so a cleanup phase must occur afterward to erase all copies of a key except the first.

Compacting hash tables extend sets, counting the number of unique keys in the input and assigning a unique ID to each as their value, effectively "compacting" the input. The compacting hash table consists of a hash table and a compacted list of the unique keys; this combination allows $O(1)$ translation between the IDs and the keys in both directions. It is most useful for memory-intensive applications where a lot of data is stored on a per-key basis: it determines how big an array is needed to store the data and directs each unique key to a different location in the array.

The cuckoo hash table is built just as they are for sets, but during the cleanup phase the first copy of each key in the table is assigned a value of one, with all other slots in the table filled with $\varnothing$. A prefix sum is then performed over the values, creating a unique value from 0 to $n-1$ for every unique key stored in the hash table, where n is the number of unique keys. We use another pass to interleave the keys with their values in the table, and finally create the compacted list by writing out each key to a separate array into the slot identified by its ID.

Multivalue hash tables are generalizations of the basic hash table that store multiple values for each key. As input, they take in one array of keys and one array of values, where each of a key's values is represented as different key-value pairs with the same key. Intuitively, the main goal during construction is to boil down the input to a single value for each key so that it can be stored using a basic hash table. The value here is a unique ID that indexes into an auxiliary array that stores more information about the key. This process can be adapted to store data other than 32-bit integers.

The multivalue hash table stores two auxiliary arrays: *sortedValues*[ ], which stores each key's values contiguously, and *keyInfo*[ ], which stores the location of every key's values and the number of values each has. Construction of the table is detailed in Algorithm 1; the majority of the algorithm is spent preprocessing the input. We first use a radix sort on the input pairs to rearrange the data, placing all copies of the same key adjacent in memory. Additionally, all values of each key end up in a contiguous location within their array; this array is stored as *sortedValues*[ ].

Next, we examine the sorted keys array to find the indices of the first instance of each key; these indices also indicate where in *sortedValues*[ ] each key's values start, and they can be differenced to determine how many values each key has. This information is stored in *keyInfo*[ ] as uint2s.

We then create a scratch array of flags indicating whether each key was unique, then perform a prefix sum to assign each key a unique ID. These unique IDs are used to index into *keyInfo*[ ] and to

---

Algorithm 1: Multivalue hash table construction

1: radix sort the input key and value arrays
2: determine what and where the unique keys are in the sorted key array
3: determine how many values each key has by differencing the locations of consecutive unique keys
4: perform a prefix sum to assign each key a unique ID
5: create an auxiliary array *keyInfo*[ ] to store the location and number of each key's values
6: create a basic hash table using the unique keys and their IDs

---

compact down the unique keys. The compacted list and their IDs serve as the input for the creation of a cuckoo hash table using the basic algorithm.

Querying the structure with a valid key first performs a retrieval using the hash table. The result is then used as an index into *keyInfo*[ ] to return information about the key's values.

4.5 ANALYSIS

4.5.1 Performance of the Basic Hash Table

To measure the performance of our hash table, we repeatedly measured the time taken to build and query it using the parameters we chose in Section 4.3. Our inputs consisted of increasingly larger sets of random 32-bit keys and values. Retrieval rates measured how long it took to retrieve all of the input data, with each retrieval performed by a different thread to mimic applications randomly accessing the data. We ran the same tests with two alternative GPU data structures: a array sorted with Merrill's radix sort implementation [6], and the two-level hash tables produced using our previous method [1]. Our tests were performed on a machine using CUDA 3.2 and the NVIDIA 260.24 drivers on an EVGA GTX 470 SC (Figure 4.4).

The sorted array uses exactly N space for N pairs and can be built at much higher rates than either hash table for large inputs. However, it is queried using $O(\lg N)$ binary searches; performance depends greatly on how well ordered the queries are. Retrieval times grow increasingly worse for larger sets because the memory reads were uncoalesced and many threads required the full set of probes.

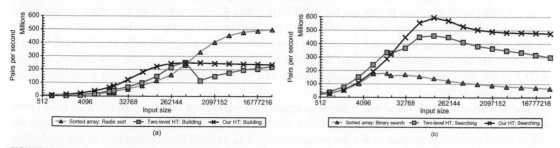

FIGURE 4.4

Comparison between insertion rates (left) and retrieval rates (right) for increasingly larger sets of random pairs of keys and values on the GTX 470. Higher rates are better.

The two-level hash table uses a total of $1.42N$ space. Its construction is faster than a radix sort for smaller inputs, but it becomes increasingly slower with larger inputs. However, it guarantees $O(1)$ random access into the structure, keeping the average number of probes required to retrieve an item below three. This method provides retrieval rates that are much faster than using binary searches, even though the probes are all uncoalesced.

Our single-level hash table has similar construction rates to the two-level hash table for large N, but uses only $1.25N$ space. However, ours is able to build at higher rates than the two-level hash table for smaller inputs (Figure 4.4). Moreover, when both tables occupy $1.42N$ space, the single-level hash table has a significantly higher construction rate for all input sizes since the algorithm encounters shorter eviction chains.

Except for inputs of size 16K or less, our retrievals complete more quickly than two-level hash table retrievals when the query keys all exist within the hash table. The likeliest reason is that the average number of probes for our retrieval is lower: the two-level hash table artificially limits the number of items that can be found with fewer probes, raising the average number of probes required to find an item.

The higher average is advantageous for the two-level hash table as its retrieval performance does not degrade significantly for failed queries. To test this performance, we built hash tables containing 10 million items then queried them with increasingly higher percentages of keys not in the table. The two-level hash table's retrieval timings linearly increase from 30 ms (when all queries are found) to 33.7 ms (when none are found). In contrast, our retrievals linearly increase from 20.5 ms to 41.6 ms because we use four probes in the worst case. When we use the same number of hash functions as the two-level hash table, our retrievals linearly increase from 19 ms to only 31.4 ms.

4.5.2 Hash Table Specializations

We tested the performance of our compacting and multivalue hash tables by repeatedly building them with datasets of a fixed size, but with an increasingly higher average number of times a key is repeated.

The compacting hash table was compared against two equivalent data structures: a structure based around sorted arrays and compacted lists, and our previous two-level compacting hash table [1] (Figure 4.5).

Both the single-level and two-level compacting hash tables take longer to build than the radix sorted structure; the biggest gap occurs when there are no duplicates in the list. These differences arise from the extra work required to process the input keys. Once there is some key repetition, construction times for both methods drop sharply. Although our single-level compacting hash table uses nearly the same algorithm, our faster cuckoo hashing procedure results in significantly smaller build times. Our retrievals also complete faster than the two-level version; until each key is repeated an average of 512 times, the combination of our construction and retrieval times is faster than using the sorted structure equivalent.

The multivalue hash table was compared against the equivalent two-level multivalue hash table, and a sorted structure based around sorted and compacted lists (Figure 4.6). To build the latter, we follow the construction procedure for the multivalue hash table until the construction of the hash table itself. Accessing the information for each key can then be done by employing binary searches rather than querying our hash table.

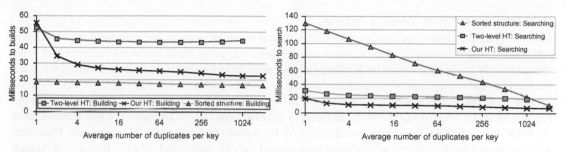

FIGURE 4.5

Compacting hash table timing comparison of construction (left) and retrievals (right) for inputs consisting of 10 million keys with increasing multiplicity on the keys. Each key was queried once for every time the key appeared in the input. Lower times are better.

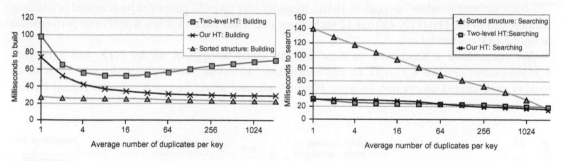

FIGURE 4.6

Multivalue hash table timing comparison of construction (left) and retrievals (right) for inputs consisting of 10 million pairs with increasing multiplicity on the keys. Each key was queried once for every time the key appeared in the input. Lower times are better.

Because construction of our hash table requires an additional step beyond construction of the sorted structure, our construction times are always slower. However, our retrievals are consistently faster than binary-searching the structure. Moreover, our hash table's size is dependent on the number of unique input keys, while the two-level version's size depends on the total number of input keys; as the average multiplicity of each key increases, the two-level multivalue hash table becomes more and more sparse.

4.5.3 Analysis of Performance Limits

We now focus our attention on the performance limits of our cuckoo hashing implementation. Because our implementation generates memory traffic that is largely random, we begin by discussing the performance bounds of random memory accesses on a GPU, then apply those lessons to our implementation. Finally, we compare our construction performance against that of radix sort.

How Fast Is Random Memory Access?

Modern dynamic random access memory (DRAM) and memory systems are optimized for workloads with substantial amounts of data access locality. However, good hash functions scatter input keys independently across the entire hash table, yielding very little locality. Given little locality, what are the limits to the throughput of our memory system?

Our hash tables are much larger than the GPU's cache, so given a random address stream, cache hits are unlikely. Thus (to first order), all memory accesses must go to DRAM. The pin bandwidth of the GTX 480 is 177.4 GB/s, so we could access 64-bit data no faster than 22.2 Gaccesses/s. However, with no spatial locality every access must be wrapped into an individual 32-byte transaction, which limits throughput to 5.5 Gaccesses/s.

From the DRAM side, the expected performance is even worse. With no spatial locality, we expect that each memory request will access a different page within each DRAM yielding an even tighter bound on the throughput of random memory accesses. For example, the 1 Gb GDDR5 DRAM from Hynix,[2] a DRAM of the same generation as the Samsung DRAMs used on the GTX 480, has a "32-bank activate window" (t_{32AW}) of 184 ns, meaning only up to 32 pages can be activated in a sliding window of 184 ns. The GTX 480 has 12 such chips, so DRAM page switches would limit performance to only 2.1 Gaccesses/s.

We constructed a benchmark to show that the actual throughput on the GTX 480 is roughly 1.3 Gaccesses/s (Figure 4.7, left). In this benchmark, we mimic successful hash insertion with no locality with strided access into an array. For an N-element array, we run N threads. Thread k reads

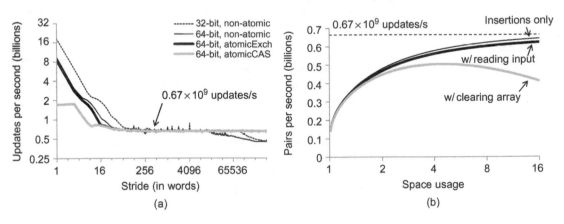

FIGURE 4.7

Left: Memory performance for strided access on the GTX 480. The array size is 512 MB. We used the `-Xptxas -cg` compiler option to enable 32 B memory transactions on reads. 32-bit `atomicInc`, `atomicExch` and `atomicCAS` performed similarly. The performance drop for nonatomic operations on the right side of the graph does not appear when the array size is under 256 MB. Right: Theoretical hash table construction updates per second on the GTX 480; our experimental results are consistent with these theoretical results.

[2]Hynix, "1Gb (32Mx32) GDDR5 SGRAM H5GQ1H24AFR", Rev. 1.0 / Nov. 2009.

an entry at location $k \cdot stride$ mod N of the array and overwrites it with a new value. Performing the read and write involves two memory accesses; we call this an "update." We choose a large stride that delivers no spatial locality and see that the access rate quickly converges to 0.67 Gupdates/s for both 32-bit/64-bit and atomic/nonatomic accesses. This GPU has an arithmetic throughput of 650 Ginstructions/s, so we can run up to 1000 instructions per memory update and remain memory bound. Consequently, arithmetic utilization and thread divergence have only marginal impact on hash performance.

How Many Random Accesses Does Our Hash Implementation Generate?

Most hashes, such as those based on chaining and open addressing, require at least one read and one write per hash-table element insertion. The read ensures that no previously inserted data is overwritten. The results of our benchmark suggests an upper performance bound of 0.67 Gpairs/s on the GTX 480.

In our cuckoo hashing implementation, we repeat insertions until no previously inserted key-value pair is evicted. How many iterations are done in total?

As an approximation, let us assume that parallel hashing does not involve more collisions than serial hashing. Then, for a table of size m, the probability of collision when inserting the kth entry is $p_k = (k-1)/m$. Using the well-known result for Bernoulli trials, we find that the expected value of the number of attempts required to find an empty slot is $1/(1-p_k)$. Summing this for $k = 1 \ldots N$ and approximating this sum with an integral, we conclude that roughly $-m \ln(1 - N/m)$ attempts are required to insert N entries. For example, only $2N$ attempts are needed if running in space $m = 1.25N$, i.e., twice the minimum.

To see how well this theory matches practice, we use it to estimate the runtime of the hash construction. Our runtime also includes reading N input pairs and initializing m table entries, both with aligned, unit-stride access. We extract the access costs from Figure 4.7, left, and get $T_{\text{uncoalesced}} = 1.5$ ns for an update operation and $T_{\text{coalesced}} = 0.05$ ns for a unit-stride read or write access. The estimate is then:

$$T_{\text{construction}} = -m \ln \left(1 - \frac{N}{m} \right) T_{\text{uncoalesced}} + (m + N) T_{\text{coalesced}}$$

The resulting rate $T_{\text{construction}}/N$ depends only on space usage m/N. This data is plotted in Figure 4.7, right, and is visually identical with our experimental results for N in the range of millions. The best performance (78% of the upper bound) is achieved with $4.5N$ space; half of the upper bound is achieved with $1.3N$ space.

Comparison with Radix Sort

Thus with these assumptions, hashing cannot sustain more than 670 Mpairs/s on the GTX 480. Surprisingly, radix sort achieves a higher rate of 775 Mpairs/s. Why is sorting, which does so much more work overall than hashing, faster than our hash table?

The answer lies in better spatial locality. Radix sort runtime is dominated by two kernels: the first reads keys contiguously and builds histograms, and the second reads the entire data set in contiguous blocks of 1024 entries and writes it out into 16 bins. Given that keys and values are in separate arrays, the average contiguous write size is 256 bytes per bin. This is substantially better than the 8 contiguous bytes per access we see in our hash table construction. The result is a radix sort implementation that achieves 70% of the theoretical maximum pin bandwidth, whereas our hash insertions sustain only 6% of this maximum.

4.5.4 **Limitations**

The algorithm we described and the parameters we chose strike a good balance between construction rates, retrieval times, and memory usage. However, there are still some drawbacks.

Retrieving a sorted set of queries can be optimized when using a sorted list structure because threads in the same warp will be likely to follow the same branches and are likely to have coalesced memory reads. Hash tables, in general, can't be optimized for these situations because they are designed to distribute items as evenly as possible across the structure.

Restarts are uncommon, but expensive because the entire table must be rebuilt from scratch effectively multiplying construction time by the number of attempts needed to build the table. If a consistent construction time is important, the parameters can be changed to make the table easier to build.

The maximum number of iterations can be hard to pin down. As the table size approaches the theoretical minimum for the given number of hash functions, the average number of iterations performed by the construction algorithm rises very quickly.

The compacting hash table becomes extremely sparse with high key multiplicity. If space usage is an issue, a procedure similar to the one followed for the multivalue hash table can be used, where the input is preprocessed using a radix sort. However, our construction can actually beat the radix sort times with smaller datasets; performing a radix sort beforehand will guarantee that construction is always slower.

4.6 **CONCLUSION**

We have presented a GPU hash table with a fast and parallel construction that provides random access at higher rates than binary searches through sorted arrays, despite the uncoalesced memory accesses inherent in hashing. Our design is more flexible than previous work on GPU hashes, allowing it to be tailored for different situations; the parameters we chose work well for general cases, striking a careful balance between the constraints of retrieval efficiency, construction time, and memory usage.

We see three major avenues for future work that will make GPU-based hash tables more useful for the community:

- We hope future work will use other hashing algorithms to address different tradeoffs, particularly to address building dense hash tables at fast rates and to optimize for the fastest possible lookup times.

- Our construction procedure could be extended to allow insertions into the table after the initial construction, but we avoided this in our implementation because of cases where an insertion fails. This would require rebuilding the entire table from scratch with the new items and could cause unpredictably large insertion times. Designing complex incremental parallel data structures for GPUs remains an active and interesting problem.

- We do not know how to handle input that exceeds the memory capacity of a single graphics card. Extending the algorithm to handle out-of-core input and multiple graphics cards is a challenging problem.

Acknowledgments

This research is supported by the National Science Foundation (Award IIS-0964473), Microsoft (Award 024263), and Intel (Award 024894), with matching funding by U.C. Discovery (Award DIG07-10227), and equipment donations by NVIDIA. Additional support comes from Par Lab affiliates National Instruments, NEC, Nokia, NVIDIA, Samsung, and Sun Microsystems. We also thank Daniel Vlasic for the 3D models.

References

[1] D.A. Alcantara, A. Sharf, F. Abbasinejad, S. Sengupta, M. Mitzenmacher, J.D. Owens, N. Amenta, Real-time parallel hashing on the GPU, ACM Trans. Graph. 28 (5) (2009) 154:1–154:9.

[2] S. Lefebvre, H. Hoppe, Perfect spatial hashing, ACM Trans. Graph. 25 (3) (2006) 579–588.

[3] R. Pagh, F.F. Rodler, Cuckoo hashing, in: 9th Annual European Symposium on Algorithms, in: F. Meyer auf der Heide (Ed.), vol. 2161 of Lecture Notes in Computer Science, Springer-Verlag, London, 2001, pp. 121–133.

[4] M. Mitzenmacher, S. Vadhan, Why simple hash functions work: exploiting the entropy in a data stream, in: S.-H. Teng (Ed.), SODA '08: Proceedings of the Nineteenth Annual ACM-SIAM Symposium on Discrete Algorithms, Society for Industrial and Applied Mathematics, Philadelphia, PA, 2008, pp. 746–755.

[5] M. Dietzfelbinger, A. Goerdt, M. Mitzenmacher, A. Montanari, R. Pagh, M. Rink, Tight thresholds for cuckoo hashing via XORSAT, in: P. Spirakis (Ed.), 37th International Colloquium on Automata, Languages and Programming, Springer-Verlag, Berlin, 2010, pp. 213–225.

[6] D. Merrill, A. Grimshaw, Revisiting Sorting for GPGPU Stream Architectures, Technical Report CS2010-03, Department of Computer Science, University of Virginia, 2010.

Acknowledgments

This research is supported by the National Science Foundation Award US 0926721, NSF Career Award 0133942, a CRA-W Distinguished Engineer...

References

Efficient CUDA Algorithms for the Maximum Network Flow Problem

5

Jiadong Wu, Zhengyu He, and Bo Hong

In this chapter, we present graphical processing unit (GPU) algorithms for the maximum network flow problem. Maximum network flow is a fundamental graph theory problem with applications in many areas. Compared with data-parallel problems that have been deployed onto GPUs, the maximum network flow problem is more challenging for GPUs owing to intensive data and control dependencies. Two GPU-based maximum flow algorithms will be presented in this chapter — the first one is asynchronous and lock free, whereas the second one is synchronized through the precoloring technique. We will demonstrate in this chapter that, with careful considerations in algorithm design and implementation, GPUs are also capable of accelerating intrinsically data-dependent problems.

5.1 INTRODUCTION, PROBLEM STATEMENT, AND CONTEXT

The maximum network flow problem is a fundamental graph theory problem. Given a directed graph with two distinct nodes, source and sink, and the capacity constraints on each edge, the problem aims to maximize the amount of flow that can be sent from the source to the sink. The maximum flow problem has many applications in different areas. For example, as a fundamental graph problem, it can be used to solve other graph problems such as disjoint paths, bipartite matching, and circulation with demand. It can also be used in some industrial applications like segmentation in image processing, routing in very large scale integration (VLSI) design and scheduling in air transportation.

Historically, multiple algorithms exist for the problem. Early solutions to the maximum flow problem are based on the augmenting path method due to Ford and Fulkerson [1], which was pseudo-polynomial and was later improved by carefully choosing the order in which augmenting paths are selected (e.g., the $O(|V||E|^2)$ algorithm by Edmonds and Karp [2] and the $O(|V|^2|E|)$ algorithm by Dinitz [3]). The concept of preflow was introduced by Karzanov in [4], which leads to an $O(|V|^3)$ algorithm. Goldberg et al. designed the push-relabel algorithm [5] with $O(|V|^2|E|)$ operations and further improved the complexity bound by using various techniques. Among those solutions, Goldberg's push-relabel algorithm is relatively easier to parallelize than other augmenting path-based algorithms, thus a few attempts have been made to parallelize it such as Anderson et al. [6] and Bader et al. [7]. Although these algorithms have demonstrated good execution speed on multicore processors, they share the common feature of using locks to protect every push and relabel operation in its entirety, which makes the algorithms unsuitable for the CUDA programming model.

The simplicity of CUDA's programming model, in fact, projects a number of challenges to design maximum flow algorithms for the multicore CUDA platform. First, CUDA does not natively provide a critical code section construct, which is essential to the correctness of the existing parallel maximum flow algorithms. It is possible to implement locks and critical sections in CUDA by explicitly using atomic memory operations. However, a study is needed to investigate the performance of such an approach. Second, multiprocessors in CUDA work in an Single Instruction Multiple Data (SIMD) fashion, where best performance is achieved when a warp of threads always takes the same execution path. Divergence among cores in the same multiprocessor results in serialization of the different paths taken and hence can cause performance penalties. The SIMD execution model becomes a significant challenge for any inherently divergent task, including the maximum flow problem.

To efficiently solve the maximum flow problem on CUDA, the algorithm should avoid using locks. In this chapter, we present two novel lock-free variations of the parallel push-relabel algorithm. The first algorithm solves the maximum flow problem by using atomic operations to perform the push and relabel operations asynchronously. The second algorithm works on precolored graphs and avoids race condition through barriers. Experiments using the NVIDIA C1060 GPU show that, despite the intrinsic challenges of data dependencies and divergent execution paths, both algorithms are able to achieve at least 3 times, and up to 8 times, speed-ups over implementations on a quad-core Intel Xeon CPU.

In this chapter we demonstrate that, with carefully designed algorithms and implementation techniques, we can use CUDA to accelerate complicated applications.

5.2 CORE METHOD

Maximum flow algorithms based on the push-relabel technique typically consist of two stages. The first stage searches for a minimum cut and the value of a maximum flow. The second stage constructs a valid maximum flow by returning possible excessive flows back to the source (the vertices may have excessive flow upon completion of the first stage). The complexity of the first stage is $O(|V|^3)$ or $O(|V|^2|E|)$ depending on the vertex processing order. The second stage uses $O(|E|log|V|)$ operations, which takes much less time than the first stage. For applications searching for the minimum cut such as some computer vision applications [8], the second stage is not needed at all. Because the first stage dominates the execution time, the study in this chapter will focus on the first stage. Before presenting the CUDA algorithms for solving the max-flow problem, we first present the problem formulation and briefly review the sequential push-relabel algorithm.

Given a direct graph $G(V, E)$ with source $s \in V$ and sink $t \in V$, in which every edge has capacity c_{uv}, the function f is called a flow if it satisfies $f(u, v) \leq c_{uv}, f(u, v) = -f(v, u)$ for $u, v \in V$. The residual capacity $c_f(u, v)$ is given by $c_{uv} - f(u, v)$, and the residual graph of G induced by f is $G_f(V, E_f)$ for $E_f = \{(u, v)|u, v \in V, c_f(u, v) > 0\}$: the same vertex set but only edges with residual capacity. Example of flows on a simple graph and its residual graph is given in Figure 5.1. The maximum flow problem is to search for function f which maximizes the value of $|f| = \sum_{v \in V} f(s, v)$.

The sequential push-relabel algorithm, due to Goldberg [5], moves flows from the source to the sink using localized operations. The source first *pushes* as much flow as possible to its neighbor vertices causing those vertices to temporarily have more incoming flows than outgoing flows. In the algorithm, a vertex v is called *active* when it has excessive incoming flows (i.e., $\sum_{u \in V} f(u, v) > 0$). The active

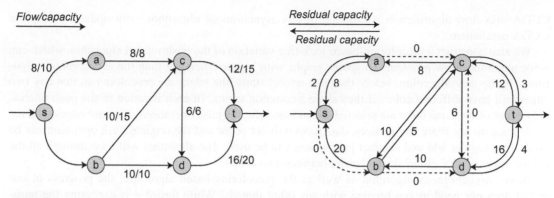

FIGURE 5.1

A flow f in graph G and the residual graph G_f. Dotted edges have 0 residual capacity and are therefore not part of the residual graph (see color insert).

vertices will be selected one at a time, in certain order, to push the excessive flows to their neighbors, thus *activating* more vertices. In this algorithm, each vertex is assigned an integer valued *label*, which is an estimate of the vertex's distance to the sink. The labels of the source and the sink are fixed at $|V|$ and 0, respectively. All the other nodes have an initial label of 0. Vertex labels are used to guide the push operations to move the flows towards the sink. A push operation always pushes to a neighbor with a lower label. If an active vertex cannot push any flow because it has a lower label than all its neighbors in the residual graph, the vertex will be *relabeled* to be one plus the minimum of all its neighbors. The algorithm repeatedly applies the push and relabel operations until there are no active vertices. When the algorithm terminates, flows will either be delivered to the sink or returned to the source, and the flows at the sink is the maximum flow of the graph.

The original push-relabel algorithm is a sequential algorithm designed for single-threaded execution. A straight-forward parallelization of this algorithm is to assign one thread for each node and let the threads do push-relabel simultaneously, but there will be race conditions if push and relabel operations are simultaneously applied to the same vertex. When such race condition occurs, two push operations may simultaneously and incorrectly modify the excessive flow of a single vertex, or a push operation may send flow to a vertex that is simultaneously being relabeled, thus violating the requirement that flow is always pushed to neighbors with a lower label.

To efficiently implement CUDA max-flow algorithms, the race conditions need to be handled without using locks. In a recent study, we proposed an asynchronous lock-free push-relabel algorithm targeting multicore processors, which will serve as a good starting point for a CUDA port. The algorithm differs from the original push-relabel algorithm in the following three aspects: (1) the push operation sends flow to the lowest neighbor rather than to an arbitrary lower neighbor; (2) each push and relabel operation is redesigned with multiple atomic instructions, thus eliminating the needs of locking the vertices; and (3) the termination condition examines the value of $e(s) + e(t)$ instead of the existence of overflowing vertices. These modifications allow the algorithm to be executed asynchronously by multiple threads, while the complexity $O(|V|^2|E|)$ stays the same as that of the original push-relabel algorithm. Detailed proof of correctness and complexity can be found in [9]. Our first

CUDA max-flow algorithm is a variation of this asynchronous algorithm, with updates to explore CUDA parallelism.

We also construct a precoloring-based lock-free variation of the push-relabel algorithm, which can solve maximum flow problems on spares graphs with higher efficiency than the asynchronous algorithm. In the new algorithm, before the push-relabel starts, the edges are precolored so that any two edges will have different colors if they share a common vertex. In each iteration of the push relabel, only edges of the same color are selected as candidates for the push operations. Because edges with the same color do not share any vertices, data races will not occur and the original push operation can be used; thus, regular add and subtract instructions can be used. The algorithm will loop through all the colors and execute a global thread barrier between two colors.

In our asynchronous algorithm as well as the precoloring-based algorithm, the progress at one thread does not need to synchronize with any other threads. While thread u is executing the push-relabel code for vertex u, all the other threads are executing the same code for their own vertices. Such properties expose maximum parallelism in the execution of the algorithm and makes the algorithm suitable for the CUDA programming model.

5.3 ALGORITHMS, IMPLEMENTATIONS, AND EVALUATIONS

The CUDA-based parallel push-relabel algorithm is presented in Algorithm 1, which has two important functions: push relabel and global relabel. Push relabel runs on CUDA. Global relabel is the heuristic running periodically on CPU, which improves the overall effectiveness of push and relabeling. We discuss the details of global relabel later in this section.

The initialization stage of the algorithm is to prepare c_f, h, and e based on the target graph. The algorithm will then enter the main loop (lines 3–8 in Algorithm 1), where the required data are first transferred to the GPU, and the CUDA kernel is then launched to concurrently execute the push and relabel operations. After the kernel executes a certain number of cycles, c_f, h, and e are transferred back to the CPU's main memory. The CPU will perform the global relabeling by calling global–relabel–CPU. The global variable *ExcessTotal* is used to track the total amount of excessive flow in the residual graph. The algorithm terminates when $e(s) + e(t)$ becomes equal to *ExcessTotal*, which is equivalent to the condition that no active vertices exist in the graph (except for the source and sink). The loop will be iterated repeatedly until the termination condition is satisfied. When the algorithm terminates, $e(t)$ stores the value of the maximum flow.

Algorithm 1: Implementation of the parallel push-relabel algorithm using CUDA

1: Initialize e, h, c_f, and *ExcessTotal*
2: Copy e and c_f from the CPU's main memory to the CUDA device global memory
3: **while** $e(s) + e(t) < ExcessTotal$ **do**
4:     copy h from the CPU main memory to the CUDA device global memory
5:     call push-relabel() kernel on CUDA device
6:     copy c_f, h, and e from CUDA device global memory to the CPU's main memory
7:     call global-relabel() on CPU
8: **end while**

The asynchronous push-relabel is presented in Algorithm 2. It uses read-modify-write atomic instructions that are supported by CUDA. The kernel launches one thread for every vertex (except for the source and the sink) and concurrently executes the push and relabel operations. Every thread will continuously perform push or relabel operations until the vertex u becomes inactive: $e(u) = 0$ or $h(u) > n$.

Algorithm 2 augments the original push-relabel algorithm by pushing to the lowest neighbor (whereas in the original algorithm, it pushes to any lower neighbor). It can be shown that even though different threads may execute their push and relabel operations in an arbitrary order, the kernel in Algorithm 2 eliminates the impact of data races and finds the maximum flow with $O(|V|^2|E|)$ operations.

Although the asynchronous lock-free algorithm is compatible with CUDA, the parallelization efficiency is affected by three factors: (1) the number of available push and relabel operations, (2) the overheads of data transfer between the CPU and the GPU, and (3) the efficiency of atomic operations on CUDA. In fact, the number of active vertices is often small for sparse graphs. Experiment results show that, for a Genrmf graph (see Section 5.4 for a description of the graph) with 262,144 vertices and 1,276,928 edges, although 262,144 threads can be launched simultaneously, there are at most 1,400 active vertices at a time. Most of the time, especially when the algorithm initially starts, only hundreds

---

Algorithm 2:   Implementation of asynchornous push-relabel kernel on CUDA device

---

1: $cycle = \text{KERNEL\_CYCLES}$
2: **while** $cycle > 0$ **do**
3:      **if** $e(u) > 0$ and $h(u) < n$ **then**
4:          $e' = e(u)$
5:          $h' = \infty$
6:          **for all** $(u,v) \in E_f$ **do**
7:              $h'' = h(v)$
8:              **if** $h'' < h'$ **then**
9:                  $v' = v$
10:                 $h' = h''$
11:             **end if**
12:         **end for**
13:         **if** $h(u) > h'$ **then**
14:             $d = \min(e', c_f(u,v))$
15:             $\text{AtomicAdd}(c_f(v',u), d)$
16:             $\text{AtomicSub}(c_f(u,v'), d)$
17:             $\text{AtomicAdd}(e(v'), d)$
18:             $\text{AtomicSub}(e(u), d)$
19:         **else**
20:             $h(u) = h' + 1$
21:         **end if**
22:     **end if**
23:     $cycle = cycle - 1$
24: **end while**

---

of vertices are active. Thus, many CUDA threads will be idle during the computation. In addition, Algorithm 2 needs to execute AtomicAdd and AtomicSub through the global memory, which is slower than the regular add and subtraction instructions executing inside the stream processors.

To overcome these limitations, another algorithm for push relabel is presented in Algorithm 3. Before the kernel starts, the edges are precolored so that any two edges will have different colors if they share a common vertex. In each iteration of the push-relabel kernel, only edges of the same color are selected as candidates for the push operations. Because edges with the same color do not share any vertices, data races will not occur, and the original push operation can be used; thus, regular add and

---

Algorithm 3: Implementation of precoloring-based synchronized push-relabel kernel

---

1: $cycle = KERNEL\_CYCLES$
2: **while** $cycle > 0$ **do**
3:    **if** $e(u) > 0$ and $h(u) < n$ **then**
4:       $lflag = 1$
5:       $e' = e(u)$
6:       $h' = \infty$
7:       **for all** $(u,v) \in E_f$ **do**
8:          $h'' = h(v)$
9:          **if** $h'' < h'$ **then**
10:            $lflag = 0$
11:            $v' = v$
12:            break
13:          **end if**
14:       **end for**
15:    **else**
16:       $lflag = 0$
17:    **end if**
18:    barrier();
19:    **for all** $cr \in COLORS$ **do**
20:       **if** $color(v') = cr$ and $lflag = 0$ **then**
21:          $d = \min(e', c_f(u,v))$
22:          $c_f(v',u) = c_f(v',u) + d$
23:          $c_f(u,v') = c_f(u,v') - d$
24:          $e(v') = e(v') + d$
25:          $e(u) = e(u) - d$
26:       **end if**
27:       barrier();
28:    **end for**
29:    **if** $lflag = 1$ **then**
30:       $h(u) = h(\text{the lowest neighborer of } u) + 1$
31:    **end if**
32:    $cycle = cycle - 1$
33: **end while**

---

subtract instructions can be used. The algorithm will loop through all the colors and execute a global thread barrier between two colors.

A graph can be colored using a simple greedy heuristic with $O(VE)$ operations. A reasonable amount of time will be saved in the later push-relabel stage. For example, a Genrmf graph with 2,515,456 vertices and an average vertex degree of 5 can be colored in 2 seconds with 11 colors, and the precoloring-based push-relabel algorithm takes about 60 seconds to compute its maximum flow, while the asynchronous push-relabel algorithm takes about 80 seconds to do it.

The efficiency of the global thread barrier (between two colors) needs some special consideration. Currently, CUDA threads within a block can communicate via shared memory or the global memory. In the CUDA programming model, the __syncthreads() function ensures in-block synchronization. However, there is no explicit support for inter-block barriers. Therefore, such a global thread barrier can be implemented only indirectly. CUDA enforces an implicit barrier between kernel launches. During kernel launch, a CUDA thread synchronize function is called implicitly on the CPU, which waits for all the threads in the previous kernel to complete. Alternatively, inter-block barriers can be achieved within the GPU by allowing threads to communicate via the global memory. Both lock-based and lock-free algorithms can be used for such a barrier. In the study by Shucai Xiao et al. [10], in-GPU barriers demonstrate relatively better performance over kernel-launch barriers only if the __threadfence() function is omitted. However, without a __threadfence() function, a thread arriving at the barrier may still have some pending memory operations waiting to be updated to the global memory, which breaks the correctness guarantee of barriers. In addition, according to the experimental results in [10], in-GPU barriers, even without using __threadfence() (which renders the barriers incorrect), will still be outperformed by kernel-launch barriers when the number of blocks exceeds the number of streaming processors. In the precoloring-based maximum flow algorithm, the correctness of the global barrier is critical, and the number of blocks needed is fairly large. As a result, in the implementation of precoloring-based algorithm, the global thread barrier is implemented by iteratively launching the kernels.

Previous studies suggested two heuristics — global relabeling and gap relabeling — to improve the practical performance of the push-relabel algorithm. The height h of a vertex helps the algorithm to identify the direction to push the flow towards the sink or the source. The global relabeling heuristic updates the heights of the vertices with their shortest distance to the sink. This process can be performed by a backward breadth-first search (BFS) from the sink or the source in the residual graph [11]. The gap relabeling heuristic developed by Cherkassky also improves the practical performance of the push-relabel method (though not as effective as global relabeling [11]).

In sequential push-relabel algorithms, the global relabeling heuristic and gap relabeling heuristic are executed by the same single thread that executes the push and relabel operations. Race conditions therefore do not exist. For parallel implementation of the push-relabel algorithms, the global relabeling and gap relabeling have been studied by Anderson [6] and Bader [7], respectively. Both implementations lock the vertices to avoid race conditions. The global or gap relabeling, push, and relabel operations are therefore pairwise mutually exclusive. Unfortunately, the lack of efficient locking primitives on CUDA makes such technology infeasible for the CUDA-based algorithms. Hussein [8] proposed a lockstep BFS to perform parallel global relabeling, but it was shown in [8] that this design was very slow. To overcome these obstacles, global relabeling is performed on the CPU side in this chapter. This is presented in Algorithm 4.

Algorithm 4: Implementation of global-relabel function on CPU

1: **for all** $(u,v) \in E$ **do**
2:     **if** $h(u) > h(v) + 1$ **then**
3:         $e(u) = e(u) - c_f(u,v)$
4:         $e(v) = e(v) + c_f(u,v)$
5:         $c_f(v,u) = c_f(v,u) + c_f(u,v)$
6:         $c_f(u,v) = 0$
7:     **end if**
8: **end for**
9: do a backwards BFS from sink and assign the height function with each vertex's BFS tree level
10: **if** not all the vertices are relabeled **then**
11:     **for all** $u \in V$ **do**
12:         **if** u is not relabeled or marked **then**
13:             mark u
14:             $ExcessTotal = ExcessTotal - e(u)$
15:         **end if**
16:     **end for**
17: **end if**

In Algorithm 4, global relabeling is performed by the CPU periodically. The frequency of global relabeling can be adjusted by changing the value of KERNEL_CYCLES. After every thread finishes KERNEL_CYCLES of push or relabel operations, c_f will be transferred from the CUDA global memory to the main memory of CPU along with h and e. If the termination condition is not satisfied, the global-relabel function will assign a new label for each vertex based on this topology of the residual graph (derived from c_f).

5.4 FINAL EVALUATION

To evaluate the performance of the presented maximum flow algorithms, we tested the CUDA algorithms on an NVIDIA Tesla C1060 GPU card and tested the pthread-based CPU algorithm on an Intel Xeon E5520 processor with four threads. The software environment is a Linux kernel version 2.6.18 with CUDA toolkit version 3.1. Both implementations were tested with five typical types of graphs which were also used in the first DIMACS Implementation Challenge [12].

1. Acyclic-dense graphs: These graphs are complete directed acyclic-dense graphs: each vertex is connected to every other vertex. Graphs of 2,000, 4,000, and 6,000 vertices were tested.
2. Washington-RLG-long graphs: These graphs are rectangular grids of vertices with w rows and l columns. Each vertex in a row has three edges connecting to random vertices in the next row. The source and the sink are external to the grid, the source has edges to all vertices in the top row, and all vertices in the bottom row have edges to the sink. We tested the graphs of $w = 512$, $l = 1,024$ (524,290 vertices and 1,572,352 edges), $w = 768$, $l = 1,280$ (983,042 vertices and 2,948,352 edges) and $w = 1,024$, $l = 1,536$ (1,572,866 vertices and 4,717,568 edges).

3. Washington-RLG-wide graphs: These graphs are the same as Washington-RLG-long graphs except for the values of w and l. Each row in the Washington-RLG-wide graphs is wider. We tested the graphs of $w = 512$, $l = 512$ (262,146 vertices and 785,920 edges), $w = 768$, $l = 768$ (589,826 vertices and 1,768,704 edges) and $w = 1,024$, $l = 1,024$ (1,048,578 vertices and 3,144,704 edges).

4. Genrmf-long graphs: These graphs are comprised of $l1$ square grids of vertices (frames) each having $l2 \times l2$ vertices. The source vertex is at a corner of the first frame, and the sink vertex is at the opposite corner of the last frame. Each vertex is connected to its grid neighbors within the frame and to one vertex randomly chosen from the next frame. We tested the graphs of $l1 = 24$, $l2 = 192$ (110,592 vertices and 533,952 edges), $l1 = 32$, $l2 = 256$ (262,144 vertices and 1,276,928 edges), $l1 = 44$, $l2 = 352$ (681,472 vertices and 3,342,472 edges), $l1 = 56$, $l2 = 448$ (1,404,928 vertices and 6,921,152 edges) and $l1 = 68$, $l2 = 544$ (2,515,456 vertices and 12,424,688 edges).

5. Genrmf-wide graphs: The topology is the same as Genrmf-long graphs except for the values of $l1$ and $l2$. Frames are bigger in Genrmp-wide graphs than in Genrmp-long graphs. We tested the graphs of $l1 = 48$, $l2 = 48$ (110,592 vertices and 541,440 edges), $l1 = 64$, $l2 = 64$ (262,144 vertices and 1,290,240 edges), $l1 = 84$, $l2 = 84$ (292,704 vertices and 2,928,240 edges), $l1 = 108$, $l2 = 108$ (1,259,712 vertices and 6,240,240 edges) and $l1 = 136$, $l2 = 136$ (2,515,456 vertices and 12,484,800 edges).

The experimental results are illustrated in Figures 5.2–5.4. In the figures, cpu-async stands for CPU-based asynchronous algorithm; gpu-async and gpu-color stand for asynchronous CUDA algorithm and precoloring-based CUDA algorithm, respectively.

Figure 5.2 shows the results on acyclic-dense graphs. gpu-async outperforms cpu-async by about three times. Better results of 4 times speed-ups are observed on Washington-RLG graphs as shown in Figure 5.3.

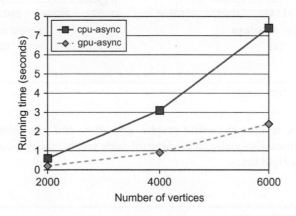

FIGURE 5.2

Experimental results on Acyclic-Dense graphs.

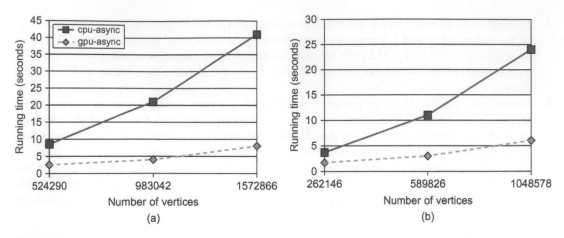

FIGURE 5.3

Experimental results on Washington-RLG graphs.

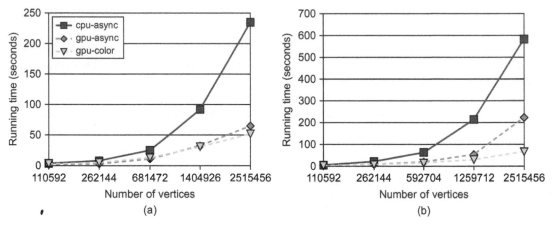

FIGURE 5.4

Experimental results on Genrmf graphs.

Figure 5.4 shows the results on Genrmf graphs. gpu-async and gpu-color still outperform cpu-async by at least three times. Especially on the Genrmf-wide graphs, the gpu-color algorithm achieved a speed-up of more than eight times.

5.5 FUTURE DIRECTIONS

In this chapter, we presented two efficient CUDA algorithms to solve the maximum network flow problem. The asynchronous lock-free algorithm exhibits good performance. And the precoloring-based algorithm is a reliable alternative, it outperforms the asynchronous algorithm for certain sparse graphs. This chapter presents a good example of the capacity and potential of multicore GPU parallel platforms in accelerating graph theory problems as well as other complex data-dependent applications. The performance can be further improved by incorporating various graph-specific techniques and by carefully allocating the vertex data in the global memory to coalesce memory accesses. Because a vertex may push flow to an arbitrary neighbor in a general graph, which will result in a random memory access pattern, we expect memory coalescing to be difficult for such graphs. However, we expect memory coalescing to work well for highly regular graphs with low-vertex degrees (where the storage of the adjacency list/matrix can be compact and regular).

The precoloring-based algorithm, as expected, does achieve higher efficiency and better scalability over the asynchronous algorithm for some sparse graphs. However, limitation also exists. For any graph, if the maximum degree of vertices is large, then we have to color it with a large numbers of colors. In such case, we will get little parallelism within each one of the colors, which affects the performance of this algorithm adversely. For example, although the Washington RLG graphs have an average vertex degree of 5, the source and sink in these graphs always have extrodinary large degrees. So, we cannot effectively apply the general precoloring-based algorithm on it. A possible way to overcome this limitation is to weigh the colors. Each color has a weight indicating how many vertices it has, and the weight is proportionally connected to the number of push-relabel iterations that will be applied.

References

[1] L.R. Ford, D.R. Fulkerson, Flows in Networks, Princeton University Press, Princeton, NJ, 1962.
[2] J. Edmonds, R.M. Karp, Theoretical improvements in algorithmic efficiency for network flow problems, J. ACM 19 (1972) 248–264.
[3] E. Dinic, Algorithm for solution of a problem of maximum flow in networks with power estimation, Sov. Math. Dokl. 11 (1970) 1277–1280.
[4] A.V. Karzanov, Determining the maximal flow in a network by the method of preflows, Sov. Math. Dokl. 15 (1974) 434–437.
[5] A.V. Goldberg, Recent developments in maximum flow algorithms (invited lecture), in: SWAT '98: Proceedings of the 6th Scandinavian Workshop on Algorithm Theory, Springer-Verlag, London, UK, 1998, pp. 1–10.
[6] R.J. Anderson, J.C. Setubal, On the parallel implementation of Goldberg's maximum flow algorithm, in: SPAA '92: Proceedings of the fourth annual ACM symposium on Parallel algorithms and architectures, ACM, New York, 1992, pp. 168–177.
[7] D. Bader, V. Sachdeva, A cache-aware parallel implementation of the push-relabel network flow algorithm and experimental evaluation of the gap relabeling heuristic, in: ISCA International Conference on Parallel and Distributed Computing Systems, Phoenix, AZ, 2005, pp. 41–48.
[8] M. Hussein, A. Varshney, L. Davis, On Implementing Graph Cuts on CUDA, in: First Workshop on General Purpose Processing on Graphics Processing Units, Boston, MA, 2007.
[9] B. Hong, Z. He, An asynchronous multi-threaded algorithm for the maximum network flow problem with non-blocking global relabeling heuristic, IEEE Trans. Parallel Distrib. Syst. 22 (6) (2011) 1025–1033, doi: 10.1109/TPDS.2010.156, ISSN: 1045-9219.

[10] S. Xiao, W. Feng, Inter-block GPU communication via fast barrier synchronization, in: IPDPS 09: IEEE International Parallel and Distributed Processing Symposium, Atlanta, GA, 2005, pp. 1–12, doi: 10.1109/IPDPS.2010.5470477, ISSN: 1530–2075.

[11] A.V. Goldberg, Recent developments in maximum flow algorithms (invited lecture), in: SWAT '98: Proceedings of the 6th Scandinavian Workshop on Algorithm Theory, Springer-Verlag, London, UK, 1998, pp. 1–10.

[12] D.S. Johnson, E.C.C. McGeoch (Eds.), Network Flows and Matching: First Dimacs Implementation Challenge, DIMACS Ser. Discrete Math. Theor. Comput. Sci. 12 (1993), American Mathematical Soc., Providence, RI.

Optimizing Memory Access Patterns for Cellular Automata on GPUs

6

James Balasalle, Mario A. Lopez, and Matthew J. Rutherford

A *cellular automaton* (CA) is a discrete mathematical model used to calculate the global behavior of a complex system using (ideally) simple local rules. The space of interest is tessellated into a grid of cells, and the behavior of each cell is captured in state variables whose values at any instant are functions of a small neighborhood around the cell. The dynamic behavior of the system is modeled by the evolution of cell states that are computed repeatedly for all cells in discrete time steps. CA-based models are highly parallelizable as, in each time step, the new state is determined completely by the neighborhood state in the previous time step. When parallelized, these calculations are generally memory bound because the number of arithmetic operations performed per memory access is relatively small (i.e., the arithmetic intensity is low). In this article, we present a series of progressively sophisticated techniques for improving the memory access patterns in CA-based calculations, and hence the overall performance. We utilize some common techniques encountered when developing CUDA code, including the use of shared memory, memory alignment, minimizing halo bytes, and ways to increase the computational intensity.

6.1 INTRODUCTION, PROBLEM STATEMENT, AND CONTEXT

CA-based simulations are common in fields as varied as mathematics, economics, earth sciences, public health, and biology, with applications ranging from models of bone erosion to the behavior of floods or forest fires, and from epidemic propagation to population growth [1–6]. Additionally, data access patterns similar to those required by CA are common in image processing and computer vision algorithms, such as the Gaussian blur and sharpening filters [7]. Because a cell's state is a function of a small number of neighbor values from the previous time step, CA calculations are highly parallelizable. Global dependencies among distant cells arise "spontaneously," as enough iterations of the local computations allow each cell to affect distant cells. Impressive speed-ups can be realized on high-performance platforms such as modern graphical processing units (GPUs), even using a straightforward, naïve port from a sequential CA implementation. However, as the arithmetic intensity (the ratio of arithmetic instructions to words of memory accessed) is low, the performance bottleneck of a CA-based calculation is typically memory bandwidth (the rate at which memory can be read from or written to global memory). Therefore, the main goal of this chapter is to describe different techniques for efficient memory access in memory-bound computations. Every CA will have a different specific set of calculations; here we are dealing with accessing the data upon which the calculations will operate.

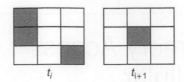

t_i t_{i+1}

FIGURE 6.1

Game of Life Cellular Automaton.

Figure 6.1 shows a simple 3-by-3 grid illustrating the states of the nine cells in two sequential time steps. The CA rules depicted in this figure are from Conway's Game of Life [8], a well-known and simple CA that we use as an example throughout this chapter. In the Game of Life, cells exist in one of two states: *alive* (black) or *dead* (white). The "neighborhood" of a cell consists of the eight cells immediately adjacent to it. Four simple rules determine the state of a cell in the Game of Life:[1]

1. Live cells with fewer than two live neighbors die (underpopulation);
2. Live cells with more than three live neighbors die (overcrowding);
3. Live cells with exactly two or three live neighbors live to the next generation; and
4. Dead cells with exactly three live neighbors become alive (reproduction).

In Figure 6.1, the cell in the center transitions from *dead* to *alive* through the application of rule number 4 while the alive cells at t_i transition to *dead* at t_{i+1} due to underpopulation (assuming cells outside the boundary are *dead*). As with all CAs, these rules are applied to each cell for every generation that is calculated — typically using two memory regions: one for the "current" state and one for the "next" state that are swapped as the system evolves over many generations. In the simple CUDA implementation of this algorithm, each thread calculates the state of one cell in the *next* array by accessing values in the *current* array (handling boundary values appropriately).

We are interested in cellular automata because of their use in many areas of science and engineering. In this chapter we use Conway's Game of Life (GoL) as an example because it is relatively simple to understand, has a compact rule implementation, and may be somewhat familiar to the reader. There are very fast GoL implementations (e.g., Hashlife [9]), that take advantage of patterns in the discrete cell states to avoid computing the states for all generations. Most CA applications in science and engineering use real numbers to store state values, and therefore, we do not explore this optimization here. Similarly, because the cell state for GoL can be represented using a single bit of information (i.e., alive or dead), dedicating an entire `unsigned int` to its storage is not optimal, but helps make the presentation more generally applicable.

6.2 CORE METHODS

Because of their inherent parallelism, CA-based computations translate quite easily to a straightforward GPU implementation that will immediately exhibit better performance than a conventional sequential or multithreaded implementation. However, in this chapter we are interested in improving the basic

---

[1]http://en.wikipedia.org/wiki/Conway's_Game_of_Life

implementation to make better use of the available hardware. The improvements presented here are targeted at several main aspects of the implementation: (1) utilizing shared memory to reduce redundant global memory accesses, (2) aligning memory for more efficient memory-bus usage, (3) minimizing halo bytes (bytes loaded to fill in the neighborhood around the cells being calculated) with non-square thread blocks and (4) improving the arithmetic intensity by computing multiple values per thread. These techniques are naturally applied in the order listed (e.g., before dealing with memory alignment, shared memory should first be utilized).

The basic CA implementation involves two global memory regions for each state value representing the **current** and **next** states for the region. For each generation, the kernel reads values from **current**, performs the necessary calculations using those values, and writes the new state value for one cell into the appropriate element of **next**. For the Game of Life, this means that nine values will be read (the cell's current state, plus the state of the eight surrounding cells), and one value will be written. For cells in the middle of the region, these values are accessed using straightforward array index calculations, but for cells on the boundary, either special logic to account for the fewer neighbors or a "halo" frame of cells must be provided. Although an implementation using conditionals to handle boundary cases may seem initially attractive, the conditionals do not actually reduce the memory transactions, but they do add instructions and branching. Therefore, using conditionals is not recommended. For simplicity of exposition, we consider only the scenario in which the boundary state values are constant, but some CA calculations instead use a region that "wraps," and boundary cell values come from the corresponding cell on the other side of the region (this calculation amounts to treating the domain as a torus). With a constant boundary, the main implementation technique involves storing these values in global memory in the halo around the actual data. This baseline implementation is discussed in Section 6.3.1. Given the overlap between cells accessed by threads in the same block, it is natural to use shared memory arrays to reduce these redundant loads. We explore shared memory in Section 6.3.2, and Section 6.3.3 addresses the performance benefits of properly aligning memory accesses of global memory. One effect of properly aligning memory access is that halo values on the sides of a thread block's region are loaded in their own memory bus transaction — a wasteful operation because a 32-byte transaction only supplies 4 bytes to the application. Reducing the number of rows in a thread block, but keeping the same overall size improves this situation. The performance impact of minimizing halo bytes is explored in Section 6.3.4. Finally, for a memory-bound calculation, it is logical to consider implementations that reuse index calculations and update multiple values per thread. This process is described in Section 6.3.5.

6.3 ALGORITHMS, IMPLEMENTATIONS, AND EVALUATIONS

In this chapter we are primarily concerned with what happens within the kernel execution. We ignore the overhead of memory copies between host and device as the small performance differences (for transfers of different size data arrays) is negligible for simulations involving a large number of generations.

6.3.1 Baseline Global Memory Implementation

In this chapter, the baseline implementation of GoL utilizes a single-cell halo around the entire region that, in our case, is initialized to "dead," and never updated. Listing 6.1 shows the kernel code for

```
1   __global__ void golPadded(unsigned int* current, unsigned int* next, int rWidth)
2   {
3     unsigned int row = blockIdx.y * blockDim.y + threadIdx.y;
4     unsigned int col = blockIdx.x * blockDim.x + threadIdx.x;
5     unsigned int idx = row * rWidth + col;
6
7     unsigned int liveCount
8       = current[idx - rWidth - 1] + current[idx - rWidth]
9       + current[idx - rWidth + 1] + current[idx - 1] + current[idx + 1]
10      + current[idx + rWidth - 1] + current[idx + rWidth]
11      + current[idx + rWidth + 1];
12
13    next[idx] = ( liveCount==3 ) || ( liveCount==2 && current[idx] );
14  }
```

Listing 6.1. Baseline GoL kernel using global memory and a one-cell halo around the region of interest. The halo eliminates the need for conditionals to handle edge cases.

this implementation. Lines 3–5 contain the common calculations for the row and column in the output matrix and then convert to the index in the one-dimensional arrays. Lines 7–11 calculate the number of living neighbors, and Line 13 implements the Boolean expression corresponding to the GoL rules. The benefit of the halo is evident in the simplicity of the live neighbor calculation — there is no danger of accessing memory outside the allocated region, so the positive and negative offsets can be calculated and used without further checking. This kernel accesses 10 memory locations per thread: 9 reads of the *current* array and a single write when updating the *next* state value.

When this kernel is used in a series of 100-generation simulations with region dimensions ranging from 160×160 to 1600×1600 cells, the Compute Visual Profiler reports a global memory overall throughput of about 145 GB/s and an instruction throughput ratio of 0.39, indicating that this kernel is, as expected, memory bound.[2] Note: the profiler reports the bandwidth seen on the memory bus that can be quite different from what is seen by the application code; we will return to this topic shortly.

6.3.2 Shared Memory Implementation

Building on the baseline implementation presented in the previous section, the first improvement is to reduce the number of redundant loads from global memory by utilizing shared memory as a user-managed cache. Within a rectangular memory region, most state values are used in the calculation of approximately nine cells (cells in the halo and on the edges are used to compute fewer than 9) so an implementation calculating 16×16 cells per thread block will need to perform 2,304 loads from global memory. In contrast, loading the values for the same 16×16 thread block into shared memory enables

---

[2]All performance numbers reported in this chapter are from a Linux server with dual quad-core Intel Xeon processors, 8 GB of RAM, and an NVIDIA GTX 285 GPU. The NVIDIA driver version is 256.35, and CUDA Toolkit version 3.1 is installed. The theoretical peak memory bandwidth of the GTX 285 is 155 GB/s.

the same 256 output values to be computed by reading only 384 (18^2) values from global memory — a sixfold reduction. We implement the loading of the shared arrays in a straightforward manner in which each thread loads its corresponding value, cells on the top and left side of the block load the halo values directly adjacent to them, and a few threads are selected to load the corner values.

Figure 6.2 shows the execution time and application bandwidth for 100-generation calculations of varying width. The baseline implementation is significantly slower, in absolute terms, than the shared memory implementation, as expected. The baseline application bandwidth is much higher than the shared implementation highlighting the memory pressure induced by this implementation owing to redundant loading of values from global memory.

6.3.3 Aligned Memory Implementation

The profiler reports a memory throughput of about 67 GB/s for the shared memory implementation, whereas Figure 6.2 indicates that the bandwidth seen by the application peaks at just over 30 GB/s. The profiler reports throughput seen on the memory bus, while our instrumentation computes the number of bytes read and written in the kernel per unit time. A large discrepancy between these numbers indicates that the interactions between the application code and the memory system are inefficient. Inspection of the alignment of the implementation confirms this inefficient interation as the culprit. Memory system transactions take place in chunks of 32, 64, and 128 bytes, so aligning the application access to these boundaries is critical (see Section 5.3 of NVIDIA's CUDA C Programming Guide [10] for more details). The addresses returned from cudaMalloc() (and related functions) are already aligned to 128-byte boundaries, but the use of the one-cell halo throws this off for the region at the core of computation. In order to align this region we do two things: (1) pad the beginning of the memory region so that the memory location associated with cell (0,0) falls on a 128-byte boundary, and (2) add padding to each row so that the beginning of subsequent rows also begins on a 128-byte boundary. These manipulations take place entirely in host code, and are therefore simple to apply.

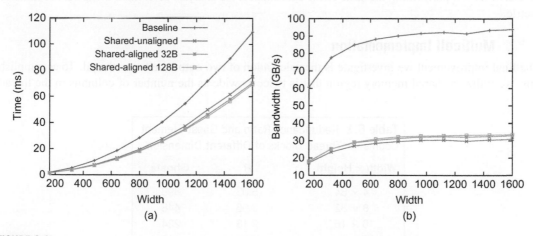

FIGURE 6.2

Plots of (a) total execution time and (b) application bandwidth for 100-generation calculations.

In Figure 6.2, data for three different alignments are shown: unaligned, aligned to 32-byte boundaries, and aligned to 128-byte boundaries. All three are significantly better than the global implementation, but the aligned versions are clearly superior to the unaligned one, with the 128-byte aligned implementation exhibiting the best performance.

6.3.4 Minimizing Halo Bytes

When we are aligning memory in the manner described in the preceding section, the main body of the memory region and the top and bottom halo rows are transferred across the bus in efficient 128-byte transactions, while the halo values on the sides are transferred inefficiently with an entire 32-byte transaction dedicated to each 4-byte halo value. This indicates that square thread blocks, those with the same number of rows and columns, may not be the most efficient way to utilize the memory bus.

In [11], Micikevicius introduces the concept of *memory access redundancy* as the ratio between the number of elements accessed and the number of elements processed. In a thread block with m columns and n rows, the redundancy ratio is calculated as:

$$R = \frac{m \times (n+2) + 2 * 8 * n}{m \times n} \tag{1}$$

In this equation, the 8 in the second numerator term represents the eight 4-byte values that come across with the left and right halo values, seven of which are "ghosts" that are not used by the application. Table 6.1 provides the redundancy values for thread-block dimensions that result in 256 threads. This table also lists the number of ghost elements transferred.

Although square thread blocks are typically the first thing tried by programmers, they actually are not optimal in terms of the memory bus utilization in this application. To investigate the impact of this, we implemented different shared-memory kernels for 256-thread blocks of the dimensions listed in Table 6.1. The performance data for the same series of 100-generation runs are shown in Figure 6.3. Clearly, the thread-block dimension makes a significant difference in terms of performance, with thread blocks of 64×4 performing the best. These data support the analysis performed using the redundancy metric.

6.3.5 Multicell Implementation

The final improvement we investigate is the calculation of two output cells per thread. To accomplish this, we utilize a shared memory region that is twice as wide as the number of columns in the thread

Table 6.1 Redundancy Ratio and Ghost Element Counts for Thread Blocks of Different Dimension

Width × Height	R	Ghosts
4 × 64	5.03	896
8 × 32	3.06	448
16 × 16	2.13	224
32 × 8	1.75	112
64 × 4	1.75	56

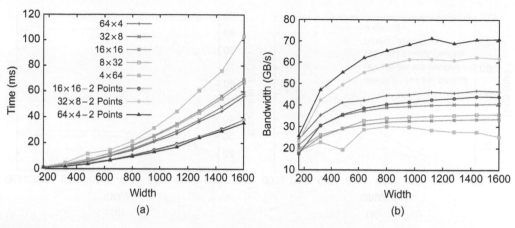

FIGURE 6.3

Plots of (a) total execution time and (b) application bandwidth for 100-generation calculations utilizing shared memory and 256-thread blocks of different dimensions (see color insert).

block — the results from the non-square region discourage the use of a shared region that is twice as high. In order to populate this larger shared memory region, each thread loads twice as many values from global memory, in the same pattern as described earlier. Once the data are in shared memory, each thread simply calculates two output cells, reusing virtually all of the index calculations. In concrete terms, the visual profiler reports that the 2-cell kernel executes just under 60% of the instructions that the 1-cell kernel does. This technique is scalable, as long as there is shared memory available to handle the wider regions.

Figure 6.3 shows the time and achieved bandwidth values for the 64×4, 32×8, and 16×16 2-cell implementations, the bandwidth is significantly higher, and the overall execution time for 100-generation calcuations is lower.

6.4 FINAL RESULTS

Figure 6.4 contains the performance numbers for each major incremental implementation described in this chapter. In absolute terms, the jump from global to shared results in a 30% faster execution of 100-generation calcuations. Aligning memory is a relatively minor improvement by itself, but it provides a means to minimize the halo bytes which results in a 20% reduction over the square thread block. Finally, going to the calculation of 2 output cells per thread results in a further 35% reduction. All told, the fastest implementation (64×4–2 Cell) is about 65% faster than the baseline implementation utilizing global memory.

In absolute terms, the global implementation has the highest memory bandwidth (and highest memory pressure owing to loading six times as many values from global memory), and the worst throughput, indicating once again, that these calculations are memory bound. Of the shared memory implementations, the 64×4–2 cell implementation has the highest memory bandwidth and exhibits the best throughput.

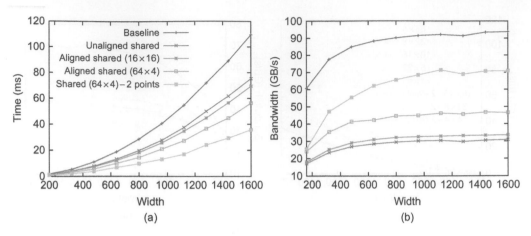

FIGURE 6.4

Plots of (a) total execution time and (b) application bandwidth for 100-generation calculations utilizing the various improvements described.

6.5 FUTURE DIRECTIONS

In this report we have described in some detail the specifics of the Game of Life. Applications of cellular automata are numerous and in widely different disciplines. In practice, each model has its own computational and memory requirements. In the future we need to evaluate the impact of CUDA on more application areas. In addition, the techniques outlined here may have an impact in other areas, such as computer vision, image processing, and finite element methods, all of which employ similar algorithmic "design patterns." For instance, various filters employed in image processing can be viewed as cellular automata with a limited number of iterations. Finite element methods, which are used to model complex physical systems, most often operate on irregular triangular lattices where the areas of greater interest are modeled using a finer mesh. In all of these, the need for keeping track of per-cell state based on that of a restricted neighborhood remains as the essential characteristic of the model. Finally, other computational paradigms, such as random walks, which on the surface may appear different from CA, may likewise benefit from the techniques outlined here. In a random walk, an entity navigates the space of interest by taking small steps whose nature is ruled by an underlying probability model. Such models are routinely used to simulate physical systems ranging from the behavior of porous materials to the distribution of photons in exploding stars. Because the models are usually computationally demanding, significant speed-ups enabled by multicore technologies would allow the scientist to efficiently explore different "what if" scenarios.

References

[1] J. Gómez, G. Cantor, A population scheme using cellular automata, cambrian explosions and massive extinctions, in: GECCO '09: Proceedings of the 11th Annual Conference on Genetic and Evolutionary Computation, ACM, New York, 2009, pp. 1849–1850.

[2] J. van Vliet, R. White, S. Dragicevic, Modeling urban growth using a variable grid cellular automaton, Comput. Environ. Urban Syst. 33 (1) (2009) 35–43.

[3] S. Al-kheder, J. Wang, J. Shan, Fuzzy inference guided cellular automata urban-growth modelling using multi-temporal satellite images, Int. J. Geogr. Inf. Sci. 22 (11) (2008) 1271–1293.

[4] J.L. Schiff, Cellular Automata: A Discrete View of the World, John Wiley & Sons, Inc., Hoboken, New Jersey, 2008.

[5] M.A. Fonstad, Cellular automata as analysis and synthesis engines at the geomorphology-ecology interface, Geomorphology 77 (2006) 217–234.

[6] G. Sirakouli, I. Karafyllidis, A. Thanailakis, A cellular automaton model for the effects of population movement and vaccination on epidemic propagation, Ecol. Modell. 133 (3) (2000) 209–223.

[7] M. Nixon, A. Aguado, Feature Extraction and Image Processing, second ed., Academic Press, London, 2008.

[8] M. Gardner, Mathematical games: the fantastic combinations of John Conway's new solitaire game "life", Sci. Am. 223 (1970) 120–123.

[9] B. Gosper, Exploiting regularities in large cellular spaces, Physica D 10 (1) (1984) 75–80.

[10] NVIDIA CUDA C Programming Guide, Version 3.1, 2010.

[11] P. Micikevicius, 3D finite difference computation on GPUs using CUDA, in: D. Kaeli, M. Leeser (Eds.), GPGPU-2: Proceedings of 2nd Workshop on General Purpose Processing on Graphics Processing Units, ACM, New York, 2009, pp. 79–84.

Fast Minimum Spanning Tree Computation

7

Pawan Harish, P.J. Narayanan, Vibhav Vineet, and Suryakant Patidar

In this chapter we present a GPU implementation of the minimum spanning tree (MST) algorithm for undirected graphs. Our application follows Boruvka's approach to MST computation in a recursive manner and lays irregular data-dependent steps in terms of primitive operations using parallel scan, segmented scan, and split to achieve the reported high performance. The adaptation also provides an outlook on exploiting data-parallel primitives for nontrivial data-dependent algorithms.

7.1 INTRODUCTION, PROBLEM STATEMENT, AND CONTEXT

Minimum spanning tree (MST) algorithms are useful as they find many tasks such as finding a minimum connected path across various components in very large scale integration (VLSI) design and several network routing problems [16, 20]. MST computation also aids in approximating solutions to the traveling salesman problem [12]. Consequently, this problem has attracted much attention of researchers, and several algorithms have been proposed for it.

The best sequential time complexity for MST computation, due to Chazelle, is $O(E\alpha(E, V))$, where α is the functional inverse of Ackermann's function [6]. Boruvka's approach to MST computation takes $O(E \log V)$ time [4]. Several parallel variations of this algorithm have been proposed [15]. Chong et al. [7] report an EREW PRAM algorithm with $O(\log V)$ time and $O(V \log V)$ work. Bader et al. [1] propose an algorithm for symmetric multiprocessors with $O((V + E)/p)$ memory accesses and local operations using p processors. Chung et al. [5] efficiently implement Boruvka's approach on an asynchronous distributed memory machine by reducing communication costs. Dehne and Götz implement three variations on the BSP model [9]. Blelloch [2] formulates a solution using the scan primitive. And Johnson and Metaxas [14] propose a variation of Boruvka's approach eliminating the need of supervertex graph generation. A GPU implementation similar to that of Johnson and Metaxas [14] using CUDA is also reported from our group [13], using irregular kernel calls.

In this work we formulate Boruvka's approach in a recursive framework, with each step implemented using a series of basic primitives [10, 19]. We reconstruct the supervertex graph in each step, which is given as an input to the next level of recursion. Boruvka's approach to MST is not data parallel and has irregular data access; a direct GPU implementation can thus suffer performance penalties. Mapping such steps to data-parallel primitives is central to the high performance gained in our implementation. We gain a speed-up of nearly 50 times over CPU execution and 8–10 times over our own irregular GPU implementation for various graph models and sizes. In the rest of this chapter, we introduce our approach and provide detailed information on each step. The use of efficient primitives to organize data for MST edge selection and supervertex graph generation is emphasized primarily. Experiments compare a sequential algorithm on the CPU, the irregular GPU algorithm, and our algorithm on various graph models.

7.2 THE MST ALGORITHM: OVERVIEW

Figure 7.1 summarizes Boruvka's approach to MST. Our recursive algorithm has two basic steps: marking MST edges and graph construction. Each step uses several data-parallel primitive operations. We primarily use three data-parallel primitives in our implementation: scan, segmented scan, and split. Scan and segmented scan implementations are taken from CUDPP [18]. We use our own implementation of the split primitive that scales linearly in the length of the key as well as the number of elements [17]. Split is a standard database primitive, bringing records of same key value together. This is a milder form of sorting. We use our implementation which handles arbitrary key/record lengths. We need to use a 64 bit split for MST.

- **Find MST edges:** The minimum outgoing edge from each vertex will be part of the final MST. We can identify this using a kernel that finds the minimum edge for each vertex in a loop as done in our previous work [13]. It can also be computed using a segmented minimum scan over an appended

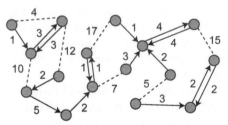

Each vertex finds the min. weighted edge to another vertex. Dotted edges are not selected.

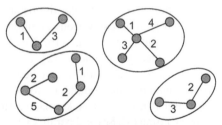

Vertices are merged into connected components called supervertices.

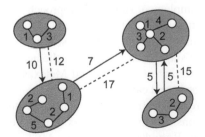

Supervertices are treated as vertices for next level of recursion.

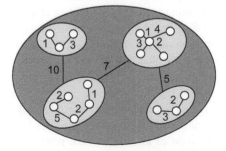

Terminates when one supervertex remains.

Cycle making edges are explicitly removed from the MST in each level of recursion.

FIGURE 7.1

Boruvka's approach to MST.

array that combines for each edge its weight and the id of the vertex it connects. This returns the minimum-weighted edge to the minimum vertex id for every vertex.

- **Remove cycles:** Cycles can form during the edge selection process, but only of length two. We break the cycles by eliminating one of the edges. No preference is given while selecting the eliminating edge since both edges have equal weights.
- **Create supervertices:** Vertices are combined to create a supervertex by traversing through their selected edges. Each vertex iteratively traverses its successor's sucessor until no further successor can be found. The terminating vertices are representatives of their respective connected components that form supervertices. We separate the vertices using their representative vertex id using the split primitive, to bring all vertices belonging to a same connected component together. Ordinal numbers are assigned to each supervertex using a scan on the output of the split operation.
- **Create the supervertex graph:** Next, we create the supervertex graph, which acts as input to the next level of recursion. Self and duplicate edges are pruned in order to create this representation. Self edges are removed by examining the supervertex id of both end points of each edge. Duplicate edges are removed using split operation on a list consisting of supervertex ids of both end vertices appended with the edge weight. A simple compaction, by selecting the first unique entry of the split operation output, results in new edge and weight lists. The vertex list is formed by scanning the new edge list followed by another compaction.

The new graph is given to the next level of recursion and the process is repeated until one supervertex remains.

7.3 CUDA IMPLEMENTATION OF MST

7.3.1 Graph Representation

We represent the graph using a compressed adjacency list format. We store vertices of the graph in an array V. We pack edges of all vertices into an array E, with each vertex pointing to the starting index of its edge list as shown in Figure 7.2. The weights are stored in an array W that is parallel to E. The initial graph is expected to be in this form. We create this representation in each recursive step for the supervertex graph.

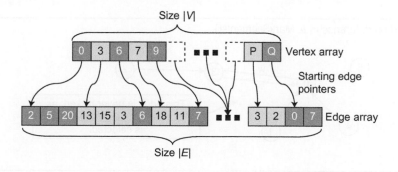

FIGURE 7.2

Graph representation.

7.3.2 Finding Minimum Weighted Edge

In the first step, each vertex u finds the minimum weighted edge to another vertex v. We use a segmented min scan for this step. We append the weight to the vertex ids of v, with weights placed in the most significant bits. We assume that weights are small, needing 8–10 bits, leaving 22–24 bits for vertex id of v. The limitation is due to the CUDPP scan primitive, which works only on 32-bit quantities today. A 64-bit scan primitive, however, would remove this limitation, resulting in greater range for both weights and vertex ids. The resulting integer array, X, is scanned with a flag array, F, specifying the segments. We use a kernel that runs over edges and computes F. It marks the first edge in the contiguous edge list for each u as shown in Figure 7.3. We use this operation, named *MarkSegments()*, at other places of the algorithm to mark discontinuities in other lists. A segmented min scan on X returns the minimum weighted edge and the minimum vertex id v for every vertex u. We store the index of this edge in the temporary array *NWE*.

7.3.3 Finding and Removing Cycles

Since there are $|V|$ vertices and $|V|$ edges, at least one cycle is formed during this step. Multiple cycles can also form, one for each connected component of vertices. Cycles in an undirected graph can be only of length 2, connecting two vertices in a connected component, because each vertex is given a unique id initially and the minimum of (*weight, v*) is chosen by the segmented scan (Figure 7.4). We use this property to eliminate cycles. We create a successor array S using the *NWE* array to hold the outgoing v for each u (Figure 7.5). Vertices with $S(S(u)) = u$ form cycles. We remove the edge from the lower of the ids of u and then remove $S(u)$ from *NWE* and set its successor to itself (Figure 7.6). Remaining vertices mark their selected edges in the output *MST* array as they will all be part of the final minimum spanning tree.

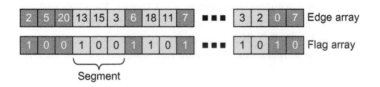

FIGURE 7.3

Segments based on difference in u, MarkSegments().

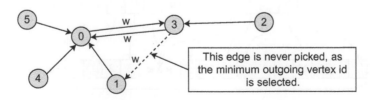

FIGURE 7.4

Cycles can only result between two vertices.

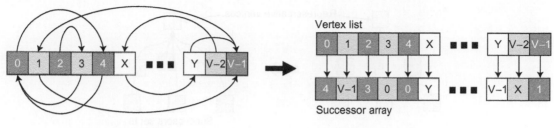

Per vertex successor

FIGURE 7.5

Creating the successor array.

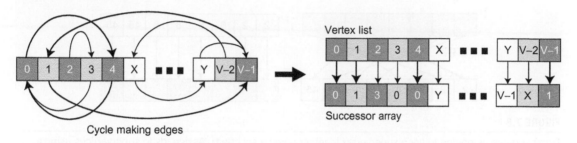

Cycle making edges

FIGURE 7.6

Updating successor array for cycle making vertices.

7.3.4 Merging Vertices

Next, we combine vertices to form a supervertex. We employ pointer doubling to achieve this result, iteratively setting $S(u) = S(S(u))$ until no further change occurs in S. Each vertex sets its value to its successor's successor, converging to the end vertex after a maximum of $log(l)$ steps, where l is longest distance of any vertex from its representative (Figure 7.7). The vertices whose successors are set to themselves are representatives for each supervertex. Each vertex points to its representative vertex after this step.

7.3.5 Assigning IDs to Supervertices

Each vertex of a supervertex now has a representative, but the supervertices are not numbered in order. The vertices assigned to a supervertex are also not placed in order in the successor array. We bring all vertices of a supervertex together and assign new unique ids to supervertices. We form a size $|V|$ list, L, of width 64 bits, with the vertex ids placed in the less significant word and the representative vertex ids in the more significant word. L is split using the representative vertex id as the key. This process results in vertices with same representatives coming together (Figure 7.8). This process, however, does not change the ids of representative vertices. We create a flag to mark the boundaries of representative vertices using *MarkSegments()*. A sum scan of the flag assigns new supervertex ids (Figure 7.8). These values are stored in an array C.

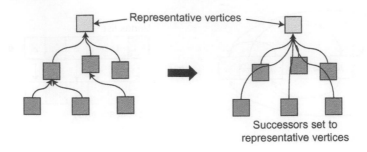

FIGURE 7.7

Pointer doubling gets to the representative vertex.

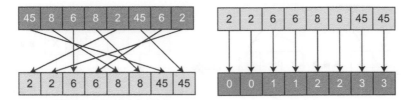

FIGURE 7.8

Bring vertices belonging to each supervertex together using a split (left). Assign ids to supervertices using a scan.

7.3.6 Removing Edges and Forming the New Edge List

We shorten the edge list by removing self edges in the new graph. Each edge examines the supervertex id of both end vertices and removes itself if the id is the same using a special kernel that runs on a grid of length $|E|$. For an edge (u, v), the supervertex id of v can be found directly by indexing C using the value part of the split output of v. The supervertex id of u requires another scan of size $|E|$ because the vertex list does not store the original id of u explicitly. To do this, we create a flag using *MarkSegments*() over the original edge list. Scanning the flag gives the original id for u, using which we can look up its supervertex id in the C array.

Duplicate edges between two supervertices may exist in the new set of edges even after removing edges belonging to the same supervertex. We eliminate nonminimal duplicate edges between supervertices to reduce the edge list further. We use a split operation on the remaining edge list for duplicate removal. We append the supervertex ids of u and v along with weight w into a single 64-bit array *UVW*, consisting of the new id of u (most significant 24 bits), the new id of v (next 24 bits), and the weight w (least significant 16 bits). We apply a 64-bit split on *UVW* array and pick the fist distinct entry for each uv combination. A sort operation can replace the split. The CUDPP radix sort doesn't support 64-bit sorting, but the split from our group scales to arbitrary key sizes [17].

We create a flag on the output of the split based on the difference in uv pair using *MarkSegments*(). This step gives the minimum weighted edge from the supervertex of u to supervertex of v. Scanning the flag array demarcating uv values returns the location of each entry in the new edge list. A simple compaction produces a new edge list (Figure 7.9), removing duplicate edges. We create a corresponding

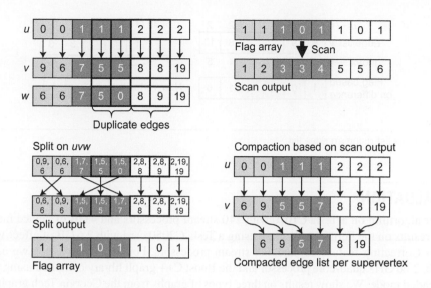

FIGURE 7.9

Removing duplicate edges based on a *uvw* split.

weight list in parallel to the edge list. We also store the original edge id of each edge while compacting entries into the new edge list. This mapping is used while marking an edge in the output MST array in subsequent recursive applications. The newly created edge list and the weight list act as inputs for the next recursive application of the MST algorithm.

Duplicate edge elimination is an optional operation because the MST algorithm works correctly even in the presence of multiple edges. However, the initial iterations usually have a large number of multiple edges, thus increasing the length of the edge list and making all edge-based operations slower. We therefore remove duplicate edges in the initial iterations. Later iterations do not require this step because the edge-list size decreases with iteration number.

7.3.7 Constructing the Vertex List

To create the vertex list, we need the starting index of each supervertex in the new edge list. We create a flag based on difference in *u* on the new edge list using *MarkSegments*(). Scanning this flag gives us the index of the location to which the starting index must be written (Figure 7.10). Compacting these entries gives us the desired vertex list.

7.3.8 Recursive Invocation

The vertex, edge, and weight lists constructed in the preceding sections represent the compact graph of supervertices. The same MST procedure can now be applied recursively on it. Because all edges in the reduced graph correspond to an edge in the original input graph, a mapping is maintained through all the recursive invocations. This mapping is used to mark a selected edge in the output MST array. The recursive invocations continue until a single vertex remains.

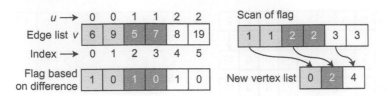

FIGURE 7.10

Creating the vertex list using an edge list.

7.4 EVALUATION

We test our algorithm on a Tesla C1070 with 240 stream processors and 4 GB of device memory. We also show results on the Fermi architecture using a Tesla C2050 card with 2.6 GB of effective memory (with Error Correcting feature on) and 448 stream processors. For CPU comparison we use an Intel Corei7 920, 2.66 GHz quad-core processor and the Boost C++ graph library compiled using gcc -O4 in single-threaded mode. We show results on three types of graphs from the Georgia Tech graph generator suite [3] and on the DIMACS USA road networks [11]:

- **Random graphs:** These graphs have a short band of degree where all vertices lie, with a large number of vertices having similar degrees.
- **R-MAT/Scale Free/Power law:** Large numbers of vertices have a small degree with a few vertices having a large degree. Performance on such graphs is of interest because they represent the structure of several real-life problems like social networks and virus multiplication [8].
- **SSCA#2:** These graphs are made of random-sized cliques of vertices with a hierarchical distribution of edges between cliques based on a distance metric.

We show results for graphs up to 5 million vertices with 30 million edges with a maximum weight range 1 to 1000 for the Tesla C1070 and up to 2 million vertices on the Tesla C2050 card, which has a smaller memory. We compare our results with a previous implementation from our group that uses irregular operations in place of the data-parallel primitives [13]. We achieve a speed-up of 2 to 3 for random and SSCA#2 graphs, and of 8 to 10 for R-MAT graphs on Tesla C1070 over the irregular implementation. A further speed-up by a factor of 2 is observed for C2050 over C1070. A speed-up of nearly 30 to 50 times over the CPU is seen on all graph models.

Section (a) of Figure 7.11 presents results for different graph sizes for the random graph model. The speed-up over the irregular algorithm is due to the elimination of atomic operations on the global memory. Comparing C1070 with C2050 timings, we see the irregular GPU algorithm performing well on Fermi. Section (b) of Figure 7.11 shows the behavior on varying degrees for the random graphs with 1M vertices. Increase in average degree per vertex does not slow down our implementation because the segmented scan scales logarithmically with the size of the longest segment.

Section (c) of Figure 7.11 shows the times on varying sizes of R-MAT graphs. The GPU implementation gains a speed-up of nearly 50 over the CPU and 8–10 over the irregular algorithm on C1070. The segmented scan finds the minimum weighted edge quickly even if there is large variation in segment sizes as is the case with R-MAT graphs. Varying the average degree of R-MAT graphs for a 1M vertex graph shows a similar speed gain (section [d] of Figure 7.11). Sections (e) and (f) of Figure 7.11 show results on the SSCA#2 graph model for different numbers of vertices and average degree, respectively.

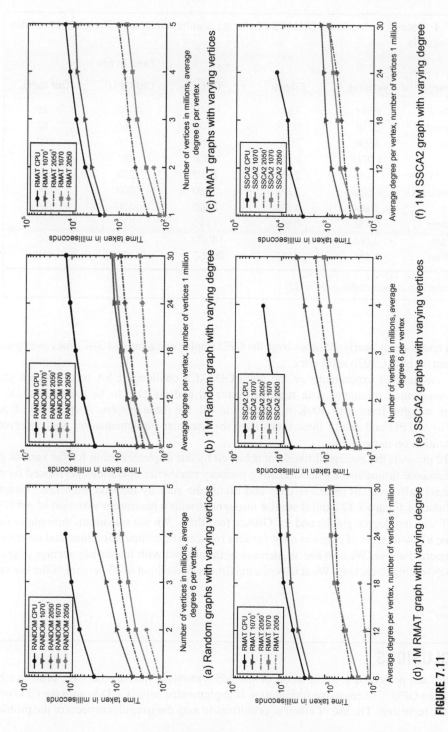

FIGURE 7.11

Running times on different sizes and average degrees for three types of graphs.

Table 7.1 Results on the Ninth DIMACS Challenge Graphs, Weights in Range 1–1K, Times in Milliseconds

USA Graph	Vertices	Edges	Time in ms		
			CPU	Old GPU[1]	Our GPU
New York	264K	733K	440	76	39
San Francisco	321K	800K	700	85	57
Colorado	435K	1M	750	116	62
Florida	1.07M	2.7M	3050	261	101
Northwest USA	1.2M	2.8M	2510	299	124
Northeast USA	1.52M	3.8M	3550	383	126
California	1.8M	4.6M	4560	435	148
Great Lakes	2.7M	6.8M	7140	671	204
USA - East	3.5M	8.7M	14000	1222	253
USA - West	6.2M	15M	26060	1178	412

[1] *Comparison with implementation given in [13].*

We achieve a speed-up of nearly 30 times over the CPU implementation and 3–4 times over previous implementation on both C1070 and Fermi.

Table 7.1 summarizes experiments on the ninth DIMACS challenge USA road network graphs. Because the segmented minimum scan requires vertex id and weights to be packed into 32 bits, we reduce the weights from 1 to 300K to range 1 to 1K for these graphs. A speed-up of nearly 10–50 times over CPU and nearly three times over the irregular implementation was observed for our implementation on these graphs.

Figure 7.12 presents the average throughput achieved by our implementation for the various graph models. We compute throughput by accumulating memory read/write operations performed by primitives and kernel calls over all recursive calls and divide the sum by the execution time. Graphs in a vertical column of Figure 7.12 exhibit similar throughput with a maximum variation of ±5 GB/sec for the RMAT varying degree graphs and ±2 GB/sec for others. We see maximum throughput for the RMAT graphs; a low number of edges at most vertices reduces the computation time and produces the throughput reported above. We also see an increase in throughput with increasing average degree per vertex on C2050 owing to caching. We achieved a maximum throughput of 43 percent of the theoretical bound.

7.5 CONCLUSIONS

In this chapter, we presented a formulation of the MST problem into a recursive, primitive-based framework on the GPU. The recursive formulation is implemented using CUDA, with the CPU used to synchronize the recursion. The use of efficient primitives to map the irregular aspects of the problem to

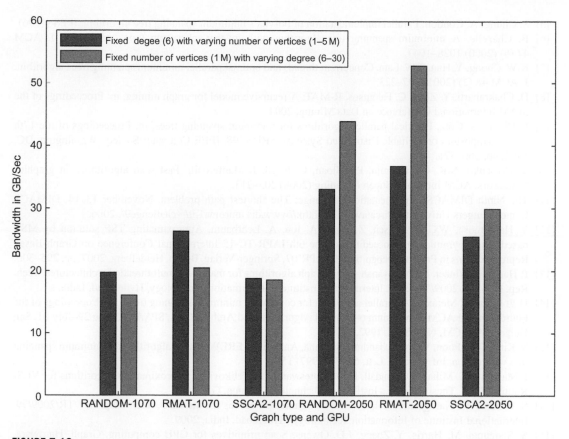

FIGURE 7.12

Average throughput achieved for various graph models on the C1070 and C2050 GPUs.

the data-parallel architecture of these massively multithreaded architectures is central to performance obtained. Optimized primitives can provide high speed-ups on such architectures. We achieved a speed-up of nearly 50 times over the CPU and 8–10 times over an irregular implementation on the GPU. We are likely to see more general graph algorithms implemented using such primitives in the near future.

References

[1] D.A. Bader, G. Cong, A fast, parallel spanning tree algorithm for Symmetric Multiprocessors (SMPs), J. Parallel Distrib. Comput. 65 (9) (2005) 994–1006.

[2] G.E. Blelloch, Scans as primitive parallel operations, IEEE Trans. Comput. 38 (11) (1989) 1526–1538.

[3] D.A. Bader, K. Madduri, GTgraph: A Synthetic Graph Generator Suite, https://sdm.lbl.gov/~kamesh/software/GTgraph/.

[4] O. Boruvka, O. Jistem, Problemu Minimalnım (About a Certain Minimal Problem) (in Czech, German summary), Prace Mor. Prirodoved. Spol. vBrne III (1926).

[5] S. Chung, A. Condon, Parallel implementation of borvka's minimum spanning tree algorithm, IPPS (1996).

[6] B. Chazelle, A minimum spanning tree algorithm with inverse-ackermann type complexity, J. ACM 47 (6) (2000) 1028–1047.

[7] K.W. Chong, Y. Han, T.W. Lam, Concurrent threads and optimal parallel minimum spanning trees algorithm, J. ACM 48 (2) (2001) 297–323.

[8] D. Chakrabarti, Y. Zhan, C. Faloutsos, R-MAT: A recursive model for graph mining, in: Proceedings of the SIAM International Conference on Data Mining, 2004.

[9] F. Dhene, S. Götz, Practical parallel algorithms for minimum spanning trees, in: Proceedings of the 17th IEEE Symposium on Reliable Distributed Systems, SRDS '98, IEEE Computer Society, Washington, DC, 1998, pp. 366–371.

[10] Y. Dotsenko, N.K. Govindaraju, P.J. Sloan, C. Boyd, J. Manferdelli, Fast scan algorithms on graphics processors, ACM Int. Conf. Supercomputing (2008) 205–213.

[11] The Ninth DIMACS implementation challenge: The shortest path problem, November 13–14, DIMACS Center, Rutgers University, Piscataway, NJ. http://www.dis.uniroma1.it/~challenge9/, 2006.

[12] Y. Haxhimusa, W.G. Kropatsch, Z. Pizlo, A. Ion, A. Lehrbaum, Approximating TSP solution by MST based graph pyramid, in: Proceedings of the 6th IAPR-TC-15 International Conference on Graph-Based Representations in Pattern Recognition, GbRPR'07, Springer-Verlag, Berlin, Heidelberg, 2007, pp. 295–306.

[13] P. Harish, V. Vineet, P.J. Narayanan, Large graph algorithms for massively multithreaded architectures, Tech. Rep. IIIT/TR /2009/74, 2009, International Institute of Information Technology, Hyderabad, India.

[14] D. Johnson, P. Metaxas, A parallel algorithm for computing minimum spanning trees, in: Proceedings of the Fourth Annual ACM Symposium on Parallel Algorithms and Architectures, SPAA'92, June 29–July 01, San Diego, CA, ACM, New York, 1992.

[15] V. King, C.K. Poon, V. Ramachandran, S. Sinha, An optimal EREW PRAM algorithm for minimum spanning tree verification, Inf. Process. Lett. 62 (3) (1997) 153–159.

[16] I. Mandoiu, K. Mihail, D. Randall, H. Venkateswaran, A. Zelikovsky, Approximation Algorithms for VLSI Routing, PhD. Thesis, Georgia Institute of Technology, Atlanta, GA, 2000.

[17] S. Patidar, P.J. Narayanan, Scalable split and gather primitives for the GPU, Tech. Rep. IIIT/TR/2009/99, International Institute of Information Technology, Hyderabad, India, 2009.

[18] S. Sengupta, M. Harris, Y. Zhang, J.D. Owens, Scan primitives for GPU computing, Graph. Hardware, (2007) 97–106.

[19] E. Sintorn, U. Assarsson, Fast parallel GPU sorting using a hybrid algorithm, J. Parallel Distrib. Comput. 68 (10) (2008) 1381–1388.

[20] P. Wan, G. Cǎlinescu, C. Wei Yi, Minimum-power multicast routing in static Ad Hoc wireless networks, IEEE/ACM Trans. Netw. 12 (3) (2004) 507–514.

Comparison-Based In-Place Sorting with CUDA

8

Hagen Peters and Ole Schulz-Hildebrandt

Although there are many efficient sorting algorithms and implementations for graphics processing units (GPUs) (merge sort [1], radix sort [1, 2], sample sort [3], quick sort [4], ...) none of them are both comparison-based and work in-place. The sorting algorithm presented in this chapter is a sorting algorithm for NVIDIA's GPUs that is both comparison-based and works in-place. It outperforms all other comparison-based algorithms known to the authors (all of them working out of place) for a wide range of sequence lengths and key types. Furthermore, it is also competitive to noncomparison-based algorithms. Because this algorithm is based on sorting networks, its performance is also independent of key distribution.

8.1 INTRODUCTION

The algorithm used in the implementation presented here is bitonic sort [5] invented by K. Batcher in 1967. Although the time complexity of this algorithm is $O(n \log^2 n)$, it is a widely used parallel sorting algorithm. Bitonic sort can be efficiently parallelized since it is based on a sorting network. Processing a sorting network in parallel requires a mechanism for synchronization and communication between parallel processing units. Using CUDA, those units are typically implemented by CUDA-threads.

In general, synchronization between arbitrary threads is not possible in CUDA; thus, to ensure a specific order of tasks, these tasks have to be executed in consecutive kernel launches. "Communication" among consecutive kernel launches is obtained by writing to (persistent) global GPU memory.

We focused on two main aspects when implementing bitonic sort for NVIDIAs GPUs:

1. Reducing communication and synchronization induced by bitonic sort in order to reduce the number of kernel launches and accesses to global memory.
2. Extensively using the shared memory and efficient inner-block synchronization. This results in a decreased number of kernel launches and global memory accesses.

8.2 BITONIC SORT

Figure 8.1 shows the bitonic sorting network for input sequences of length 8. The numbered horizontal lines represent data lanes, and the arrows represent the compare/exchange operations. A compare/exchange operation compares the data of two lanes, and the greater data is shifted to the

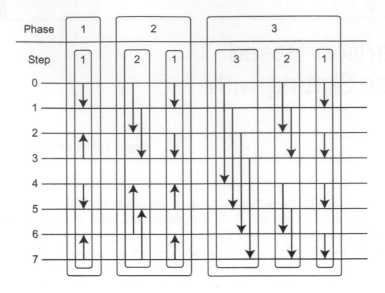

FIGURE 8.1

Bitonic sorting network.

arrowhead. A bitonic sorting network for sequences of length 2^k consists of k phases $1,\ldots,k$ and each phase p consists of p steps $p, p-1, \ldots, 1$, thus the total number of steps is

$$\sum_{i=1}^{k} i = \frac{k \cdot (k+1)}{2} \tag{1}$$

Roughly speaking the data traverses from the left to the right on the lanes and is compared and exchanged by each arrow it encounters. The number and order of operations processed in sorting networks is independent of data values, thus sorting networks can easily be implemented on parallel architectures. The only assertion that has to be ensured is that before a compare/exchange operation relating to data elements x_i and x_j in any step s is processed, both compare/exchange operations relating to x_i and x_j in the preceding step $s+1$ must have been processed. In bitonic sort each step consists of $\frac{n}{2}$ compare/exchange operations.

8.3 IMPLEMENTATION

8.3.1 Basic Approach

In a basic CUDA-implementation one thread processes one compare/exchange operation of one step of one phase. In this case the assertion mentioned in the preceding section is ensured by stepwise processing the steps of the sorting network; that is, processing all compare/exchange operations of any step s before any compare/exchange operation of the next step $s-1$ is processed. After each step s, all threads have to be synchronized and data has to be communicated between threads. Because synchronization between arbitrary threads is not possible in CUDA, this results in using multiple kernel launches and storing temporary data in global memory to ensure a specific order of computations.

Thus, sorting a sequence of length $n = 2^k$ residing in GPU global memory results in a sequence of $(k \cdot (k+1))/2$ kernel launches, each launch processing all compare/exchange operations of one step of one phase. Each of these kernel launches consists of 2^{k-1} threads, each thread processing one compare/exchange operation, reading and writing related data elements from and to global memory.

Figure 8.2a illustrates this approach. Step 3 in phase 3 is processed in one single-kernel launch using four threads, each thread reading two data-elements (lanes {0,4}, {1,5}, {2,6}, {3,7}) from global memory and processing one out of the four compare/exchange operations. After processing, the data-elements are written to global memory.

This basic implementation provides a good utilization of the GPU because many threads can process in parallel, and memory accesses and workload are uniformly distributed among threads. The main disadvantage is a high number of global memory accesses that increases the runtime of the algorithm. All operations of one step are processed in an individual kernel launch, and thus, each step implies n read/write accesses to global memory. Therefore the total number of accesses to global memory is

$$2 \cdot n \cdot \frac{k \cdot (k+1)}{2} = n \cdot k \cdot (k+1) \tag{2}$$

Thus, the basic implementation is memory bandwith bound (e.g., when sorting a sequence of length 2^{20} there are 420 accesses per element). Furthermore, the access pattern to global memory is awkward in smaller steps causing non-coalesced memory accesses. That results in a lower memory throughput from an application point of view than from a hardware point of view (e.g., 77 GB/s vs. 110 GB/s when sorting 2^{20} 32-bit integer using a GTX280).

8.3.2 Reducing Global Memory Accesses

Our approach to reduce communication and synchronization is to let one thread process compare/exchange operations of more than one consecutive step. To ensure correctness one thread has to process a set of compare/exchange operations of a particular step such that there exist compare/exchange operations in the following step that are related to exactly the same data elements. We define a *job* to be such a set of compare/exchange operations of one or more steps.

Figure 8.2b illustrates for this approach. The compare/exchange operations of steps 3 and 2 of phase 3 are divided into two jobs, one marked by dashed lines and arrows, the other marked by dotted lines and arrows. Each job consists of two compare/exchange operations in both steps 3 and 2 relating to exactly the same four data elements. The data elements of the one job are not accessed by the other job and vice versa. Thus, a thread that processes both operations of one job in step 3 can afterward also process both operations in step 2. Using this approach there is no synchronization or communication among threads needed between step 3 and step 2. While the thread processes four operations of two steps, the elements reside in thread-local registers; thus, the elements are read and written only once from and to global memory for processing two steps (and not twice as in the basic implementation, Figure 8.2a).

In the example in Figure 8.2b the compare/exchange operations of two consecutive steps are partitioned into jobs such that these two consecutive steps can be executed within one single-kernel launch. This approach can be extended. In case of sorting 32- or 64-bit keys, we used jobs allowing up to

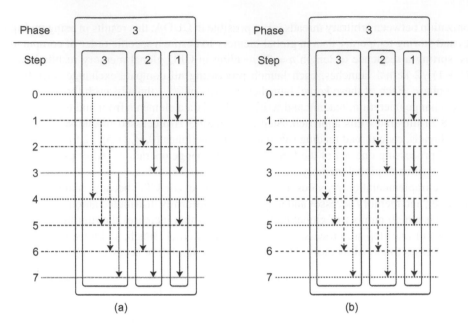

FIGURE 8.2

(a) Basic implementation. (b) Advanced implementation.

four consecutive steps to be executed within one single-kernel launch, nearly quartering the number of accesses to global memory.

Hypothetically speaking, we note that this approach could be extended to allow any number t of consecutive steps to be executed in one kernel launch. However, given a sequence of length $n = 2^k$, executing t consecutive steps in one kernel launch uses $\frac{n}{2^t}$ threads, each thread storing 2^t data elements in thread local registers. On the one hand the number of thread local registers is limited, and on the other hand a relatively high number of threads is needed to utilize the GPU. Due to this reasons t is limited to a small number.

8.3.3 Using Shared Memory

The approach described could also be extended to threadblocks: A single job is processed by one block instead of one thread, storing its elements in shared memory instead of registers and distributing the compare/exchange operations of the job among the threads.

The amount of shared memory available to one block is much greater than the amount of register memory of one thread; thus, processing a higher number t of consecutive steps in a single kernel-launch. Unfortunately, the elements that belong to one job do not lie consecutive in global memory in general (Figure 8.2b); that is, accessed memory does not lie in the same memory segment. For this reason it is not possible to coalesce these memory transactions, making this approach impractical.

There is another way to benefit from shared memory: Consider an input sequence of length 2^k. Because of the recursive definition of bitonic sort it holds, that in the steps $s, s-1, \ldots, 1$ of any phase p, 2^{k-s} sequences of length 2^s are processed completely independently. For example, in Figure 8.2b the input sequence is of length 8, whereas in steps 2 and 1 two sequences of length 4 $((0,1,2,3)$ and $(4,5,6,7))$ are processed independently.

If such a subsequence of length 2^s processed in step s completely fits into shared memory, a block first transfers its subsequence into shared memory. Afterward the threads of the block process the steps $s, s-1, \ldots, 1$ using the approach described in the Section 8.3.2, but accessing shared instead of global memory and using efficient block-synchronization mechanisms instead of synchronization by multiple kernel launches.

In our implementation we process, depending on key type of the sequence to sort and whether it is key-value sorting, up to $s = 9$ steps completely in the shared memory. Because the first nine phases consist of nine or fewer steps each, it is possible to process the first nine phases within a single-kernel launch using shared memory.

8.3.4 Analytical Results

Reducing communication and synchronization needed in bitonic sort reduces the number of necessary kernel launches and global memory accesses. In addition, the use of shared memory in some phases and steps, respectively, allows for the use of efficient inner-block synchronization and high-performance communication among threads, additionally avoiding kernel launches and accesses to global memory. Algorithm 1 is the pseudocode of our optimized implementation. The first `firstPh` phases are processed within `BS_firstPh`. In greater phases, `BS_4_step` is called repeatedly, each call processing four consecutive steps, and the last `lastSt` steps are processed by `BS_lastSt`. In case of sorting

---

Algorithm 1: Pseudocode for bitonic sort with CUDA

```
BS(key* lo, int n, int dir, int phases, int firstPh,
   int lastSt)
{
  BS_firstPh<<<grid, block, 0, 0>>>(lo, firstPh, n, dir);

  for (int ph = firstPh + 1; ph <= phases; ph++)
  {
    for (int st = ph; st > lastSt; st -= 4)
    {
      BS_4_step<<<grid,block, 0, 0>>>(lo, ph, st, dir);
    }

    BS_lastSt<<<grid,block, 0, 0>>>(lo, ph, lastSt, dir);
  }
}
```

32-bit integers, we use $\mathtt{lastSt} = 9$, $\mathtt{firstPh} = 9$. Thus the total number of accesses to global memory when sorting a sequence of length $n = 2^k$ is

$$n \cdot 2 \cdot \left(1 + \sum_{i=10}^{k} 1 + \left\lceil \frac{i-9}{4} \right\rceil\right) \tag{3}$$

As an example, when sorting a sequence of length 2^{20} the number of global memory accesses per element is $2 \cdot (1 + 4 \cdot 2 + 4 \cdot 3 + 3 \cdot 4) = 60$ as opposed to 420 when using the basic implementation. In addition, smaller steps are processed in shared memory, so there are no more awkward access patterns to global memory in smaller steps, and all accesses to global memory are coalesced (in case of 32-bit, 64-bit, or 128-bit keys). Thus, the memory throughput from an application point of view and from a hardware point of view are the same (e.g., 51.2 GB/s when sorting 2^{20} 32-bit integer using a GTX280). Altogether this significantly increases performance as shown in the next section.

8.4 EVALUATION

We tested our implementation of bitonic sort using a GTX 280. Because we consider sorting to be just a part of a larger computation, we did not include the time needed to transfer data to or from the GPU in our tests. Because bitonic sort is based on sorting networks, its performance is independent of key distribution; thus, we only used uniformly distributed key sequences in our tests.

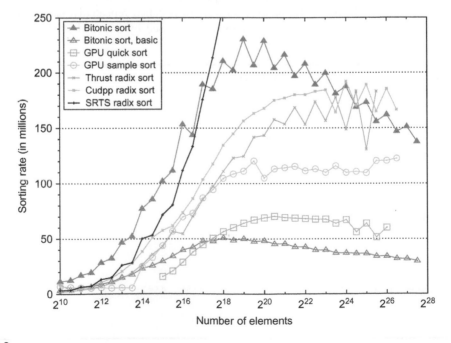

FIGURE 8.3

32-bit integer (see color insert).

In all figures presented here, on the y-axis the sorting rate is shown; that is, the length of a sequence that has been sorted divided by the runtime of the algorithm. The x-axis presents the length of the input sequence.

We compared our bitonic sort to the best-performing algorithms for GPUs: the quick sort implementation from Cederman et al. [4], the radix sort implementation in the CUDPP library [6], the radix sort from Satish et al. [1] from the Thrust library, the sample sort algorithm from Leischner et al. [3] and the recently published radix sort (SRTS radix sort) from Merrill et al. [7]. None of these algorithms works in-place, and all the radix sort implementations are not comparison-based. Consequently, the maximum length of a sequence that can be sorted differs for each algorithm.

Figure 8.3 presents the sorting rates for 32-bit integer sequences. Although we focused on comparing comparison-based algorithms, we also included the noncomparison-based radix sorts in Figure 8.1. Bitonic sort is faster than the other comparison-based sorting algorithms GPU quick sort and GPU sample sort and it is also competitive to the radix sort from the CUDPP library and the radix sort from Satish et al. However, it is outperformed by the radix sort from Merrill et al. by more than a factor of 3 times for larger sequences.

In Figure 8.4 the results for sorting 64-bit integer keys are shown (including all implementations that are able to sort 64-bit integers). Bitonic sort again is the fastest comparison-based algorithm and is even faster then the radix sort from Satish et al. but it is outperformed by the radix sort from Merrill et al. by more than a factor 2 times for larger sequences.

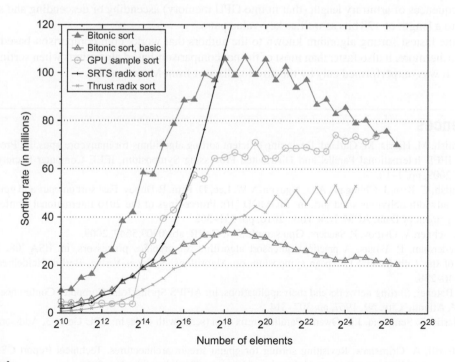

FIGURE 8.4

64-bit integer.

Compared with other algorithms, the sorting rate of bitonic sort strongly depends on the length of the input sequence due to the complexity $O(n \log^2 n)$ of bitonic sort, causing the number of compare/exchange operations and global memory accesses per element to increase for larger sequences (c.f. equation [3]).

Recently Satish et al. presented a novel sorting algorithm [2] that is based on merge sort. It is comparison-based, but does not work in-place. Comparing the results given in their paper bitonic sort seems to perform better for smaller sequences. The (sequential) time complexity of a merge sort $(0(n \log n))$ is better than that of a bitonic sort $(0(n \log^2 n))$. Parallelization using a constant number of processors, as in the case of a GPU, can improve performance by a constant factor only. Therefore there always exists (theoretically) a cross-over point from which on a merge sort based implementation performs better than a bitonic sort based one. In case of the merge sort from Satish et al. and our bitonic sort implementation, this cross-over point seems to be at 2^{25} when sorting 32-bit integers.

We also tested the basic implementation of bitonic sort. The results show that the obtained speed-up of the optimized implementation compared with the basic implementation is about 4 when sorting 32-bit integers and about 3 when sorting 64-bit integers.

8.5 CONCLUSION

In this chapter we present a novel comparison-based sorting algorithm for NVIDIA's GPUs. It is able to sort sequences of arbitrary length (that fit into GPU memory) ascending or descending and supports keys up to a length of 128 bits as well as key-value pairs.

It is the fastest sorting algorithm known to the authors that works both comparison-based and in-place. Furthermore, it also faster than most of the noncomparison-based algorithms when sorting 64-bit integers. It was outperformed only by the novel radix sort from Merrill et al.

References

[1] N. Satish, M. Harris, M. Garland, Designing efficient sorting algorithms for manycore gpus, in: Proceedings 23rd IEEE International Parallel and Distributed Processing Symposium, IEEE Computer Society, Rome, Italy, 2009, pp. 1–10.

[2] N. Satish, C. Kim, J. Chhugani, A.D. Nguyen, V.W. Lee, D. Kim, P. Dubey, Fast sort on cpus and gpus: a case for bandwidth oblivious simd sort, in: SIGMOD '10: Proceedings of the 2010 International Conference on Management of Data, ACM, New York, 2010, pp. 351–362.

[3] N. Leischner, V. Osipov, P. Sanders, Gpu sample sort, CoRR, abs/0909.5649, 2009.

[4] D. Cederman, P. Tsigas, A practical quicksort algorithm for graphics processors, in: ESA '08: Proceedings of the 16th Annual European symposium on Algorithms, Springer-Verlag, Berlin, Heidelberg, 2008, pp. 246–258.

[5] K.E. Batcher, Sorting networks and their applications, in: AFIPS Spring Joint Computer Conference, vol. 32, ACM, Atlantic City, NJ, 1967, pp. 307–314.

[6] M. Harris, S. Sengupta, J.D. Owens, Parallel prefix sum (scan) with cuda, in: GPU Gems 3, Addison-Wesley, 2007.

[7] D. Merrill, A. Grimshaw, Revisiting sorting for gpgpu stream architectures, Technical Report CS2010-03, Department of Computer Science, University of Virginia, Charlottesville, VA, 2010.

SECTION

Numerical Algorithms

Frank Jargstorff (NVIDIA)

2

STATE OF GPU-BASED NUMERICAL ALGORITHMS

Deployment of GPUs in high-performance computing depends on the availability of efficient numerical algorithms running on this new generation of super computers. Over the past years a number of GPU-based libraries of numerical algorithms as well as software products for numerical analysis with dedicated GPU support have emerged.

Three factors specific to GPU computing necessitate continued research and development of numerical algorithms in this otherwise well-established field:

- The GPU hardware architecture and the GPU programming model are substantially different from previous generations of parallel computer architectures.
- The GPUs' capabilities continue to be expanded from hardware generation to hardware generation. Limitations of previous generations of hardware get lifted.
- As GPUs evolve performance characteristics shift and what used to be an optimal implementation may need to be readjusted.

IN THIS SECTION

This section's content was chosen based on universal applicability and general relevance as well as creative use of the GPU architecture.

"Interval Arithmetic in CUDA" and "Approximating the `erfinv` Function" fall into the latter category.

"A Hybrid Method for Solving Tridiagonal Systems on the GPU" and "Accelerating CULA Linear Algebra Routines with Hybrid GPU and Multicore Computing" were chosen for their general relevance and universal applicability.

"GPU Accelerated Derivative-Free Mesh Optimization" fits both categories.

Interval Arithmetic in CUDA

Sylvain Collange, Marc Daumas, and David Defour

Every now and then some headlines question the confidence we may have in results obtained from computers. In the past, failures to deliver an accurate result were caused by exceptions (division by zero for example [6]) or situations that are now characterized as catastrophic (cancellation) [1], ill-posed or ill-conditioned [7]. Peak performance of GPUs typically counts in teraflops, and they are used in peta-scale systems. Most applications running on such systems can be considered as ill-conditioned, and no catastrophic or exceptional event may be blamed for computed results that fall too far from their target.

One solution is to spend some of the impressive computing power offered by GPUs to compute a validated range for the results instead of the uncontrolled estimation delivered by regular floating-point arithmetic. Interval arithmetic (IA) accounts for uncertainties in data at operator level and returns reliable bounds that include the correct result of an expression [8]. The basic principle of IA is to replace approximate floating-point numbers by intervals enclosing the results. Expressions and programs are then evaluated on intervals instead of points.

Naïve use of IA often provides very little insights, but common techniques of IA are profitably used in computer graphics [10] (including ray tracing of implicit surfaces [3]), root finding [2], and in various other fields to estimate and reduce the effects of rounding errors [4] and characterize tolerance on parameters [9].

In this chapter, we present a simple, but powerful implementation of IA on CUDA GPUs. The implementation is written in C for CUDA using C++ features such as operator overloading and templates, leading to an intuitive interface.

9.1 INTERVAL ARITHMETIC

Regular floating-point arithmetic rounds the exact result of any arithmetic operation. The result returned by a single operation is either the greatest floating-point number smaller than the mathematical result, or the smallest floating-point number greater than the mathematical result. In some cases, providing an approximation is not enough, especially with long computations where rounding errors accumulate. The exact result has to be bounded. IA operations take into account rounding errors introduced by floating-point operations.

The most common encoding of intervals uses two floating-point numbers to store a lower bound l and an upper bound u. Valid intervals are defined for $l \leq u$. We represent intervals as $[l, u]$ for

$\{x \in \mathbb{R} : l \leq x \leq u\}$. An alternative encoding stores their centers and their radii. Both encodings are roughly equivalent, though the center-radius representation is sometimes used to take advantage of existing readily optimized BLAS libraries when IA is used in linear algebra.

As IA operations are validated, we round down the lower bound of the resulting interval, and we round up its upper bound. We can extend the usual operations $(+, -, \times, 1/\cdot)$ from reals to intervals and define:

$$[a,b] + [c,d] = [\underline{a+c}, \overline{b+d}],$$

$$[a,b] - [c,d] = [\underline{a-d}, \overline{b-c}],$$

$$[a,b] \times [c,d] = [\min(\underline{a \times c}, \underline{b \times d}, \underline{a \times d}, \underline{b \times c}),$$

$$\max(\overline{a \times c}, \overline{b \times d}, \overline{a \times d}, \overline{b \times c})],$$

$$1 / [c,d] = [\underline{1/d}, \overline{1/c}] \text{ when } 0 \notin [c,d],$$

$$[-\infty, \overline{1/c}] \text{ and } [\underline{1/d}, +\infty] \text{ otherwise.}$$

In the preceding formula, $\underline{a * b}$ is the operation $a * b$ rounded toward $-\infty$ and $\overline{a * b}$ is the operation rounded toward $+\infty$, for $* \in \{+, -, \times, /\}$.

9.2 IMPORTANCE OF ROUNDING MODES

Development of IA has been hindered so far by the lack of portable support in mainstream programming languages and the poor performances of Naïve implementations. The IEEE-754 standard on floating-point arithmetic mandates that each operation is rounded to the nearest floating-point value or using one of the directed rounding modes (up or down, among others). Most existing CPUs store the active rounding mode as a part of the processor state for backward compatibility with decisions made early in the 1980s. The previous section suggests that we switch between rounding modes at least once every IA operation. Each change of the rounding mode typically requires the CPU to flush the execution pipeline, which causes a dramatic performance drop.

Workarounds based on flipping signs have been devised to alleviate this problem. Such implementations keep the same rounding mode toward $+\infty$ for all IA operations [11]. However, they still incur some overhead. They also require strict compliance of the system to IEEE-754 rules, which may require disabling some compiler optimizations, if not all. Finally, they still have to switch between rounding modes in many cases, for instance, when IA is intermixed with regular floating-point operations rounded to the nearest.

Having to restore the rounding mode after every IA operation significantly increases the cost of IA, especially on traditional CPUs. A possible optimization is to provide two execution modes. In the default mode, the original rounding mode is saved and restored upon each IA operation. An unprotected mode is used for code blocks involving several consecutive IA operations. The rounding direction can be set once at the beginning of the block and restored at the end. The Boost Interval library [11] is based on this optimization.

9.3 INTERVAL OPERATORS IN CUDA

Latest generations of NVIDIA processors provide correctly rounded double-precision addition and multiplication in both directed rounding modes. Starting with GT200 (Compute Capability 1.3), CUDA GPUs offer support for all IEEE-754 rounding modes in double precision. This support is extended to single precision on the Fermi architecture (Compute Capability 2.x). Contrary to most CPU implementations, this support is stateless, and the rounding direction can be selected independently for each machine instruction instead of through one global rounding mode. This implementation complies with the new IEEE-754:2008 floating-point standard, which allows static *rounding attributes* to replace the former *dynamic rounding modes*.

In CUDA, rounding attributes are accessible through rounding modifiers at the PTX level or through compiler intrinsics in C for CUDA, thereby eliminating completely the overhead associated with switching rounding modes. Consequently, GPUs may reach their peak performance regardless of the rounding directions in use, allowing implementations of IA that are both simple and efficient.

Yet, state-of-the-art libraries of IA rely on advanced features of processors, including efficient branch prediction mechanisms. Naïve ports of these libraries to GPU architectures would yield poor results. On the other hand, the support of rounded operations throughout the whole CUDA software stack makes the compiler fully aware of their semantics, allowing for optimizations like instruction reordering, constant propagation, and copy propagation to be safely performed.

We propose an implementation of IA in CUDA that aims at being compatible with the Boost Interval C++ library [11, 12]. We will present the library through a top-down approach, starting from the interface and digging through the implementation.

9.3.1 Interval Class

The Interval template class is the user-visible component (Listing 9.1).

It is parameterized by the underlying datatype T, which is typically float or double. It contains the higher and lower bounds, which constitute the only state associated with an interval. Interval objects can be constructed and manipulated in both host and device code. The meanings and implementations of class members are straightforward, with the exception of empty, which builds the empty interval containing by convention the special values [NaN, NaN].

9.3.2 Arithmetic

Standard C arithmetic operators are overloaded to operate on the interval class: unary $+$ and $-$, binary $+$, $-$ and $*$. These arithmetic operations require support for directed rounding, which is provided by the `rounded_arith` template (Listing 9.2).

The `rounded_arith` template class contains all platform-dependent code. The operators themselves are generic, although the algorithms employed are optimized for GPU execution.

The addition, subtraction, and multiplication operators follow directly the textbook implementations from Section 9.1. For instance, Listing 9.3 presents the implementation of interval addition. These algorithms are branch free and are well suited to GPU architectures. For example, we replace the nested conditional blocks involved in common multiplication implementations used to tell apart the 13 different cases, depending on the sign of each input interval, by using the IEEE-754:2008 compliant min

```
template<class T>
class interval
{
public:
    __device__ __host__ interval();
    __device__ __host__ interval(T const & v);
    __device__ __host__ interval(T const & l, T const & u);

    __device__ __host__ T const & lower() const;
    __device__ __host__ T const & upper() const;

    static __device__ __host__ interval empty();

private:
    T low;
    T up;
};
```

Listing 9.1. Interval template class.

```
template<class T>
struct rounded_arith
{
    __device__ T add_down (const T& x, const T& y);
    __device__ T add_up   (const T& x, const T& y);
    __device__ T sub_down (const T& x, const T& y);
    __device__ T sub_up   (const T& x, const T& y);
    __device__ T mul_down (const T& x, const T& y);
    __device__ T mul_up   (const T& x, const T& y);
    __device__ T div_down (const T& x, const T& y);
    __device__ T div_up   (const T& x, const T& y);
    __device__ T median   (const T& x, const T& y);
    __device__ T sqrt_down(const T& x);
    __device__ T sqrt_up  (const T& x);
    __device__ T int_down (const T& x);
    __device__ T int_up   (const T& x);
};
```

Listing 9.2. Rounding.

and max functions available on the GPU as follows:

$$[a,b] \times [c,d] = [\min(\underline{a \times c, b \times d, a \times d, b \times c}),\ \max(\overline{a \times c, b \times d, a \times d, b \times c})].$$

The implementation of IA division operator is more involved, as it has to consider two cases, depending on whether zero is included or not in the divisor interval. Two helper functions are proposed

```
template<class T> inline __device__
interval<T> operator+(interval<T> const & x,
    interval<T> const & y)
{
    rounded_arith<T> rnd;
    return interval<T>(rnd.add_down(x.lower(), y.lower()),
                        rnd.add_up(x.upper(), y.upper()));
}
```

Listing 9.3. Interval addition operator.

```
template<>
struct rounded_arith<float>
{
    __device__ float add_down (const float& x, const float& y) {
        return __fadd_rd(x, y);
    }
    ...
}
```

Listing 9.4. Specialization of rounding implementation for the float type.

for that purpose: `division_part1` and `division_part2`. They are used to obtain both parts of the result, following the convention set by the Boost Interval library.

9.3.3 Rounding Modes

The `rounded_arith` template class is responsible for the datatype-specific and platform-specific implementation of directed rounding. The base class does not provide any implementation by itself. However, two template specializations are provided for float and double.

Each of these specializations is based on the rounded arithmetic intrinsics provided by CUDA (Listing 9.4), with the exception of division, which is not supported by CUDA in all rounding modes on Compute Capability 1.3 devices. We implement it in software at the CUDA source level on these GPUs.

9.4 SOME EVALUATIONS: SYNTHETIC BENCHMARK

Listing 9.5 describes a possible implementation of an AXPY micro-benchmark computing $a \times x + y$ on intervals using the proposed library. We compare in Figure 9.1 the performance of this micro-benchmark on several software and hardware configurations.

```
#include "cuda_interval_lib.cuh"

template<class T>
__global__ void interval_test(int iters, interval<T> * output,
                                interval<T> a, interval<T> b) {
    interval<T> c = a;

    for(int i = 0; i < iters; i++) {
        c = a * c + b;
    }

    output[blockIdx.x * blockDim.x + threadIdx.x] = c;
}

int main(){
    interval<T> * d_result;
    cudaMalloc((void**)&d_result, ...);
    interval_test<float><<<512, 128>>>(1000, d_results,
        interval<float>(1.0f, 1.1f),
        interval<float>(2.3f, 2.4f));
    ...
    return 0;
}
```

Listing 9.5. CUDA Implementation of AXPY with IA.

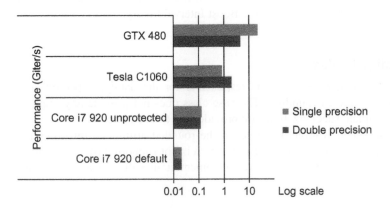

FIGURE 9.1

AXPY synthetic benchmark (see color insert).

The single-thread CPU implementation uses the Boost Interval library and runs on one core of a Core i7 920 processor, while the GPU implementation is based on the proposed CUDA interval library and runs on a Tesla C1060 and a GeForce GTX 480. We consider the default and unprotected modes of the Boost Interval library, as described in Section 9.2.

Results are representative of peak throughput, that is, the number of IA operations per second that can be achieved. We expect the performance of real applications to be comprised between the *default* and the *unprotected* figures for the CPU implementation.

In single precision, we observe that the GTX 480 is able to execute 1165 times more AXPY iterations per second than one Core i7 CPU core with IA in default mode.

The CPU version exhibits a slowdown of more than seven times when we enforce the necessary changes in rounding modes. The same benchmark (not shown in Figure 9.1) shows an even greater impact (around 20 times slowdown) on a Xeon 5148 (Core 2 based). On the other hand, a five-year old Pentium 4 630 is able to run the default implementation with a minimal performance impact of 10% over the unprotected version, and ends up being faster than both the Xeon and the Core i7.

The GT200 GPU used in the Tesla C1060 board does not support directed rounding modes in single precision. As these operations are emulated in software, it is not surprising that it suffers from a large overhead in single precision. When taking the difference in peak performance into account, we note that the efficiency of IA on the GTX 480 is slightly below the efficiency of the unprotected mode in CPU and much better than the default implementation, still on the CPU.

Raw performance drops on the GTX 480 when going from single precision to double precision, as there are fewer usable double-precision units on the GeForce. It still performs twice as fast as the GT200-based Tesla. We expect Fermi-based Tesla boards to perform significantly better in this test.

To sum up, speed-ups vastly higher than the theoretical ratio of peak performance of the systems are possible. This is owing to the ability of CUDA GPUs to alternate between different rounding attributes with no penalty.

9.5 APPLICATION-LEVEL BENCHMARK

As an example, these interval operators can be used for root finding of one-dimensional equations using an interval Newton method as in [5]. In our parallel implementation, each thread is responsible for solving its own equation.

We consider an interval Newton method that searches the roots of univariate functions. It consists in a tree traversal algorithm. Intermediate results are stored in a stack in local memory. The results show the benefit of using a GPU for IA.

For this evaluation, we use the toy example of the family of polynomials $x^2 + (\alpha - 2)x + 1$, where $\alpha = \text{threadID}/\text{threadCount}$ (or loop index / iteration count for the sequential version).

This application exhibits a large amount of divergent branches and irregular memory accesses. Hence, performance of the Tesla C1060 GPU is comparatively lower than in the previous benchmark (Figure 9.2). In particular, it suffers from the high latency of its uncached local memory. On the other hand, the caches of the Fermi architecture mitigate the impact of irregular memory accesses.

A working set of intervals to be refined is maintained as a stack in local memory. The top entry cached in registers to improve performance. At each step, the interval at the top of the stack is refined to yield either no solution, one smaller interval, or two smaller intervals. If one of the produced intervals satisfies a given accuracy criterion, it is appended to a thread-specific result list in global memory. Otherwise, intervals are pushed back into the working stack in order to be refined further.

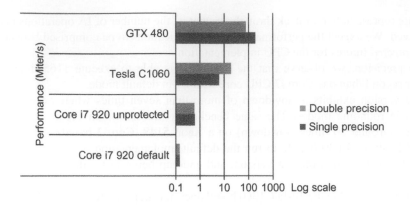

FIGURE 9.2

Interval Newton benchmark (see color insert).

In some cases, the refinement may not significantly decrease the width of the interval, causing a slow rate of convergence. When such a case is detected, a bisection method is applied to split the interval into two halves. Each half is then recursively refined and/or bisected.

9.6 CONCLUSION

Interval Arithmetic brings reliability in floating-point computations by bounding every calculation. The implementation of IA operations can be significantly accelerated thanks to hardware support of static rounding attributes. The latest CUDA GPUs offer such features.

We have presented how to implement IA in CUDA and take advantage of the latest features of NVIDIA GPUs. The proposed implementation is easier to use than an equivalent CPU implementation such as the Boost Interval package as there is no need to deal with different executions mode, and it is faster and more work efficient as it increases arithmetic intensity.

References

[1] M. Daumas, D.W. Matula, Validated roundings of dot products by sticky accumulation, IEEE Trans. Comput. 46 (1997) 623–629.

[2] T. Duff, Interval arithmetic recursive subdivision for implicit functions and constructive solid geometry, in: J.J. Thomas (Ed.), Proceedings of the 19th Annual Conference on Computer Graphics and interactive Techniques, SIGGRAPH 92, ACM, New York, 1992, pp. 131–138.

[3] J. Flórez, M. Sbert, M.A. Sainz, J. Vehi, Improving the interval ray tracing of implicit surfaces, Lect. Notes Comput. Sci. 4035 (2006) 655–664.

[4] E.R. Hansen, Global optimization using interval analysis: The one-dimensional case, J. Optim. Theory Appl. 29 (3) (1979) 331–334.

[5] E.R. Hansen, R.I. Greenberg, Interval Newton method, Appl. Math. Comput. 12 (2–3) (1983) 89–98.

[6] A.M. Hayashi, Rough sailing for smart ships, Sci. Am. Mag. 11 (1998) 26.

[7] N.J. Higham, Accuracy and Stability of Numerical Algorithms, SIAM ed. Philadelphia, PA, 2002.

[8] L. Jaulin, M. Kieffer, O. Didrit, E. Walter, Applied Interval Analysis, Springer-Verlag, London, 2001.

[9] B. Kearfott, V. Kreinovich, Applications of Interval Computations: An Introduction, Kluwer Academic Publishers, Dordrecht, 1992.

[10] J.M. Snyder, Interval analysis for computer graphics, SIGGRAPH Comput. Graph. 26 (2) (1992) 121–130.

[11] H. Bronnimann, G. Melquiond, S. Pion, The design of the Boost interval arithmetic library, Theor. Comput. Sci. 351 (1) (2006) 111–118.

[12] S. Collange, J. Flórez, D. Defour, A GPU interval library based on Boostinterval, in: J.D. Bruguera, M. Daumas (Eds.), Real Numbers and Computers, Santiago de Compostela, 2008, pp. 61–72.

Approximating the erfinv Function

10

Mike Giles

The inverse error function erfinv is a standard component of mathematical libraries, and particularly useful in statistical applications for converting uniform random numbers into Normal random numbers. This chapter presents a new approximation of the erfinv function, which is significantly more efficient for GPU execution due to the greatly reduced warp divergence.

10.1 INTRODUCTION

Like $\cos x$, $\sin x$, e^x and $\log x$, the error function

$$\mathrm{erf}(x) = \frac{2}{\sqrt{\pi}} \int_0^x e^{-t^2}\, dt,$$

and its inverse $\mathrm{erfinv}(x)$ are a standard part of libraries such as Intel's MKL, AMD's ACML and NVIDIA's CUDA math library.

The inverse error function is a particularly useful function for Monte Carlo applications in computational finance, as the error function is closely related to the Normal cumulative distribution function

$$\Phi(x) = \frac{1}{\sqrt{2\pi}} \int_{-\infty}^x e^{-t^2/2}\, dt = \frac{1}{2} + \frac{1}{2}\,\mathrm{erf}\left(\frac{x}{\sqrt{2}}\right)$$

so

$$\Phi^{-1}(x) = \sqrt{2}\,\mathrm{erfinv}(2x - 1).$$

If x is a random number uniformly distributed in the range $(0, 1)$, then $y = \Phi^{-1}(x)$ is a Normal random variable, with zero mean and unit variance. Other techniques such as the polar method and Marsaglia's Ziggurat method are usually used to transform pseudorandom uniforms to psuedorandom Normals, but $\Phi^{-1}(x)$ is the preferred approach for quasirandom uniforms generated from Sobol sequences and lattice methods, as it preserves the beneficial properties of these low-discrepancy sequences [4].

Like trigonometric functions, $\mathrm{erfinv}(x)$ is usually implemented using polynomial or rational approximations [1, 7, 8]. However, these approximations have been designed to have a low

Table 10.1 Pseudo code to Compute $y = \mathtt{erfinv}(x)$, with $p_n(t)$ Representing a Polynomial Function of t

$a = |x|$

if $a > 0.9375$ **then**
    $t = \sqrt{\log(a)}$
    $y = p_1(t) / p_2(t)$

else if $a > 0.75$ **then**
    $y = p_3(a) / p_4(a)$

else
    $y = p_5(a) / p_6(a)$
end if

if $x < 0$ **then**
    $y = -y$
end if

computational cost on traditional CPUs. The single precision algorithm from [1] which was used in the CUDA 3.0 math library has the form shown in Table 10.1.

If the input x is uniformly distributed on $(-1, 1)$, there is a 0.75 probability of executing the third branch in the code, and only a 0.0625 probability of executing the expensive first branch, which requires the computation of $\log(a)$ and its square root.

However, on an NVIDIA GPU with 32 threads in a warp, the probability that all of them take the third branch is $0.75^{32} \approx 0.0001$, while the probability that none of them take the first branch is $0.9375^{32} \approx 0.13$. Hence, in most warps there will be at least one thread taking each of the three branches, and so the execution cost will approximately equal the sum of the execution costs of all three branches.

The primary goal of this paper is to improve the execution speed of erfinv(x) through constructing single and double precision approximations with greatly reduced warp divergence, i.e., with most warps executing only one main branch in the conditional code. The technique which is used can be easily adapted to other special functions. The MATLAB code which generates the approximations is provided on the accompanying website, along with the CUDA code for the erfinv approximations, and test code which demonstrates its speed and accuracy.

The efficiency of the new approximations is demonstrated in comparison with the implementations in CUDA 3.0. While this chapter was being written, CUDA 3.1 was released. Its single precision erfinv implementation incorporates the ideas in this chapter, although the code is slightly different from that shown in Table 10.5. The double precision implementation is still the same as in CUDA 3.0, but a new version is under development.

These approximations were originally developed as part of a commercial maths library providing Numerical Routines for GPUs [2, 5]. Similar approximations have also been developed independently for the same reasons by Shaw and Brickman [6].

The CUDA source code, the MATLAB code used to create the approximations, and the test code for the evaluation are all freely available [3].

10.2 NEW `erfinv` APPROXIMATIONS

10.2.1 Single Precision

The new single precision approximation $\mathtt{erfinv}_{\mathrm{SP}}$ is defined as

$$
\mathtt{erfinv}_{\mathrm{SP}}(x) = \begin{cases} x p_1(w), & w \le w_1 \qquad \text{central region} \\[2mm] x p_2(s), & w_1 < w \qquad \text{tail region} \end{cases}
$$

where $w = -\log(1 - x^2)$, $s = \sqrt{w}$, and $p_1(w)$ and $p_2(s)$ are two polynomial functions. The motivation for this form of approximation, which in the tail region is similar to one proposed by Strecok [7], is that

- `erfinv` is an odd function of x, and has a Taylor series expansion in odd powers of x near $x = 0$, which corresponds to $p_1(w)$ having a standard Taylor series at $w = 0$;
- `erfinv` is approximately equal to $\pm\sqrt{w}$ near $x = \pm 1$.

Using $x = \sqrt{1 - e^{-w}}$, the left part of Figure 10.1 plots $\mathtt{erfinv}(x)/x$ versus w for $0 < w < 16$ which corresponds to the entire range of single precision floating point numbers x with magnitude less than 1. The right part of Figure 10.1 plots $\mathtt{erfinv}(x)/x$ versus $s \equiv \sqrt{w}$ for $4 < w < 36$. The extension up to $w \approx 36$ is required later for double precision inputs.

Using polynomials P_n of degree n, a standard L_∞ approximation for the central region would be defined by

$$
p_1 = \arg\min_{p \in P_n} \max_{w \in (0, w_1)} \left| p(w) - \frac{\mathtt{erfinv}(x)}{x} \right|.
$$

However, what we really want to minimize is the relative error defined as $(\mathtt{erfinv}_{\mathrm{SP}}(x) - \mathtt{erfinv}(x))/\mathtt{erfinv}(x)$, so it would be better to define p_1 as

$$
p_1 = \arg\min_{p \in P_n} \max_{w \in (0, w_1)} \left| \frac{x}{\mathtt{erfinv}(x)} \left(p(w) - \frac{\mathtt{erfinv}(x)}{x} \right) \right|.
$$

Since this weighted L_∞ minimization is not possible using MATLAB, p_1 is instead approximated by performing a weighted least-squares minimization, minimizing

$$
\int_0^{w_1} \frac{1}{\sqrt{w(w_1 - w)}} \left(\frac{x}{\mathtt{erfinv}(x)} \left(p(w) - \frac{\mathtt{erfinv}(x)}{x} \right) \right)^2 dw.
$$

The weighting is a standard one under which Chebyshev polynomials are orthogonal, and is introduced to control the errors near the two ends of the interval. A similar construction is used for p_2.

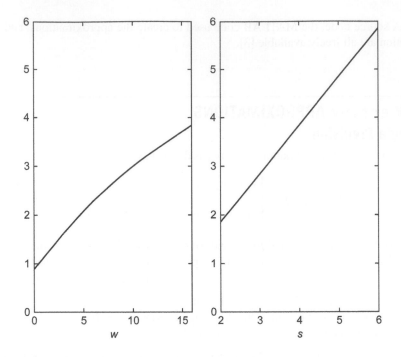

FIGURE 10.1

`erfinv(x)/x` plotted versus w and $s \equiv \sqrt{w}$.

Table 10.1 shows the degree of polynomial required for p_1 and p_2, to reduce the relative approximation error to less than 10^{-7}, depending on the choice of the dividing point w_1. The fourth column gives the approximate probability that a random input x, uniformly distributed on $(-1, 1)$, will lie in the tail region. Multiplying this by 32 gives the approximate probability that one or more inputs in a CUDA warp of 32 threads will lie in the tail region, and hence that a CUDA implementation will have a divergent warp.

Using $w_1 = 5$, there is roughly a 10% probability of a divergent warp, but the cost of the central region approximation is the least since it requires only a degree 8 polynomial for p_1. On the other hand, using $w_1 = 16$, there is no tail region; the central region covers the whole interval. However, p_1 is now of degree 14 so the cost has increased. The second option uses $w_1 = 6.25$, for which p_1 needs to be of degree 9. In this case, there is only a 3% probability of a divergent warp.

10.2.2 Double Precision

The double precision approximation `erfinv`$_{\text{DP}}$ is defined similarly, but it is defined with up to two tail regions as it needs to extend to $w \approx 36$ to cover the full double precision range for x.

$$\text{erfinv}_{\text{DP}}(x) = \begin{cases} x p_1(w), & w \leq w_1 & \text{central region} \\ x p_2(s), & w_1 < w \leq w_2 & \text{tail region 1} \\ x p_3(s), & w_2 < w & \text{tail region 2} \end{cases}$$

Table 10.2 Three Alternatives for Single Precision Approximation of `erfinv`

w_1	p_1 degree	p_2 degree	Tail prob.
5.00	8	8	0.3%
6.25	9	7	0.1%
16.00	14	n/a	0%

Table 10.2 shows the degree of polynomial required for p_1, p_2, and p_3 to reduce the relative approximation error to less than 2×10^{-16}, depending on the choice of the dividing points w_1 and w_2. The last column again gives the approximate probability that a uniformly distributed random input x is not in the central region.

In constructing the weighted least-squares approximation using MATLAB, variable precision arithmetic (an extended precision feature of the Symbolic Toolbox) is required to evaluate the analytic error function to better than double precision in order to compute the accuracy of the approximation.

10.2.3 Floating Point Error Analysis

In this section we look at the errors due to finite precision arithmetic. The floating point evaluation of $(1 - x)(1 + x)$ will yield a value equal to

$$(1 - x)(1 + x)(1 + \varepsilon_1)$$

where ε_1 corresponds to at most 1 `ulp` (unit of least precision) which is roughly 10^{-7} for single precision and 10^{-16} for double precision. Computing w by evaluating the log of this will yield, approximately,

$$w + \varepsilon_1 + \varepsilon_2$$

where ε_2 is the error in evaluating the log function, which is approximately $5 \times 10^{-8} \max(1, 3w)$ when using the CUDA fast single precision function `__logf()`, and $10^{-16}w$ when using the double precision function `log()`.

Computing $p_1(w)$ will then yield, approximately

$$p_1(w) \left(1 + (\varepsilon_1 + \varepsilon_2) \frac{p'_1(w)}{p_1(w)} + \varepsilon_3 \right)$$

where ε_3 is the relative error in evaluating p_1. The relative error in the final product $xp_1(w)$ will then be approximately

$$(\varepsilon_1 + \varepsilon_2) \frac{p'_1(w)}{p_1(w)} + \varepsilon_3 + \varepsilon_4,$$

where ε_4 is again of order 10^{-7}.

Since $p_1(w) \approx 1 + 0.2w$, the combined contributions due to ε_1 and ε_2 are about 1.5 `ulp` in single precision, and about 0.5 `ulp` in double precision. The errors due to ε_3 and ε_4 will each contribute another 0.5 ulp. These are in addition to a relative error of roughly 1 ulp due to the approximation of erfinv. Hence, the overall error is likely to be up to 4 ulp for single precision and up to 3 ulp for double precision.

In the tail region, there is an extra step to compute $s = \sqrt{w}$. Since

$$\sqrt{w+\varepsilon} \approx \sqrt{w} + \frac{\varepsilon}{2\sqrt{w}}$$

the value which is computed for s is approximately

$$s + \frac{1}{2s}(\varepsilon_1 + \varepsilon_2) + \varepsilon_5 s$$

where ε_5 is the relative error in evaluating the square root itself, which for the CUDA implementation is 3 ulp in single precision and less than 0.5 ulp in double precision. Noting also that $p_2(s) \approx s$, the relative error in the final result is

$$\frac{1}{2w}(\varepsilon_1 + \varepsilon_2) + \varepsilon_5 + \varepsilon_3 + \varepsilon_4.$$

In single precision, ε_2/w is about 3 ulp and ε_5 is also 3 ulp, so the overall error, including the p_2 approximation error, will be about 6 ulp. In double precision, ε_2/w and ε_5 are about 1 ulp and 0.5 ulp, respectively, so the overall error is 2 to 3 ulp.

10.3 PERFORMANCE AND ACCURACY

Table 10.4 gives the performance of the first of the new approximations in Tables 10.2 and 10.3, compared to the existing ones in CUDA 3.0. Table 10.5 gives the code for the new single precision approximation. The times are in milliseconds to compute 100M values, using 28 blocks with 512 threads, and each thread computing 7000 values.

There are two conditions for the tests, "uniform" and "constant." In the uniform case, the inputs x for each warp are spread uniformly in a way which ensures 100% warp divergence for the existing implementation. This worst case scenario is slightly worse than the 87% divergence which would result from random input data, as discussed in the Introduction. The constant case represents the best case scenario in which all of the threads in each warp use the same input value, though this value is varied during the calculation so that overall each conditional branch is exercised for the appropriate fraction of cases.

Table 10.3 Two Alternatives for Double Precision Approximation of `erfinv`

w_1	w_2	p_1 degree	p_2 degree	p_3 degree	Tail prob.
6.25	16.0	22	18	16	0.1%
6.25	36.0	22	26	n/a	0.1%

Table 10.4 Times in Milliseconds to Compute 100M Single Precision (SP) and Double Precision (DP) Values Using CUDA 3.0 on C1060 and C2050

Time (ms)	C1060		C2050	
	SP	DP	SP	DP
Uniform, old	24	479	31	114
Uniform, new	8	219	10	49
Constant, old	8	123	11	30
Constant, new	8	213	9	48

Table 10.5 CUDA Code for Single Precision Implementation

```
_inline_ _device_ float MBG_erfinv(float x) {
float w, p;

w = - _logf((1.0f-x)*(1.0f+x));

if ( w < 5.000000f ) {
    w = w - 2.500000f;
    p =    2.81022636e-08f;
    p =    3.43273939e-07f + p*w;
    p =   -3.5233877e-06f + p*w;
    p =   -4.39150654e-06f + p*w;
    p =     0.00021858087f + p*w;
    p =    -0.00125372503f + p*w;
    p =    -0.00417768164f + p*w;
    p =      0.246640727f + p*w;
    p =      1.50140941f + p*w;
}
else {
    w = sqrtf(w) - 3.000000f;
    p =   -0.000200214257f;
    p =    0.000100950558f + p*w;
    p =    0.00134934322f + p*w;
    p =   -0.00367342844f + p*w;
    p =    0.00573950773f + p*w;
    p =    -0.0076224613f + p*w;
    p =    0.00943887047f + p*w;
    p =      1.00167406f + p*w;
    p =      2.83297682f + p*w;
}

return p*x;
}
```

The results show a factor 3 or more difference in the performance of the existing implementation on the two test cases. This reflects the penalty of warp divergence, with a cost equal to the sum of all branches which are taken by at least one thread, plus the fact that the execution of the main branch (the one which is taken most often) is significantly less costly because it does not require a log calculation.

The cost of the new approximations varies very little in the two cases, because even in the "uniform" case almost all warps are nondivergent. On the other hand, all warps have to perform a log calculation, and therefore in double precision the new implementation is slower than the existing one for the constant case.

Regarding accuracy, the maximum error of the new single precision approximation, compared to the existing double precision version, is around 7×10^{-7}, which is better than the existing single precision version, and the maximum difference between the new and existing double precision implementations is approximately 2×10^{-15}.

10.4 CONCLUSIONS

This chapter illustrates the cost of warp divergence, and the way in which it can sometimes be avoided by redesigning algorithms and approximations which were originally developed for conventional CPUs.

It also illustrates the dilemma which can face library developers. Whether the new double precision approximations are viewed as better than the existing ones depends on how they are likely to be used. For random inputs they are up to 3 times faster, but they can also be slower when the inputs within each warp are all identical, or vary very little.

References

[1] J.M. Blair, C.A. Edwards, J.H. Johnson, Rational Chebyshev approximations for the inverse of the error function, Math. Comput. 30 (136) (1976) 827–830.

[2] T. Bradley, J. du Toit, M. Giles, R. Tong, P. Woodhams, Parallelisation techniques for random number generators, in: GPU Computing Gems, vol. 1, Morgan Kaufmann, Boston, MA, 2010.

[3] M.B. Giles, Approximating the erfinv function (source code). http://gpucomputing.net/?q=node/1828, 2010.

[4] P. Glasserman, Monte Carlo Methods in Financial Engineering, Springer, New York, 2004.

[5] Numerical Algorithms Group, Numerical routines for GPUs. http://www.nag.co.uk/numeric/GPUs/, 2009.

[6] W.T. Shaw, N. Brickman, Differential equations for Monte Carlo recycling and a GPU-optimized normal quantile, Working paper. Available from: arXiv:0901.0638v3, 2009.

[7] A.J. Strecok, On the calculation of the inverse of the error function, Math. Comput. 22 (101) (1968) 144–158.

[8] M.J. Wichura, Algorithm AS 241: the percentage points of the normal distribution, Appl. Stat. 37 (3) (1988) 477–484.

A Hybrid Method for Solving Tridiagonal Systems on the GPU

11

Yao Zhang, Jonathan Cohen, Andrew A. Davidson, and John D. Owens

Tridiagonal linear systems are of importance to many problems in numerical analysis and computational fluid dynamics, as well as to computer graphics applications in video games and computer-animated films. Typical applications require solving hundreds or thousands of tridiagonal systems, which takes a majority part of total computation time. Fast parallel solutions are critical to larger scientific simulations, interactive computations of special effects in films, and real-time applications in video games. In this chapter, we study the performance of multiple tridiagonal algorithms on a GPU. We design a novel hybrid algorithm that combines a work-efficient algorithm with a step-efficient algorithm in a way well-suited for a GPU architecture. Our hybrid solver achieves $8\times$ and $2\times$ speed-up, respectively, in single precision and double precision over a multithreaded highly-optimized CPU solver, and a $2\times$–$2.3\times$ speedup over a basic GPU solver.

11.1 INTRODUCTION

We wish to solve a system of n linear equations of the form $Ax = d$, where A is a tridiagonal matrix

$$
A = \begin{pmatrix}
b_1 & c_1 & & & & & \\
a_2 & b_2 & c_2 & & & 0 & \\
& a_3 & b_3 & c_3 & & & \\
& & \ddots & \ddots & \ddots & & \\
& & & \ddots & \ddots & \ddots & c_{n-1} \\
& 0 & & & & a_n & b_n
\end{pmatrix}.
$$

The classic sequential Thomas algorithm requires $O(n)$ computation steps to solve this system. Since the 1960s, a variety of parallel algorithms have been developed for vector supercomputers to solve a tridiagonal system in $O(\log_2 n)$ steps, at the cost of more computational work per step. Notable among these algorithms are cyclic reduction (CR) [3], parallel cyclic reduction (PCR) [3], recursive doubling [10], and partition methods [11].

We notice that tridiagonal algorithms can be characterized by their step and work complexity, and a high-performance algorithm suitable for vector architecture should not only require fewer algorithmic steps, but also perform less work per step. Based on this observation, we propose a hybrid method to combine the merits of the step-efficient and the work-efficient algorithms.

11.1.1 Related Work

The tridiagonal solver was first implemented on a GPU by Kass et al. [4] to perform efficient depth-of-field blurs. Their solver was based on CR and was written in a GPU shading language. Sengupta et al. implemented CR with CUDA, and applied it to real-time shallow water simulation [5, 8]. Sakharnykh simulated 3D viscid incompressible fluid on the GPU by using the serial Thomas algorithm to solve thousands of tridiagonal systems in parallel [6]. His solver achieves high performance when there are a large number of systems available. Göddeke et al. developed a bank-conflicts-free GPU implementation of CR at the expense of 50% more on-chip storage, and employed it as a line relaxation smoother in a multigrid solver [2]. Egloff developed a GPU-based PCR solver to solve one dimensional PDEs with finite difference schemes [1]. The work by Sakharnykh [7] is most similar to ours in nature. He designed a hybrid solver based on the Thomas algrithm and PCR, and applied it to the simulation of depth-of-field effects. In this chapter, we expand on and extend our previous work on hybrid tridiagonal solvers [12] in two aspects: (1) we introduce new techniques to avoid branches and bank conflicts, and (2) we conduct a comprehensive performance comparison between various optimization and hybrid techniques.

11.2 CORE METHOD

We first characterize the complexity of three tridiagonal algorithms in terms of algorithmic steps and work per step as shown in Table 11.1. The Thomas algorithm is essentially sequential Gaussian elimination, which requires the most algorithmic steps, but the least amount of work per step. Cyclic reduction (CR) consists of $2\log_2 n$ algorithmic steps, and can perform up to $n/2$ parallel units of work per step. Parallel cyclic reduction (PCR) requires the fewest algorithmic steps and the most parallel units of work per step.

Which algorithm is most efficient for a vector architecture depends on the length of vector arithmetic unit. In the case of a vector length of one, which is equivalent to a scalar arithmetic unit, the Thomas algorithm is most efficient because it has the least amount of total work. If the vector length is larger than n, PCR is most efficient because it has the fewest algorithmic steps. If the vector length is between 1 and n, it is not clear which algorithm is the best, because the Thomas algorithm and CR may not fully utilize the vector unit, while PCR requires more than n units of work per step.

This observation motivates a hybrid method that is both step-efficient and work-efficient, while at the same time keeping the vector arithmetic unit fully utilized. The hybrid method works by making

Table 11.1 Complexity Comparison of Algorithms in Terms of Algorithmic Steps and Work per Step. n is the System Size

Algorithm	Algorithmic Steps	Work Per Step
The Thomas Algorithm	$2n$	1
Cyclic Reduction	$2\log_2 n$	$(1, n/2)$
Parallel Cyclic Reduction	$\log_2 n$	n

a switch between the basic algorithms at a point when the combined cost of two algorithms is lowest. There are two variants of hybrid algorithm, CR-PCR and PCR-Thomas. Sengupta et al. use a similar idea to combine a step-efficient scan algorithm with a work-efficient one for implementation on a GPU [9]. Figure 11.1 illustrates the step and work complexity of various algorithms, as well as their utilization of vector arithmetic unit, for solving an 8-equation system with a vector length of 4.

(a) Thomas: $2*8 = 16$ steps.
The vector unit has a utilization rate of 25% through all steps.
Less work per step, more steps.

(b) CR: $2\log_2 8 = 6$ steps.
The vector unit is partially idle during the middle three steps.
Less work per step, more steps.

 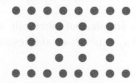

(c) PCR: $\log_2 8 = 3$ steps.
The vector unit is fully utilized across all steps.
More work per step, fewer steps.

(d) CR-PCR: $2 + \log_2 4 = 4$ steps.
The vector unit is fully utilized across all steps.
Less work per step than PCR, fewer steps than CR.

(e) PCR-Thomas: $2 + 2*2 = 6$ steps.
The vector unit is fully utilized across all steps.
Less work per step than PCR, fewer steps than the Thomas algorithm.

FIGURE 11.1

Comparison between the CR, PCR, and hybrid algorithms in terms of algorithmic steps and work per step for solving an 8-equation system. A dot stands for a unit of work, and a row of dots stands for an algorithmic step. We assume the length of vector arithmetic unit is 4 in this example (see color insert).

11.3 ALGORITHMS

In this section, we review three basic algorithms: the Thomas algorithm, CR, and PCR, and their two hybrid variants: CR-PCR and PCR-Thomas.

11.3.1 The Thomas Algorithm

The Thomas algorithm is Gaussian elimination in the tridiagonal system case. The algorithm has two phases, forward elimination and backward substitution. In the first phase, we eliminate the lower diagonal by

$$c_1' = \frac{c_1}{b_1}, \; c_i' = \frac{c_i}{b_i - c_{i-1}'a_i}, \; i = 2,3,\ldots,n$$

$$d_1' = \frac{d_1}{b_1}, \; d_i' = \frac{d_i - d_{i-1}'a_i}{b_i - c_{i-1}'a_i}, \; i = 2,3,\ldots,n.$$

The second phase solves all unknowns from last to first:

$$x_n = d_n', \; x_i = d_i' - c_i'x_{i+1}, \; i = n-1,\ldots,2,1.$$

The algorithm is simple, but inherently serial and takes $2n$ computation steps, because the calculation of c_i', d_i', and x_i depends on the result of the immediately preceding calculation of c_{i-1}', d_{i-1}', and x_{i+1}.

11.3.2 Cyclic Reduction (CR)

CR consists of two phases, forward reduction and backward substitution. The forward reduction phase successively reduces a system to a smaller system with half the number of unknowns, until a system of 2 unknowns is reached. The backward substitution phase successively determines the other half of the unknowns using the previously solved values.

In each step of forward reduction, we update all even-indexed equations in parallel with equation i of the current system as a linear combination of equations i, $i+1$, and $i-1$, so that we derive a system of only even-indexed unknowns. Equation i has the form $a_ix_{i-1} + b_ix_i + c_ix_{i+1} = d_i$. The updated values of a_i, b_i, c_i, and d_i are

$$a_i' = -a_{i-1}k_1, \; b_i' = b_i - c_{i-1}k_1 - a_{i+1}k_2$$

$$c_i' = -c_{i+1}k_2, \; d_i' = d_i - d_{i-1}k_1 - d_{i+1}k_2$$

$$k_1 = \frac{a_i}{b_{i-1}}, \; k_2 = \frac{c_i}{b_{i+1}}$$

In each step of backward substitution, we solve all odd-indexed unknowns x_i in parallel by substituting the already solved x_{i-1} and x_{i+1} values to equation i,

$$x_i = \frac{d_i' - a_i'x_{i-1} - c_i'x_{i+1}}{b_i'}.$$

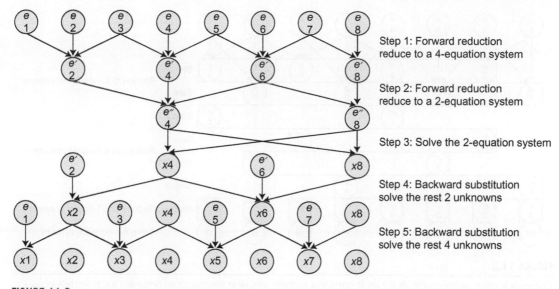

Step 1: Forward reduction
reduce to a 4-equation system

Step 2: Forward reduction
reduce to a 2-equation system

Step 3: Solve the 2-equation system

Step 4: Backward substitution
solve the rest 2 unknowns

Step 5: Backward substitution
solve the rest 4 unknowns

FIGURE 11.2

Communication pattern of CR for an 8-equation system, showing the dataflow between each equation, labeled $e1$ to $e8$. Letters e' and e'' stand for updated equation.

Note that for the sake of simplicity, in the above description, we disregard the special treatment of the last equation and the first unknown respectively, in the two algorithm phases. Also, we solve a 2-equation system between the two algorithm phases. Figure 11.2 shows the communication pattern of the algorithm for an 8-equation system.

Both the parallel CR algorithm and the serial Thomas algorithm perform a number of operations that are linear in the number of unknowns. The Thomas algorithm performs $8n$ operations while CR performs $17n$ operations. However, on a parallel computer with n processors, CR requires $2\log_2 n$ steps while the Thomas algorithm requires $2n$ steps.

11.3.3 Parallel Cyclic Reduction (PCR)

PCR is a variant of CR. In contrast to CR, PCR only has the forward reduction phase. Although the reduction mechanism and formula are the same as those of CR, in each reduction step, PCR reduces each of the current systems to two systems of half size. For example, for an 8-equation system as shown in Figure 11.3, PCR first reduces it from one 8-equation system to two 4-equation systems in step 1, from two 4-equation systems to four 2-equation systems in step 2, from four 2-equation systems to eight 1-equation systems in step 3, and finally solves eight 1-equation systems. PCR takes $12n\log_2 n$ operations and $\log_2 n$ steps to finish. PCR requires fewer algorithmic steps than CR but does asymptotically more work per step.

11.3.4 CR-PCR

CR-PCR first reduces the system to a certain size using the forward reduction phase of CR, then solves the reduced (intermediate) system with PCR, and finally substitutes the solved unknowns back

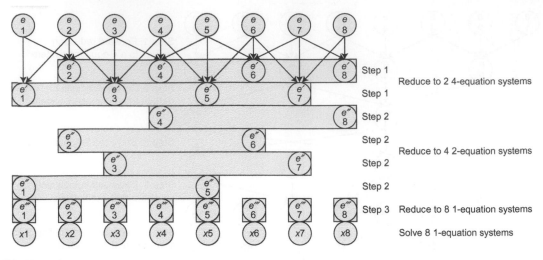

FIGURE 11.3

Communication pattern of PCR for an 8-equation system, showing the dataflow between each equation, labeled $e1$ to $e8$. Letters e', e'' and e''' stand for updated equation. Equations in the gray sections form a system. We omit the dataflow arrows in step 2 and step 3 for clarity.

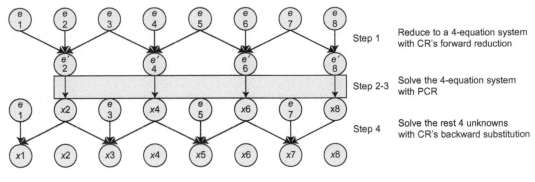

FIGURE 11.4

The CR-PCR algorithm for an 8-equation system. Letter e stands for equation, and e' stands for updated equation.

into the original system using the backward substitution phase of CR. Figure 11.4 shows the hybrid CR-PCR schematically. In this example, we switch to PCR before the forward reduction has reached a 2-equation system, which enables us to skip the inefficient CR steps where the vector arithmetic unit is not fully utilized.

11.3.5 PCR-Thomas

PCR-Thomas first reduces a single large system to many smaller systems, then solves these smaller systems in parallel with the Thomas algorithm. Figure 11.5 shows PCR-Thomas for solving an 8-equation

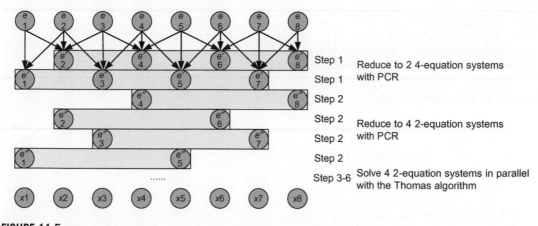

FIGURE 11.5

The PCR-Thomas algorithm for an 8-equation system. Letter e stands for equation. Letters e' and e'' stand for updated equation.

system. PCR-Thomas allows us to use an algorithm of lower computational cost than PCR, when the PCR stage has created a sufficient number of smaller systems to be solved in parallel by the sequential Thomas algorithms.

11.4 IMPLEMENTATION

To solve hundreds of tridiagonal systems simultaneously, we map the solver to the GPU's two-level hierarchical architecture with systems mapped to blocks and equations mapped to threads. We use shared memory to keep most communication between threads on chip. Although all parallel algorithms are general for any system size, our solvers only handle a power-of-two system size, which makes thread numbering and address calculation simpler. In the following subsections, we will walk through the implementation details of the tridiagonal solvers.

11.4.1 Cyclic Reduction

We first set up the kernel execution parameters as shown in Listing 11.1. The number of CUDA blocks is the number of systems, since every single system is mapped to one CUDA block. The number of threads per block is half the number of equations per system, since we start with updating only even-indexed equations in the first algorithmic step. The template parameter T allows us to choose either single precision or double precision floating-point arithmetic.

We use five global arrays to store three matrix diagonals (a: lower diagonal, b: main diagonal, c: upper diagonal), one right-hand side d, and one solution vector x. These five arrays store the data of all systems continuously, with the data of the first system stored at the beginning of the arrays, followed by the second system, the third system, and so on. The amount of shared memory we allocate for each CUDA block or each tridiagonal system is sizeSystem * 5 * sizeof(T) bytes.

```
dim3  grid(numSystems, 1, 1);
dim3  threads(sizeSystem/2, 1, 1);
int   sizeSharedMemory = sizeSystem * 5 * sizeof(T);
crKernel<<< grid, threads, sizeSharedMemory>>>(a, b, c, d, x);
```

Listing 11.1. Kernel setup for CR.

```
int stride = 1;
for (int j = 0; j < numSteps; j++)
{
    __syncthreads();
    stride *= 2;
    int delta = stride / 2;
    if (threadIdx.x < numThreads)
    {
        int i = stride * threadIdx.x + stride - 1;
        int iLeft  = i - delta;
        int iRight = i + delta;
        if (iRight >= sizeSystem) iRight = sizeSystem - 1;

        T tmp1 = a[i] / b[iLeft];
        T tmp2 = c[i] / b[iRight];
        b[i]   = b[i] - c[iLeft] * tmp1 - a[iRight] * tmp2;
        d[i]   = d[i] - d[iLeft] * tmp1 - d[iRight] * tmp2;
        a[i]   = -a[iLeft]  * tmp1;
        c[i]   = -c[iRight] * tmp2;
    }

    numThreads /= 2;
}
```

Listing 11.2. Forward reduction in CR.

The forward reduction phase (Listing 11.2) takes ($\log_2$ sizeSystem/2) algorithmic steps. All five arrays a, b, c, d, and x are shared memory arrays with data loaded from global memory. The stride starts with 1, and doubles its value every algorithmic step. The number of active threads decreases by half every algorithmic step. We always enable contiguously ordered threads as active threads so that we do not have unnecessary divergent branches within a SIMD unit.

To unify the special treatment to the last equation, we set iRight to sizeSystem $-$ 1 if iRight is equal or larger than sizeSystem. This technique takes the advantage of the fact that c[sizeSystem $-$ 1] $=$ 0, and more and more zeros are introduced to the array c along the algorithmic steps.

At the beginning of the backward substitution phase (Listing 11.3), we solve a 2-equation system produced at the final stage of forward reduction. Then we have ($\log_2$ sizeSystem/2) algorithmic steps to solve all of the rest unknowns. We double the number of active threads every algorithmic step.

```
if (threadIdx.x < 2)
{
    int addr1 =  stride − 1;
    int addr2 =  2 * stride − 1;
    T tmp     =  b[addr2] * b[addr1] − c[addr1] * a[addr2];
    x[addr1]  = (b[addr2] * d[addr1] − c[addr1] * d[addr2]) / tmp;
    x[addr2]  = (d[addr2] * b[addr1] − d[addr1] * a[addr2]) / tmp;
}

numThreads = 2;
for (int j = 0; j < numSteps; j++)
{
    int delta = stride/2;
    __syncthreads();
    if (threadIdx.x < numThreads)
    {
        int i = stride * threadIdx.x + stride / 2 − 1;
        if(i == delta − 1)
            x[i] = (d[i] − c[i] * x[i + delta]) / b[i];
        else
            x[i] = (d[i] − a[i] * x[i − delta] − c[i] * x[i+delta]) / b[i];
    }
    stride /= 2;
    numThreads *= 2;
}
```

Listing 11.3. Backward substitution in CR.

```
dim3  grid(numSystems, 1, 1);
dim3  threads(sizeSystem, 1, 1);
int   sizeSharedMemory = sizeSystem * 5 * sizeof(T);
pcrKernel<<< grid, threads, sizeSharedMemory>>>(a, b, c, d, x);
```

Listing 11.4. Kernel setup for PCR.

11.4.2 Parallel Cyclic Reduction

As in CR, we set the number of CUDA blocks to the number of systems. But in contrast to CR, we set the number of threads per block to the number of equations per system, since in PCR we update all equations, rather than half equations, during an algorithmic step (Listing 11.4). Furthermore, the number of active threads keeps constant as the number of equations through all algorithmic steps (Listing 11.5).

To unify the special treatment to the first equation and the last equation, we set iRight to sizeSystem − 1 if iRight is equal or larger than sizeSystem, and iLeft to 0 if iLeft is equal or less than 0 (Listing 11.5). This technique takes the advantage of the fact that a[0] = 0

```
for (int j = 0; j <numSteps; j++)
{
    int i = threadIdx.x;
    int iRight = i + delta;
    if (iRight >= sizeSystem) iRight = sizeSystem - 1;
    int iLeft = i - delta;
    if (iLeft < 0) iLeft = 0;

    T tmp1 = a[i] / b[iLeft];
    T tmp2 = c[i] / b[iRight];
    bNew  = b[i] - c[iLeft] * tmp1 - a[iRight] * tmp2;
    dNew  = d[i] - d[iLeft] * tmp1 - d[iRight] * tmp2;
    aNew  = -a[iLeft]  * tmp1;
    cNew  = -c[iRight] * tmp2;

    __syncthreads();
    b[i] = bNew;
    d[i] = dNew;
    a[i] = aNew;
    c[i] = cNew;
    delta *= 2;

    __syncthreads();
}

if (threadIdx.x < delta)
{
    int addr1 =  threadIdx.x;
    int addr2 =  threadIdx.x + delta;
    T tmp3    = b[addr2] * b[addr1] - c[addr1] * a[addr2];
    x[addr1] = (b[addr2] * d[addr1] - c[addr1] * d[addr2]) / tmp3;
    x[addr2] = (d[addr2] * b[addr1] - d[addr1] * a[addr2]) / tmp3;
}
```

Listing 11.5. PCR.

and c[sizeSystem - 1] = 0, and more and more zeros are introduced to the array a and c along the algorithmic steps.

11.4.3 CR-PCR

The implementation of hybrid solver is straightforward once we have the implementations of CR and PCR. To prepare for the PCR stage, we copy the data of the intermediate system to another contiguous space in shared memory. The copy takes little time and extra storage space for the intermediate system, but makes the solver more modular, so that we can directly plug the PCR solver into the intermediate system.

11.4.4 PCR-Thomas

The PCR-Thomas solver first reduces a system to many smaller systems, and then solves all systems in parallel with each system mapped to a CUDA thread. Since the equations of the reduced systems are interleaved as shown in step 2 of Figure 11.5, the Thomas solver needs to access these systems in a strided fashion. Figure 11.6 redraws the memory layout of four 2-equation systems reduced from an 8-equation system. A bonus of strided access is that it is free of any bank conflicts, which would have been a serious problem if all equations of a system are stored in a continuous fashion. Listing 11.6

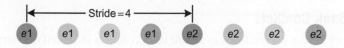

FIGURE 11.6

The memory layout of four 2-equation systems reduced from an 8-equation system by PCR. A dot stands for an equation. Equations of the same color belong to the same system.

```
__device__ void thomas(T *a, T *b, T *c, T *d, T *x, int sizeSmallerSystem)
{
    // Forward elimination
    c[threadIdx.x] = c[threadIdx.x] / b[threadIdx.x];
    d[threadIdx.x] = d[threadIdx.x] / b[threadIdx.x];
    int startLocationSystem = stride + threadIdx.x;
    for (int i = startLocationSystem; i < sizeSmallerSystem; i += stride)
    {
        T tmp = (b[i] - a[i] * c[i - stride]);
        c[i]  = c[i] / tmp;
        d[i]  = (d[i] - d[i - stride] * a[i]) / tmp;
    }

    // Backward substitution
    int endLocationSystem = sizeSmallerSystem - stride + threadIdx.x;
    x[endLocationSystem] = d[endLocationSystem];
    for (int i = endLocationSystem - stride; i >= 0; i -= stride)
    {
        x[i] = d[i] - c[i] * x[i + stride];
    }
}
```

Listing 11.6. The Thomas solver.

```
__device__ int addressTranslater(int address)
{
    int n = address >> 4;
    int m = address & 15;
    int addressPadded = n * 17 + m;
    return addressPadded;
}
```

Listing 11.7. Address translator.

shows the Thomas solver as a GPU device function which can be plugged into the PCR solver to form the PCR-Thomas hybrid solver.

11.4.5 Avoid Bank Conflicts

CR's strided memory access pattern leads to severe bank conflicts in shared memory. As the algorithm doubles its access stride every step as shown in the Figure 11.2, the number of bank conflicts are doubled as well, from 2-way bank conflicts in step one, to 4-way in step two, to 8-way in step three, and so on. We use a padding technique to avoid bank conflicts. Since there are 16 shared memory banks, we pad 1 element per 16 elements, which redirects all conflicted accesses to available banks. Compared to the interleaving technique by Göddeke et al. [2], which requires 50% more shared memory usage and complex addressing, this padding technique is simple and only costs 1/16 extra storage space. The technique can be easily integrated to the existing CR solver by translating all original addresses to padded addresses with an address translater as shown in Listing 11.7.

11.5 RESULTS AND EVALUATION

Our test platform uses a 2.8 GHz Intel Core i7 quad-core CPU, a GTX 480 graphics card with 1.5 GB video memory, CUDA 3.1 and the Windows 7 operating system.

11.5.1 Hybrid Solvers

We tune the performance of hybrid solvers by experimenting with various sizes of intermediate systems to find the sweet spot for algorithm switching. Figure 11.7 shows the performance of hybrid solvers respectively for single precision and double precision floating-point arithmetic. For solving 1024 1024-equation systems, the tuned performance of a hybrid solver is up to 2× faster than a basic solver. The best switch point turns out to be around 128, which is far larger than the warp size 32.[1] This is because it is preferable to have more than a warp of threads active so that multiple warps can be executed simultaneously in a interleaved way to keep the GPU busy.

---

[1] A warp is a group of 32 threads that execute in lockstep in a SIMD fashion. The warp size is the effective vector length for the GPU.

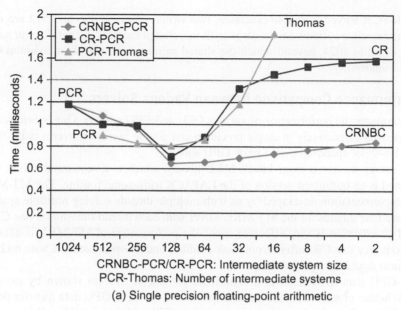

(a) Single precision floating-point arithmetic

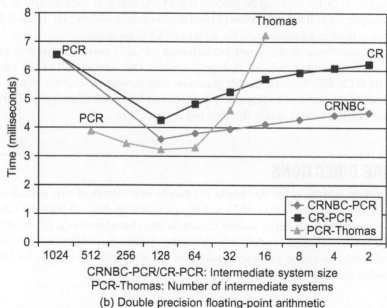

(b) Double precision floating-point arithmetic

FIGURE 11.7

Timings for the hybrid solvers with various switch points for solving 1024 1024-equation systems. CRNBC is the CR solver optimized for no bank conflicts. We label the algorithm names in the figure. The nearer a switch point is to a labeled algorithm, the more proportion that algorithm takes in the hybrid solver.

For the CR-PCR solver in double precision, two switch points at 256 and 512 are not available, because the intermediate systems are too large to fit into shared memory. Generally, our solvers support a system size of up to 1024, beyond which the shared memory size and the maximum CUDA block size become limitations.

11.5.2 Performance Comparison between Various Solvers

Figure 11.8 compares the performance of various GPU and CPU solvers. Our hybrid solver achieves $8\times$ and $2\times$ speedup respectively in single precision and double precision over a multi-threaded CPU solver, and a $2\times$–$2.3\times$ speed-up over a basic GPU solver.

The CPU solver we use is from Intel's MKL library, which is a sequential solver based on LU factorization and is an optimized version of the LAPACK tridiagonal routine. The MT-MKL solver is an OpenMP implementation developed by us with multiple threads solving multiple systems simultaneously. We use four threads for the MT-MKL solver with each thread running on one CPU core. The multithreaded acceleration is very effective, since the performance of MT-MKL is about $4\times$ that of MKL. We also notice that CR suffers from bank conflicts and an optimized CR with no bank conflicts (CRNBC) almost doubles its performance.

The CPU-GPU data transfer takes a significant amount of time as shown by the PCI-E bar in Figure 11.8. Whether or not we should include the cost of the CPU-GPU data transfer depends on the application scenario. Transfer time can be ignored if the GPU solver is used locally as a part of a GPU program (for example, GPU fluid simulation [8] and depth-of-field effects [4]). It should be considered if the GPU solver is used as an accelerator for a part of a CPU program.

Several factors contribute to the lower performance of GPU solvers in double precision. First, the number of enabled double precision arithmetic units is only one eighth of the number of single precision units on GTX 480. Second, double precision data consumes doubled shared memory bandwidth and the major data traffic of tridiagonal solvers comes from shared memory. Third, note that the PCI-Express data transfer time is nearly doubled too as expected.

11.6 FUTURE DIRECTIONS

We see several future directions for this work: (1) handle non–power-of-two system sizes, (2) effectively support a system size larger than 1024 and design solutions that can partially take advantage of shared memory even though the entire system cannot fit into shared memory, (3) overlap PCI-Express data transfer and the GPU kernel execution by grouping systems to chunks and pipelining the PCI-E data transfer and kernel execution of these chunks, and (4) generalize the solvers for block tridiagonal systems and banded systems.

SOURCE CODE

We have integrated the solvers into CUDA Data Parallel Primitives Library (CUDPP). The source code is available at:

http://cudpp.googlecode.com/ or
http://tridiagonalsolvers.googlecode.com/

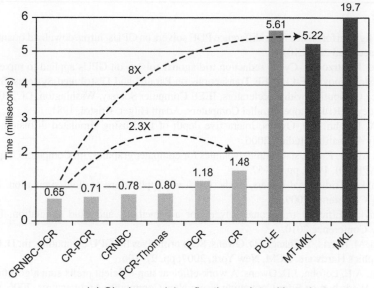

(a) Single precision floating-point arithmetic

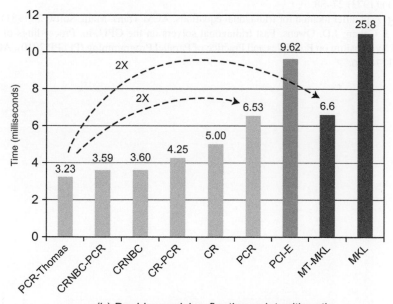

(b) Double precision floating-point arithmetic

FIGURE 11.8

Performance comparison of various GPU and CPU solvers for solving 1024 1024-equation systems. PCI-E: CPU-GPU PCI-Express data transfer. CRNBC: a CR solver optimized for no bank conflicts. MKL: a sequential tridiagonal routine from Intel's MKL library. MT-MKL: a multithreaded MKL solver.

References

[1] D. Egloff, High performance finite difference PDE solvers on GPUs. http://download.quantalea.net/fdm_gpu.pdf, 2010 (accessed 28.02.10).

[2] D. Göddeke, R. Strzodka, Cyclic reduction tridiagonal solvers on GPUs applied to mixed precision multigrid, in: I. Stojmenovic (Ed.), IEEE Transactions on Parallel and Distributed Systems, Special Issue: High Performance Computing with Accelerators, IEEE Computer Society, Washington, DC, 2010.

[3] R.W. Hockney, C.R. Jesshope, Parallel Computers, Adam Hilger, Bristol, 1981.

[4] M. Kass, A. Lefohn, J.D. Owens, Interactive depth of field using simulated diffusion, Technical Report 06-01, Pixar Animation Studios, 2006.

[5] M. Kass, G. Miller, Rapid, stable fluid dynamics for computer graphics, in: Computer Graphics (Proceedings of SIGGRAPH 90), 1990, pp. 49–57.

[6] N. Sakharnykh, Tridiagonal solvers on the GPU and applications to fluid simulation, in: NVIDIA GPU Technology Conference 2009.

[7] N. Sakharnykh, Efficient tridiagonal solvers for adi methods and fluid simulation, in: NVIDIA GPU Technology Conference 2010.

[8] S. Sengupta, M. Harris, Y. Zhang, J.D. Owens, Scan primitives for GPU computing, in: D. Fellner, S. Spencer (Eds.), Graphics Hardware, ACM, New York, 2007, pp. 97–106.

[9] S. Sengupta, A.E. Lefohn, J.D. Owens, A work-efficient step-efficient prefix sum algorithm, in: Proceedings of the 2006 Workshop on Edge Computing Using New Commodity Architectures, 2006, pp. D-26–D-27.

[10] H.S. Stone, An efficient parallel algorithm for the solution of a tridiagonal linear system of equations, J. ACM 20 (1) (1973) 27–38.

[11] H.H. Wang, A parallel method for tridiagonal equations, ACM Trans. Math. Softw. 7 (1981) 170–183.

[12] Y. Zhang, J. Cohen, J.D. Owens, Fast tridiagonal solvers on the GPU, in: Proceedings of the 15th ACM SIGPLAN Symposium on Principles and Practice of Parallel Programming (PPoPP 2010), ACM, New York, 2010, pp. 127–136.

Accelerating CULA Linear Algebra Routines with Hybrid GPU and Multicore Computing

12

John Humphrey, Daniel Price, Kyle Spagnoli, and Eric Kelmelis

The LU decomposition is a popular linear algebra technique with applications such as the solution of systems of linear equations and calculation of matrix inverses and determinants. Central processing unit (CPU) versions of this routine exhibit very high performance, making the port to a graphics processing unit (GPU) a challenging prospect. This chapter discusses the implementation of LU decomposition in our CULA library for linear algebra on the GPU, describing the steps necessary for achieving significant speed-ups over the CPU.

12.1 INTRODUCTION, PROBLEM STATEMENT, AND CONTEXT

The modern GPU found in many standard personal computers is a highly parallel math processor capable of nearly 1 TFLOPS peak throughput at a cost similar to a high-end CPU and an excellent FLOPS (floating point operations per second)/watt ratio. There is a strong desire to utilize such power, but it can be difficult to harness given the features and limitations of the platform. Therefore, libraries can be of great utility, allowing novices and experts alike to access high computational performance without knowledge of GPU programming. Some routines such as FFTs are quite common in scientific and numerical computing and it would be wasteful for each user to implement such routines that could instead be provided in a centralized library. Moreover, a library routine that is tuned by an expert will often outperform and be more feature robust, allowing users to instead focus on their particular areas of expertise. In this paper we present CULA, a library of linear algebra routines developed using a hybrid computation model employing both CPU and GPU power.

When you are performing numerical analysis, there are numerous recurring building blocks, many of which fall under the umbrella term of "linear algebra." At the lowest level, important fundamental operations deal with the manipulation of matrices and vectors, typically in simple ways, such as multiplication and addition. Building a level upward are a series of algorithms that cover a broad scope of concepts, including linear system solution, various decompositions (QR, SVD (singular value decomposition)), eigenproblem analysis, and least squares solution. Such operations have nearly limitless applications, such as electromagnetic analysis, financial computations, image processing, and statistics.

Over time, the numerical computing community has settled on a tiered representation of linear algebra operations. This scheme is embodied in the Basic Linear Algebra Subprograms (BLAS) [1] and

Linear Algebra Package (LAPACK) [2] libraries. These have also become standardized interfaces, with the typical usage scenario being to use a separate offering that has been specially tuned or completely rewritten for a given platform. Our offering, CULA, is a product of this nature. Specifically, it is a unified BLAS/LAPACK package that is tuned for the hybrid CPU/GPU machine.

CULA [3] is a high-performance linear algebra library that executes in a unified CPU/GPU hybrid environment. In this section, we discuss the functions that CULA provides and the interfaces through which a developer can integrate CULA into his or her code. We follow this with an introduction to some of the specialized techniques employed by CULA to obtain significant speed-ups over existing packages.

CULA features a wide variety of linear algebra functions, including least squares solvers (constrained and unconstrained), system solvers (general and symmetric positive definite), eigenproblem solvers (general and symmetric), singular value decompositions, and many useful factorizations (QR, Hessenberg, etc.). All such routines are presented in the four standard data types in LAPACK computations: single precision real (S), double precision real (D), single precision complex (C), and double precision complex (Z).

We support a number of methods for interfacing with CULA. The two major interfaces are host and device, and they accept data via host memory and device memory, respectively. The host interface features high convenience, whereas the device interface is more manual, but can avoid data transfer times. Additionally, there are facilities for interfacing with MATLAB and the Fortran language. Lastly, a special interface, called the Bridge interface, assists in porting existing codes that employ Intel MKL (Math Kernel Library), AMD ACML (AMD Core Math Library), and Netlib CLAPACK.

CULA employs several specialized techniques to attain its speed-ups. In the following sections, we describe several of these. Most notable are hybrid overlapped CPU/GPU processing, algorithm refactoring for performance, and the avoidance of partition camping on pre-Fermi architectures. All work will be described in terms of our LU decomposition routine, which is a popular algorithm in linear algebra for the solution of systems of linear equations.

12.2 CORE METHODS

Although CULA features linear algebra routines constituting a survey of the field, this chapter will focus on one routine in particular, the LU decomposition. LU factorizes a matrix into two triangular matrices: L is a lower triangular, and U is an upper triangular. The product of the matrices L and U is the original matrix, A. The applications of LU include solving systems of linear equations, inverting a matrix, and calculating the determinant and condition. The mathematical basis of the decomposition is Gaussian Elimination, modified to record the pivot value as each entry is eliminated.

In practice, LU must be pivoted for stability. The partial pivoting process selects the maximum subdiagonal element each time a division operation is executed to avoid division by zero or a small number. The resulting form is $P^*A = L^*U$. Performing the subdiagonal scan and row interchanges can take a significant amount of time; our solution will be described later.

Direct ports of the LU algorithm are not suitable to parallel computations because the operations would appear to work on vectors within the matrix. The algorithm is instead cast in terms of matrix multiplication, which has highly performing parallel implementations, especially on GPUs. Therefore, this chapter will describe a blocked, partially pivoted LU based on matrix multiplication.

Adhering to common LAPACK naming conventions, we discuss the routine known as GETRF (standing for General Matrix Triangular Factorization). There are four variants: SGETRF (single precision), DGETRF (double precision), CGETRF (single precision complex), and ZGETRF (double precision complex), all of which are equally implementable based on this chapter.

12.3 ALGORITHMS, IMPLEMENTATIONS, AND EVALUATIONS
12.3.1 Overview

A base implementation of a matrix multiply-based LU decomposition will show performance that does not exceed a highly tuned CPU implementation, such as Intel's MKL. This might be surprising, given that matrix multiply performs the bulk of the work and NVIDIA makes available an excellent matrix multiply in their CUBLAS library.

The following specific techniques required to achieve strong performance are described in this section:

- Employing a look-ahead hybrid CPU/GPU processing model for areas of limited parallelism
- Minimizing ill-performing sections caused by performing row swaps
- Avoiding partition camping prior to Fermi GPUs

In pseudocode, the base blocked algorithm for a square matrix is:

```
1  For j=1:blockSize:N
2          Factorize the panel A(j:N,j:j+blockSize)
3          Swap rows to the left and right of the factorized panel in the same manner
                  as the panel
4          Backsolve the area A(j:j+blockSize,j+blockSize:N) using the upper
                  triangular section of the panel
5          Perform the operation c = c - a*b, where
6                  c = A(j+blockSize:N,j+blockSize:N)
7                  a = A(j+blockSize:N, j:j+blockSize)
8                  b = A(j:j+blockSize, j+blockSize:N)
```

The algorithm described here performs all work on the input A matrix. This matrix is destroyed in the process of factorization and is replaced with the L and U matrices, both of which are packed into a single matrix (their shapes are complementary, and all zeros are omitted). L is chosen to be a unit lower triangular matrix, and its diagonal is omitted and implicit.

Following the decomposition, the main application is to use the factorized matrix to solve a system of equations. As the two matrices are triangular, the backward and forward solves are a straightforward process requiring $O(N^2)$ operations, making this stage significantly less intense than the $O(N^3)$ required by the LU. Moreover, the LU can be reused for solutions to multiple right-hand sides that can be performed serially or in parallel. In LAPACK and CULA terms, the backsolve portion of the algorithm is implemented in the GETRS routines, and the GESV routine combines the LU and the backsolve into one convenient call.

12.3.2 Hybrid Processing Model

In the GPU computing field, a hybrid code such as CULA is one that utilizes both a CPU and a GPU for its computation. CULA, as it exists today, differs somewhat from our original intent at the outset of development, which was to create a purely GPU-based library. We discovered that the GPU's poor performance for certain types of operations made it very difficult to achieve speed-ups over the CPU. For example, the LU decomposition features a number of "panel factorizations" and a number of BLAS routines. The panel factorized when implemented on the GPU would often result in the GPU being a *slowdown* compared with the CPU.

As suggested in the literature [4], it proves worthwhile to bring the panel back to the CPU for processing compared to an optimal CPU implementation. The total time of *transfer + factorize + transfer* will often be shorter than the time for the pure GPU version because the GPU will be asked to perform operations that it does not excel at — for example, the scan to find the appropriate pivot element for the LU pivoting operation.

Using the CPU for processing these operations introduces a second chance for optimization — overlapping the operations. We have produced a thorough treatment on this topic in [5], but it is also mentioned here for completeness. The notion is that while the panel is being transferred to and factorized by the CPU, the GPU can continue doing other operations. This is possible as long as there is work that doesn't immediately depend on the CPU results, but for many linear algebra algorithms this is often the case. The result is that the work shifted to the CPU essentially becomes free in terms of overall time.

In the end, these two concepts are key to performance. By allowing the CPU and GPU to perform operations for which they are naturally well suited, we can avoid a bottleneck. Furthermore, by overlapping these we can then leverage the power of both platforms simultaneously.

This method of operation requires the realization that the CUDA kernel launches (as well as CUBLAS function calls) are asynchronous. In addition, memory transfers can be made explicitly asynchronous, although they are not naturally asynchronous as kernels are. Asynchronous memory transfers and kernel launches can be used as shown in Figure 12.1 to hide some of the cost of computation and transfer. Asynchronous transfers require the use of pinned memory and the *cudaMemcpyAsync* function. Pinned memory is contiguous in host physical memory that allows for high-throughput

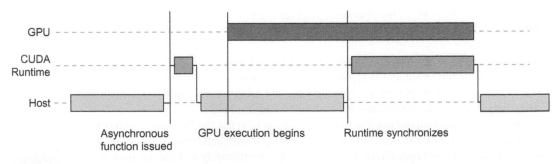

FIGURE 12.1

Overlapped computation. The host issues an asynchronous command to the CUDA runtime, which returns control to the host thread. At a later time, GPU execution begins, and the host may complete work during this execution. Upon request of the GPU's results, the CUDA runtime synchronizes, waiting for the GPU to ensure that these results are coherent.

asynchronous transfers. Each asynchronous operation is placed into a *stream*, which is the CUDA term describing task-level parallelism — operations in the same stream are executed in order; there is no order nor relationship guaranteed or provided for different streams. Streams are allocated and managed with the CUDA API functions: *cudaStreamCreate* and *cudaStreamSynchronize*. The function of the former should be clear, and the latter does not return until all the operations in a certain stream have completed.

In practice for LU, there are certain obvious overlaps that can be achieved. For instance, if we are executing Operation 2 of the pseudocode on the CPU, while the resulting panel transfers to the GPU, Operation 3 can be performed on GPU memory. The code for such a method would appear as:

1. *cudaMemcpy* (synchronous) the area of *panel* to the host
2. Factorize the panel
3. Initiate asynchronous transfer of *panel* to the GPU
4. Initiate asynchronous row swap operations
5. Synchronize

The key point is that steps 3 and 4 must be in different streams. Otherwise, CUDA will force them to serialize rather than to execute concurrently.

To this point, we have hidden the one-way transfer overhead of *panel*, but have not yet hidden the operation's CPU time nor the transfer from the GPU to the CPU of the data. Such changes require a restructuring of the algorithm.

It is useful to observe the output areas of Operations 3 and 5 of the pseudocode for the LU algorithm. The output area wholly contains the *next* panel to be factorized, plus much more. By carefully applying asynchronous operations, we can first perform Operations 3 through 5 for only the areas that affect the *next panel*, then synchronize that stream, begin an asynchronous transfer, and continue to process the remaining area. The result is that the CPU portion of the code, including both execution and transfers is completely hidden while the GPU performs the highly parallel sections of the code.

Figures 12.2 through 12.4 demonstrate, in pictures, the progression from traditional blocked code to hybrid GPU/CPU code is as follows:

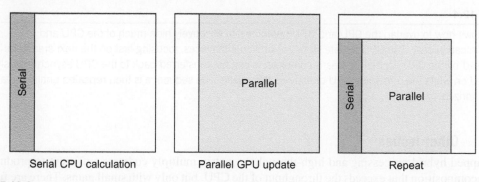

Serial	Parallel	Serial Parallel
Serial CPU calculation	Parallel GPU update	Repeat

FIGURE 12.2

Many blocked linear algebra algorithms share a similar structure where largely serial operations are performed on a section of the matrix ("panel"), and then the results of that operation are broadcast to some other larger area of the matrix via highly serial operations.

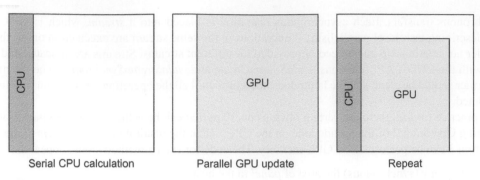

FIGURE 12.3

A typical first pass GPU implementation of a blocked algorithm will be as above, with the serial portions mapped to the CPU and the parallel portions mapped to the GPU. This can produce speed-ups, but is likely to be nonoptimal use of the hardware. Also noteworthy is that mapping the more serial panel operations to the GPU will often lead to a slowdown compared with a good CPU implementation.

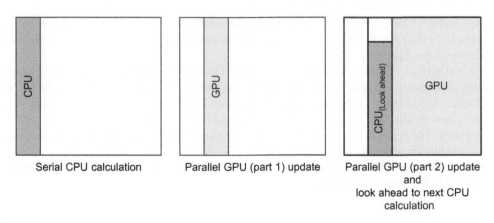

FIGURE 12.4

This shows how to overlap the CPU and GPU operations to effectively hide much of the CPU and communication cost. The GPU update steps are broken into pieces, focusing first on the next area to be processed by the CPU. Once this area is complete, is can be transferred back to the CPU asynchronously and operated on while the remaining GPU operations take place. The sequence is then repeated until the matrix is fully factorized.

12.3.3 Other Issues

Overlapped hybrid processing and high-throughput matrix multiply code are sufficient to produce an LU Decomposition that exceeds the throughput of the CPU, but only with small gains. There are further optimizations that will be discussed in this section.

A first profiling of the code described in the preceding section reveals that a new bottleneck has been formed; namely, the row interchange operations following the panel factorization. This bottleneck occurs because LAPACK routines store data in column major order, and therefore, sequential row elements are far in memory. Swapping rows leads to highly divergent memory accesses. A working solution, when possible, is to work in row major order, but that is contrary to LAPACK conventions. Our answer is to employ a transpose to convert from column major order to row major. The time for such an operation is trivial for what it gains in performance of the other operations. The NVIDIA GPU Computing SDK has a good example showing out-of-place transpose (one in which data is copied to a new matrix, albeit in transposed order). This bloats the memory usage at the cost of simplicity. For square matrices, an efficient in-place transpose can be written to avoid the memory usage increase.

The effect on other code is significant, though not insurmountable. Mostly, modifications to the arguments of CUBLAS routines is sufficient (i.e., TRSM "Left" "Lower" becomes TRSM "Right" "Upper" to represent the new data layout, indices are switched to represent transposed, and sizes are also swapped). Similarly, transfers of *panel* back to the CPU must be transposed prior to departing from the GPU to arrive in CPU memory in column major order; this can be handled using the sample NVIDIA code.

In prior literature, it was decided that replacing CUBLAS calls with custom BLAS routines was necessary for performance owing to the specific size and job combinations required by LU Decomposition. As of CUDA 3.1, this is no longer the case because the performance of CUBLAS has been increased considerably.

12.3.4 Fermi Architecture GPUs

Prior to the Fermi GPU architecture, a major source of ill performance from GPU routines was partition camping. LU relies on many blocked column memory transactions that could easily end in a partition camped memory access pattern.

The memory of an NVIDIA graphic card is grouped into multiple partitions of various widths. The number and width of these partitions depends on the model of the GPU and has changed between generations. Figure 12.5 shows the partitions of the G200 series of processors, which has eight partitions each of 256-byte width.

To efficiently access this memory, the memory transactions of all active threads should be spread evenly across the different memory partitions to fully utilize each of the partitions. In the case where the memory access is unbalanced, partition camping will occur, and memory bandwidth will be limited because several partitions are not utilized.

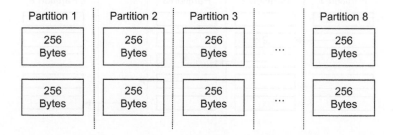

FIGURE 12.5

G200 Memory Partitioning. Memory is organized into 8 partitions of 256-byte width.

For many common usage scenarios, threads will naturally be spread out among the memory partitions, leading to full performance, as shown in Figure 12.6. For example, a kernel might read in multiple floating-point vectors from a matrix where each vector has a length of 64. If these vectors, each 256 bytes in size, are accessed in a row-wise pattern, they will be evenly accessed between partitions. There will be no partition camping, and memory throughput will be maximized. If these same vectors are accessed in a column-wise pattern, however, severe partition camping will occur because all memory accesses will be within the same memory partition. This partition camping will adversely affect memory throughput because only one of the eight memory units will be employed to service the request, limiting the bandwidth to an eighth of its full potential.

In many cases, using padded memory helps you avoid the problem of partition camping. As shown in Figure 12.7, if the memory in the column-wise access pattern was padded by the width of one vector, the memory requested would now be spread out between all of the partitions, rather than all targeting the same partitions, because this padding offsets the target partition for each vector request by one. For most applications and problem sizes, this memory overhead is small (2–3%) and is an acceptable sacrifice for the drastic increase in GPU memory throughput.

On Fermi machines, this problem is largely abated by the more sophisticated memory scheduler, but we mention this for completeness because pre-Fermi systems are still common as of this writing.

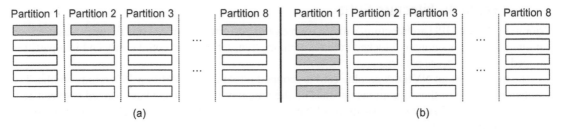

FIGURE 12.6

Partition access and conflicts. In (a), requests are spread across all available partitions, leading to full performance. In (b), several threads target the same partition, leading to several reduced throughputs.

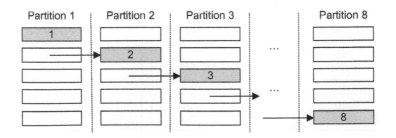

FIGURE 12.7

Padding to avoid partition camping. An additional vector forces memory requests to be spread out across all partitions by offsetting the target partition by one.

12.4 FINAL EVALUATION AND VALIDATION OF RESULTS, TOTAL BENEFITS, AND LIMITATIONS

In this section we present collected benchmarking statistics for the LU decomposition in CULA. The performance of this routine over a wide range of problem sizes and in singe/double precision is presented in Figures 12.8 and 12.9. The benchmark system contains a NVIDIA Tesla C2050 GPU and Intel Core i7 920 processor. All problems fit within memory.

Our CULA LU routine was compared against the Intel MKL 10.3 offering (S/DGETRF), running all four processor cores in the system. Note that MKL 10.3 has been fully optimized for the Core i7 processor on which it was running. Therefore, this benchmark is of the highest possible quality. Although not specifically pictured, the performance of the complex versions trends similarly to their real single/double counterparts.

The CULA version is for our device pointer interface, which ignores the overhead of transfer time of the original and result matrices to/from the GPU. Data was allocated using the routine *culaDevice-Malloc*, which may pad the leading dimension for performance reasons. At large problem sizes, the transfer overhead is as small as 5–10%, so the host interface is also usable for convenience. The device interface is for users who know the lifetime of data on the GPU; that is, if they are following the decomposition with some number of follow-up operations such as system solves, it will make sense to leave the factorized matrix on the GPU and potentially the factorized matrix itself is never returned to CPU memory, thereby saving time.

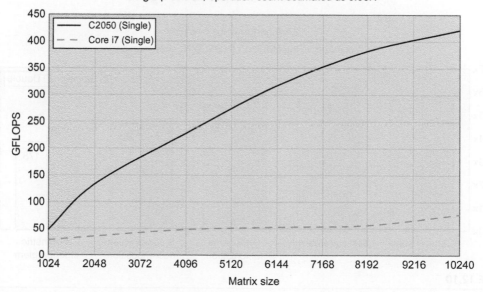

FIGURE 12.8

Performance of LU Decomposition in Single Precision.

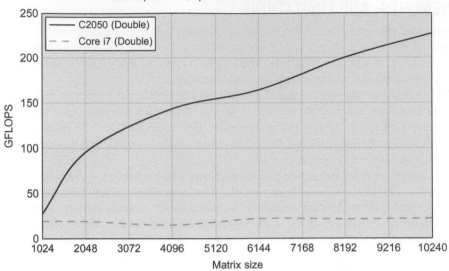

FIGURE 12.9

Performance of LU Decomposition in Double Precision.

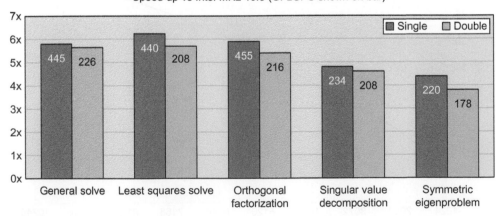

FIGURE 12.10

Showing performance for a wide range of CULA routines. The GFLOPS measure is shown in the bar, and the speed-up versus the CPU is represented by the height of the bar.

It is an exercise to the user to determine the appropriate precision (single/double) for their particular problem. In each case, the LU decomposition's accuracy matches that of the CPU. Such testing is carried out via a reconstruction test; that is, performing the multiplication of $L*U$ (permuted by the pivot array) and checking against the original A matrix using a relative norm test. This test is robust and standard, but it is worth mentioning that the individual L and U matrices will in general not match those produced by the CPU because there will be divergent decisions when choosing the locations of the pivots. This type of performance is expected because the LU decomposition for a given matrix is only unique in an infinite precision environment.

As for overall performance of CULA, performance is similar across the range of routines present. Figure 12.10 shows speed-ups for a variety of routines, on the same test system as described earlier in this section. In all test cases, the data and inputs to both the CULA solver and the CPU solver were identical.

12.5 FUTURE DIRECTIONS

The future work for this routine expands capability in several directions:

- Multi-GPU processing for large scale processing
- Sparse matrix computations; work in this area is described in [6].

References

[1] J.J. Dongarra, J. Du Croz, I.S. Duff, S. Hammarling, A set of level 3 basic linear algebra subprograms, ACM Trans. Math. Soft. 16 (1990) 1–17.

[2] E. Anderson, Z. Bai, C. Bischof, S. Blackford, J. Demmel, J. Dongarra, et al., LAPACK user's guide, third ed., Society for Industrial and Applied Mathematics, Philadelphia, PA, 1999.

[3] J.R. Humphrey, D.K. Price, K.E. Spagnoli, A.L. Paolini, E.J. Kelmelis, CULA: Hybrid GPU Accelerated Linear Algebra Routines, Presented at SPIE Defense, Security, and Sensing, April 2010.

[4] V. Volkov, J. Demmel, Benchmarking GPUs to tune dense linear algebra, in: SC'08 Proceedings of the 2008 ACM/IEEE Conference on Supercomputing, IEEE Press, Piscataway, NJ, 2008.

[5] D.K. Price, J.R. Humphrey, K.E. Spagnoli, A.L. Paolini, Analyzing the Impact of Data Movement on GPU Computations, Presented at SPIE Defense, Security, and Sensing, April 2010.

[6] K.S. Spagnoli, J.R. Humphrey, D.K. Price, E.J. Kelmelis, Accelerating Sparse Linear Algebra Using Graphics Processing Units, Presented at SPIE Defense, Security, and Sensing, April 2011.

CHAPTER

GPU Accelerated Derivative-Free Mesh Optimization

13

Eric Shaffer and George Zagaris

In this chapter, we present a GPU-based implementation of a derivative-free optimization method. The utility of derivative-free optimization is demonstrated in a mesh optimization algorithm that improves the element quality of a surface mesh. The parallelism afforded by the GPU is exploited to optimize a large number of elements simultaneously, resulting in a significant speed-up as compared with serial optimization.

13.1 INTRODUCTION, PROBLEM STATEMENT, AND CONTEXT

Numerical optimization is one of the most prolific scientific computing activities. It is employed in incredibly diverse fields, finding applications in logistics, computational finance, and medicine, among many others. Amidst this diversity of applications, problems frequently arise for which it is infeasible or impossible to compute derivatives of the objective function. Therefore, these problems cannot be attacked using the preferred derivative-based line-search methods such as conjugate gradient. Instead, derivative-free methods must be employed.

One example of an application requiring derivative-free optimization is the problem of mesh improvement formulated for per-vertex parallelism. Meshes are frequently used in computational simulation to model physical objects. As an example, Figure 13.1 shows a fan disk modeled using a triangulated surface mesh. It is known that meshes with poorly shaped elements degrade both the accuracy and efficiency of a simulation [3]. One popular method for improving mesh quality is to change the positions of the mesh vertices to optimize some measure of mesh quality.

We can formalize the mesh optimization problem as having three components: the quality metric, the objective function, and the optimization algorithm. The quality metric is a continuous function that measures one or more geometric properties of an element and provides a measure of how "good" the shape of an element is. Our focus is on triangulated surface meshes, meaning the mesh elements are triangles embedded in three-dimensional space. We will use the minimum angle in a triangle as the quality metric, with larger minimum angles indicating higher element quality. Although minimum angle is not necessarily the best quality metric available, it is reasonably effective and has the benefit of being very intuitive and widely used in engineering practice [3].

The quality metric measures the quality of individual mesh elements. An objective function is needed to combine these individual values into one for the domain of the optimization problem. In

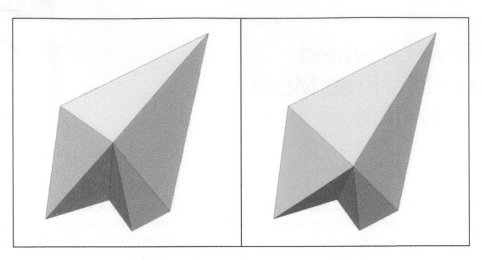

FIGURE 13.1

A vertex before and after optimizing its position to maximize the minimum angle.

optimizing the vertex positions in a surface mesh, one must adhere to the constraint that the new vertex positions remain close to the original surface. Enforcing this constraint is a significant complication for global optimization. Local optimization is an attractive alternative because it is relatively easy to approximate a surface locally and constrain the optimization domain accordingly. Local optimization also has the advantage of letting us exploit the massive parallelism of a GPU. We will optimize the mesh on a per-vertex basis similar to the approach taken in [2] for parallel optimization of two-dimensional meshes. When we are optimizing the position of a single vertex p, the domain of the optimization problem becomes the set of triangles T_p neighboring p. The objective function we choose is the minimum angle among all of the neighboring triangles of p, yielding an objective function $Q(p) = \min \theta_t$ where $t \in T_\mathbf{p}$. Our goal is to position the vertex so that the value of $Q(p)$ is maximized. An example of this operation, as applied to a single vertex, can be seen in Figure 13.1. As formulated, the objective function $Q(p)$ is clearly nonsmooth as discontinuities occur when the minimum angle shifts from one triangle to another as the vertex v is moved. Given this, a derivative-free optimization method is the natural choice for optimizing the objective function. We have chosen to employ the Nelder-Mead Simplex method [1]. The Nelder-Mead method has enjoyed enduring popularity in the scientific community and is one of the fundamental derivative-free optimization algorithms found in most numerical packages. The reasons for the popularity of the Nelder-Mead algorithm are mostly practical in nature. Chief among these is the ease of implementation of the simplex transformations employed by the algorithm. Additionally, although there are no theoretical convergence guarantees, the algorithm is reputed to converge quite often in practice. One of the known disadvantages of the algorithm is that it requires a large number of objective function evaluations. Optimizing a large number of variables clearly exacerbates this shortcoming, leading to very slow serial performance. GPU acceleration provides an unprecedented opportunity for improving the performance of the simplex search algorithm in such a setting.

13.2 CORE METHOD

The core technology presented in this work is the GPU implementation of the Nelder-Mead Simplex search algorithm using the CUDA application program interface (API). The implementation is best understood by first describing the general steps of the Nelder-Mead Simplex search algorithm. As generally formulated, the goal is to *minimize* the function $Q(p)$, where $Q{:}\mathbb{R}^N \to \mathbb{R}$, by searching through the domain for the optimal point p. The algorithm starts by generating a nondegenerate simplex, $\mathbf{S_p}$ in $\mathbb{R}^N$, consisting of $N+1$ vertices. Hence, $\mathbf{S_p}$ is a triangle in $\mathbb{R}^2$, a tetrahedron in $\mathbb{R}^3$, etc. Next, the objective function Q is evaluated at each of the $N+1$ vertices of the simplex $\mathbf{S_p}$ and the "worst," "good," and "best" vertices of the simplex are identified, where the "worst" vertex has the least desirable objective value Q. Then, the simplex is iteratively transformed to improve the "worst" vertex as follows:

1. First, the worst vertex is *reflected* to point $\mathbf{R}$ along the edge composed by the two other vertices (i.e, the edge formed by the best and good vertices), as illustrated in the left-most simplex in Figure 13.2.
2. If the objective function $Q(\mathbf{R})$ is better than the value at the best vertex $Q(\mathbf{B})$, then $\mathbf{R}$ is *expanded* along the same direction to $\mathbf{E}$, as illustrated in Figure 13.2. If $Q(\mathbf{E})$ yields a better objective value than $Q(\mathbf{R})$, then $\mathbf{E}$ replaces $\mathbf{W}$ and the algorithm moves to the next iteration.
3. Otherwise, a *contraction* of $\mathbf{R}$ at $\mathbf{C_1}$ and $\mathbf{W}$ at $\mathbf{C_2}$ is constructed. The best value of these two points according to the objective function Q, defined as the minimum of $Q(\mathbf{C_1})$ and $Q(\mathbf{C_2})$, determines which of $\mathbf{C_1}$ and $\mathbf{C_2}$ is chosen to replace $\mathbf{W}$.
4. Last, if all the preceding steps fail to provide an improvement on $\mathbf{W}$, the simplex is shrunk toward the "best" vertex $\mathbf{B}$, as depicted in Figure 13.2.

Expansion allows the search to move through the domain when it appears a minimum lies outside the simplex. The contraction transformation is used when it appears a minimum is somewhere within the original or reflected simplex. The shrinking operation handles the case where none of the previous

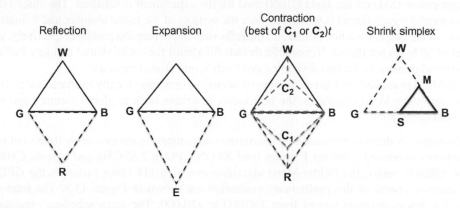

FIGURE 13.2

Nelder-Mead Simplex search transformations where **B** is the best vertex, **G** is the good vertex, and **W** is the worst vertex.

transformations achieved an improvement and seeks to facilitate the convergence of the algorithm in subsequent iterations. The algorithm terminates after the simplex shrinks below a user-specified size or some maximum number of iterations have been performed.

The parallelization strategy that we employed in this work is based on the classical single-instruction multiple-data (SIMD) approach in which each thread executes the Nelder-Mead algorithm on different data. Given a set of M variables to be optimized, our implementation is capable of applying the Nelder-Mead algorithm on each of the M variables in parallel on the GPU.

13.3 ALGORITHMS, IMPLEMENTATIONS, AND EVALUATIONS

A preliminary benchmark to evaluate the performance of the implementation consisted of the optimization of a point-set $\mathbf{P}$ in $\mathbb{R}^2$ where the objective function Q was defined as the Euclidean distance from a circle with radius r centered at the origin.

The Nelder-Mead algorithm was implemented for the CPU in C++ and the GPU using CUDA (CUDA 2.3). All the simplex transformation routines, as well as the routine for the objective function calculation, were implemented as device functions. Data within the scope of these functions reside in registers, and shared memory is used for global data. The implementation is based on the SIMD approach where each thread is assigned a single point and executes the iterative Nelder-Mead algorithm. The basic steps in the GPU implementation are as follows:

1. The point-set array is copied to the GPU device global memory using CPU-to-device memory copy.
2. The Nelder-Mead kernel is invoked with a block size of 256 and the number of blocks given by the formula:

```
NBLOCKS = NPOINTS / BLKSIZE + ( (NPOINTS%BLKSIZE == 0) ? 0:1 )
```

Here the block size is chosen such that the 16 KB shared memory limitation of each streaming multiprocessor (SM) on the Tesla C1060 used for the experiment is satisfied. The shared memory requirement for each thread is 6 floats to store the vertices of the initial simplex and 8 floats for the vertices of the two contraction points and the reflection and expansion points, respectively, yielding a total of 56 bytes per thread. Hence, 256 threads fill almost the entire shared memory buffer.

3. Each thread constructs the initial simplex and loads it into shared memory.
4. Nelder-Mead is applied for a given number of iterations, operating locally in shared memory space.
5. After the Nelder-Mead completes, the best vertex is written back to global memory and replaces the initial query point.

Our performance evaluation proceeded by measuring and comparing the execution time(s) of optimizing a randomly generated point-set $\mathbf{P}$ on an Intel XEON CPU at 2.67 GHz and a Tesla C1060 GPU card. For 450,000 points, the Nelder-Mead algorithm executed 118 times faster on the GPU. Sample performance results of this preliminary evaluation are shown in Figure 13.3. The total number of points for this experiment ranged from 150,000 to 450,000. The large speed-up obtained using this simple benchmark is an artifact of the embarrassingly parallel nature of the iterative optimization algorithm. The Nelder-Mead algorithm typically requires a large number of function evaluations to converge. Hence, processing 450,000 independent variables serially dwarfs the transfer-time of the

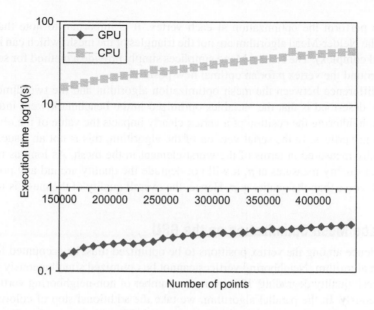

FIGURE 13.3

Comparative execution time of Nelder-Mead optimization on the CPU and on the GPU.

data to the GPU device where each independent variable can be processed simultaneously. This is a substantial performance boost for applications requiring the optimization of many input variables such as our motivating application: implementing a derivative free optimization for parallel mesh quality optimization.

13.3.1 Basic Surface Mesh Optimization Algorithm

The input to the mesh quality optimization algorithm is a triangulated surface mesh. The algorithm uses a tangent plane at each vertex as a local approximation to the surface at that point. In order to construct these tangent planes, the algorithm begins by computing a normal vector to the surface at each vertex p. This is accomplished by simply averaging the area-weighted unit normals of the triangles neighboring p. Once this is done, the normal and the vertex p define the tangent plane. An orthonormal basis for this plane is then constructed by finding vectors u and v [6]. This basis together with p as the origin forms a *local frame*. This local frame defines a two-dimensional space in which the optimization of p will occur. Movement within this local frame must be further constrained to prevent neighboring triangles from folding over on one another. This step is accomplished by projecting the neighboring vertices of p to the tangent plane and then finding the minimum distance d from p to a projected neighbor. The new position of p is then constrained to be less the αd from the original position, where α is a user-supplied parameter with $0 < \alpha < 1$. In our experiments, we have used $\alpha = 0.5$ with good results.

The objective function we seek to optimize for each vertex is the same as described in Section 13.1 with one amendment. Because we employ a traditional implementation of Nelder-Mead, which seeks to minimize a function, we will use $Q(p) = 1/\min \theta_t$ where $t \in T_p$. Minimizing $Q(p)$ should result in maximizing the minimum angle among the triangles incident on p. We employ two-dimensional

Nelder-Mead to perform the optimization at each vertex. It is important to note that the simplices constructed by the Nelder-Mead algorithm are not the triangles of the mesh (which can itself be thought of as a simplicial complex). The Nelder-Mead simplices simply provide a method for searching a small neighborhood around the vertex p for an optimal new position.

The signal difference between the mesh optimization algorithm and the two-dimensional benchmark previously described is that the variables optimized in the benchmark were independent. With mesh optimization, altering the position of a vertex clearly impacts the value of the objective function at the neighboring vertices. In the serial version of the algorithm, this is not an issue. The quality of a mesh is typically measured in terms of the worst element in the mesh. As long as moving a vertex p results in better quality measures at p, it will not degrade the quality around any previously moved vertex to a level worse than the quality at p. Hence, the overall quality of the mesh is not degraded.

13.3.2 Surface Mesh Optimization on the GPU

The interdependence among the vertex positions to be optimized must be accounted for to parallelize the optimization algorithm. Neighboring vertices cannot be optimized simultaneously without the risk of the overall mesh quality degrading. However, any number of non-neighboring vertices can be optimized simultaneously. In the parallel algorithm, we take the additional step of coloring (or labeling) the vertices of the mesh so that no two neighboring vertices have the same color. Computing an optimal coloring, one in which the fewest possible colors are used, is NP-Hard. However, a number of heuristics exist that do a reasonable job [4]. We implemented a First Fit heuristic that runs on the CPU. This algorithm is essentially just a greedy one that colors each vertex in turn with a color not used by any currently colored neighbors. Our "colors" are simply integer labels, and we always choose the lowest possible integer not represented among the neighbors. As can be seen in Table 13.1, in our experiments, the time required for coloring is tiny compared with the optimization time. Moreover, the number of colors used was always close to the minimum possible, which would be the maximum degree of a vertex in the mesh. Each set of identically colored vertices constitutes an independent set that can be optimized simultaneously.

Overall, the CUDA version of the mesh optimization procedure is broken down into three main steps:

1. Project the Cartesian xyz coordinates of a vertex to the tangent plane.
2. Optimize the projected uv coordinates using the Nelder-Mead method.
3. Unproject the optimized uv coordinates and update the mesh on the host.

These steps, illustrated in Figure 13.4, are implemented as separate kernels that the host code invokes. Although it is not shown, evaluation of the objective function inside the optimization step requires unprojection as well in order to evaluate the angles that would be generated by moving p to the various candidate locations examined by Nelder-Mead.

After the initial step of coloring the mesh vertices, the host transfers all the information required about the mesh to the GPU. Specifically, there are three pieces of information needed for a given vertex: its coordinates in Cartesian xyz space, the local frame at the vertex, and the neighboring vertices forming the triangles incident on the given vertex. Note that the neighbor information and the local frames require only read access. Thus, texture memory may be used for storing this information to reduce latency. However, in this implementation global memory was used to store all the information.

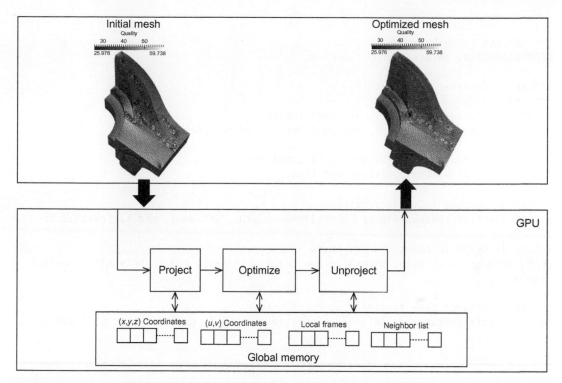

FIGURE 13.4

Basic component architecture of GPU mesh optimization kernel (see color insert).

Next, the host uses the vertex coloring to determine the independent sets consisting of the mesh vertex IDs that can be optimized in parallel without conflict. For each independent set, the mesh vertex IDs are passed to the card and the kernels are invoked as illustrated in Listing 13.1 to optimize the mesh on the GPU. The updated vertex coordinates are then transferred back to the host and the mesh is updated.

13.4 FINAL EVALUATION

The performance data for three different meshes are shown in Table 13.1. The serial version of the code uses the GNU Scientific Library (GSL) to perform the Nelder-Mead optimization and was run on an Intel Core i7 920 2.67 GHz CPU. The GPU timings were made on a system with an Intel Xeon 2.67 GHz CPU and an NVIDIA Tesla C2050 GPU. The Nelder-Mead optimization was implemented using CUDA 3.0.

Even with the overhead of coloring the graph, transferring the mesh data to the GPU, and limiting the parallelism to multiple independent sets, we still see significant speed-ups, between 10 and 40 times faster than serial. As is typical, the GPU clearly exhibits greater speed-up on the larger problems, as more computation further hides latency. Also, it is interesting to see that the First Fit graph coloring

```
...
int nBlocks = N/blocksize;
If(N%blockSize) nBlocks++;

//Step 1: Transfer the point IDS
int *pntids_d;
cudaMalloc((void**)&pntids_d, N*sizeof(int));
cudaMemcpy(pntids_d, pontids, N*sizeof(int), cudaMemcpyHostToDevice);

//Step 2: Allocate space for the (u,v) coordinates
cudaMalloc((void**)&uv_d, 2*N*sizeof(float));

//Step 3: Compute (u,v)coordinates
pointProjectToFrames<<<nBlocks, blockSize>>>( uv_d, pntids_d, xyz_d, frames_d );

//Step 4: Optimize points in u-v space
gpnNelderMead<<< nBlocks, blockSize >>>( uv_d, pntids_d, xyz_d, triangles_d,neis_d,
frames_d );

//Step 5: Project back to cartesian coordinates
pointProjectFromFrames<<< bBlocks, blockSize >>>( uv_d, pntids_d, xyz_d, frames_d );

....
```

Listing 13.1. Kernel invocations in the CUDA version of the mesh optimization algorithm.

Table 13.1 Comparative Performance of the Serial and GPU-Based Mesh Optimization Algorithms

Mesh	Number of Vertices	Time to Color (s)	CPU Optimization Time (s)	GPU Optimization Time (s)	Speed-up	Original Min Angle	Min Angle CPU	Min Angle GPU
FanDisk	6,475	0.007	11.1	1.08	10	17	25.9	25.9
Blade	882,954	0.952	634.7	34.8	18	0.31	2.02	2.02
Dragon	3,609,600	3.902	5910.2	147.5	40	0.14	3.54	5.15

has an essentially insignificant time cost compared with the optimization. The resulting mesh quality from the GPU and CPU codes was the same for the two smaller meshes, but differed on the largest with the GPU code producing a markedly better mesh. The source of this anomaly is currently unknown, but it seems likely to stem from a difference in the GSL version of Nelder-Mead and our CUDA-based implementation.

Figure 13.5 shows a close-up of the original and optimized FanDisk meshes. One can see that the surface shapes are very similar, indicating that the optimization process has not deformed the surface significantly. It should be noted that the mesh optimization algorithm can perform poorly in areas where a tangent plane is a poor approximation of the surface. Design discontinuities, often called

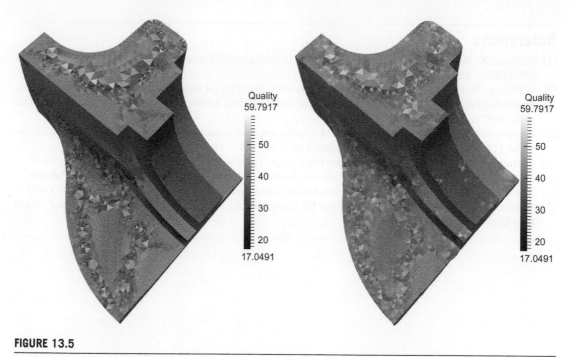

FIGURE 13.5

FanDisk mesh before and after optimization colored by element quality with higher values indicating better quality.

feature edges, and corners of the physical object being modeled can be degraded by the algorithm. This shortcoming could be remedied fairly easily by employing a feature detection algorithm [7] and locking in place the vertices determined to lay on features.

13.5 FUTURE DIRECTION

There are several ways in which the present mesh optimization implementation can be improved. Recall, the two main arrays that the algorithm operates on are the *xyz*-coordinates array and the *uv*-coordinates array. These are the only two arrays that need to be read writable. Read-only access is all that is required for the mesh connectivity, neighbor connectivity, and tangent plane information. On Tesla cards, storing the read-only information in texture memory can offer substantial performance improvements over global memory because the hardware automatically caches reads from texture memory. On newer Fermi cards, exploiting the L1 cache capability of the configurable memory attached to each streaming multiprocessor should yield a similar speed-up. Lastly, reducing the total cost to transfer data from host to the GPU device can be achieved by computing more of the required mesh information on the GPU. For example, the tangent planes could be computed directly and more efficiently on the GPU instead of transferring the data from the CPU. Similarly, the graph coloring could be performed in parallel [5] as well, although the speed-up would be very modest.

References

[1] A. Conn, K. Scheinberg, L. Vicente, Introduction to derivative-free optimization, Soc. Ind. Appl. Math. 59 (271) (2009) 1867–1869.

[2] L. Freitag, M. Jones, P. Plassmann, An efficient parallel algorithm for mesh smoothing, in: T.J. Tautges (Ed.), Proceedings of the 4th International Meshing Roundtable (4IMR), Sandia National Laboratories, Alberquerqe, NM, 1997, pp. 47–58.

[3] J. Shewchuk, What is a good linear element? Interpolation, conditioning, and quality measures, in: Proceedings of the 11th International Meshing Roundtable, Ithaca, NY, 2002, pp. 115–126.

[4] D. Brelaz, New methods to color the vertices of a graph, Commun. ACM 22 (4) (1979) 251–256.

[5] M. Jones, P. Plassmann, A parallel graph coloring heuristic, SIAM J. Sci. Comput. 14 (3) (1993) 654–669.

[6] J. Hughes, T. Möller, Building an orthonormal basis from a unit vector, J. Graph. Tools 4 (4) (1999) 33–35.

[7] X. Jiao, N. Bayyana, Identification of C1 and C2 discontinuities for surface meshes in CAD, Comput. Aided Des. 40 (2) (2008) 160–175.

158   SECTION 3   Engineering Simulation

SECTION

Engineering Simulation

Peng Wang (NVIDIA)

3

STATE OF GPU COMPUTING IN ENGINEERING SIMULATIONS

In engineering simulation, there is a strong quest for more computational power in order to run larger models and get shorter turn-around time. The massively parallel architecture of GPU has been proven to be suitable for many of the key algorithmic patterns used in engineering simulations such as structured grids, unstructured grids, dense and sparse matrix operations, spectral methods, particle methods, and so on.

In the past few years, GPU computing techniques are beginning to be widely adopted in production engineering simulation codes. In the near future, research will be needed on porting more complex numerical algorithms and codes to GPU, some of which are not very suitable for GPU today. In order to be successful in those endeavors, radical redesign of the algorithms or new development tools will likely be needed. The methods and experiences reported in the chapters of this section help set the foundation for addressing those challenges.

IN THIS SECTION

Chapter 14 by Brandvik and Pullan describes the porting of a multiblock structured grid computational fluid dynamics code to GPU. To avoid redundant kernel development efforts for many similar stencil computations, they developed a stencil CUDA kernel generator based on high-level specifications of the stencil computations. Such an approach enables rapid development of complex and high performance CUDA code.

Chapter 15 by Frezzotti, Ghiroldi, and Gibelli describes the GPU implementation of a two-dimensional kinetic equation solver using the semiregular methods. They use a finite difference kernel to handle the streaming part. For the expensive collision part, they use the one-thread-per-cell approach for the Monte Carlo evaluation and distribution function update.

Chapter 16 by Cecka, Lew, and Darve describes strategies to perform finite element matrix assembly on GPU. The main techniques are careful mapping of threads to the computational tasks and efficient utilization of shared memory by fine-grained grid partitioning. Coupled with a GPU linear solver, those results enable the implementation of a finite element code fully on GPU.

Chapter 17 by Trompoukis, Asouti, Kampolis, and Giannakoglou describes the GPU implementation of an unstructured grid finite volume Navier-Stokes flow solver, using both the point-implicit Jacobi and Runge-Kutta methods. Both a one-kernel approach and a two-kernel approach for the flux computation are discussed and can be chosen depending how memory-demanding the method is. New GPU data structures for unstructured grids are also discussed to enable coalesced memory access.

Chapter 18 by Klöckner, Warburton, and Hesthaven describes the GPU implementation of discontinuous Galerkin methods on unstructured grids. The authors discussed trade-offs in various ways of mapping the degrees of freedom and elements into threads and blocks. Other key techniques discussed are proper data layout, how to utilize the GPU memory hierarchy and avoiding padding waste using data aggregation. Furthermore, code written in PyCUDA is provided as a clear demonstration of those techniques.

Chapter 19 by Li, Chang, and Lomakin describes the GPU implementation of a nonuniform grid interpolation method for evaluating electromagnetic fields. The main techniques include mapping one thread to one observer, computing all the fields on the fly and rearranging data layout to enable coalesced memory access.

CHAPTER

14

Large-Scale Gas Turbine Simulations on GPU Clusters

Tobias Brandvik and Graham Pullan

In this chapter, we present a strategy for implementing solvers for partial differential equations (PDEs) that rely heavily on stencil computations on three-dimensional, multiblock structured grids. As a starting point, a simple stencil computation arising from the discretization of the three-dimensional heat diffusion equation is considered. Building on this example, the steps taken to redevelop a complete computational fluid dynamics solver originally written in Fortran 77 that consists of many complicated stencil computations are then described. The new solver makes extensive use of automatic source code generation for the implementation of its stencil computations. This capability is provided by a recently developed software framework called SBLOCK and a description of this framework and the strategies it uses to achieve good performance on NVIDIA GPUs is also included. As a final demonstration of the performance and scalability of the new solver, we include both single-GPU and multi-GPU benchmarks obtained on a 64-GPU cluster.

14.1 INTRODUCTION, PROBLEM STATEMENT, AND CONTEXT

Solvers for PDEs that use stencil computations on three-dimensional, multiblock structured grids are one of the main workhorses of scientific computing. In particular, they are frequently used in fields where the relevant equations can be solved using finite difference, finite element or finite volume techniques on structured grids. Examples of such fields are numerous and include fluid dynamics, computational finance and general relativity.

This chapter presents a strategy for how to best implement such solvers on computers with multiple GPUs. The motivation for the work comes from the field of computational fluid dynamics (CFD) for flows in turbomachines such as jet engines and land-based gas turbines. We aim to describe how a widely used legacy Fortran 77 code called TBLOCK [1] was completely reimplemented through the use of a new software framework called SBLOCK [2] to become a highly parallel solver that is capable of running on a variety of modern multicore processors, including NVIDIA GPUs.

The work described in this chapter makes two main contributions:

- Demonstrating that stencil-based PDE solvers can be efficiently implemented on a range of multicore processors by using a combination of automatic source code generation and a runtime library for memory management. Although automatic source code generation has previously been used

FIGURE 14.1

A model turbine with six blade rows. Mach number (left) and entropy function (right) (see color insert).

by others for simple stencils [3, 4], the solver presented here is the first example in this field that makes heavy use of this technique for a production-quality application with many complicated stencils that span hundreds of lines of code, have multiple input and output and output arrays and include conditional branching in their inner loops.

- Showing that GPUs can offer almost an order of magnitude increase in performance for stencil codes, even compared to fully threaded and SSE-enabled CPU implementations. In the authors' field of turbomachinery CFD, such speed-ups have a significant impact on the design process. Routine simulations that previously took hours on a single CPU can now be done in a few minutes on a GPU-enabled desktop. In addition, more ambitious simulations that were previously only performed on large clusters in a research environment can now form part of the routine design process in industry by using clusters of GPUs. As an example of the latter, Figure 14.1 shows a snapshot of the unsteady flow in a model turbine.

14.2 CORE METHOD

The fundamental algorithm used in this work is called a stencil computation, which arises from approximating the derivatives in a PDE by finite differences. As an example, consider the three-dimensional heat diffusion equation:

$$\frac{\partial T}{\partial t} = \alpha \nabla^2 T, \tag{1}$$

where T is temperature, t is time and α is a constant.

This equation can be solved on a structured grid with uniform spacing by a Jacobi iteration and a centred finite difference approximation to the derivative:

$$T_{i,j,k}^{n+1} = T_{i,j,k}^n + \frac{\alpha \Delta t}{\Delta l^2} \left(T_{i+1,j,k}^n - 2T_{i,j,k}^n + T_{i-1,j,k}^n \right.$$
$$+ T_{i,j+1,k}^n - 2T_{i,j,k}^n + T_{i,j-1,k}^n$$
$$\left. + T_{i,j,k+1}^n - 2T_{i,j,k}^n + T_{i,j,k-1}^n \right), \tag{2}$$

where Δt is the time-step, Δl is the grid spacing, the subscripts refer to the grid node and the superscripts refer to the time index. Implementing the finite difference approximation on a computer leads to a stencil computation, in which the output value at every grid node is a linear combination of the values at that node and the nodes surrounding it in space. A naive implementation of the stencil computation would consist of three nested loops, one for each grid direction, with the inner loop containing the stencil computation itself:

$$Y[i,j,k] = AX[i,j,k] + B(X[i-1,j,k] + X[i+1,j,k]$$
$$+ X[i,j-1,k] + X[i,j+1,k] + X[i,j,k-1]$$
$$+ X[i,j,k+1]), \tag{3}$$

where X and Y are three-dimensional arrays, and A and B are scalar constants.

14.3 ALGORITHMS, IMPLEMENTATIONS, AND EVALUATIONS

In this section, we first describe the overall structure of a typical stencil-based PDE solver, using the legacy Fortran 77 flow solver TBLOCK as an example. We then present the design of the SBLOCK software framework that can be used to implement such solvers on parallel processors, focusing specifically on how it uses automatic source code generation for the implementation of stencil computations on GPUs. To aid this discussion, a source code example based on the stencil computation in Eq. (3) is given. Finally, we describe a new flow solver called Turbostream [5], which is a reimplementation of the TBLOCK flow solver using the SBLOCK framework. Several different stencil computations taken from the flow solver are considered, all of which are significantly more complex than the model stencil in Eq. (3).

14.3.1 Stencil-Based PDE Solvers

We will use Eq. (3) as our model stencil computation throughout this chapter as it is one of the simplest stencils that still correspond to a physical problem. However, most problems of interest are more complicated than this simple diffusion case. Usually, several variables (e.g., mass, momentum, and energy) and additional physical phenomena (e.g., convection) are involved. Solving such problems requires a series of stencil computations with multiple inputs and outputs, as well as a range of different boundary conditions. In addition, if the problem involves a large range of length scales, the use of additional algorithms such as multigrid is often required. As a final difficulty, the underlying geometry can be both complicated and in relative motion, which requires multiple structured grids with some form of interpolation between them.

The Turbostream solver presented in this chapter contains all the above complications. Turbostream is a reimplementation of the old solver TBLOCK that is a typical example of many current multiblock structured grid PDE solvers. It was originally a scalar code that was based on previous solvers first developed in the 1970s and 1980s. Around the turn of the century, it was parallelized using MPI to take advantage of clusters of commodity single-core x86 processors. With the recent switch to multicore, however, it faces several challenges. In particular, its parallelization approach is coarse-grained and operates on the block level by assigning a discrete number of blocks to each core. Although this approach scales well across the multiple cores of current CPUs, we expect that it will have insufficient granularity to take advantage of future CPUs that will have tens of cores within a few years.

An additional problem is that TBLOCK relies on the compiler to automatically vectorize the code to take advantage of single instruction multiple data (SIMD) instruction sets such as the Streaming SIMD Extensions (SSE) found on the x86 architecture, which often leads to unsatisfactory results.

Finally, the solver is unable to take advantage of novel processors such as GPUs that require a more fine-grained approach to parallelism and the use of different languages and runtime libraries. It is worth pointing out at this point that the challenges posed by the current class of GPUs in many ways mirror those that we expect to face from future generations of CPUs.

Although we have raised these issues in the context of the TBLOCK solver, they are, to varying degrees, also applicable to many other multiblock structured grid PDE solvers. In the authors' field of turbomachinery CFD alone, similar points could be made about most popular codes currently used in industry and academia.

14.3.2 SBLOCK Framework

The SBLOCK framework consists of two components: a runtime library and a source code generator. The runtime library provides an API that is used by the application for functions such as memory management, kernel invocation, and MPI communication between processors in a cluster. In addition, it can perform reductions and parallel sparse matrix vector multiplications (SpMV). In this chapter, we do not describe the runtime library further, choosing instead to concentrate on the source code generator.

14.3.2.1 *Source Code Generation*

From the point of view of an application developer, a stencil kernel is a single file written in the Python scripting language. The file defines the inputs and outputs of the kernel, as well as the expressions that constitute the computation performed by it. At compile time, the definition is passed through the source code generator which outputs source code that can be further compiled into object code for the target processor.

The source-to-source compilation performed by the code generator uses the Cheetah templating system [6]. Cheetah is most commonly used to insert dynamic content into predefined HTML templates for web pages, but it is equally applicable to automatic source code generation. The underlying idea is to create a template which contains the static content of a kernel implementation — i.e., everything that is common for all kernels on a particular device. In addition to this static content, small snippets of code written in the Cheetah templating language are also included. These take information from the kernel definition and insert them into the appropriate places to generate a valid source file that can be compiled into machine code. A different template has to be created for each different platform — i.e., there is one template that produces normal C code for multicore CPUs and another that produces CUDA code for NVIDIA GPUs.

While simple, this approach achieves two important goals:

1. It enables multiple platforms to be supported using only a single, high-level definition of the computations performed by the solver.
2. Since the actual kernel implementation is hidden from the developer, SBLOCK is free to use any optimization strategy it wants without worrying about code readability.

14.3.2.2 *Implementation Strategy*

On all processors, the primary way of achieving high performance is through the use of domain decompositioning on multiple levels. At the highest level, each MPI process (which corresponds to a multicore CPU or a single GPU) is responsible for an integer number of the blocks in the whole multiblock domain (Figure 14.2 shows a 2-D slice through a typical six-block grid around a turbine blade). The distribution of blocks to MPI processes is the responsibility of the application and typically involves a consideration of the cost of the computation required for each block versus the cost of the communication between the blocks. The Turbostream flow solver uses the third-party package METIS [7] for this purpose and the load imbalance between processors is usually within 10%.

At the processor level, each block is further split into several smaller "sub-blocks" that can be computed independently. The implementation strategy at this level is based on that studied extensively by Datta et al. [3]. On the CPU, the sub-blocks are distributed to a pool of POSIX worker threads. Each of these threads iterates over the three directions in the sub-block, performing the stencil computation at each grid node. For the innermost loop over the unit-stride direction, the framework is capable of producing vectorized code that takes advantage of the CPU's SSE units. This feature requires the creation

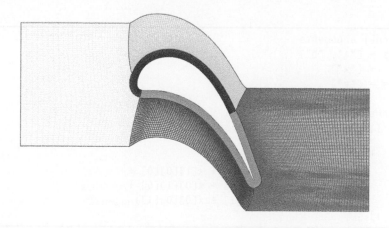

FIGURE 14.2

A 2-D slice through a multiblock grid around a turbine blade (see color insert).

of an abstract syntax tree representation of the stencil computation, a task which is accomplished using the freely available *pycparser* [8] Python module.

On the GPU, each sub-block corresponds to a CUDA thread block, which is executed on a CUDA multiprocessor. The implementation strategy here is based on the "cyclical queue" strategy described by Williams et al. [9] for the IBM Cell processor. This procedure involves starting one thread for each grid node in a plane of a sub-block (Figure 14.3). These threads then iterate upwards in the sub-block together, each time discarding one plane of data and fetching a new one to be stored in its place. At each iteration, the threads compute the specified stencil operation using data stored in the on-chip memory planes and write out the result.

14.3.2.3 *Source Code Example*

To further describe the process of source code generation and the resulting CUDA implementation, we will consider the stencil computation in Eq. (3). Listing 14.1 shows the high-level definition of the kernel in the Python scripting language. The kernel is simply a Python module containing variables

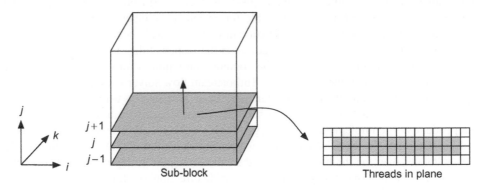

FIGURE 14.3

The iteration procedure for a stencil kernel.

```
# stencil kernel arguments
input_scalars = ["a", "b"]
input_arrays  = ["x"]
output_arrays = ["y"]

# stencil kernel computation
inner_loop = [{
            "lvalue": "y",
            "rvalue": a*x[0][0][0] +
                    b*(x[-1][0][0] + x[1][0][0] +
                        x[0][-1][0] + x[0][1][0] +
                        x[0][0][-1] + x[0][0][1])
            }]
```

Listing 14.1. High-level SBLOCK definition of the stencil computation in Eq. (3).

that describe the input and output arguments to the kernel, as well as the stencil computation itself. In this case, there are four arguments: two scalar value inputs, one array input, and one array output. The arrays are four-dimensional, indexed by the block number and the three grid indices. The stencil computation is contained in the Python list called **inner_loop**. This list contains a series of **(lvalue, rvalue)** pairs that define the left- and right-hand sides of a computation. Here, the list contains only a single pair due to the simplicity of the stencil computation, but more complex stencils may contain hundreds of such pairs. In the **rvalue** variable, it is permissible to index into the input arrays in order to access the grid nodes used in the stencil computation. The indices are relative to the grid node, which is being computed, and the computation is implicitly defined to be across all the grid nodes in all the blocks.

Listing 14.2 shows a simplified version of the resulting CUDA implementation produced by the source code generator. In this example, each sub-block has a size **(NI-2, NJ-2, NK-2)**. To compute this sub-block, it is necessary to read in the grid nodes for a block of size **(NI, NJ, NK)** due to the stencil access pattern extending one grid node in each direction. The extra grid nodes that pad the sub-block being computed are referred to as "halo nodes." The CUDA thread block that computes the sub-block is a plane in the **I** and **K** directions and contains **(NI, NK)** threads. Regarding the source code itself, the following points should be noted:

- A 3-D array in shared memory is used as local storage for the input arrays to maximize the amount of data reuse.
- The variables **i0m10**, **i000**, **i0p10** are indices into the global memory arrays **a_d** and **b_d** which are the input and output to the stencil computation. For brevity, the calculation of these indices is not shown, but it involves a 4-D to 1-D index transformation based on which block in the multiblock domain is being computed, the position of the current sub-block within this block, and the position of the current CUDA thread within the sub-block.
- The variables **jm1**, **j**, and **jp1** are used to hold the offsets to the j−1, j, and j+1 planes in shared memory. These are cycled at the end of each iteration so that the new plane that is loaded during the next iteration replaces the one that is no longer required by the stencil operation.
- The threads corresponding to the halo nodes in the plane of the sub-block only load data from the global memory into the shared memory and do not participate in the computation.

14.3.2.4 *GPU Optimizations*

The strategy described in the previous section is usually sufficient to achieve high performance for simple stencils such as that in Eq. (3). However, implementing more complicated stencils that need to access data from multiple input arrays is more challenging. The main trade-off involves the sub-block size versus the amount of available shared memory. Increasing the sub-block size is desirable because it reduces the ratio of grid nodes that have to be read in comparison to the number of grid nodes that are actually computed. Specifically, for a stencil that requires SI, SJ, SK halo nodes for the I, J, and K directions, respectively, the memory traffic overhead O for a sub-block of size $NI - SI$, $NJ - SJ$, $NK - SK$ is

$$O = \frac{Data\ in}{Data\ out} = \frac{NI \cdot NJ \cdot NK}{(NI - SI) \cdot (NJ - SI) \cdot (NK - SK)}, \tag{4}$$

```
__global__ void kernel(float a, float b, float *x_d, float *y_d) {

// shared memory indices
int i, j, jm1, jp1, k, jplane, tmp;

// shared memory for three planes
__shared__ float x[NI][3][NK];

// indices into global memory arrays
int i000, i010, i020; // j, j+1, j+2;

// current thread index in plane
i = (int)threadIdx.x;  k = (int)threadIdx.y;

// set initial shared memory and global memory indices
jm1 = 0; j = 1; jp1 = 2;
i0m10 = ...; i000 = ...; i0p10 = ...;

// fetch the first planes into shared memory
a[i][0][k] = a_d[i0m10]; a[i][1][k] = a_d[i000];

// iterate upwards in j-direction
for (j_plane=1; j_plane < NJ-1; j_plane++) {

// read the next plane into the jp1 slot
x[i][jp1][k] = x_d[i0p10]; __syncthreads();

// halo node threads d o n t compute
if (i>0 && i<ni-1 && k>0 && k<nk-1) {

   // compute stencil and write out result
   y_d[i000] = a*x[i][j][k] +
          b*(x[i-1][j][k] + x[i+1][j][k] +
             x[i][jm1][k] + x[i][jp1][k] +
             x[i][j][k-1] + x[i][j][k+1]);
} __syncthreads();
// cycle j indices
tmp = jm1; jm1 = j; j = jp1; jp1 = tmp;

// update global memory indices;
i0m10 = ...; i000 = ...; i0p10 = ...;
}
}
```

Listing 14.2. CUDA implementation of the stencil computation in Eq. (3).

which reduces with increasing sub-block size. Unfortunately, the amount of shared memory severely constrains the sub-block size for kernels with a large number of input arrays. For example, consider a stencil computation with a similar access pattern to that in Eq. (3) ($SI = SJ = SK = 2$), but with 10 input arrays. A typical sub-block size that can fit in the GT200's 16-KB shared memory is $NI = 16, NJ = 20$, $NK = 8$, which would require $NI \cdot NK \cdot 3 \cdot 10 \cdot 4 = 15{,}360$ bytes (i.e., 3 planes of size $NI \cdot NK$ for 10 arrays of single-precision floats). The memory traffic overhead as calculated by Eq. (4) is then 52.4%, which is clearly significant.

In order to reduce the pressure on the shared memory, we try to use the other forms of on-chip memory as much as possible through the following optimizations:

- An input array can be defined as a 1-D texture, which means that parts of it will reside in the on-chip texture cache. Although using the texture cache is slower than using shared memory, this strategy can win out overall if the sub-block size can be increased sufficiently.
- For stencils with access patterns such as that in Eq. (3), it is only necessary to store one plane in shared memory since the stencil only requires neighboring grid nodes with offsets in the I and K directions for a single J-plane, allowing the $J - 1$ and $J + 1$ planes to be stored in registers instead.

A final optimization relates to the number of threads that are created for each sub-block. In the example in the previous section, we created threads both for the grid nodes that we were computing the stencil *and* for the halo nodes which only read in data. Clearly, only the former group of threads is strictly necessary. Omitting the halo threads means that each computing thread must perform several memory reads, and nontrivial control logic in required to coordinate these reads. However, in practice it is found that this optimization yields a minor performance boost for most kernels.

14.3.3 Turbostream Solver

The Turbostream solver is a reimplementation using the SBLOCK framework of an older solver called TBLOCK which was originally developed by Denton [1]. The solvers are aimed primarily at predicting flows in turbomachines, but are also applicable to other types of flow such as that around wings and propellers. The TBLOCK solver is widely used in both industry and in academia, and is the latest in a long line of previous codes by Denton that are known collectively as the "Denton codes." A complete description of the algorithm used by the solver is given by Klostermeier [10] while shorter overviews and examples of its application to turbomachinery research have been published by Reid et al. [11] and Rosic et al. [12]. In addition, the motivation for the current method can be traced through a series of papers by Denton [13–15]. Here, we give a basic overview of the original solver, focusing particularly on the aspects relevant to its reimplementation using the SBLOCK framework.

14.3.3.1 *Solver Overview*

Turbomachines, whether for propulsion or for power generation, consist of many rows of airfoils (referred to as "blades"). Typically, alternating rows are either stationary or rotating, and each row has between 10 and 200 blades. The aim of the flow solver is to predict the flow between the blades by solving the compressible Navier-Stokes equations, so that more efficient blades can be designed. The solver uses a finite volume approach in which the space between the blades is divided into many small hexahedra (referred to as "cells"). The algorithm starts with an initial guess of the flow and iterates forward in time, each time evaluating the equations for each cell. This process is done by evaluating the fluxes of mass, momentum, and energy through the faces of the cell, and hence computing a change in these properties for that cell.

Conceptually, we split the kernels of the algorithm into two different groups. The first group are the stencil kernels — these fit neatly into the SBLOCK framework and are handled by the SBLOCK source code generator. The second group contains kernels with more complicated data access patterns — we call these "nonstencil" kernels. The nonstencil kernels typically implement boundary conditions or multigrid operations, and have to be dealt with separately. It should also be noted here that the stencil and the nonstencil kernels, both in the original TBLOCK implementation and in the new Turbostream implementation, use only single precision.

14.3.3.2 *Stencil Kernels*

The main stencil kernels are those that evaluate the fluxes through the faces of each cell; these fluxes have two components — convective and diffusive. The diffusive flux is further split into two parts, one is due to physical diffusion while the other is due to "artificial diffusion" that is added to stabilize the numerical scheme. Once the fluxes through each face are set, another kernel is then used to sum the fluxes through the faces of each cell.

Here, we consider the kernels for the convective fluxes, flux summation, and the artificial diffusion. Although the full algorithm also requires other stencils, these three make up approximately 60% of the total runtime. Table 14.1 summarizes the properties of each stencil; we focus on the amount of arithmetic (flops) and memory traffic (bytes) required by each kernel, as well as the arithmetic intensity (AI), which is the ratio of flops to bytes. The stencil access patterns themselves are also shown.

14.4 FINAL EVALUATION

In this section we consider the performance of the generated stencil kernel implementations for the model stencil in Eq. (3), as well as the three kernels taken from Turbostream. In addition, we present

Table 14.1 Properties of the Most Important Stencils in the Solver

Kernel	Stencil	SP FLOPS	Bytes	AI
Convective fluxes		260	139	1.87
Flux summation		8	28	0.29
Artificial diffusion		242	44	5.5

Table 14.2 Details of Systems Used

System	Intel CPU	AMD CPU	NVIDIA GPU
Processor	Core i7 920	Phenom II X4 940	GTX 280
Clock freq. (GHz)	2.67	3.00	1.30
GFLOP/s (DP/SP)	42.6/85.1	48.0/96.0	933.1/77.8
DRAM BW (GB/s)	25.6	17.1	141.7
Power* (Watts)	130	95	165
OS	CentOS 5.3	CentOS 5.3	CentOS 5.3
Compiler	gcc 4.1.2	gcc 4.1.2	nvcc 2.3

Based on the thermal design power from manufacturers' datasheet.

the overall speed-up of Turbostream as compared to TBLOCK. Finally, results are presented for Turbostream running on a GPU cluster.

The details of the processors used are shown in Table 14.2. Instead of using the full model names of the processors, we will in the following sections refer to the Intel, AMD, and NVIDIA processors as "Nehalem," "Phenom II," and "GT200," respectively.

The GPU cluster results were obtained on the University of Cambridge's GPU cluster. It consists of 32 Dell Precision T5500 servers with dual Intel Xeon 5550 2.66-GHz CPUs, connected through PCI-Express 2.0 to 32 NVIDIA Tesla S1070 GPU units, for a total of 64 CPUs and 128 GPUs. The servers communicate with each other using Mellanox QDR Infiniband.

14.4.1 Model Stencil Performance

To demonstrate the effectiveness of the kernel generator, we first consider its performance for the model stencil in both single and double precision (Figure 14.4). The grid used consists of a single 256^3 block, which is much larger than that which would fit in the on-chip memory of any of the processors. We aim primarily to show the effectiveness of multithreading by comparing the performance of the parallelized version to the scalar case. For the two CPUs, the impact of the use of SSE is also shown. It should be noted that for the GT200 there is no simple scalar implementation due to the multithreaded nature of the CUDA programming model and the use of software-managed caches, so only the parallel case is shown. The power efficiency of each processor is also shown. Here, we have chosen to simply use the thermal design power (TDP) as quoted by the manufacturers themselves, with the understanding that the effective real-world power consumption of a whole system is a factor of many other variables that we do not account for (e.g., idle power vs. peak power, cooling requirements, and power for memory modules).

Comparing the scaling across cores for the non-SSE CPU implementations, we achieve a performance increase of around 200–230% for both single and double precision when using all available cores as compared to the single-core case. This result comes from utilizing more of the available bandwidth when running on multiple cores. The effect of SSE vectorization is significant if there is enough bandwidth available to make the stencil compute-bound. However, since the total bandwidth utilization does not scale linearly with core count, SSE is less effective when using multiple threads.

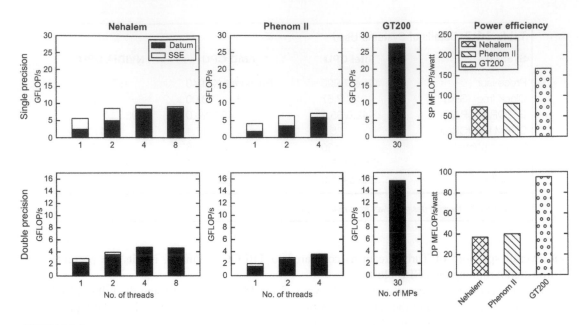

FIGURE 14.4

Performance for model stencil in single and double precision.

The top performance of the Nehalem is 30% higher than that of the Phenom II, which is in accordance with the difference in the processors' peak bandwidth. The performance advantage of the GT200 is in the range of 300–440% of the CPUs, which comes as a result of its unrivaled bandwidth of 141.7 GB/s. In terms of power efficiency, the two CPUs are similar while the GT200 is better by around a factor of two, which is lower than its raw performance advantage because it also consumes more power.

For all processors, the performance penalty of using double precision instead of single precision is significant: a 98% reduction is seen for the fully threaded and SSE-optimized CPU implementations, and 76% for the GPU implementation. This result demonstrates the importance for applications to only use double precision if it is necessary.

14.4.1.1 *Turbostream Stencil Kernel Performance*

By comparing the arithmetic intensity to the peak FLOP/s and peak GB/s offered by each processor (see Table 14.2), we expect all the kernels to be memory-bound on all processors. The one possible exception is the artificial diffusion kernel which has a high AI of 5.5, which is slightly higher than the flops/byte ratio of the two CPUs. However, the large size of the stencil requires additional memory bandwidth, so we still expect it to be memory-bound.

Table 14.3 lists the performance of each of the Turbostream stencil kernels. As pointed out by Kamil et al. [4], the maximum possible performance of a memory-bound kernel is the product of the kernel's arithmetic intensity and the peak bandwidth of the processor. In reality, the useful bandwidth will be lower than the peak due to the extra halo nodes that have to be fetched for each sub-block.

Table 14.3 Properties and Performance of the Most Important Stencils in the Solver

Kernel	Performance (SP GFLOP/s, GB/s)					
Processor	Nehalem		Phenom II		GT200	
Convective fluxes	10.7	5.71	5.62	3.00	71.7	38.3
Flux summation	3.55	12.2	2.83	9.76	13.6	47.0
Artificial diffusion	16.92	3.08	10.75	1.95	99.4	18.1

Table 14.4 Overall Performance of Solvers, Relative to TBLOCK on Phenom II

Processor	TBLOCK Performance	Turbostream Performance
Nehalem	1.21	1.48
Phenom II	1	0.89
GT200	–	10.2

Since the number of halo nodes grows with the size of the stencil, we expect large stencils to have a worse bandwidth utilization than small ones, and this is indeed the trend seen in Table 14.3. The flux summation kernel, which has the smallest stencil, achieves the highest useful bandwidth of the three kernels, obtaining 12.2 GB/s on the Nehalem, 9.76 GB/s on the Phenom II, and 47 GB/s on the GT200. The convective flux kernel has a slightly larger stencil, and consequently a lower bandwidth. Finally, the artificial dissipation kernel achieves the lowest bandwidth of all three, but also has a much larger stencil than the others.

Comparing the three processors against each other, the results echo those for the model kernel. The main difference is that the GT200 has a larger performance advantage over the CPUs for the real solver kernels than for the model kernels.

14.4.2 Overall Performance

Table 14.4 shows the overall performance of the new Turbostream solver compared to that of the old TBLOCK solver. We have chosen to normalize all results by the slowest TBLOCK performance, which is that on the Phenom II. The most important metric is the speed-up of Turbostream running on the GT200 compared to that of TBLOCK running on the two CPUs. It should be noted that the TBLOCK results were obtained with the solver running on all cores of the CPUs using MPI. Compared to the Phenom II, Turbostream has a performance increase of 10.2, while compared to the Nehalem the performance increase is 8.42. This speed-up is significant for the application of the solver to practical design work. In typical usage, obtaining the flow field around a single turbine blade takes around an hour using the TBLOCK solver on a single CPU. Using Turbostream on the GT200, the time to solution is reduced by roughly an order of magnitude, changing it to just a few minutes.

Turbostream running on the two CPUs achieves comparable performance to the TBLOCK solver. This result is mainly a demonstration of the ability of current quad-core CPUs to offer good scaling across cores for traditional MPI-based PDE solvers using a block-based decomposition strategy. How long this will continue to be the case as CPU core counts continue to increase remains to be seen, but it seems likely that the threaded approach used by Turbostream will eventually win out.

14.5 TEST CASE AND PARALLEL PERFORMANCE

In the last ten years, large-scale, time-accurate simulations with multiple blade-rows have become more common during the turbomachinery design process. Such simulations require more memory than that which is typically available on a single desktop, making the efficient use of clusters an important requirement of any solver. To demonstrate the effectiveness of the SBLOCK framework in such situations, both weak and strong scaling benchmarks have been performed across 64 GPUs on the University of Cambridge's GPU cluster (Figure 14.5). The benchmarks use the three-stage model turbine shown in Figure 14.1. The baseline configuration contains 27 million nodes, but can be scaled up as required — the largest case for the weak scaling on 64 GPUs contains 432 million grid nodes. As can be seen, the strong scaling tails off significantly after 16 GPUs. The weak scaling is excellent up to 32 GPUs, but more work remains to improve it for 64 GPUs.

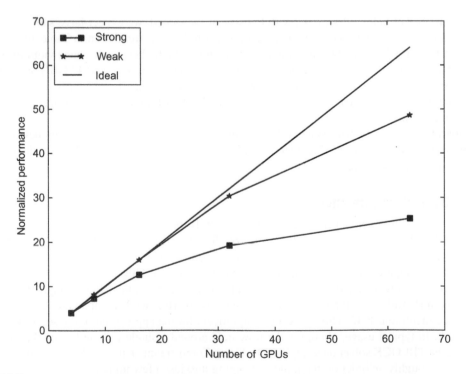

FIGURE 14.5

Multi-GPU performance.

14.6 FUTURE DIRECTIONS

Although both the SBLOCK framework and the Turbostream solver are now mature, several directions for future work would be interesting to pursue. The first is to add support for OpenCL to SBLOCK. The second is to further validate the generality of SBLOCK by using it to port other solvers to parallel processors, and there are several in-house solvers in the University of Cambridge Engineering Department that are currently being considered for this purpose.

References

[1] J.D. Denton, The effects of lean and sweep on transonic fan performance, TASK Quart. 1 (2002) 7–23.

[2] T. Brandvik, G. Pullan, SBLOCK: a framework for efficient stencil-based PDE solvers on multi-core platforms, in: Frontiers of GPU Computing, 2010 IEEE 10th International Conference on Computer and Information Technology, 2010, pp. 1181–1188.

[3] K. Datta, M. Murphy, V. Volkov, S. Williams, J. Carter, L. Oliker, et al., Stencil computation optimization and autotuning on state-of-the-art multicore architectures, in: Proceedings of 2008 ACM/IEEE Conference on Supercomputing, 2008, pp. 1–12.

[4] S. Kamil, C. Chan, S. Williams, L. Oliker, J. Shalf, M. Howison, et al., A generalized framework for auto-tuning stencil computations, in: Proceedings of Cray User Group Conference, 2009.

[5] T. Brandvik, G. Pullan, An accelerated 3D navier-stokes solver for flows in turbomachines, ASME Paper GT 2009-60052, 2009.

[6] The Cheetah Templating System. http://www.cheetahtemplate.org/

[7] G. Karypis, V. Kumar, Multilevel algorithms for multi-constraint graph partitioning, in: Proceeding of 1998 IEEE/ACM Conference on Supercomputing, 1998, p. 28.

[8] E. Bendersky, Pycparser. http://code.google.com/p/pycparser/

[9] S. Williams, J. Shalf, L. Oliker, S. Kamil, P. Husbands, K. Yelick, Scientific computing kernels on the cell processor, Int. J. Parallel Program. 35 (3) (2007) 263–298.

[10] C. Klostermeier, Investigation into the capability of large eddy simulation for turbomachinery design, Ph.D. dissertation, University of Cambridge, 2008.

[11] K. Reid, J.D. Denton, G. Pullan, E. Curtis, J. Longley, The interaction of turbine inter-platform leakage flow with the mainstream flow, ASME J. Turbomach. 129 (2) (2007) 303–310.

[12] B. Rosic, J.D. Denton, G. Pullan, The importance of shroud leakage modeling in multistage turbine calculations, ASME J. Turbomach. 128 (4) (2006) 699–707.

[13] J.D. Denton, An improved time marching method for turbomachinery flow calculation, ASME Paper 82-GT-239, 1982.

[14] J.D. Denton, The use of a distributed body force to simulate viscous effects in 3D flow calculations, ASME Paper 86-GT-144, 1986.

[15] J.D. Denton, The calculation of three dimensional viscous flows through multistage turbines, ASME Paper 90-GT-19, 1990.

CHAPTER

GPU Acceleration of Rarefied Gas Dynamic Simulations

15

Aldo Frezzotti, Gian Pietro Ghiroldi, and Livio Gibelli

Kinetic equations are used to mathematically model gas flows that are far from equilibrium due to their more general applicability than typical hydrodynamic equations. However, their complex mathematical structure requires time consuming algorithms to obtain accurate numerical solutions for realistic flow geometries. In this chapter, we show GPU-accelerated algorithms for direct solutions of kinetic equations. The efficiency of the GPU-accelerated codes is demonstrated on the two-dimensional driven cavity flow. Experimental results show that the GPU-accelerated codes run about two orders of magnitude faster than their sequential counterparts whose execution time is comparable to those reported in the literature. The algorithms described can be extended to three-dimensional flows and gas mixtures.

15.1 INTRODUCTION, PROBLEM STATEMENT, AND CONTEXT

The conventional continuum approach to gas dynamics, based on Navier-Stokes equations with no-slip boundary conditions, is justified when the molecular mean free path λ, i.e., the average distance travelled by molecules between two successive collisions, is much smaller than a characteristic length L associated to the flow geometry. This condition breaks down in several physical situations ranging from the reentry of spacecraft in upper planetary atmospheres, characterized by large λ, to fluid-structure interaction in small-scale micro-electro-mechanical systems (MEMS), characterized by small L [1]. In such situations, a macroscopic description of the gas is no longer possible and a microscopic description has to be adopted by means of the distribution function, $f(r, v, t)$, which gives the number of molecules with position r and velocity v at time t. The distribution function evolves in space and time according to a kinetic equation which, in absence of external force field, can be written in the form

$$\frac{\partial f}{\partial t} + v \cdot \frac{\partial f}{\partial r} = \left(\frac{\partial f}{\partial t} \right)_c \tag{1}$$

Equation (1) is a conservation law for $f(r, v, t)$ in the six-dimensional space (three physical space dimensions and three velocity space dimensions). The left-hand side is analogous to the substantial derivative in fluid dynamics, but here the molecular velocity is also an independent variable. The right-hand side, known as the collision integral, represents a source term due to intermolecular collisions whose precise structure depends on the assumed atomic interaction forces [1]. Obtaining numerical solutions of

Eq. (1) for realistic flow conditions is a challenging task because, in general, it is a complex integro-differential equation and the unknown function, f, depends on seven variables. For a long time, the Direct Simulation Monte Carlo (DSMC) [2] has been the only effective method to solve Eq. (1) numerically. DSMC has been extremely successful in simulating high-speed rarefied gas flows; however, the computational efficiency of its traditional implementation is very poor for low Mach number unsteady flows, typical of microfluidics application to MEMS. Moreover, the standard form of DSMC algorithm is not efficiently portable to SIMD architectures [3]. Unlike DSMC, direct solution methods discretize the distribution function on a regular grid in the phase space. The existing implementations adopt similar strategies to approximate the streaming term on the left-hand side of Eq. (1) by finite difference schemes. However, they differ in the way the collision integral is evaluated. In semiregular methods $(\partial f/\partial t)_c$ is computed by Monte Carlo or quasi Monte Carlo quadrature methods [4, 5] whereas deterministic integration schemes are used in regular methods [6]. Whatever method is chosen to compute the collision term, the adoption of a grid in the phase space has limited the direct solution of kinetic equations to problems where particular symmetries reduce the number of spatial and velocity variables. The availability of low cost GPUs, however, has changed the situation. Actually, direct solution methods are ideally suited for the parallel architecture provided by commercially available GPUs since the locality of the collision term allows the concurrent execution of the time consuming evaluation of the collision integral at each spatial grid point by a massive number of independent, non-diverging threads. Therefore, GPUs make direct methods of solution a viable alternative to DSMC in simulating unsteady and/or low Mach number flows [7].

15.2 CORE METHODS

The direct solution methods described in this chapter are based on the time-splitting of the evolution operator into a free streaming step, in which the right-hand side of Eq. (1) is neglected (collisionless molecular flow) and a purely collisional step (homogeneous relaxation), in which spatial motion is frozen and only the effect of the collision integral is taken into account. The free streaming step is performed according to a first order explicit upwind scheme whereas the collision integral is computed by either a Monte Carlo quadrature method (semi-regular method) [4, 5] or a deterministic integration scheme (regular method) [6] depending on its structure. The streaming and the collision steps are executed as separate kernels since both steps do possess an intrinsic, although different, parallel structure. In the streaming step the distribution function values associated to different velocity grid nodes are independently transported across the computational domain. The key performance enhancing strategies are then allowing threads to cooperate in the shared memory and accessing the global memory in a coalescent manner by properly organizing the discretized distribution function. On the other hand, the relaxation step in each cell of the physical space does not involve any information from nearby cells, whatever form of the collision integral is adopted. This naturally fits to the parallel architecture of GPUs where one may use as many threads as the number of cells in the physical space. Although in the following we restrict our discussion to a two-dimensional space geometry, the extension to three-dimensional problems is straightforward since the three-dimensional streaming kernel may proceed as discussed in Ref. [8], whereas the collision kernel is independent on the dimensionality of the physical space.

15.3 ALGORITHMS, IMPLEMENTATIONS, AND EVALUATIONS

15.3.1 Mathematical Background

The two-dimensional driven cavity flow has been chosen as a test problem since, in spite of its simple geometry, it contains most of the features of more complicated problems described by kinetic equations. The problem can be stated as follows. A monatomic gas is confined in a two-dimensional square cavity with side length L. All the walls are isothermal with temperature T_0. The gas flow is driven by a uniform translation of the top with velocity V_w and is assumed to be governed by the two-dimensional kinetic equation

$$\frac{\partial f}{\partial t} + v_x \frac{\partial f}{\partial x} + v_y \frac{\partial f}{\partial y} = \left(\frac{\partial f}{\partial t}\right)_c \tag{2}$$

Initially, the gas is in uniform equilibrium with density n_0, and molecules which strike the walls are supposed to be reemitted at the same space location according to the Maxwell's scattering kernel with complete accommodation [1]. Two different forms of the collision term have been considered, namely the Boltzmann hard sphere (BHS) collision integral and the Bathnagar-Gross-Krook-Welander (BGKW) kinetic model [1]. The BHS collision integral reads

$$\left(\frac{\partial f}{\partial t}\right)_c = \frac{\sigma^2}{2} \int_{\mathcal{R}^3} d\mathbf{v}_1 \int_{\mathcal{S}^2} d^2\widehat{\mathbf{k}} \left[f(\mathbf{r}, \mathbf{v}_1^*, t)f(\mathbf{r}, \mathbf{v}^*, t) - f(\mathbf{r}, \mathbf{v}_1, t)f(\mathbf{r}, \mathbf{v}, t)\right] |\widehat{\mathbf{k}} \cdot \mathbf{v}_r| \tag{3}$$

where σ is the hard sphere diameter, $\mathbf{v}_r = \mathbf{v}_1 - \mathbf{v}$ is the relative velocity between two colliding atoms and $\widehat{\mathbf{k}}$ is a vector, belonging to the unit sphere $\mathcal{S}^2$, used to specify the relative position of two atoms at the time of their impact. The postcollisional velocities of two colliding atoms, $\mathbf{v}^*$ and $\mathbf{v}_1^*$, are obtained from the precollisional velocities, $\mathbf{v}$ and $\mathbf{v}_1$, by a binary collision through the relationships:

$$\mathbf{v}^* = \mathbf{v} + (\mathbf{v}_r \cdot \widehat{\mathbf{k}})\widehat{\mathbf{k}}, \qquad \mathbf{v}_1^* = \mathbf{v}_1 - (\mathbf{v}_r \cdot \widehat{\mathbf{k}})\widehat{\mathbf{k}} \tag{4}$$

Both from the theoretical and computational point of view, it is often convenient to use the simpler BGKW kinetic model [1]

$$\left(\frac{\partial f}{\partial t}\right)_c = \nu \left(\Phi - f\right) \tag{5}$$

where $\Phi(\mathbf{r}, \mathbf{v}, t)$ is the local Maxwellian

$$\Phi(\mathbf{r}, \mathbf{v}, t) = \frac{n}{(2\pi RT)^{3/2}} \exp\left[-\frac{(\mathbf{v} - \mathbf{u})^2}{2RT}\right] \tag{6}$$

In Eq. (5), $v(n, T)$ is the collision frequency and $n(r, v, t), u(r, v, t), T(r, v, t)$ are the local values of density, bulk velocity, and temperature, which are obtained from f through the relationships

$$n(r, t) = \int_{\mathcal{R}^3} f(r, v, t) \, dv \tag{7}$$

$$u(r, t) = \frac{1}{n} \int_{\mathcal{R}^3} vf(r, v, t) \, dv \tag{8}$$

$$T(r, t) = \frac{1}{3Rn} \int_{\mathcal{R}^3} (v - u)^2 f(r, v, t) \, dv \tag{9}$$

being R the specific gas constant. The above expressions show that Eq. (5) is a strongly nonlinear integro-differential equation, in spite of the linear appearance of its right-hand side. However, its numerical evaluation only requires computing the five moments $n(r, t), u(r, t), T(r, t)$ defined above. On the contrary, the more realistic Boltzmann collision term requires the calculation of a fivefold integral at each spatial location.

15.3.2 Outline of the Numerical Methods

The two-dimensional physical space is divided into $N_r = N_x \times N_y$ rectangular cells. Likewise, the three-dimensional velocity space is replaced by a parallelepiped box divided into $N_v = N_{v_x} \times N_{v_y} \times N_{v_z}$ cells. Size and position of the velocity box in the velocity space have been chosen so as to contain the significant part of $f(r, v, t)$ at any spatial position. The distribution function is assumed to be constant within each cell of the phase space, i.e., f is represented by the array $f_{i,j}(t) = f(x(i_x), y(i_y), v_x(j_x), v_y(j_y), v_z(j_z), t)$ where $x(i_x), y(i_y)$ and $v_x(j_x), v_y(j_y), v_z(j_z)$ are the values of the spatial coordinates and velocity components in the center of the phase space cell and $i = (i_x, i_y), j = (j_x, j_y, j_z)$. The algorithm that advances $f_{i,j}^n = f_{i,j}(t_n)$ to $f_{i,j}^{n+1} = f_{i,j}(t_n + \Delta t)$ is constructed by time-splitting the evolution operator into a free streaming step, in which the right-hand side of Eq. (2) is neglected and a purely collisional step, in which spatial motion is frozen and only the effect of the collision integral is taken into account. The free-streaming step is solved by a simple first order explicit upwind conservative scheme. For later reference, we here report the difference scheme for $v_x > 0$ and $v_y > 0$

$$\tilde{f}_{i_x, i_y, j}^{n+1} = (1 - C_x - C_y) f_{i_x, i_y, j}^n + C_x f_{i_x - 1, i_y, j}^n + C_y f_{i_x, i_y - 1, j}^n \tag{10}$$

In Eq. (10) $C_x = v_x(j_x) \Delta t / \Delta x$ and $C_y = v_y(j_y) \Delta t / \Delta y$ are the Courant numbers along the x and y axis, respectively. After completing the free streaming step, $f_{i,j}^{n+1}$ is obtained by solving the homogeneous relaxation equation. The method of solution is different depending on the collision integral, Eq. (3) or (5). When the collision integral is given by Eq. (3), the relaxation step is solved with a semiregular method. The solution is advanced from the nth time level to the next according to the explicit scheme

$$f_{i,j}^{n+1} = \tilde{f}_{i,j}^{n+1} + \tilde{Q}_{i,j}^{n+1} \Delta t \tag{11}$$

In Eq. (11), $\widetilde{\mathcal{Q}}_{i,j}^{n+1}$ is obtained by evaluating the integral given by Eq. (3) with a low-variance Monte Carlo quadrature method since a regular quadrature formula would be too demanding in term of computing time [4, 5]. The solution of the homogeneous relaxation equation is much simpler when the collision integral is given by Eq. (5). Since n, $\boldsymbol{u}$, and T are conserved during homogeneous relaxation, the collision integral can be evaluated with a regular quadrature formula

$$f_{i,j}^{n+1} = [1 - \exp(-\widetilde{\nu}_i^{n+1}\Delta t)]\widetilde{\Phi}_{i,j}^{n+1} + \exp(-\widetilde{\nu}_i^{n+1}\Delta t)\widetilde{f}_{i,j}^{n+1} \tag{12}$$

in each cell (i, j) of the phase space [6]. A drawback of both semiregular and regular methods of solution is that, due to the discretization in the velocity space, momentum and energy are not exactly conserved across the collision step. In order to enforce their conservation, a proper correction procedure has thus been adopted [4, 5].

15.3.3 CUDA™ Implementation

The codes that implement the direct solution methods described above are organized into a host program, which deals with all memory management and other setup tasks, and a number of kernels running on the GPU. One performs the streaming step and the others perform the collision step. Because of their different impact on the code performance, we distinguish the slow global memory accesses, ⇐, from the fast reads and writes, ←, from local registers and shared memory.

Algorithm 1 lists the pseudo-code of the streaming kernel. For clarity of presentation, it refers to one cell of the velocity space with $v_x > 0$ and $v_y > 0$. For each cell of the velocity space, the streaming step, Eq. (10), involves the distribution function evaluated at different space locations. The key performance enhancing strategy is to allow threads to cooperate in the shared memory [8]. In order to fit into the device's resources, blocks are composed by a two-dimensional grid of threads with dimension $B_x \times B_y$ having each thread associated with one cell of the physical space. When a block becomes active, each thread loads one element of the distribution function from global memory, stores it into shared memory (line 5), updates its value according to Eq. (10) (line 21) and then saves it back to the global memory (line 22). This procedure is repeated sequentially $N_x/B_x \times N_y/B_y$ times. To ensure non-overlapping access, threads are synchronized at the onset of both reading from and writing to the global memory (lines 20 and 23). In order to obtain coalesced accesses to the global memory, values of the discretized distribution function of cells which are adjacent in the physical space are stored in contiguous memory locations. However, not all the threads in a block can read data in a coalescent manner. In fact, in order to update $f_{i,j}^n$, the values of the distribution function of two upwind neighboring nodes, often referred to as "halo" nodes [8], are required. The halos in one physical direction can be read in with coalesced accesses (lines 6–12) while the others have to be read in with noncoalesced accesses (lines 13–19). Threads that update boundary points perform calculations which are slightly different to account for the incoming Maxwellian flux from the boundaries of the domain (lines 8 and 15).

The relaxation step in a cell of the phase space does not involve any information from nearby physical cells, whatever the collision operator employed, Eqs. (3) and (5). This naturally matches the GPU's execution model, where one may define as many threads as the number of cells in the physical space. Moreover, by having one thread for each cell of the physical space, potentially dangerous conflicts between threads are avoided and the accesses to the global memory may be coalesced.

Algorithm 1: GPU pseudo-code of the two-dimensional streaming kernel

---

Require: t_x, thread index in x direction within the block
Require: t_y, thread index in y direction within the block
Require: f_{sh}, matrix $(B_x + 1) \times (B_y + 1)$ in the shared memory
  1: **for** $I_{by} = N_y/B_y - 1$ to 0 **do**
  2:    **for** $I_{bx} = N_x/B_x - 1$ to 0 **do**
  3:       $i_x \leftarrow t_x + B_x I_{bx}$
  4:       $i_y \leftarrow t_y + B_y I_{by}$
  5:       $f_{sh}(t_x + 1, t_y + 1) \Leftarrow f^n_{i_x, i_y, j}$
  6:       **if** $t_y == 0$ **then**
  7:          **if** $i_y - 1 < 0$ **then**
  8:             $f_{sh}(t_x, t_y) \leftarrow \mathrm{BoundaryFlux}$
  9:          **else**
10:             $f_{sh}(t_x, t_y) \Leftarrow f^n_{i_x, i_y - 1, j}$
11:          **end if**
12:       **end if**
13:       **if** $t_x == 0$ **then**
14:          **if** $i_x - 1 < 0$ **then**
15:             $f_{sh}(t_x, t_y) \leftarrow \mathrm{BoundaryFlux}$
16:          **else**
17:             $f_{sh}(t_x, t_y) \Leftarrow f^n_{i_x - 1, i_y, j}$
18:          **end if**
19:       **end if**
20:       syncthreads
21:       $f_{rg} \leftarrow (1 - C_x - C_y) f_{sh}(t_x + 1, t_y + 1) + C_x f_{sh}(t_x, t_y + 1) + C_y f_{sh}(t_x + 1, t_y)$
22:       $\widetilde{f}^{n+1}_{i_x, i_y, j} \Leftarrow f_{rg}$
23:       syncthreads
24:       $I_{bx} \leftarrow I_{bx} - 1$
25:    **end for**
26:    $I_{by} \leftarrow I_{by} - 1$
27: **end for**

The relaxation step for the BHS equation, Eq. (11), is organized into two kernels whose pseudo-codes are listed in Algorithms 2 and 3. The first kernel computes the sequence of collisions used in the Monte Carlo evaluation of the collision integral, whereas the second kernel updates the discretized distribution function, executes the correction procedure, and computes the macroscopic quantities of interest as well.

Algorithm 2 reports the pseudo-code of the sampling kernel. Here, there are as many threads as the number of the collision samples, N_t. Firstly, each thread generates the precollisional velocities v and v_1 by sampling the Maxwellian distribution function with the Box-Muller algorithm (lines 1–2) and the unit vector $\widehat{k}$ by sampling the uniform distribution on the unit sphere (line 3). Afterwards, the postcollisional velocities are evaluated (lines 4–6). Finally the index of the velocity cells containing the velocities of the colliding atoms as well as parameters to be used in the Monte Carlo evaluation of

---

Algorithm 2: GPU pseudo-code of the sampling kernel

Require: i, global thread index in the grid
1: $\mathbf{v} \leftarrow$ BoxMulller
2: $\mathbf{v}_1 \leftarrow$ BoxMulller
3: $\widehat{\mathbf{k}} \leftarrow$ UnitSphere
4: $\mathbf{v}_r \leftarrow \mathbf{v}_1 - \mathbf{v}$
5: $\mathbf{v}^* \leftarrow \mathbf{v} + (\mathbf{v}_r \cdot \widehat{\mathbf{k}})\widehat{\mathbf{k}}$
6: $\mathbf{v}_1^* \leftarrow \mathbf{v}_1 - (\mathbf{v}_r \cdot \widehat{\mathbf{k}})\widehat{\mathbf{k}}$
7: $[I(i), C(i)] \Leftarrow$ CollisionParam$(\mathbf{v}, \mathbf{v}_r)$
8: $[I_1(i), C_1(i)] \Leftarrow$ CollisionParam$(\mathbf{v}_1, \mathbf{v}_r)$
9: $[I^*(i), C^*(i)] \Leftarrow$ CollisionParam$(\mathbf{v}^*, \mathbf{v}_r)$
10: $[I_1^*(i), C_1^*(i)] \Leftarrow$ CollisionParam$(\mathbf{v}_1^*, \mathbf{v}_r)$

Algorithm 3: GPU pseudo-code of the collision kernel: semiregular method

---

Require: i, global thread index in the two-dimensional grid of threads
1: **for all** j **do**
2: $\quad f_{rg} \Leftarrow \widetilde{f}_{i,j}^{n+1}$
3: $\quad n_i \leftarrow n_i + f_{rg}\, d\mathbf{v}$
4: $\quad \mathbf{q}_i \leftarrow \mathbf{q}_i + \mathbf{v}_j f_{rg}\, d\mathbf{v}$
5: $\quad e_i \leftarrow e_i + |\mathbf{v}_j|^2 f_{rg}\, d\mathbf{v}$
6: **end for**
7: **for** $m = 1$ to N_t **do**
8: $\quad f_{rg} \Leftarrow \widetilde{f}_{i,I(m)}^{n+1}$
9: $\quad f_{rg,1} \Leftarrow \widetilde{f}_{i,I_1(m)}^{n+1}$
10: $\quad f_{rg}^* \Leftarrow \widetilde{f}_{i,I^*(m)}^{n+1}$
11: $\quad f_{rg,1}^* \Leftarrow \widetilde{f}_{i,I_1^*(m)}^{n+1}$
12: $\quad \widetilde{f}_{i,I(m)}^{n+1} \Leftarrow$ Update$(f_{rg}, f_{rg}, f_{rg,1}, C(m))$
13: $\quad \widetilde{f}_{i,I_1(m)}^{n+1} \Leftarrow$ Update$(f_{rg,1}, f_{rg}, f_{rg,1}, C_1(m))$
14: $\quad \widetilde{f}_{i,I^*(m)}^{n+1} \Leftarrow$ Update$(f_{rg}^*, f_{rg}, f_{rg,1}, C^*(m))$
15: $\quad \widetilde{f}_{i,I_1^*(m)}^{n+1} \Leftarrow$ Update$(f_{rg,1}^*, f_{rg}, f_{rg,1}, C_1^*(m))$
16: **end for**
17: $f_{i,j}^{n+1} \Leftarrow$ Correction$(\widetilde{f}_{i,j}^{n+1}, n_i, \mathbf{q}_i, e_i)$
18: **for all** j **do**
19: $\quad f_{rg} \Leftarrow f_{i,j}^{n+1}$
20: $\quad n_i \leftarrow n_i + f_{rg}\, d\mathbf{v}$
21: $\quad \mathbf{q}_i \leftarrow \mathbf{q}_i + \mathbf{v}_j f_{rg}\, d\mathbf{v}$
22: $\quad e_i \leftarrow e_i + |\mathbf{v}_j|^2 f_{rg}\, d\mathbf{v}$
23: $\quad \vdots$
24: $\quad$ // others moments of the distribution function
25: $\quad \vdots$
26: **end for**

Algorithm 4: GPU pseudo-code of the collision step: regular method

---

Require: i, global thread index in the two-dimensional grid of threads

1: **for all** j **do**
2:   $f_{rg} \Leftarrow \tilde{f}_{i,j}^{n+1}$
3:   $n_i \leftarrow n_i + f_{rg}\, dv$
4:   $q_i \leftarrow q_i + v_j\, f_{rg}\, dv$
5:   $e_i \leftarrow e_i + |v_j|^2\, f_{rg}\, dv$
6: **end for**
7: $u_i \leftarrow q_i / n_i$
8: $T_i \leftarrow (e_i / n_i - |u_i|^2)/(3R)$
9: **for all** j **do**
10:   $f_{rg} \Leftarrow \tilde{f}_{i,j}^{n+1}$
11:   $f_{rg} \leftarrow \left[1 - \exp(-\tilde{v}_i^{n+1}\Delta t)\right] \tilde{\Phi}_{i,j}^{n+1} + \exp(-\tilde{v}_i^{n+1}\Delta t) f_{rg}$
12:   $f_{i,j}^{n+1} \Leftarrow f_{rg}$
13: **end for**

---

the collision integral are calculated and stored in the global memory as vectors I, I_1, I^*, I_1^* and C, C_1, C^* C_1^*, respectively (lines 7–10). Algorithm (3) shows the pseudo-code of the relaxation kernel. Here there are as many threads as the number of physical cells, N_r. Firstly each thread computes the macroscopic quantities that are subsequently needed to enforce the conservation of mass, momentum, and energy (lines 1–6). Afterwards, the Monte Carlo evaluation of the collision integral is performed by using the velocity samples produced by the sampling kernel (lines 7–16). Since the same set of collisions is used to evaluate the collision integral at different space locations, all threads need to access the vectors I, I_1, I^*, I_1^* and $C, C_1, C^*\, C_1^*$. In this respect, reading these data from the texture memory improves the performance considerably. More precisely, a reduction of the overall computing time in the range of 7%–22% is achieved depending on the Knudsen number. As Kn decreases, in fact, a greater number of collisions are needed in the Monte Carlo evaluation of the collision and hence the use of texture memory becomes increasingly important. The distribution function is then corrected (line 17) and the macroscopic quantities of interest computed (lines 18–26).

Algorithm (4) shows the pseudo-code of the relaxation kernel when the regular method for the BGKW collision integral is used. According to Eq. (12), the collision step in a cell of the phase space seems not to involve information exchange from nearby cells. However, coupling is produced by the Maxwellian, Φ, which depends on the local density, bulk velocity, and temperature. In order to reduce data transfers from and to the global memory, the computation of the macroscopic quantities (lines 1–8) and the collision step (lines 9–13) are performed in the same kernel, by having a thread associated to each cell of the physical space. Although this choice reduces the overall number of threads, it is not quite limiting since for realistic two- or three-dimensional problems, one would probably refine the physical grid more than the velocity grid.

It is worth observing that alternative parallelization schemes are possible. For instance, the relaxation step could be organized by assigning a block of threads to each spatial cell, having each thread associated to a phase space cell. However, the choice presented here seems to possess a few advantages. Actually, the concurrent execution of relaxation in the phase space can be performed only after the evaluation of macroscopic quantities at each spatial location. Such evaluation is more naturally performed by the adopted scheme which reduces the number of memory I/O operation and avoids using parallel reduction algorithms [10].

15.4 FINAL EVALUATION

15.4.1 Codes Validation

In Ref. [9], the driven cavity flow problem has been solved by assuming that $V_w \ll \sqrt{2RT_0}$ and Eq. (2), with the collision integral given by Eq. (5), has been linearized around the equilibrium state at rest. In order to reproduce these results, the dimensionless lid velocity has been set to $V_w/\sqrt{2RT_0} = 0.01$. The gas is thus in a weakly nonequilibrium state and the solution of the nonlinear kinetic equations approach the linearized results. Moreover, the linearized results are largely independent of the details of the collision integral and hence the solutions of the nonlinear BHS and BGKW equations are expected to agree each other. The cavity flow has been solved over a wide range of the Knudsen numbers, $Kn = \lambda_0/L$, defined on the basis of the mean free path at equilibrium $\lambda_0 = \mu_0/p_0(2RT_0)^{1/2}$, with μ_0 the viscosity of the hard sphere gas and p_0 the gas pressure [1]. The square cavity, $[0, 1/Kn] \times [0, 1/Kn]$, has been divided into $N_r = 160 \times 160$ cells with uniform width and the number of velocity cells have been set $N_v = 20 \times 20 \times 20$ with $v_x, v_y, v_z \in [-3\sqrt{2RT_0}, 3\sqrt{2RT_0}]$. The velocity samples, N_t, employed in the Monte Carlo evaluation of the BHS collision integral Eq. (3), has been varied from a minimum of 1024 for $Kn = 10$ to a maximum of 16,384 for $Kn = 0.1$. Finally, the time step has been determined by requiring that $\text{Max}(|C_x|, |C_y|) = 0.5$. In order to have a first qualitative picture of the cavity flow results, some velocity streamlines superimposed to the dimensionless temperature fields T/T_0 are presented in Figure 15.1 for $Kn = 0.1$ with $V_w/\sqrt{2RT_0} = 0.01$ (left panel) and $V_w/\sqrt{2RT_0} = 0.7$ (right panel). For the lower lid velocity, the flow is symmetric about the vertical line crossing the center of the cavity. A vortex forms and its center is located at about one-third of the cavity depth from the top. Instead, the temperature profile is antisymmetric with the maximum gradients close to the moving lid. As the lid velocity increases, nonlinear effects cause the vortex to move in the direction of the lid velocity and the gas temperature to increase considerably. Table 15.1 compares the predictions of the stationary values of the dimensionless flow rate of the main vortex which forms in the cavity, G, and the mean dimensionless shear stress along the moving plate, D, with the results reported in Ref. [9]. The overall agreement is quite good, with small discrepancies at low Knudsen numbers mainly due to the physical and velocity discretizations adopted.

15.4.2 Performance Evaluation

The performance analysis has been performed on a commercially available GPU GeForce GTX 260 using CUDA version 2.0. The GTX 260 GPU model consists of 24 streaming multiprocessors with 8 streaming processors (SP) clocked at 1.242 GHz each for a peak theoretical performance of 715.4 GFLOP/s in single precision. The GPU has 896 MB of device memory with a memory bandwidth of 111.9 GB/s. The graphic processing unit has been hosted by a personal computer equipped with 4 GB of main memory with a memory bandwidth of 12.8 GB/s and an Intel Core Duo Quad Q9300 CPU, running at 2.5 GHz for a peak theoretical performance of a single core of 20 GFLOP/s. The host

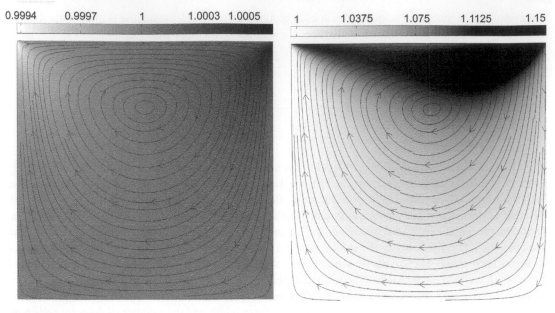

FIGURE 15.1

Velocity streamlines and dimensionless temperature field T/T_0 for Kn $= 0.1$. Left panel: $V_w/\sqrt{2RT_0} = 0.01$. Right panel: $V_w/\sqrt{2RT_0} = 0.7$ (see color insert).

Table 15.1 Flow Rate of the Main Vortex, G, and Drag Coefficient, D, Versus the Knudsen Number, Kn, for the BHS and BGKW Collision Integral

	G			D		
Kn	BHS	BGKW	Ref. [9]	BHS	BGKW	Ref. [9]
10	0.0970	0.0975	0.0973–0.0976	0.675	0.675	0.676–0.678
1	0.102	0.103	0.104–0.105	0.627	0.624	0.625–0.631
0.1	0.142	0.143	0.145–0.145	0.396	0.393	0.412–0.415

code has been compiled using the gcc/g++ compiler with optimization option "-O3" whereas no SSE instructions have been used.

The efficiency of the BHS and BGKW numerical codes has been assessed by computing the speed-up factor $S = T_{CPU}/T_{GPU}$, where T_{CPU} and T_{GPU} are the times used by the CPU and GPU, respectively. Times are measured after initial setup and do not include the initial and final execution times required to transfer data between the disjoint CPU and GPU memory spaces. Figure 15.2 shows the time in seconds which is spent on the streaming step and on the collision step by the BHS code and the BGKW code for Kn $= 1$. For the BHS code, the collision step is more time consuming than the streaming step,

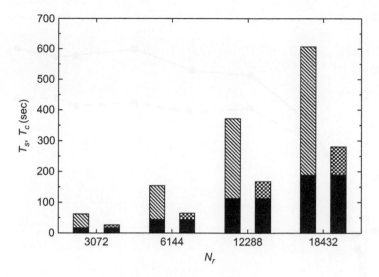

FIGURE 15.2

Time in seconds spent on the streaming step (dark bar) and on collision step for the BHS code with $N_t = 6144$ (striped bar) and for the BGKW code (checked bar). $N_v = 8000$.

which takes at most 31% of overall computing time. This is not the case for the BGKW code where the evaluation of the collision integral is less computationally demanding.

Figure 15.3 reports the obtained speed-up factors, S, as a function of the number of spatial grid points, N_r. They grow rapidly with the number of cells, till N_r approximately exceeds 10^4. Afterwards, the speed-up factors level up at about 440 and 350 for the BHS and the BGKW equations, respectively. As shown by the speed-up curves, the GPU power is not fully exploited till the number of concurrent threads reaches a threshold. Beyond, the speed-up saturates and the computing time approximately behaves as a linear function of N_r.

The GPU-based codes can be further analyzed by carrying out a simplified evaluation of their ideal performance. A single application of the upwind scheme requires the execution of 7 floating point operations and 2.3 accesses to the global memory. The GPU delivers 715.4 GFLOP/s but the transfer rate to/from the main memory is limited to 111.9 GB/s. Since the ratio of number of floating point operations to the number of bytes accessed is low (7 : 9.2), it is reasonable to obtain the number of floating point operation per second from the transfer rate alone. Hence, the ideal number of GFLOP/s can be obtained by assuming that 7 floating point operations will be executed in the time required to transfer 9.2 bytes from the main memory. Accordingly, this simple argument yields an ideal performance of 85.1 GFLOP/s. Using similar arguments leads to an estimate of the ideal performance of the collision step of 153.8 GFLOP/s and 270.4 GFLOP/s for the BHS and BGKW codes, respectively. Timing the execution of the separate kernels and counting the number of associated floating point operations provides the real kernel's GFLOP/s. As shown by Figure 15.4, it results that the performance of the streaming kernel grows with N_r and quickly levels at about 23 GFLOP/s, approximately one fourth of the estimated ideal performance. The difference can be justified by observing that the real

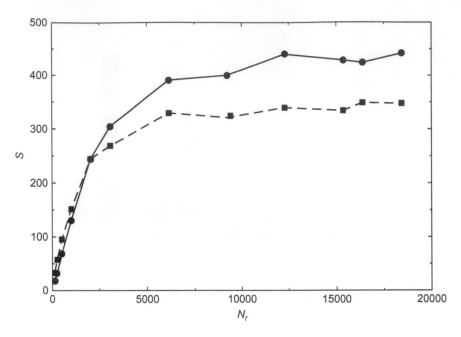

FIGURE 15.3

Speed-up, S, versus the number of cells in the physical space, N_r. Circles: BHS code with $N_t = 6144$. Squares: BGKW code. $N_v = 8000$.

CUDA implementation of the finite difference scheme is not free from thread divergence and ancillary tasks whose effects can be evaluated with difficulty [8]. For both the BHS and BGKW collision integrals, the collision kernel's performance closely patterns the speed-up behavior. They rapidly grow in the range $N_r < 10^4$ and then level up at about 130 GFLOP/s and 190 GFLOP/s, respectively. The main reason why the collision kernel performs better than the streaming kernel is its higher FLOPs to memory operation ratio which allows a more efficient use of GPU computing power. Altogether, the codes which solve the BHS and BGKW equations show a performance of 100 and 75 GFLOP/s, respectively.

A similar analysis can be performed for the CPU-based codes. The time required by the CPU to execute the floating point operations, however, is not negligible with respect to the time required to transfer data to/from the main memory and, hence, it has to be taken into account in the estimate of the ideal number of GFLOP/s. The number of accesses to the global memory are supposed to be the same as above whereas the CPU maximum bandwidth and the computing performance per single core are about 12.8 GB/s and 20 GFLOP/s, respectively. Therefore the sequential codes which solve the BHS and the BGKW equations may ideally deliver 9.9 GFLOP/s and 11.1 GFLOP/s, respectively, in marked contrast with the effective performance which are about 0.28 GFLOP/s and 0.34 GFLOP/s. This analysis would suggest that the high speed-up factors shown in Figure 15.3 are mainly due to the fact that the sequential codes are not fully optimized. However, it is worth noticing that the ideal analysis discussed above is less accurate for the CPU than for the GPU. For instance, as indicated by benchmark

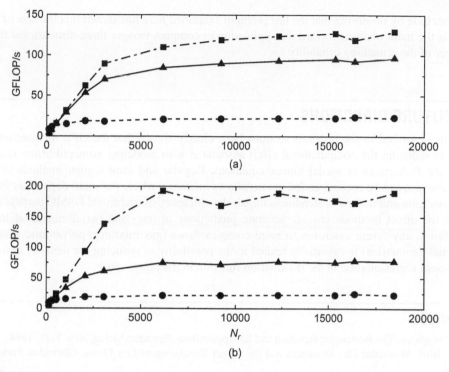

FIGURE 15.4

Real GFLOP/s versus the number of cells in the physical space, N_r. (a) BHS code with $N_t = 6144$; (b) BGKW code. $N_v = 8000$. Dashed lines with circles: streaming step. Dot-dashed lines with squares: collision step. Solid lines with triangles: overall code.

tests, the CPU effective bandwidth is approximately one-half of the maximum bandwidth whereas this is not the case for the GPU. Accordingly, the above ideal GFLOP/s of the CPU-based codes should be halved. Moreover, the performance of the sequential codes here developed are comparable to the performance of similar codes described in literature. For instance, in Ref. [9] the solution of the cavity flow problem is obtained by integrating the linearized BGKW equation in about 3 hours. Using the execution time of this sequential code to compute the speed-up factor yields a result as high as 265. It is worth noticing that in Ref. [9] the number of velocity variables has been reduced by a standard projection method [1]. The value of the speed-up factor given above has been obtained by modifying the parallel code to take advantage of the same reduction technique. To the best of the authors' knowledge, no direct solutions of the cavity flow problem based on the BHS equation have been provided until now. However, a similar reasoning can be applied to the one-dimensional unsteady Couette flow. In Ref. [11] its solution is achieved in approximately 9 hours, which gives a speed-up factor of the BHS code of about 54. This results is still lower than the speed-up factor reported in Figure 15.3, but this is due to the fact that the discretizations used to provide solutions as accurate as the ones reported in Ref. [11] does not allow to fully exploit the computational power of the GPU.

We conclude by observing that the test problem examined here has shown that the size of physical memory is the main obstacle toward the application to complex two- or three-dimensional flows, not the number of the crunching capability.

15.5 FUTURE DIRECTIONS

The results described in the previous sections have clearly shown that the GPU architecture is very effective in reducing the computational effort associated with modeling nonequilibrium rarefied gas flows by the Boltzmann or model kinetic equations. Regular and semi-regular methods of solution outlined above are to be recommended in microflows modeling where the small departures from equilibrium condition and/or flow unsteadiness impair the efficiency of traditional DSMC particle schemes. Although the direct methods provide accurate predictions of one- and two-dimensional low Mach number flows, any future extension to more complex flows (gas mixtures, polyatomic gases, three-dimensional geometries) is essentially related to the possibility of reducing the memory demand by a more efficient representation of the distribution function in the phase space.

References

[1] C. Cercignani, The Boltzmann Equation and Its Applications, Springer-Verlag, New York, 1988.
[2] G.A. Bird, Molecular Gas Dynamics and the Direct Simulation of Gas Flows, Clarendon Press, Oxford, 1994.
[3] L. Dagum, Three-dimensional direct particle simulation on the Connection Machine, AIAA Paper No. 91-1365, 1991, pp. 1–11.
[4] A. Frezzotti, Numerical study of the strong evaporation of a binary mixture, Fluid Dyn. Res. 8 (1991) 175–187.
[5] F. Tcheremissine, Direct numerical solution of the Boltzmann equation, RGD24 AIP Conf. Proc. 762 (2005) 677–685.
[6] V.V. Aristov, Direct Methods for Solving the Boltzmann Equation and Study of Nonequilibrium Flows, Springer-Verlag, New York, 2001.
[7] A. Frezzotti, G.P. Ghiroldi, L. Gibelli, Direct solution of the Boltzmann equation for a binary mixture on GPUs, RGD27 AIP Conf. Proc. 1333 (2011) 884–889.
[8] P. Micikevicius, 3D finite difference computation on GPUs using CUDA, ACM Int. Conf. Proc. Ser. 383 (2009) 79–84.
[9] S. Varoutis, D. Valougeorgis, F. Sharipov, Application of the integro-moment method to steady-state two-dimensional rarefied gas flows subject to boundary induced discontinuities, J. Comput. Phys. 227 (2008) 6272–6287.
[10] E. Elsen, P. LeGresley, E. Darve, Large calculation of the flow over a hypersonic vehicle using a GPU, J. Comp. Phys. 227 (2008) 10148–10161.
[11] L.L. Baker, N.G. Hadjiconstantinou, Variance-reduced Monte Carlo solutions of the Boltzmann equation for low-speed gas flows: A discontinuous Galerkin formulation, Int. J. Numer. Meth. Fluids 58 (2008) 381–402.

Application of Assembly of Finite Element Methods on Graphics Processors for Real-Time Elastodynamics

16

Cris Cecka, Adrian Lew, and Eric Darve

In this chapter, we discuss multiple strategies to perform general computations on unstructured grids, with specific application to the assembly of matrices in finite element methods (FEMs). We review and apply two methods, discussed in depth in [1], for assembly of FEMs to produce and accelerate a FEM model for a nonlinear hyperelastic solid where the assembly, solution, update, and visualization stages are performed solely on the GPU, benefiting from speed-ups in each stage and avoiding costly GPU-CPU transfers of data. For each method, we discuss the NVIDIA GPU hardware's limiting resources, optimizations, key data structures, and dependence of the performance with respect to problem size, element size, and GPU hardware generation. This chapter will inform potential users of the benefits of GPU technology, provide guidelines to help them implement their own FEM solutions, give potential speed-ups that can be expected, and provide source code for reference.

16.1 INTRODUCTION, PROBLEM STATEMENT, AND CONTEXT

In the domain of partial differential equations (PDEs), finite difference methods naturally fit into the GPU computing environment. Finite difference approaches have regular, vectorizable data access patterns, making them a natural candidate for execution on GPUs. When solving PDEs in complex domains or when adaptive mesh refinement strategies are needed, unstructured grids are often more convenient and the method of finite elements is appealing. In this section, we introduce elementary notions on finite elements and the important primitive operations and data flow. For more detail, we recommend any FEM textbook, such as [2].

Unstructured meshes are common in many engineering and graphics applications to create versatile discretizations of PDEs. To illustrate this, consider the problem of finding a function $u: \Omega \to \mathbb{R}$ that satisfies

$$\mathcal{L}u = f \quad \text{in} \quad \Omega \tag{1}$$

and subject to some boundary conditions. Here, Ω is a domain, $\mathcal{L}$ is a general linear differential operator, and f is a scalar-valued function over Ω.

A standard finite element method begins by constructing a finite dimensional space $\mathcal{V}_h$ of functions over Ω. The numerical approximation of the solution is then written as

$$u_h(x) = \sum_j u_j \varphi_j(x),$$

where $\{u_j\}$ are the components of u_h in the basis $\{\varphi_j\}$ of $\mathcal{V}_h$. Then Eq. (1) is multiplied by φ_i and integrated over Ω to obtain a weak formulation:

$$a(u_h, \varphi_i) := \sum_j u_j \int_\Omega \varphi_i \, \mathcal{L}\varphi_j \, d\Omega = \int_\Omega \varphi_i f \, d\Omega, \qquad \forall \varphi_i. \tag{2}$$

These equations are then further transformed (using integration by parts, the boundary conditions of the problem, etc.) to yield a linear system of equations:

$$Au = F,$$

where A is the so-called stiffness matrix and F is the forcing vector. The numerical approximation, u_h, follows by solving this system for the vector of components $u = [u_i]$.

In the finite element method, the basis functions $\{\varphi_i\}$ are constructed using a partition of the domain into a set $\mathcal{E}$ of disjoint domains, $\Omega^e \subset \Omega$, $e \in \mathcal{E}$, termed *elements* (see Figure 16.1). Then, the bilinear form defined in Eq. (2) can be split as

$$A_{ij} = a(\varphi_i, \varphi_j) = \sum_{e \in \mathcal{E}} a^e(\varphi_i, \varphi_j),$$

where a^e is the bilinear form that results from restricting the integral in Eq. (2) to Ω^e.

Typically, finite element formulations introduce a set, $\mathcal{N}$, of nodes $x_i \in \Omega$, and basis functions are often chosen such that $\varphi_j(x_i) = \delta_{ij}$, so that u_h is uniquely determined by its values at the nodes. In the simplest case, the set $\mathcal{N}$ is the set of vertices of the polyhedral elements. Furthermore, in most cases, the finite element basis functions $\{\varphi_i\}$ are nonzero only over the elements containing x_i. Then, the elemental contribution

$$A_{ij}^e = a^e(\varphi_i, \varphi_j)$$

to A_{ij} from element $e \in \mathcal{E}$ is different from zero if and only if the points x_i and x_j are both in or on the boundary of e. Consequently, during assembly A_{ij}^e needs to be computed only for a few values of i and j, independent of the size of the mesh. These elemental contributions are then accumulated into matrix A.

Usually, the computation of the numerical solution is performed in two steps: the assembly of matrix A and vector F, and the solution of the linear system $Au = F$. Matrix-free iterative methods, which do not assemble and store the system explicitly, are advocated in [3]. Many applications require the assembly and solution to be performed many times, such as when $\mathcal{L}$ is nonlinear and/or time-dependent.

Although the computational cost of the assembly procedure is smaller than the computational cost of solving the resulting system of equations, we show in this chapter that with emerging research in adapting the conjugate gradient method [4–6] and sparse matrix-vector multiplication (SpMV) [7–10]

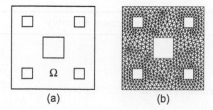

FIGURE 16.1

Illustration of a domain and associated finite element mesh. Each vertex is a node and each triangle is an element of the finite element mesh.

to the GPU, the assembly stage becomes a bottleneck. Devising and implementing algorithms for FEM assembly on the GPU not only prevents costly CPU-GPU transfers of data, but can also provide a significant speed-up to the application.

16.2 CORE METHOD

16.2.1 Finite Element Assembly

The assembly procedure partitions the integrals over Ω in Eq. (2) as a sum of integrals over the elements, so that each entry A_{ij} or F_i is computed as a sum of elemental contributions,

$$A_{ij} = a(\varphi_i, \varphi_j) = \sum_{e \in \mathcal{E}} a^e(\varphi_i, \varphi_j) = \sum_{e \in \mathcal{E}} A_{ij}^e,$$

A typical finite element assembly program relies on given *element subroutines* to compute element matrices A^e and element forcing vectors F^e. These element subroutines change with the PDE, the element type, and the basis functions, and are functions of the nodal coordinates, any nodal fields, forces, or boundary conditions, and other element parameters.

Three types of data structures are then important for computations over unstructured meshes:

1. The nodal data matrix $C(n)$, which yields the field values of the nth node, with n, $0 \le n < |\mathcal{N}|$, referred to as the *global node number*. The first fields are often the coordinates of the node, followed by nodal values of other fields, such as a force. In the case of nonlinear problems, the system of equations depends on u. Hence, nodal data will also include the values of the required degrees of freedom, such as temperature or displacement.

2. The supplemental data matrix $S(e)$, which yields supplemental data for the eth element. For example, inhomogeneous problems may require spatially varying element subroutines that are parameterized by some value, i.e., permeability, conductivity, material constants, etc.

3. The connectivity matrix $E(e, a)$, which yields the global node number of the ath node of the eth element. Here, e, $0 \le e < |\mathcal{E}|$, is referred to as the *global element number* and a, $0 \le a < e_n$, where e_n denotes the number of nodes per elements, is referred to as the *local node number*.

The input arguments for element e are the nodal data contained in $C(n)$, for each global node number n in the element, and the supplemental data $S(e)$. The nodal data is generally retrieved from

---

Algorithm 1: The direct stiffness method of finite element assembly

---

1: Initialize A and F to zero;
2: **for** *all elements $e \in \mathcal{E}$* **do**
3:      $(A^e, F^e) \leftarrow \text{elem}(e)$;   /* element subroutine */
4:      **for** *all local degrees of freedom d_1 of e* **do**
5:          $F(L(e,d_1)) + = F^e(d_1)$;
6:          **for** *all local degrees of freedom d_2 of e* **do**
7:              $A(L(e,d_1), L(e,d_2)) + = A^e(d_1, d_2)$;

---

memory and arranged following a local node numbering scheme for the element. Similarly, after the element data A^e and F^e are computed, these data are accumulated in A and F following a map from local to global degrees of freedom.

This mapping information is stored in the *location matrix L*. For the dth degree of freedom of the eth element, $L(e,d)$ is the corresponding global degree of freedom number. This mapping allows us to write and store A^e and F^e densely so that

$$A(i,j) = \sum_{\substack{e,d_1,d_2 \\ L(e,d_1)=i \\ L(e,d_2)=j}} A^e(d_1,d_2) \qquad\qquad F(i) = \sum_{\substack{e,d \\ L(e,d)=i}} F^e(d), \qquad (3)$$

where we have adopted the notation $A_{ij} = A(i,j)$ and $F_i = F(i)$. An implementation is given in Algorithm 1. This is known as the direct stiffness method and is the most common implementation of finite element assembly.

16.3 ALGORITHMS, IMPLEMENTATIONS, AND EVALUATIONS

Previous studies on finite element methods (FEMs) on GPUs have largely focused on the solution of the sparse linear system of equations resulting from a FEM discretization [4, 6, 11], mainly because the solution stage is often the most computationally intensive step. Some assembly strategies for the GPU have been mentioned as well. However, specific applications have often allowed special approaches for FEM assembly. The methods, described in [11] for geometric flow on an unstructured mesh and in [12] for FEM cloth simulation, derive relatively simple expressions for each nonzero entry in the system of equations. This relative simplicity and the inherent parallelism of computing each nonzero entry independently makes these approaches well suited to GPUs.

In this section, we review, update, and apply methods for finite element assembly from [1] that are general enough to be used for a wide range of finite element models. Consequently, we attempt to make few, unrestrictive assumptions about the properties of the problem, the element subroutine, and the sparse matrix format. The following assumptions are nonetheless made:

- The element subroutine is provided as a black box intended to be executed by a single thread on the GPU. This may be the case for a wide range of low-order finite element methods that are ideal for acceleration. Problem-dependent optimizations like those found in [11, 13, 14] and high-order optimizations such as parallelizing the element subroutine [15] can also be investigated for additional performance improvement.

- The sparse matrix format provides a one-to-one mapping $K : \mathbb{N} \times \mathbb{N} \to \mathbb{N}$ which takes a row-column pair, (i,j), corresponding to a nonzero of the matrix and returns the index into a value array where this nonzero entry is stored.

- The connectivity, $E(e,a)$, and supplemental data, $S(e)$, are constant over the course of the computation. This allows significant precomputation to be performed, which greatly accelerates the methods. This prevents the easy application of these methods to dynamically changing or adaptive meshes.

The first method, in Section 16.3.1, consists of decomposing the calculation into two phases: all the element data are computed and written to global memory. It is then assembled into the matrix A in any number of ways. The advantages of this method include its relative ease of implementation and its potential for further improvement since it is primarily limited by the second stage: the reduction of the element data into the system of equations.

The second method, in Section 16.3.2, is more complex and uses the shared memory space to stage the element data and reduce the number of transactions with global memory. The nodes and elements are partitioned into subdomains wherein some set of nonzeros of the system of equations can be safely computed. A thread block computes all the element data required for a subdomain and then accumulates and assembles all possible nonzero entries in the matrix A and vector F. This can reduce the number of passes through global memory while avoiding excessive recomputation of the element data. However, this method is restricted by the size of the shared memory space, the size of the element data A^e and F^e, and the connectivity of each node.

Both of these methods are slightly modified from those found in [1], where more detail on each method may be found as well as additional methods not considered in this chapter. In this chapter, the methods are updated to account for the need to include supplemental data, $S(e)$ — that are associated with an element rather than a node. The supplemental data appear in the application of these methods to a nonlinear elastic model at the end of this chapter. Additionally, we discuss the use of these methods on more modern hardware than was available for [1], and how this affects their performance.

16.3.1 Assembly by Nonzero Entries Using Global Memory

This approach, deemed GlobalNZ, assigns one thread to compute the element data for one element at a time and, to avoid race conditions, writes the element data in coalesced memory transactions to global memory for later reduction into the system of equations. Since the reduction stage then operates on element data stored in global memory and there are no global synchronization primitives, the computation and assembly of the element data must be performed using separate kernels.

A significant optimization is made by exploiting the fact that elements can be grouped to share many nodes. The total number of transactions with global memory can be reduced by prefetching all the nodal data a thread block will require and sharing it between the set of elements to be computed.

Thus, we precompute the set of nodes $\mathcal{N}_k$ that thread block k will require for all the elements $\mathcal{E}_k$ that it is responsible for computing. The nodal data corresponding to the nodes of $\mathcal{N}_k$ are prefetched into shared memory. Each thread is then assigned to compute the element data for an element using the nodal data in shared memory. To do this, each thread reads from a precomputed array telling it which

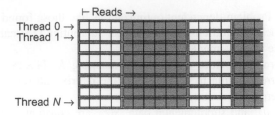

FIGURE 16.2

The column-major block element matrix E_k in the case $e_n = 4$. Each white entry stores a block node number $E_k(e,a)$, which can be used to find the nodal data in shared memory. Each group of 4 entries defines an element to be computed. Followed, in gray, are any constant supplemental data to be given to the element. A thread block will read down a column of the array in coalesced memory transactions.

nodes to retrieve from shared memory. That is, for each thread block k, we precompute block element matrices, E_k, defined by

$$E_k(e,a) = \sigma_k(E(e,a)) \qquad \forall\, e \in \mathcal{E}_k,\ a = 1, \ldots, e_n$$

where $\sigma_k : \mathcal{N}_k \rightarrow \{1, \ldots, |\mathcal{N}_k|\}$ is a mapping of global node number $E(e,a)$ to block node number $E_k(e,a)$ within block k, which can be used to find the nodal data in shared memory. Although not considered in [1], constant supplemental data should also be appended to this list. This results in the data structure shown in Figure 16.2. A thread will read $e_n + |S(e)|$ values, where e_n is the number of nodes per element, in coalesced memory transactions. It then passes to the element subroutine the supplemental data and indices into shared memory pointing to the required nodal data. The element subroutine computes the element data and stores it into global memory using coalesced memory writes.

It is mentioned in [1] that the assembly of the element data from global memory can be expressed as the sparse matrix vector multiplication

$$[A\,;F] = SG$$

where A and F define the system of equations, G is the element data stored in global memory, and $S_{ij} \in \{0,1\}$ is a matrix appropriately constructed to perform the summation in Eq. (3). Thus, this stage of the global assembly method should take advantage of the emerging research in sparse matrix-vector multiplication (SpMV) methods on GPUs. However, it should be noted that in practical tests, we find that the reduction array method presented in [1] outperforms many SpMV routines, including CSR, HYB, and ELLPACK-R, to preform this reduction. This may be simply due to the superfluous lookup of the "1"s in the SpMVs, and this is under ongoing research.

Our approach to the reduction step involves determining the indices into the element data array previously computed and stored in global memory that contribute to each nonzero entry (NZ) of the system of equations. Each one of these lists is appended with the index into the system of equations of the NZ in question. Thus, for each NZ of the system, we have an NZ reduction list of the form where the light entries represent indices into the element data array (source indices) and the final dark entry is the index of the NZ in the system of equations (target index), which can be distinguished by the sign of the integer. Each NZ of the system of equations has an associated reduction list of this form. However, the lists may have significantly differing lengths. Assigning one thread to one list could lead to unbalanced workloads. Furthermore, we need to coalesce the access to these lists. To efficiently perform these reduction operations in parallel, we pack these lists into a *reduction array*. First, we decide the number of NZs to compute per block. For each block, we then pack the NZ reduction lists into an array that will be read fully coalesced in the kernel. Simple packing algorithms such as Largest-Processing-Time (LPT) [16] appear to suffice and result in only small amounts of wasted space provided there are enough reduction lists per block. The result is a column-major matrix with *blockSize* rows and data profile shown in Figure 16.3 and the parallel algorithm using this structure is given in Algorithm 2.

For efficiency and simplicity, we assemble contiguous entries of the matrix value array in shared memory. That is, we map contiguous entries of a matrix to the shared memory space, and perform coalesced writes into matrix's value array when all NZs have been computed. Thus, the only memory reads

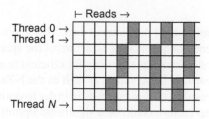

FIGURE 16.3

The column-major reduction matrix with *blockSize* rows. The light entries represent source indices and the dark entries represent target indices. A thread block will read down a column of the array in coalesced memory transactions.

Algorithm 2: Reduction operation from reduction array. In this case, the source array S is the element data array in global memory and the target array T is the system of equations stored in global memory.

1: $k \leftarrow blockID$;
2: $tid \leftarrow blockThreadID$;
3: $t \leftarrow 0$;
4: **while** $tid < end_k$ **do**
5:     $i \leftarrow reductionArray_k[tid]$;
6:     **if** $i > 0$ **then**
7:         $t \leftarrow t + S[i - 1]$;
8:     **else if** $i < 0$ **then**
9:         $T[-i - 1] \leftarrow t$;
10:         $t \leftarrow 0$;
11:     $tid \leftarrow tid + blockSize$;

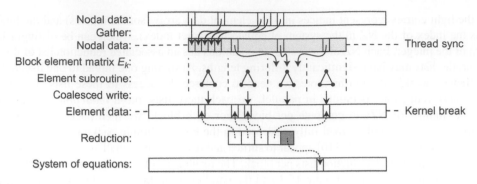

FIGURE 16.4

The global assembly by NZ on the GPU. Global memory is depicted in white and shared memory is depicted in light gray. Solid black arrows represent memory reads and writes and dotted arrows represent references to memory. The kernel break denotes the end of the element computation kernel and the beginning of the assembly kernel.

that are not coalesced are the retrievals of the element data. This approach proves to be quite efficient, but also causes a slight dependency on the storage structure of the sparse matrix. If there is significant padding in the sparse matrix's value array (presumably for efficient matrix-vector multiplication), then this approach will be uselessly writing these values as well as the NZs. However, the matrix format is presumably designed to be accessed in coalesced reads in order to optimize the SpMV kernel. Assembling the NZs in this same access pattern could be a significant optimization to this stage — although this is difficult to recognize and perform in the general case.

The entire assembly algorithm by NZ using global memory is diagrammed in Figure 16.4.

16.3.2 Assembly by Nonzero Entries Using Shared Memory

The second approach, deemed SharedNZ, uses shared memory to stage the element data and perform the assembly/reduction step on-chip. First, a thread block is assigned responsibility for assembling a set of nonzero entries (NZs) of the system of equations. For the NZs to be assembled from element data in shared memory, we must guarantee that all of the element data that contribute to the set of NZs are available in shared memory.

Thus, we first partition the nodes and assign a thread block to be responsible for assembling all NZs associated with a node in that partition. Although [1] recommends METIS [17] to perform the partition, METIS failed in [1] to define partitions small enough to allow the 5th order triangular element test case to proceed. We find METIS to be insufficient for the partitioning that SharedNZ requires and, instead, wrote a simple greedy algorithm to determine nodal partitions. This greedy algorithm is initialized with each partition containing one node. At each iteration, a node finds an adjacent partition which, if added to its partition, would result in the smallest number of elements that would be required to assemble all nodes of the unioned partition. If the shared memory constraint is satisfied, the two partitions are unioned and we move on to the next node until no more partitions can be unioned. We find this acceptable and note that it actually outperforms METIS's partitions in most cases.

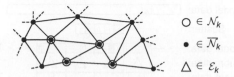

FIGURE 16.5

Example of sets $\overline{\mathcal{N}}_k$, $\mathcal{N}_k$, and $\mathcal{E}_k$. As $|\mathcal{E}_k|$ increases, the ratio $|\overline{\mathcal{N}}_k| / |\mathcal{N}_k|$ decreases, which improves the efficiency of the algorithm.

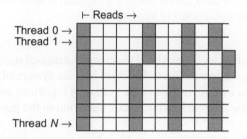

FIGURE 16.6

The column-major scatter matrix with *blockSize* rows. The dark entries represent source indices and the light entries represent target indices. A thread block will read a column of the array in coalesced memory transactions.

For thread block k, let $\mathcal{N}_k$ be the set of nodes it is responsible for assembling. We denote $\mathcal{E}_k$ the set of elements required to compute the associated NZs. In order to compute elemental data for $\mathcal{E}_k$, a thread block must retrieve the data for any node adjacent to elements of $\mathcal{E}_k$. We call this set of nodes $\overline{\mathcal{N}}_k$. Figure 16.5 shows an example of the sets $\mathcal{N}_k$, $\overline{\mathcal{N}}_k$, and $\mathcal{E}_k$.

The nodes of $\overline{\mathcal{N}}_k$ are to be fetched from global memory once and stored in shared memory as input for the element subroutines. For each node in $\overline{\mathcal{N}}_k$, we define the list of elements in $\mathcal{E}_k$ that require the data from that node. For each node we create a list of the form

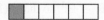

where the dark entry represents the node number (source index) to be retrieved from global memory and the light entries represent the block element number that requires the data from that node (target index). Again, the lists associated to different nodes in $\overline{\mathcal{N}}_k$ may have significantly different lengths, but we can pack these lists into a *scatter array* using a packing algorithm such as LPT [16]. The result is a column-major matrix with *blockSize* rows and data profile shown in Figure 16.6. The parallel algorithm using this structure is similar to Algorithm 2.

In addition to the nodal data, the element subroutines also require the element-wise supplemental data. In contrast to the approach taken in Section 16.3.1, we have simply adopted computing a separate array in global memory of the supplemental data that are ordered such that they can be read by the elements with coalesced reads.

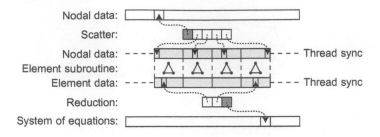

FIGURE 16.7

The shared assembly by NZ on the GPU. Global memory is depicted in white and shared memory is depicted in light gray. Dotted arrows represent references into memory.

After the element subroutines have calculated the element data and stored them into shared memory (overwriting the nodal data), we need to assemble them into the system of equations. By construction, all of the element data needed by a set of NZs of the system of equations are now in the shared memory space and we can use a similar approach to the scatter operation in the previous section to perform the reduction operation.

The entire procedure is diagrammed in Figure 16.7. Note that the shared assembly by NZ algorithm is heavily constrained by the size of the shared memory space.

16.4 EVALUATION AND VALIDATION OF RESULTS, TOTAL BENEFITS, LIMITATIONS

16.4.1 Benchmark Problem — Nonlinear Elastodynamics

We wish to apply the above methods for finite element assembly to a realistic problem which depends critically on the efficiency of the finite element assembly stage. For this purpose, we chose to simulate the dynamics of a nonlinear elastic model in three dimensions; see, e.g., [18]. The essential details of this model are introduced below.

We consider a body occupying a reference configuration $\Omega \subset \mathbb{R}^3$. The motion of this body is described through a smooth map $\phi \colon \Omega \times \mathbb{R} \to \mathbb{R}^3$, so that $\phi(\mathbf{X}, t)$ describes the position at time t of the material particle at $\mathbf{X} \in \Omega$. This motion may be a consequence of the elasticity of the body, of forces or constraints acting on $\partial\Omega$, or of a system of body forces $\boldsymbol{b} \colon \Omega \times \mathbb{R} \to \mathbb{R}^3$. The elasticity of the body is described by the strain energy density per unit volume of a neo-Hookean material extended to the compressible range, namely,

$$W(\mathcal{F}; X) := \frac{\mu}{2}(\mathcal{F}^T \mathcal{F} - \boldsymbol{I}) : \boldsymbol{I} + \frac{\lambda}{2}\ln^2(J) - \mu \ln(J),$$

where $\mathcal{F} = \nabla\phi(\boldsymbol{X}, t)$ is the spatial gradient of ϕ, or deformation gradient, μ and λ are elastic constants, and J is the determinant of $\mathcal{F}$. Then the first Piola-Kirchhoff stress tensor is given by

$$\boldsymbol{P} := \mu \mathcal{F} + (\lambda \ln(J) - \mu)\mathcal{F}^{-T}.$$

Variational time-integrators for these systems are discussed, for example, in [19]. The traditional midpoint rule is an example of such an integrator, and takes the form

$$p^k = m \frac{\phi^{k+1} - \phi^k}{\Delta t} + \frac{\Delta t}{2} f\left(\frac{\phi^{k+1} + \phi^k}{2}\right) =: h(\phi^{k+1}) \tag{4}$$

$$p^{k+1} = m \frac{\phi^{k+1} - \phi^k}{\Delta t} - \frac{\Delta t}{2} f\left(\frac{\phi^{k+1} + \phi^k}{2}\right) \tag{5}$$

where p^k and ϕ^k are the vector of nodal momentum and positions at time t^k, and m and f are the mass matrix and the force vector given by

$$(m)_{a_i b_j} = \int_\Omega \rho\, \varphi_a\, \varphi_b\, d\Omega \quad (f)_{a_i} = \int_\Omega (P)_{iK}\, \varphi_{a,K}\, d\Omega - \int_\Omega b\, \varphi_a\, d\Omega$$

where ρ is the material density and a_i denotes the ith degree of freedom of the ath node. We use a lumped mass matrix diagonalized by using a Lobatto quadrature. To solve for ϕ^{k+1}, we solve the nonlinear Eq. (4) via the Newton-Raphson iteration

$$\phi_{p+1}^k = \phi_p^k + [\nabla h(\phi_p^k)]^{-1} [p^k - h(\phi_p^k)], \qquad p = 0, 1, \ldots, P$$

where the tangent matrix is given by

$$(\nabla h)_{a_i b_j} = \frac{1}{\Delta t} (m)_{a_i b_j} + \frac{\Delta t}{2} \int_\Omega (\partial_\mathcal{F} P)_{iKjL}\, \varphi_{a,K}\, \varphi_{b,L}\, d\Omega \tag{6}$$

$$(\partial_\mathcal{F} P)_{ijkl} = \mu \delta_{ik} \delta_{jl} + \lambda \mathcal{F}_{ij}^{-T} \mathcal{F}_{kl}^{-T} - (\lambda \ln(J) - \mu) \mathcal{F}_{li}^{-T} \mathcal{F}_{jk}^{-T} \tag{7}$$

Once $\phi^{k+1} = \phi_P^k$ has been computed within tolerance $\|p^k - h(\phi_P^k)\| \le \epsilon$, we determine p^{k+1} using Eq. (5). For more information on variational integrators, hyperelasticity, and neo-Hookean materials, see [20].

For simplicity, we use tetrahedral elements and affine basis functions. This makes computation of the deformation gradient particularly simple and compact. For each element,

$$\mathcal{F}_{ij} = \frac{\partial \phi_i}{\partial X_j} = \frac{\partial \phi_i}{\partial \xi_k} \left[\frac{\partial X_j}{\partial \xi_k}\right]^{-1} = \phi_{ai} \frac{\partial \varphi_a}{\partial \xi_k} \left[X_{bj} \frac{\partial \varphi_b}{\partial \xi_k}\right]^{-1}$$

$$= [\phi_1 - \phi_4, \phi_2 - \phi_4, \phi_3 - \phi_4][X_1 - X_4, X_2 - X_4, X_3 - X_4]^{-1}$$

where X_a is the position of node a in the reference configuration, and $\phi_a = \phi(X_a, t)$ is the position of the same node as a result of the deformation. The second matrix can be precomputed and stored as supplemental data to be passed to the element subroutine.

Thus, this problem requires multiple assemblies and sparse matrix solves per time step: one assembly and one sparse matrix solve per Newton-Raphson iteration. In the following sections we use the conjugate gradient method as our linear solver. Indeed, we will show that, with a GPU accelerated diagonally preconditioned conjugate gradient solver, a standard assembly stage run on the CPU is the bottleneck. Thus, this problem can benefit greatly from a GPU accelerated assembly, which we provided in this chapter, to yield significant additional speed-up. As we show later, this and other time-integration schemes implemented in GPUs can yield stable, large time-step, real-time integrators for meshes of unprecedented size.

16.4.2 Implementation

The source code which accompanies this chapter is written in a modular fashion to accommodate testing and optimizing (see Figure 16.8). Each stage of the code has a CPU and a GPU version, which will perform the CPU-GPU transfers for the previous/subsequent stages as necessary, and all stages interface with a general sparse matrix class, allowing many sparse matrix formats to be tested easily.

The COO and CSR matrix structures are common sparse matrix formats and the HYB format from [8, 9] is a hybrid of the ELL and COO formats. The CSR_Vector and HYB matrix-vector product on the GPU both performed very well in tests in [8, 9] for matrices assembled from finite element models. Clearly though, this chapter's study should be extended to other formats, such as ELLPACK-R, PKT, DIA, and block-structured versions [7–9, 21].

16.4.2.1 *Optimizations and Assumptions*

The implemented matrices all have DXXX versions, which reserve the first portion of the matrix value array for the diagonal NZs of the matrix. For many sparse matrix formats and SpMV kernels, this

- Newton-Raphson
  - `NR_CPU`
  - `NR_GPU`
- Assembly
  - `AssemblyCPU`
  - `AssemblyCPU_Opt`
  - `AssemblyGlobalNZ`
  - `AssemblySharedNZ`
- Conjugate gradient
  - `CG_CPU`
  - `CG_GPU`
  - `DCG_CPU`
  - `DCG_GPU`
- Sparse matrix format
  - `CCU_Matrix`
  - `CSR_Matrix`
  - `HYB_Matrix`
  - `DCOO_Matrix`
  - `DCSR_Matrix`
  - `DHYB_Matrix`
- All SpMVs on CPU and GPU.

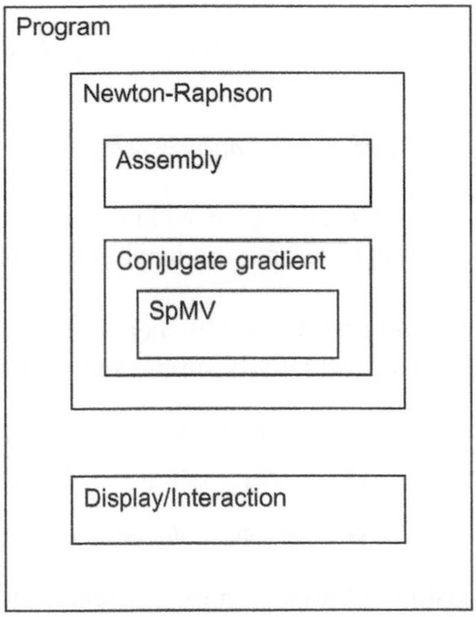

FIGURE 16.8

The structure of the program and some of the modular components available. `NR` denotes the Newton-Raphson iteration, `CG` denotes the conjugate gradient method, and `DCG` denotes the diagonally preconditioned conjugate gradient method. Multiple sparse matrix formats are available as well as their associated sparse matrix-vector multiplication (SpMV) implementations on the CPU and GPU.

is a small modification. This allows the diagonally preconditioned conjugate gradient method and the summation with the diagonal, lumped mass matrix in Eq. (6) to be implemented trivially and efficiently.

Rather than read in the reference configuration nodes for each assembly, we precompute the supplemental data

$$S(e) = \left[X_1^e - X_4^e, X_2^e - X_4^e, X_3^e - X_4^e \right]^{-1}$$

where X_a^e, $a = 1, 2, 3, 4$, denote the local reference configuration node for element e. Note that ∇h^e and f^e, the restriction of ∇h and f to the domain of element e, are rotationally invariant when the material is isotropic, as in our construction. Thus, the supplemental data can be compressed from 9 values (3×3 matrix) to 6 values by performing an orientation-preserving QR decomposition and storing only the upper triangular part.

16.4.3 Validation

In this section, we validate the finite element assembly procedures by comparing the output of the single-precision GlobalNZ, SharedNZ, and a host implementation against a trivially implemented double-precision assembly on the host for a number of meshes. The validation is performed by assembling the tangent matrix ∇h for a tetrahedral mesh of a unit sphere with various levels of refinement.

Table 16.1 lists the L^2 relative error between the entries of the system of equations constructed in double-precision on the host and single-precision on the device. As shown in Table 16.1, all of the device methods agree and exhibit the expected floating point accuracy, which increase with the inverse of the characteristic mesh size of the grid, $h \sim |\mathcal{N}|^{-1/3}$. This is expected since the entries of the system are functions of the distance between nodes, which have relative errors from the truncation of the nodal data proportional to $1/h$.

16.4.4 Performance Analysis

Our experimental setup is composed of an NVIDIA GeForce GTX 480 and Tesla C1060 processor installed on the PCI Express 2 bus (8 GB/s bandwidth) of a Intel Core 2 Quad CPU Q9450 2.66 GHz with 8 GB of RAM and running Linux kernel 2.6.32. The GTX 480 card has 15 multiprocessors, 480 cores, 1536 MB of memory, with a memory bandwidth of 177.4 GB per second. The C1060 card

Table 16.1 The L^2 Error of the Nonzeros in the System of Equations, $\left[\sum_{ij} |A_{ij}^s - A_{ij}^d|^2 / \sum_{ij} |A_{ij}^d|^2 \right]^{1/2}$, between the Single-Precision Matrix, A^s, and the Double-Precision Matrix, A^d

		Sphere Mesh (Nodes, Elems)			
		63,120	305,960	1.7K, 7.1K	3.6K, 16.5K
Assembler and Matrix	CPU (float) COO	9.15e−8	1.05e−8	1.45e−7	1.77e−7
	SharedNZ CSR	8.75e−8	1.14e−8	1.45e−7	1.77e−7
	SharedNZ HYB	8.75e−8	1.14e−8	1.45e−7	1.77e−7
	GlobalNZ CSR	8.75e−8	1.14e−8	1.45e−7	1.77e−7
	GlobalNZ HYB	8.75e−8	1.14e−8	1.45e−7	1.77e−7

has 30 multiprocessors, 240 cores, 4 GB of memory, with a memory bandwidth of 102 GB per second. We use CUDA version 3.1, driver 256.35, gcc version 4.4.3, and nvcc release 3.1 version 0.2.1221.

Figure 16.9 shows the surface of a volumetric tetrahedral mesh consisting of 28,796 nodes and 125,127 elements representing a hand. (This mesh is available online at aimatshape.net and is commonly used to test graphics and physics applications.)

We now present benchmarks that illustrate that a GPU accelerated assembly provides a significant benefit for engineering applications, and is necessary if the goal is either graphics or real-time simulations. The GPU kernels are timed using CUDA events [22].

To begin, we run a system solely on the CPU using $\Delta t = 0.2$, $\mu = 5$, $\lambda = 2$, $\rho = 1$, and strict single-precision convergence – the Newton-Raphson tolerance is $\left\| p^k - h(\phi_p^k) \right\|_2 < 10^{-5}$ and the conjugate gradient tolerance is $\left\| r_p \right\|_2 < 10^{-6} \left\| r_0 \right\|_2$, where r_p is the residual at iteration p. The breakdown of the total time executing each stage is shown on the left of Figure 16.10. Clearly, at 70% of the total runtime, the SpMV is the bottleneck of this configuration and should be optimized. This stage can be optimized by implementing the conjugate gradient and sparse matrix-vector multiplication on the GPU and switching to the HYB matrix format, which is more efficient on the GPU. Running the same

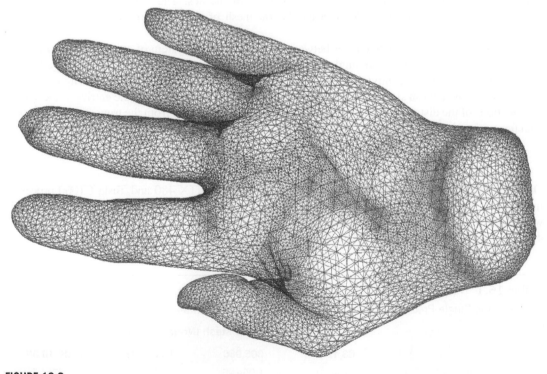

FIGURE 16.9

The surface of the tetrahedral mesh used in the validation and benchmarking sections. This mesh contains 28,796 nodes and 125,127 elements, resulting in a sparse linear system of size 86,388 and a matrix with 3.3M nonzeros.

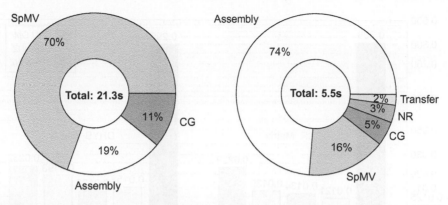

FIGURE 16.10

Optimizing only the conjugate gradient and SpMV for the GPU yields very good results, but ultimately has diminishing returns. (Left) All stages optimized and run on the CPU: `NR_CPU`, `AssemblyCPU_Opt`, `DCSR_Matrix`, `DCG_CPU`. (Right) Same run with SpMV and CG optimized and executed on the GPU: `NR_CPU`, `AssemblyCPU_Opt`, `DHYB_Matrix`, `DCG_GPU`.

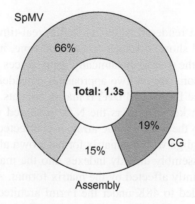

FIGURE 16.11

The breakdown of the total time spent in each stage when all components are optimized for and run on the GPU: `NR_GPU`, `AssemblyGlobalNZ`, `DHYB_Matrix`, `DCG_GPU`.

simulation with the optimized CG configuration, the new bottleneck is now the assembly on the CPU and the focus should no longer be on optimizing the SpMV on the GPU. Together with the 2% of time taken to perform the CPU-GPU transfers of data, the assembly now takes up 76% of the total runtime, while the entire conjugate gradient stage has been reduced to only 21%.

Using the methods in this chapter to implement the assembly on the GPU, a time profile similar to the pure CPU version is retrieved, as shown in Figure 16.11. The entire computation of the time step has been accelerated by over 16× from the CPU version. This is certainly beneficial for the engineering community, but by slightly relaxing the time step and convergence criteria, over 7 frames

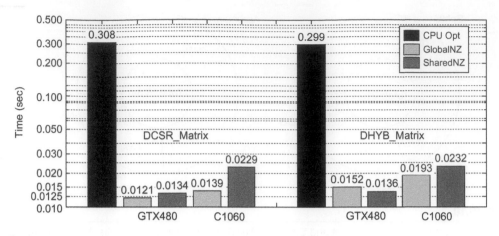

FIGURE 16.12

Comparison of the assembly operations with respect to hardware and matrix format. The `CPU_Opt` and `SharedNZ` assembly are not affected by the matrix format since they use direct indexing to write NZs. The `GlobalNZ` buffers the NZs in shared memory before writing coalesced blocks into the matrix (see color insert).

per second can be computed and rendered, allowing stable, real-time elastodynamics for meshes of unprecedented size. Figure 16.13 shows 4 frames from a real-time, interactive simulation which uses an OpenGL renderer and allows the user to dynamically apply forces to the mesh with the mouse.

Finally, in Figure 16.12 we compare the two approaches considered in this chapter with the optimized CPU assembly for both the DCSR and DHYB matrix formats. It is important to point out that, because the GlobalNZ reduction kernel buffers the NZs in shared memory before writing them in coalesced memory transaction to the matrix value array, it is affected by the DHYB's padded matrix format. Optimizing this stage to align with the matrix format's own alignment may be worthwhile. On the other hand, the SharedNZ assembly directly indexes into the matrix value array, sacrificing coalesced writes, but is not significantly affected by the matrix format. Additionally, the shared memory space on the GTX480 is expanded to 48K under the Fermi architecture, while the C1060 has only 16K per streaming multiprocessor, which disproportionately affects the performance of the SharedNZ method on the C1060.

16.4.5 Comparison with Previously Published Results

In the case of linear tetrahedral elastodynamics, each element has 4 nodes with 3 degrees of freedom each. Thus, the size of the elemental forcing vector F^e is 12 ($= 4 \cdot 3$) and the size of the symmetric elemental matrix A^e is 78 ($= \frac{1}{2}4 \cdot 3(4 \cdot 3 + 1)$), so each element subroutine will compute 90 values.

In [1], the performance of the assembly routines were tested against the polynomial order of triangular elements, and therefore the size of the element data. Table IV of [1] shows that third order triangular elements compute 65 values and fourth order triangular elements compute 135 values. Thus, we may expect the performance of GlobalNZ and SharedNZ to be comparable to their third or fourth order performance values in [1]. However, the connectivity of the mesh plays an important role in the performance of these assembly algorithms. Specifically, nodes in the 2-dimensional mesh used in [1]

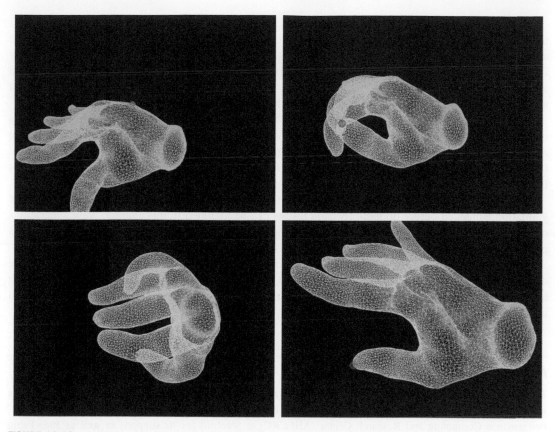

FIGURE 16.13

Sequence of images from elastodynamic simulation using the hand mesh with interactive user input forcing. The simulation is run at approximately 7–14 frames per second with $\Delta t = 0.01$, $\mu = 5$, $\lambda = 2$, $\rho = 1$, and single-precision convergence – the Newton-Raphson tolerance is $\left\| p^k - h(\phi_p^k) \right\|_2 < 2 \cdot 10^{-5}$, and the conjugate gradient tolerance is $\left\| r_p \right\|_2 < 10^{-4} \left\| r_0 \right\|_2$. Each time-step typically requires 3–6 NR iterations.

had, at most, only 9 adjacent triangular elements, whereas nodes in the 3-dimensional mesh shown in Figure 16.9 can have up to 42 adjacent tetrahedral elements. This seriously limits the size of the SharedNZ partitions, and is reflected in the relatively poor performance of SharedNZ on the C1060. On the GTX 480, this effect is reasonably offset by the expanded shared memory space, which offers a 48K shared memory space rather than the 16K on the C1060 and GTX 8800 used in [1].

16.5 FUTURE DIRECTIONS

There are a number of further optimizations that can be made in this problem, and which would likely have broader application.

First, also not considered in [1] is the recognition that, if n_f is the number of degrees of freedom per node and the degrees of freedom are numbered consecutively by node in the system of equations, then almost all NZs in the system appear in $n_f \times n_f$ blocks. These blocks can be assembled straightforwardly from the corresponding blocks in the element matrix, A^e. This would compress the reduction array and allow for easier coalescing of data reads and writes. Similarly, in the SpMV, blocked versions of almost all matrix formats are possible and offer similar benefits.

Although the system of equations is symmetric, this is not taken advantage of in any of the methods in this chapter. Neither the assembly nor the SpMV use the symmetry as an optimization. Indeed, the authors are aware of only a few sparse matrix formats which are designed for symmetric matrices. Using an extra flag in the reductions arrays may allow an assembled NZ to be stored to two locations in the system of equations, potentially speeding up the reduction stage by almost a factor of two.

Although the code is templated to facilitate both single- and double-precision computing, more validation is needed before double-precision results can be included in this chapter. New generations of NVIDIA GPU hardware, such as the Tesla generation, which includes the GTX 480 used in this chapter, have greatly improved the architecture for computing with double-precision.

Testing double-precision versions of each stage on the GTX 480, with its new Fermi architecture designed with double-precision computing in mind, is an important new step. The code is written with templated classes to facilitate this. This is slightly more difficult to do on the GPU and more validation is needed before results can be included.

Acknowledgments

This work was partially supported by a research grant from the Academic Excellence Alliance program between King Abdullah University of Science and Technology and Stanford University. We also thank the Army High-Performance Computing and Research Center (AHPCRC) at Stanford for its support, as well as Juan-Pablo Samper-Mejia and Vivian Nguyen for their contribution during the 2010 AHPCRC Summer Institute.

References

[1] C. Cecka, A. Lew, E. Darve, Assembly of finite element methods on graphics processors, Int. J. Num. Meth. Eng. (2009).

[2] T.J.R. Hughes, The Finite Element Method: Linear Static and Dynamic Finite Element Analysis, Prentice-Hall, Englewood Cliffs, NJ, 1987.

[3] M. Rumpf, R. Strzodka, Graphics processor units: new prospects for parallel computing, in: A.M. Bruaset, A. Tveito (Eds.), Numerical Solution of Partial Differential Equations on Parallel Computers, vol. 51 of Lecture Notes in Computational Science and Engineering, Springer, 2005, pp. 89–134.

[4] D. Göddeke, R. Strzodka, J. Mohd-Yusof, P. McCormick, H. Wobker, C. Becker, et al., Using GPUs to improve multigrid solver performance on a cluster, Int. J. Comput. Sci. Eng. 4 (1) (2008) 36–55.

[5] R. Strzodka, D. Göddeke, Pipelined mixed precision algorithms on FPGAs for fast and accurate PDE solvers from low precision components, in: IEEE Symposium on Field-Programmable Custom Computing Machines 2006, 2006, pp. 259–268.

[6] D. Göddeke, R. Strzodka, S. Turek, Accelerating double precision FEM simulations with GPUs, in: Proceedings of ASIM 2005, 2005.

[7] L. Buatois, G. Caumon, B. Lévy, Concurrent number cruncher: an efficient sparse linear solver on the GPU, in: HPCC, 2007.

[8] N. Bell, M. Garland, Efficient sparse matrix-vector multiplication on CUDA, in: NVIDIA Technical Report, NVR-2008-004, 2008.

[9] N. Bell, M. Garland, Implementing sparse matrix-vector multiplication on throughput-oriented processors, in: Proceedings Supercomputing '09, 2009.

[10] M. Baskaran, R. Bordawekar, Optimizing sparse matrix-vector multiplication on GPUs using compile-time and run-time strategies, Technical Report, Research Report RC24704, IBM TJ Watson Research Center, 2008.

[11] J. Bolz, I. Farmer, E. Grinspun, P. Schröder, Sparse matrix solvers on the GPU: conjugate gradients and multigrid, ACM Trans. Graph. 22 (2003) 917–924.

[12] J. Rodriguez-Navarro, A. Susin, Non structured meshes for cloth GPU simulation using FEM, in: VRIPHYS, 2006, pp. 1–7.

[13] E. Tejada, T. Ertl, Large steps in GPU-based deformable bodies simulation, Simul. Model. Pract. Th. 13 (8) (2005) 703–715.

[14] E. Elsen, P. LeGresley, E. Darve, Large calculation of the flow over a hypersonic vehicle using a GPU, J. Comput. Phys. 227 (24) (2008) 10148–10161.

[15] D. Komatitsch, D. Micha, G. Erlebacher, Porting a high-order finite-element earthquake modeling application to NVIDIA graphics cards using CUDA, J. Parallel Distr. Com. 69 (5) (2009) 451–460.

[16] R.L. Graham, Bounds on multiprocessing timing anomalies, SIAM J. Appl. Math. 17 (1969) 263–269.

[17] G. Karypis, V. Kumar, MeTiS 4.0: Unstructured Graph Partitioning and Sparse Matrix Ordering System, 1998.

[18] J.E. Marsden, T.J.R. Hughes, Mathematical Foundations of Elasticity, Dover, Mineola, New York, 1994.

[19] A. Lew, J.E. Marsden, M. Ortiz, M. West, Variational time integrators, Int. J. Numer. Methods Eng. 60 (1) (2004) 153–212.

[20] J. Bonet, R.D. Wood, Nonlinear Continuum Mechanics for Finite Element Analysis, Cambridge University Press, 1997.

[21] F. Vázquez, E.M. Garzón, J.A. Martinez, J.J. Fernádez, The sparse matrix vector product on GPUs, Technical Report, University of Almeria, 2009.

[22] NVIDIA Corporation, NVIDIA CUDA Programming Guide 3.0. 2010.

CHAPTER

17

CUDA Implementation of Vertex-Centered, Finite Volume CFD Methods on Unstructured Grids with Flow Control Applications

X.S. Trompoukis, V.G. Asouti, I.C. Kampolis, and K.C. Giannakoglou

This chapter presents the graphical processing unit (GPU) implementation of a Navier-Stokes equations solver for steady and unsteady flows and its use for the analysis and optimization of flow control problems based on active control mechanisms. The developed software solves the flow (mean-flow and turbulence model) equations using the vertex-centered, finite volume method on unstructured grids. This is the worst case in memory handling, which is known to be the most important parameter affecting speed-up. Thanks to the use of GPUs, the analysis and, in particular, the optimization, which is based on stochastic, population-based (evolutionary) algorithms, is carried out in affordable wall-clock time.

17.1 INTRODUCTION, PROBLEM STATEMENT, AND CONTEXT

Over the last 10 years, there is an increased interest in the use of graphics processing units (GPUs) for scientific computations. Modern GPUs offer high performance, while a number of programming languages are available to develop software running on them. In the beginning, GPUs were almost exclusively used in computational physics, and just a few works in the field of computational fluid dynamics (CFD) appeared. The latter were limited to the solution of 2-D and 3-D Euler equations on structured grids and relied on *single precision arithmetic* (SPA) because, by that period of time, the available GPUs could not support *double precision arithmetic* (DPA) computations [3–6]. Only recently, a few CFD applications on unstructured grids were brought to light [1, 2, 7]. Furthermore, last-generation GPUs support DPA computations, thereby allowing the extension from the Euler to the Navier-Stokes simulations [1, 2] where DPA is, in fact, a prerequisite.

An important issue that affects the GPU performance is related to the memory access. Structured grids are associated with organized memory accesses and, thus, high speed-ups. On the other hand, unstructured grid solvers running on GPUs achieve inevitably lower speed-ups depending, among others, on the discretization scheme used (Figure 17.1). For instance, in cell-centered finite volume

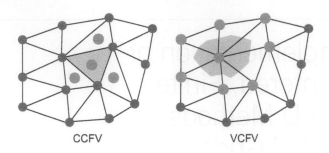

CCFV   VCFV

FIGURE 17.1

Application of cell- (left) and vertex-centered (right) finite volumes for the numerical solution of p.d.e.'s, on unstructured grids with triangular elements. Working with a CCFV method, the computation of flow variables requires the communication/interaction of three adjacent cell centers. On the other hand, in the VCFV method, the number of adjacent vertices affecting the finite volume under consideration may vary.

(CCFV) schemes, [7], the number of neighbors to each cell barycenter, where the flow variables are stored, is fixed (for instance, equal to three or four in grids with triangular or tetrahedral elements, respectively, etc.), and these fixed numbers are advantageous regarding memory access. In contrast, in vertex-centered finite volume (VCFV) schemes [1, 2], the number of neighbors to each finite volume is variable and, therefore, the corresponding software requires delicate memory management owing to highly noncoalesced memory accesses.

This chapter focuses on GPU implementations of Navier-Stokes VCFV schemes for unstructured/hybrid grids. A *mixed precision arithmetic* (MPA) scheme, as proposed in [1], which employs DPA for computing residuals and the parsimonious SPA for the left-hand-side (l.h.s.) coefficient matrices, contributes to increasing the performance of the GPU-enabled code, without damaging the accuracy of the numerical prediction. Recall that the latter is determined only by the accuracy with which residuals are computed. Using the developed software, we demonstrate active flow control studies (steady suction and synthetic jets, [11–14]) aiming at reducing the flow separation effects over aerodynamic shapes. On the GPU, these demanding computations are made ~ 51 times faster, allowing parametric and optimization studies to be performed within reasonable wall-clock time. The latter becomes more important when evolutionary algorithms, which require a great number of calls to the evaluation software (i.e., the CFD tool) before reaching the optimal solution, are used as optimization method.

CFD code developers who wish to make the right decision regarding the features of their GPU-enabled Navier-Stokes solver will certainly benefit from this chapter because this may help them maximize the efficiency of their codes. However, this chapter does not exclusively target the CFD community; software developers in different fields (electromagnetism, structural analysis, etc.), governed by "similar" p.d.e.'s with similar discretization schemes, may also be interested in the programming techniques described later in this chapter and our findings. Finally, from the application viewpoint, the target audience includes scientists working on the development/design of active flow control systems for suppressing or reducing separation in high- or low-speed aerodynamics (aircrafts, cars, turbomachines, etc.).

17.2 CORE (CFD AND OPTIMIZATION) METHODS

For the analysis of flow control problems, a steady (in case of steady suction or blowing) or unsteady (when employing synthetic jets) Navier-Stokes equations solver for turbulent compressible flows, coupled with a turbulence model, is used. Steady-state solvers are concerned with the numerical modeling of flows with properties that do not change in time. As it will be explained later in this chapter, an efficient way of computing steady-state flows is by adding a pseudo-time derivative and, then, marching in pseudo-time to reach the steady-state solution as the asymptotic limit in pseudo-time. The numerical solution of any unsteady flow field, such as the unsteadiness caused by the use of pulsating/synthetic jets, requires time-accurate discretization and integration schemes, leading to flow fields that vary in time. However, the pulsating jet is periodic and, therefore, the CFD code suffices to predict the flow during a single time period. For the cases presented herein, air flows at high speeds and compressibility effects cannot be neglected; thus, the flow is characterized as compressible.

The solver employs a VCFV technique with a second-order upwind scheme for the spatial discretization on unstructured grids. For the more accurate prediction of the viscous layers developed in the vicinity of solid walls, unstructured/hybrid grids with structured layers of quadrilaterals close to the wall and triangular elements elsewhere are generated and used. The solution is based on the time-marching method with dual-time stepping for time-accurate computations. The dual-time stepping technique, apart from the real-time step, employs also a pseudo-time step for the integration of the governing equations within each real-time step.

The design optimization of the steady suction control parameters for minimum boundary layer separation is based on evolutionary algorithms (EAs, [15–17]), in the context of which the aforementioned Navier-Stokes flow solver undertakes the evaluation of each candidate solution. Population-based methods (such as EAs) used for the search of the optimal solution(s) are inherently parallel. The evaluation of several population members can be carried out simultaneously, and the reduction in the elapsed time for each evaluation reflects directly on the reduction of the overall wall-clock time of the optimization.

17.2.1 Numerical Solution of the Navier-Stokes Equations

The Navier-Stokes equations for unsteady compressible flows are written as

$$\frac{\vartheta \vec{U}}{\vartheta t} + \frac{\vartheta \vec{U}}{\vartheta \tau} + \frac{\vartheta \vec{f_i}}{\vartheta \vec{x_i}} = 0 \tag{1}$$

where $\vec{U} = [\rho, \rho \vec{u}, E]^T$ is the vector of the mean-flow conservative variables, $\vec{f_i}$ the inviscid and viscous fluxes, t the physical time and τ the pseudo-time. Closure of Eq. (1) is achieved using the one-equation Spalart-Allmaras turbulence model.

In the VCFV scheme, the discrete form of the above equations written for node P (Figure 17.2), which expresses the balance of fluxes $\vec{\Phi}$ crossing the finite volume boundaries plus two temporal terms, can be written as follows:

$$\Omega_P \left(\frac{3\vec{U}_P^{k+1,n+1} - 4\vec{U}_P^k + 4\vec{U}_P^{k-1}}{2\Delta t} + \frac{\vec{U}_P^{k+1,n+1} - \vec{U}_P^{k+1,n}}{\Delta \tau_P} \right) + \sum_{Q \in nei(P)} \vec{\Phi}^{k+1} \Delta \partial \Omega_P = 0 \tag{2}$$

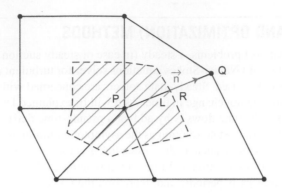

FIGURE 17.2

Finite volume Ω_P (hatched area) formed around node P, on a hybrid grid.

By omitting the term depending on the physical time-step Δt (index k), we make this equation valid for steady flows, too. Δt is determined by the required resolution of the flow solution in time, whereas the pseudo-time step $\Delta \tau_P$ (index n) is computed by means of stability criteria. According to the dual-time stepping approach, for each physical time-step the Navier-Stokes equations are integrated/solved in pseudo-time until convergence. $\vec{U}_P$ denotes the mean-flow variables at P, $\vec{\Phi} = \vec{\Phi}\left(\vec{U}_p, \vec{U}_Q, \nabla \vec{U}_p, \nabla \vec{U}_Q\right)$ are the numerical inviscid/viscous fluxes crossing the interface $\Delta \partial \Omega_P$ between the finite volumes defined around nodes P, Q; $nei(P)$ denotes the set of neighboring nodes of P. The discretized flow equations 2 are solved using either the point-implicit Jacobi (PIJ) or the Runge-Kutta (RK) iterative methods. The RK method is a representative CFD solver based on explicit discretizations of space and time derivatives. Because the flow variables at one grid point are expressed in terms of the flow variables at the adjacent grid points, at previous time (or pseudo-time) steps, no matrix inversion is involved and RK is appropriate for use on both serial and parallel computers. In contrast, the use of implicit discretizations, where the $\vec{U}$ values at each grid point are expressed in terms of $\vec{U}$ values at the adjacent points, at the current time step, calls for matrix inversions and increases the programming complexity, on multiprocessing platforms in particular [18]. The PIJ method, used also in this chapter, is the "standard" iterative solver; it is euphemistically referred to as a "point-implicit" method because matrix inversion is replaced by a small number of "internal iterations" (successive updates of nodal $\vec{U}$ values by "freezing" the adjacent $\vec{U}$ values at any node; see Eq. (3)).

The PIJ method employs the following iterative scheme to update the flow variables,

$$\Delta \vec{U}_P^{n+1,j+1} = (D_P^n)^{-1}\left[-\vec{R}_P^n - \sum_{Q \in nei(P)} Z_Q^n \Delta \vec{U}_Q^{n+1,j}\right] \qquad (3)$$

In Eq. (3), j is the PIJ iteration counter whereas the physical-time counter K has been omitted. $\Delta \vec{U}$ is the correction to the flow variables $\left(\vec{U}_P^{n+1} = \vec{U}_P^n + \Delta \vec{U}_P^{n+1}\right)$. $D(\vec{U})$, $Z(\vec{U})$ are the diagonal and nondiagonal l.h.s. coefficient matrices, respectively, and $\overrightarrow{R}_P$ is the right-hand-side term (r.h.s.; i.e., the residual of the discretized equations at node P). The latter is formed by accumulating the inviscid and viscous fluxes crossing the boundary ($\partial \Omega_P$) of the control volume centered at node P, Figure 17.2. D, Z and the residuals are all recalculated once $\overrightarrow{U}$ is updated, i.e., in each new pseudo-time step.

In the (fourth-order) RK method, the flow variables are updated at each pseudo-time step through $r_{max} = 4$ steps, as follows:

$$\overrightarrow{U}_P^{n+1,r} = \overrightarrow{U}_P^n + a_r \overrightarrow{R}_P^{n+1,r-1} \qquad r = 1, \ldots, r_{max} \tag{4}$$

where $[a_1, a_2, a_3, a_4] = [0.11, 0.2766, 0.5, 1.0]$. Note that, compared with the PIJ method, the RK one requires no more than the residuals of the discretized equations.

In the sake of completeness, let us also describe briefly the grid data structure required to cope with unstructured grids. As in all similar codes, data input to the code comprises the IDs of the nodes forming all elements as well as the nodal coordinates. Based on them, geometrical and topological data are computed that include the IDs of the two nodes forming each grid edge, the number of nodes linked to each node by an edge as well as their IDs, the areas/volumes (2-D/3-D) associated with each node (Ω_p, Figure 17.2), the components of the normal vectors to the part of the finite volume contour associated with each grid edge scaled by the corresponding $\Delta \partial \Omega_p$ arc-length/area (2-D/3-D), etc.

17.2.2   Optimization Method — Evolutionary Algorithms (EAs)

EAs [15–17] are stochastic optimization methods based on the evolution theory. They handle a population of candidate solutions (offspring) that evolves according to the principles of natural selection; that is, using selection, recombination, and mutation processes. During the evolution, individuals compete, and the fittest among them mate for creating the offspring population.

EAs are able to locate the global optimum and are widely used in engineering optimization problems because they may accommodate any ready-to-use evaluation software. However, EAs call for a great number of fitness function evaluations before reaching the global optimum.

In this chapter, the optimization of the flow control parameters is carried out using EASY (Evolutionary Algorithms System) software [9]. EASY is based on EAs, implements optionally surrogate evaluation models, allows the parallelization of evaluations on the available processing units (CPUs and GPUs) and so on, and may solve single- or multi-objective optimization problems. EASY handles the evaluation tool as a "black-box"; that is, in the form of script or batch file. In the present studies, the EA runs on the CPU and the evaluations of the candidate solutions are performed on the GPU.

17.3   IMPLEMENTATIONS AND EVALUATION

This section focuses on the efficient porting of an existing CPU code to the NVIDIA GPUs; GPU programming issues are discussed and the speed-up of the GPU implementation, related to the CPU one, is quantified.

17.3.1 Programming on GPUs

A typical way of programming the iterative part of a Navier-Stokes solver for unstructured grids is by looping over grid edges, computing the associated fluxes and scattering-adding flux contributions to their two end nodes within the same loop. However, for a GPU-enabled code, this is prone to shared memory conflicts because concurrently executed threads may likely try to simultaneously store data in the same global memory space. To avoid these conflicts and also manage the limited GPU cached memory, the CPU code had to be restructured. A single node-based kernel (one-kernel scheme, Figure 17.3) was tried instead, according to which, for each grid node (i.e., for each finite volume), all of its edges are swept one by one, and their contributions to the balance of fluxes at the central node are collected. The one-kernel scheme computes all fluxes twice. Alternatively, a two-kernel scheme was devised, too. The first (edge-based) kernel computes the fluxes associated with the edges, whereas the second (node-based) one accumulates the so-computed fluxes (Figure 17.4). As a third alternative, groups of edges that do not share the same nodes are identified (edge coloring). When we are sweeping edges of the same group (same "color"), fluxes can safely and simultaneously be accumulated to their end nodes.

The first two flux computing schemes were employed and evaluated, as it will be discussed later in this chapter, with the PIJ and the RK solution methods. Because at least for the coloring schemes we tried, edge coloring proved to be less efficient than the previous two methods, this was abandoned.

17.3.2 Memory Handling

It is clear that the performance of any GPU implementation is strongly related to the handling of global, texture, constant, and shared memories. In all cases, it is strongly recommended to minimize the access to the noncached global (device) memory within a kernel. Thus, in both one- and two-kernel schemes, threads associated with nodes, sweeping the emanating edges, accumulate contributions using the per-thread local memory, before storing the cumulative sum of computed fluxes to the global memory.

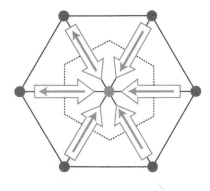

FIGURE 17.3

Schematic representation of the one-kernel scheme. Each thread associated with a single grid node (central node in the middle of the figure) computes and simultaneously accumulates flux contributions associated with the edges emanating from it. Thin arrows correspond to fluxes. Thick arrows indicate summation of contributions to the central node residual.

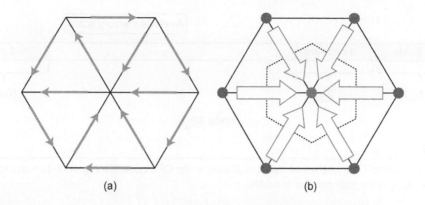

(a)   (b)

FIGURE 17.4

Schematic representation of the two-kernel scheme. In the first kernel, each thread undertakes the computation of the flux associated with a single edge (a) (thin arrows). The computed fluxes are accumulated (thick arrows) by the second, node-based kernel (b).

In the VCFV schemes for unstructured grids, two of the main obstacles in programming an efficient GPU-enabled flow solver are the random (index) numbering of nodes and the variable number of edges emanating from each node. Both result in noncoalesced global memory accesses damaging the speed-up. However, the fixed and known number of edges emanating from each node (in structured grids) or number of adjacent elements to each element (CCFV schemes for unstructured grids) ensures coalesced global memory accesses and, thus, high memory bandwidth. In addition, in structured grids, the nodal IDs follow the standard pattern, making the efficient porting of the CPU code to the GPU much easier, as coalesced global memory assesses can readily be achieved.

Determining the global memory access pattern is very important, regarding especially the memory demanding l.h.s. coefficient matrices D and Z, in case these are really required by the solution method. These matrices are computed anew within each pseudo-time step and stored in the global memory as shown in Figures 17.6 and 17.7 because concurrently executed threads may have access to nearby global memory spaces.

Concerning the diagonal terms D, Figures 17.5 and 17.6 illustrate two alternative ways of storage; both require almost the same memory space, but with different access patterns. According to Figure 17.5, adopted in the CPU-enabled code we are comparing with, the diagonal terms are stored as series of 4×4 matrices (in 2-D cases). This access pattern is appropriate for the sequential CPU code, but leads to noncoalesced global memory accesses if employed in the parallel multithreaded GPU-enabled code. The alternative way (Figure 17.6) shows that concurrently executed threads access data grouped in 128B segments of the global memory, maximizing, thus, the effective memory bandwidth. This pattern indicates grouping the diagonal terms D in blocks (similar to the threads) and storing them per element. The maximum memory bandwidth reported in reading-writing D on the global memory based on the proposed pattern is 115 GB/sec, whereas based on the alternative CPU storage, this bandwidth is reduced to 15 GB/sec. Note that according to the specifications of the GTX 285 graphics card (used herein) its memory bandwidth is 159 GB/sec [10]. Using the bandwidth test problem (NVIDIA CUDA C SDK code Samples, [10]) the device-to-device bandwidth was measured at 123 GB/sec.

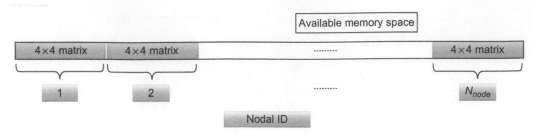

FIGURE 17.5

Storage of the diagonal l.h.s. coefficient matrices D used in the CPU code. Each grid node is associated with a 4×4 matrix. N_{node} is the total number of nodes.

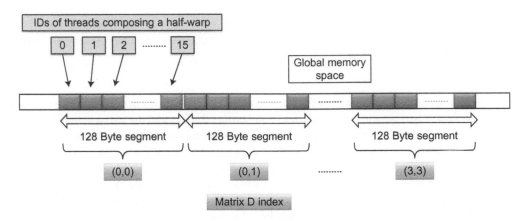

FIGURE 17.6

Storage of the diagonal l.h.s. coefficient matrices D in the GPU global memory space. These matrices (4×4 for each node in a 2-D case) are stored so that concurrently executed threads, comprising a half-warp, access a 128B (for DPA) segment of the global memory space, for each D element. For MPA/SPA, a 128B segment corresponds to a pair of D elements (for instance (0,0) and (0,1), i.e., using float2 type variables).

Since the nondiagonal l.h.s. coefficient matrices Z are associated with the largest allocated part of the GPU memory space, its proper treatment noticeably improves the overall performance of the GPU implementation. According to Figure 17.7, concurrently executed threads associated with nodes, access data related to the edges emanating from these nodes in a "structured" manner, as determined by the local edge numbering system. These data, in the form of 4×4 nodal matrices (in a 2-D case) are stored in a way similarly to D. According to this access pattern, the memory bandwidth is not affected by the random numbering of nodes because threads comprising a half-warp access a sequence of 128B global memory segments, thus maximizing the memory bandwidth. The misaligned access to the global memory by concurrently executed threads, caused by the variable number of edges emanating from each node, is avoided at the expense of slightly extra memory requirements. All nodes associated with threads of the same block are assumed to have the same number of emanating edges (being equal to the

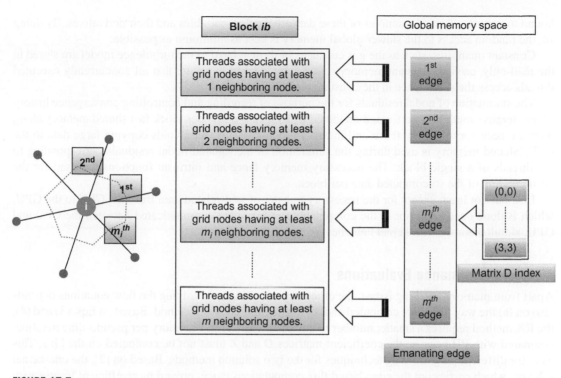

FIGURE 17.7

Nondiagonal l.h.s. coefficient matrices Z access pattern. Let the i_{th} thread of block ib correspond to a node with m_i surrounding edges. Also, let m be the highest m_i value within this block and NT_{m_i} be the total number of threads of block ib associated with nodes having at least m_i surrounding edges. NT_{m_i} threads of block ib access m_i^{th} emanating edge-related data. Synchronization occurs upon completion of all reads/writes. Data related to the emanating edges are in the form of 4×4 matrices stored in a way similar to D (Figure 17.6). Simultaneously executed threads, adhering to this pattern, access nearby global memory spaces.

maximum number among them). Thus, concerning the l.h.s. terms memory access, the performance of the developed software is almost identical to that of any software employing the CCFV technique on structured or unstructured grids. In particular, the maximum obtained memory bandwidth of a kernel copying Z is 118 GB/sec. On the other hand, if the number of emanating edges per node is assumed to be fixed and a priority known, which is the case of structured grids or CCFV schemes on unstructured grids, the corresponding maximum memory bandwidth is 120 GB/sec. The difference is very small and can be ignored. The CPU-code addresses the nondiagonal terms in memory based on edge IDs as it loops over edges, adding contributions to their end nodes. Because of the aforementioned memory conflicts, this technique is not applicable to the GPUs, and this memory access pattern is not illustrated herein.

Additional gain was achieved using the read-only cached texture memory. In the unstructured grid topology, frequently and randomly accessed data, updated at the end of each pseudo-time step, are bound to textures. Typical examples of these data are the flow variables and their derivatives. By doing so, the random access to the slower global memory is kept as minimum as possible.

Constant quantities, such as the gas constants or those related to the turbulence model are stored in the read-only, cached, constant memory space. Care is taken to ensure that all concurrently executed threads access the same space in the constant memory.

The summation of nodal residuals for the purpose of recording and controlling convergence history of the iterative method is performed on the GPU, by means of the per-block fast shared memory along with the necessary memory fence and intrinsic functions. This step avoids copying large data to the CPU. Shared memory is used during the summation of the squared nodal residuals corresponding to the threads of a single block. The necessary memory fence and intrinsic functions are used for the accumulation of the so-computed data per block.

Last but not least, except for the necessary transfer of grid-related data from the CPU to the GPU, which is done once and prior to the computations, all data are communicated between the CPU and GPU, simultaneously with kernel launches.

17.3.3 Performance Evaluations

Apart from memory-handling issues, the efficiency of a GPU code solving the flow equations depends also on (a) the way fluxes are computed and (b) the iterative solution method. Based on Eqs. (3) and (4), the RK method requires a smaller number of computations and less memory per pseudo-time iteration, compared with PIJ because the coefficient matrices D and Z must not be computed on the l.h.s. This calls for different programming techniques for the two solution methods. Based on [2], the one-kernel scheme, which carries out the edge-based flux computations twice, proved more efficient for use with the PIJ method owing to the limited noncoalesced memory accesses. However, the two-kernel scheme performs better if used with the less memory-demanding RK method that avoids computing the l.h.s. coefficient matrices.

Compared with a conventional CPU code, significant speed-ups of the GPU-enabled CFD code have been reported for both RK and PIJ [1, 2] (Figure 17.8). To further improve the performance of the PIJ method, the work presented in [1] investigates also the combined use of SPA and DPA within the same software. The basic idea is to use DPA for the storage of r.h.s. terms (i.e., the residuals of the governing equations at the grid nodes) and SPA for the l.h.s. coefficient matrices (D, Z). This gave rise to the so-called *mixed precision arithmetic* (MPA) scheme with less memory related operations and, thus, higher speed-up compared with the code that exclusively uses DPA. It is evident that DPA and MPA produce flow predictions of the same accuracy (Figure 17.9).

In Figure 17.8, the speed-up values achieved by the RK and PIJ methods are plotted. The performances of the PIJ flow solver with MPA, SPA, and DPA, for the prediction of a turbulent flow around an isolated airfoil, are compared (Figure 17.8a). The outcome of a number of runs using unstructured grids of different sizes is shown. All computations were carried out on NVIDIA's Ge-Force GTX 285 graphics card and a 2xQuad Core Intel Xeon CPU (2.00 GHz, 6144KB cache size). The CPU code (sequential run on a single core) was based on DPA and compiled using the GNU Fortran compiler version 4.1.2 with full optimization options. MPA and DPA yield almost the same convergence plot (Figure 17.9). In the absence of l.h.s. terms, programming the MPA GPU code for the RK method was meaningless. Moreover, given that the GPU code variant with PIJ (DPA) yielded significantly higher speed-ups compared with that of the RK, the SPA code variant with the RK solver was not programmed.

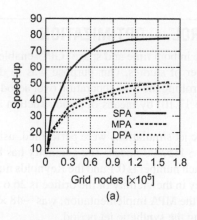 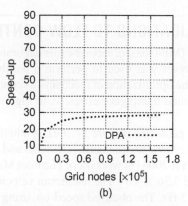

(a)   (b)

FIGURE 17.8

Speed-up curves for (a) the PIJ and (b) the RK solution method for the prediction of the turbulent flow around an isolated airfoil. The comparison of the speed-ups achieved by the DPA, MPA, and SPA GPU implementations are shown only for the PIJ method for the reasons exposed in the text. It should be stated that, compared with [2] (in which, for the same case, lower speed-up values are shown), in the present method the nondiagonal l.h.s. data to be accessed concurrently have been coalesced into 128B global memory segments. This led to higher speed-up values at the expense of slightly increased memory requirements.

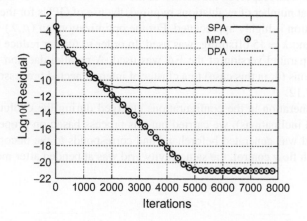

FIGURE 17.9

Convergence history of the continuity equation residual obtained by the DPA, MPA and SPA GPU implementations, using PIJ. This plot corresponds to the prediction of the turbulent flow around an isolated airfoil.

Lessons learned from Figures 17.8 and 17.9 can readily be generalized to other case studies. Therefore, a high-performance Navier-Stokes equations solver with MPA, running on GPUs, was made available for the flow control studies presented in the next section.

17.4 APPLICATIONS TO FLOW CONTROL — OPTIMIZATION

The developed (MPA-based, second-order accurate in both time and space) GPU-enabled code variant with the PIJ solver was used to perform a number of studies. Our purpose was to demonstrate its application in the optimization of mechanisms controlling the flow separation over aerodynamic shapes (two wall-mounted hump geometries, as in Figure 17.10) by means of steady suction and (unsteady) synthetic jets.

On the first geometry (Figure 17.10a), synthetic jet simulations were performed, using an unstructured grid with $\sim$230,000 triangular elements and $\sim$115,000 nodes. The geometry has been borrowed from the CFD-Val 2004 [8] workshop. The inlet Mach number is 0.1 and the Reynolds number based on the hump chord 9.36×10^5. The maximum velocity in the vicinity of the orifice is 26.6 m/s and the jet frequency 138.5 Hz. The obtained speed-up, using the MPA implementation, was $\sim$48$\times$. Figure 17.11 shows the Mach number field at four instants during the synthetic jet period.

The optimization of the steady suction control parameters (jet position, its inclination, and the orifice width) for minimum boundary layer separation was performed next. These studies were based on the second hump geometry (Figure 17.10b) and the following flow conditions: inlet Mach number equal to 0.3, the Reynolds number based on the hump chord equal to 6.35×10^6, and suction mass flow rate normalized by the inlet mass flow rate (i.e., the mass per time unit entering the computational area with height equal to one hump chord) equal to 5.48×10^{-4}. The jet position was allowed to vary between 60% and 70% of the hump chord, the orifice width between 0.15% and 0.25% of the chord, and the jet inclination (with respect to the normal to the wall) between $-70°$ and $70°$.

Because of the great number of evaluations required, the use of GPUs for the reduction of the wall-clock time per evaluation is highly appreciated. For the optimization, an $(\mu, \lambda) = (10, 15)$ EA; that is, with $\mu = 10$ parents and $\lambda = 15$ offspring, was used. In order to further reduce the wall-clock time of the optimization, the parallel version of the EA was used. A parallel daemon spawned a number of simultaneous evaluations (4, in this case) to a cluster of interconnected processors (CPUs with GPUs) as shown in Figure 17.12.

Regarding grid generation in the configurations emerged during the evolution (with different jet locations, widths, and inclinations), we carried out this process based on proper modifications of the starting grid. This grid was generated beforehand and corresponds to the uncontrolled case. For each new configuration with flow control, the same cavity grid was appended after modifying a patch of the

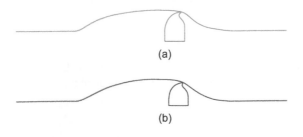

(a)

(b)

FIGURE 17.10

(a) First hump and cavity geometry: the CFD-Val 2004 [8] Workshop benchmark. (b) Second hump and cavity geometry: new shape.

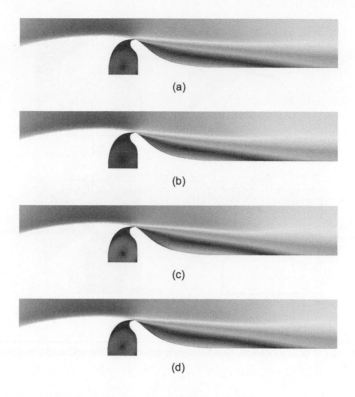

FIGURE 17.11

Flow over the CFD-Val 2004 [8] hump geometry. Mach number field at (a) $T/4$, (b) $T/2$, (c) $3T/4$, and (d) T, where T denotes the period of the synthetic jet actuator.

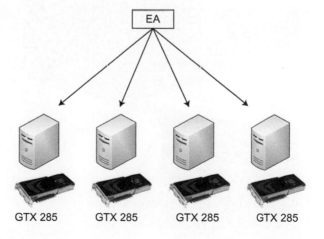

GTX 285   GTX 285   GTX 285   GTX 285

FIGURE 17.12

Parallel deployment of the EA-based optimization to four interconnected CPUs with the corresponding GPUs.

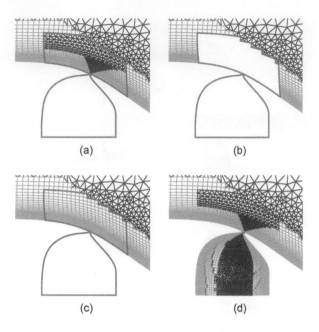

FIGURE 17.13

Grid adaptation close to the orifice location. Quadrilaterals adjacent to the wall and triangles elsewhere were used (see color insert).

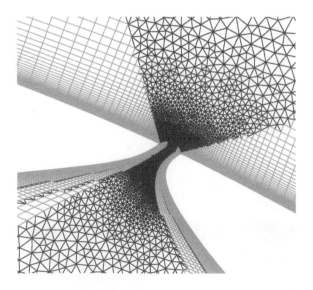

FIGURE 17.14

Close-up view of the final grid ((d), in Figure 17.13) at the junction of the main and cavity grids.

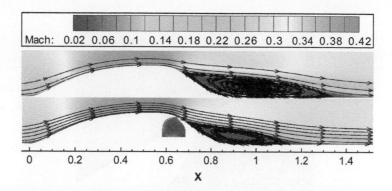

FIGURE 17.15

~31% reduction in the separation length downstream a wall-mounted hump using the steady suction technique. Results from the GPU-enabled Navier-Stokes solver, without (top) and with (bottom) flow control.

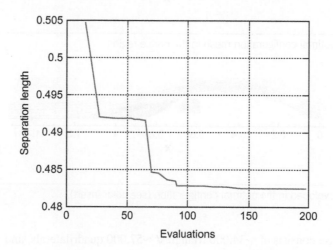

FIGURE 17.16

Convergence of the EA-based optimization.

starting grid in the vicinity of the jet. This modification was necessary for generating a sufficiently fine grid in this area, as shown in Figures 17.13 and 17.14.

Before we proceed to the optimization, both the uncontrolled case and an indicative controlled case were studied. Figure 17.15 shows the Mach number contours for these cases. It should be made clear that the controlled case (with the jet arbitrarily positioned at 65% of the hump chord, 50° inclination and orifice width equal to 0.189% of chord) does not necessarily correspond to the optimal configuration. For the configuration presented in Figure 17.15, the separation region was reduced by ~31%. For the uncontrolled case study, a hybrid grid with ~20,000 triangles/ ~35,000 quadrilaterals, and ~46,000 nodes was generated yielding a speed-up value of ~37 times. The hybrid grid used

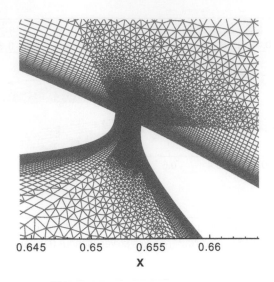

FIGURE 17.17

Close-up view of the optimal configuration mesh in the orifice region.

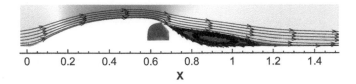

FIGURE 17.18

Mach number field developed in the optimal configuration (see color insert).

for the controlled case consists of ~34,000 triangles/ ~57,000 quadrilaterals, and ~75,000 nodes and the achieved speed-up was ~42 times.

The convergence of the EA is presented in Figure 17.16. The optimal configuration is achieved for jet position 65.21% of the hump chord, inclination −19.22° and orifice width 0.234% of the hump chord (Figure 17.17). This optimal configuration yields a nondimensional separation length of 0.482 or ~34% reduction in the separation length compared with the uncontrolled case. The Mach number field developed in the optimal configuration is also shown in Figure 17.18.

References

[1] I. Kampolis, X. Trompoukis, V. Asouti, K. Giannakoglou, CFD-based analysis and two-level aerodynamic optimization on Graphics Processing Units, Comput. Methods Appl. Mech. Eng. 199 (9–12) (2010) 712–722.

[2] V. Asouti, X. Trompoukis, I. Kampolis, K. Giannakoglou, Unsteady CFD computations using vertex-centered finite volumes for unstructured grids on Graphics Processing units, Int. J. Numer. Method. Fluids (2011) doi: 10.1002/fld.2352.

[3] T. Hagen, K. Lie, J. Natvig, Solving the euler equations on graphics processing units, Comput. Sci. – ICCS 3994 (2006) 220–227.

[4] T. Bradvik, G. Pullan, Acceleration of a 3D Euler solver using commodity graphics hardware, in: AIAA Paper 2008-607, 46th AIAA Aerospace Sciences Meeting and Exhibit, Curran Associates, Inc., Reno, Nevada, 2008.

[5] E. Elsen, P. LeGresley, E. Darve, Large calculation of the flow over a hypersonic vehicle using a GPU, J. Comput. Phys. 227 (24) (2008) 10148–10161.

[6] J. Cohen, M. Molemaker, A fast double precision CFD code using CUDA, in: Biswas, R. (Ed.), Proceedings of Parallel CFD 2009, Moffett Field, California, 2009.

[7] A. Corrigan, F. Camelli, R. Löhner, J. Wallin, Running unstructured grid based CFD solvers on modern graphics hardware, in: AIAA Paper 2009-4001, 19th AIAA Computational Fluid Dynamics, San Antonio, Texas, 2009.

[8] http://cfdval2004.larc.nasa.gov.

[9] http://velos0.ltt.mech.ntua.gr/EASY/.

[10] http://www.nvidia.com/page/home.html.

[11] M.H. Buschmanna, M. Gad-El-Hak, Recent developments in scaling of wall-bounded flows, Prog. Aerosp. Sci. 42 (5–6) (2006) 419–467.

[12] J. Ekaterinaris, Active flow control of wing separated flow, in: ASME FEDSM'03 Joint Fluids Engineering Conference, Honolulu, Hawai, 2003.

[13] R. Duvigneau, M. Visonneau, Optimization of a synthetic jet actuator for aerodynamic stall control, Comput. Fluids 35 (2006) 624–638.

[14] A. Seifert, A. Darabi, I. Wygnanski, Delay of airfoil stall by periodic excitation, AIAA J. 33 (4) (1996) 691–707.

[15] D. Goldberg, Genetic Algorithms in Search, Optimization and Machine Learning, Addison–Wesley, 1989.

[16] K. Giannakoglou, Design of optimal aerodynamic shapes using stochastic optimization methods and computational intelligence, Prog. Aerosp. Sci. 38 (1) (2002) 43–76.

[17] I. Kampolis, K. Giannakoglou, A multilevel approach to single- and multiobjective aerodynamic optimization, Comput. Methods Appl. Mech. Eng. 197 (33–40) (2008) 2963–2975.

[18] G. Karniadakis, R. Kirby, Parallel Scientific Computing in C++ and MPI, Cambridge University Press, UK, 2003.

Solving Wave Equations on Unstructured Geometries

18

Andreas Klöckner, Timothy Warburton, and Jan S. Hesthaven

Waves are all around us — be it in the form of sound, electromagnetic radiation, water waves, or earthquakes. Their study is an important basic tool across engineering and science disciplines. Every wave solver serving the computational study of waves meets a trade-off of two figures of merit — its computational speed and its accuracy. Discontinuous Galerkin (DG) methods fall on the high-accuracy end of this spectrum. Fortuitously, their computational structure is so ideally suited to GPUs that they also achieve very high computational speeds. In other words, the use of DG methods on GPUs significantly lowers the cost of obtaining accurate solutions. This article aims to give the reader an easy on-ramp to the use of this technology, based on a sample implementation which demonstrates a highly accurate, GPU-capable, real-time visualizing finite element solver in about 1500 lines of code.

18.1 INTRODUCTION, PROBLEM STATEMENT, AND CONTEXT

At the beginning of our journey into high-performance, highly accurate time-domain wave solvers, let us briefly illustrate by a few examples how common the task of simulating wave phenomena is across many disciplines of science and engineering, and how accuracy figures into each of these application areas. Consider the following examples:

- An engineer needs to understand the time-domain response of an oscillating structure such as an accelerator cavity. Real-life measurement of the desired properties is extremely costly, if it is possible at all. Accuracy is important because wrong results may lead to wrong conclusions.

- A seismic engineer has time-domain data from a sounding using geophones and needs to model an underground structure, characterized by different wave propagation speeds. Doing so requires a solver for the "forward problem," i.e., a code that, given data about the location of the sources and wave propagation speeds throughout the underground domain, can model the propagation of the waves. Accuracy is important because these simulations often inform potentially very costly enterprises such as drilling or mining.

- An electrical engineer wants to model the stealth properties of a new airplane involving complicated nonlinear materials. Physical prototyping is expensive, and accurate predictions of scattering properties help minimize its necessity.

In the field of time-domain wave simulation, the main competitors of the discontinuous Galerkin method include finite-difference, finite-volume and continuous finite-element methods. In a nutshell, finite-difference solvers have trouble representing complicated geometric boundaries, finite-volume methods become very difficult (and very expensive) to implement at a high order of accuracy,[1] and continuous finite-element methods typically assemble large, sparse matrices, whose application to a vector is necessarily memory-bound and thus unable to make use of the massive compute bandwidth available on a GPU.

In addition, while finite-difference methods have relatively benign implementation properties on GPUs [1, 2], we will see that the computational structure of DG methods is even better suited to GPU implementation at high accuracy because they largely avoid the wide "halo" of outside values that must be fetched in order to apply a large (high-order) stencil to three-dimensional volume data.

This chapter complements an article [3] which we have recently published that, in its spirit, is probably more like the other chapters in this volume in that it exposes all the technicalities and tricks that have enabled us to demonstrate high-speed DG on the GPU. To avoid redundancy between [3] and this chapter, we have instead chosen to focus our treatment here on easing a prospective user's entry into using our technology. While [3] is very technical and not entirely suited as an introduction to the subject, in this chapter we will be applying a number of simplifications to facilitate understanding and promote ease-of-use.

18.2 CORE METHOD

Discontinuous Galerkin (DG) methods for the numerical solution of partial differential equations have enjoyed considerable success because they are both flexible and robust: They allow arbitrary unstructured geometries and easy control of accuracy without compromising simulation stability. Lately, another property of DG has been growing in importance: The majority of a DG operator is applied in an element-local way, with weak penalty-based element-to-element coupling.

The resulting locality in memory access is one of the factors that enables DG to run on off-the-shelf, massively parallel graphics processors (GPUs). In addition, DG's high-order nature lets it require fewer data points per represented wavelength and hence fewer memory accesses, in exchange for higher arithmetic intensity. Both of these factors work significantly in favor of a GPU implementation of DG.

Readers wishing a deeper introduction to the numerical method are referred to the introductory textbook [4].

18.3 ALGORITHMS, IMPLEMENTATIONS, AND EVALUATIONS

18.3.1 Background Material

18.3.1.1 A Precise Mathematical Problem Statement

Discontinuous Galerkin methods are most often used to solve hyperbolic systems of conservation laws in the time domain. This rather general class of partial differential equation (PDE) can be

---

[1]The order of accuracy refers to the power with which the error decreases as the discretization is refined — for example, if the distance between neighboring mesh points is halved, a fourth-order scheme would decrease the error by a factor of sixteen.

written in the form

$$\frac{\partial q}{\partial t} + \nabla_x \cdot F(q) = f. \tag{1}$$

DG methods generally solve the *initial boundary value problems* (IBVPs) of these equations on a bounded domain Ω. This means that in addition to the PDE (Eq. (1)), one needs to specify the finite geometry of interest, an initial value of the solution q at an initial time T_0 (which we will assume to be zero) as well as which (potentially time-dependent) conditions prevail at the boundary $\partial \Omega$ of the domain. In addition, source terms may be present. These are represented in Eq. (1) by f.

Classes of partial differential equations more general than Eq. (1), such as parabolic and elliptic equations, can be solved using DG methods. In this chapter, we will focus on hyperbolic equations, and for the sake of exposition, on one particularly important example of these equations, the second-order wave equation in two dimensions. To emphasize the equation's grounding in reality, we will cast this equation as (the transverse-magnetic version of) the linear, isotropic, constant-coefficient Maxwell's equations in two dimensions and show the method's development by its example. The equation itself is given by

$$0 = \mu \frac{\partial H_x}{\partial t} + \frac{\partial E_z}{\partial y}, \tag{2a}$$

$$0 = \mu \frac{\partial H_y}{\partial t} - \frac{\partial E_z}{\partial y}, \tag{2b}$$

$$0 = \epsilon \frac{\partial E_z}{\partial t} - \frac{\partial H_y}{\partial x} + \frac{\partial H_x}{\partial y}. \tag{2c}$$

One easily verifies that this equation can be rewritten into the more well-known second-order form of the wave equation,

$$\frac{\partial^2 E_z}{\partial t^2} = c^2 \Delta E_z$$

with $c^{-2} = \epsilon \mu$. For simplicity, we may assume $c = \epsilon = \mu = 1$. Together with an initial condition as well as perfectly electrically conducting (PEC) boundary condition

$$E_z(x,t) = 0 \quad \text{on } \partial \Omega.$$

Observe that no value is prescribed for the magnetic fields H_x, H_y, which we leave to obey *natural boundary conditions*. In terms of the second-order wave equation, PEC corresponds to a Dirichlet boundary.

18.3.1.2 *Construction of the Method*

To begin the discretization of Eq. (2), we assume that the domain Ω is polyhedral, so that it may be represented as a union $\Omega = \biguplus_{k=1}^{K} D_k \subset \mathbb{R}^2$ consisting of disjoint, straight-sided, face-conforming triangles D_k.

We demonstrate the construction of the method by the example of Eq. (2c). We begin by multiplying Eq. (2c) with a test function ϕ and integrating over the element D_k:

$$0 = \int_{D_k} \frac{\partial E_z}{\partial t} \phi \, dV - \int_{D_k} \frac{\partial H_y}{\partial x} \phi \, dV + \int_{D_k} \frac{\partial H_x}{\partial y} \phi \, dV$$

$$= \int_{D_k} \frac{\partial E_z}{\partial t} \phi \, dV + \int_{D_k} \nabla_{(x,y)} \cdot \underbrace{(-H_y, H_x)^T}_{F=} \phi \, dV.$$

Observe that the vector-valued F indicated here assumes the role of the flux F in Eq. (1). Integration by parts yields

$$0 = \int_{D_k} \frac{\partial E_z}{\partial t} \phi \, dV - \int_{D_k} (-H_y, H_x)^T \cdot \nabla_{(x,y)} \phi \, dV + \int_{\partial D_k} \widehat{n} \cdot (-H_y, H_x)^T \phi \, dS, \tag{3}$$

where $\widehat{n}$ is the unit normal to $\partial \Omega$. Now a key feature of the method enters. Because no continuity is enforced on H_x and H_y between D_k and its neighbors, the value of H_x and H_y on the boundary is not uniquely determined. For now, we will record this fact by a superscript asterisk, denote these chosen values the *numerical flux*, and leave a determination of what value should be used for later.

To revert the so-called *weak form* Eq. (3) to a shape more closely resembling the original Eq. (2c), we integrate by parts again, obtaining the so-called *strong form*

$$0 = \int_{D_k} \frac{\partial E_z}{\partial t} \phi \, dV + \int_{D_k} \nabla_{(x,y)} \cdot (-H_y, H_x)^T \phi \, dV - \int_{\partial D_k} \widehat{n} \cdot (-(H_y - H_y^*), H_x - H_x^*)^T \phi \, dS \tag{4}$$

where we carefully observe that the boundary term obtained in the last step has stayed in place.

To determine the values of H^*, we note that in many cases a simple average across neighboring faces, i.e., $H^* := (H^+ + H^-)/2$ leads to a stable and accurate numerical method, where H^- denotes the values on the local face. This is termed a *central flux*. We choose a more dissipative (but less noisy) *upwind flux* [5], given by

$$\widehat{n} \cdot (F - F^*) = \begin{bmatrix} \widehat{n}_y[E_z] + \alpha \widehat{n}_x (\widehat{n}_x[H_x] + \widehat{n}_y[H_y] - [H_x]) \\ -\widehat{n}_x[E_z] + \alpha \widehat{n}_y (\widehat{n}_x[H_x] + \widehat{n}_y[H_y] - [H_y]) \\ \widehat{n}_y[H_x] - \widehat{n}_x[H_y] - \alpha[E_z] \end{bmatrix}. \tag{5}$$

The value to be used for $\widehat{n} \cdot (-(H_y - H_y^*), H_x - H_x^*)^T$ in Eq. (4) can be read from the third entry of the right-hand side of Eq. (5), and the first two entries apply to Eqs. (2a) and (2b). We have used the common notation $[q] = q^- - q^+$ for the inter-element jumps. α is a parameter, commonly chosen as 1. Obviously, $\alpha = 0$ recovers a central flux.

We expand E, H, and ϕ into a basis of N_p Lagrange interpolation polynomials l_i spanning the space P^N of polynomials of total degree N, where the Lagrange interpolation points are purposefully chosen for numerical stability [6]. Substituting the expansions into Eq. (4) combined with Eq. (5) yields a numerical scheme that is discrete in space, but not yet in time.

18.3.1.3 *Implementation Aspects*

To actually implement this scheme, we express Eq. (4) in matrix form. To do so, first note that in our setting, each element $\mathsf{D}_k \subset \Omega$ can be obtained by an affine map $\Psi(r,s) = A_k(r,s)^T + b_k$ from a reference element I. Now define the mass matrix

$$\mathcal{M}_{ij}^k := \int_{\mathsf{D}_k} l_i l_j \, dV = |A_k| \mathcal{M} := |A_k| \int_{\mathsf{I}} l_i l_j \, dV.$$

$|A_k|$ is the determinant of the matrix A_k. Also let $\mathcal{D}^{\partial v}$ be the matrix that realizes polynomial differentiation along the reference element's vth axis in Lagrange coefficients. Polynomial differentiation along *global* coordinates is realized as a linear combination of these local differentiation matrices, according to, e.g.,

$$\mathcal{D}^{k,\partial x} = \left(A_k^{-1}\right)_{11} \mathcal{D}^{\partial 1} + \left(A_k^{-1}\right)_{12} \mathcal{D}^{\partial 2}. \tag{6}$$

This allows us to express an implementation of the volume part of Eq. (4):

$$0 = |A_k| \mathcal{M} \frac{\partial (E_z)_N}{\partial t} + |A_k| \mathcal{M} \left(\mathcal{D}^{k,\partial x}(-H_y)_N + \mathcal{D}^{k,\partial y}(H_x)_N \right)$$
$$- \int_{\partial \mathsf{D}_k} \widehat{n} \cdot (-(H_y - H_y^*), H_x - H_x^*)^T \phi \, dS. \tag{7}$$

For numerical stability at increasing N, the matrices $\mathcal{M}^k$ and $\mathcal{D}^{\partial v}$ are computed by ways of orthogonal polynomials on the triangle [7, 8].

To implement the surface terms, define the surface mass matrix for a single face Γ of the reference triangle I:

$$M_{ij}^\Gamma := \int_{\Gamma \subset \partial \mathsf{I}} l_i l_j \, dS.$$

Suppose we compute values of $\widehat{n} \cdot (F - F^*) = \widehat{n} \cdot (-(H_y - H_y^*), H_x - H_x^*)^T$ along all faces and concatenate these into one vector. Then the sum over all facial integrals may be computed through a carefully assembled matrix:

$$\int_{\partial \mathsf{D}_k} \widehat{n} \cdot (F - F^*) \phi \, dS = \boxed{\begin{matrix} M^{\Gamma_1} & \\ & M^{\Gamma_3} \\ M^{\Gamma_2} & \end{matrix}} \left(J_1 \widehat{n} \cdot (F - F^*)|_{\Gamma_1} \Big| \cdots \Big| J_3 \widehat{n} \cdot (F - F^*)|_{\Gamma_3} \right). \tag{8}$$

We denote this matrix $\mathcal{M}^{\partial \mathsf{I}}$ and the vector to which we are applying it $\mathbf{f}^k$. The factors J_n are the determinants of the affine maps parametrizing the faces of D_k with respect to the faces of I.

Returning to Eq. (7), we left-multiply by $|A_k|^{-1} \mathcal{M}^{-1}$ to obtain

$$0 = \frac{\partial (E_z)_N}{\partial t} + (\mathcal{D}^{k,\partial x}(-H_y)_N + \mathcal{D}^{k,\partial x}(H_x)_N) - |A_k|^{-1} \mathcal{M}^{-1} \mathcal{M}^{\partial \mathsf{I}} \mathbf{f}^k \tag{9}$$

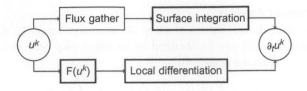

FIGURE 18.1

Decomposition of a DG operator into subtasks. Element-local operations are highlighted with a bold outline.

Despite all the machinery involved, Eq. (9) is strikingly simple, consisting of three data-local element-wise matrix-vector multiplications (two differentiations, one combined face mass matrix) and a surface flux exchange term. A view of the flow of data is provided by Figure 18.1.

Even better, the time derivative $\frac{\partial(E_z)_N}{\partial t}$ occurs on its own, making it possible to use simple, explicit Runge-Kutta methods for integration in time.

18.3.2 A Minimal Implementation

After this very quick (but mostly self-contained) introduction to discontinuous Galerkin methods, we will now discuss how Eq. (9) and its analogous extension to Eqs. (2a) and (2b) may be brought onto the GPU to form a solver for the 2-D TM variant of Maxwell's equations.

18.3.2.1 Introduction

To make the discussion both more tangible and easier to follow, we have created a simple implementation of the ideas presented here. This implementation may be downloaded from the URL http://tiker.net/gcg-dg-code-download. As improvements are made, the code at this address may change from time to time. The source code may also be browsed online at http://tiker.net/gcg-dg-code-browse.

We will begin by briefly discussing the construction of this package. The solver is written in Python. We feel that this allows for clearer code that, in both notation and structure, closely resembles the MAT-LAB codes of [4], and yet allows a simple and concise GPU implementation to be added using, in this case, PyOpenCL (PyCUDA, whose use is demonstrated in another chapter of this volume, would have been another obviously possible implementation choice). In addition, the solver is designed for clarity, not peak performance. What we mean here is that the compute kernels we show are rather simple and lack a few performance optimizations. The solver's performance is not related to its implementation language. High-performance GPU codes can easily be constructed using PyOpenCL (and PyCUDA), which is demonstrated below and in a number of other chapters of this volume. Finally, we would like to remark that the kernels as shown below are optimized for NVIDIA GPUs and run well on chips ranging from the G80 to the GF100.

In discussing the solver, we focus on the performance-relevant kernels running on the GPU. There are other, significant parts of the solver that deal with preparation and administrative issues such as mesh connectivity and polynomial approximation. These parts are obviously also important to the success of the method, but they are beyond the scope of this chapter. The interested reader may find them explained more fully in the introductory book [4]. Once we have discussed the functioning of the basic solver, we will describe any additional steps that may be taken to improve performance. Lastly, we will discuss a set of features that may be added to this rather bare implementation to make it more useful. In the next chapter, we close by showing performance numbers first for this solver, and then for our production solver, which is a more complete implementation of the ideas to follow.

18.3.2.2 *Computing the Volume Contribution*

First in our examination of implementation features is what we call the "volume kernel," which achieves element-local differentiation as described in Eqs. (6) and (7). The key parts of the kernel's OpenCL C source are given in Listing 18.1.

One key objective of this subroutine is the multiplication of the local differentiation matrices $\mathcal{D}^{\partial\nu}$ by a large number of right-hand sides, each representing degrees of freedom ("DOFs") on an element. This is a suitable point to realize that matrix-vector multiplication by a large number of vectors is

```
const int n = get_local_id(0);
const int k = get_group_id(0);

int m = n+k*BSIZE;
int id = n;

l_Hx[id] = g_Hx[m];
l_Hy[id] = g_Hy[m];
l_Ez[id] = g_Ez[m];


barrier(CLK_LOCAL_MEM_FENCE);

float dHxdr=0,dHxds=0;
float dHydr=0,dHyds=0;
float dEzdr=0,dEzds=0;

float Q;
for(m=0; m<p_Np; ++m)
{
  float4 D = read_imagef(i_DrDs, samp, (int2)(n, m));

  Q = l_Hx[m]; dHxdr += D.x*Q; dHxds += D.y*Q;
  Q = l_Hy[m]; dHydr += D.x*Q; dHyds += D.y*Q;
  Q = l_Ez[m]; dEzdr += D.x*Q; dEzds += D.y*Q;
}

const float drdx = g_vgeo[0+4*k];
const float drdy = g_vgeo[1+4*k];
const float dsdx = g_vgeo[2+4*k];
const float dsdy = g_vgeo[3+4*k];

m = n+BSIZE*k;
g_rhsHx[m] = -(drdy*dEzdr+dsdy*dEzds);
g_rhsHy[m] =  (drdx*dEzdr+dsdx*dEzds);
g_rhsEz[m] =  (drdx*dHydr+dsdx*dHyds
  - drdy*dHxdr-dsdy*dHxds);
```

Listing 18.1. OpenCL kernel implementing element-local volume contribution in the discontinuous Galerkin method, consisting of element-local polynomial differentiation.

equivalent to matrix-matrix multiplication by a very fat, moderately short matrix that encompasses all elemental vectors glued together. Perhaps the most immediate approach to such a problem might be to use NVIDIA's CUBLAS. Unfortunately, while CUBLAS successfully covers a great many use cases, the matrix sizes in question here resulted in uninspiring performance in our experiments [3]. We are thus left considering the choices for a from-scratch implementation.

In the design of computational kernels for GPUs, perhaps *the* key defining factor is the work decomposition into thread blocks (in CUDA terminology) or work groups (in OpenCL terminology). In our demonstration solver, we choose a very simple alternative, a one-to-one mapping between elements and work groups, and a one-to-one mapping between output degrees of freedom and threads (CUDA) or work items (OpenCL). This choice is simple and expedient, but it can be improved upon in a number of cases, as we will discuss in Section 18.3.3.3.

The next key decision is the memory layout of the data to be worked on. Again, we make a simple choice and describe possible improvements later. As was discussed in Section 18.3.1.2, the data we are working on consists of N_p coefficients of Lagrange interpolation polynomials for each of the K elements. Observe that, by their being coefficients of interpolation polynomials, they each represent the exact value of the represented solution at a point in space belonging to a certain element.

To ensure that each work group can fetch element data in the least number of memory transactions, we choose to pad each element up to $\lceil N_p \rceil_{16}$ floating point values, where the notation $\lceil x \rceil_y$ represents x rounded up to the nearest multiple of y.

With data layout and work decomposition clarified, we can now examine the implementation itself, as shown in Listing 18.1. After getting the element number k and the number of the elemental degree of freedom n from group and local IDs, respectively, first the elemental degrees of freedom for all three fields (H_x, H_y, E_z) are fetched into local memory for subsequent multiplication by the differentiation matrix.

As indicated above, the work being performed is effectively matrix-matrix multiplication, and therefore existing best practices suggest that also fetching the matrix into local memory might be a good idea. At least on pre-Fermi chips, this does not turn out to be true. We will take a closer look at the trade-offs involved in Section 18.3.3.2. For now, we simply state that the matrix is streamed into core through texture memory, and its fetch cost amortized by reusing it for not just one, but all three fields (H_x, H_y, and E_z).

Once the derivatives along each element's axes are computed by matrix multiplication, they are converted to global x and y derivatives according to Eq. (6), using separate per-element geometric factors. Finally, the results are stored, where our memory layout and work decomposition permit a fully coalesced write.

18.3.2.3 *Computing the Surface Contribution*

The second (and slightly more complicated) part of our sample implementation of the DG method is what we call the "surface kernel," which, as part of the same subroutine, achieves both the extraction of the flux expression of Eq. (5) and the surface integration of Eq. (8). The key parts of the OpenCL C source code of the kernel are shown in Listing 18.2 and continued in Listing 18.3.

We use the same one-work-group-per-element work partition as in the previous section, and obviously the memory layout of the element data is likewise unchanged. It is, however, important to note that the kernel in question here operates on two different data formats during its lifetime. First, the output of the flux gather results in a vector of facial degrees of freedom as displayed in Eq. (8). The number

```
const int n = get_local_id(0);
const int k = get_group_id(0);

__local float l_fluxHx[p_Nafp];
__local float l_fluxHy[p_Nafp];
__local float l_fluxEz[p_Nafp];

int m;

/* grab surface nodes and store flux in shared memory */
if (n < p_Nafp)
{
  /* coalesced reads (maybe) */
  m = 6*(k*p_Nafp)+n;

  const   int    idM = g_surfinfo[m]; m += p_Nafp;
  int            idP = g_surfinfo[m]; m += p_Nafp;
  const  float   Fsc = g_surfinfo[m]; m += p_Nafp;
  const  float   Bsc = g_surfinfo[m]; m += p_Nafp;
  const  float   nx  = g_surfinfo[m]; m += p_Nafp;
  const  float   ny  = g_surfinfo[m];

  float dHx=0, dHy=0, dEz=0;
  dHx = 0.5f*Fsc*(    g_Hx[idP] - g_Hx[idM]);
  dHy = 0.5f*Fsc*(    g_Hy[idP] - g_Hy[idM]);
  dEz = 0.5f*Fsc*(Bsc*g_Ez[idP] - g_Ez[idM]);

  const float ndotdH = nx*dHx + ny*dHy;

  l_fluxHx[n] = -ny*dEz + dHx - ndotdH*nx;
  l_fluxHy[n] =  nx*dEz + dHy - ndotdH*ny;
  l_fluxEz[n] =  nx*dHy - ny*dHx + dEz;
}

/* make sure all element data points are cached */
barrier(CLK_LOCAL_MEM_FENCE);
```

Listing 18.2. Part 1 of the OpenCL kernel implementing inter-element surface contribution in the discontinuous Galerkin method, consisting of the calculation of the surface flux of Eq. (5).

of entries in this vector is $3N_{fp}$, where three is the number of faces in a triangle, and $N_{fp} = N + 1$ is the number of degrees of freedom required to discretize each face. In general $3N_{fp} \neq N_p$, where we recall that N_p is the number of volume degrees of freedom. At each of the two stages of the algorithm, we employ a design that uses one work item per degree of freedom. The number of work items required per work group is therefore $\max(N_p, N_{fp})$, and at the start of each stage of the algorithm, we need to

```
if (n < p_Np)
{
  float rhsHx = 0, rhsHy = 0, rhsEz = 0;
  int col = 0;

  /* can manually unroll to 3 because there are 3 faces */
  for (m=0;m < p_Nfaces*p_Nfp;)
  {
    float4 L = read_imagef(i_LIFT, samp, (int2)(col, n));
    ++col;

    rhsHx += L.x*l_fluxHx[m];
    rhsHy += L.x*l_fluxHy[m];
    rhsEz += L.x*l_fluxEz[m];
    ++m;

    rhsHx += L.y*l_fluxHx[m];
    rhsHy += L.y*l_fluxHy[m];
    rhsEz += L.y*l_fluxEz[m];
    ++m;

    rhsHx += L.z*l_fluxHx[m];
    rhsHy += L.z*l_fluxHy[m];
    rhsEz += L.z*l_fluxEz[m];
    ++m;
  }

  m = n+k*BSIZE;

  g_rhsHx[m] += rhsHx;
  g_rhsHy[m] += rhsHy;
  g_rhsEz[m] += rhsEz;
}
```

Listing 18.3. Part 2 of the OpenCL kernel implementing inter-element surface contribution in the discontinuous Galerkin method, consisting of the lifting of the surface flux contribution, as described in Eq. (8).

verify whether the local thread number is less than the number of outputs required in that stage, to avoid computing (and perhaps storing) spurious extra outputs. This is necessary in both stages because either of N_p or $3N_{fp}$ may be larger.

After fixing the DOF and element indices n and k, the kernel begins by allocating $3N_{fp}$ degrees of freedom of local storage (N_{fp} per face) for each of the three fields (H_x, H_y, and E_z). This local memory serves as a temporary storage for the facial vector of Eq. (8). Next, index and geometry information is read from a surface descriptor data structure called surfinfo. For each facial degree of freedom and, hence, for each work item, this data structure contains the index of the volume degree of freedom the work item processes, as well as the index of its facial neighbor (idM and idP, respectively). In addition, surfinfo contains geometry information, namely the surface unit normal of the face being integrated over (nx and ny), the surface Jacobian divided by the element's volume Jacobian (Fsc), and a boundary indicator (Bsc) used for the implementation of boundary conditions which takes values of ± 1. Based on this information, the kernel computes jump terms $[H_x]$, $[H_y]$, $[E_z]$, which are then scaled with the geometry scaling Fsc and stored as dHx, dHy, and dEz. The computation of the flux expression (Eq. (5)) and its temporary storage in local memory concludes the first part of the kernel, displayed in Listing 18.2.

The second part of the kernel, of Listing 18.3, is much like local polynomial differentiation as discussed in Section 18.3.2.2 in that it represents an element-local matrix multiplication. We have applied the same design decisions as above for simplicity, mainly based on the facial flux data already being resident in local memory. Again, data for the matrix is streamed in using the texture units, and the streamed matrix is reused for each of the three fields. One trick we were able to apply here is the three-fold unrolling of the loop. This is valid because we know that the combined face mass matrix $\mathcal{M}^{\partial l}$ covers three faces and hence must have a column count that is divisible by three. Naturally, the same applies to the lifting matrix $\mathcal{L} := \mathcal{M}^{-1}\mathcal{M}^{\partial l}$. The result of this matrix-vector product is then added to global destination arrays in which the volume contribution to the right-hand side $\partial(H_x, H_y, E_z)^T/\partial t$ is already stored, completing the computation the entire right-hand side of Eq. (9).

This concludes our description of the basic kernel implementing the computation of the ODE right-hand side for nodal discontinuous Galerkin methods. What is missing to complete the implementation of the method is a simple Runge-Kutta time integrator, which we have implemented using PyOpenCL's built-in array operations. We now proceed to discuss a number of ways in which performance of these basic kernels can be improved.

18.3.3 Improving Performance

18.3.3.1 Avoiding Padding Waste: Data Aggregation

In the above codes, each element is represented by $\lceil N_p \rceil_{16}$ floating point values for alignment and fetch efficiency reasons. Especially in two dimensions, or in three dimensions for elements of relatively small polynomial order N, this extra padding can be rather inefficient — not just in terms of GPU memory use, but especially also in computational resources. All of our kernels adopt a one-work-item-per-output design and, hence, wasted memory has a one-to-one correspondence to wasted computational power. This is all the more true once one realizes that NVIDIA hardware schedules computations in units of 32-wide *warps*, such that a rounding to 16 has a chance of 50 percent of leaving the trailing half-warp of the computation unused. An obvious remedy for this problem is the aggregation of multiple elements into a single unit. This aggregation represents a trade-off against the work partition flexibility of all kernels operating on the data, and should therefore be chosen as small as possible, while still minimizing waste.

In [3], we pursue a compromise strategy, where we choose a granularity that combines enough elements so that less than a given percentage (e.g., 10) of waste occurs. All further occurring granularities are then required to operate integer multiples of this smallest possible granularity. To differentiate this granularity from the generally larger work group size (or "block size" in CUDA terminology), we have introduced the term *microblock* to denote it.

18.3.3.2 *Which Memory for What?*

On-chip memory in a GPU setting is always somewhat scarce, and we foresee that this will remain so for the foreseeable future. As already discussed in Section 18.3.2, it is far from clear which portions of the GPU's on-chip memory should be used for what data. In discussing this question, we focus on the element-local matrix-vector polynomial differentiation as this asymptotically (and practically) dominates runtime as the polynomial degree N increases.

In [3], we discuss two possible strategies for element-local matrix multiplication, the first of which proceeds by loading the matrix into local memory, and the second of which loads field data into local memory, as we have done above.

To allow the flexibility of being able to choose which strategy to use for each each of the two element-local matrix products (differentiation and lift), the surface kernel of Section 18.3.2.3 may have to be split into its two constituent parts, necessitating an extra store-load cycle. We find that this disadvantage is entirely compensated by the advantage of being able to use a more immediately suitable work partition for each part.

The enumeration of the two strategies begs an immediate question — why is the strategy of loading *both* quantities into local memory not considered? The reason for this lies rooted in a number of important practicalities. While generic matrix multiplication routines are free to optimize for the case of large, square matrices, the matrices we are faced with are small. A generic blocking strategy would therefore leave us with many inefficient corner cases which would come to dominate our run time. In addition, in the case of three-dimensional geometry, the three differentiation matrices of size $N_p \times N_p$ exhaust the local memory on NVIDIA hardware even for moderate N.

We find that, at low-to-moderate N and in general in two dimensions, we can derive a gain of about 20 percent by making the matrix-in-local strategy available in addition to the field-in-local strategy shown above. Nonetheless, the latter strategy has fewer size restrictions than the former, is thus more generally applicable, and it successfully uses register and texture memory to avoid many redundant matrix fetches. This justifies our choice of the strategy in our demonstration code. In these codes, we amortized matrix fetch costs by operating on three fields at once. Note that even in a scalar (i.e., single-field) case, such amortization is possible, simply by operating on multiple elements within the same work item.

18.3.3.3 *Rethinking the Work Partition*

Because of the inherent advantages of using one work item per output value, the question of work partitioning into work groups and work items on GPU hardware is never far removed from that of memory use and data layout, as discussed above. The work partition chosen in the demonstration code was purposefully simple — one work item per degree of freedom, one work group per element. Moving beyond that, while taking into account the lessons of Section 18.3.3.1, one naturally arrives at a partition of one microblock per work group. But even this can be further generalized, as one may work on more than one microblock in each work group. We assume here that the work on each work item is independent, but may depend on some preparation, such as fetching matrix data into on-chip memory. This opens up a number of possible avenues: One may ...

- process microblocks in parallel, adding more work items to each work group, to achieve better usage of individual compute units.

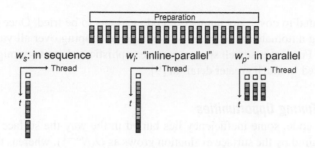

FIGURE 18.2

Possibilities for partitioning a large number of independent work units, potentially requiring some preparation, into work groups. Each work unit consists of multiple stages, symbolized by different colors. Preparation is shown in a white color. An example of this would be multiple independent matrix-vector multiplications, each consisting of individual multiply-add cycles (see color insert).

- process microblocks in sequence, leaving the number of work items unchanged, but doing more work in each work item, thus amortizing preparation work.
- process multiple work items along with each other, reusing auxiliary data (such as matrices) that is already present in machine registers. We term this usage "*in-line parallel.*"
- use any combination of the above.

Figure 18.2 illustrates these possibilities.

If a strategy is chosen that exploits the parallel processing of multiple microblocks in one work group (the first option) above, subtle questions of thread ordering arise that may influence the number of local memory bank conflicts. In [3], we discuss one such question in more detail.

Note that all combinations of parallel, sequential, and in-line parallel do the same amount of work, and should, in theory, require similar time to complete. In practice, this is not the case. This begs the question of how to decide between the numerous different possibilities. It is of course possible to explore manually which combination yields the best performance, but this is tedious, error-prone, and needs to be repeated for nearly every change to the hardware on which the code is run. This is clearly undesirable, but a potential solution is described in the next section.

18.3.3.4 *Using Run-Time Code Generation*

In [9], we discuss the numerous benefits of being able to generate computational code immediately before it is used, i.e., being able to perform C-level *run-time code generation*. We are delighted that OpenCL has this capability built into its specification. We do note, however, that the feature can be retrofitted onto CUDA through the use of the *PyCUDA* Python package. In our DG demonstration code, we already make simple use of this facility, by using string substitution on the source code of our kernels to make certain problem size parameters known to the compiler at compilation time. This helps decrease register pressure and allows the compiler to use a number of optimizations such as static loop unrolling for loops whose trip counts are now known.

But this is far from the only benefit. Another immediate advantage is the ability to perform automated tuning to answer questions such as the one raised at the end of the last section, where individual kernels can be generated to cover any number of code variants to be tried. Once this has been accomplished, implementing automated tuning can be as simple as looping over all variants and comparing timing data for each. For larger search spaces, a more sophisticated strategy might be desirable. This entire topic is discussed in much greater detail in [9].

18.3.3.5 *Further Tuning Opportunities*

In the demonstration code, some inefficiency lies buried in the way the surface fluxes are evaluated. Because the data required by the surface evaluation grows as $O(N^{d-1})$, whereas the volume data's size grows as $O(N^d)$, this is mainly felt at low-to-moderate N, which are particularly relevant for practical purposes.

First, the index data loaded into idM and idP has significant redundancy and can easily be compressed by breaking it down into element offsets added to one particular entry from a list of subindex lists. This list of subindex lists is comparatively small and has better odds of being able to reside in on-chip memory.

Second, data for faces lying opposite to each other is fetched twice — once for each side — in our current implementation. Through a blocking strategy (which, unfortunately, introduces significant complexity) these redundant fetches can be avoided. The strategy is discussed in detail in [3].

The last opportunity for tuning we will discuss in this setting is the use of multiple GPUs through MPI or Pthreads. Since only facial data for flux computation needs to be exchanged between GPUs, such a code is cheap in communications bandwidth and relatively easy to implement. We will now turn our discussion here from opportunities for speed increase to ways of making the technology more useful and more broadly applicable.

18.3.4 **Adding Generality**

GPU-DG as demonstrated in the demonstration code in this chapter can be extended in a number of ways to address a larger number of application problems.

Three Dimensions Perhaps the most gentle, but also the most immediately necessary generalization is the use of three-dimensional discretizations. The main complexity here lies in adapting the set-up code that generates matrices and computes mesh connectivity. The GPU kernels only require mild modification, although a number of complexity trade-offs change, requiring different tuning decisions. It is further helpful to generate general, n-dimensional code from a single source through run-time code generation, to reduce the amount of code that needs to be maintained and debugged.

Double Precision We have found that for most engineering problems, single precision calculations are more than sufficient. We do, however, acknowledge that some problems *do* require double precision, and our methods can be easily adapted to accommodate it.

General Boundary Conditions Our demonstration code only provided facilities for a single (Dirichlet) boundary condition. In nearly all practical problems, multiple boundary conditions (BCs) are needed, ranging from Neumann to absorbing BCs to even more complicated conditions arising in fluid dynamics.

General Linear Systems of Conservation Laws In addition to more general BCs, one obviously often wants to solve more general PDEs than the 2-D wave/Maxwell equation discussed here — this might include Maxwell's equations in 3-D or the equations of aeroacoustics. Again, making these adaptations to the demonstration code is relatively straightforward and mainly entails implementing a different local differentiation operator along with a new flux expression.

Nonlinear Systems of Conservation Laws Once general *linear* systems are treated by GPU-DG, it is, conceptually, not a very big step to also treat *nonlinear* systems of conservation laws, such as Euler's equations of gas dynamics or the even more complicated Navier-Stokes equations, potentially along with various turbulence models. The good news is that the methods presented so far again generalize seamlessly and work well for simple problems.

However, due to the subtle subject matter, a number of refinements of the method may be required to successfully treat real application problems.

The first issue revolves around the evaluation of nonlinear terms on a nodal grid and the aliasing error thus introduced into the method. One possibility of addressing this is filtering, which is easily implemented, but impacts accuracy. Another is overintegration using quadrature and cubature rules to more accurately approximate the integrals involved in the method. A more detailed discussion of these subjects is beyond the scope of this chapter and can be found in [4].

Shocks, i.e., the spontaneous emergence of very steep gradients in the solution, are another complication that only arises in nonlinear problems. Some initial ideas on using GPU-DG in conjunction with shock-laden flow computations are available in [10].

Curved Geometries While finite element methods already offer much greater flexibility in the approximation of geometry than solvers on structured grids, the demonstration solver shown here is restricted to geometries that consist of straight surfaces. A cost-efficient way to extend this solver to curved geometries is shown in [11].

Local Time Integration Lastly, as the solvers described in this chapter all employ explicit marching in time, time step restrictions may become an issue if the mesh involves very small elements. [12, Chapter 8] describes a number of time stepping schemes that can help overcome this problem.

As we have seen, a simple solver employing discontinuous Galerkin methods on the GPU can be written without much effort. On the other hand, far more effort can be spent on performance tuning and adaptation to more general problems. A free solver that implements nearly all of the improvements described here is available at http://mathema.tician.de/software/hedge under the GNU Public License.

18.4 FINAL EVALUATION

In the present chapter, we have shown that, even with limited effort, large performance gains are realizable for discontinuous Galerkin methods using explicit time integration. Figure 18.3 shows a live snapshot of the simulation of a wave propagation problem on a moderately complex domain as shown during run time by the solver if the mayavi2[2] visualization package is installed.

Figure 18.4 shows the performance of the demonstration solver developed here and compares it to the performance of hedge, our (freely available) production solver. Note that these graphs should not be compared directly, as one shows the result of a 2-D simulation, while the other portrays the

[2]http://code.enthought.com/projects/mayavi/

FIGURE 18.3

Screen shot of the demonstration solver showing a live snapshot of the simulation of a wave propagation problem on a moderately complex domain (see color insert).

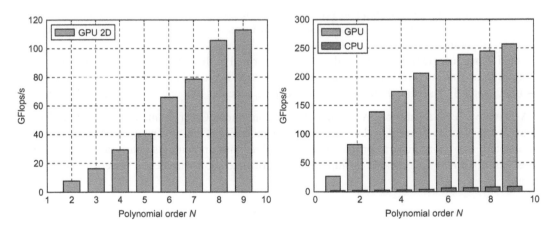

FIGURE 18.4

Performance figures for the demonstration solver (2-D) and the full-featured (3-D) solver "hedge," both executing solvers for the Maxwell problem on an NVIDIA GTX 295 in single precision.

performance of a three-dimensional computation. With some care, a few observations can be made however.

It is possible to observe that, as the element-local matrices grow with the third power of the degree in three dimensions (as opposed to the second power in 2-D), they constitute a larger part of the computation and contribute many more floating point operations, leading to higher performance. For the same reason, performance increases as the polynomial degree N increases.

Many of the tuning ideas described in Section 18.3.3 (such as microblocking and matrix-in-local) are designed to help performance in the case of lower N and, hence, smaller matrices. Without comparing absolute numbers, we observe that the initial performance increase at low N is much faster in the production solver than in the demonstration solver. We attribute this to the implementation of these extra strategies, that lead to markedly better performance at moderate N. In [3], we also briefly study the individual and combined effects of a few of these performance optimizations.

As a final observation, we would like to remark that the performance obtained here is very close to to the performance obtained in a C-based OpenCL solver written for the same problem — the use of Python as an implementation language does not hamper the speed of the solver at all. In particular, this facilitates a very logical splitting of computational software into performance-critical, low-level parts written in OpenCL C, and performance-uncritical set-up and administrative parts written in Python.

18.5 FUTURE DIRECTIONS

We have shown that, using our strategies, high-order DG methods can reach double-digit percentages of published theoretical peak performance values for the hardware under consideration. This computational speed translates directly into an increase of the size of the problem that can be reasonably treated using these methods. A single compute device can now do work that previously required a roomful of computing hardware — even using the simplistic implementation demonstrated here.

It is our stated goal to further broaden the usefulness of the method through continued investigation of the treatment of nonlinear problems, improved time integration characteristics, and coupling to other discretizations to optimally exploit the characteristics of each. GPUs present a rare opportunity, and it is fortuitous that a method like DG, which is known for highly accurate solutions, can benefit so tremendously from this computational advance.

Acknowledgments

We would like to thank Xueyu Zhu, who performed the initial Python port of the Matlab codes from which the demonstration solver is derived.

TW acknowledges the support of AFOSR under grant number FA9550-05-1-0473 and of the National Science Foundation under grant number DMS 0810187. JSH was partially supported by AFOSR, NSF, and DOE. AK's research was partially funded by AFOSR under contract number FA9550-07-1-0422, through the AFOSR/NSSEFF Program Award FA9550-10-1-0180 and also under contract DEFG0288ER25053 by the Department of Energy. The opinions expressed are the views of the authors. They do not necessarily reflect the official position of the funding agencies.

References

[1] P. Micikevicius, 3D finite difference computation on GPUs using CUDA, in: D. Kaeli, M. Leeser (Eds.), Proceedings of 2nd Workshop on General Purpose Processing on Graphics Processing Units, ACM, New York, 2009, pp. 79–84.

[2] J. Cohen, OpenCurrent. http://code.google.com/p/opencurrent/.

[3] A. Klöckner, T. Warburton, J. Bridge, J.S. Hesthaven, Nodal discontinuous Galerkin methods on graphics processors, J. Comp. Phys. 228 (2010) 7863–7882.

[4] J.S. Hesthaven, T. Warburton, Nodal Discontinuous Galerkin Methods: Algorithms, Analysis, and Applications, first ed., Springer, Heidelberg, 2007.

[5] A.H. Mohammadian, V. Shankar, W.F. Hall, Computation of electromagnetic scattering and radiation using a time-domain finite-volume discretization procedure, Comput. Phys. Commun. 68 (1–3) (1991) 175–196.

[6] T. Warburton, An explicit construction of interpolation nodes on the simplex, J. Eng. Math. 56 (2006) 247–262.

[7] T. Koornwinder, Two-variable analogues of the classical orthogonal polynomials, in: Theory and Applications of Special Functions, Proceedings of an Advanced Seminar sponsored by the Mathematics Research Center, The University of Wisconsin-Madison, March 31–April 2, 1975, pp. 435–495.

[8] M. Dubiner, Spectral methods on triangles and other domains, J. Sci. Comput. 6 (1991) 345–390.

[9] A. Klöckner, N. Pinto, Y. Lee, B.C. Catanzaro, P. Ivanov, A. Fasih, Pycuda: Gpu run-time code generation for high-performance computing, Technical Report 2009-40, Scientific Computing Group, Brown University, Providence, RI, 2009, submitted.

[10] A. Klöckner, T. Warburton, J.S. Hesthaven, Viscous shock capturing in a time-explicit discontinuous galerkin method, Math. Model. Nat. Phenom. 6 (2011) 57–83

[11] T. Warburton, A low storage curvilinear discontinuous Galerkin time-domain method for electromagnetics, in: Electromagnetic Theory (EMTS), 2010 URSI International Symposium on, pp. 996–999, 2010.

[12] A. Klöckner, High-Performance High-Order Simulation of Wave and Plasma Phenomena, PhD thesis, Brown University, Providence, RI, 2010.

Fast Electromagnetic Integral Equation Solvers on Graphics Processing Units

Shaojing Li, Ruinan Chang, and Vitaliy Lomakin

In this chapter, we present volumetric and surface integral equation (IE) electromagnetic solvers implemented on graphics processing units (GPUs). The IEs are discretized into a set of algebraic equations that are solved iteratively. The matrix-vector product in the iterative solution is evaluated via the nonuniform grid interpolation method (NGIM), which allows evaluating the electromagnetic field from N sources at N observers in $O(N)$ or $O(N \log N)$ operations. We describe how the NGIM and IE solvers can be implemented on GPUs. Specifically, we present a "one-thread-per-observer" "on-fly" approach allowing for an efficient utilization of the GPU architectures, including shared memory, coalesced global memory access, and massive parallelization. We demonstrate that the presented approaches allow achieving significant GPU speed-up rates for problems of a large computational size. The presented methods and approaches can be used not only for electromagnetic problems but also for many other problem types.

19.1 PROBLEM STATEMENT AND BACKGROUND

Computational methods for the electromagnetic analysis of large-scale and complex systems are essential for our ability to design and characterize practical devices and systems. Integral equation (IE) solvers are a powerful tool for the electromagnetic analysis. IEs allow focusing the solution only on the structure of interest (without a need to discretize the surrounding volumes), incorporate exact radiation conditions, and do not lead to numerical dispersion. These properties make IEs attractive for simulating complex and large-scale structures.

Several integral equation formulations can be used. Volumetric integral equations represent the structure's volume in terms of equivalent unknown currents or fields. For example, assuming that the structure under consideration comprises only bulk dielectric (nonmagnetic) materials, a volume integral equation can be written in the following form

$$\frac{\mathbf{D}(\mathbf{r})}{\varepsilon_r} - \nabla \iiint_V \frac{e^{-jk_0|\mathbf{r}-\mathbf{r}'|}}{|\mathbf{r}-\mathbf{r}'|} \nabla' \bullet (k_e \mathbf{D}(\mathbf{r}')) dV' - k_0^2 \iiint_V \frac{e^{-jk_0|\mathbf{r}-\mathbf{r}'|}}{|r-r'|} k_e \mathbf{D}(\mathbf{r}') dV' = 4\pi \varepsilon_0 \mathbf{E}^{inc}(\mathbf{r}); \ \mathbf{r} \in V,$$

(1)

where k_0 is the free space wavenumber, $\mathbf{E}^{inc}$ is the incident field, $\mathbf{D}$ is the electric flux density, $|\mathbf{r} - \mathbf{r}'|$ is the distance between the source point $\mathbf{r}'$ and observation point $\mathbf{r}$, ε_r is the relative permittivity of the material under consideration, and $k_e = 1 - 1/\varepsilon_r$ represents the contrast between the free space permittivity and the material permittivity.

Surface integral equations define equivalent unknown currents on the structure's surface only. For example, for a surface problem comprising a structure made of a perfect electric conductor residing in free space, an electric field IE can be written for an unknown surface current $\mathbf{J}_s$ distributed on the surface S of the structure in the following mixed potential form

$$\widehat{\mathbf{n}} \times \left(j\omega\mu \iint_S \frac{e^{-jk_0|\mathbf{r}-\mathbf{r}'|}}{|\mathbf{r}-\mathbf{r}'|} \mathbf{J}_s\left(\mathbf{r}'\right) ds' - \nabla \iint_S \frac{e^{-jk_0|\mathbf{r}-\mathbf{r}'|}}{j\omega\varepsilon|\mathbf{r}-\mathbf{r}'|} \nabla' \cdot \mathbf{J}_s\left(\mathbf{r}'\right) ds' \right) = 4\pi\widehat{\mathbf{n}} \times \mathbf{E}^i\left(\mathbf{r}\right); \ \mathbf{r} \in S. \quad (2)$$

To solve Eqs. (1) and (2), the structure under consideration is meshed over volume or surface elements, which typically are tetrahedrons volumes or triangles for surfaces. The unknowns are expanded via a number N of basis function [1]. These expansions are substituted in the IE and are subsequently tested (i.e., integrated) with testing functions (that may be chosen the same as the basis functions). The IE is then transformed into a set of algebraic equations

$$\sum_{n=1}^{N_s} Z_{mn} j_n = V_m, \quad (3)$$

where Z_{mn} are elements of the impedance matrix that represent a discretized form of the integro-differential operators in Eqs. (1) and (2) and V_m is the tested (known) incident field. For example, for the surface integral equation, Z_{mn} and V_m are given by

$$Z_{mn} = k_0 \iint_{Sm} d\mathbf{r} \mathbf{f}_m(\mathbf{r}) \bullet \iint_{S_n} \frac{\mathbf{f}_n(\mathbf{r}')e^{-jk_0|\mathbf{r}-\mathbf{r}'|}}{|\mathbf{r}-\mathbf{r}'|} d\mathbf{r}' - \frac{1}{k_0} \iint_{Sm} d\mathbf{r} \nabla \bullet \mathbf{f}_m(\mathbf{r}) \iint_{S_n} \frac{\nabla' \bullet \mathbf{f}_n(\mathbf{r}')e^{-jk_0|\mathbf{r}-\mathbf{r}'|}}{|\mathbf{r}-\mathbf{r}'|} d\mathbf{r}',$$

$$V_m = j\frac{4\pi}{\eta} \iint_{Sm} \mathbf{f}_m(\mathbf{r}) \bullet \mathbf{E}^{inc} d\mathbf{r}, \quad (4)$$

where $\mathbf{f}_m$ are vector basis and testing functions. Similar expressions for the impedance matrix can be given also for the volume integral equation (Eq. (1)). For nonoverlapping basis and testing functions, the integrals in Eq. (4) are computed using quadrature rules of a certain order, whereas for overlapping basis and testing functions, the singular behavior of the integral kernel is accounted for via an analytical integration.

Solving the system (Eqs. (3)–(4)) iteratively requires evaluating the Helmholtz type field potential via the following discrete transformation

$$u(\mathbf{r}_m) = \sum_{n=1; n \neq m}^{N} \frac{e^{-jk_0|\mathbf{r}_m-\mathbf{r}_n|}}{|\mathbf{r}_m-\mathbf{r}_n|} Q_n, \quad m = 1, 2, \ldots, N \quad (5)$$

Here, the potential $u(\mathbf{r}_m)$ at the observation locations $\mathbf{r}_m$ is evaluated by a discrete convolution of the Green's function $G(\mathbf{r}_m, \mathbf{r}_n) = \exp\left(-jk_0|\mathbf{r}_m - \mathbf{r}_n|\right)/|\mathbf{r}_m - \mathbf{r}_n|$ and the sources Q_n are colocated with the observers. In the framework of the above IE, the potential $u(\mathbf{r}_m)$ represents each one of the three components of the vector potential and the scalar potential (i.e., four components total), which result from the sources Q_n representing the three components of the current and the charge together with proper quadrature weights. The total number of sources is N, and it is proportional to the number of discretization elements. In the low-frequency regime, the computational domain is small in terms of the wavelength ($D \ll \lambda$, or $D \sim \lambda$) and the source density is prescribed by the particular problem (e.g., by the geometrical). In the special case of $k_0 = f = 0$, the potential satisfies the Poisson equation, and the problem is considered to be static. In the high-frequency regime, the computational domain is large in terms of the wavelength ($D \gg \lambda$), and the source density is determined by the wavelength according to the Nyquist criterion. In the mixed-frequency regime, the computational domain is large in terms of the wavelength, and it has dense source constellations, typically representing sharp geometrical features.

Rapidly evaluating the potential in the form of Eq. (5) is important for solving electromagnetic IEs, but it also is applied in many other areas, including micromagnetics, acoustics, and elastodynamics. Moreover, the methods presented here can be directly applied, without any modification, to other potential types with many additional applications (e.g., London or Van-der-Waals potentials).

Accelerating the direct evaluation of Eq. (5) through parallelization on either CPU clusters or GPU-CPU heterogeneous hardware platforms has been investigated in various research fields, such as a standard "N-body" problem in astrophysics and molecular dynamics [2, 3] or a matrix-vector multiplication problem in electromagnetics [4]. However, the $O(N^2)$ computational complexity essentially prevents the simulation of a reasonable large problem on desktop machines or even midsize clusters. Fast methods, such as Fast Multipole Methods (FMMs) [5–14], Fast-Fourier-Transforms (FFT)-based methods [15–18], H- or H2-matrices-based methods [19–22], or interpolation-based methods [23–28], reduce the computational complexity to $O(N)$ or $N \log(N)$. However, porting these methods to GPUs is not a trivial task and a relatively small number of works have reported on their implementations [29–31].

The goal of this work is to introduce a method that evaluates the potential in Eq. (5) efficiently using CUDA on graphics processor units (GPUs) with computational complexity (i.e., the computational time of number of operation) of $O(N)$ or $O(N \log N)$. This method is further coupled with an integral equation solver to rapidly solve the EFIE equation.

19.2 ALGORITHMS INTRODUCTION

This section describes a highly efficient GPU implementation of a modification of the nonuniform grid interpolation method (NGIM) [32], for the fast evaluation of the potential $u(\mathbf{r}_m)$ in Eq. (5). The NGIM exploits the fact that the field potential far from a source distribution is a function with a known asymptotic behavior. This behavior allows smoothing the fast spatial variations of the potential, computing it on a sparse grid, and interpolating to the required observation points. The algorithm is implemented using a hierarchical domain decomposition method in which the domain is subdivided via an octal tree into a hierarchy of levels comprising subdomains of different sizes. Near- and far-field subdomains are identified, and the interpolation procedures are implemented for the sufficiently separated subdomains. This algorithm achieves the computational cost of $O(N)$ in the low-frequency regime, $O(N \log N)$ in the high-frequency regime, and between these costs in the mixed-frequency regime.

Similar to the FMMs, NGIMs can handle nonuniform geometries and can have the same asymptotic cost for volumetric and surface problems. The NGIM differs from the FMMs in that it relies on direct spatial interpolations, which are natural operations for GPUs so can be better adapted to GPU architectures and achieve higher computational throughput. Moreover, the same NGIM can be applied to static ($k_0 = 0$) and dynamic ($k_0 \neq 0$) problems, as well as to problems with other kernels without major changes in its structure and mathematical operations, as opposed to FMMs. In addition, NGIM has a simple structure and does not require any special function evaluations, which facilitates its implementations on GPU systems, as will be shown in the section titled "GPU Implementations."

19.3 ALGORITHM DESCRIPTION

In this section we present a description of the NGIM and its implementation scheme. The presentation is given in a summary form. A more complete description of the algorithm can be found in [23–27] and [32].

19.3.1 Grid Construction

The NGIM divides the computational domain into a hierarchy of boxes containing sources and observers. At any subdivision level, each box is treated as a "parent" box and recursively is divided into eight "child" boxes at lower level. This process stops until boxes at the finest level contain less than a prescribed number of sources. Then, for a certain observation point, near-field and far-field boxes are identified for a distance larger or smaller than a predefined value (e.g., for distances twice the box diameter). The field potentials contributed by sources in the near-field boxes are evaluated one by one directly via superposition. The fields due to the sources in far-field boxes are aggregated to the box center and had their field interpolated on observer through several grids of sample points across different levels. This procedure, illustrated in Figure 19.1, is similar to other multilevel algorithms.

The field outside a group of sources is amplitude- and phase-compensated with respect to the common distance from the group center. The resulting slowly varying field can then be sampled at a sparse nonuniform grid (NG) and calculated at all desirable observation locations via inexpensive local (e.g., Lagrange) interpolation. The density and specific position of NG samples points are determined mathematically [26, 32] in preprocessing stage and remain the same in the entire algorithm or IE solver. In a low-frequency regime, a total of $O(N)$ NG samples are required to sample the field across all levels of the boxes, but in a high-frequency regime, this number is $O(N \log N)$. Generally speaking, in either domain, the higher the accuracy requirement, the denser the NG grid.

The frequency of the computations also affects another aspect of the algorithm. If the frequency of the problem is low, the field transition from NG samples to the final observation points are not done directly, but via another set of intermediate Cartesian Grids (CGs). The CGs can save the computational cost because in low-frequency applications, a small number of sampling points are sufficient to sample a slow varying field generated by sources outside a computational domain. In a high-frequency regime, the density of CGs should be the same as the density of the observers so that using CGs would not lead to any computational savings; therefore, CGs are not used in the high-frequency regime. In the mixed-frequency regime, CGs are built for lower levels with sufficiently small boxes (low-frequency levels)

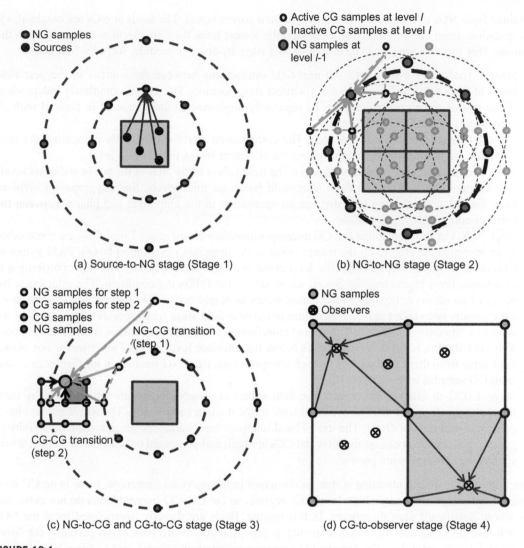

FIGURE 19.1

The 2-D illustration of the far-field stages of NGIM (see color insert).

and are omitted for higher levels where the field between boxes varies too rapid even when they are well separated from each other (high-frequency levels).

19.3.2 Algorithm

From the preceding section, the fields at observers are obtained via a sequence of interpolations. In the low-frequency regime, for example, the field at observers is interpolated via CGs, which is in turn obtained from NGs of certain boxes and CGs of their parent boxes. The fields at NGs are obtained, via interpolation, from their child boxes, except on the lowest level they are calculated directly from the sources. This process, which can be described as a stage-by-stage procedure, includes four stages:

- Stage 0 (near-field evaluation): All near-field interactions between the sources in the near-field boxes at the finest level are computed via direct superposition. This step is completely independent of the rest of the algorithm and can be separately implemented and executed in parallel with all other stages on multi-GPU systems.
- Stage 1 (finest level NG construction): The computation starts with directly computing the field values on an NGs serving as sample points for all source boxes in the finest level.
- Stage 2 (aggregation of NGs/upward pass): The field values at the NGs of the boxes at coarser levels are computed by aggregation from their child boxes on finer levels. Such aggregation involves local interpolation and common distance compensation in the amplitude and phases between the corresponding NGs.
- Stage 3 (NG to CG transitions and CG decomposition/downward pass): Local CGs are constructed as an intermediate step to do the interpolation in the desirable observation boxes. Field values at CGs of an observer box on a specific level come from two contributions. The first contribution is from same level interaction-list boxes, which satisfy the following condition. The interaction-list boxes of an observer box have their parent boxes as neighbors of the observer box, except those have already been taken into considerations in the near-field stage (corresponds to influences of the source of "medium distance"). The second contribution of field at CGs comes from the parent box. This contribution is valid only for boxes below the interface level. CGs of an observer box obtain field value from these two sources through interpolations, from NG samples in the former case, and from CG samples in the latter case.
- Stage 4 (CG to observation point): The field values at observation points are obtained by local interpolations from the CGs on the finest level of the domain subdivision. The whole process has a computational cost of $O(N)$. The use of local interpolation guarantees the automatic adaptivity to geometrical features because the NGs and CGs are built and processed only around locations where sources and observers are present.

One thing worth special attention is that, as discussed in the previous paragraph, there is no CG constructed for computations in a high-frequency regime, so the CG-CG interpolations do not exist, and the whole downward pass disappears. In this regime, fields are directly interpolated from the NGs at each level to observers. In mixed-frequency regime, the downward pass exists partially, for "low-frequency" levels only; thus, the downward pass possesses a hybrid scheme of the "direct NG-observer interpolation" and "NG-CG-observer interpolation."

19.4 GPU IMPLEMENTATIONS

In the implementation of the NGIM, the unique programming mechanisms and hardware arrangement of GPUs are critical to the efficiency of the algorithm. These include the coalesced accessing of the global memory, the utilization of shared memory, and the minimal atomic parallelization unit, *"warp."* All these concepts and mechanisms have been discussed extensively in NVIDIA [33] as well as many other works related to scientific computing on GPUs [34]. These concepts have significant effects on the time and memory consumption of the NGIM on GPUs and result in a number of important modifications in the data structure of the code as compared with the CPU implementations. The implementation of the NGIM on GPUs follows the same "stage-by-stage" protocol as that on CPUs, yet extensive changes are made to parallelize the operations and utilize tools provided by CUDA.

19.4.1 Preprocessing and Initialization Stages

In the preprocessing stage, all vectors, matrices, and other data structures used by the NGIM are initiated. The initialization includes memory allocation in global memory of GPU and copying coordinates of sources and observers to the allocated matrices as well as reshaping and copying auxiliary matrices — for example, indexing and storing the near-field boxes and interaction-list boxes for each observer box. This task is done only once in standard IE application because the geometry of the computational domain usually remains the same during the whole problem-solving process.

In addition to the memory transfer operations, one crucial task done in the preprocessing stage specifically for GPU is rearranging the source storage so that sources belong to the same box are situated contiguously in the memory. This is critical for the GPU to adopt "coalesced accessing" to accelerate the memory handling, which will be described in detail later in this chapter. Fortunately, the hierarchical structure of boxes still allows this to be done once for all levels as sources belong to the same box on lower levels always belong to the same box on higher levels, too.

In the GPU implementation of NGIM, grid tabulation is significantly shortened compared with its CPU sequential counterparts. The position of NG or CG samples and their mutual interpolation coefficient are computed *on-fly* where needed. This *on-fly* approach reduces the memory consumption and the total memory access time. As a result, the preprocessing time of the GPU code is reduced, making the code more efficient and practical. In addition, the overall code speed may increase in spite of a larger number of operations. It is noted that using a similar approach for FMM type methods is also possible, but it may be somewhat less efficient owing to more complex operations involved (e.g., these methods require computing special functions).

19.4.2 Near-Field Computation

In this stage, the fields at the observers are evaluated directly via Eq. (5) by adding up the field contributions from sources belonging to the level L boxes in the near-field region of the observer's box. Methods to parallelize this stage also apply to direct evaluations of the classical "n-body" problems [2]. Because the computational domain has already been divided into boxes with sources and observers arranged box by box, the traversing within the list of observers and sources are done in a box-by-box manner.

Mathematically, the near-field computation is a sparse matrix-vector multiplication. However, for large problem sizes the memory limitations may be an obstacle. Therefore, instead of defining sparse matrix-vector products, we compute all the fields on-fly by direct superposition. Figure 19.2 shows the flowchart diagram of CPU and GPU implementation of NGIM, respectively, and Figure 19.3 shows the thread arrangement and assignment during the memory loading and the computation of the same stage. The key points are summarized here.

(1) We adopted "one-thread-per-observer" type of parallelization in which one thread is responsible for calculating the field value at one observer.

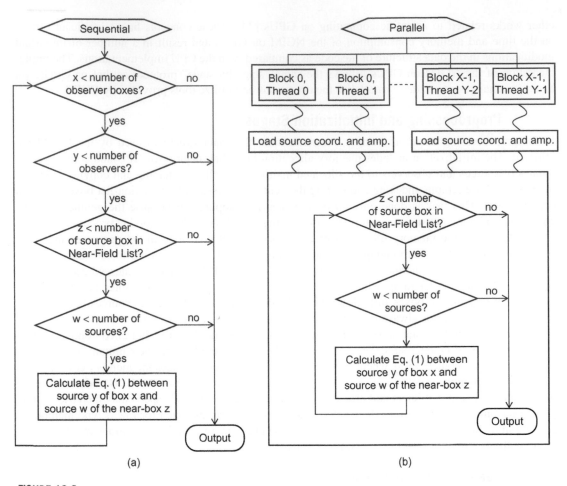

FIGURE 19.2

The flow chart of CPU and GPU NGIM. (a) The sequential version of the near-field stage of the NGIM involves a four-level loop that takes into account that each source-observer pair satisfies the Near-Field criterion. (b) In the corresponding parallel version of the near-field stage of the NGIM, two levels of loop are spread onto parallel stream processors of GPU. X and Y are the number of observer boxes and number of observers in each box, respectively. Coalesced memory loading is utilized and shown in detail in Figure 19.3.

(2) The number of threads per block can be chosen by the user or determined by properties of the hardware, number of unknowns of the problem, and the source/observer distribution automatically. However, only threads for observers of the same box are bundled to form a block. One or several thread blocks may be launched to handle a certain box when the number of observers within the box exceeds the user-defined number or the hardware limitation. To achieve a better performance, the number of threads per block should be greater than 32 because this is the size of a warp.

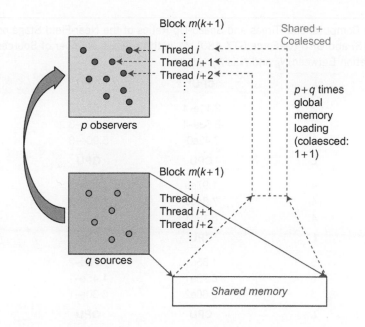

FIGURE 19.3

Memory access pattern of threads within the same block. Coalesced global memory is utilized to accelerate the memory loading.

(3) The exact same source information (coordinates and amplitudes) is required to compute the near field of the observers in the same box, so threads assigned for these observers first cooperatively load the source information they all need before they synchronize their progress and distribute themselves into the task they are assigned. Because the information of any sources in the same box is located contiguously in the global memory, coalesced loading can always be utilized.

(4) One-, two-, or three-dimensional grids of blocks can be used to handle all nonempty boxes. In the current implementation, we use two-dimensional grids of blocks because they allow any practical number of blocks to be launched for each individual kernel.

(5) Some intrinsic mathematical functions are used to accelerate the computations. These functions include single precision versions of sin and cos functions, used to evaluate the complex exponential in the Greens' function in Eq. (5). Other instruction level techniques include replacing the integer division and modulo operations with bitwise shifting and AND operations when the dividend is power of 2 [33].

(6) The data type "float2" is used in the near-field and following stages because it can be directly mapped to the "complex" data type we use in our CPU code written in Fortran. In the CUDA compiler, the operator overload mechanism is introduced so that the operations on float2 can be defined exactly as those for complex numbers.

Table 19.1 shows the computational time of the near-field stage on CPU and GPU. The CPU timing results were obtained on a single core of an Intel Xeon X5248 with a 3.2-GHz CPU using Intel Fortran

Table 19.1 The Computational Times and Speed-Up Ratios of the Near-Field Stage on CPU (Xeon X5248) and GPU (GeForce GTX 480). N_p is the Average Number of Sources per Box on Level L. The Relation Between N_p and N is $N_p = N/8^L$

N_p	L	CPU*	GPU	Ratio
16	3	2.11e–1	1.02e–3	206.9
32	3	8.63e–1	2.22e–3	388.7
64	3	3.42e0	5.90e–3	579.7
N_p	L	CPU	GPU	Ratio
16	4	1.97e0	7.49e–3	263.0
32	4	7.84e0	1.74e–2	450.6
64	4	3.13e1	4.84e–2	646.7
N_p	L	CPU	GPU	Ratio
16	5	1.85e1	7.76e–2	238.4
32	5	6.75e1	1.45e–1	465.5
64	5	2.66e2	5.30e–1	501.9
N_p	L	CPU	GPU	Ratio
16	6	1.43e2	6.38e–1	224.1
32	6	5.66e2	1.19e0	475.6
64	6	2.22e3	4.37e0	508.0

All timing results shown in this table are in seconds.

Compiler v10 with –O3 optimization (there was around 20-fold speed-up of a -O3 optimized CPU code over a nonoptimized one). At the GPU end, an NVIDIA GTX480 running at 700 MHz with 1.5 GB of memory was used. The GPU implementation was written and compiled using CUDA Toolkit v3.0 from NVIDIA. Both CPU and GPU versions of the code used the *on-fly* approach, and the positions of source and observer were random with a uniform probability distribution function.

It is evident that the speed-up ratios of the GPU code compared with that of the CPU one are very high, varying between 200 and 650. The speed-ups are higher for larger N_p, that is, for a larger number of sources and observers per box, when the massive parallelization is fully exploited. Taking into account the fact that the number of the GPU cores in the considered case is 480 and they are run at the clock rate around 4.5 times lower than that of the CPU, achieving the acceleration rates higher than 600 is impressive. Such high rates are obtained because of not only massive floating-point computing power and memory bandwidth of GPUs but also the memory sharing between threads and the coalesced memory access of the global memory.

A comment should be made on the timing results shown Table 19.1. For a fixed number of levels, the complexity of the near-field calculation stage scales approximately as $O(N^2)$ with increasing N as the number of near-field evaluations is proportional to N_p^2. The complexity of $O(N)$ of the near-field stage is achieved because the number of levels L increases with an increase of N. Indeed, the computational time behaves as $O(N)$ when the number of level L is properly chosen, balancing the near- and far-field computation time.

19.4.3 Outward Computation from Sources to NG Samples (Stage 1)

The NG construction stage computes the field values at NGs, which is the first step of the upward pass of the algorithm. The core operations in this stage are (a) the construction of NGs of each nonempty box at the finest level L and (b) the direct calculation of the field values at these NGs via Eq. (5).

The sequential version of code consists of two nested loops to deal with all pairs of sources and NG samples for individual boxes and another loop to account for all boxes at level L (Eq. (5)). Because the relative positions of NG samples and sources do not change during the whole process of IE solver, their interaction coefficients can be calculated beforehand in the preprocessing stage and stored for later use (i.e., the interacting matrix filling). However, this task is only done in our CPU version of code. For GPU, no coefficient matrices are used for the reasons mentioned in previous sections.

Before the fields on NG samples can be calculated, the positions of the NG samples have to be calculated first. The construction process follows the "one-thread-per-observer" approach described in the section titled "Algorithms Introduction." However, here the "observers" are in their broader definition, referring to NG samples. One or several blocks of threads are allocated for each observation box. For calculation in the low-frequency regime without very high accuracy, the number of NG samples per box is not large, and one block of threads would be enough to achieve the maximal parallel efficiency. In the high- and mixed-frequency regimes, however, the boxes at high-frequency levels can have a large number of NG samples. This requires assigning multiple blocks for each box. Regardless of the number of blocks assigned for each box, the "coalesced" memory-reading technique is always employed to accelerate the loading of source coordinates and amplitudes.

The computational times of Stage 1 are presented in Table 19.2 (these results are frequency regime independent for the same N, L, and the number of NG samples per smallest box). It is evident that the speed-up ratio increases significantly with an increase of the number of sources per box.

It should be mentioned that generally, the computation time of Stage 1 is about 1–5% of the total time. Therefore, the influence of this stage is relatively insignificant provided other stages are implemented efficiently.

19.4.4 NG Upward Aggregation (Stage 2)

In this stage, the field values at the NG samples of the parent boxes at levels from $L-1$ to 2 are computed by interpolating from the NG samples of the corresponding nonempty child boxes. In this chapter, we use spatial tri-linear interpolations for phase- and amplitude-compensate fields.

Similar to other stages, the GPU implementation follows the "one-thread-per-observer" parallelization, in which one thread handles one observer, and threads handling observers of the same box are bundled to form one or more blocks. The interpolation process includes calculating coordinates of the NG samples of parent boxes, transforming them into the coordinate system of their child boxes, extracting coordinates and amplitudes of the nearest grid samples around the observers, calculating the interpolation coefficients, and finally evaluating the fields. All these operations are done by a single thread for a single observer. This process seems to be burdensome, but the vast computational power of even a single-stream processor on a GPU handles the jobs with ease.

Table 19.2 The Computational Times and Speed-Up Ratios of the Source-to-NG Stage (Stage 1) on CPU (Xeon X5248) and GPU (GeForce GTX 480) for Different N_p, L, and Oversampling Rates. N_p is the Average Number of Sources per Box on the Level L. The Relation Between N_p and N is $N_p = N/8^L$

Accuracy Requirement	N_p	L	CPU*	GPU	Ratio
L_1 error $= 1 \times 10^{-3}$ for domain size $D = \lambda/2$	16	3	5.89e–3	1.33e–4	44
	32	3	1.55e–2	1.00e–4	155
	64	3	3.16e–2	1.33e–4	238
	N_p	L	CPU	GPU	Ratio
	16	4	5.01e–2	6.31e–4	79
	32	4	1.21e–1	9.28e–4	130
	64	4	2.45e–1	1.66e–3	148
	N_p	L	CPU	GPU	Ratio
	16	5	4.74e–1	3.99e–3	119
	32	5	1.16e0	6.73e–3	172
	64	5	2.44e0	1.24e–2	197
	N_p	L	CPU	GPU	Ratio
	16	6	5.49e0	2.99e–2	184
	32	6	1.07e1	5.23e–2	205
	64	6	2.14e1	9.78e–2	219

* All timing results shown in this table are in seconds.

Table 19.3 shows the computational time results of Stage 2 for the low-frequency case. Note that the results are not shown for different N because this stage is solely grid operations that do not depend on N for a fixed L. (We assume all boxes are active, which means at least one source/observer is presenting in any boxes.) The speed-up ratios are in the same range as those of Stage 1 for most problem sizes. It is noted that in the low-frequency regime, Stage 2 takes only less than 2% of the total computational time.

Table 19.4 shows the computational time for the high-frequency regime for the GPU code. The absolute computational time is noticeably larger than that for the low-frequency case in Table 19.3, but it still shows a gain taking into account the number of more operations required for high-frequency calculations. Note that no CPU results are shown for this case because the increased grid density for high-frequency calculation makes the "precomputation approach" used in the CPU not able to produce results for problems in the comparable range. To allow for larger problem sizes would require implementing the on-fly approach also in the CPU code, making it significantly slower. The rest of the results in this chapter for the high-frequency regime are also presented only for the GPU code. The GPU code efficiency is accessed by comparing with the GPU code for the same N for low-frequency problems.

Table 19.3 The Computational Times and Speed-Up Ratios for the NG Aggregation Stage (Stage 2) on CPU (Xeon X5248) and GPU (GeForce GTX 480) for Different L and Oversampling Rates. The Number of NG Samples per Box is Chosen as 64 Due to the Accuracy Requirement

Accuracy Requirement	L	CPU	GPU	Ratio
L_1 error $= 1 \times 10^{-3}$ for domain size $D = \lambda/2$	3	2.70e–3	1.33e–4	20
	4	2.74e–2	3.96e–4	69
	5	2.25e–1	1.77e–3	127
	6	1.81e0	8.33e–3	217

Table 19.4 The Computational Times and Speed-Up Ratios for the NG Aggregation Stage (Stage 2) in High-Frequency Regime for Different L on GPU (GeForce GTX 480). No CGs are Constructed. The Number of NG Samples per Box at Level l is $64 \times 8^{L-l}$, and the Frequency for a Given is Chosen as $D = \lambda(L-2)$

Accuracy Requirement	L	GPU
L_1 error $= 5 \times 10^{-2}$	3	4.14e–4
	4	2.92e–3
	5	3.59e–2
	6	3.89e–1

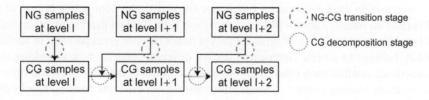

FIGURE 19.4

The relation of two sub-stages: NG-CG transition stage and CG decomposition stage in calculating the field values on CG samples of boxes at each computational level in the low-frequency regime.

19.4.5 Evaluation of Field Values on CG Samples (Stage 3)

In Stage 3, the field values at the samples of CGs are calculated. This stage can conceptually be treated as a two-step process in low-frequency regime as shown in Figure 19.4, but a one-step process in high-frequency regime with some variation. In the two sub-stages in low-frequency regime, each of the two origins of fields, as mentioned in Section 3, on CG samples are computed. In the high-frequency regime, fields on observers are directly obtained via similar interpolation as in low-frequency regime.

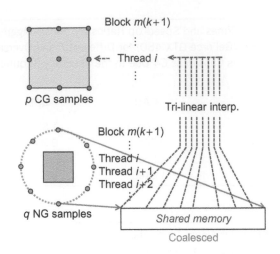

FIGURE 19.5

Memory access scheme of the NG-CG substage. Eight NG samples are required by the trilinear interpolation through which the field values on CG samples are obtained.

In mixed-frequency regime, the process is a hybrid of those two as described in [32]. The "one-thread-per-observer" approach is still adopted as shown in Figure 19.5, where "observers" now are CG samples for in low-frequency regime and actual observers in high-frequency regime.

This substage, evaluating fields of the CG samples from the NG samples in the interacting far-field boxes, is the most time-consuming part of the far-field calculation. The major reason for this larger time, besides a large number of operations needed to be executed, is that the source information required by observers in each observation box is not situated in the contiguous region of the global memory. This random memory access pattern is the result from the fact that "interaction-list" boxes of an observer box belong to a number of different parent boxes or even great parents. In addition to that, one box usually belongs to several "interaction-list" of different observer boxes, making the memory accessing sometimes conflict each other. This "random" relation between source and observer boxes and possible memory loading request of same information from different running blocks may lead to the reduced efficiency of memory handling.

The CG decomposition step is executed for CGs in all observation boxes at the low-frequency levels after the NG-CG transition step. At each such level the CG samples in the child boxes are obtained via trilinear interpolations from the CGs samples in the parent boxes. This step is the NG-NG aggregation stage (Stage 2) in opposite direction, but even simpler as no spherical-Cartesian coordinate transformations are required to account for the relative shift of source (parent) and observer (child) boxes. The total contribution of this substage to the total computational time is low, accounting for only about 1–2%.

Table 19.5 shows the computational time of Stage 3 (NG-CG transition stage and CG decomposition combined) for different L in the low-frequency regime. Similar to the results in Table 19.3 (for Stage 2), for a fixed number of levels L, the speed of Stage 3 is independent of the number of source and observer points N and hence no dependence of N is shown. The obtained computational times

Table 19.5 The Computational Times and Speed-Up Ratios of Stage 3 in the Low-Frequency Regime, on CPU (Xeon X5248) and GPU (GeForce GTX 480) for Different L and Oversampling Rates

Accuracy Requirement	L	CPU	GPU	Ratio
L_1 error $= 1 \times 10^{-3}$ for domain size $D = \lambda/2$	3	2.68e–1	2.44e–3	110
	4	3.02e0	2.32e–2	130
	5	2.95e1	2.11e–1	140
	6	2.43e2	1.82e0	134
	L	CPU	GPU	Ratio
L_1 error $= 2.5 \times 10^{-4}$ for domain size $D = \lambda/2$	3	3.23e0	2.10e–2	154
	4	4.16e1	2.32e–1	179
	5	3.38e2	2.18e0	155

depend on the oversampling ratios of both NGs and CGs, particularly CG. The smallest speed-up ratio list in the table is at the 100+ level, which is in the same order to other far-field stages (comparing with significantly lower speed-up for similar stages in GPU implementation of MLFMA [29, 31]). The speed-up ratios increase for increasing oversampling rates as GPU is less vulnerable to the computational burden owing to the larger number of interpolations. In addition, from our tests on different generations of GPUs, we found that the new Fermi generation (GeForce GTX 480) GPU better handles kernels with access to relatively "random" sets of data in the memory, which results in about three-fold computational time reduction on GeForce GTX 480 as compared with the Tesla C1060. This time reduction is interesting, taking into account that the number of stream processors in GTX 480 is only twice as large (480 vs. 240).

Table 19.6 shows the computational time of Stage 3 in the high-frequency regime. The time increases compared with the low-frequency case in Table 19.5, but this increase is relatively insignificant (on the order of the number of levels L), which demonstrates the efficiency of the code in the high-frequency regime.

19.4.6 CG Grids to Observers (Stage 4)

In this stage, the fields at actual observers are interpolated from the CG samples of the finest level L boxes to which the observers belong. This stage is only valid in low- and mixed-frequency regime. This stage is conceptually the Stage 1 in opposite direction. All critical programming strategies in Stage 1 are adopted, including "one-thread-per-observer," coalesced loading of source information, and so on. The computational time of this stage is smaller than that of Stage 1 because only interpolations from the CGs are involved, and no direct evaluations shown in Eq. (5) are needed.

Timing results of Stage 4 are presented in Table 19.7. The computational time behavior is similar to that of Stage 1 (Table 19.2). The GPU computational times are constant for smaller problem sizes. For larger problems sizes, after all stream processor are utilized, the speed-up ratio increases up to a saturation point of around 150. We have also tested more cases with an increase in CG oversampling rates. We found that the increase of the CG oversampling rates barely affects the computational time

Table 19.6 The Computational Times and Speed-Up Ratios of Stage 3 in the High-Frequency Regime on GPU (GeForce GTX 480) for Different L and Oversampling Rates. The Number of NG Samples per Box at Level l is $64 \times 8^{L-l}$, and the Frequency for a Given L is Chosen as $D = \lambda(L-2)$

Accuracy Requirement	L	GPU
L_1 error $= 5 \times 10^{-2}$	3	3.33e-3
	4	4.79e-2
	5	6.16e-1
	6	6.97e0
	L	**GPU**
L_1 error $= 1.5 \times 10^{-2}$	3	2.84e-2
	4	4.39e-1
	5	5.33e0

Table 19.7 The Computational Times and Speed-Up Ratios of CG-to-Receiver Stage (Stage 4) on CPU (Xeon X5248) and GPU (GeForce GTX 480) for Different N_p and L. There are 64 CG Samples per Box. N_p is the Average Number of Sources per Box on the Level L. The Relation Between N_p and N is $N_p = N/8^L$

N_p	L	CPU	GPU	Ratio
16	3	1.18e-3	1.50e-4	8
32	3	1.99e-3	1.50e-4	13
64	3	3.62e-3	1.70e-4	21
N_p	**L**	**CPU**	**GPU**	**Ratio**
16	4	9.77e-3	3.30e-4	30
32	4	1.68e-2	3.30e-4	51
64	4	3.53e-2	5.06e-4	70
N_p	**L**	**CPU**	**GPU**	**Ratio**
16	5	1.03e-1	1.50e-3	69
32	5	1.84e-1	1.50e-3	123
64	5	3.51e-1	2.60e-3	135
N_p	**L**	**CPU**	**GPU**	**Ratio**
16	6	9.01e-1	9.90e-3	91
32	6	1.58e0	1.01e-2	156
64	6	2.95e0	1.79e-2	165

on CPU or GPU, even though with more CG samples per box, more data has to be loaded before doing the interpolations. For the CPU version, the memory-loading time is negligible compared with calculations, whereas for the GPU, the memory-loading time is small owing to coalescent access.

It should be mentioned that, generally, the computational time of Stage 4 is below 1% of the total time. Therefore, the influence of this stage is insignificant provided other stages are implemented efficiently.

19.5 RESULTS
19.5.1 Computational Time

First, we study the computations time in the low-frequency regime. The overall performance of CPU and GPU implementations of NGIM in this regime is shown in Figure 19.6 and Table 19.8. The GPU implementations have been tested on two generations of NVIDIA's GPUs: older generation Tesla C1060 with 4 GB of memory and new-generation Geforce GTX 480 with 1.5 GB of memory. Because the acceleration provided by GPUs varies across stages and is closely related to the problem size, optimal performance of the CPU or GPU is achieved under different parameters. Therefore, similar to [29], we define "effective" speed-up ratio as the ratio between computational times of the CPU and GPU codes when each implementations uses its optimal settings.

In Figure 19.6, the computational time of the direct calculation (i.e., the evaluation of each source-observer pair on CPU and GPU) are provided as a reference. For the direct calculations, the

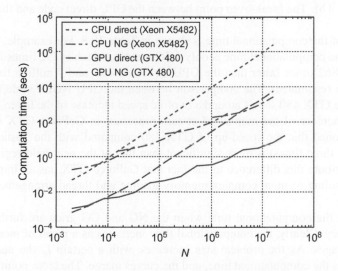

FIGURE 19.6

Computational time of the direct method and multilevel NGIM on CPU and GPU as a function of N. The time of all necessary memory transfer between the hosts and the GPU devices are included, as will be the case for all other timing results in this section. The size of the computational domain is $D = \lambda/2$. The relative L_1 error is approximately 5×10^{-3}.

Table 19.8 Computational Times and Speed-Up Ratios of the GPU and CPU Implementations of the NGIM and the Direct Method for $\Omega_r = \Omega_a = \Omega_x = 2$. The Size of the Computational Domain is $D = \lambda/2$. The Relative L_1 Error is Approximately 5×10^{-3}

# of Unknowns		16K	64K	256K	1M	4M	16M	64M
CPU	Time	1.15e0	4.84e0	2.69e1	9.66e1	3.67e2	2.49e3	N/A
GPU	Time	5.19e-3	3.09e-2	7.49e-2	3.69e-1	2.33e0	6.36e0	N/A
(GTX480)	Speed-up	222	157	359	262	152	392	N/A
GPU	Time	1.15e-2	5.29e-2	1.53e-1	8.14e-1	3.85e0	1.18e1	8.49e1
(C1060)	Speed-up	100	90	176	119	95	211	N/A

computational time scales as $O(N^2)$. The computational time of the NGIM scales as $O(N)$ for both CPU and GPU implementations when optimal L is chosen, respectively, but the GPU code is significantly faster and can handle larger N. The largest problem size N that GeForce GTX 480 can handle is 28 million (1.5-GB memory), while Tesla C1060 can handle $N = 64$ million (4-GB memory). As a comparison, the CPU code can run up to 16 million with 32 GB of RAM. As the acceleration ratio of the near-field components increases within each curve while that of the far-field component remains almost the same, the cross point of curves with different L shifts toward larger N on GPU. It is remarkable that the computational time break-even point between the GPU direct code and the NGIM CPU code is around $N = 4$ M. The break-even point between the GPU direct code and the NGIM GPU code is only $N = 4000$.

A detailed list of the computational time is shown in Table 19.8. For example, for a problem with $N = 16,777,072$, the computational time is only 6.36 seconds, which is 392 times faster than the CPU version of NGIM, 862 times faster than the GPU direct version, and 7 million times faster than the CPU direct version (estimated). The comparison between the GPU NGIM code running on a Tesla C1060 and GeForce GTX 480 shows around a twofold speed increase of the latter, which is consistent with the twofold increase of the number of stream processor in GeForce GTX 480 (480 vs. 240). It should be mentioned that the speed-up of GTX 480 compared with the Tesla C1060 of the far-field regime (about three times) is more significant than that of the near-field regime (slightly below two times). We attribute this difference to the fact that GeForce GTX has an improved architecture allowing easier handling of more complex memory loading and thread arrangement required for the far-field calculation.

Table 19.9 lists the computational time when the NG and CG grids are further oversampled to improve the accuracy. Clearly, the computational time increases as a result of more operations being done in far-field stages. As the problem size increases, with a certain L, the near-field component gradually dominates the computational time, and the curves merge. The cross points between different L moves for both GPU and CPU cases. Qualitatively, the performance of the CPU and GPU versions is similar to the low oversampling case, but the adverse effect of oversampling in computational time is much lesser for the GPU code. In fact, the "L_1 error $= 2 \times 10^{-2}$ case" runs at the same speed as "L_1 error $= 5 \times 10^{-3}$" case because our current version of the GPU code launches at least one warp to handle one observer box, as explained in Section 17.4. Therefore, further decreasing of NG/CG samples per box below 32 would not reduce the computational resources consumption on GPUs.

Table 19.9 Computational Times and Speed-Up Ratios of the GPU and CPU Implementations of NGIM with Different Oversampling Rates. The Size of the Computational Domain is $D = \lambda/2$

# of Unknowns			1,048,576	8,388,608
L_1 error $= 2 \times 10^{-2}$	CPU NG	Time (sec)	5.29e1	4.46e2
	GPU NG	Time (sec)	3.69e−1	3.11e0
		Speed-up	143	143
L_1 error $= 5 \times 10^{-3}$	CPU NG	Time (sec)	9.66e1	8.14e2
	GPU NG	Time (sec)	3.69e−1	3.11e0
		Speed-up	262	262
L_1 error $= 1 \times 10^{-3}$	CPU NG	Time (sec)	3.43e2	N/A**
	GPU NG	Time (sec)	1.02e0	8.87e0
		Speed-up	336	N/A

Table 19.10 Computational Times and Speed-Up Ratios of the GPU and CPU Implementations of NGIM for the Surface Source-Observer Distribution of the "inverse-T" Structure in Figure 19.7

# of Unknowns		8,192	32,768	131,072	524,288
CPU NG	Time (sec)	4.35e−1	2.03e0	8.34e0	4.41e1
GPU NG	Time (sec)	2.22e−3	6.33e−3	2.16e−2	1.12e−1
	Speed-up	196	321	386	394

*The size of the computational domain is $D = \lambda/2$, L_1 error $= 5 \times 10^{-3}$.

Finally, the performance of the GPU and CPU implementations of the NGIM in the low-frequency regime is illustrated for a surface problem in Figure 19.2. All sources are placed on the surface of an "inverse T-structure." For this problem, FFT-based methods would require sampling the empty volume using excessive zero padding, resulting in a significant increase of the computational time and memory consumption. As evident from Table 19.10, the CPU and GPU implementations of the NGIM have performance similar to (and even better than) that obtained for the source/observer distribution in a box. The GPU-CPU speed-up ratios are high as well.

Next, we show the computational time results for the GPU NGIM code in the high- and mixed-frequency regimes. The general behavior of the code performance is similar to that for the low-frequency regime and hence many conclusions and discussions for the low-frequency regime apply here as well. In Table 19.11 and 19.12 we present a quantitative summary of the results in the format similar to that in Table 19.1. Table 19.11 shows the computational time in the high-frequency regime for the number of sources up to $N = 14$ million and domain sizes up to $D = 12\lambda$. The computational time is consistent with the time of the low-frequency regime taking into account the anticipated increase related to L. As in the low-frequency case, the speed increase for the newer-generation GPU is around twofold.

Table 19.12 shows the computational time in the mixed-frequency regime with the hybrid NG-CG transformation scheme. It is evident that the code is efficient in handling this case. The computational

Table 19.11 Computational Time of the NGIM on GPUs in the High-Frequency Regime. The Number of Sources N is Taken such that there are Around 20 Sources per Linear Wavelength. The Density of NGs are to Keep the L_1 Error Less than 5.0e-2 for all Problem Sizes

# of Unknowns	8K	64K	216K	512K	1M	4M	8M	14M
Domain size (D/λ)	1.0	2.0	3.0	4.0	5.0	8.0	10.0	12.0
Level L	3	3	3	4	4	5	5	5
GPU Time GTX 480	5.0e-3	2.8e-2	2.0e-1	4.1e-1	9.6e-1	4.9e0	1.0e1	2.1e1
GPU Time TESLA C1060	1.4e-2	6.1e-2	3.8e-1	8.9e-1	1.8e0	1.0e1	2.0e1	4.4e1

Table 19.12 Computational Time in the Mixed-Frequency Regime. The Domain Size is Set to be $D = 2\lambda$. The L_1 Error is 6.0e-2 for All Cases. For the Case $N = 64$M, the Optimal Level L should be 7, but Owing to the Memory Limitations, the Results are Shown for $L = 6$

# of Unknowns	64K	256K	512K	1M	4M	8M	32M	64M*
Level L	3	4	4	5	5	6	6	6
GPU Time GTX 480	2.6e-2	9.2e-2	2.1e-1	3.7e-1	1.8e0	3.1e0	N/A	N/A
GPU Time TESLA C1060	4.4e-2	1.7e-1	3.7e-1	8.6e-1	3.1e0	7.0e0	1.2e1	8.0e1

time for the same N is noticeably smaller for the results in Table 19.12 as compared with those in Table 19.11 because the grid density for the low-frequency levels is a constant of $O(1)$, and the number of high-frequency levels is reduced.

19.5.2 Memory Usage

The memory usage is a very important factor affecting the applicability of a GPU-based algorithm because GPUs typically have smaller amounts of memory than CPU-based systems. For example, in the Dell Precision T7400 workstation used to test our algorithm, two Xeon processors share 32 GB of RAM, but our GPU, an NVIDIA GeForce GTX 480, has 1.5 GB of global memory. In our current version of the code, the memory usage of GPU is determined by both L and N.

With 1.5 GB of memory, the NVIDIA GeForce GTX 480 can handle up to $L = 6$ and up to $N = 28,000,000$ using NGIM code presented in this chapter. The memory consumption of our CPU code used for comparison is significantly larger (while at the same time, much slower). For example, the memory required by NGIM CPU implementation for a problem of $N = 8,388,632$ is 18.1 GB for the same accuracy requirements. This is almost 50 times more than that of the GPU code. Most of the CPU memory is used for storing the coefficient matrices, which if eliminated would cause the computation time of the CPU code to be significantly longer.

19.6 INTEGRATING THE GPU NGIM ALGORITHMS WITH ITERATIVE IE SOLVERS

We have coupled the CUDA NGIM accelerator with our volumetric and surface electric field IE solver. In these solvers the NGIM implemented on GPUs is run four times for each one of the three vector

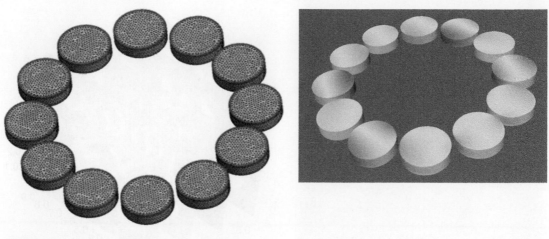

FIGURE 19.7

The mesh figure and solved flux density in 12 dielectric resonators (see color insert).

components of the vector potential and one scalar potential in Eq. (2). The solution was iterative via tfqmr iterative solver, which evaluates a single iteration with three field evaluations, totaling 12 scalar matrix-vector products per iteration. All other operations, which have a complexity of $O(N)$, are implemented in a Fortran CPU code. The solver can handle a large scattering problem very efficiently. All results in this section are obtained on an inexpensive desktop with an Intel i7-920 CPU operating at 2.66 GHz and an NVIDIA GTX 280.

Figure 19.7 demonstrates the performance of our general-purpose volume integral equation solver accelerated with NGIM and GPUs. The figure shows the color map of the electric flux density distribution in an array of single-mode optical resonators. Each resonator is a cylinder of a diameter of 200 nm and a height of 50 nm. The number of resonators is 12. The resonators are arranged in a circle with the smallest distance between the resonators of approximately 25 nm. The whole structure was meshed with a tetrahedral mesh of 201,958 elements. The structure was excited by a y-polarized plane wave propagating in the x-direction with the free-space wavelength of $1\,\mu m$. The total computational time of the simulation was 81 sec. The simulation was completed in 17 iterations with 4.7 sec per iteration. The preprocessing time was 4.7 sec.

Figure 19.8 demonstrates the performance of our surface integral equation solver. The figure shows the structure and the equivalent current distribution on a structure comprising 4 perforated films, which is excited by a plane wave propagating in the z-direction with the free-space wavelength of $1\,\mu m$. Each film is of size of $1 \times 1\,\mu m$, thickness of 20 nm, and is made of gold with assumed Drude model for permittivity. The films are modeled via their corresponding surface impedance, which is taken into account in the IE. This structure supports plasmonic resonances due to the interactions between the holes and between the plates. Respectively, the current exhibits bright spots. Because of the plasmonic resonances, the structure needs to be discretized densely. The number of unknowns in this example was above $N = 500,000$. There were 300 iterations to converge. The total time for a single iteration on a GTX GeForce 280 was 5 secs. This time was dominated by the local operations running on the CPU, whereas the time of the N to N superposition evaluated via NGIM on GPUs was only 0.5 second, i.e., 10% of the total time.

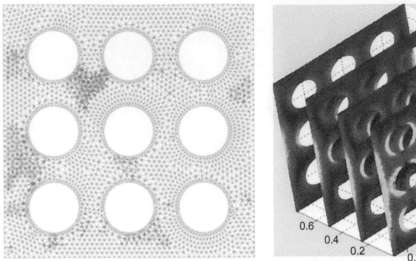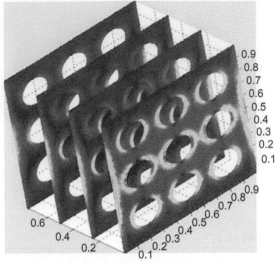

FIGURE 19.8

The mesh figure and solved current distributions on 4 parallel plates (see color insert).

The resulted computational performance of the volume and surface solvers on GPUs is much smaller than that corresponding to the same solvers running on a CPU. It is also compares favorably to many other results reported for similar structures.

19.7 FUTURE DIRECTIONS

Our future work will focus on the following directions. First, we will port the entire electromagnetic solver to the GPU platform. This step will result in a faster and more robust code. Second, we will improve and extend the NGIM implementations. In particular, we will incorporate higher order interpolations to result in better error control. Because of the massive parallelization, the computational time of the code with higher order interpolations will not be significantly different as compared with the times quoted here. However, the GPU-CPU speed-ups will be more significant as the CPU time for higher order interpolations is noticeably larger. Second, we will improve the way the grids are constructed. In the current version of the code, the grids are constructed for all directions in space. In the future codes, the grids will be constructed only around the structure of interest, thus reducing the computational time. Third, we will implement the code in heterogeneous systems with multiple nodes comprising multiple GPUs. This will involve using MPI and Open-MP to parallelize across multiple GPUs. It should be mentioned that we also use the NGIM (assuming a static kernel with $k_0 = 0$) to accelerate micromagnetic solvers and achieve a very high overall performance of the micromagnetic codes [8, 9].

References

[1] A.F. Peterson, S.L. Ray, R. Mittra, Computational Methods for Electromagnetics, IEEE Press, New York, 1998.

[2] R.G. Belleman, J. Bdorf, S.F. Portegies Zwart, High performance direct gravitational N-body simulations on graphics processing units II: an implementation in CUDA, New Astron. 13 (2008) 103–112.

[3] J.E. Stone, J.C. Phillips, P.L. Freddolino, D.J. Hardy, L.G. Trabuco, K. Schulten, Accelerating molecular modeling applications with graphics processors, J. Comput. Chem. 28 (2007) 2618–2640.

[4] S. Peng, Z. Nie, Acceleration of the method of moments calculations by using graphics processing units, IEEE Transa. Antennas Propag. 56 (2008) 2130–2133.

[5] L. Greengard, V. Rokhlin, A fast algorithm for particle simulations, J. Comput. Phys. 73 (1987) 325–348.

[6] V. Rokhlin, Rapid solution of integral equations of scattering theory in two dimensions, J. Comput. Phys. 86 (1990) 414–439.

[7] L. Greengard, J. Huang, V. Rokhlin, S. Wandzura, Accelerating fast multipole methods for the Helmholtz equation at low frequencies, IEEE Comput. Sci. Eng. 5 (1998) 32–38.

[8] S. Li, B. Livshitz, V. Lomakin, Graphics processing unit accelerated O(N) micromagnetic solver, IEEE Trans. Magn. 46 (2010) 2373–2375.

[9] R. Chang, S. Li, M. Lubarda, B. Livshitz, V. Lomakin, FastMag: Fast micromagnetic solver for large-scale simulations, J. Appl. Phys. 109 (2011) 07D358.

[10] V. Jandhyala, E. Michielssen, B. Shanker, W.C. Chew, A combined steepest descent-fast multipole algorithm for the analysis of three-dimensional scattering by rough surfaces, IEEE Trans. Geosci. Remote Sens. 36 (1998) 738–748.

[11] H. Cheng, L. Greengard, V. Rokhlin, A fast adaptive multipole algorithm in three dimensions, J. Comput. Phys. 155 (1999) 468–498.

[12] G. Brown, T.C. Schulthess, D.M. Apalkov, P.B. Visscher, Flexible fast multipole method for magnetic simulations, IEEE Trans. Magn. 40 (2004) 2146–2148.

[13] H.W. Cheng, W.Y. Crutchfield, Z. Gimbutas, L.F. Greengard, J.F. Ethridge, J.F. Huang, et al., A wideband fast multipole method for the Helmholtz equation in three dimensions, J. Comput. Phys. 216 (2006) 300–325.

[14] B. Shanker, H. Huang, Accelerated Cartesian expansions — A fast method for computing of potentials of the form R-[nu] for all real [nu], J. Comput. Phys. 226 (2007) 732–753.

[15] E. Bleszynski, M. Bleszynski, T. Jaroszewicz, AIM: adaptive integral method for solving large-scale electromagnetic scattering and radiation problems, Radio Sci. 31 (1996) 1225–1251.

[16] J.R. Phillips, J.K. White, A precorrected-FFT method for electrostatic analysis of complicated 3-D structures, IEEE Trans. Comput. Aided Des. Integr. Circuits Sys. 16 (1997) 1059–1072.

[17] A.E. Yilmaz, J. Jian-Ming, E. Michielssen, Time domain adaptive integral method for surface integral equations, IEEE Trans. Antennas Propag. 52 (2004) 2692–2708.

[18] H. Bagci, A. Yilmaz, V. Lomakin, E. Michielssen, Fast solution of mixed-potential time-domain integral equations for half-space environments, IEEE Trans. Geosci. Remote Sens. 43 (2005) 269–279.

[19] W. Hackbusch, B. Khoromskij, A sparse matrix arithmetic based on H-matrices. Part I: Introduction to H-matrices, Computing 62 (1999) 89–108.

[20] W. Hackbusch, B. Khoromskij, A sparse H-matrix arithmetic. Part II: Application to multi-dimensional problems, Computing 64 (2000) 203–225.

[21] W. Chai, D. Jian, An H-Matrix-based method for reducing the complexity of integral-equation-based solutions of electromagnetic problems, in: Presented at the IEEE International Symposium on Antennas and Propagation, San Diego, CA, 2008.

[22] W. Chai, D. Jian, An H2-Matrix-based integral-equation solver of reduced complexity and controlled accuracy for solving electrodynamic problems, IEEE Trans. Antennas Propag. 57 (2009) 3147–3159.

[23] A. Boag, E. Michielssen, A. Brandt, Nonuniform polar grid algorithm for fast field evaluation, IEEE Antennas Wirel. Propag. Lett. 1 (2002) 142–145.

[24] A. Boag, U. Shemer, R. Kastner, Hybrid absorbing boundary conditions based on fast non-uniform grid integration for non-convex scatterers, Microw. Opt. Technol. Lett. 43 (2004) 102–106.

[25] A. Boag, B. Livshitz, Adaptive nonuniform-grid (NG) algorithm for fast capacitance extraction, IEEE Trans. Microw. Theory Tech. 54 (2006) 3565–3570.

[26] A. Boag, V. Lomakin, E. Michielssen, Nonuniform grid time domain (NGTD) algorithm for fast evaluation of transient wave fields, IEEE Trans. Antennas Propag. 54 (2006) 1943–1951.

[27] B. Livshitz, A. Boag, H.N. Bertram, V. Lomakin, Nonuniform grid algorithm for fast calculation of magnetostatic interactions in micromagnetics, J. Appl. Phys. 105 (7) (2009) 07D541.

[28] J. Meng, A. Boag, V. Lomakin, E. Michielssen, A multilevel Cartesian non-uniform grid time domain algorithm, J. Comput. Phys. 229 (22) (2010) 8430–8444, ISSN 0021-9991, doi: 10.1016/j.jcp.2010.07.026.

[29] N.A. Gumerov, R. Duraiswami, Fast multipole methods on graphics processors, J. Comput. Phys. 227 (2008) 8290–8313.

[30] J. Mahaffey, K. Sertel, J.L. Volakis, On the implementation of the fast-iterative solvers on graphic processor units, in: Presented at the 2010 National Radio Science Meeting, Boulder, CO, 2010.

[31] M. Cwikla, J. Aronsson, V. Okhmatovski, Low-frequency MLFMA on graphics processors, IEEE Antennas Wirel. Propag. Lett. 9 (2010) 8–11.

[32] S. Li, B. Livshitz, V. Lomakin, Fast evaluation of Helmholtz potential on graphics processing units (GPUs), J. Comput. Phys. 229 (2010) 8430–8444.

[33] NVIDIA, CUDA Compute Unified Device Architecture Programming Guide, V2.3, Santa Clara, CA, 2009.

[34] A. Brodtkorb, E.C. Dyken, T.R. Hagen, J.M. Hjelmervik, O.O. Storaasli, State-of-the-art in heterogeneous computing, Sci. Program. 18 (2010) 1–33.

STATE OF GPU COMPUTING IN INTERACTIVE PHYSICS AND AI

SECTION

4

Interactive Physics and AI for Games and Engineering Simulation

Richard Tonge (NVIDIA)

STATE OF GPU COMPUTING IN INTERACTIVE PHYSICS AND AI

Interactive physics and artificial intelligence have diverse applications in fields from mechanical engineering and medical training to video games. All involve a set of discrete physical objects interacting with each other and with the static environment. As the number of simulated objects and the level of geometric detail per object increases, the computation resources required increase as does the level of exploitable parallelism. Efficiency is especially important when the application requires real-time simulation at interactive rates. As a result, such simulations benefit from the high throughput and bandwidth available on GPUs. Implementing these algorithms on GPU can be challenging however, as these simulations are usually sparse, have varying workload per object, and require irregular data accesses. Although the use of GPUs in this area is a fairly recent development, a large amount of progress has already been made, examples of which can be found in this section.

I expect that the demand for computation power will continue to increase for a long time. Game players would like virtual worlds to have the freedom and detail of the real world. Mechanical engineers would like to simulate in real time the frictional interaction of complex mechanisms in environments with billions of discrete parts, such as tank tracks on sand. Surgical trainers would like to be able to visually simulate the human body at a realistic level of detail. At the same time, simulations will become more widely used, often on mobile devices, requiring maximum performance per dollar and performance per watt. With these scaling demands, I expect the GPU to become widely used in this area.

IN THIS SECTION

Chapter 20 by Negrut et al. describes a simulator for large numbers of rigid bodies interacting through frictional contact. Like previous methods used in engineering and games, the method in this chapter models the dynamics as a complementarity problem. This chapter extends the model to utilize a continuous friction cone and describes its efficient implementation on the GPU.

Chapter 21 by Allard et al. describes a simulator for deformable bodies. The method is unconditionally stable, and only generates elements of the system matrix as needed, reducing memory and bandwidth consumption. It is also a good example of how a scatter operation can be turned into a gather operation to increase performance on the GPU.

Chapter 22 by Erra et al. describes a path planning method that could be used in video games, AI, or robotics applications. The method is a GPU implementation of the Real Time A* algorithm that operates with a small memory footprint per thread.

Solving Large Multibody Dynamics Problems on the GPU

20

Dan Negrut, Alessandro Tasora, Mihai Anitescu,
Hammad Mazhar, Toby Heyn, and Arman Pazouki

This paper describes an approach for the dynamic simulation of large collections of rigid bodies interacting through millions of frictional contacts and bilateral mechanical constraints. Thanks to the massive parallelism available on modern GPUs, we are able to simulate sand, granular materials, and other complex physical scenarios with one order of magnitude speed-up when compared to a sequential CPU–based implementation of the discussed algorithms.

20.1 INTRODUCTION, PROBLEM STATEMENT, AND CONTEXT

The ability to efficiently and accurately simulate the dynamics of rigid multibody systems is relevant in computer-aided engineering design, virtual reality, video games, and computer graphics. Devices composed of rigid bodies interacting through frictional contacts and mechanical joints pose numerical solution challenges because of the discontinuous nature of the motion. Consequently, even relatively small systems composed of a few hundred parts and constraints may require significant computational effort. More complex scenarios such as vehicles running on pebbles and sand as in Figures 20.1 and 20.2, soil and rock dynamics, and flow and packing of granular materials are particularly challenging and prone to very long simulation times. Results reported in [3] indicate that the most popular rigid body software for engineering simulation, which uses an approach based on the so-called Discrete Element Method, runs into significant difficulties when handling problems involving thousands of contact events.

Until recently, the high cost of parallel computing limited the analysis of such large systems to a small number of research groups. This is rapidly changing owing in large part to general-purpose computing on the GPU. Another example of commercially available rigid body dynamics software is NVIDIA's PhysX [4]. This software is commonly used in real-time applications where performance is the primary goal. The requirements of our application placed somewhat less emphasis on efficiency and instead prioritized generality, suitability for GPU implementation, numerical accuracy, and an open source code development philosophy [1].

Unlike the so-called penalty or regularization methods, where the frictional interaction can be represented by a collection of stiff springs combined with damping elements that act at the interface of the two bodies [5], the approach embraced here draws on time-stepping procedures producing weak solutions of the differential variational inequality (DVI) problem, which describes the time evolution of

FIGURE 20.1

Chrono::Engine [1] simulation of a complex, rigid multibody mechanism with contacts and joints (see color insert).

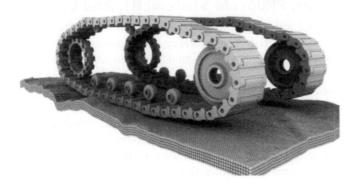

FIGURE 20.2

Chrono::Engine simulation of a tracked vehicle on a granular soil. The GPU was used for both dynamics and collision detection between tracks, sprockets, and pebbles [2].

rigid bodies with impact, contact, friction, and bilateral constraints. Early numerical methods based on DVI formulations can be traced back to the early 1980s and 1990s [6–8]. Recent approaches based on time-stepping schemes have included both acceleration-force linear complementarity problem (LCP) approaches [9, 10] and velocity-impulse, LCP-based time-stepping methods [11–13]. The LCPs, obtained as a result of the introduction of inequalities accounting for nonpenetration conditions in time-stepping schemes, coupled with a polyhedral approximation of the friction cone, must be solved at each time step in order to determine the system state configuration as well as the Lagrange multipliers representing the reaction forces [7, 11]. If the simulation entails a large number of contacts and rigid bodies, as is the case for granular materials, the computational burden of classical LCP solvers can become significant. Indeed, a well-known class of numerical methods for LCPs based on *simplex methods*, also known as *direct* or *pivoting* methods [14], may exhibit exponential worst-case complexity [15]. Moreover, the three-dimensional Coulomb friction case leads to a nonlinear complementarity problem (NCP). The use of a polyhedral approximation to transform the NCP into an LCP introduces unwanted anisotropy in friction cones and significantly augments the size of the numerical problem [11, 12].

In order to circumvent the limitations imposed by the use of classical LCP solvers and the limited accuracy associated with polyhedral approximations of the friction cone, a parallel fixed-point iteration method with projection on a convex set has been developed [16]. The method is based on a time-stepping formulation that solves at every step a cone-constrained quadratic optimization problem [17]. The time-stepping scheme has been proved to converge in a measure differential inclusion sense to the solution of the original continuous-time DVI. This paper illustrates how this problem can be solved in parallel by exploiting the parallel computational resources available on NVIDIA's GPU cards.

20.2 CORE METHOD

The formulation of the equations of motion, that is, the equations that govern the time evolution of a multibody system, is based on the so-called absolute, or Cartesian, representation of the attitude of each rigid body in the system. The state of the system is denoted by the generalized positions $\mathbf{q} = \left[\mathbf{r}_1^T, \epsilon_1^T, \ldots, \mathbf{r}_{n_b}^T, \epsilon_{n_b}^T \right]^T \in \mathbb{R}^{7n_b}$ and their time derivatives $\dot{\mathbf{q}} = \left[\dot{\mathbf{r}}_1^T, \dot{\epsilon}_1^T, \ldots, \dot{\mathbf{r}}_{n_b}^T, \dot{\epsilon}_{n_b}^T \right]^T \in \mathbb{R}^{7n_b}$, where n_b is the number of bodies, $\mathbf{r}_j$ is the absolute position of the center of mass of the jth body, and the quaternions (Euler parameters) ϵ_j are used to represent rotation and to avoid singularities. Instead of using quaternion derivatives in $\dot{\mathbf{q}}$, it is more advantageous to work with angular velocities expressed in the local (body-attached) reference frames; in other words, the method described will use the vector of generalized velocities $\mathbf{v} = \left[\dot{\mathbf{r}}_1^T, \overline{\omega}_1^T, \ldots, \dot{\mathbf{r}}_{n_b}^T, \overline{\omega}_{n_b}^T \right]^T \in \mathbb{R}^{6n_b}$. Note that the generalized velocity can be easily obtained as $\dot{\mathbf{q}} = \mathbf{L}(\mathbf{q})\mathbf{v}$, where $\mathbf{L}$ is a linear mapping that transforms each $\overline{\omega}_i$ into the corresponding quaternion derivative $\dot{\epsilon}_i$ by means of the linear algebra formula $\dot{\epsilon}_i = \frac{1}{2}\mathbf{G}^T(\mathbf{q})\overline{\omega}_i$, with 3×4 matrix $\mathbf{G}(\mathbf{q})$ as defined in [18]. We denote by $\mathbf{f}^A(t, \mathbf{q}, \mathbf{v})$ the set of applied, or external, generalized forces.

Bilateral constraints represent kinematic pairs, for example spherical, prismatic or revolute joints, and can be expressed as algebraic equations constraining the relative position of two bodies. Assuming a set $\mathcal{B}$ of constraints is present in the system, they lead to the scalar equations $\Psi_i(\mathbf{q}, t) = 0$, $i \in \mathcal{B}$. Assuming smoothness of constraint manifold, $\Psi_i(\mathbf{q}, t)$ can be differentiated to obtain the Jacobian $\nabla_q \Psi_i = [\partial \Psi_i / \partial \mathbf{q}]^T$. The notation $\nabla \Psi_i^T = \nabla_q \Psi_i^T \mathbf{L}(\mathbf{q})$ will be used in what follows.

Given a large number of rigid bodies with different shapes, modern collision-detection algorithms are able to find efficiently a set of contact points, that is, points where a *gap function* $\Phi(\mathbf{q})$ can be defined for each pair of near-enough shape features. Where defined, such a gap function must satisfy the nonpenetration condition $\Phi(\mathbf{q}) \geq 0$ for all contact points.

When a contact i is active, that is, $\Phi_i(\mathbf{q}) = 0$, a normal force and a tangential friction force act on each of the two bodies at the contact point. In terms of notation, $\mathcal{A}$ will denote the set of all active contacts for a given configuration $\mathbf{q}$ of the system at time t_l. In fact, $\mathcal{A}(\mathbf{q}, \epsilon)$ includes even potential contacts between bodies that are at t_l within a distance ϵ of each other and might collide during the time step from t_l to t_{l+1}. If no collision occurs, the algorithm will lead to zero normal/tangential forces for inactive collisions that were conservatively added to $\mathcal{A}(\mathbf{q}, \epsilon)$.

We use the classical Coulomb friction model to define these forces [12]. If the contact is not active, that is, $\Phi_i(\mathbf{q}) > 0$, no contact or friction forces exist. This implies that the mathematical description of the model leads to a complementarity problem [11]. Consider two bodies A and B in contact. Let $\mathbf{n}_i$ be the normal at the contact pointing toward the exterior of the body of lower index, which by convention is considered to be body A. Let $\mathbf{u}_i$ and $\mathbf{w}_i$ be two vectors in the contact plane such that $\mathbf{n}_i, \mathbf{u}_i, \mathbf{w}_i \in \mathbb{R}^3$ are mutually orthonormal vectors. The frictional contact force is impressed on the system by means of multipliers $\widehat{\gamma}_{i,n} \geq 0$, $\widehat{\gamma}_{i,u}$, and $\widehat{\gamma}_{i,w}$, which lead to the normal component of the force $\mathbf{F}_{i,N} = \widehat{\gamma}_{i,n}\mathbf{n}_i$ and the tangential component of the force $\mathbf{F}_{i,T} = \widehat{\gamma}_{i,u}\mathbf{u}_i + \widehat{\gamma}_{i,w}\mathbf{w}_i$. The Coulomb model is expressed by using the maximum dissipation principle:

$$\left(\widehat{\gamma}_{i,u}, \widehat{\gamma}_{i,w}\right) = \underset{\sqrt{\widehat{\gamma}_{i,u}^2 + \widehat{\gamma}_{i,w}^2} \leq \mu_i \widehat{\gamma}_{i,n}}{\operatorname{argmin}} \mathbf{v}_{i,T}^T \left(\widehat{\gamma}_{i,u}\mathbf{u}_i + \widehat{\gamma}_{i,w}\mathbf{w}_i\right). \tag{1}$$

The time evolution of the dynamical system is governed by the following differential variational inequality [16]:

$$\dot{\mathbf{q}} = \mathbf{L}(\mathbf{q})\mathbf{v}$$

$$\mathbf{M}\dot{\mathbf{v}} = \mathbf{f}(t, \mathbf{q}, \mathbf{v}) + \sum_{i \in \mathcal{B}} \widehat{\gamma}_{i,b} \nabla \Psi_i + \sum_{i \in \mathcal{A}} \left(\widehat{\gamma}_{i,n} \mathbf{D}_{i,n} + \widehat{\gamma}_{i,u} \mathbf{D}_{i,u} + \widehat{\gamma}_{i,w} \mathbf{D}_{i,w}\right)$$

$$i \in \mathcal{B} : \Psi_i(\mathbf{q}, t) = 0$$

$$i \in \mathcal{A} : \widehat{\gamma}_{i,n} \geq 0 \perp \Phi_i(\mathbf{q}) \geq 0, \quad \text{and} \tag{2}$$

$$\left(\widehat{\gamma}_{i,u}, \widehat{\gamma}_{i,w}\right) = \underset{\mu_i \widehat{\gamma}_{i,n} \geq \sqrt{\widehat{\gamma}_{i,u}^2 + \widehat{\gamma}_{i,w}^2}}{\operatorname{argmin}} \mathbf{v}^T \left(\widehat{\gamma}_{i,u} \mathbf{D}_{i,u} + \widehat{\gamma}_{i,w} \mathbf{D}_{i,w}\right).$$

The tangent space generators $\mathbf{D}_i = [\mathbf{D}_{i,n}, \mathbf{D}_{i,u}, \mathbf{D}_{i,w}] \in \mathbb{R}^{6n_b \times 3}$ are sparse and are defined given a pair of contacting bodies A and B as

$$\mathbf{D}_i^T = \begin{bmatrix} \mathbf{0} & \cdots & -\mathbf{A}_{i,p}^T & \mathbf{A}_{i,p}^T \mathbf{A}_A \widetilde{\mathbf{s}}_{i,A} & \mathbf{0} & \cdots \\ \mathbf{0} & \cdots & \mathbf{A}_{i,p}^T & -\mathbf{A}_{i,p}^T \mathbf{A}_B \widetilde{\mathbf{s}}_{i,B} & \mathbf{0} & \cdots \end{bmatrix}, \tag{3}$$

where $\mathbf{A}_A$ is the orientation matrix associated with body A, $\mathbf{A}_{i,p} = [\mathbf{n}_i, \mathbf{u}_i, \mathbf{w}_i]$ is the $\mathbb{R}^{3 \times 3}$ matrix of the local coordinates of the ith contact, the vectors $\bar{\mathbf{s}}_{i,A}$ and $\bar{\mathbf{s}}_{i,B}$ are the contact point positions in body coordinates. A tilde $\widetilde{\mathbf{x}}$ over a vector $\mathbf{x} \in \mathbb{R}^3$ represents the skew symmetric matrix associated with the outer product of two vectors [18].

20.3 THE TIME-STEPPING SCHEME

Given a position $\mathbf{q}^{(l)}$ and velocity $\mathbf{v}^{(l)}$ at the time step $t^{(l)}$, the numerical solution is found at the new time step $t^{(l+1)} = t^{(l)} + h$ by solving the following optimization problem with equilibrium constraints [19]:

$$\mathbf{M}(\mathbf{v}^{(l+1)} - \mathbf{v}^{(l)}) = h\mathbf{f}(t^{(l)}, \mathbf{q}^{(l)}, \mathbf{v}^{(l)}) + \sum_{i \in \mathcal{B}} \gamma_{i,b} \nabla \Psi_i + \sum_{i \in \mathcal{A}} \left(\gamma_{i,n} \mathbf{D}_{i,n} + \gamma_{i,u} \mathbf{D}_{i,u} + \gamma_{i,w} \mathbf{D}_{i,w} \right), \quad (4)$$

$$i \in \mathcal{B} \ : \ \frac{1}{h} \Psi_i(\mathbf{q}^{(l)}, t) + \nabla \Psi_i^T \mathbf{v}^{(l+1)} + \frac{\partial \Psi_i}{\partial t} = 0 \quad (5)$$

$$i \in \mathcal{A} \ : \ 0 \le \frac{1}{h} \Phi_i(\mathbf{q}^{(l)}) + \mathbf{D}_{i,n}^T \mathbf{v}^{(l+1)} \perp \gamma_n^i \ge 0, \quad (6)$$

$$(\gamma_{i,u}, \gamma_{i,w}) = \operatorname*{argmin}_{\mu_i \gamma_{i,n} \ge \sqrt{\gamma_{i,u}^2 + \gamma_{i,w}^2}} \mathbf{v}^{(l+1),T} \left(\gamma_{i,u} \mathbf{D}_{i,u} + \gamma_{i,w} \mathbf{D}_{i,w} \right) \quad (7)$$

$$\mathbf{q}^{(l+1)} = \mathbf{q}^{(l)} + h\mathbf{L}(\mathbf{q}^{(l)})\mathbf{v}^{(l+1)}. \quad (8)$$

Here, γ_s represents the constraint impulse of a contact constraint; that is, $\gamma_s = h\widehat{\gamma}_s$, for $s = n, u, w$. The $\frac{1}{h}\Phi_i(\mathbf{q}^{(l)})$ term achieves constraint stabilization; its effect is discussed in [20]. Similarly, the term $\frac{1}{h}\Phi_i(\mathbf{q}^{(l)})$ achieves stabilization for bilateral constraints. The scheme converges to the solution of a measure differential inclusion [17] when the step size $h \to 0$.

The proposed approach casts the problem as a monotone optimization problem through a relaxation over the complementarity constraints, replacing Eq. (6) with

$$i \in \mathcal{A}: 0 \le \frac{1}{h} \Phi_i(\mathbf{q}^{(l)}) + \mathbf{D}_{i,n}^T \mathbf{v}^{(l+1)} - \mu_i \sqrt{(\mathbf{v}^T \mathbf{D}_{i,u})^2 + (\mathbf{v}^T \mathbf{D}_{i,w})^2} \perp \gamma_n^i \ge 0. \quad (12)$$

The solution of the modified time-stepping scheme will approach the solution of the same measure differential inclusion for $h \to 0$ as the original scheme [17], yet, in some situations, for large h, μ, or relative velocity $\mathbf{v}^{(l+1)}$; i.e., when not in an asymptotic regime, this relaxation can introduce motion oscillations. It was shown in [16] that the modified scheme is a cone complementarity problem (CCP), which can be solved efficiently by an iterative numerical method that relies on projected contractive maps. Omitting for brevity some of the details discussed in [16, 21], we note that the algorithm makes use of the following vectors:

$$\widetilde{\mathbf{k}} \equiv \mathbf{M}\mathbf{v}^{(l)} + h\mathbf{f}(t^{(l)}, \mathbf{q}^{(l)}, \mathbf{v}^{(l)}) \quad (9)$$

$$\mathbf{b}_i \equiv \left\{ \tfrac{1}{h} \Phi_i(\mathbf{q}^{(l)}), 0, 0 \right\}^T \quad i \in \mathcal{A}, \quad (10)$$

$$b_i \equiv \tfrac{1}{h} \Psi_i(\mathbf{q}^{(l)}, t) + \tfrac{\partial \Psi_i}{\partial t}, \quad i \in \mathcal{B}. \quad (11)$$

The solution, in terms of dual variables of the CCP (the multipliers), is obtained by iterating the following contraction maps until convergence [19]:

$$\forall i \in \mathcal{A} : \gamma_i^{r+1} = \Pi_{\Upsilon_i} \left[\gamma_i^r - \omega \eta_i \left(D_i^T \mathbf{v}^r + \mathbf{b}_i \right) \right] \tag{12}$$

$$\forall i \in \mathcal{B} : \gamma_i^{r+1} = \Pi_{\Upsilon_i} \left[\gamma_i^r - \omega \eta_i \left(\nabla \Psi_i^T \mathbf{v}^r + b_i \right) \right]. \tag{13}$$

At each iteration r, before repeating Eqs. (12) and (13), also the primal variables (the velocities) are updated as

$$\mathbf{v}^{r+1} = \mathbf{M}^{-1} \left(\sum_{z \in \mathcal{A}} D_z \gamma_z^{r+1} + \sum_{z \in \mathcal{B}} \nabla \Psi_z \gamma_z^{r+1} + \tilde{\mathbf{k}} \right). \tag{14}$$

Note that the superscript $(l + 1)$ was omitted. Interested readers are referred to [16] for a proof of the convergence of this method.

20.4 ALGORITHMS, IMPLEMENTATIONS, AND EVALUATIONS

The GPU dynamics solver data structures are implemented as large arrays (*buffers*) to match the execution model associated with NVIDIA's CUDA. Four main buffers are used: the contacts buffer, the constraints buffer, the reduction buffer, and the bodies buffer. The data structure for the contacts has been mapped into columns of four floats. Each contact will reference its two touching bodies through the two pointers B_A and B_B, in the fourth and seventh rows of the contact data structure. There is no need to store the entire $\mathbf{D}_i$ matrix for the ith contact because it has zero entries for most of its part, except for the two 12×3 blocks corresponding to the coordinates of the two bodies in contact. In fact, once the velocities of the two bodies $\dot{\mathbf{r}}_{A_i}$, ω_{A_i} and $\dot{\mathbf{r}}_{B_i}$, ω_{B_i} have been fetched, the product $\mathbf{D}_i^T \mathbf{v}^r$ in Eq. (12) can be performed as

$$\mathbf{D}_i^T \mathbf{v}^r = \mathbf{D}_{i,v_A}^T \dot{\mathbf{r}}_{A_i} + \mathbf{D}_{i,\omega_A}^T \omega_{A_i} + \mathbf{D}_{i,v_B}^T \dot{\mathbf{r}}_{B_i} + \mathbf{D}_{i,\omega_B}^T \omega_{B_i} \tag{15}$$

with the adoption of the following 3×3 matrices:

$$\begin{aligned} \mathbf{D}_{i,v_A}^T &= -\mathbf{A}_{i,p}^T, & \mathbf{D}_{i,\omega_A}^T &= \mathbf{A}_{i,p}^T \mathbf{A}_A \tilde{\mathbf{s}}_{i,A} \\ \mathbf{D}_{i,v_B}^T &= \mathbf{A}_{i,p}^T, & \mathbf{D}_{i,\omega_B}^T &= -\mathbf{A}_{i,p}^T \mathbf{A}_B \tilde{\mathbf{s}}_{i,B}. \end{aligned} \tag{16}$$

Since $\mathbf{D}_{i,v_A}^T = -\mathbf{D}_{i,v_B}^T$, there is no need to store both matrices. Therefore, in each contact data structure only a matrix $\mathbf{D}_{i,v_{AB}}^T$ is stored, which is then used with opposite signs for each of the two bodies. The velocity update vector $\Delta \mathbf{v}_i$, needed for the sum in Eq. (14) also is sparse: it can be decomposed into small subvectors. Specifically, given the masses and the inertia tensors of the two bodies m_{A_i}, m_{B_i} and $\mathbf{J}_{A_i}$, $\mathbf{J}_{B_i}$, the term $\Delta \mathbf{v}_i$ will be computed and stored in four parts as follows:

$$\begin{aligned} \Delta \dot{\mathbf{r}}_{A_i} &= m_{A_i}^{-1} \mathbf{D}_{i,v_A} \Delta \gamma_i^{r+1}, & \Delta \omega_{A_i} &= \mathbf{J}_{A_i}^{-1} \mathbf{D}_{i,\omega_A} \Delta \gamma_i^{r+1} \\ \Delta \dot{\mathbf{r}}_{B_i} &= m_{B_i}^{-1} \mathbf{D}_{i,v_B} \Delta \gamma_i^{r+1}, & \Delta \omega_{B_i} &= \mathbf{J}_{B_i}^{-1} \mathbf{D}_{i,\omega_B} \Delta \gamma_i^{r+1}. \end{aligned} \tag{17}$$

Note that those four parts of the $\Delta \mathbf{v}_i$ terms are not stored in the ith contact data structure or in the data structure of the two referenced bodies (because multiple contacts may refer the same body, they would overwrite the same memory position). These velocity updates are instead stored in the reduction buffer used to efficiently perform the summation in Eq. (14).

The constraints buffer is based on a similar concept. Jacobians $\nabla \Psi_i$ of all scalar constraints are stored in a sparse format, each corresponding to four rows $\nabla \Psi_{i,v_A}$, $\nabla \Psi_{i,\omega_A}$, $\nabla \Psi_{i,v_B}$, $\nabla \Psi_{i,\omega_B}$. Therefore the product $\nabla \Psi_i^T \mathbf{v}^r$ in Eq. (13) can be performed as the scalar value $\nabla \Psi_i^T \mathbf{v}^r = \nabla \Psi_{i,v_A}^T \dot{\mathbf{r}}_{A_i} + \nabla \Psi_{i,\omega_A}^T \omega_{A_i} + \nabla \Psi_{i,v_B}^T \dot{\mathbf{r}}_{B_i} + \nabla \Psi_{i,\omega_B}^T \omega_{B_i}$. Also, the four parts of the sparse vector $\Delta \mathbf{v}_i$ can be computed and stored as

$$\Delta \dot{\mathbf{r}}_{A_i} = m_{A_i}^{-1} \nabla \Psi_{i,v_A} \Delta \gamma_i^{r+1}, \quad \Delta \omega_{A_i} = \mathbf{J}_{A_i}^{-1} \nabla \Psi_{i,\omega_A} \Delta \gamma_i^{r+1}$$
$$\Delta \dot{\mathbf{r}}_{B_i} = m_{B_i}^{-1} \nabla \Psi_{i,v_B} \Delta \gamma_i^{r+1}, \quad \Delta \omega_{B_i} = \mathbf{J}_{B_i}^{-1} \nabla \Psi_{i,\omega_B} \Delta \gamma_i^{r+1}. \tag{18}$$

Each body is represented by a data structure containing the state (velocity and position), the mass moments of inertia and mass values, and the external applied force $\mathbf{F}_j$ and torque $\mathbf{C}_j$. We store the inverse of the mass and inertias rather than their original values because the operation $\mathbf{M}^{-1} \mathbf{D}_i \Delta \gamma_i^{r+1}$ must be performed multiple times.

A parallelization of computations in Eq. (12) and Eq. (13) is easily implemented, by simply assigning one contact per thread (and, similarly, one constraint per thread). In fact the results of these computations would not overlap in memory, and two parallel threads will never need to write in the same memory location at the same time. These are the two most numerically intensive steps of the CCP solver, called the *CCP contact iteration kernel* and the *CCP constraint iteration kernel*.

However, the sums in Eq. (14) cannot be performed with embarrassingly-parallel implementations: it may happen that two or more contacts need to add their velocity updates to the same rigid body. A possible approach to overcome this problem is presented in [22]. We adopted an alternative method, with higher generality, based on the *parallel segmented scan* algorithm [23] that operates on an intermediate reduction buffer; this method sums the values in the buffer using a binary-tree approach that keeps the computational load well balanced among the many thread processors.

The following pseudocode shows the sequence of main computational phases at each time step, for the most part executed as parallel kernels on the GPU.

Algorithm 1: Time Stepping Using GPU

1: (*GPU, see [24, 25]*) Perform collision detection between bodies, obtaining n_A possible contact points within a distance δ, as contact positions $s_{i,A}$, $s_{i,B}$ on the two touching surfaces, and normals $\mathbf{n}_i$.

2: (*GPU, body-parallel*) **Force kernel**. For each body, compute forces $\mathbf{f}(t^{(l)}, \mathbf{q}^{(l)}, \mathbf{v}^{(l)})$, if any (for example, gravity). Store these forces and torques into F_j and C_j.

3: (*GPU, contact-parallel*) **Contact preprocessing kernel**. For each contact, given contact normal and position, compute in place the matrices $\mathbf{D}_{i,v_A}^T$, $\mathbf{D}_{i,\omega_A}^T$, and $\mathbf{D}_{i,\omega_B}^T$. Then compute η_i and the contact residual $\mathbf{b}_i = \{\frac{1}{h} \Phi_i(\mathbf{q}), 0, 0\}^T$.

4: (*GPU, body-parallel*) **CCP force kernel**. For each body j, initialize body velocities: $\dot{\mathbf{r}}_j^{(l+1)} = h \, m_j^{-1} \mathbf{F}_j$ and $\omega_j^{(l+1)} = h \, \mathbf{J}_j^{-1} \mathbf{C}_j$.

(Continued)

Algorithm 1: (*Continued*)

5: (*GPU, contact-parallel*) **CCP contact iteration kernel**. For each contact i, do
$\gamma_i^{r+1} = \lambda \, \Pi_{\Upsilon_i} \left(\gamma_i^r - \omega \eta_i \left(\mathbf{D}_i^T \mathbf{v}^r + \mathbf{b}_i \right) \right) + (1-\lambda)\gamma_i^r$. Note that $\mathbf{D}_i^T \mathbf{v}^r$ is evaluated with sparse data, using
Eq. (15). Store $\Delta \gamma_i^{r+1} = \gamma_i^{r+1} - \gamma_i^r$ in the contact buffer. Compute sparse updates to the velocities of the
two connected bodies A and B, and store them in the $R_{i,A}$ and $R_{i,B}$ slots of the reduction buffer.

6: (*GPU, constraint-parallel*) **CCP constraint iteration kernel**. For each constraint i, do
$\gamma_i^{r+1} = \lambda \left(\gamma_i^r - \omega \eta_i \left(\nabla \Psi_i^T \mathbf{v}^r + b_i \right) \right) + (1-\lambda)\gamma_i^r$. Store $\Delta \gamma_i^{r+1} = \gamma_i^{r+1} - \gamma_i^r$ in the contact buffer. Compute
sparse updates to the velocities of the two connected bodies A and B, and store them in the $R_{i,A}$ and $R_{i,B}$ slots
of the reduction buffer.

7: (*GPU, reduction-slot-parallel*) **Segmented reduction kernel**. Sum all the $\Delta \dot{\mathbf{r}}_i$, $\Delta \omega_i$ terms belonging to the
same body, in the reduction buffer.

8: (*GPU, body-parallel*) **Body velocity updates kernel**. For each j body, add the cumulative velocity updates
that can be fetched from the reduction buffer, using the index R_j.

9: Repeat from step 5 until convergence or until number of CCP steps reached $r > r_{max}$.

10: (*GPU, body-parallel*) **Time integration kernel**. For each j body, perform time integration as $\mathbf{q}_j^{(l+1)} = \mathbf{q}_j^{(l)} + h \mathbf{L}(\mathbf{q}_j^{(l)})\mathbf{v}_j^{(l+1)}$.

11: (*Host, serial*) If needed, copy body, contact, and constraint data structures from the GPU to host memory.

20.5 FINAL EVALUATION

The GPU iterative solver outlined herein and the GPU collision detection, see [24, 25], have been
embedded in our C++ simulation software Chrono::Engine. We tested the GPU-based parallel method
with benchmark problems and compared it with the serial implementation in terms of efficiency.

For the results in Table 20.1, we simulated densely packed spheres that flow from a silo. The CPU
was an Intel Xeon 2.66 GHz; the GPU was an NVIDIA Tesla C1060. The simulation time increases
linearly with the number of bodies in the model. The GPU algorithm is at least one order of magnitude
faster than the serial algorithm.

The test of Figure 20.3 simulates 1 million rigid bodies inside a tank being shaken horizontally. This represents to date the largest multibody dynamics problem solved on one GPU card using
Chrono::Engine. The track system shown in Figure 20.2 was exercised on granular terrain that was
made up of more than 480,000 bodies.

A set of numerical experiments was carried out to gauge the efficiency of the parallel CD algorithm
developed [24, 25]. The reference used was the sequential CD implementation from Bullet Physics

Table 20.1 Benchmark Test of the GPU CCP Solver and GPU Collision Detection

Number of Bodies	CPU CCP [s]	GPU CCP [s]	Speedup CCP	Speedup CD
16,000	7.11	0.57	12.59	4.67
32,000	16.01	1.00	16.07	6.14
64,000	34.60	1.97	17.58	10.35
128,000	76.82	4.55	16.90	21.71

FIGURE 20.3

Light ball floating on 1 million rigid bodies moving around in a tank while interacting through friction and contact.

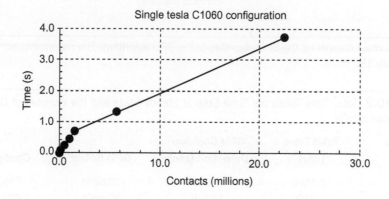

FIGURE 20.4

Collision time vs. contacts detected. This graph shows that when the algorithm is executed on a single GPU it scales linearly.

Engine [26]. The CPU used in this experiment (relevant for the Bullet implementation) was AMD Phenom II Black X4 940, a quad core 3.0-GHz processor with 16 GB of RAM. The GPU used was NVIDIA's Tesla C1060. The operating system used was the 64-bit version of Windows 7. Two scenarios were considered. The first scenario determined how many contacts a single GPU could determine before running out of memory. As Figure 20.4 shows, approximately 22 million contacts were determined in less than 4 seconds. The second scenario gauged the relative speed-up gained with respect to a serial implementation. The first test stopped when dealing with about 6 million contacts (see horizontal axis of Figure 20.5), when Bullet ran into memory management issues. Our specialized sphere based collision system running on the GPU was up to 180 times faster than Bullet's general purpose collision code running on the CPU. Specializing the collision detection code increased our opportunities for parallelization and optimization, so the speed-up was partly due to algorithm choice and partly due to the power of the GPU.

A final set of experiments was designed to illustrate the scaling of the parallel numerical solution and collision detection. The vehicle used to this end was the simulation of a cylindrical tank that had a constant height with the radius varying with the number of spheres added to the tank. Specifically, the number of spheres in the tank was increased with each simulation without increasing the fill-in depth

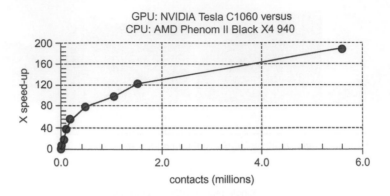

FIGURE 20.5

Overall speedup when comparing the CPU algorithm to the GPU algorithm. The maximum speed-up achieved was approximately 180 times.

Table 20.2 Total Time Taken per Time Step at Steady State and the Number of Contacts Associated with It

Objects [$\times 10^6$]	Total Time [sec]	GPU Collision Detection [sec]	GPU Solver	Contacts
0.2	12.1190	1.0758	10.5881	718,377
0.4	23.2806	1.9746	20.4606	1,403,784
0.6	35.0433	2.9785	30.7971	2,124,639
0.8	46.9516	4.0234	41.2297	2,838,832
1.0	58.1518	4.9473	51.1686	3,548,594

of the tank. Instead, the radius of the cylinder was increased for each simulation based on the number of spheres and their packing factor. Each test was run using an NVIDIA Tesla C1060 until the number of collisions and the compute time per solution time step reached steady state. The results presented in Table 20.2 and graphed in Figure 20.6 indicate that the overall algorithm scales linearly. Furthermore, the results suggest that the bulk of the computation at each time step was taken by the GPU dynamics solver, with a small amount of time taken up by the collision detection. These collision detection times are longer than the raw times presented earlier due to the pre- and post-processing required by the physics engine as it organizes data on the GPU for use between the solver and collision detection.

20.6 FUTURE DIRECTIONS

The GPU dynamics engine proposed is more than one order of magnitude faster than a previously developed sequential implementation. The largest GPU simulation run to date had approximately 1.1 million bodies. Two barriers prevented the simulation of larger systems. First, we exhausted the GPU

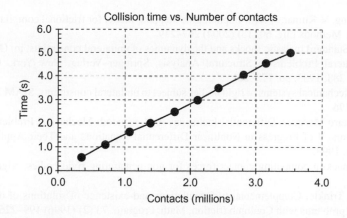

FIGURE 20.6

Scaling, collision time.

memory; second, we noticed a convergence stalling in the Gauss-Jacobi algorithm for CCP problems with more than 15 million variables. In order to address these aspects we are developing a distributed computing framework that leverages multiple GPUs, and we are investigating a minimal residual type Krylov method for the CCP solution. It is an open question whether adding a GPU sparse preconditioner would be advantageous in this case.

Acknowledgments

We would like to thank Richard Tonge for the substantial feedback and assistance he provided in generating this paper. Financial support for D. Negrut was provided in part by the National Science Foundation Award CMMI–0840442. Financial support for A. Tasora was provided in part by the Italian Ministry of Education under the PRIN grant 2007Z7K4ZB. Mihai Anitescu was supported by the Office of Advanced Scientific Computing Research, Office of Science, U.S. Department of Energy, under Contract DE-AC02-06CH11357. We thank NVIDIA and Microsoft for sponsoring our research programs in the area of high-performance computing.

References

[1] A. Tasora, Chrono: Engine, An Open Source Physics–Based Dynamics Simulation Engine, http://www .chronoengine.info, 2006 (accessed 01.08.11).

[2] T. Heyn, Simulation of Tracked Vehicles on Granular Terrain Leveraging GPU Computing, M.S. thesis, Department of Mechanical Engineering, University of Wisconsin–Madison, http://sbel.wisc.edu/documents/TobyHeynThesis_final.pdf, 2009 (accessed 01.08.11).

[3] J. Madsen, N. Pechdimaljian, D. Negrut, Penalty versus complementarity-based frictional contact of rigid bodies: A CPU time comparison, Technical Report TR-2007-06, Simulation-Based Engineering Lab, University of Wisconsin, Madison, 2007.

[4] PhysX.NVIDIA PhysX for Developers. http://developer.nvidia.com/object/physx.html, 2010 (accessed 01.08.11).

[5] P. Song, J. Pang, V. Kumar, A semi-implicit time-stepping model for frictional compliant contact problems, Int. J. Numer. Methods Eng. 60 (13) (2004) 267–279.

[6] J.J. Moreau, Standard inelastic shocks and the dynamics of unilateral constraints, in: G.D. Piero, F. Macieri (Eds.), Unilateral Problems in Structural Analysis, Springer–Verlag, New York, CISM Courses and Lectures No. 288, 1983, pp. 173–221.

[7] P. Lotstedt, Mechanical systems of rigid bodies subject to unilateral constraints, SIAM J. Appl. Math. 42 (2) (1982) 281–296.

[8] M.D.P. Monteiro Marques, Differential Inclusions in Nonsmooth Mechanical Problems: Shocks and Dry Friction, volume 9 of Progress in Nonlinear Differential Equations and Their Applications, Birkhäuser Verlag, Basel, 1993.

[9] D. Baraff, Issues in computing contact forces for non-penetrating rigid bodies, Algorithmica 10 (1993) 292–352.

[10] J. Pang, J.C. Trinkle, Complementarity formulations and existence of solutions of dynamic multi-rigid-body contact problems with Coulomb friction, Math. Program. 73 (2) (1996) 199–226.

[11] D.E. Stewart, J.C. Trinkle, An implicit time-stepping scheme for rigid-body dynamics with inelastic collisions and Coulomb friction, Int. J. Numer. Methods Eng. 39 (1996) 2673–2691.

[12] M. Anitescu, F.A. Potra, Formulating dynamic multi-rigid-body contact problems with friction as solvable linear complementarity problems, Nonlinear Dyn. 14 (1997) 231–247.

[13] D.E. Stewart, Rigid-body dynamics with friction and impact, SIAM Rev. 42 (1) (2000) 3–39.

[14] R.W. Cottle, G.B. Dantzig, Complementary pivot theory of mathematical programming, Linear Algebra. Appl. 1 (1968) 103–125.

[15] D. Baraff, Fast contact force computation for nonpenetrating rigid bodies, in: Computer Graphics Proceedings, Annual Conference Series, ACM, New York, 1994, pp. 23–34.

[16] M. Anitescu, A. Tasora, An iterative approach for cone complementarity problems for nonsmooth dynamics, Comput. Opt. Appl. 47 (2) (2010) 207–235.

[17] M. Anitescu, Optimization-based simulation of nonsmooth rigid multibody dynamics, Math. Program. 105 (1) (2006) 113–143.

[18] E.J. Haug, Computer-Aided Kinematics and Dynamics of Mechanical Systems Vol. I, Prentice-Hall, Englewood Cliffs, NJ, 1989.

[19] A. Tasora, M. Anitescu, A matrix-free cone complementarity approach for solving large-scale, nonsmooth, rigid body dynamics, Comput. Meth. Appl. Mech. Eng. 200 (2011) 439–453.

[20] M. Anitescu, G.D. Hart, A constraint-stabilized time-stepping approach for rigid multibody dynamics with joints, contact and friction, Int. J. Numer. Meth. Eng. 60 (14) (2004) 2335–2371.

[21] A. Tasora, D. Negrut, M. Anitescu, Large-scale parallel multi-body dynamics with frictional contact on the graphical processing unit, J. Multibody Dyn. 222 (4) (2008) 315–326.

[22] T. Harada, Real-time rigid body simulation on GPUs, GPU Gems. 3 (2007) 611–632.

[23] S. Sengupta, M. Harris, Y. Zhang, J.D. Owens, Scan primitives for GPU computing, in: Proceedings of the 22nd ACM SIGGRAPH/EUROGRAPHICS Symposium on Graphics Hardware, Eurographics Association, San Diego, CA, 2007, p. 106.

[24] H. Mazhar, T. Heyn, D. Negrut, A parallel method for large scale collision detection on the GPU, Multibody Syst. Dyn. (2010).

[25] A. Pazouki, H. Mazhar, D. Negrut, Parallel ellipsoid collision detection with application in contact dynamics DETC2010-29073, in: S. Fukuda, J. G. Michopoulos (Eds.), Proceedings to the 30th Computers and Information in Engineering Conference, ASME International Design Engineering Technical Conferences (IDETC) and Computers and Information in Engineering Conference (CIE), Montreal, 2010.

[26] Physics Simulation Forum, Bullet Physics Library. http://www.bulletphysics.com/Bullet/wordpress/bullet, 2008.

Implicit FEM Solver on GPU for Interactive Deformation Simulation

Jérémie Allard, Hadrien Courtecuisse, and François Faure

We present a set of methods to implement an implicit Finite Element solver on the GPU. In contrast to previous FEM implementations on the GPU which only address explicit time integration, our method allows large time steps for arbitrarily stiff objects. Unlike previous GPU-based sparse solvers, we avoid the assembly of the system matrix, and parallelize the matrix operations directly on the original object mesh. This considerably reduces the number of operations required, and more importantly the consumed bandwidth, enabling the method to be fast enough for highly complex interactive stiff body simulations. The presented methods can be applied in game and visual effects simulations, as well as medical and physics applications, where FEM is well established but currently limited by its computational cost. The core of the method can also be applied to many other scientific applications where a large irregular sparse system of equations is solved using an iterative method.

21.1 PROBLEM STATEMENT AND CONTEXT

The Finite Element Method (FEM) is broadly used to simulate deformable materials in physics simulations (Figure 21.1).

Recently, co-rotational linear FEM was applied successfully in interactive games [1] and medical simulations [2]. However, interactive CPU implementations are limited to coarse meshes due to the high computational cost of FEM. Existing GPU-based methods implement FEM only with explicit time integrators [3], which are simple and easy to parallelize. However, these methods suffer from stability issues and require very small time steps to simulate stiff materials [4]. Many real-world materials are stiff, such as the in-plane viscoelastic response of cloth or the volumetric response of deformable organs. The penalty forces typically used to avoid deep intersections between objects also require a high stiffness to avoid visible artifacts. Implicit time integration is thus necessary to maintain stability, but can require the solution of a nonlinear equation system at each time step. In this chapter, we explain how to apply backward Euler integration and solve the linearized equation system using a Conjugate Gradient solver [4] on the GPU.

We present a set of methods to implement an implicit FEM solver on the GPU. However, in contrast to existing GPU-based sparse solvers [5, 6], we optimize this step so that the system matrix does not have to be explicitly assembled. The matrix is only multiplied with vectors, and this operation is parallelized directly using the original mesh. This considerably reduces the computations required, and, more importantly, the consumed bandwidth, enabling the method to be fast enough for interactive soft bodies simulations. For conciseness, we focus on the core components of the method. Straightforward

FIGURE 21.1

A deformable object (top) and its FEM mesh (bottom), subjected to an external force (gray line) and constraints (gray points) (see color insert).

extensions to damping and constraints are possible, as explained in [4]. A well-written and detailed introduction to FEM can be found in [7].

21.1.1 Implicit Time Integration

In this section, we briefly outline the implicit integration method. More detail can be found in [4].

Consider the deformable dinosaur shown in Figure 21.1. Its body is discretized using a finite number of particles with positions, velocities, forces, and accelerations encoded in vectors $\mathbf{p}$, $\mathbf{v}$, $\mathbf{f}$, and $\mathbf{a}$, respectively. The size of the vectors is $3n$, where n is the number of particles. Each point models a particle with a given mass encoded in a diagonal matrix $\mathbf{M}$. At a given time t, accelerations and forces are related by Newton's second law: $\mathbf{a}_t = \mathbf{M}^{-1}\mathbf{f}_t$. The forces may have a constant value, such as gravity, but generally they are a function $\mathbf{f}(\mathbf{p}, \mathbf{v})$ of the positions and velocities. The simplest method for physically based animation is the *explicit* Euler integration scheme:

$$\mathbf{p}_{t+h} = \mathbf{p}_t + h\,\mathbf{v}_t, \quad \mathbf{v}_{t+h} = \mathbf{v}_t + h\,\mathbf{a}_t \tag{1}$$

where h is the length of the time step. Acceleration $\mathbf{a}_t$ is directly computed based on the forces in the current state. A popular, more accurate alternative is the *symplectic* Euler integration scheme, where the positions are updated using the new velocities:

$$\mathbf{v}_{t+h} = \mathbf{v}_t + h\,\mathbf{a}_t, \quad \mathbf{p}_{t+h} = \mathbf{p}_t + h\,\mathbf{v}_{t+h} \tag{2}$$

These methods and all their variants suffer from the well-known instability problem, due to the fact the acceleration at the beginning of the time step is considered constant during the whole time step, thereby neglecting the possibly important force changes across the time step. As a result, the simulation of elastic objects diverges unless damping forces are used and sufficiently small time steps are applied. Stiff objects can require such small time steps that real-time simulation is impossible, even with very fast computations. To avoid this problem, the *implicit* Euler integration scheme updates the velocities based on the acceleration at the *end* of the time step:

$$\mathbf{v}_{t+h} = \mathbf{v}_t + h\,\mathbf{a}_{t+h}, \quad \mathbf{p}_{t+h} = \mathbf{p}_t + h\,\mathbf{v}_{t+h} \tag{3}$$

As the forces at the end of the time step are not known, a first-order approximation is used:

$$\mathbf{f}(\mathbf{p}_{t+h}, \mathbf{v}_{t+h}) \approx \mathbf{f}(\mathbf{p}_t, \mathbf{v}_t) + \mathbf{K}\,(\mathbf{p}_{t+h} - \mathbf{p}_t) \tag{4}$$

where $\mathbf{K} = \delta\mathbf{f}/\delta\mathbf{p}$ is the stiffness matrix which describes the change in force given a displacement. Eq. (4) and Newton's law expressed at time $t + h$ allows us to set up the final linear system of equations:

$$(\mathbf{M} - h^2\mathbf{K})\mathbf{a}_{t+h} = \mathbf{f}(\mathbf{p}_t, \mathbf{v}_t) + h\,\mathbf{K}\,\mathbf{v}_t \tag{5}$$

The solution of this equation system is then used to update the velocities and positions (Eq. (3)). Baraff and Witkin noticed [4] that a good approximation of this solution can be found efficiently using a relatively small number of iterations of a conjugate gradient solver. This iterative method can be tuned to trade-off accuracy for speed by controlling the number of iterations and residual error threshold. In practice, ten to fifty iterations are used to obtain a stable and visually satisfying simulation.

21.1.2 Corotational Finite Elements

The finite element method provides a means for discretizing and solving volumetric models of deformable materials. Unlike springs, the elements are easily adjustable to model real-world materials. The object volume is represented by a mesh which is divided into contiguous, nonoverlapping cells (or faces in 2-D). The mesh vertices are the degrees of freedom of the discretized model. At each point in space, the local material deformation is modeled by three stretch values ϵ_{ii} in orthogonal directions, and three shear values ϵ_{ij} in orthogonal planes ($i, j \in (1, 2, 3)$). These values are the six entries of the strain vector $\epsilon_{\mathbf{e}}$. We use subscript $\mathbf{e}$ to denote values associated with a single element, as opposed to the global vectors and matrices used in Section 21.1.1.

In this article we focus on the simplest volumetric finite elements, tetrahedral cells, where each point inside a cell can be represented as a linear combination of the vertex positions. The strain is constant across each element, and is a nonlinear function of the vertex displacements. The linear approximation of the strain function can be used for small displacements: $\epsilon_{\mathbf{e}} = \mathbf{S}_{\mathbf{e}}\,\mathbf{u}_{\mathbf{e}}$ where $\mathbf{u}_{\mathbf{e}}$ is a 12×1 vector encoding the displacement of the four vertices and $\mathbf{S}_{\mathbf{e}}$ is a 6×12 matrix. Vector $\mathbf{D}_{\mathbf{e}}\epsilon_{\mathbf{e}}$ represents volume forces opposed to deformation. $\mathbf{D}_{\mathbf{e}}$ is a 6×6 matrix characteristic of the element material and size. This allows us to compute the vertex forces in each tetrahedron as:

$$\mathbf{f}_{\mathbf{e}} = \mathbf{K}_{\mathbf{e}}\mathbf{u}_{\mathbf{e}}, \quad \mathbf{K}_{\mathbf{e}} = \mathbf{S}_{\mathbf{e}}^{\mathsf{T}}\mathbf{D}_{\mathbf{e}}\mathbf{S}_{\mathbf{e}}. \tag{6}$$

The 12×12 matrix $\mathbf{K}_{\mathbf{e}}$ is called the stiffness matrix of the element. The net force on each vertex of a mesh can be computed by looping over the tetrahedra and accumulating the element forces at the vertices.

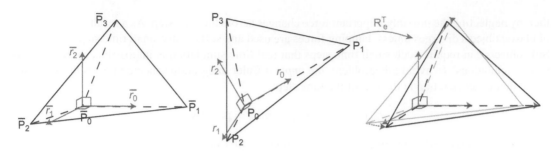

FIGURE 21.2

Corotational FEM. Left: a tetrahedral element in the reference configuration with its local frame. Middle: the deformed tetrahedron and its local frame. Right: deformation (dashed arrows) as measured after aligning the frames.

When large rotations occur, the linear approximation of the strain function leads to well-known inflation artifacts. The popular corotational method [8] solves this problem by computing displacements in a rotated local coordinate system (Figure 21.2).

In each tetrahedron, the local frame is represented by a rigid rotation matrix $\mathbf{R_e}$, and its transpose is used to align the deformed tetrahedron with its reference, undeformed shape. The displacements and forces are computed in the rotated coordinate system, then transformed back to world coordinates. Using this formulation, the forces $\mathbf{f_e}$ applied to the element vertices, and the change in force $\mathbf{df_e}$ due to vertex displacements $\mathbf{u_e}$, are, respectively:

$$\mathbf{f_e} = \widetilde{\mathbf{R}}_\mathbf{e} \mathbf{S_e}^\top \mathbf{D_e} \mathbf{S_e} \left(\widetilde{\mathbf{R}}_\mathbf{e}^\top \mathbf{p_e} - \overline{\mathbf{p_e}} \right), \quad \mathbf{df_e} = \widetilde{\mathbf{R}}_\mathbf{e} \mathbf{S_e}^\top \mathbf{D_e} \mathbf{S_e} \widetilde{\mathbf{R}}_\mathbf{e}^\top \mathbf{u_e} \tag{7}$$

where the 12×1 vectors $\mathbf{p_e}$ and $\overline{\mathbf{p_e}}$ are the vertices in the deformed and undeformed state, respectively, and $\widetilde{\mathbf{R}}_\mathbf{e}$ is the block-diagonal matrix used to apply rotation $\mathbf{R_e}$ to the four 3-D vectors. Several methods have been proposed to compute the local reference frames [2, 8]. Ours is presented in Section 21.3.4, along with the corresponding matrix expressions.

21.2 CORE METHOD

The overall algorithm is presented in Listing 21.1. It is split into a set of tasks (Figure 21.3) that can be executed on CPU or GPU. While an explicit integration scheme can be implemented with very few tasks (Figure 21.3b), a lot more are required for implicit integration (Figure 21.3c). Most tasks are standard linear vector algebra, except for **Force** and **dForce** (force evaluation and stiffness matrix/displacement vector product, i.e., lines 1 and 8 in Listing 21.1). These two tasks are the most expensive. We avoid constructing the large system matrix explicitly, instead computing matrix-vector products for each element in the original unstructured finite element mesh. The implementation of this step is based on the following techniques.

Parallelization Strategy While the actual computations depend on the specific FEM formulation, their parallelization only depends on the mesh. Several elements are connected to each vertex, causing

```
1   f₀ = f(p,v);      // Force
2   b = f₀ + h K v;
3   a = 0;
4   // Solve (M − h²K) a = b
5   d = r = b;
6   δ₀ = dot(r,r);
7   for( i=1; i ≤ i_max; ++i ) {
8     df = K d;       // dForce
9     q = M d − h²df; // mass
10    α = δ_{i−1} / dot(d,q);
11    a = a + α d;
12    r = r − α q;
13    δ_i = dot(r,r);
14    β = δ_i / δ_{i−1};
15    d = r + β d;
16    if( δ_i > ε²δ₀ ) break;
17  }
18  v = v + h a; // use solution
19  p = p + h v;
```

Listing 21.1. Euler implicit + CG.

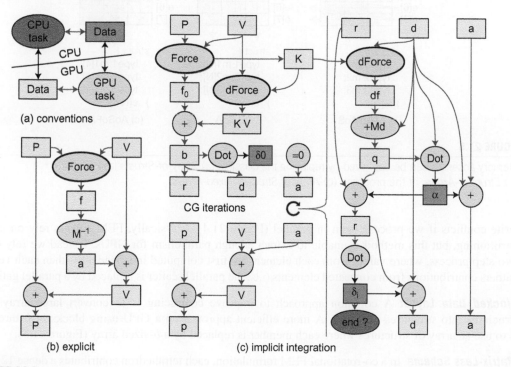

(a) conventions

CG iterations

(b) explicit

(c) implicit integration

FIGURE 21.3

CPU/GPU task graphs.

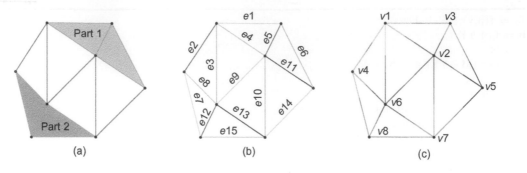

FIGURE 21.4

Parallel write conflicts can be removed by (a) mesh partitioning, (b) graph coloring, or (c) transforming scatter into gather.

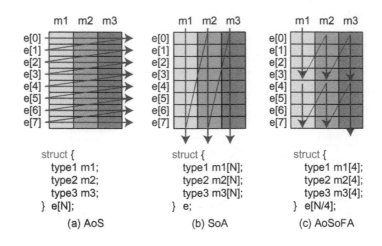

FIGURE 21.5

Memory accesses can be optimized by replacing the classical (a) *Array-of-Structs* layout into (b) *Struct-of-Arrays*, or the proposed (c) *Array-of-Struct-of-Fixed-Arrays*.

write conflicts if we process them in parallel (Figure 21.4). Classically, FEM solvers rely on mesh partitioning, but this method is unable to extract enough parallelism for GPUs. Instead we rely on a two-step process, where values from each element are first computed independently, then each vertex gathers contributions from connected elements (i.e., the parallel scatter is replaced by a parallel gather).

Blocked Data Layout A common approach to improve coalescing is to convert large arrays-of-structures into structures-of-arrays. A more efficient approach on a GPU using blocks of b threads, is to use an array of structures where each member is replaced by a b-sized array (Figure 21.5).

Matrix-Less Scheme In a co-rotational FEM formulation, each tetrahedron contributes a dense 12×12 matrix, the result of a product of five smaller matrices, some of which change at each step. Instead of computing and storing the final matrix, we store the few scalars that are required to express the small matrices, and each matrix-vector product is decomposed into five successive but simpler products. There is a trade-off between the number of stored values and the number of operations required to recreate the matrices. We can vary the number of stored values, depending on the ratio between bandwidth and compute power of each GPU architecture.

Reducing Launch Overheads In an interactive application, only a few milliseconds are available to compute one full time step, which can involve hundreds of different computation steps. In such a context, the achieved performance can be greatly affected by the launch overheads of each kernel. It is thus important to merge as many steps as possible into a single kernel.

21.3 ALGORITHMS AND IMPLEMENTATIONS

In this section, we present the key ideas used to implement our method on the GPU. A basic sample implementation is also provided, and we invite readers to try it and play with its source code. A more general implementation with additional features (such as collisions and preconditioning) and more complex demos, including medical scenarios, are also available within SOFA [9].

21.3.1 Matrix-Less Iterative Solver

The system matrix $(\mathbf{M} - h^2\mathbf{K})$ in Eq. (5) doesn't need to be explicitly computed, as only matrix-vector multiplications are used in the iterative solver (lines 8–9 of Listing 21.1). This property is leveraged in the SOFA [9] physics engine to build a modular yet efficient implementation of soft body simulations.

Each physical object contains its own state and associated vectors (which for the CG algorithm are **f, a, b, r, d, q**). The internal forces are computed and accumulated locally. In the iterative solver, the only operation combining data from all the objects is the vector dot product (lines 10 and 13). Each object performs it internally, and the overall dot product is the sum of the scalar values computed by the objects. Each object also has to implement vector sums and products, as well as the product **M u** of its mass matrix by one of its vectors. Each internal force field has to implement its force computation $\mathbf{f}(x,v)$ (the **Force** task) and the product **K u** of its stiffness with a position change (the **dForce** task).

Interestingly, within this framework it is straightforward to simulate some objects on the GPU while others are executed on the CPU. Interaction forces (such as contact forces) implement the same **Force** and **dForce** operations as internal force fields, but access state vectors from two objects instead of one. These are the only operations that require the object state to be communicated between the GPU and CPU. The only other information that needs to be transferred is the scalar results of the dot products.

In the case of our co-rotational FEM implementation, the stiffness matrix K is decomposed into per-element 12×12 matrices K_e. Each of these matrices contribute a 3-D force at the four vertices of an element, based on the displacements of the same vertices. In other words, the global matrix K can be constructed by dispatching the 16 3×3 blocks of each K_e matrices into the global rows and columns corresponding to the pair of indices from the four vertices of each tetrahedron. Therefore, the sparsity structure of K is exactly the same as the tetrahedral mesh, i.e., a 3×3 block if K is present in row $3i$ and column $3j$ if and only if there is an edge connecting vertices i and j in the mesh. This property is the basis of our parallelization strategy, as explained below.

21.3.2 Parallelization of FEM Computation on GPU

To parallelize a given set of computations on the GPU it is necessary to extract a massive level of parallelism, on the order of tens of thousands of threads. In many cases, the computations are independent except that they need to scatter their results onto a set of shared variables. This happens for instance when computing FEM elements accumulating forces to particles (i.e., lines 1 and 8 of Listing 21.1), or when computing a sparse matrix–vector product. Such operations can be represented as a graph, where nodes represent shared variables and edges the computations between them.

A very common technique [10] to parallelize such a graph is to partition it into a set of subgraphs (Figure 21.4a), each computed by a different processor. Edges that cross partition borders must be computed in a separate pass to the main computation, increasing runtime. The partitioning thus tries to minimize the size of these borders. This method is efficient only if the number of processors is small compared to the number of nodes in the graph, as otherwise most edges will be on borders. This method is used in many large-scale FEM simulation solvers running on distributed CPU platforms [11].

An alternative method, *graph-coloring* (Figure 21.4b), partitions the graph into sub-graphs such that the arity of all nodes with each sub-graph is at most one, i.e., a node is never shared between edges. This allows all edges within each subgraph to be executed in parallel, but requires $n - 1$ synchronizations, where n is the number of partitions (colors) necessary. This method is often used on the GPU to solve contact constraints in large stacks of objects [12].

Finally, another method involves transforming the parallel scatter operation into a parallel gather. Instead of computing edges in parallel, the nodes are processed in parallel, each gathering the results from the connected edges (Figure 21.4c). This requires either duplicating the computations of each edge in the threads of the two connected nodes, or using a temporary buffer to store the result of each edge computation, and then doing the gather step reading from this buffer.

This final method is used to implement the FEM force computation, as it is able to extract more parallelism than the previous two. A temporary vector is used to store four 3-D vectors for each tetrahedron, and the algorithm is based on the following two steps:

1. First, using one thread per tetrahedron, all per-element computations are done in parallel, and the result is stored independently for each element in the temporary vector.
2. Then, using one thread per vertex, we accumulate the results on each vertex, using a precomputed array storing for each vertex the indices of all connected tetrahedra.

A possible optimization for the second step is to use 4 or more threads per vertex instead of one, as volumetric meshes contain fewer vertices than elements. The resulting CUDA kernel is shown in Listing 21.2.

Note that on recent GPU architectures, it is possible to remove the second step by using floating-point atomic operations to accumulate the results directly in the first step. However, this is not yet supported for double-precision, and could lead to non-deterministic results (as accumulations might not occur in the same order between runs).

21.3.3 Data Layout for Memory Accesses Coalescing

To achieve maximum performance it is critical to design data layouts to optimize memory access. A common approach to improve cache efficiency of memory access patterns is to convert large arrays of structures (Figure 21.5a) into a structure of arrays (Figure 21.5b). To access the variable **m** inside

```
1   __global__ void addForce4(int nbVertex, int nb4ElemPerVertex,
2       const float4* eforce, const int* velems, float* f) {
3       int index1 = threadIdx.x;
4       __shared__  float temp[BSIZE*3]; // Shared memory buffer
5       float3 force = {0,0,0};
6       int entry = blockIdx.x*nb4ElemPerVertex*BSIZE+index1;
7       for (int s = 0; s < nb4ElemPerVertex; ++s) {
8           int i = velems[entry];
9           if (i == -1) break;
10          float3 fe = getElemForce(i,eforce); // using memory access or texture
11          force.x += fe.x; force.y += fe.y; force.z += fe.z;
12          entry += BSIZE;
13      }
14      int iout = (index1/4)*3 + (index1&3)*((BSIZE*3/4));
15      temp[iout] = force.x;  temp[iout+1] = force.y;  temp[iout+2] = force.z;
16      __syncthreads(); // BARRIER
17      if (index1 < (BSIZE*3/4)) { // we need to merge 4 values together
18          float res = temp[index1] + temp[index1 + (BSIZE*3/4)] +
19              temp[index1 + 2*(BSIZE*3/4)] + temp[index1 + 3*(BSIZE*3/4)];
20          f[blockIdx.x*(BSIZE*3/4) + index1] += res;
21      }
22  }
```

Listing 21.2. Parallel gather with 4 threads per node.

element **i**, **e.m[i]** will be used instead of **e[i].m**. On a CPU, this is useful if only a subset of the member of the structure are read or written in a given pass. However, n pointers will have to be stored (and incremented within each loop) instead of just one.

A more efficient approach, specially for SIMD processors or when loop unrolling with blocks of b values, is to use an array of structures where each member is replaced by an array of fixed size b (Figure 21.5c). Accesses to a variable **m** of element **i** will be converted from **e[i].m** to **e[i/b].m[i%b]**. If b is a power of two this can be done by simple bit swizzling operations, and on the GPU if b corresponds to the size of the thread blocks, then the block index directly provides the index to use within **e**, and the thread index the index to use within **m**. This method requires the minimal number of memory accesses (coalesced parallel operations, or cache line fetches), even if only a subset of values is used, and only a single pointer or iterator is necessary.

This approach is used to store all internal data-structures of the FEM elements, except vectors that sometimes require random access, such as positions and velocities.

21.3.4 Optimized FEM Elements

In this section we present our fast implementation of the corotational FEM introduced in Section 21.1.2. The fastest method to compute the local frame of an element (Figure 21.2), although not the most accurate one, is to set the origin at vertex $\mathbf{p}_0$ and use its adjacent edges [2]. The first vector, $\mathbf{r}_0$, is set parallel to the first edge $\mathbf{p}_0\mathbf{p}_1$, the second vector, $\mathbf{r}_1$, perpendicular to the first one in the plane of the first and the second edge $\mathbf{p_0 p_2}$, and the third vector, $\mathbf{r_2}$, perpendicular to this plane:

$$\mathbf{r_0} = \frac{(\mathbf{p_1}-\mathbf{p_0})}{\|(\mathbf{p_1}-\mathbf{p_0})\|}, \quad \mathbf{r_2} = \frac{(\mathbf{p_1}-\mathbf{p_0})\times(\mathbf{p_2}-\mathbf{p_0})}{\|(\mathbf{p_1}-\mathbf{p_0})\times(\mathbf{p_2}-\mathbf{p_0})\|}, \quad \mathbf{r_1} = \mathbf{r_2} \times \mathbf{r_0}$$

The 3×3 element rotation matrix $\mathbf{R_e} = [\mathbf{r_0}\ \mathbf{r_1}\ \mathbf{r_2}]$ is used to compute the undeformed vertex positions $(a\ b\ c\ d)$ in the rotated frame, with the origin on $\mathbf{p_0}$, as follows:

$$
\begin{aligned}
a &= \mathbf{R_e}^\mathsf{T}(\mathbf{p_0} - \mathbf{p_0}) = (0 \quad 0 \quad 0)^\mathsf{T}\\
b &= \mathbf{R_e}^\mathsf{T}(\mathbf{p_1} - \mathbf{p_0}) = (b_x \quad 0 \quad 0)^\mathsf{T}\\
c &= \mathbf{R_e}^\mathsf{T}(\mathbf{p_2} - \mathbf{p_0}) = (c_x \quad c_y \quad 0)^\mathsf{T}\\
d &= \mathbf{R_e}^\mathsf{T}(\mathbf{p_3} - \mathbf{p_0}) = (d_x \quad d_y \quad d_z)^\mathsf{T}
\end{aligned}
\tag{8}
$$

Using these points, the 6×12 strain-displacement matrix $\mathbf{S_e}$ is defined in the local frame as follows:

$$
\mathbf{S_e} =
\begin{pmatrix}
-p_x(bcd) & 0 & 0 & -p_y(bcd) & 0 & -p_z(bcd)\\
0 & -p_y(bcd) & 0 & -p_x(bcd) & -p_z(bcd) & 0\\
0 & 0 & -p_z(bcd) & 0 & -p_y(bcd) & -p_x(bcd)\\
p_x(cda) & 0 & 0 & p_y(cda) & 0 & p_z(cda)\\
0 & p_y(cda) & 0 & p_x(cda) & p_z(cda) & 0\\
0 & 0 & p_z(cda) & 0 & p_y(cda) & p_x(cda)\\
-p_x(dab) & 0 & 0 & -p_y(dab) & 0 & -p_z(dab)\\
0 & -p_y(dab) & 0 & -p_x(dab) & -p_z(dab) & 0\\
0 & 0 & -p_z(dab) & 0 & -p_y(dab) & -p_x(dab)\\
p_x(abc) & 0 & 0 & p_y(abc) & 0 & p_z(abc)\\
0 & p_y(abc) & 0 & p_x(abc) & p_z(abc) & 0\\
0 & 0 & p_z(abc) & 0 & p_y(abc) & p_x(abc)
\end{pmatrix}^\mathsf{T}
\tag{9}
$$

$$p(uvw) = u\times v + v\times w + w\times u$$

Given the zeros in $(a\ b\ c\ d)$, we have:

$$S_b = p(cda) = \begin{pmatrix} c_y d_z \\ -c_x d_z \\ c_x d_y - c_y d_x \end{pmatrix}, \quad S_c = -p(dab) = \begin{pmatrix} 0 \\ b_x d_z \\ -b_x d_y \end{pmatrix}, \quad S_d = \begin{pmatrix} 0 \\ 0 \\ b_x c_y \end{pmatrix}
\tag{10}$$

Since the sum of applied forces must be zero, we know that:

$$S_a + S_b + S_c + S_d = 0 \quad \Leftrightarrow \quad S_a = -S_b - S_c - S_d$$

The material stiffness is represented by a 6×6 matrix $\mathbf{D_e}$ as follows:

$$
\mathbf{D_e} =
\begin{pmatrix}
\gamma+\mu & \gamma & \gamma & 0 & 0 & 0\\
\gamma & \gamma+\mu & \gamma & 0 & 0 & 0\\
\gamma & \gamma & \gamma+\mu & 0 & 0 & 0\\
0 & 0 & 0 & \mu/2 & 0 & 0\\
0 & 0 & 0 & 0 & \mu/2 & 0\\
0 & 0 & 0 & 0 & 0 & \mu/2
\end{pmatrix}, \quad
\begin{aligned}
\gamma &= \frac{1}{36\mathcal{V}_e}\frac{E\nu}{(1+\nu)(1-2\nu)}\\
\mu &= \frac{1}{36\mathcal{V}_e}\frac{E}{1+\nu}\\
\mathcal{V}_e &= \tfrac{1}{6}b \cdot (c\times d)
\end{aligned}
\tag{11}
$$

where E is the Young's modulus, representing stiffness, $0 < \nu < 0.5$ is the Poisson's ratio, related to volume conservation, and $\mathcal{V}_e$ is the element volume.

Given the above matrices, the forces and their derivatives are computed using Eq. (7). We want to find the smallest number of values that can be used to compute the matrix–vector product $\tilde{\mathbf{R}}_e \mathbf{S}_e^{\mathsf{T}} \mathbf{D}_e \mathbf{S}_e \tilde{\mathbf{R}}_e^{\mathsf{T}} \mathbf{u}_e$:

- $\mathbf{R}_e$ can be applied using 9 values (the full matrix), or 6 values (two vectors) and a cross-product to compute the last (giving 9 operations), or 4 values (a quaternion) and 30 operations to get the matrix.
- $\mathbf{D}_e$ can be applied using 2 values (γ, μ).
- $\mathbf{S}_e$ can be applied using 6 values (Sb_x, Sb_y, Sb_z, Sc_y, Sc_z, Sd_z), or 1 value (Sb_z) and 4 operations. Another alternative is to divide S_e by b_x, if we multiply D_e by its square: $\tilde{\mathbf{R}}_e \left(\frac{1}{b_x}\mathbf{S}_e^{\mathsf{T}}\right) (b_x^2 \mathbf{D}_e)$ $\left(\frac{1}{b_x}\right)\mathbf{S}_e \tilde{\mathbf{R}}_e^{\mathsf{T}} \mathbf{u}_e$. This allows us to store only 3 values $\left(\frac{Sb_x}{b_x}, \frac{Sb_y}{b_x}, \frac{Sb_z}{b_x}\right)$ without needing additional operations to compute the other 3.

In our current implementation, we store the rotation using six values in a separate buffer (as it needs to be updated at each time step), and the rest of the values in the structure shown in Listing 21.3. This structure is stored in a buffer with one instance for each thread block (see Section 21.3.3).

21.3.5 Overheads Reduction with Kernel Merges

Merging kernels not only removes some launch overheads, it can also reduce the consumed bandwidth, as data computed by one step can be directly used by the next without going through the global device memory. The computation of FEM force $\mathbf{f}_0$ and its derivative $\mathbf{df}$ is handled in two CUDA kernels that cannot be merged, as they rely on a global synchronization. However quite a few other steps in the overall algorithm could benefit from being combined. Within the main loop of the CG algorithm (Figure 21.3c and Listing 21.1), we can see 5 simple vector operations (lines 10–13 and 15) in addition to the matrix-vector products (lines 8 and 9).

The simplest cases concern successive linear algebra operations, such as the update of both **v** and **p** vectors at the end of the time step (lines 18–19), or **a** and **r** within each CG iteration (lines 11–12). These steps can be merged very easily. The two dot products in lines 10 and 13 require two parallel reductions, each including a global synchronization. We could merge them if we can evaluate **r·r** before

```
1   struct GPUElement {
2       /// index of the 4 connected vertices
3       int ia[BSIZE], ib[BSIZE], ic[BSIZE], id[BSIZE];
4       /// initial position of the vertices in the local frame
5       float bx[BSIZE];
6       float cx[BSIZE], cy[BSIZE];
7       float dx[BSIZE], dy[BSIZE], dz[BSIZE];
8       /// Values to compute the strain—displacement matrix S
9       float Sbx_bx[BSIZE],Sby_bx[BSIZE],Sbz_bx[BSIZE];
10      /// Values to compute the material stiffness matrix D
11      float gamma_bx2[BSIZE], mu_bx2[BSIZE];
12  };
```

Listing 21.3. GPU data layout for FEM elements.

knowing the value of α used to update $\mathbf{r}$ by subtracting $\alpha\mathbf{q}$ from its previous value (which we will note as $\mathbf{r}'$ in the following). As the dot product is linear, we can express it as:

$$\mathbf{r} \cdot \mathbf{r} = (\mathbf{r}' - \alpha\mathbf{q}) \cdot (\mathbf{r}' - \alpha\mathbf{q}) = (\mathbf{r}' \cdot \mathbf{r}') - 2\alpha(\mathbf{r}' \cdot \mathbf{q}) + \alpha^2(\mathbf{q} \cdot \mathbf{q}) \tag{12}$$

Therefore, we can compute in a single step the parallel reductions for $\mathbf{d}\cdot\mathbf{q}$, $\mathbf{r}'\cdot\mathbf{q}$, and $\mathbf{q}\cdot\mathbf{q}$ ($\mathbf{r}'\cdot\mathbf{r}'$ being known from the previous iteration). After a single synchronization, we can compute both α and δ_i. Finally, we can update all vectors (lines 11, 12, and 15) at once in a second step.

Another optimization concerns the **dForce** task. In typical applications, there are many contributions to the total force (including FEM forces, boundary conditions, collisions, and user interactions). Most simple forces can be computed in parallel on all particles, and as such they should be merged within one kernel. However, merging all forces in a single kernel is only possible if we know them in advance. The sample code included with this article includes this optimization, while the version in use within the SOFA framework does not, as in a generic physics framework it is too restrictive.

21.4 RESULTS AND EVALUATION

Figure 21.6 presents the improvements achieved by successive optimizations, on both the GPU and CPU versions when applicable, depending on the number of tetrahedra, and using the initial CPU FEM implementation from SOFA [9] as a reference. We measured the computation time per time step of the dinosaur example (Figure 21.1), using 25 conjugate gradient iterations.

On the CPU version, using the compact element representation (**V1**, Section 21.3.4) provides a significant improvement (1.7×) over the initial FEM implementation. Also, a good ordering of the vertices and elements is useful to improve coalescing on GPU and cache usage on CPU, as is visible by comparing the versions with a **u** prefix (up to 1.3× on CPU and 2× on GPU). A simple ordering such as sorting particles along a spatial axis already provides good performance (**sV1**), however more

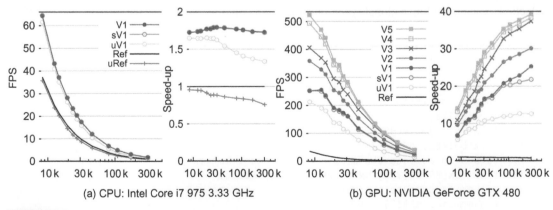

(a) CPU: Intel Core i7 975 3.33 GHz   (b) GPU: NVIDIA GeForce GTX 480

FIGURE 21.6

Performances of several versions of a FEM simulation: **Ref**: reference CPU implementation; **V1**: optimized matrices (Section 21.3.4); **uRef & uV1**: using unordered meshes; **V2**: 4 threads per particle for parallel gather (Section 21.3.2); **V3**: textures accesses for positions and element forces; **V4 & V5**: merge of resp. linear algebra & stiffness kernels (Section 21.3.5).

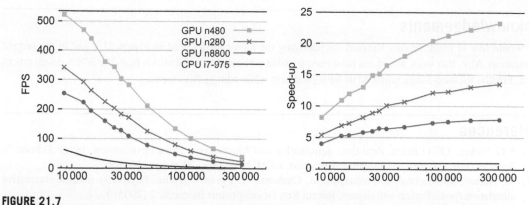

FIGURE 21.7

Performance comparison between CPU and GPU in interactive FEM simulations with varying object complexity (number of tetrahedra).

complex methods such as [13] (which we use for **V1**) can provide additional improvements for large meshes (+16%).

The parallel force gather (Section 21.3.2) is a critical step for the performance of the overall algorithm, as it consumes around half of the computation time. The use of 4 threads per particles (**V2**) significantly reduces this time by extracting more parallelism, providing an overall improvement of 1.3×. The use of texture units is essential on earlier architectures such as the G80 and is beneficial (up to +20%) on the Fermi GPU architecture. On Fermi there is a benefit from accessing the parallel gather buffer through the texture cache, but not the particles positions.

The last optimizations (**V4 & V5**) are implemented by merging successive kernels (Section 21.3.5). This is most useful for small meshes (+37%), as it reduces launch overhead, but it is also beneficial for large meshes (+7%) as it also reduces memory bandwidth. Overall, combining all optimizations allows to reach a speed-up of 39× compared to the reference CPU implementation.

The final CUDA-based implementation is able to simulate a deformable object with 45K tetrahedral elements (Figure 21.1) at 212 FPS on a NVIDIA GeForce GTX 480, 18× faster than our most optimized sequential implementation on an Intel Core i7 975 3.33GHz CPU. We ran benchmarks to evaluate the speed-up on several GPUs with varying mesh sizes (Figure 21.7). With the largest meshes, the speed-up can reach 23× on a GeForce GTX 480, and 13.5× with the previous generation GTX 280.

21.5 **FUTURE DIRECTIONS**

The method as presented in this article could be extended to other FEM variants (hexahedral elements, shells, etc.). For advanced applications, medical simulations for example, it would be beneficial to add support for dynamic topologies (cutting), more complex materials and haptics. Regarding the numerical sparse solver, an interesting avenue of work is to study the use of preconditioners on the GPU.

In our opinion the most interesting direction would be to combine this method with existing GPU methods for rigid bodies [12, 14], fluids [15, 16], and collision detection and response [14, 17]. This would allow interactive multi-physics simulations to run entirely on the GPU.

Acknowledgements

We would like to thank Jeremy Ringard for providing the raptor model used in Figure 21.1 and in the sample application. Also, this work would not have been possible without the contributions from the SOFA development team. Finally, Richard Tonge provided us with great help while editing this chapter.

References

[1] E.G. Parker, J.F. O'Brien, Real-time deformation and fracture in a game environment, in: D. Fellner, S. Spencer (Eds.), Symp. on Computer Animation, ACM, New York, 2009, pp. 156–166.

[2] M. Nesme, M. Marchal, E. Promayon, M. Chabanas, Y. Payan, F. Faure, Physically realistic interactive simulation for biological soft tissues, Recent Res. Developments Biomech. 2 (2005) 1–22.

[3] O. Comas, Z. Taylor, J. Allard, S. Ourselin, S. Cotin, J. Passenger, Efficient nonlinear FEM for soft tissue modelling and its GPU implementation within the open source framework SOFA, in: F. Bello, P.J. Edwards (Eds.), ISBMS, Springer, Berlin, series, LNCS, vol. 5104, 2008, pp. 28–39.

[4] D. Baraff, A. Witkin, Large steps in cloth simulation, in: Proc. of SIGGRAPH 98, ACM, New York, 1998, pp. 43–54.

[5] J. Krüger, R. Westermann, A GPU framework for solving systems of linear equations, in: M. Pharr, R. Fernando (Eds.), GPU Gems 2, Addison-Wesley, Reading, MA, 2005, pp. 703–718 (Chapter 44).

[6] L. Buatois, G. Caumon, B. Lévy, Concurrent number cruncher—a GPU implementation of a general sparse linear solver, Int. J. Parallel Emerg. Distrib. Syst. 24 (3) (2009) 205–223.

[7] C. Mendoza, M. Garcia, Soft bodies using finite elements, in: G. van den Bergen, D. Gregorius (Eds.), Game Physics Pearls, A.K. Peters, Mellesley, MA, 2010, pp. 217–250 (Chapter 10).

[8] M. Müller, M. Gross, Interactive virtual materials, in: W. Heidrich, R. Balakrishnan (Eds.), GI '04: Proc. of Graphics Interface 2004, Canadian Human-Computer Communications Society, School of Computer Science, University of Waterloo, Waterloo, Ontario, Canada, 2004, pp. 239–246.

[9] Simulation open framework architecture (SOFA). http://sofa-framework.org.

[10] K. Schloegel, G. Karypis, V. Kumar, A unified algorithm for load-balancing adaptive scientific simulations, in: Supercomputing, 2000.

[11] W.J. Camp, S.J. Plimpton, B.A. Hendrickson, R.W. Leland, Massively parallel methods for engineering and science problems, Commun. ACM, 37 (4) (1994) 30–41.

[12] R. Tonge, B. Wyatt, N. Nicholson, PhysX GPU rigid bodies in Batman: Arkham Asylum, in: A. Lake (Ed.), Game Programming Gems 8, Cengage, Florence, KY, 2010, pp. 590–601 (Chapter 7).

[13] M. Tchiboukdjian, V. Danjean, B. Raffin, Binary mesh partitioning for cache-efficient visualization, IEEE Trans. on Vis. and Comp. Graph. 16 (5) (2010) 815–828.

[14] T. Harada, Real-time rigid body simulation on GPUs, in: H. Nguyen (Ed.), GPU Gems 3, Addison-Wesley, Reading, MA, 2007, pp. 611–632 (Chapter 29).

[15] K. Crane, I. Llamas, S. Tariq, Real-time simulation and rendering of 3d fluids, in: GPU Gems 3, Addison-Wesley, 2007, pp. 633–675 (Chapter 30).

[16] Y. Zhang, B. Solenthaler, R. Pajarola, Adaptive sampling and rendering of fluids on the GPU, in: H.-C. Hege, D. Laidlaw, R. Pajarola, and O. Staadt (Eds.), Proc. of Symp. on Point-Based Graph., Eurographics Association, Aire-la-Ville, Switzerland, 2008, pp. 137–146.

[17] J. Allard, F. Faure, H. Courtecuisse, F. Falipou, C. Duriez, P.G. Kry, Volume contact constraints at arbitrary resolution, in: H. Hoppe (Ed.), ACM, New York, 2010.

Real-Time Adaptive GPU Multiagent Path Planning

Ugo Erra and Giuseppe Caggianese

This chapter presents a GPU path planning algorithm that is derived from the sequential A* algorithm to allow massively parallel, real-time execution. The new algorithm employs a limited lookahead strategy similar to the wave fronts of a breath-first-search algorithm. Using a heuristic to estimate the most profitable direction for moving along a particular direction at each step, the algorithm strikes a balance between work set size and optimality. The implementation of the algorithm further employs a windowed strategy to reduce the amount of information that needs to be maintained for fast access. We show that the resulting algorithm indeed achieves high efficiency while yielding good quality movement paths.

22.1 INTRODUCTION

Many types of computer games involve player and nonplayer characters moving over terrain. In some types of game, the player directly controls a main character while the nonplayer characters are controlled by path planning algorithms. In real-time strategy games the player doesn't control any characters directly. Instead, the player selects a group of characters (or agents) and then selects a target position with the mouse. The target position can be in a known position (a position that the agents have observed before) or an unknown position. The agents then have to find their own way to the target position. The characters do not know the whole terrain in advance, instead they observe a certain range around them and remember the positions they've observed for future use. If they observe that their current trajectory is blocked after they have started moving, they have to search for another path. A fast path planning algorithm is therefore essential for the agents to move smoothly around obstacles.

A* [1] is the most famous algorithm for finding cost-minimal paths in state spaces, which are usually represented as graphs. Given a start state (start node) and a goal state (goal node) A* finds the least-cost path by using a distance-cost heuristic function to determine the order in which the search visits states. The search performed by A* is ideal for off-line artificial intelligence applications, but it is not suitable for computer games where agents have to search paths in real time.

This work proposes an efficient multiagent planning approach for the GPU. The implementation is based on a previous algorithm called Real-Time Adaptive A* (RTAA*) [2]. In RTAA*, the search is restricted to a small part of the state space that can be reached from the current state using a single A* search episode. For each search episode, the agent determines a local search space, searches it, updates the distance-cost heuristics, and moves along the resulting trajectory. The agent repeats this process until it reaches a goal state. RTAA* is efficient in real-time applications but has a major drawback; the large amount of memory required for each agent limits the number of simultaneous searches. Our approach reduces the amount of memory for each agent, enabling the design of a parallel implementation of RTAA* for the GPU architecture. This offers a simple and powerful way to accelerate simultaneous path planning in real-time applications such as computer games and robotics.

22.2 CORE METHOD

Before explaining the GPU implementation, we give a brief overview of the A* and RTAA* algorithms. In A* (Algorithm 1), for every state s, the user supplies a heuristic $h[s]$ that estimates the goal distance, which is the cost of a minimal path from the state s to a goal state. Classical heuristics are based on Manhattan, diagonal, or Euclidian distance calculations. During its execution, A* maintains two values, $g[s]$ and $f[s]$. The value $g[s]$ is the smallest cost of any discovered path from the start state s_{start} to state s. The value $f[s] = g[s] + h[s]$ estimates the distance from s_{start} to the goal state via state s. The algorithm maintains two lists, the open list and the closed list. The open list is a priority queue and

---

Algorithm 1: A*

1: $ClosedList \Leftarrow \emptyset$
2: $OpenList \Leftarrow start$
3: $g[start] \Leftarrow 0$
4: $h[start] \Leftarrow$ HEURISTICESTIMATE($start, goal$)
5: $f[start] \Leftarrow h[start]$
6: **while** $OpenList \neq \emptyset$ **do**
7:      $x \Leftarrow$ EXTRACTLOWERVALUE($OpenList$)
8:      **if** $x = goal$ **then**
9:          **return** RECONSTRUCTPATHFROM($goal$)
10:     **end if**
11:     **for all** $s \in$ NEIGHBORNODES(x) **do**
12:         $newg \Leftarrow g[x] +$ COST(x, s)
13:         **if** $s \in OpenList$ **and** $newg < g[s]$ **then**
14:             REMOVE($OpenList, s$)
15:         **end if**
16:         **if** $s \in ClosedList$ **and** $newg < g[s]$ **then**
17:             REMOVE($ClosedList, s$)
18:         **end if**
19:         **if** $s \notin OpenList$ **or** $s \notin ClosedList$ **then**
20:             $parent[s] \Leftarrow x$
21:             $g[s] \Leftarrow newg$
22:             $h[s] \Leftarrow$ HEURISTICESTIMATE($s, goal$)
23:             $f[s] \Leftarrow g[s] + h[s]$
24:             ADD($OpenList, s$)
25:         **end if**
26:         ADD($ClosedList, x$)
27:     **end for**
28: **end while**

---

contains the most recently discovered states. Initially, it contains only the start state s_{start}. The closed list contains the expanded states, those from which all adjacent states have been explored and inserted into open list. At each iteration, A* removes the state s with the smallest $f[s]$ value from the open list. If state s is a goal state, it terminates. Otherwise, it explores the adjacent states and updates the g-value of each visited state. If the g-value decreases, it updates the g-value and the corresponding f-value in the open list. It then repeats the process. Finally, the g-value of every visited state s will be the distance from the start state s_{start} to state s.

For real-time applications, A* has two main drawbacks. The first is the computational time required to perform a search from the start state to the goal state. The second disadvantage relates to memory footprint during the execution of the algorithm. Each agent must store and update the $h[s]$, $g[s]$, and $f[s]$ values for each state s. This makes A* unsuitable for multiagent path planning in large state spaces when memory is limited.

Real-Time Adaptive A* (Algorithm 2) is a real-time heuristic search method that chooses its local search spaces in a very fine-grained way. The main idea is to update the heuristics of all states in the local search space very quickly and to save the heuristics to speed up future A* searches. This approach uses a variable called lookahead, which specifies the largest number of states to expand during an A* search. After the A* search, we define $\bar{s}$ to be the state that was about to be expanded when the A* search terminated. At this point, RTAA* updates the heuristic of all the expanded states s in the closed list by setting $h[s] = g[\bar{s}] + h[\bar{s}] - g[s]$. RTAA* then executes the plan along the trajectory found by the A* search until state $\bar{s}$ is reached. Koenig et al. [2] have proven that this heuristic becomes more informed over time and that it is consistent, ensuring a trajectory of smaller cost for a given time-limited search episode.

The key aim in designing and implementing a RTAA* multiagent path plan in the GPU is to reduce the memory required for $g[s]$, $h[s]$, and $g[s]$ for all states s. Table 22.1 shows the main input and output variables handled by RTAA* for each agent. Note that, for each search episode, we need a START state variable, and the queues for OPEN LIST, CLOSED LIST, and PARENT LIST that must be sufficiently large

---

Algorithm 2: RTAA*

1: *lookahead* $\Leftarrow$ any integer greater than zero
2: *movements* $\Leftarrow$ any integer greater than zero
3: **while** $s_{curr} \neq goal$ **do**
4:     A*() {Expand lookahead states in A*}
5:     **if** $\bar{s} = FAILURE$ **then**
6:         **return** FAILURE
7:     **end if**
8:     **for all** $s \in$ CLOSEDLIST **do**
9:         $h[s] \Leftarrow g[\bar{s}] + h[\bar{s}] - g[s]$
10:         **while** $s_{curr} \neq \bar{s}$ and *movements* > 0 **do**
11:             $a \Leftarrow$ ACTIONONTRAJECTORY()
12:             $s_{curr} \Leftarrow succ(s_{curr}, a)$
13:             *movements* $\Leftarrow$ *movements* $- 1$
14:             CHANGECOSTS()
15:         **end while**
16:     **end for**
17: **end while**

Table 22.1 INPUT and OUTPUT Data for RTAA*. The Variables in a Search Episode Keep State Expansion Information for the Current A* Search

INPUT			
Used	**Variable**	**Description**	**Init**
PER SEARCH EPISODE	START	Start state	USER
	OPEN LIST	List of discovered states	ZERO
	CLOSED LIST	List of expanded states	ZERO
	PARENT LIST	List of successors	ZERO
FOR ALL SEARCH EPISODES	GOAL	Goal state	USER
	G_{cost}	Cost of any discovered path $g[s]$, for each state s	∞
	H_{cost}	Estimated goal distance $h[s]$, for each state s	Heuristic function
	F_{cost}	Cost of estimated path $f[s]$, for each state s	ZERO
OUTPUT			
Used	**Variable**	**Description**	**Init**
PER SEARCH EPISODE	$\bar{s}$	Start state for the next A* search	ZERO
	PATH LIST	Path state list	ZERO

to handle the number of lookahead states. Moreover, for each search episode we need a GOAL state variable and the arrays G_{cost}, H_{cost}, and F_{cost} to keep updated the values of any discovered path $g[s]$, estimated cost distance $h[s]$, and the cost of the estimated path $f[s]$, respectively, of each state s. The amount of memory required for G_{cost}, H_{cost}, and F_{cost} depends on the number of states.

The proposed implementation is based on the observation that after each search episode G_{cost}, H_{cost}, and F_{cost} values only in the surrounding area of an agent's current position are updated. In addition, as the agent moves along the path toward the goal state, values related to explored states will not be required in the current search episode. Thus, we do not maintain these values after a certain number of search episodes. In our GPU implementation, we exploit the variable lookahead in order to take into account only those values in the surrounding area of the agent's current position and then to reduce the memory footprint required for each agent.

22.3 IMPLEMENTATION

In this section, we describe a path planning system for many thousands of agents that use RTAA*. NVIDIA's CUDA is the platform chosen for exploiting data parallelism in the GPU. The following subsections discuss parallel pathfinding implementation on the GPU.

22.3.1 Grid Map

Our implementation is suitable for games that are based on a grid map. In these games, the world is subdivided into small regular zones called tiles. Each tile represents a state s of the state space and is connected to all nearby tiles. These connections form a tile-graph as illustrated in Figure 22.1.

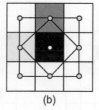

FIGURE 22.1

(a) Grid map. An integer indicates a terrain element. (b) Tile-graph. A light grey tile indicates a hill, the dark gray a mountain, and the black tile an obstacle which is unreachable.

The cost of moving from a tile to each of its neighbors is specified by an integer. This can be used to model terrain elements that are difficult or impossible to pass, for example hills and lakes. A common metric used on grid maps, which we adopt for this work, is the Manhattan distance. The memory footprint for each grid map is $4 \times h \times w$ words, where h and w are the height and width of the map, respectively. At the initial phase of planning, the grid map is copied from host memory to the device's global memory region and processed by a grid of threads.

22.3.2 Lookahead and Movements Array

In order to perform searches for many thousands of agents in parallel we need a way to reduce the working set per thread. Our solution exploits the `lookahead` parameter of the RTAA* algorithm, and this parameter allows us to store for each agent the G_{cost}, H_{cost}, and F_{cost} values only for a limited area surrounding the current agent position. This area is tracked by using two overlay arrays, called the **lookahead array** and the **movements array** (Figure 22.2).

The lookahead array is centered on the agent start position at the beginning of a search episode and tracks all the tiles that are discoverable during the search episode. Its size is $(\text{lookahead} \times 2 + 1)^2$ because during the search episode an agent can explore, at the most, `lookahead` tiles in all directions. These tiles are inserted in the queues OPEN LIST and CLOSED LIST as illustrated in Section 22.2. Thus, the memory required for OPEN LIST and CLOSED LIST is $(\text{lookahead} \times 2 + 1)^2$ words. However, the memory required for PARENT LIST is `lookahead` words, because for each search episode we need only to store lookahead expanded tiles from which all adjacent tiles have been explored and inserted in the OPEN LIST.

The movements array is used to keep track of those tiles that are explorable during a certain number of successive search episodes. Each agent, by using the movement arrays, keeps a cost list for G_{cost}, H_{cost}, and F_{cost} only for those tiles contained in the movements array. When an agent performs a search episode, it stores and updates $g[s]$, $h[s]$, and $f[s]$, where s is a tile in the movements array. This array enables us to avoid maintaining an array of the same size as the grid map to store G_{cost}, H_{cost}, and F_{cost} values for each agent. The inspiration for this arises from the observation that an agent rarely requires or updates the values $g[s]$, $h[s]$, and $f[s]$ for some tile s discovered in past search episodes. In our implementation the size of the movement array is $(\text{lookahead} \times 4 + 1)^2$. Thus, the memory layout required for the three cost lists is $(\text{lookahead} \times 4 + 1)^2 \times 3$ words.

According to the positions of the lookahead and movements arrays for each agent, we update only those values in the agent's surrounding area. Initially, both arrays are centered on a start tile

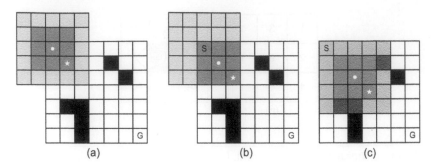

FIGURE 22.2

The dark-gray array is the lookahead array. The light-gray array is the movements array. Behavior of the arrays during a search episode with `lookahead=1`. The white dot is the start tile. The white star is the next start tile. (a) The lookahead array position is always centered on the start position. (b) After each search episode, the lookahead array will move according to the next start tile. As long as the movements array contains the lookahead array, it does not change its current position. (c) When the lookahead array moves out from the movements array then we must shift both arrays and center them on the new start tile (see color insert).

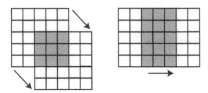

FIGURE 22.3

Two examples of movements array motion. The gray cells show that values $g-$, $h-$, and $f-$ are still valid when the movements array is moved. These values must be retained and then copied.

(Figure 22.2a). After a search episode the lookahead array will move according to the next start tile (Figure 22.2b). As long as the movements array contains the lookahead array, it does not change its current position. When the lookahead array moves out from the movements array, both arrays must be moved and centered on a new start tile (Figure 22.2c).

Note that before the movements array moves into a new position, the same values may still be valid and must be retained for the next search episode. In Figure 22.3, we show valid values in the movements array between two positions. Based on the direction these values must be copied to another part of the movements array. This operation is performed by simple read and write operations inside the same block of memory with negligible overhead.

22.3.3 The Working Set

The implementation of a search episode is designed using four kernels that have several inputs and two outputs. The input for all agents is a grid map. Whereas, the inputs for each agent include:

- A START and a GOAL tile. Initialized by the user.
- A NEXTSTARTTILE value to keep track of the next starting tile $g[\overline{s}]$.

- A STATE value to maintain the state of the search.
- The OPEN LIST, PARENT LIST, and CLOSED LIST. Initialized to zero.
- A cost list of updated heuristics H_{cost}. Initialized the first time by the host.
- A cost list of discovered paths G_{cost}. Initialized to ∞.
- A cost list of estimated paths F_{cost}. Initialized to zero.
- A COUNTER value to keep track of the current search episode.
- A list of values $search(s) = i$ if state s has been generated last by the ith A* search. This list is used to check if a tile has been generated in the previous search episodes. In the case $search(s) \neq$ COUNTER we set $g[s] = \infty$, enable us to rediscover this tile and improve the trajectory. Initialized to zero.

The pair of outputs for each agent are:

- A trajectory found in the last search episode without obstacles.
- The start tile $\bar{s}$ for the next A* search.

All input data structures reside in global memory. Static data structures, e.g., the grid map, are kept in cached constant global memory. While any modifiable data structures are kept in non-cached read-write global memory locations. All data structures are stored in an efficient collection of Structure-of-Arrays (SoA) that improves the probability of coalesced memory transactions across a half-warp.

22.3.4 **The CUDA Kernels**

Each agent is processed by a thread on the GPU. In order to improve the distribution of resources in the streaming multiprocessors, we implement the search episode process in four sequential CUDA kernels:

- `InitializeArray`: moves the lookahead array in the current tile $\bar{s}$ and moves the movements array when necessary.
- `InitializeSearch`: initializes $g[\bar{s}]$ and $f[\bar{s}]$ for the current tile $\bar{s}$ and inserts it in the OPEN LIST.
- `SearchEpisode`: performs the A* search from $\bar{s}$ expanding lookahead tiles. The priority queue is implemented in a similar way to that proposed in [3].
- `UpdateAndCheck`: updates the heuristics $h[s]$ of the tiles s contained in the CLOSED LIST, creates the path using the PARENT LIST, and checks the presence of obstacles along the path.

22.4 **RESULTS**

In this section, we show the results of two types of experiments. The first experiment demonstrates the efficiency of our approach, the second is related to the quality of the trajectory found using the lookahead and movements arrays.

The experiments were performed on six grid maps of sizes ranging from 20×20 to 1024×1024. Start and goal tiles were randomly chosen, and `lookahead` was set to 3. For each grid map, we launched several groups of agents, of size 128 to 294,912, and each CUDA block had 128 threads.

Table 22.2 Left: the Size of the Grid Maps and the GPU Memory Footprint for Each One. Right: the Number of Agents (Threads), the Number of Thread Blocks (128 Threads per Block), and the Memory Footprint for Each Group of Agents with Lookahead = 3. In the Worst-Case Scenario (T5 Grid Map and 294,912 Agents) the Total Amount of Memory Used is Below 5MB

	Map	States	Memory KB		Agents	Blocks	Memory MB
T0	20 × 20	400	1600	G0	128	1	0.39
T1	40 × 40	1600	6400	G1	8192	64	24.72
T2	80 × 80	6400	25600	G2	28800	225	86.69
T3	160 × 160	25600	102400	G3	80000	625	241.39
T4	320 × 320	102400	409600	G4	139392	1089	420.61
T5	1024 × 1024	1048576	4194304	G5	294912	2304	889.88

Table 22.3 Average Path Lengths and Average Search Episodes in Planning All Groups of Agents on Each Grid Map

	Average Path Lengths	Average Search Episodes
T0	10	7
T1	20	13
T2	38	27
T3	77	53
T4	151	105
T5	478	336

The GPU memory footprint for the grid maps and agent groups can be seen in Table 22.2. Our tests were performed on an Intel Core i7 CPU 1.6GHz, NVIDIA Fermi GTX 470 1.28GB, Windows 7. All the kernels were written in CUDA 2.1 and Microsoft's Visual C++ 2008 compiler.

Table 22.3 lists the average path lengths and the average number of search episodes that occurred for all groups of agents. Figure 22.4 shows the performance of the GPU. The absolute running time for the benchmarks executed on the GPU ranges from 458 milliseconds for T0 to 21,717 milliseconds for T5 and an average time per search episode of 65 milliseconds for T0, up to 63 milliseconds for T5. The smallest value, as observed for G5, arose because as the number of search episodes in T5 increases, the average time per search episode decreases, although the number of agents is greater than G0 (see Table 22.3). At the bottom of Figure 22.4, we can see the total average time taken for agent to reach its goal. Figure 22.5 supports the GPU CUDA performance scale compared to multithreading CPU implementation in running one, two, and four threads.

A GPU implementation of the A* algorithm has been presented by Bleiweiss [3]. Although the results of this work cannot be directly compared owing to the different hardware generation used, we can note the difference in terms of memory footprint. In Bleiweiss's work, with a map of 340 nodes and 115,600 agents, the working set memory (about 1.5GB) exceeds the available GPU global memory, and searches are thereby broken into multiple pathfinding passes, each one responsible for a subset of the total agents. In our work, a comparable configuration with T0 grid map and G4 agent configuration, the memory footprint is below 500 MB.

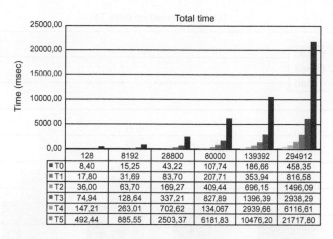

Total time	128	8192	28800	80000	139392	294912
■ T0	8,40	15,25	43,22	107,74	186,66	458,35
■ T1	17,80	31,69	83,70	207,71	353,94	816,58
■ T2	36,00	63,70	169,27	409,44	696,15	1496,09
■ T3	74,94	128,64	337,21	827,89	1396,39	2938,29
■ T4	147,21	263,01	702,62	134,067	2939,66	6116,61
■ T5	492,44	885,55	2503,37	6181,83	10476,20	21717,80

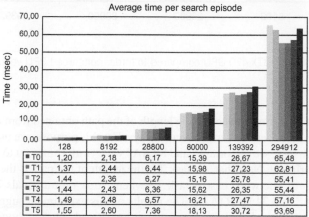

Average time per search episode	128	8192	28800	80000	139392	294912
■ T0	1,20	2,18	6,17	15,39	26,67	65,48
■ T1	1,37	2,44	6,44	15,98	27,23	62,81
■ T2	1,44	2,36	6,27	15,16	25,78	55,41
■ T3	1,44	2,43	6,36	15,62	26,35	55,44
■ T4	1,49	2,48	6,57	16,21	27,47	57,16
■ T5	1,55	2,60	7,36	18,13	30,72	63,69

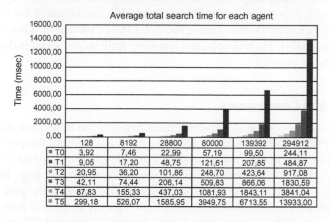

Average total search time for each agent	128	8192	28800	80000	139392	294912
■ T0	3,92	7,46	22,99	57,19	99,50	244,11
■ T1	9,05	17,20	48,75	121,61	207,85	484,87
■ T2	20,95	36,20	101,86	248,70	423,64	917,08
■ T3	42,11	74,44	206,14	509,83	866,06	1830,59
■ T4	87,83	155,33	437,03	1081,93	1843,11	3841,04
■ T5	299,18	526,07	1585,95	3949,75	6713,55	13933,00

FIGURE 22.4

GPU performance for all group of agents run over all six grid maps. We measured the total time to search the paths for all six groups of agents, the average time per search episode, which is critical for real-time applications, and average total search time per agent, which measures parallelism efficiency on the GPU.

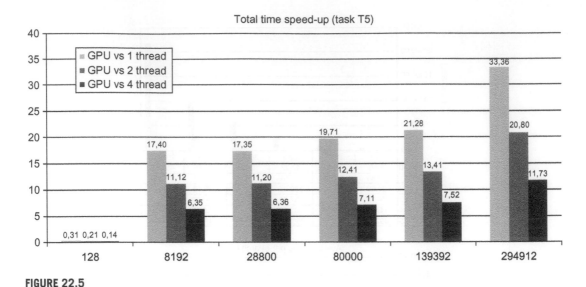

FIGURE 22.5

T5 performance of the NVIDIA GTX 470 GPU compared to three multithread CPU versions, using an Intel Core i7 CPU 1.6 GHz.

The second type of experiment concerns the length of the path obtained from our approach owing to the introduction of the lookahead and movements arrays. For this purpose, we use the five tasks shown in Figure 22.6. For each task, we perform A* and RTAA* with lookahead set to 3–7. Table 22.4 shows the results of this experiment. Note that, for task T1, the length of the path is the same, independent of the value of lookahead. The worst case is task T3 where lookahead equals 7. In this scenario, the path length is 19 for A* and 34 for RTAA*. The results of this experiment suggest that in some cases the approach finds paths whose lengths are worse than the optimal solution though the difference from the optimal path length is not significant. This deficiency is compensated for in terms of efficiency as shown in performance experiments. Tuning the lookahead parameter allows the user to trade off speed against path optimality. For example, in a real-time application, speed is the highest priority and suboptimal paths may be acceptable.

22.4.1 Results and Conclusions

In this chapter, we have shown that an implementation based on the Real-Time Adaptive A* algorithm fits well with the GPU parallel architecture. By using a limited memory footprint per thread, it offers a simple and powerful way to plan trajectories for many thousands of agents in parallel. The implementation manages only static and known obstacles reported in the grid map. In future research, we plan to implement the management of unknown obstacles that occur in the grid map. Once an agent recognizes the presence of an unknown obstacle, it will report it in the grid map and share this information with other agents. The unknown obstacle will become visible and will be taken into account in subsequent search episodes. This approach can easily be extended to cope with the presence of dynamic obstacles.

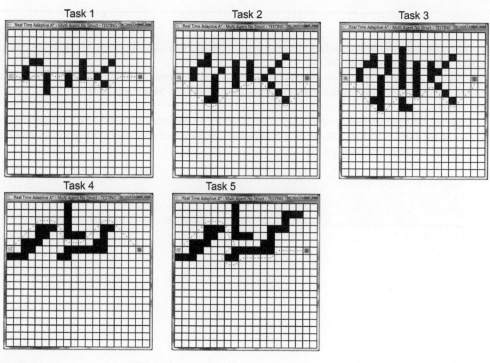

FIGURE 22.6

In each task the start position is on the left and the end position is on the right. The sketched line is the optimal path.

Table 22.4 For All the Tasks, the A* Row Reports the Least-Cost Paths, While GPU RTAA* Rows Report the Path Lengths and the Search-Episode Counts with Increasing `lookahead` Values

Pathfinding		Task 1	Task 2	Task 3	Task 4	Task 5
A*	Length	**18**	**19**	**19**	**19**	**23**
RTAA*-3	Length	18	28	33	26	31
	Search episodes	10	18	18	13	16
RTAA*-4	Length	18	23	40	20	29
	Search episodes	6	10	23	7	12
RTAA*-5	Length	18	25	23	20	27
	Search episodes	5	10	8	6	9
RTAA*-6	Length	18	21	32	20	26
	Search episodes	5	8	14	5	6
RTAA*-7	Length	18	19	34	22	27
	Search episodes	4	4	11	6	7

References

[1] P.E. Hart, N.J. Nilsson, B. Raphael, A formal basis for the heuristic determination of minimum cost paths, SIGART Bull. 4 (37) (1972) 28–29.

[2] S. Koenig, M. Likhachev, Real-time adaptive A*, in: G. Weiss, P. Stone (Eds.), AAMAS '06: Proceedings of the Fifth International Joint Conference on Autonomous Agents and Multiagent Systems, ACM, New York, 2006, pp. 281–288.

[3] A. Bleiweiss, GPU accelerated pathfinding, in: S. Spencer, D. Fellner (Eds.), GH '08: Proceedings of the 23rd ACM SIGGRAPH/EUROGRAPHICS Symposium on Graphics hardware, Eurographics Association, Aire-la-Ville, Switzerland, 2008, pp. 65–74.

Computational Finance

Thomas Bradley (NVIDIA)

STATE OF GPU COMPUTING IN COMPUTATIONAL FINANCE

The ever-increasing sophistication of financial instruments and trading strategies, as well as strict regulatory requirements, leads to an enduring demand for faster and more accurate models. Computational finance encompasses the spectrum of algorithms to provide these models in applications such as options pricing, risk management, portfolio optimization, and algorithmic trading; GPUs are providing extraordinary performance benefits in the acceleration of the underlying numerical methods for calibration, pricing, and analytics. These benefits are frequently dispensed not only on reducing the time to get a result but also on improving the accuracy of the computation, reducing the cost of the hardware, and reducing the cost of running the hardware.

The increased performance as well as the scalability provided by GPUs means that institutions are able to increase business at the same time as having tighter control on their exposure. In addition the GPU opens new opportunities, for example, by making it tractable to evaluate larger baskets in a short period of time or by enabling analysts to model more complex risk relationships, and as new algorithms are developed, so yet more advanced models and strategies will be deployed on the GPU.

IN THIS SECTION

Chapter 23 develops a finite difference approach to value financial derivatives. Starting with a single-factor model, the author develops the model to a two-factor model using the alternating direction implicit scheme. Building on the tri-diagonal solver techniques introduced in Chapter 11, the author develops a PDE solver and shows how it can be applied in financial applications to accelerating pricing and risk calculations.

Chapter 24 uses a Monte Carlo simulation to model credit risk, creating a loss distribution for a large portfolio and enabling detailed analytics in the tail of the distribution. Deviating from the normal one-thread-per-scenario method for embarrassingly parallel algorithms, the authors use multiple threads cooperating on a single scenario to improve the memory characteristics. As a result the performance scales very well and large problem sizes are easily accommodated, enabling significant power and hardware cost saving.

Chapter 25 applies Monte Carlo simulation to market value-at-risk calculation and considers the application from a variety of perspectives to understand where performance can be improved. The authors evolve the application from a naïve implementation by applying algorithmic and high-level optimizations to achieve a significant speedup, thereby enabling such calculations to be performed on-demand rather than overnight.

Pricing Financial Derivatives with High Performance Finite Difference Solvers on GPUs

23

Daniel Egloff

The calculation of the fair value and the sensitivity parameters of a financial derivative requires special numerical methods, which are often computationally very demanding. In this chapter we discuss the design and implementation of efficient GPU solvers for the partial differential equations (PDEs) of derivative pricing problems.

For derivatives on a single asset like a stock or an index we consider a massively parallel PDE solver which simultaneously prices a large collection of similar or related derivatives with finite difference schemes. We achieve a speedup of a factor of 25 on a single GPU and up to a factor of 40 on a dual GPU configuration against an optimized CPU version.

Often derivatives are written on multiple underlying assets, e.g., baskets, or the future asset price evolution is modeled with additional risk factors, like for instance stochastic volatilities. The resulting PDE is defined on a multidimensional state space. For these kinds of derivatives it is not necessary to pool multiple pricing calculations: alternating direction implicit (ADI) schemes for PDEs on two or more state variables have enough parallelism for an efficient GPU implementation. We benchmark a specific ADI solver for the Heston stochastic volatility model against a fully multithreaded and optimized CPU implementation. On a recent C2050 Fermi GPU we attain a speedup of a factor of 70 and more for a sufficiently large problem size.

Our results demonstrate the importance of the effective use of GPU resources such as fast on-chip memory and registers.

23.1 INTRODUCTION, PROBLEM STATEMENT, AND CONTEXT

Under the assumption of no arbitrage, the fair value of a European derivative with maturity T is given by the expectation

$$\mathbb{E}_{\mathbb{Q}}[P(0,T)f(X_T)], \tag{1}$$

where X_T is usually a vector valued stochastic process modeling the evolution of the market uncertainty, $P(0,T)$ is the price of a zero bond of face value one at maturity, $\mathbb{Q}$ is a suitable risk-neutral probability measure, and $f(X_T)$ is the payoff at maturity. Analytical expressions for the expectation (Eq. (1)) can only be derived under very stringent conditions; almost all practically relevant models must be solved with numerical techniques.

Existing numerical methods can be broadly classified into three groups: Monte Carlo simulation, partial differential equation (PDE) methods, and numerical integration methods. Monte Carlo simulation is the most direct approach to calculate the expectation (Eq. (1)). It is very versatile and can handle complex and high dimensional models. Monte Carlo methods fall in the category of embarrassingly parallel problems and are usually parallelized on a per sample basis. As such, a GPU implementation is relatively straightforward — typically the most challenging component is the random number generator, which must be capable of producing independent streams of random numbers for every thread. Because GPU programs should be designed in such a way that a very large number of threads can be executed in parallel, the implementation of the random number generator has to carefully balance the quality and the size of the internal state of the random number generator. Impressive performance benefits from using GPUs for Monte Carlo simulations are already documented in several places. An early contribution is made by [1], a more recent work for Asian options is [2]. The principal disadvantages of Monte Carlo simulations are its significant computational cost, even on GPUs, and a possibly large simulation error, which often require special purpose or variance reduction schemes tuned to the specific payoff or product category.

Numerical integration techniques rely on a transformation to the Fourier domain. The idea is to express the expectation (Eq. (1)) as an integral with respect to the probability density function of the random variable X_T. For several important processes, including the Heston stochastic volatility model, the Bates model, and also Levy models, the Fourier transform of the density or the characteristic function is available in analytical form. Hence, a suitable transform of the integral can be calculated analytically and transformed back to obtain the option price. These methods are often used for path-independent options and in the context of model calibration. Recently, some progress has been achieved to extend transform techniques also to American and some path-dependent options. An interesting implementation on GPUs can be found in [3].

The Feynman-Kac theorem links the expectation (Eq. (1)) under the risk-neutral measure to the solution of a partial differential equation (see for instance [4], Sections 4.4 and 5.7, or [5], Section 8.2), which then can be solved with numerical methods such as finite difference or finite element schemes. The advantage of the PDE approach is its accuracy and generality. Moreover, handling the optimal stopping problem for American options and early exercise features is significantly less complicated than with Monte Carlo methods. The main drawback is the curse of dimensionality. PDE methods become computationally intractable at high dimensionality, and therefore PDE methods are mainly used for one and two-factor models, and to some extent for three-factor models.

PDEs in dimension two or higher can be solved with so called operator splitting methods, of which alternating direction implicit schemes are particular versions. The main idea of an ADI scheme is best explained in two dimensions with coordinates x and y under the assumption of no mixed spatial derivative terms. The discretized PDE operator is split into two parts, each representing only the discretization in one coordinate direction. Starting with the initial conditions, every time step is handled in two stages: the first half-step is taken implicitly in the x-direction and explicitly in the y-direction, followed by a second half-step taken implicitly in the y-direction and explicitly in the *x*-direction. The presence of a mixed spatial derivative term requires further steps to guarantee the stability of the solution.

23.2 CORE METHOD

The partial differential equation to calculate the arbitrage free price of a derivative, as derived from the Feynman-Kac theorem, is a parabolic convection diffusion equation

$$\frac{\partial u}{\partial t} - \mathcal{L}_t u(t,x) = 0. \tag{2}$$

In one-factor models *x* is a suitable transform of the underlying asset. An example of a two-factor model is a stochastic volatility model, where $x = (s, v)$, with *s* the underlying asset and *v* the unobservable stochastic volatility.

We solve the PDE (Eq. (2)) by finite difference schemes on variable time and state grids. Inhomogeneous grids lead to more complicated expressions for the finite difference discretization of derivatives but are indispensable to achieve good stability and accuracy. For instance, payoff discontinuities and steep gradients lead to spurious oscillations and a significant loss in accuracy. A reasonably effective approach is to increase the finite difference approximation accuracy with locally refined grids in both the time and state dimensions, properly aligned to the points of singularities. For example, the mesh must be concentrated at barriers and the time grid must be exponentially refined after payoff singularities or time window barriers. For additional details we refer the reader to [6], Chapter 5.

For one-dimensional PDEs and implicit/mixed-time discretization schemes of Crank Nicolson type, a linear system of equations must be solved at every time step. The alternating direction implicit (ADI) schemes of Douglas or Craig-Sneyd [7, 8] and the more recent one of Hundsdorfer-Verwer [9, 10] also lead to many independent linear systems for every direction and at every time step. For the commonly used finite difference approximation of the spatial derivatives, these linear systems are essentially tridiagonal, up to a suitable permutation of the grid points.

The commonly used tridiagonal systems solver is Gaussian elimination without pivoting. It solves diagonally dominant tridiagonal system of *n* linear equations with $8n$ arithmetic operations. Because the algorithm minimizes the number of arithmetic operations, and because all vector elements are accessed with unit stride, it is optimal for a serial computer. Conversely, the algorithm displays no parallelism at all because all loops are serial recurrences, and therefore it is unsuitable for a parallel architecture with more than one processor.

Solving tridiagonal systems efficiently on parallel computers is very challenging, because of the inherent dependency between the rows of the system and the low computation to communication ratio. Fortunately, the architecture of modern GPUs, with memory close to the ALU and very fast thread synchronization, allows us to implement a fine grained parallel tridiagonal solver based on the parallel cyclic reduction algorithm and opens the door to very efficient PDE solvers on GPUs.

For a GPU implementation we restrict ourselves to the CUDA parallel computing architecture and refer the reader to [11] for basic CUDA terms and concepts. The adjustments for an OpenCL implementation should be straightforward and are not further discussed.

23.3 ALGORITHMS, IMPLEMENTATIONS, AND EVALUATIONS

23.3.1 No-Arbitrage Pricing PDEs

The most commonly used single-factor model in the equity domain is the local volatility model with dynamics

$$dS_t = S_{t-}(r_t - q_t)dt + S_{t-}\sigma_{loc}(t, S_{t-})dW_t - \sum_{0 < t_i \leq T} \{S_{t_i-}b_i + a_i\}\delta_{t=t_i} dt \tag{3}$$

for the underlying asset S_t, where r_t is the risk free rate, q_t a continuous dividend yield, and a_i, b_i discrete/proportional cash dividends at times t_i. In between the time points t_i, the arbitrage free price $V(t, s)$ of a derivative security with payoff $g(s)$ at maturity T satisfies the PDE

$$\frac{\partial V}{\partial t} + (r_t - q_t)s\frac{\partial V}{\partial s} + \frac{1}{2}\sigma_{loc}^2(t, s)s^2\frac{\partial^2 V}{\partial s^2} - r_t V = 0, \tag{4}$$

with final value $V(T, s) = g(s)$ and has the jump discontinuity

$$V(t_i-, s) = V(t_i+, s(1 - b_i) - a_i) \tag{5}$$

across every discrete dividend time t_i. By a financially motivated coordinate transformation as described in [12] we can remove the jump discontinuities (Eq. (5)) across discrete dividends. The PDE (Eq. (4)) is of the general form (Eq. (2)), with $\mathcal{L}_t$ a second-order differential operator

$$\mathcal{L}_t u(t, x) = a(t, x)\frac{\partial^2 u}{\partial x^2}(t, x) + b(t, x)\frac{\partial u}{\partial x}(t, x) + c(t, x)u(t, x) + d(t, x). \tag{6}$$

Single-factor convertible bond models, as studied in [13] and [14], for example, and one-factor interest rate models, such as the Hull-White, Vasicek, Cox-Ingersoll-Ross, or Black-Derman-Toy model [15], Chapter 3, lead to similar no-arbitrage PDEs.

In (Eq. (3)) the volatility is a state dependent function. It can also be modelled with a separate stochastic process, which results in a two-factor model. A prominent example is the Heston stochastic volatility model introduced in [16], with dynamics

$$dS_t = S_t(r_t - q_t)dt + S_t\sqrt{v_t}dW_t^1, \tag{7}$$

$$dv_t = \kappa(\eta - v_t)dt + \sigma\sqrt{v_t}dW_t^2, \tag{8}$$

where $dW_t^1 dW_t^2 = \rho dt$ with correlation $\rho \in [-1, 1]$. The model parameters are the initial volatility $v_0 > 0$, the mean reversion rate κ, long run variance η, volatility of variance σ, and correlation ρ. The corresponding no-arbitrage PDE is given by

$$\frac{\partial V}{\partial t} + \frac{1}{2}vs^2\frac{\partial^2 V}{\partial s^2} + \rho\sigma vs\frac{\partial^2 V}{\partial s\partial v} + \frac{1}{2}\sigma^2 v\frac{\partial^2 V}{\partial v^2} + (r_t - q_t)s\frac{\partial V}{\partial s}$$

$$+ (\kappa(\eta - v) - \Lambda(t, s, v))\frac{\partial V}{\partial v} - r_t V = 0 \tag{9}$$

where $\Lambda(t, s, v) = \lambda v$ is the (affine) market price of volatility risk and singles out a specific risk neutral measure. We note that the model structure allows us to re-parameterize it in such a way that $\lambda = 0$.

23.3.2 Finite Difference Discretization

23.3.2.1 *Single-Factor Models*

We formulate the finite difference discretization of the PDE (Eq. (2)) with differential operator (Eq. (6)) on variable time and state grids. To this end, let $[0, T] \times [x_{\min}, x_{\max}]$ be a truncated domain and

$$\mathcal{T} = \{t_0, \ldots, t_{n_t-1}\}, \quad \mathcal{X} = \{x_0, \ldots, x_{n_x-1}\}, \tag{10}$$

be (possibly inhomogeneous) grids for the time and state variables. Also let

$$\Delta_t^n = t_{n+1} - t_n, \quad \Delta_x^i = x_{i+1} - x_i. \tag{11}$$

For any function $a(t, x)$, $a_i^n = a(t_n, x_i)$ is the value at the grid point (t_n, x_i). Likewise, u_i^n denotes an approximate solution of (Eq. (2)) at (t_n, x_i).

The finite difference approximations on $\mathcal{T} \times \mathcal{X}$ can be conveniently derived using the technique described in [17] and [18]. Fornberg's algorithm allows us to derive the finite difference weights; a version for symbolic calculus is implemented in the Mathematica function `FiniteDifferenceDerivative`. For instance, the second-order-accurate finite difference approximation of the first derivative is given by

$$\frac{\partial u}{\partial x}(t_n, x_i) \approx -\frac{\Delta_x^i}{\Delta_x^{i-1}\left(\Delta_x^{i-1} + \Delta_x^i\right)} u_{i-1}^n + \left(\frac{1}{\Delta_x^{i-1}} - \frac{1}{\Delta_x^i}\right) u_i^n + \frac{\Delta_x^{i-1}}{\Delta_x^i\left(\Delta_x^{i-1} + \Delta_x^i\right)} u_{i+1}^n, \tag{12}$$

whereas the first-order-accurate finite difference approximation of the second derivative is

$$\frac{\partial^2 u}{\partial x^2}(t_n, x_i) \approx \frac{2}{\Delta_x^{i-1}\left(\Delta_x^{i-1} + \Delta_x^i\right)} u_{i-1}^n - \frac{2}{\Delta_x^{i-1}\Delta_x^i} u_i^n + \frac{2}{\Delta_x^i\left(\Delta_x^{i-1} + \Delta_x^i\right)} u_{i+1}^n. \tag{13}$$

Both approximations are central finite differences, yielding, for all interior nodes $x_1, \ldots, x_{n_x-2}$, the approximation

$$\mathcal{L}_{t_n} u(t_n, x_i) \approx (\mathcal{L}^n \mathbf{u}^n)_i = a_i^n \sum_{k=-1}^{1} w_k^2 u_{i+k}^n + b_i^n \sum_{k=-1}^{1} w_k^1 u_{i+k}^n + c_i^n u_i^n + d_i^n, \tag{14}$$

with weights w_k^l determined from Eqs. (12), (13) and $\mathbf{u}_n = (u_0^n, \ldots, u_{n_x-1}^n)^\top$. Equation (14) defines a tridiagonal operator on all interior nodes. To fully specify the operator we must supply boundary conditions. Depending on the payoff, we choose either Dirichlet, Neumann or asymptotically linear boundary conditions

$$s^2 \frac{\partial^2 V}{\partial s^2} = 0 \quad \text{for} \quad s \to \infty. \tag{15}$$

We refer to [19] and also [6] page 122. Note that asymptotically linear boundary conditions are formulated in the underlying coordinates and must be properly transformed if the PDE is solved in any other coordinate system, for example in log-spot coordinates.

Using a one-sided forward difference for the time derivative and the usual mixed scheme for $\theta \in [0,1]$ gives

$$\frac{u_i^{n+1} - u_i^n}{\Delta_t^n} = (1-\theta)(\mathcal{L}^n \mathbf{u}_n)_i + \theta(\mathcal{L}^{n+1} \mathbf{u}_{n+1})_i, \tag{16}$$

For every time step $n = n_t - 2, \ldots, 0$ this is a tridiagonal system

$$\left(\mathrm{id} + (1-\theta)\Delta_t^n \mathcal{L}^n\right)\mathbf{u}_n = \left(\mathrm{id} - \theta\Delta_t^n \mathcal{L}^{n+1}\right)\mathbf{u}_{n+1} \tag{17}$$

for the unknown $\mathbf{u}_n$, in terms of $\mathbf{u}_{n+1}$ determined in the previous time step or from the terminal payoff condition $\mathbf{f}$ at time step $n_t - 1$. The algorithm to find the solution $\mathbf{u}_0$ is now as follows:

Algorithm 1: PDE solver pseudo code

---

input: discretized operators $\mathcal{L}^n$, terminal condition f, time steps Δ_t^n, parameter θ
result: value curve $\mathbf{u}_0$ at time t_0

1: $\mathbf{A}_r \leftarrow \mathcal{L}^{N+1}$;
2: $\mathbf{u}_{n_t-1} \leftarrow \mathbf{f}$;
3: **for** $n \leftarrow n_t - 2$ **to** 0 **do**
4:     $\mathrm{rhs} \leftarrow \left(\mathrm{id} - \theta\Delta_t^n \mathbf{A}_r\right)\mathbf{u}_{n+1}$;
5:     $\mathbf{A}_l \leftarrow \mathcal{L}^n$;
6:     $\mathbf{u}_n \leftarrow$ solution of $\left(\mathrm{id} + (1-\theta)\Delta_t^n \mathbf{A}_l\right)\mathbf{x} = \mathrm{rhs}$;
7:     swap $\mathbf{A}_r \leftrightarrow \mathbf{A}_l$;

Once the matrices $\mathcal{L}^n$ are assembled, the most performance critical section of Algorithm 1 is to solve the tridiagonal system (Eq. (17)).

23.3.2.2 *Two-Factor Models*

For a two-factor model the Crank-Nicolson time discretization and finite difference discretization of the differential operator $\mathcal{L}_t$ in Eq. (2) leads to a linear system of equations as in Eq. (17). However, the matrices $\mathcal{L}^n$ are no longer tridiagonal but instead have a bandwidth proportional to the minimum of the number of grid points along the coordinate axes of the two factors. The system can be solved with LU factorization, but this becomes ineffective for larger numbers of grid points.

We therefore consider ADI-style splitting schemes. We restrict our exposition to the particular case of the Heston stochastic volatility model, and only briefly explain the ideas and introduce the required notations to discuss the GPU implementation. Further details can be found in [20].

Let $[0, T] \times [s_{\min}, s_{\max}] \times [v_{\min}, v_{\max}]$ be a truncated domain and

$$\mathcal{T} = \{t_0, \ldots, t_{n_t-1}\}, \quad \mathcal{S} = \{s_0, \ldots, s_{n_s-1}\}, \quad \mathcal{V} = \{v_0, \ldots, v_{n_v-1}\}, \tag{18}$$

be suitable grids. Let $\mathbf{v}_n = (V(t_n, s_i, v_j), i = 0, \ldots, n_s - 1, j = 0, \ldots, n_v - 1)^\top$ be an approximation of the solution of Eq. (9) on the discretization nodes (Eq. (18)) at time t_n. We approximate the PDE (Eq. (9))

with finite differences, complement it with the proper boundary conditions and decompose the resulting linear operator $\mathcal{L}^n$ into three submatrices

$$\mathcal{L}^n = \mathcal{L}_0^n + \mathcal{L}_1^n + \mathcal{L}_2^n, \tag{19}$$

where $\mathcal{L}_0^n$ is the part of $\mathcal{L}^n$ coming from the mixed derivative term, $\mathcal{L}_1^n$ is the part that contains all the spacial derivatives, and $\mathcal{L}_2^n$ collects all the derivatives in direction of the variance coordinate v. The zero-order term $r_t V$ is evenly distributed to $\mathcal{L}_1^n$ and $\mathcal{L}_2^n$. In contrast to [20], we apply finite difference approximations such that the resulting operators $\mathcal{L}_1^n$ and $\mathcal{L}_2^n$ are essentially tridiagonal in a suitable permutation of the grid points.

The Douglas scheme successively calculates the solution at time t_0 by

$$\mathbf{y}_0 = \mathbf{v}_{n+1} + \Delta_t^n \mathcal{L}^{n+1} \mathbf{v}_{n+1} \tag{20}$$

$$\mathbf{y}_j = \mathbf{y}_{j-1} + \Delta_t^n \theta \left(\mathcal{L}_j^n \mathbf{y}_j - \mathcal{L}_j^{n+1} \mathbf{v}_{n+1} \right), \quad j = 1,2 \tag{21}$$

$$\mathbf{v}_n = \mathbf{y}_2 \tag{22}$$

A forward Euler predictor step is followed by two implicit but unidirectional corrector steps, which stabilize the predictor step. The Douglas scheme is a direct generalization of the classical ADI scheme for two-dimensional diffusion equations applied to the situation of a non-vanishing mixed spatial derivative term. It is first-order-accurate, and only stable when applied to two-dimensional convection-diffusion equations with a mixed derivative term if $\theta \geq \frac{1}{2}$. A more refined scheme is the Hundsdorfer-Verwer scheme given by

$$\mathbf{y}_0 = \mathbf{v}_{n+1} + \Delta_t^n \mathcal{L}^{n+1} \mathbf{v}_{n+1} \tag{23}$$

$$\mathbf{y}_j = \mathbf{y}_{j-1} + \Delta_t^n \theta \left(\mathcal{L}_j^n \mathbf{y}_j - \mathcal{L}_j^{n+1} \mathbf{v}_{n+1} \right), \quad j = 1,2 \tag{24}$$

$$\tilde{\mathbf{y}}_0 = \mathbf{y}_0 + \frac{1}{2} \Delta_t^n \left(\mathcal{L}^n \mathbf{y}_2 - \mathcal{L}^{n+1} \mathbf{v}_{n+1} \right) \tag{25}$$

$$\tilde{\mathbf{y}}_j = \tilde{\mathbf{y}}_{j-1} + \Delta_t^n \theta \left(\mathcal{L}_j^n \tilde{\mathbf{y}}_j - \mathcal{L}_j^n \mathbf{y}_2 \right), \quad j = 1,2 \tag{26}$$

$$\mathbf{v}_n = \tilde{\mathbf{y}}_2 \tag{27}$$

The Hundsdorfer-Verwer scheme is an extension of the Douglas scheme, performing a second predictor step, followed by two unidirectional corrector steps. The advantage of the Hundsdorfer-Verwer scheme is that it attains order of consistency two for general operators $\mathcal{L}_0^n$, $\mathcal{L}_1^n$, $\mathcal{L}_2^n$. Further alternatives are given by the Craig-Sneyd and its modified version, for which we refer to [20].

23.3.3 Tridiagonal Solver

The implicit time step updates (Eqs. (17) and (21), (24), (26)) require linear systems of equations to be solved. However, efficiently solving tridiagonal systems in parallel is a demanding task and requires specialized algorithms. The first parallel algorithm for the solution of tridiagonal systems was cyclic reduction developed by [21], which is also known as the odd-even reduction method. Later

[22] introduced the recursive doubling algorithm. Both cyclic reduction and recursive doubling are designed for fine-grained parallelism, where each processor owns exactly one row of the tridiagonal matrix. For further details we refer to Section 5.4, page 470, in [23] and [24]. For a description of the cyclic reduction, the parallel cyclic reduction and some hybrid schemes on the GPU please refer to A Hybrid Method for Solving Tridiagonal Systems on the GPU, Numerical Algorithms, Chapter 11.

A highly optimized GPU based parallel cyclic reduction solver is also introduced in [12]. The implementation slightly differs from the parallel cyclic reduction presented earlier in this book. The main difference is that it can handle systems of any number of dimensions, not necessarily a power of two, uses registers instead of shared memory for temporary variables, and uses preprocessor techniques to unroll loops. Finally it uses a problem size dependent kernel dispatching method to call the optimal algorithm for a given dimension. The solver is tuned for systems of dimension 128 to 512 because these dimensions are relevant in practical applications. Its performance is comparable to those presented in [25] and in A Hybrid Method for Solving Tridiagonal Systems on the GPU, Numerical Algorithms, Chapter 11.

23.3.4 GPU Implementation

One-Factor PDE Solver

Pricing a single derivative in a one-factor model context with Algorithm 1 does not lead to enough parallel work to keep a modern GPU busy. Fortunately, in a realistic financial application it is often the case that many derivative prices must be recalculated at the same time. If an underlying change, usually a large collection of options with different strikes, maturities, and payoff profiles needs to be repriced. Another example comes from risk management, where whole books of derivatives have to be priced under multiple scenarios.

We therefore design the GPU PDE solver for single-factor models based on Algorithm 1 to price a large collection of similar, or related, derivatives in parallel on one or multiple GPUs. The overall collection of pricing problems is split into subsets according to a suitable load balancing strategy. Each subset is scheduled for execution on one of the available GPUs. For every GPU a dedicated CPU thread is responsible for the scheduling and execution of subsets of pricing problems. This thread also performs the data transfer to and from the GPU and launches the data preparation and pricing kernels.

A single PDE pricing problem out of a subset is solved with a block of threads, where each thread is handling a discretization node of the finite difference scheme. This thread organization optimally utilizes the hierarchical hardware structure of the GPU. It allows us to use shared memory for the data exchange between threads and to synchronize threads working on the same PDE, and we can apply the fine-grained parallel tridiagonal solver from Section 23.3.3 for implicit or Crank Nicolson time stepping schemes. Because thread blocks are executed on one of the available streaming multiprocessors of the GPU we can process several PDE pricing problems in parallel on a single GPU. Note that if we assign more pricing problems to a GPU than numbers of multiprocessors on the GPU, the hardware utilization can be further optimized because the hardware thread manager can switch between different PDE pricing problems, thereby hiding memory latency more efficiently.

Some design and implementation considerations are worth mentioning. A good overall GPU utilization for the one-factor PDE solver can only be achieved with a large problem set. Therefore, in order to maximize the number of derivatives which can be bundled for parallel execution, the PDE solver is designed to handle all kinds of payoff features, including single and double barriers, time window barriers, as well as early exercise of Bermudan or American type. On the implementation side, we must pay attention to scalability within a GPU and across multiple GPUs, with sophisticated data management to reuse common data and ensure efficient data transfer.

For a multi-GPU configuration the splitting strategy is important to achieve scalability in the number of GPUs. A fairly simple and still efficient approach is to first group pricing problems of the same underlying and sort them according to the computational cost, measured in terms of the product of time steps and discretization nodes. The idea is to build subsets of pricing problems of roughly the same computational cost and with as much common input data as possible.

Because the transfer of data from CPU host memory to GPU device memory and back can easily cost a significant amount of the overall processing time, an optimized data management is indispensable for high performance and low latency. We design our data management along the following guidelines:

1. Keep the data on the GPU as long as possible and reuse it for multiple computations;
2. Avoid lots of small data transfers — instead, pack data into blocks before sending it to the GPU device memory;
3. Optimize the layout of the packed data by introducing padding, memory alignment, or interleaving, such that the data structure allows for efficient memory access patterns from multiple blocks of threads.

A further optimization is achieved by asynchronous data transfer such that memory transfer and computations can overlap. For additional details we refer to [26].

Two-Factor PDE Solver

In contrast to single-factor models, the ADI schemes for two-factor models offer sufficient parallelism for an effective GPU implementation of a single pricing problem; i.e., there is no need to pool multiple pricing problems in order to increase the data parallelism.

We decompose every time step into multiple kernel calls. The Douglas scheme requires three kernel calls per time step. The first kernel performs the explicit forward Euler predictor step (Eq. (20)) by exploiting the decomposition (Eq. (19)). Because the operators $\mathcal{L}_j^n, j = 0, 1, 2$ are only used in matrix vector operations, we are free to use a discretization of the spatial derivatives, which does not necessarily lead to tridiagonal operators. This is particularly convenient for the mixed derivative terms in $\mathcal{L}_0^n$ at the boundary, where we can use second-order forward and backward difference approximations. This kernel also calculates $\mathcal{L}_j^{n+1}\mathbf{v}_{n+1}$, which will be reused in next two kernel calls to perform Eq. (21).

The second kernel calculates $\mathbf{y}_1$ in Eq. (21) for $j = 1$ by sweeping over the n_v slices $v = v_0, \ldots, v = v_{n_v-1}$. In the inner nodes the kernel solves a tridiagonal system, and at the face nodes $v = v_0$ and $v = v_{n_v-1}$ it uses the proper boundary conditions. Finally the third kernel determines $\mathbf{y}_2$ from Eq. (21) for $j = 2$ by sweeping over the n_s slices $s = s_0, \ldots, s = s_{n_s-1}$. For these two kernels we must pay attention that the operators $\mathcal{L}_j^n, j = 1, 2$, which are used to solve the system of equations, are essentially tridiagonal such that we can apply the parallel cyclic reduction solver or a variation thereof.

The implementation of the Hundsorfer-Verwer scheme is similar, but slightly more complex.

23.4 FINAL EVALUATION

23.4.1 One-Factor PDE Solver

All benchmarks for the one-factor PDE solver are compiled with the Microsoft 32-bit C++ compiler and CUDA version 3.1, and executed on an Intel Core 2 Quad CPU Q6602 system, running at 2.4 GHz, with two NVIDIA Tesla C1060 GPUs. The test set to benchmark the efficiency of the one-factor PDE solver consists of a large collection of European put and call options of different maturities and strikes. The finite difference scheme uses 50 time steps per year. This time we measure overall execution time, including the time required to transfer data to and from GPU device memory and the overhead for thread management in case of multiple GPUs. Tables 23.1 and 23.2 display the timings based on the fully optimized tridiagonal solver kernel, where all the vectors of the tridiagonal system fit into shared memory.

To gain further insight into the overall efficiency it is interesting to analyze the runtime cost for the data transfer. Because we minimize the number of memory copy operations by packing data into large blocks, we find that only 2% to 4% of the overall execution time is required for the data transfer, including the conversion from double to single precision.

So far we only considered the pricing of European options. The benchmark results for barrier options are very much similar. We handle the pricing of American options with a parallel operator splitting method, which resolves the nonlinear early exercise constraint independently for

Table 23.1 European Option, State Grid Size 128. Timings are Measured in Milliseconds

Problem Size	CPU	1 GPU	Speedup 1 GPU	2 GPUs	Speedup 2 GPUs	GPU Scaling
300	582	33	17.6	28	20.8	1.2
600	1149	53	21.7	45	25.5	1.2
900	1707	76	22.5	61	28.0	1.2
1200	2277	94	24.2	72	31.6	1.3
1800	3437	141	24.4	101	34.0	1.4

Table 23.2 European Option, State Grid Size 256. Timings are Measured in Milliseconds

Problem Size	CPU	1 GPU	Speedup 1 GPU	2 GPUs	Speedup 2 GPUs	GPU Scaling
300	1091	52	21.0	41	26.6	1.3
600	2204	93	23.7	72	30.6	1.3
900	3254	132	24.9	91	35.8	1.4
1200	4405	174	25.1	120	36.7	1.5

every discretization state and can therefore be implemented in a data-parallel manner. The resulting performance figures are even better than for European options.

23.4.2 PDE Solver for Heston Stochastic Volatility Model

The GPU ADI solver for the two-dimensional Heston stochastic volatility model is benchmarked against an optimized fully multithreaded CPU implementation, which we based on the Intel thread building blocks. In the following we only consider the Douglas scheme in single precision; see Figure 23.1 for a graphical illustration.

On an Intel dual core E5200 2.5 GHz with a GTX260 GPU the ADI solver runs about 40 times faster than the CPU single core version and 27 times faster than the optimized multi-core version. The shared memory requirements of the tridiagonal solver limit the GPU ADI solver on a Tesla C1060 or GTX260 to state grids of at most 1004 points. The best speedup is achieved when the state grid size is near this limit. For small scale problems the speedup is not very large, due to the cost of allocating device memory. If the problem size is growing, the time required to allocate memory on the GPU becomes less dominant and the speedup increases significantly.

Interesting performance results are obtained with a recent C2050 Fermi GPU, see Table 23.3. The ADI solver on a C2050 faces fewer hardware limitations. More registers and a larger amount of shared memory per block allow us to execute problems with up to 3056 state grid nodes. At these very large grid points we obtain a speedup factor of more than 70 against a single core implementation. Besides the capability to handle larger problem sizes, the speed increase of the C2050 against the GTX260 ranges from a factor of 1.6 up to a factor 2 for the state grid size of 896 and more, even though the C2050 has only 14 multiprocessors and no Fermi-specific optimizations were made in the code.

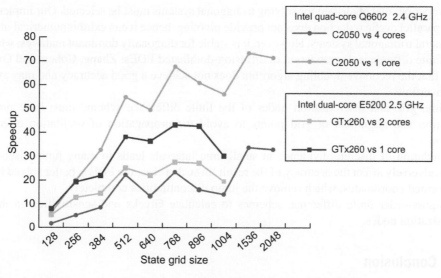

FIGURE 23.1

Speedup ADI Douglas scheme on GTX260 versus dual core and C2050 versus quad core.

Table 23.3 Timing in Seconds. Time to Maturity = 2 Years, Time Steps = 200 (Intel Quad-Core Q6602 2.4 GHz, Fermi C2050, Cuda 3.1, Windows Vista)

Problem Size (n_s, n_v)	One core	Four cores	GPU	Speedup single core	Speedup multi-core
128	2.1	0.6	0.3	6.2	1.7
256	8.5	2.2	0.4	19.9	5.2
384	19.4	5.0	0.6	32.6	8.5
512	46.8	19.0	0.9	54.7	22.2
640	55.9	15.1	1.1	49.3	13.3
768	97.9	34.0	1.4	67.5	23.4
896	111.0	29.3	1.8	60.7	16.0
1004	133.6	33.6	2.4	56.0	14.1
1536	445.8	205.2	6.1	73.2	33.7
2048	793.3	365.7	11.1	71.3	32.9

23.4.3 Single Precision versus Double Precision

The current GPU generation features substantially more throughput in single precision than in double precision. Our numerical experiments show that for practical applications, the accuracy of single precision is usually sufficient. The stability and accuracy of the solver benefits from a careful implementation:

1. The proper parallel algorithm for solving tridiagonal systems must be selected. Our implementation of the parallel cyclic reduction does not provide pivoting, hence it can exhibit numerical instabilities for general tridiagonal systems. However, it is stable for diagonally dominant matrices, which occur from finite difference discretization of diffusion-dominated PDEs. Zhang, Cohen, and Owens [25] found that the recursive doubling algorithm does not achieve a good accuracy and may even suffer from overflow.
2. The time grid and discretization nodes of the finite difference scheme must have proper concentration and alignment of grid points to avoid the propagation of oscillation effects in the solution.
3. Accumulation of discrete dividends in small time intervals leads to many jump discontinuities, which adversely affect the accuracy of the result. In such a case, the PDE is better solved in suitably transformed coordinates, which remove the jump discontinuities completely.
4. Use higher-order finite difference schemes to calculate Greeks and sensitivities on the grid of discretization nodes.

23.4.4 Conclusion

The architecture of the GPU and the hardware limitations make the development of high performance general purpose solvers for one-dimensional finite difference schemes a challenging task. Our benchmark results prove that, with the proper algorithm and a well designed GPU resource management, it is possible to implement solvers which perform exceptionally well in the range of numbers of discretization nodes from 128 to 512. Fortunately, most realistic problems can be handled within that range. For single-factor models, the performance figures clearly document the importance of a large problem set of around 300 or more pricing problems. On the other hand, ADI schemes for two-factor models are well suited for an efficient GPU implementation, even for a single pricing problem. On the new Fermi hardware architecture our ADI solver can run significantly larger problems and shows a large performance speedup of up to a factor of 70 against an optimized single core CPU implementation, even though we did not specifically tune the solver for the Fermi architecture.

23.5 FUTURE DIRECTIONS

Yet another interesting application for GPU application is the calibration of financial models.

Let us consider the local volatility model. The calibration algorithm determines the state dependent local volatility surface $(t, s) \mapsto \sigma_{loc}(t, s)$ in Eq. (3) from quoted option prices or implied volatilities. Dupire's formula (see, for example, Section 2 in [27]), expresses the local volatility as an expression of the first and second derivatives of the implied volatility surface, which must be calculated on a relatively fine grid of time and state values, either through numerical differentiation or by exploiting the analytical representation of the implied volatility surface interpolation. The calculations are fully data parallel because the grid point can be processed independently. An alternative approach is the PDE based local volatility calibration method of [27], which requires a series of tridiagonal systems to be solved for every time step. The tridiagonal systems are decoupled over time and can be solved independently.

An interesting approach is to combine a local volatility calibration algorithm with the finite difference solver for pricing on the GPU. The first advantage is that the input data is reduced significantly because instead of transferring a possibly large local volatility matrix, only a few implied volatility slices have to be copied to the GPU. Caching the local volatility surface directly on the GPU and reusing it for multiple calculation further enhances the overall performance. The advantage is even more pronounced if the Greeks are calculated by taking volatility smile dynamics into account, which would require a recalibration of the local volatilities after shifting the spot value.

A further application comes from spline interpolation and spline smoothing, which is often applied to preprocess implied volatility smiles before passing them to local volatility calibration.

Last but not least it would be interesting to explore three-factor models with ADI methods and the tridiagonal parallel cyclic reduction solver. In [28] a GPU implementation is discussed but they do not use a fine-grained parallel solver for the resulting tridiagonal systems. Instead they use a much simpler approach where individual linear systems are solved in a single thread.

References

[1] C. Bennemann, M.W. Beinker, D. Egloff, M. Gauckler, Teraflops for games and derivatives pricing, Wilmott Mag. 36 (2008) 50–54.

[2] M. Joshi, Graphical Asians, Technical Report, University of Melbourne — Centre for Actuarial Stud, 2009.

[3] C.W. Oosterlee, B. Zhang, Acceleration of option pricing technique on graphics processing units, Technical Report, Delft University of Technology, Report 10-3, 2010.

[4] I. Karatzas, S.E. Shreve, Brownian Motion and Stochastic Calculus, vol. 113 of Graduate Texts in Math, second ed., Springer, 1999.

[5] B. Oksendal, Stochastic Differential Equations, An Introduction with Applications, fifth ed., Springer, 2000.

[6] D. Tavella, C. Randall, Pricing Finanical Instruments — The Finite Difference Method, Wiley, 2000.

[7] J. Douglas, Alternating direction methods for three space variables, Numer. Math. 4 (1962) 41–63.

[8] I.J.D. Craig, A.D. Sneyd, An alternating-direction implicit scheme for parabolic equations with mixed derivative terms, Comp. Math. Appl. 16 (1988) 341–350.

[9] K.J. in 't Hout, B.D. Welfert, Stability of ADI schemes applied to convection diffusion equations with mixed derivative terms, Appl. Numer. Math. 57 (2007) 19–35.

[10] K.J. in 't Hout, B.D. Welfert, Unconditional stability of second order ADI schemes applied to multi-dimensional diffusion equations with mixed derivative terms, Appl. Numer. Math. 59 (2009) 677–692.

[11] NVIDIA, CUDA^{TM}, NVIDIA Corporation, http://developer.nvidia.com/cuda-toolkit-sdk, 2011 (accessed 14.08.11).

[12] D. Egloff, GPUs in financial computing: high performance tridiagonal solvers on GPUs for partial differential equations, Wilmott Mag. September (2010) 32–40.

[13] E. Ayache, P.A. Forsyth, K.R. Vetzal, Next generation models for convertible bonds with credit risk, Wilmott Mag. 11 (2002) 68–77.

[14] L. Andersen, D. Buffum, Calibration and implementation of convertible bond models, J. Comput. Finance 7 (2) (2004) 1–34.

[15] D. Brigo, F. Mercurio, Interest Rate Models — Theory and Practice, Springer-Verlag, 2006.

[16] S.L. Heston, A closed-form solution for options with stochastic volatility with application to bond and currency options, Rev. Financ. Stud. 9 (2) (1993) 327–343.

[17] B. Fornberg, Fast generation of weights in finite difference formulas, in: G.D. Byrne, W.E. Schiesser (Eds.), Recent Developments in Numerical Methods and Software for ODEs/DAEs/PDEs, World Scientific, Singapore, 1992, pp. 97–123.

[18] B. Fornberg, Calculation of weights in finite difference formulas, SIAM Rev. 40 (3) (1998) 685–691.

[19] H. Windcliff, P.A. Forsyth, K.R. Vetzal, Analysis of the stability of the linear boundary condition for the Black-Scholes equation, Comput. Finance 8 (1) (2004) 65–92.

[20] K.J. in 't Hout, S. Foulon, ADI finite difference schemes for option pricing in the Heston model with correlation, Int. J. Numer. Anal. Mod. 7 (2) (2010) 302–320.

[21] R.W. Hockney, A fast direct solution of Poisson's equation using Fourier analysis, J. ACM 12 (1) (1965) 95–113.

[22] H. Stone, An efficient parallel algorithm for the solution of a tridiagonal linear system of equations, J. ACM 20 (1) (1973) 27–38.

[23] R.W. Hockney, C.R. Jesshope, Parallel Computers 2: architecture, programming, and algorithms, second ed., Institute of Physics Publishing, 1988.

[24] W. Gander, G.H. Golub, Cyclic reduction — History and applications, in: G.H. Golub (Ed.), Proceedings of the Workshop on Scientific Computing, Springer Verlag, 1997.

[25] Y. Zhang, J. Cohen, J.D. Owens, Fast tridiagonal solvers on the GPU, in: Proceedings of the 15th ACM SIGPLAN Symposium on Principles and Practice of Parallel Programming (PPoPP 2010), ACM, New York, 2010, p. 10.

[26] D. Egloff, GPUs in Financial Computing Part II: Massively Parallel Solvers on GPUs, Wilmott Mag. November (2010) 50–53.

[27] L.B.G. Andersen, R. Brotherton-Ratcliffe, The equity option volatility smile: an implicit finite-difference approach, J. Comput. Finance 1 (2) (1997) 5–37.

[28] D.M. Dang, C.C. Christara, K.R. Jackson, Parallel implementation on GPUs of ADI finite difference methods for parabolic PDEs with applications in finance, Technical Report, Department of Computer Science, University of Toronto, 2010.

Large-Scale Credit Risk Loss Simulation

24

Simon J. Rees and Joseph Walkenhorst

In this chapter, we present a GPU algorithm to perform a Monte Carlo simulation of a portfolio of credit risk exposures. Multiple design paths are explored with discussion around the relative costs and benefits. The kernel implementation itself is described in detail, identifying and improving several areas of optimization to maximize the performance for demanding problem sizes. The algorithm allows us to generate a loss distribution for the portfolio, and the success of the application motivates discussion into re-simulation of the scenarios in the tail for more detailed analysis.

24.1 INTRODUCTION, PROBLEM STATEMENT, AND CONTEXT

In the wake of the credit crisis, banks are committed to maintaining sufficient capital buffers to protect against unexpected losses that arise from widespread defaults throughout their portfolios. The size of the capital buffer is intended to reflect the level of credit quality that the bank affords its clients. It is determined in terms of a confidence interval, up to which the bank claims it can absorb losses and remain solvent. As a result highly rated banks maintain large capital buffers to justify their rating. There is consequently a great deal of scrutiny over the capital calculation — estimating too little leaves the bank overly exposed to credit risk, while too much consumes valuable capital better invested elsewhere.

The capital calculation boils down to an analysis of the distributional properties of the portfolio's losses. Estimating this loss distribution is a challenging task given the size of the portfolio, the wide range of credit quality of the assets, and the default correlation driving the portfolio dynamics. It is made even more demanding when a high confidence interval is imposed, e.g., 99.95% and involves examination of the tails of the loss distribution, which are typically long and thick.

Analytical approaches have been developed to provide approximations to the tails of the loss distribution properties; however, the problem's highly complex nonlinear characteristics render such approaches limited and lacking in specificity. Instead a Monte Carlo simulation approach is adopted to generate a portfolio-specific loss distribution. These Monte Carlo simulations are very computationally expensive owing to the slow convergence properties of the tails of the loss distribution; they require no less than a CPU server farm consisting of several hundred cores running over several hours.

The motivation of GPU acceleration is to investigate the extent to which a single GPU can replicate the performance of a CPU server farm and, if so, what new capabilities does a GPU implementation offer. This application is a good fit for the GPU both algorithmically and architecturally: the parallel compute capabilities are an excellent platform for running Monte Carlo simulations, which themselves are highly parallel processes; equally, the onboard memory provides both the capacity and bandwidth to complement the frequent processing of large portfolio data sets.

24.2 CORE METHODS

In this section we describe the core methods behind our application. The target application is intended for use in a credit risk setting; however, the application is driven by a Monte Carlo simulation and is sufficiently generic to be adapted to the context of a much wider audience. The performance metric of our application will be the rate of scenario generation. To help the reader assess the relevance to their own application, Figure 24.1 illustrates the basic model mechanics, while a more detailed description is given below.

24.2.1 Simulation Framework

We demonstrate the Monte Carlo simulation using a single period, single-factor, default/non-default model, however many of the approaches taken mean that the model can be easily generalized to multiple periods and factors.

The portfolio's assets are each described in terms of: *PD*; *LGD*; *EAD*. The *probability-of-default*, *PD* is a measure of the default risk within a certain horizon, typically one year. It ranges substantially, from the highest level of credit quality — AAA, which on average equates to a $PD = 0.01\%$, to the lowest level of credit quality — C, which on average equates to a $PD = 30\%$. The *loss-given-default*, *LGD*, which is also described as $1 - r$, where r is the recovery rate, is the proportion of the *exposure-at-default*, *EAD*, expected to be lost in the event of default. These two can be combined together to give the *loss-at-default*, $LAD_i = LGD_i \cdot EAD_i$, and represents the expected loss in the case of default. Separate models are developed to calculate each of these properties and are out of the scope of this discussion.

The dynamics of the portfolio are determined by the default correlation structure, which can be defined in two different ways: either by constructing a correlation matrix or by using a factor model. The correlation matrix is not an attractive approach because of the size of the portfolio — the corresponding matrix would be enormous and consume a lot of memory to store as well as a lot of time to process. The alternative, a factor model, is attractive by comparison as it is an efficient method for reducing the dimensionality of the data to just a few factors responsible for explaining the majority of the behavior. A principal component analysis (PCA) is an example of a factor model which produces an orthogonal basis of latent variables, derived so as to explain the largest proportion of the portfolio variance. Regressing the time-series of each asset on the time-series with the principal component establishes the asset specific factor weights.

The factor model is the core component of this model and completely determines the dynamics of the portfolio. As such, while the loss simulation kernel is discussed in considerable detail in the next section of this chapter, the details relating to the factor model remain highly confidential.

Following the Merton approach, each PD_i is mapped into a corresponding *distance-to-default*:

$$DD_i = -\Phi^{-1}(PD_i) \tag{1}$$

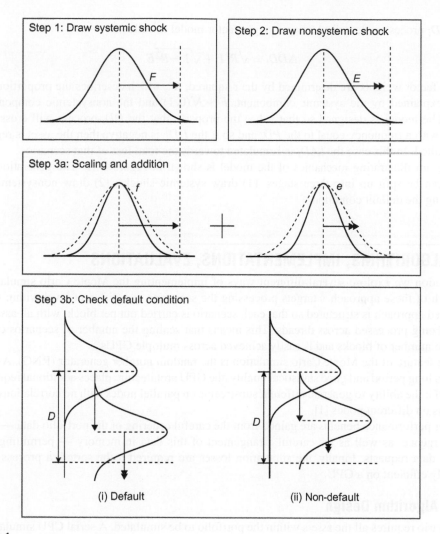

FIGURE 24.1

Three stages of scenario generation.

where Φ is the cumulative standard normal distribution function. The DD_i is an alternative measure of credit quality and is indicated by the distance from zero boundary.

Initially at time t_0 the DD_i^0 is a positive number. It is allowed to evolve over the single time period due to shocks in credit quality, ΔDD_i,

$$DD_i^1 = DD_i^0 + \Delta DD_i \qquad (2)$$

with the new DD_i^1 reflecting the new credit quality of the asset at time $t_1 = t_0 + \Delta t$.

The DD_i process is described using a single-factor model as follows:

$$\Delta DD_i = \sqrt{R^2}F + \sqrt{1-R^2}E \tag{3}$$

where the factor weights are determined by the r-squared, R^2, which describes the proportion of asset variance explained by the systemic component, $F \sim \mathcal{N}(0,1)$ and the nonsystemic component, $E \sim \mathcal{N}(0,1)$. The model is designed so that it has the property that the DD_i-process will cross the zero boundary with a frequency equal to the PD_i and so if the DD_i^1 is negative then the asset is regarded to have defaulted. In this case the LAD_i is cumulated towards the total loss of that scenario.

A diagram illustrating mechanics of the model is shown in Figure 24.1. The generation of each scenario can be split up into three stages: (1) draw systemic shocks; (2) draw nonsystemic shock; (3) checking the default condition.

24.3 ALGORITHMS, IMPLEMENTATIONS, EVALUATIONS

In this section we explore several different ways of implementing the Monte Carlo simulation on a GPU. Each of these approaches targets processing the scenarios at a different level within the GPU. The favored approach is structured so that each scenario is carried out per block, with all assets of the portfolio being processed across threads. This means that scaling the number of scenarios equates to scaling the number of blocks and is easily achieved across multiple GPUs.

A core feature of the Monte Carlo simulation is the random number generator (RNG). Aside from requiring a long period and good statistical quality, the GPU architecture places additional requirements on the RNG: the ability to generate different substreams on parallel nodes with no correlations between substreams on different nodes [1].

Further performance benefits are gained from the careful ordering of the portfolio data — reducing warp divergence, as well as the careful arrangement of this data in memory — permitting efficient coalesced data requests. Finally, the simulation losses are required to be sorted, a process which is particularly efficient on a GPU.

24.3.1 Algorithm Design

Each scenario requires all the assets within the portfolio to be simulated. A serial CPU simulates assets one after another, whereas the GPU can process them in parallel. The various levels of parallelism within a GPU offer many different ways of structuring the code so that scenarios are generated either by each thread, block, or kernel. The advantages and disadvantages of each of these approaches is considered and discussed below.

Scenario per Thread
This approach conducts a single scenario per thread, which processes the whole portfolio. The advantage of this approach is it the simple and intuitive to port the serial CPU code onto a GPU. The disadvantage is that it does not make efficient use of the GPU resources. Handling multiple scenarios per block means that a lot of shared memory is consumed storing all the different systemic shocks for each of the different scenarios; if the model is exapnded to multiple factors, shared memory is quickly exhausted.

Scenario per Block

This approach conducts a single scenario per block by distributing the assets of the portfolio across the threads. This structure has advantages over the scenario per thread approach as each block only has to store the systemic shocks and losses for a single scenario in shared memory. The independence of blocks complements the independence of scenarios and allows scaling across multiple GPUS. The required number of scenarios is achieved by declaring a grid of blocks (potentially across multiple GPUs) of the same size. In order to run a substantial number of scenarios, a two-dimensional block structures allows a single GPU to conduct up to 2^{32} scenarios. This is the preferred approach adopted in our final implementation.

Scenario per Kernel

This approach attempts to distribute the portfolio into block-sized subportfolios so that all the portfolio data can be stored in shared memory for fast read/write access. However, this solution is more complex to engineer because coordination and scheduling is required between blocks since systemic shocks and subportfolio losses need to be shared and cumulated respectively. The gains from storing the portfolio in shared memory compete with the losses due to the high level of interblock communication. Scheduling a single scenario per kernel is likely to incur a heavy cost from kernel intialization costs, relative to the computational expense this implies that multiple scenarios per kernel call are required.

24.3.2 Memory Storage and Alignment

The following discussion targets the scenario per block approach.

A large amount of data is required to describe the properties of the portfolio, O(numAssets$\times$ numFactors). This is too large to store in shared memory and hence must be stored in global memory. Each scenario must process all of this data and, as a result, optimizing the arrangement of this data in global memory is an important consideration.

The portfolio data can be described by a large matrix indexed by asset index and factor index:

$$\begin{bmatrix} (1,1) & (1,2) & \cdots & (1,M) \\ (2,1) & (2,2) & \cdots & (2,M) \\ \vdots & \vdots & \ddots & \vdots \\ (N,1) & (N,2) & \cdots & (N,M) \end{bmatrix} \tag{4}$$

where N is the numAssets and M is the numFactors. Since threads of the same warp execute in parallel and all process different assets then the data must be stored first by asset index and second by factor index, i.e., (assetIdx, factorIdx) as follows:

$$(1,1),(2,1),\ldots(N,1),(1,2),(2,2),\ldots(N,2),\ldots,(1,N),(2,N),\ldots(N,M). \tag{5}$$

This arrangement allows data requests to be efficiently coalesced.

24.3.3 Random Number Generation

Large-scale simulations require a large number of random numbers, $O(10^{15}) \sim O(2^{53})$ and consequently a high quality random number generator (RNG) is required. Popular choices such as Mersenne

Twister (MT19937), however, require lots of precious memory and as a result are not ideal as GPU RNGs.

Pseudo-Random and Quasi-Random Number Generators

Two different GPU optimized RNGs are used in this application both of which are developed by the Numerical Algorithm Group (NAG). In benchmarking the same generator is used on both the GPU and CPU.

The first is a pseudo-random number generator (PRNG) which uses an implementation of L'Ecuyer's multiple recursive random number generator (mrg32k3a) described in [2] and [3]. L'Ecuyer's mrg32k3a ports well onto the GPU because of its inherent structure of long streams and substreams, providing a substantially large period of 2^{191}. The second is a quasi-random number generator (QRNG) which uses a Sobol sequence implementation described in [4] and [5]. The block and grid structures on the GPU complement the Sobol implementation, which ports well onto the GPU and boasts a 600 times speed-up as a stand alone kernel. Both the mrg32k3a and Sobol RNGs can produce a deterministic sequence of random numbers. This is an important feature allowing each scenario to be exactly replicated.

Both RNGS produce a deterministic stream of random numbers and do not cause any warp divergence. However, the transformation required to convert from uniform to normal random numbers does cause warp divergence. This is because the transform function is split into two separate domains: the central domain and the tail domain. The transform function is described by different rational function approximations depending on which domain is executed. Recent improvements to this implementation conducted by Mike Giles mean that the central domain is executed 99.66% of the time; however, the probability that all threads execute this central domain and thus the warp executing divergence free reduces significantly to $0.9966^{32} = 89.67\%$.

Monte Carlo Convergence

Using pseudo-random (PR) numbers, offers a rate of convergence $O(N^{-1/2})$, whereas with quasi-random (QR) numbers this rate of convergence can improve to as much as $O(N^{-1})$. Making use of QR scheme would require fewer simulations to achieve the same convergence properties and effectively offer a speed-up.

The QR scheme is limited by the maximum number of independent dimensions, which is currently 19,000 in this implementation. The number required for a multiperiod simulation is $O(\text{numAssets} \times \text{numPeriods})$, which typically far exceeds this limit. This problem can be resolved by only using QR numbers to simulate the systemic components, requiring just $O(\text{numFactors} \times \text{numPeriods})$ dimensions. PR numbers would continue to be used to simulate the nonsystemic components. This hybrid scheme still offers superior convergence properties because the majority of the portfolio variance is driven by the systemic components.

Using a combination of QR and PR numbers has big implications on the algorithm design. To assist this discussion Figure 24.2 is included to illustrate the distinction between low level, high level and hybrid functional call scheme for our model. Using just PR numbers and generating them on the fly allows the code to be structured using just low level functional calls. Generating both QR and PR numbers using low level functional calls consumes a lot of additional registers which limits occupancy and impacts performance. This tends to promote the use of separate high level functional calls

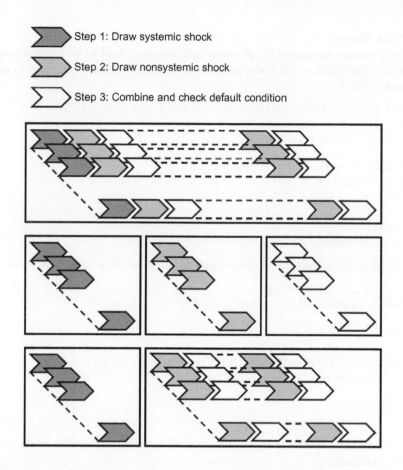

Step 1: Draw systemic shock

Step 2: Draw nonsystemic shock

Step 3: Combine and check default condition

FIGURE 24.2

Low level, high level, and hybrid functional implementations of the model (see color insert).

(i.e., separate kernels) specialized to their individual tasks. While this is not possible for nonsystemic PR numbers since far too many are generated to be stored in global memory, it is possible for the systemic QR numbers. Thus the hybrid solution aims to maintain lightweight kernels, with the systemic shocks being pregenerated and stored in global memory using a separate dedicated QRNG kernel. These are then transferred into shared memory (for fast, frequent access) at the start of each block call for each scenario at little extra cost, while the nonsystemic shocks continue to be generated on the fly.

24.3.4 Simulation Implementation

In describing the kernel implementation it is helpful to reiterate the algorithm structure of the code, namely scenarios per blocks, assets per threads.

Systemic Shock Draws

Because systemic shocks are shared by all assets and therefore need to be accessible to all threads within a block, they should be stored in shared memory. If pseudo-random numbers are used then they can be generated on the fly:

```
// generate pseudo-random systemic shocks and write into shared
// memory
if (threadIdx.x < numFactors)
{
    // draw next random normal number
    nag_gpu_mrg32k3a_next_normal(v1, v2, x1, x2);
    z[threadIdx.x] = x1;
}
__syncthreads();
...
```

alternatively if they are pregenerated quasi-random numbers they would be read from global memory:

```
// read quasi-random systemic shocks from global to shared
// memory
if (threadIdx.x < numFactors)
{
z[threadIdx.x] = d_sobolSeq[threadIdx.x+numFactors*(blockIdx.x
                +blockIdx.y*gridDim.x)];
}
__syncthreads();
...
```

The first `numFactors` threads perform this step, while other threads are made to wait using a `__syncthreads` statement.

Nonsystemic Shock Draws and Calculating DD

With the systemic factors simulated threads now work to process the portfolio. The portfolio is divided equally among threads given by `assetsPerThread` and index as follows:

```
// asset allocation between threads
for (unsigned int assetIdx = threadIdx.x; i < assetsPerThread;
    i += blockDim.x)
{
```

Threads that would attempt to access elements beyond the end of the arrays overflow will not execute any further.

The distance-to-default, DD, is initialized to DD_i^0. The nonsystemic shock is drawn and the DD_i^1 is calculated by first cumulating the nonsystemic shock and then looping over all `numFactors` to cumulate the systemic shocks.

```
// initialize distance to default
distToDef = d_distToDef[assetIdx];
```

```
// draw next random normal number
nag_gpu_mrg32k3a_next_normal(v1, v2, x1, x2);

// cumulate nonsystemic shock
distToDef += d_factorWeights[assetIdx]*x1;

// cumulate systemic shocks
for (unsigned int j=1; j<numFactors+1; j++)
{
    distToDef += d_factorWeights[assetIdx + j*numAssets]*z[j-1];
}
```

Because the systemic shocks are stored in shared memory this calculation is very quick.

Checking for Default

With the DD_i^1 calculated the default condition needs to be checked.

```
// check default condition
if (distToDef < 0)
{
    // cumulate loss to thread
    lossPerThread[threadIdx.x] += d_lossAtDef[assetIdx];
}
} ...
```

Assets default probabilistically and this presents a source of warp divergence. The nondefault branch does nothing whereas the default branch cumulates the loss to global memory. Provided that none of the assets within a warp default the default branch need not execute and consequently no global memory transaction is required. The probability of a warp making a memory transaction is given by:

$$P(\text{memory transaction}) = 1 - \prod_{i \in warp} (1 - PD_i). \qquad (6)$$

The arrangement of the assets within the portfolio can be optimized in order to minimize the probability of memory transactions across all warps. The solution is achieved by ordering the assets in ascending order by PD because the probability of all the assets not defaulting is heavily limited by the riskiest asset within a warp. This optimization benefits portfolios composed of a high proportion of low PD assets.

With a small number of simulations, several blocks will tend to be executing the same stage of the simulation and hence will be fetching asset parameters from more or less the same region. On pre-Fermi architectures this can result in accessing the same memory partition, as a result of which the performance can suffer due to an effect known as partition camping. However, the same probabilistic element described above causes each simulation, and consequently each block, to take a variable amount of time to execute. As a result, blocks will fall out of sync with each other and, with a large number of simulations, a steady rate of performance will be achieved. On Fermi architecture devices the hardware ensures that the partition camping effect is eliminated; in addition, Fermis L2 cache offers some benefit by caching the asset parameters.

Cumulating Losses

In our implementation each thread cumulates losses to its own specific entry within the lossPerThread shared memory vector. As a result a final reduction is required at the end of the kernel to efficiently cumulate all the losses per thread to produce a total scenario loss per block. This enables a single global memory write to store the result.

```
// initialize losses of each thread
lossPerThread[threadIdx.x] = 0;
...


...
// reduction to cumulate losses across threads
for(unsigned int p = blockDim.x/2; p > 0; p /= 2)
{
    __syncthreads();
    if (threadIdx.x < p) lossPerThread[threadIdx.x] +=
        lossPerThread[threadIdx.x + p];
}
// record total loss per simulation
if (threadIdx.x==0) d_lossPerSim[blockIdx.x+blockIdx.y*
    gridDim.x] = lossPerThread[0];
...
```

This implementation is simple and offers reasonable performance at the expense of shared memory consumption. An alternative would be to have a single shared memory entry that all losses reference and cumulate losses in using the atomicAdd function for safe scheduling and avoid the need for a reduction altogether. This saves shared memory at the expense of performance as multiple defaults within the same warp will incur a delay due to scheduling. Yet another alternative, which attempts to maintain performance and keep shared memory consumption low, would be to reference a lossPerThread vector of size equal to the number of threads per warp using modulo/bitshift arithmetic. This would avoid any scheduling requirements and also keep the shared memory consumption fixed irrespective of the thread structure.

24.3.5 **Sorting the Loss Distribution**

Calculating the capital buffer based on the analysis of the portfolio losses requires the loss vector to be sorted. Sorting on GPUs is particularly efficient and can be done using well established sort algorithms supplied within the Thrust library, http://code.google.com/p/thrust/. Thrust applies several optimizations to achieve high sorting performance either using a merge or radix sort algorithm.

Unsorted, the index of each loss within the loss vector indicates the scenario responsible for producing that loss and thus provides a loss-scenario mapping. Simply sorting the loss vector alone would discard this information and so to retain it a key-value pair is set up. Using a sort by key algorithm, the operations necessary to sort the loss vector (key) are also applied to a corresponding scenario index vector (value), thus preserving the loss-scenario mapping.

24.4 RESULTS AND CONCLUSIONS

In this section benchmarks are conducted between GPU and CPU implementations for portfolios of different sizes. The results are presented in Table 24.1. The specifications of the GPU and CPU setups are described as follows:

- Tesla C1060 (single card)
- CUDA Compute Capability 1.3
- 64 threads per block
- CPU: Intel Xeon X5570 @ 2.93 GHz (single thread)
- RAM: DDR3 PC-10600
- OS : 64-bit Windows Server 2008

Comparing results between the GPU and CPU results it is noted that for portfolios with 13,400 and 26,800 assets the GPU implementation experiences a 84.19 and 91.40 times speed-up, respectively, relative to the CPU.

In order to explain these results we consider how the kernel runtime can be decomposed into fixed and variable costs. Fixed costs can be further distinguished into fixed costs per scenario, e.g., systemic shock draws and reduction of losses per thread, and fixed costs per simulation, e.g., kernel initialization, which does not scale with the size of portfolio. Variable costs only occur per scenario and scale with the size of portfolio, e.g., nonsystemic draws, *DD* calculation and default condition, which are carried out for each asset in the whole portfolio. Hence the kernel runtime can be decomposed as follows:

$$\frac{\text{kernel}}{\text{runtime}} = \frac{\text{fixed cost}}{\text{per simulation}} + \frac{\text{number of}}{\text{scenarios}} \left(\frac{\text{fixed cost}}{\text{per scenario}} + \frac{\text{variable cost}}{\text{per scenario}} \right)$$

It is noted that the kernel runtimes shown in Table 24.1 only reflect the scenario calculations and do not capture fixed costs per simulation like data transfer costs on and off the GPU. This is not significant, however, since operationally a far greater number of simulations are considered which increases the second term in the above equation, marginalizing the impact of the first. Similarly fixed

Table 24.1 Simulation Results for 1,000,000 Scenarios

GPU Implementation			
numAssets	secPerRun	simsPerSec	assetsPerSec
13,400	8.78	113,864.35	$1,525.78 \times 10^6$
26,800	16.15	61,934.46	$1,659.84 \times 10^6$
CPU Implementation			
numAssets	secPerRun	simsPerSec	assetsPerSec
13,400	739.40	1,352.44	18.12×10^6
26,800	1,475.73	677.63	18.16×10^6

costs per scenario can be marginalized as the variable costs per scenario increase. This helps to explain the observation that increasing the number of assets within the portfolio increases the number of assets per second processed on the GPU but not on the CPU — while the fixed costs per scenario are fairly similar across platforms, variable costs per scenario are significantly lower on the GPU because they are shared and processed across threads run in parallel. Thus on the CPU the variable cost term already dominates the equation above offering little room for improvement, while on the GPU a near 10% improvement in performance was achieved simply by increasing the portfolio size. This consequently translated into similar improvement in the speed-up on the GPU relative to the CPU.

Overall the GPU implementation offers an encouraging $\sim100\times$ speed up that only improves relative to the CPU implementation as the problem becomes more demanding, i.e., larger portfolios and greater number of simulations. This indicates that a small cluster of GPUs could feasibly replace a server farm of CPUs, a situation with very real implications regarding power and hardware cost saving.

24.5 FUTURE DEVELOPMENTS

Beyond calculating the capital buffer, analyzing the properties of the loss distribution, particularly those resulting in tail loss scenarios, is of great interest in credit risk. However, there is no way of knowing whether a scenario loss is a tail event or not *a priori* and as a result any further diagnostics would required re-simulation. In this section we offer a short discussion surrounding re-simulation.

24.5.1 Re-Simulating Tail Loss Scenarios

Using a scenario per block approach means that resimulating a specific set of tail scenarios equates to executing the corresponding set of blocks. For the resimulation kernel the body of the code remains identical; however, an additional section of code is required at the start.

If the PRNG supports arbitrary skip-ahead to a specific subsequence then resimulation requires launching one block per tail scenario. The additional code at the start of each block uses the block index to look up the target scenario index in order to determine how to initialize the generator.

Since the NAG generator does not support arbitrary sequence selection at this time, resimulation requires launching as many blocks as the original simulation. In this case the additional code checks whether the current block index matches any of the tail scenario indices, any blocks which do not match terminate immediately.

```
__shared__ bool runTailSim;
runTailSim = false;
unsigned int numTailSimsPerThread = (numTailSims+blockDim.x-1)
                                    /blockDim.x;
for (unsigned int i=0; i<numTailSimsPerThread; i++)
{
if (threadIdx.x+i*blockDim.x<numTailSims)
{
if (blockIdx.x+gridDim.x*blockIdx.y == d_simIdxTail[threadIdx.
    x+i*blockDim.x]) runTailSim = true;
}
}
```

```
_syncthreads();
 if (runTailSim)
 ...
```

The above code is a simple example; however, a more efficient but complex algorithm would be to use the threads to conduct a multi-nomial search.

Tail Loss Diagnostics

Conducting diagnostics to collect detailed information about each scenario significantly increases the computational expense. Thus, it is too expensive to carry out diagnostics for all scenarios during the initial loss simulation. However, running diagnostics for just the tail scenarios is relatively inexpensive, since they represent only a small proportion of the total number of scenarios. The ability to resimulate only tail scenarios means that the simulation kernel can remain fast and lightweight in order to generate a rich source of tail scenarios from which the slower heavyweight resimulation kernel can feasibly collect detailed information.

In conclusion it is suggested that while the simulation kernel provides the means to conduct risk measurement, it is the resimulation kernel that provides the necessary means to conduct risk management.

Acknowledgements

This code was developed as part of a proof-of-concept exercise into investigating the applications of GPU computing in credit risk. The authors would like to thank Thomas Bradley at NVIDIA whose consultation helped stimulate and progress the project development. All ideas presented in this article are of the author and not reflected by Barclays Capital.

References

[1] D.B. Thomas, L. Howes, W. Luk, A comparison of CPUs, GPUs, FPGAs, and massively parallel processor arrays for random number generation, in: FPGA '09: Proceeding of the ACM/SIGDA International Symposium on Field Programmable Gate Arrays, ACM, New York, 2009, pp. 63–72.

[2] G.W. Fischer, Z. Carmon, D. Ariely, G. Zauberman, P. L'Ecuyer, Good parameters and implementations for combined multiple recursive random number generators, Oper. Res. 47 (1) (1999) 159–164.

[3] P. L'Ecuyer, R. Simard, E. Jack Chen, W. David Kelton, An object-oriented random-number package with many long streams and substreams, Oper. Res. 50 (6) (2002) 1073–1075.

[4] P. Bratley, B.L. Fox, Algorithm 659: implementing sobol's quasirandom sequence generator, ACM Trans. Math. Softw. 14 (1) (1988) 88–100.

[5] S. Joe, F.Y. Kuo, Remark on algorithm 659: implementing sobol's quasirandom sequence generator, ACM Trans. Math. Softw. 29 (1) (2003) 49–57.

Monte Carlo–Based Financial Market Value-at-Risk Estimation on GPUs

Matthew F. Dixon, Thomas Bradley, Jike Chong, and Kurt Keutzer

With the proliferation of algorithmic trading, derivative usage and highly leveraged hedge funds, there is increasing need to accelerate financial market Value-at-Risk (VaR) estimation to measure the severity of potential portfolio losses in real time. However, VaR estimation of portfolios uses the Monte Carlo method, which is a computationally intensive method. GPUs provide the scale of performance improvement to enable "on demand" deployment of financial market VaR estimates rather than as an overnight batch job.

This chapter allows *quantitative financial application developers* in the capital markets industry, who have some knowledge of GPU computing and finance, to gain insights into implementation challenges and solutions in risk analysis and the Monte Carlo method. *Quantitative technology researchers and managers* in the finance industry with limited knowledge of GPU computing can also get an overview of the key areas of concern in developing a high performance risk analysis engine based on the Monte Carlo method. *GPU computing researchers and developers* with no background in quantitative finance will find this chapter useful as (i) a source of guidance on leveraging the CUDA SDK for implementing Monte Carlo methods and as (ii) an entry point for applying their own work to performance critical quantitative finance applications.

25.1 INTRODUCTION, PROBLEM STATEMENT, AND CONTEXT

Financial institutions seek quantitative risk infrastructure which is able to provide "on demand" reporting of global financial market risk while managing thousands of risk factors and considering hundreds of thousands of future market scenarios [16]. A fast implementation can improve the responsiveness of risk management systems, enable risk analysts to perform more comprehensive VaR estimates on an adhoc basis (e.g., pre-deal limit checking), and can give financial institutions a competitive edge in algorithmic trading. It will also allow institutions to effectively step up to the more pervasive systematic stress testing standards recently imposed by market risk regulators.

The ability to closely monitor and control an institution's market risk exposure is critical to the performance of trading units, which rely on complex risk analysis in order to structure and execute trades. Yet, despite tightening legal requirements on market risk estimation, the industry is still far from adopting a standardized and comprehensive framework for market risk analysis. As a result, many institutions still run oversimplified portfolio risk analytics, which, although computationally efficient, misrepresent major sources of market risk affecting the prices of complex financial instruments. This may lead to unaccountable market exposures that may be difficult to close out without sizeable losses.

In a recent survey conducted by the Global Association of Risk Professionals in conjunction with SYBASE [5], only approximately 5% of the firms currently perform complex risk analysis on portfolios and global positions in real time although around 25% are able to perform real time analysis on individual trades. Going forward, over a third of these firms indicated that the current risk infrastructure wasn't fast enough for the needs of the business and that the gap between IT and business domain expertise is one of the major sources of dislocation in the deployment of risk management systems. This calls for a more comprehensive approach to the design and deployment of complex risk analytics with a stronger emphasis on using financial domain knowledge and expertise to enhance the software optimization process. By applying such a software optimization process tailored for the GPU, this chapter demonstrates an "on demand" market VaR estimate scalable to the needs of the largest financial institutions.

25.1.1 Monte Carlo Implementation

A typical implementation of the Monte Carlo method involves a simple solution structure where experiments are generated, executed, and the experimental output is assimilated to estimate the result. Figure 25.1 illustrates the general structure of the solution, where experiments are set up, estimated, then assimilated into a concise result.

The formulation of the Monte Carlo Value-at-Risk (MC-VaR) method and its software architecture has been covered extensively in the literature (see, for example, [13, 15]). MC-VaR is ideal for GPUs as it requires a small set of parameters to set up the estimation process, involves a large amount of computation, and outputs a concise set of risk profiles as the result. Furthermore, after applying the techniques described in this chapter, very little memory movement is required between intermediate steps of the algorithm.

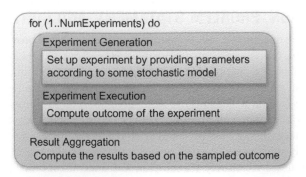

FIGURE 25.1

The general solution structure of Monte Carlo methods.

   The Solution is based on a set of considerations or perspectives for optimizing the performance critical steps in our GPU-based MC-VaR implementation: Uniform random sequence generation, parameter distribution conversion, and portfolio loss calculation (including risk factor cross-correlation). This chapter will explain seven techniques to address the challenges of implementing MC-VaR on the GPU.

25.2 CORE METHODS

We identified seven key implementation techniques in the construction of Monte Carlo–based applications by studying the implementation process from three different perspectives, namely the task-centric, numerical-centric, and data-centric perspectives:

1. **The task-centric perspective** focuses on the tasks being executed (Section 25.3.2.1):
   - Key technique 1: Minimization of the amount of necessary computation by task transformation and algorithm reformulation
   - Key technique 2: Maximization of computational efficiency by identifying opportunities to leverage existing high-performance library components

   Applied in MC-VaR as: (1) a reformulation of the loss aggregation module to avoid matrix-matrix computations, (2) an analysis of the relative performance of various linear algebra routines to take advantage of more efficient types of CUBLAS library components.

2. **The numerical-centric perspective** focuses on the numerical properties of modules and their influence on the application performance[1] (Section 25.3.2.2):
   - Key technique 3: Selection of random sequences which provide desirable convergence properties
   - Key technique 4: Selection of random sequences that enable parallel generation of sequences
   - Key technique 5: Selection of distribution conversion modules which preserve a uniformity property[2] of the random sequences

   Applied in MC-VaR as: (3) the selection of Sobol' quasi-random sequences for its uniformity property in accelerating convergence, (4) the usage of a Sobol' generator with skip-ahead capability to enable parallel generation of random sequences, (5) the selection of the Box-Muller algorithm for its ability to preserve property A, Sobol' sequences' measure of uniformity, under distribution transformation.

3. **The data-centric perspective** focuses on the data access properties of the algorithms and their influence on the application performance (Section 25.3.2.3):
   - Key technique 6: Elimination of redundant data transfers between small kernels
   - Key technique 7: Increasing utilization of data accessed in algorithm execution

---

[1]Implementation techniques for efficient generation of Gaussian random numbers in CUDA are well studied; see, for example [8].

[2]A uniformity property is a measure of how well subsequences of the random sequence cover the target distribution.

Applied in MC-VaR as: (6) the merging of random number generation and distribution conversion to eliminate redundant storage and transfer of intermediate results and the identification of key data alignment needs between parameter generation and risk estimation, (7) the application of flexible data blocking strategies that maximally leverage the shared memory resources (or local scratch-pad memory).

By combining these three perspectives we built up a comprehensive set of techniques for effectively utilizing the CUDA infrastructure in developing financial applications and demonstrated a 169× speedup in VaR estimation over the baseline GPU implementation, corresponding to a 53× speedup over the optimized CPU implementation and 1311× over the baseline CPU implementation. Examining an application from task-centric, numerical-centric and data-centric perspectives also provides clear interfaces for collaborations within research and development projects by allowing experts in different domains to focus on different aspects of the optimization process, and the modular structure of MC-VaR (as will be described in the next section) facilitates potentially faster and smoother integration across domains of expertise.

25.3 ALGORITHMS, IMPLEMENTATIONS, AND EVALUATIONS
25.3.1 The Monte Carlo Method

The Monte Carlo method is an approach where the solution to some problem is estimated by statistically sampling the problem's parameter space with thousands to millions of experiments using different parameter settings. By statistically sampling a problem's parameter space and simulating the outcome of an experiment, we gain valuable insights into complex problems that may be impossible or impractical to solve analytically or by other numerical methods. The ease and intuitiveness of setting up the experiments makes the Monte Carlo method a popular approach [7].

The Monte Carlo method has several properties that make it desirable for implementation on a high performance GPU accelerator:

1. **Experiments are independent and parallelizable:** the approach assumes that experiments are independent and identically distributed (i.i.d.), such that the set of experiments provides a statistically valid sampling of the parameter space. This independence between experiments provides significant parallelization opportunities for GPU and multi-GPU implementations.

2. **Execution is computationally expensive:** by the law of large numbers, the statistical error (standard error) in the solution is proportional to the inverse square-root of the experimental size, i.e., to achieve 10× more precision in the result, one needs to run 100× more experiments. The GPU-based implementation can provide the necessary speedup to allow many problems to become computationally feasible.

3. **Input specifications and results are concise:** the Monte Carlo method takes a small set of experiment parameter inputs, generates thousands to millions of experiments, executes them, and assimilates the results as a single solution. There is a large amount of computation consumed with little input/output data transferred. This is ideal for GPU-based implementations, as input/output data has to be transferred between the CPU and the GPUs and all computation is performed on the GPU.

25.3.2 **Value-at-Risk**

VaR estimation[3] uses the Monte Carlo method to simulate the effects of various market movement scenarios on the value of the portfolio. A comparatively small set of parameters is required to set up the estimation process, whereas experiment execution requires a large amount of computation. The VaR is output at one or more time intervals over the horizon for one or more user-defined choices of p (the percentile for VaR estimation). For ease of exposition, we consider the simplest case when the interval is the length of the time horizon. *Market Risk Factors*, R_i, where $i = 1..N$, are used to capture a market scenario that could potentially devalue the portfolio. Common examples of market risk categories include interest rates, stocks, commodities, credit, and foreign exchange. Major banks model the joint probability distribution of hundreds, or even thousands, of risk factors [16].

Experiment Generation

The Monte Carlo method simulates the correlated market risk factor log returns (value changes) over the time horizon. More precisely, each experiment k, where $k = 1..M$, is set up by first generating uncorrelated Gaussian *Random Variables*, X_{ik}, where $i = 1..N$. These are the uncorrelated Gaussian random perturbations away from the current market scenario which is defined by the current value of the risk factors R_i. The input to a Monte Carlo–based VaR estimation includes:

1. *Statistical Parameters:* the estimated means μ_i and Cholesky factor matrix $\widehat{Q}$ of the covariance matrix $\Sigma_{ij} = \widehat{Q}^T\widehat{Q}$ for the Gaussian distributed market risk factor log returns $d\ln(R_i)$, where $i = 1..N, j = 1..N$, are obtained from historical time series;
2. *Delta term:* Δ_i, where $i = 1..N$, is the sensitivity of the portfolio to a change in the log of the market risk factor R_i;
3. *Gamma term:* λ_i and U_{ij}, where $i = 1..N, j = 1..N$, are the eigenvalues and orthogonal matrix of column eigenvectors of the s.p.d. matrix $\sum_{ij}\widehat{Q}^T_{mi}\Gamma_{ij}\widehat{Q}_{jn}$, Γ_{ij} is the sensitivity of Δ_i to a change in the log of market risk factor R_j. Since the Δ from simple models of instrument prices typically only depend on one or a small number of risk factors, Γ is generally sparse and sometimes even diagonal;
4. *Percentile for VaR evaluation:* is typically either 1% or 5%; and
5. *Time horizon:* the duration of the simulation is typically at least a day and is measured in units of years.

Experiment Execution

The execution of each experiment k outputs the change of value of the portfolio dP_k using the (rotated) *delta-gamma* (Δ-Γ) approximation

$$dP_k = \sum_i \underbrace{\Delta_i Y_{ik}}_{delta} + \underbrace{\frac{1}{2}\lambda_i X_{ik}^2}_{gamma}, \tag{1}$$

---

[3]The market VaR at probability p of a portfolio is defined as the *minimum potential loss that the portfolio may suffer* due to the p % worse case market movements over a given time horizon $t - t_0$. So, for example, the daily VaR with probability $p = 0.01$ is the minimum potential loss of a portfolio due to the 1-in-100 worse case market scenario over a day (see [11] for further details).

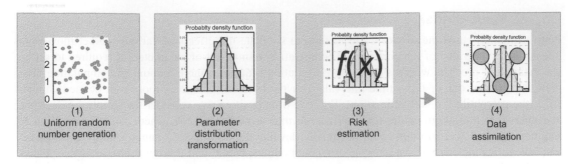

FIGURE 25.2

Solution structure for Monte Carlo–based Value-at-Risk estimation.

where $Y_{ik} = \sum_j \mu_i + Q_{ij}X_{jk}$ are the correlated Gaussian random variables obtained from multiplying the (rotated) Cholesky matrix factor $Q = \widehat{Q}U$ with the i.i.d. standard Gaussian random variables X_{ik}. Expressing the approximation in rotated random variables simplifies the expression in the gamma term.[4]

Hundreds of thousands of experiments are typically required to reduce statistical error in the estimated distribution of dP to an acceptable precision. The results of these experiments are sorted and a percentile is chosen according to user selection.

As shown in Figure 25.2, there are four key steps in a typical market VaR implementation and the parallelization involves many levels of optimization. Steps 1 and 2 implement the experimental generation, step 3 evaluates the experiments (e.g., using the Δ-Γ approximation in Eq. (1)), and step 4 assimilates (i.e., reduces) the results. A typical VaR implementation executes one step at a time, with intermediate results written out to memory.

25.3.2.1 *Task-Centric Perspective*

Statistical sampling of the parameter space with the Monte Carlo method involves running thousands to millions of independent experiments. With respect to the structure of an implementation of the Monte Carlo method, the experiment execution step often has the most amount of parallelism. For this reason, the evaluation of the delta term of the loss function (Eq. (1)) can be efficiently implemented as a dense matrix computation using existing well-parallelized CUBLAS library routines. This is illustrated in two substeps, each shown in Figures 25.3a and 25.3b, for the delta component of the loss function evaluation with N risk factors and $M >> N$ experiments.

Step 3.1 forms the correlated random $N \times M$ matrix Y using matrix-matrix multiplication of the $N \times N$ (rotated) Cholesky factor matrix and the uncorrelated Gaussian random $N \times M$ matrix in $2N \times N \times M$ FLOPs. Step 3.2 computes the M vector of the delta component of the portfolio losses dp^Δ as a matrix-vector multiplication of Y and the N vector Δ in a further $2N \times M$ FLOPs.

---

[4]Readers more familiar with the approximation in original variables should refer to [7] for further details. The problem reformulation described in Section 25.3.2.1 relies on this rotated form of the approximation in which the rotated Cholesky matrix factor is now a full matrix and no longer upper triangular.

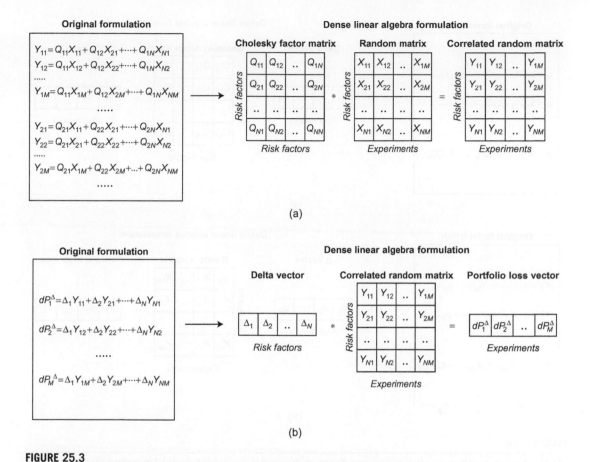

FIGURE 25.3

(a) The correlation of random variables is refactored as a dense matrix-matrix multiplication in order to use the existing well-parallelized CUBLAS library. (b) Loss function evaluation is also refactored as a dense matrix-vector multiplication in order to use the existing well-parallelized CUBLAS library.

Problem Reformulation

A key optimization reformulates the computation of the delta component of the portfolio loss function. The reformulated computation is illustrated in two steps. First, the product of the (rotated) Cholesky matrix factor Q and the Δ vector is stored in a vector $q := \Delta^T Q$ using a call to the BLAS level 2 matrix-vector multiply function $\texttt{Sgemv}$. This is shown in Figure 25.4a. Precomputation of q enables the bottleneck matrix-matrix computation to be replaced with a matrix-vector operation, reducing computation from $O(N)^3$ to $O(N)^2$, where N is the number of risk factors. This is shown in Figure 25.4b.

The Δ-Γ approximation of the portfolio loss is thus obtained using the optimized form

$$dP_k = dP_k^\Delta + dP_k^\Gamma = \sum_i q_i X_{ik} + \frac{1}{2} \lambda_i X_{ik}^2. \tag{2}$$

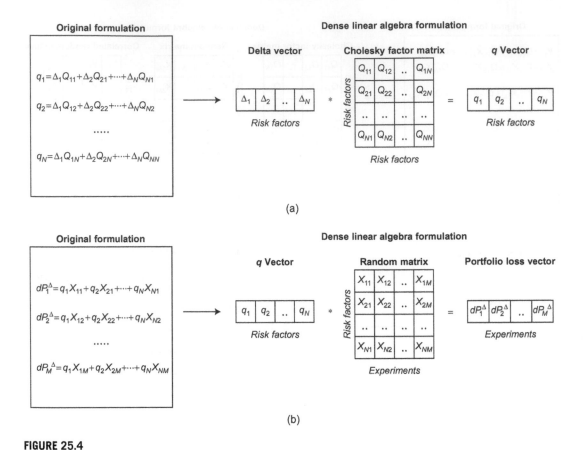

FIGURE 25.4

(a) The precomputation of q is factored as a dense matrix-vector multiplication. (b) The reformulated loss function evaluation is also factored as a dense matrix-vector multiplication.

By reformulating the computation, the deterministic component of the delta term, q, computes in $2N \times N$ FLOPs and the delta component of the loss function computes in just $2N \times M$ FLOPs (excluding terms independent of M). This reformulation achieves a factor of $N+1$ reduction in computation resulting from replacing the BLAS single precision general matrix-matrix multiplication kernel Sgemm with the matrix-vector multiplication kernel Sgemv.

The quadratic gamma term is evaluated by first scaling each row of X_{ik} by λ_i using N Saxpy evaluations totaling $N \times M$ FLOPs. This step is followed by M BLAS single precision vector-vector products Sgemv evaluations, totaling $2N \times M$ FLOPs. The evaluation of the gamma term totals $3N \times M$ FLOPs. Table 25.1 summarizes the upper bound on the FLOP count for Δ and Δ-Γ loss function approximations with and without optimization.

Performance Results

Table 25.2 compares the performance of MC-VaR on an Intel Core i7 processor and an NVIDIA GeForce GTX 480. Readers should refer to Section 25.4.1 for further system configuration details.

Table 25.1 A Comparison of the Upper Bound on the Number of FLOPs (Excluding Terms Independent of M) Required to Compute the Standard and Reformulated Δ and Δ-Γ Loss Function Approximations

	Standard	Reformulated	Speedup
Δ	$2N \times (N+1) \times M$	$2N \times M$	$N+1$
Δ-Γ	$N \times (2N+5) \times M$	$5N \times M$	$\frac{(2N+5)}{5}$

Table 25.2 The Comparative Timings(s) of the Standard and Reformulated Monte Carlo Algorithm for Evaluating Δ-Γ VaR on a NVIDIA GeForce GTX480 and an Intel Core i7 CPU Using the Box-Muller Method with 7.5×10^5 Simulations. The Parenthesized Values Represent the Times and Speedup Factors in Just the Loss Function Evaluation Step.

Timing (s)	Standard	Reformulated	Speedup
CPU	457 (384)	73.9 (1.17)	6.18× (328×)
GPU	58.9 (58.5)	0.951 (0.540)	61.9× (108×)
Speedup	7.76×(6.56×)	77.7×(31.5×)	481×(711×)

The estimate assumes a normal distribution for the joint risk factor returns. $N_b = 23$ batches of size M_b were generated using a portfolio of $N = 4000$ risk factors. With a maximum batch size of $M_b = 32{,}768$ (for the available memory), this number of batches ensures that approximately 7.5×10^5 (753,664) scenarios are generated to achieve 0.1% accuracy in the standard error of the loss distribution. Table 25.2 shows the comparative effect of the optimized Monte Carlo algorithm on the time taken to evaluate Δ-Γ VaR on the GPU and CPU. The numbers in parentheses are the loss estimating portion of execution times without the QRNG and distribution conversion steps.

Without problem reformulation, we see only a 7.76× speedup going from baseline CPU to baseline GPU implementation. With the problem reformlation, we see an additional 108× speedup for the loss estimation from baseline GPU implementation to reformulated GPU implementation, a 61.9× speedup for the Δ-Γ VaR estimation problem.

Overall, the reformulated algorithm performs 77.7× faster on the GPU than the reformulated algorithm on the CPU.

25.3.2.2 *Numerical-Centric Perspective*

A critical feature of the Monte Carlo method is the type of random number generator (RNG) used to generate the random experiments [8] in the first step of the solution structure illustrated in Figure 25.1. These generators must not only be extremely fast but also generate high dimensional sequences which lead to fast convergence in the VaR estimate. Quasi-random number generators (QRNG), also referred to as low discrepancy sequence generators, are used extensively in financial applications[5] [6] and are

---

[5]Monte Carlo methods that use QRNGs are referred to as "Quasi-Monte Carlo" methods.

the preferred choice for generating high dimensional sequences of uniformly distributed variables with respect to a measure of uniformity [17]. Many of these generators use a "skip-ahead" method [14] to efficiently generate sequences on parallel architectures. As VaR estimation typically requires Gaussian random numbers, a distribution conversion function must also be used to transform the uniform random sequence to a Gaussian random sequence. This distribution stage should preserve the uniformity properties of the initial random sequence.

The Sobol' QRNG has recently been shown by Joe and Kuo [9] to satisfy Sobol's measure of uniformity (property A) in up to $N = 16,900$ dimensions. Broadly put, this means a VaR estimate can be performed using upto $N = 16,900$ market risk factors, provided the distribution conversion stage preserves this uniformity property. The best choice of distribution conversion function isn't always obvious and the decision should be approached on a case-by-case basis.

Sobol' Sequences

The Sobol' generator produces a sequence of M N-dimensional uniformly distributed points of the form

$$X_{i,k} = 2^{-32} m_{i,k} \tag{3}$$

where i is the dimension (risk factor) index, k is the experiment index, $m_{i,k}$ is a 32-bit unsigned integer, and $X_{i,k}$ is in the interval $[0, 1)$. The CUDA implementation generates the initial value of $m_{i,k}$ for each parallel thread based on Bratley and Fox's 659 algorithm

$$m_{i,k} = g_0 v_{i,0} \wedge g_1 v_{i,1} \wedge \ldots g_{31} v_{i,31} \tag{4}$$

where g_j is the jth significant bit of the gray code g = k & $(k-1)$ and $v_{i,j}$ is the jth element of an unsigned integer direction vector for dimension (risk factor) i. If the number of experiments is $M = 2^n$, then only the first n vectors are used for $k < M$. 2^{32} is far more experiments than necessary so typically $n < 32$. An important feature of the CUDA implementation is that contiguous blocks of uniform distributed points are then generated in p-way parallel using the recursion relation

$$m_{i,k+1} = m_{i,k} \wedge v_{i,c_g}, \tag{5}$$

to "skip-ahead" from element $X_{i,k}$ in the sequence to element $X_{i,k+p}$ in $O(\log p)$ operations.[6]

Another important feature of the CUDA implementation is that it is able to generate multiple blocks of random numbers, should $N \times M$ single precision variables saturate the device memory. This is achieved by starting each block from the last point in the previous block.

Distribution Conversion

The CUDA SDK 3.1 demonstrates three Gaussian distribution conversion functions, the Box-Muller method [2], the Moro interpolation method [12], and the inverse complementary error function (inverse erfc). We just consider the first two approaches here. The former takes a pair of uncorrelated uniform random numbers, from different dimensions of the Sobol' sequence, in the product of closed unit intervals $(0, 1) \times (0, 1)$ and uses the polar coordinate transformation to generate a pair of uncorrelated

---

[6]c_g is the index of the least-significant zero bit in g.

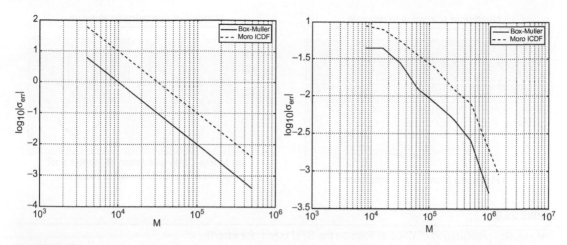

FIGURE 25.5

(Left) A comparison of the standard error (%) in the portfolio loss distribution using Moro's interpolation method and the Box-Muller method applied to Sobol' sequences. (Right) The corresponding error (%) in the simulated 1-day portfolio delta VaR ($c = 95\%$) monotonically converges to the analytic delta VaR (9.87%) with the number of scenarios. In single-precision arithmetic, approximately 1.5×10^6 or 7.5×10^5 scenarios is sufficient to estimate the delta-VaR to within 0.1% when using Moro's interpolation method or the Box-Muller method respectively.

standard Gaussian variables. The Moro interpolation method takes a single uniform random number in the open unit interval $[0, 1]$ and draws standard Gaussian variables using a polynomial interpolation of the inverse cumulative Gaussian distribution function.

The convergence rate in the standard error of the portfolio loss distribution can be used as a metric for choosing the best distribution method. It is also advisable to compare the Δ VaR estimate with the analytic estimate. In general, the Δ-Γ VaR cannot be estimated analytically, of course, but having an understanding of how the standard error compares with the delta VaR estimate error can provide some intuition into what tolerance to choose for the standard error given a target VaR estimate error.

The results of the comparison are presented in Figure 25.5. For 4000 risk factors, approximately 1.5×10^6 or 7.5×10^5 scenarios is sufficient to estimate the standard error of the loss distribution to within 0.1% when using Moro's interpolation method or the Box-Muller method respectively. This tolerance corresponds to an error in the delta-VaR of 0.1%. The study of the comparative effect of using single versus double precision arithmetic on the convergence rate is beyond the scope of this chapter.

Performance Results
The CUDA implementation of the Box-Muller method transforms $4000 \times 1.5 \times 10^6$ uniform quasi-random numbers in $0.470s$ and accounts for 20.5% of the total time of the reformulated algorithm.

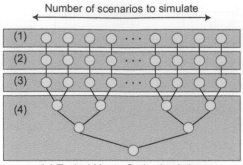

(a) Typical Monte Carlo simulation

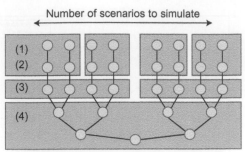

(b) Monte Carlo simulation of market VaR
optimized for GPU resource hierarchy

FIGURE 25.6

The solution organization of Value-at-Risk on the GPU (see color insert).

The primary criteria for choosing the Box-Muller method is that the standard error converges twice as fast in single precision as when using Moro's interpolation method applied to the same sequence of uniform quasi-random numbers.

25.3.2.3 *Data-Centric Perspective*

In Monte Carlo–based risk estimation, thousands to millions of experiments are generated and executed. The computation takes place according to the four steps shown in Figure 25.1. There is a significant amount of intermediate results that must be managed. In a basic implementation, as shown in Figure 25.6a, the steps are executed one step at a time. The amount of intermediate data can be 100s of MBytes. Storing them out to off-chip memory after one step and bringing them back in for the next step can be inefficient, especially when steps such as Step 1 and Step 2 require very little computation.

The need to maintain large intermediate working sets does not arise from the application. It is usually put in place to achieve function modularity in large projects. To optimize the implementation for execution on GPUs, one must re-evaluate the software architecture trade-offs and work towards minimizing the number of data movements, which can dominate the execution time of an implementation.

Kernel Merging

In the case of the VaR implementation, merging the uniform random sequence generation and the distribution conversion steps provides a significant performance boost. The distribution conversion step can be executed in place as soon as the uniform random values are generated, as illustrated in Figure 25.6b. By converting the uniform random values while they are still in the GPU's register files on-chip, we saved the execution time associated with a set of round trip memory transfers to write out the results to device memory and read them back.

Table 25.3 Implementation Cost in Seconds on a NVIDIA GeForce GTX480 for Setting Up 7.5×10^5 Experiments Each with 4000 Risk Factors

Timing (s)	Standard (Separate)	Optimized (Merged)	Speedup
Box-Muller (step 1)	0.128	0.156	2.63x
(step 2)	0.282		
Bailey (step 1)	0.128	0.441	1.16x
(step 2)	0.384		

Performance Results

Table 25.3 illustrates the performance impact on a NVIDIA GeForce GTX 480 from applying kernel merging to two similar methods — the Box-Muller and Bailey's methods.[7] The performance highlights the sensitivity of the kernel merging optimization. The implementation of the Box-Muller method and the Bailey's method are almost identical, except for two extra parameters in the Bailey's method to produce a distribution with slightly higher weights for less likely events. These extra parameters caused the compiled kernel to maintain more registers; as a result the speedup for the Bailey method is less that that of the Box-Muller method.

This optimization, however, can be sensitive to the amount of context each parallel thread of execution must maintain. It is found to be effective for the Box-Muller method, but not as effective for the Bailey's method, even though their functional form is very similar. Specifically, the merged Bailey's method resulted in a 1.16x speedup over two separate steps. This indicates some degree of register spilling, although this overhead is drastically reduced compared with the GTX200 generation of GPU architectures.

Data Blocking

In Step 3, as explained in Section 25.3.2.1, we are leveraging the CUBLAS library for experiment execution. For VaR estimation, 750,000 experiments are used. With thousands of risk factors being considered in each experiment, the experiments must be executed in batches to allow all operands and results of the CUBLAS routines to reside in a GPU's global memory. Sharing the 1.5GB GPU global memory with the Monte Carlo–based VaR estimation engine, one can fit 2^{14} experiments within one batch. The batches of experiments are executed and the outcome of each experiment is saved for later use. This batching process is illustrated by horizontally segmented Steps 1–3 in Figure 25.6b.[8]

---

[7]The Bailey's method [1] also makes use of a polar coordinate transformation of uniform random variables. Unlike the Box-Muller method, however, it produces student-t distributed random variables which give more conservative VaR estimates [10]. Performance benchmarks using the Bailey's method are based on our own implementation as is it not available in the CUDA SDK.

[8]Step 4 does not need to be batched, as its data set comfortably fits in the GPU's global memory.

25.4 FINAL RESULTS

Summary

Our baseline GPU NVIDIA GeForce GTX480 graphics processing unit (GPU) implementation of MC-VaR is a straightforward port from the CPU implementation and has a 7.76× speed advantage over a quad-core Intel i7 Q920 central processing unit (CPU)–based implementation. By reformulating the VaR estimate to reduce the amount of computation, we achieved a further 61.9× speedup. Use of a Box-Muller algorithm to convert the distribution gives an additional 2× speedup over interpolating the inverse of the Gaussian distribution function. We merged data-parallel computational kernels to remove redundant load store operations leading to an additional 2.63× speedup. Overall, we have achieved a speedup of 169× against the baseline GPU implementation, reducing the time of a VaR estimation with a standard error of 0.1% from minutes to less than one second.

25.4.1 System Configurations

The benchmark results for the CPU implementation are measured on an Intel i7 Q920 quad-core CPU, with 8MB L2 cache and 2.67-GHz clock frequency. The estimation engine is compiled with Intel ICC version 11.1 (072). We use the multi-threaded BLAS kernels implemented in the Intel Math Kernel Library (MKL) version 10.2.5 (update 35).

The benchmark results for the GPU implementation are measured on an NVIDIA GeForce GTX 480 GPU with 1.5 GB of global memory. The GTX480 has 15 multiprocessors at 1.4-GHz clock frequency, each with dual issue 16-way vector arithmetic units. The CUDA programs are compiled with NVCC release 3.1 and use BLAS routines available in the CUBLAS library version 3.1.

We have chosen algorithmically equivalent baseline CPU and GPU implementations which provide negligible differences in intermediate results and VaR estimates. In other words, the baseline implementations only provide a transparent reference point from which to trace back any differences in output between the CPU and GPU after subsequent code modifications. They are not fully optimized for performance.

The baseline CPU implementation first generates Sobol' sequences using our own OpenMP parallel implementation of the Sobol' QRNG adapted from a publicly available C++ code written by Joe and Kuo [9]. This implementation conveniently provided precomputed direction vectors to dimensions beyond our requirements. Intel's MKL provides an optimized implementation of the Sobol' QRNG (with merged distribution transformations) based on Bratley and Fox's [3] algorithm 659. This implementation, however, is only pre-configured to generate quasi-random numbers in dimensions of up to 40, although it does allow for precomputed direction vectors in higher dimensions (e.g., from [9]) to be externally referenced.

Sobol' sequences are transformed into normal random variables using a C implementation of Moro's Inverse Cumulative Distribution Function (ICDF) provided, for comparative reasons, in the NVIDIA CUDA SDK 3.1. The loss function is then evaluated with calls to the Streaming SIMD Extensions (SSE) enabled MKL cBLAS kernels `cblasSgemm`, `cblasSgemv` and `cblasSaxpy`, and the result is stored in a loss vector.

We observed that the baseline CPU implementation spends approximately half the time generating the random matrices (QRNG + distribution conversion), and half the time evaluating the loss function. Finally, the moments of the loss distribution are estimated by sorting the loss vector of length M using

Table 25.4 GPU Speedup for the Δ-Γ Approximation with 4000 Risk Factors, Simulated to Achieve a Standard Error in the Normal Loss Distribution within 0.1%

Timing (s)	QRNG	Distribution Conversion	Loss Evaluation
Baseline GPU	0.257 (0.22%)	0.564 (0.48%)	117 (99.3%)
Problem Formulation (GPU)	– (13.5%)	– (29.7%)	1.08 (56.8%)
Module Selection (GPU)	0.129 (13.6%)	0.282 (29.6%)	0.540 (56.8%)
Kernel Merging (GPU)	0.156 (22.4%)		– (77.6%)
Speedup	5.27x		217x
Total Speedup		169x	

qsort from cstdlib in $O(MlogM)$ operations on average. This is a negligible step compared to the BLAS computations which are at least $O(MN)$.

The baseline GPU implementation first generates uniform quasi-random numbers with the "embarrassingly parallel" Sobol' QRNG provided in the NVIDIA SDK 3.1. The sequence is transformed using our own optimized version of Moro's ICDF which makes extensive use of computation blocking and shared constants in the on-chip shared memory. The loss function is then evaluated using cublasSgemm, cublasSgemv, and cublasSaxpy kernels. At the final step, the loss vector is copied from device to CPU memory and sorted using qsort from cstdlib.

25.4.2 Overall Performance Results

The overall speedup from a three-stage optimization of the CUDA implementation of the Δ-Γ VaR model is presented in Table 25.4. The columns in the Table represent the three steps of execution in the VaR estimation and the Table content specifies the absolute and proportional timings of the steps.

The baseline GPU implementation is able to exploit the absence of cross thread communication in the Sobol' QRNG and Moro's ICDF by leveraging the faster native transcendental functions to significant effect. There is a 22.2× speedup for the Sobol' quasi-random number generation and a 25.8× speedup for Moro's ICDF. With a 7.97× speedup, the loss function evaluation step also benefits from being mapped to the GPU, although it becomes the performance bottleneck in the baseline GPU implementation.

We optimize the VaR computation on the GPU in three ways: using problem reformulation, module selection, and kernel merging. We briefly restate the effect of these three optimizations here:

- *Problem reformulation:* By reformulating the algorithm using task-centric techniques as described in Section 25.3.2.1, we are able to obtain a 108× speedup in the loss function evaluation — the bottleneck in the baseline implementation. This amounts to an overall speedup in the VaR estimate of 61.9×.

- *Module selection:* Using the numerical-centric techniques to choose the Box-Muller method over Moro's ICDF, as described in Section 25.3.2.2, we selected the module that gives the faster numerical convergence. As a result, we were able to reach the same VaR estimation accuracy with nearly half the number of simulations. This provides another 2× speedup.
- *Kernel merging:* Using the data-centric techniques, we merged the Sobol' and distribution conversion steps, as described in Section 25.3.2.3, to remove a pair of redundant load and store operations from the computation of each distribution conversion. This reduces the QRNG generation and distribution conversion execution time by 2.63×.

After these optimizations, we have enabled a 169× faster implementation compared to a GPU-based baseline solution, and 1311× faster implementation compared to a CPU-based baseline solution. This illustrates that using a GPU-based implementation may provide some speedup over a CPU-based implementation, but relying on the platform advantage alone would overlook significant acceleration opportunities.

25.5 CONCLUSION

This chapter has considered the implementation of Monte Carlo–based financial market Value-at-Risk estimation on GPUs from three perspectives — the task-centric, the numerical-centric and the data-centric perspectives. By combining these three perspectives, we built up a more comprehensive set of considerations for effectively utilizing the CUDA infrastructure in developing financial applications and achieved a 169× speedup (against the baseline GPU implementation) in VaR estimation through a broad range of optimizations. This approach provides clear interfaces for collaboration within a research and development project and facilitates potentially faster and smoother integration across domains of expertise. Furthermore, many of the optimizations described in this chapter are applicable to a wider range of Monte Carlo–based applications such as exotic option pricing.

Financial institutions seek to improve their market risk infrastructure so that complex risk analytics can be performed on demand. The level of performance improvement reported in this chapter suggests that GPUs can enable much faster deployment of financial market VaR estimates — allowing for global financial market risk to be estimated on demand rather than as an overnight batch job of multiple VaR estimates.

References

[1] R. Bailey, Polar generation of random variates with the t-distribution, Math. Comput. 62 (1994) 779–781.
[2] G.E.P. Box, M.E. Muller, A note on the generation of random normal deviates, Ann. Math. Statist. 29 (2) (1958) 610–611.
[3] P. Bratley, B.L. Fox, Implementing Sobol's quasirandom sequence generator, ACM Trans. Math. Softw. 14 (1) (1988) 88–100.
[4] M.F. Dixon, J. Chong, K. Keutzer, Acceleration of market value-at-risk estimation, in: D. Daly, M. Eleftheriou, J. Moreira, K. Ryu (Eds.), WHPCF '09: Proceedings of the 2nd Workshop on High Performance Computational Finance, ACM, pp. 1–8.
[5] Risk Management Systems in the Aftermath of the Financial Crisis Flaws, Fixes and Future Plans, a GARP report prepared in association with SYBASE, 2010.

[6] M.B. Giles, F.Y. Kuo, I.H. Sloan, B.J. Waterhouse, Quasi-Monte Carlo for finance applications, ANZIAM J. 50 (2008) 308–323.

[7] P. Glasserman, Monte Carlo Methods in Financial Engineering, Appl. of Math. 53, Springer, New York, 2003.

[8] L. Howes, D. Thomas, Efficient random number generation and application using CUDA, in: H. Nguyen (Ed.), GPU Gems 3, NVIDIA, Addison Wesley, Upper Saddle River, NJ, 2007 (Chapter 37).

[9] S. Joe, F. Kuo, Remark on algorithm 659: implementing Sobol's quasirandom sequence generator, ACM Trans. Math. Softw. 29 (1) (2003) 49–57.

[10] E. Jondeau, S. Poon, M. Rockinger, Financial Modeling Under Non-Gaussian Distributions, Springer Finance, New York, 2007.

[11] P. Jorion, Value-at-Risk: The New Benchmark for Managing Financial Risk, third ed., McGraw-Hill, New York, 2007.

[12] B. Moro, The full monte, Risk Mag. 8 (2) (1995) 57–58.

[13] N. Singla, M. Hall, B. Shands, R.D. Chamberlain, Financial Monte Carlo simulation on architecturally diverse systems, in: D. Daly, M. Eleftheriou, J. Moreira, K. Ryu (Eds.), Workshop on High Performance Computational Finance, Supercomputing 08, Austin, TX, 2008, pp. 1–7.

[14] A. Srinivasan, Parallel and distributed computing issues in pricing financial derivatives through Quasi Monte Carlo, in: Proceedings of the 16th International Parallel and Distributed Processing Symposium, Fort Lauderdale, FL, 2002, pp. 14–19.

[15] D.B. Thomas, W. Luk, Multivariate gaussian random number generation targeting reconfigurable hardware, ACM Trans. Reconfigurable Technol. Syst. 1 (2) (2008) 1–29, ISSN 1936–7406.

[16] P. Youngman, Procyclicality and Value-at-Risk, Bank of Canada Financial System Review Report, 2009, pp. 51–54.

[17] X. Wang, I.H. Sloan, Low discrepancy sequences in high dimensions: how well are their projections distributed? J. Comput. Appl. Math. 213 (2) (2008) 366–386.

SECTION

Programming Tools and Techniques

6

Cliff Woolley (NVIDIA)

PROGRAMMING TOOLS AND TECHNIQUES FOR GPU COMPUTING

GPU computing has become an attractive choice in many application domains, as illustrated throughout this book. Occasionally, however, applications that *should* lend themselves well to GPU computing pose implementation challenges of a purely practical nature. For example:

- How can we maximize developer productivity for both expert CUDA C developers as well as those less experienced with GPU programming?
- How can high-performance code be written using higher-level scripting or meta-languages?
- How can we use the CPU and GPU cooperatively in a manner that best suits the architectural strengths of each to solve a problem as efficiently as possible?
- How can we effectively parallelize tasks that require dynamic load balancing?

These are the questions this area seeks to address. The state of the art in this area will no doubt continue to evolve over time as new techniques, frameworks, and tools become available. With these chapters, we seek to provide both a snapshot of the current state of the art as well as inspiration for the next generation of techniques, frameworks, and tools yet to come.

IN THIS SECTION

Programming Frameworks, and Performance Tuning Tools

Chapter 26, "Thrust: A Productivity-Oriented Library for CUDA" by Bell and Hoberock, describes the Thrust parallel template library for C++. Thrust brings a familiar high-level interface similar to the C++ Standard Template Library to GPU computing, helping the developer rapidly develop concise, readable, and efficient GPU code that retains full compatibility with the rest of the CUDA software ecosystem.

Chapter 27, "GPU Scripting and Code Generation with PyCUDA" by Klöckner et al., describes the PyCUDA framework, which combines the computational speed of CUDA C/C++ with the ease of use of Python. Since many computational codes begin their life in a high-level language such as Python, PyCUDA helps bridge the gap between initial proof-of-concept code and the high-performance code that is ultimately needed in production.

Chapter 28, "Jacket: GPU Powered MATLAB Acceleration" by Larsen et al., presents Jacket, which is a software platform for offloading MATLAB computation onto CUDA-capable GPUs. This combines the productivity and simplicity of MATLAB's M-language with the performance of GPU computing without requiring the programmer to use CUDA C/C++ directly.

Chapter 29, "Accelerating Development and Execution Speed with Just-in-Time GPU Code Generation" by Eastman and Pande, describes a method for automatically generating optimized OpenCL kernels from user-supplied mathematical expressions.

Chapter 30, "GPU Application Development, Debugging, and Performance Tuning with GPU Ocelot" by Kerr et al., describes the GPU Ocelot dynamic compilation framework, which provides a rich set of profiling and correctness tools for CUDA Runtime API applications. It can be used to prototype, debug, and tune CUDA applications for efficient execution on GPUs, translate kernels to run on multicore x86 CPUs, and provide information about kernel behavior at instruction-level granularity.

Chapter 31, "Abstraction for AoS and SoA Layout in C++" by Strzodka, presents an abstraction layer for use in C++ applications that allows for easy switching between the array-of-structures (AoS) and structure-of-arrays (SoA) data layouts. This allows performance comparison of the two layouts without tedious manual code changes due to the different access syntax these layouts normally require.

Metaprogramming

Chapter 32, "Processing Device Arrays with C++ Metaprogramming" by Cohen, explains how C++ template metaprogramming can be used to simplify the development of libraries for CUDA C++ applications. By way of example, it walks the reader through the design of a high-level array-processing library for CUDA C++.

Chapter 33, "GPU Metaprogramming: A Case Study in Biologically Inspired Machine Vision" by Pinto and Cox, presents a case study on the use of metaprogramming techniques to accelerate application development and optimization. This system uses textual kernel templating in conjunction with PyCUDA to provide for easy exploration of the application design space and to enable autotuning, resulting in code that is simultaneously general and high-performance.

Scheduling and Load Balancing

Chapter 34, "A Hybridization Methodology for High-Performance Linear Algebra Software for GPUs" by Agullo et al., presents a methodology for scheduling the tasks that make up an algorithm over the computational components of a hybrid system of multicore CPUs and GPU accelerators, resulting in hybrid algorithms that are better performance-wise than corresponding homogeneous algorithms designed exclusively for either GPUs or multicore CPUs.

Chapter 35, "Dynamic Load Balancing Using Work-Stealing" by Cederman and Tsigas, presents a methodology for efficient load-balancing of the multiple tasks that make up a computational problem when it is hard to predict the computational cost of each task or when new tasks are created dynamically at runtime.

Chapter 36, "Applying Software-Managed Caching and CPU/GPU Task Scheduling for Accelerating Dynamic Workloads" by Silberstein et al., presents a pair of complementary methods: the first optimizes memory access for kernels with complex input-dependent memory access patterns; the second maps the subtasks within an application to the CPU or the GPU, accounting for the dependencies among tasks.

Thrust: A Productivity-Oriented Library for CUDA

26

Nathan Bell and Jared Hoberock

This chapter demonstrates how to leverage the Thrust parallel template library to implement high-performance applications with minimal programming effort. Based on the C++ Standard Template Library (STL), Thrust brings a familiar high-level interface to the realm of GPU Computing while remaining fully interoperable with the rest of the CUDA software ecosystem. Applications written with Thrust are concise, readable, and efficient.

26.1 MOTIVATION

With the introduction of CUDA C/C++, developers can harness the massive parallelism of the GPU through a standard programming language. CUDA allows developers to make fine-grained decisions about how computations are decomposed into parallel threads and executed on the device. The level of control offered by CUDA C/C++ (henceforth CUDA C) is an important feature: it facilitates the development of high-performance algorithms for a variety of computationally demanding tasks which (1) merit significant optimization and (2) profit from low-level control of the mapping onto hardware. For this class of computational tasks CUDA C is an excellent solution.

Thrust [1] solves a complementary set of problems, namely those that are (1) implemented efficiently without a detailed mapping of work onto the target architecture or those that (2) do not merit or simply will not receive significant optimization effort by the user. With Thrust, developers describe their computation using a collection of *high-level* algorithms and completely *delegate* the decision of how to implement the computation to the library. This abstract interface allows programmers to describe *what to compute* without placing any additional restrictions on how to carry out the computation. By capturing the programmer's intent at a high level, Thrust has the discretion to make informed decisions on behalf of the programmer and select the most efficient implementation.

The value of high-level libraries is broadly recognized in high-performance computing. For example, the widely-used BLAS standard provides an abstract interface to common linear algebra operations. First conceived more than three decades ago, BLAS remains relevant today in large part because it allows valuable, platform-specific optimizations to be introduced behind a uniform interface.

Whereas BLAS is focused on numerical linear algebra, Thrust provides an abstract interface to fundamental parallel algorithms such as scan, sort, and reduction. Thrust leverages the power of C++ templates to make these algorithms *generic*, enabling them to be used with arbitrary user-defined types and operators. Thrust establishes a durable interface for parallel computing with an eye towards generality, programmer productivity, and real-world performance.

26.2 DIVING IN

Before going into greater detail, let us consider the program in Listing 26.1, which illustrates the salient features of Thrust.

```
#include <thrust/host_vector.h>
#include <thrust/device_vector.h>
#include <thrust/generate.h>
#include <thrust/sort.h>
#include <thrust/copy.h>
#include <cstdlib>

int main(void)
{
    // generate 16M random numbers on the host
    thrust::host_vector<int> h_vec(1 << 24);
    thrust::generate(h_vec.begin(), h_vec.end(), rand);

    // transfer data to the device
    thrust::device_vector<int> d_vec = h_vec;

    // sort data on the device
    thrust::sort(d_vec.begin(), d_vec.end());

    // transfer data back to host
    thrust::copy(d_vec.begin(), d_vec.end(), h_vec.begin());

    return 0;
}
```

Listing 26.1. A complete Thrust program which sorts data on the GPU.

Thrust provides two vector *containers*: host_vector and device_vector. As the names suggest, host_vector is stored in host memory while device_vector lives in device memory on the GPU. Like the vector container in the C++ STL, host_vector and device_vector are generic containers (i.e., they are able to store any data type) that can be resized dynamically. As the example shows, containers automate the allocation and deallocation of memory and simplify the process of exchanging data between the host and device.

The program acts on the vector containers using the generate, sort, and copy algorithms. Here, we adopt the STL convention of specifying *ranges* using pairs of *iterators*. In this example, the iterators h_vec.begin() and h_vec.end() can be thought of as a pair of int pointers, where the former points to the first element in the array and the latter to the element one past the end of the array. Together the pair defines a *range* of integers of size h_vec.end() - h_vec.begin().

Note that even though the computation implied by the call to the sort algorithm suggests one or more CUDA kernel launches, the programmer has not specified a launch configuration. Thrust's interface *abstracts* these details. The choice of performance-sensitive variables such as grid and block size, the details of memory management, and even the choice of sorting algorithm are left to the discretion of the library implementor.

26.2.1 Iterators and Memory Spaces

Although vector iterators are similar to pointers, they carry additional information. Notice that we did not have to instruct the `sort` algorithm that it was operating on the elements of a `device_vector` or hint that the `copy` was from device memory to host memory. In Thrust the memory spaces of each range are automatically *inferred* from the iterator arguments and used to dispatch the appropriate implementation.

In addition to memory space, Thrust's iterators implicitly encode a wealth of information which can guide the dispatch process. For instance, our `sort` example above operates on `int`s, a primitive data type with a fundamental comparison operation. In this case, Thrust dispatches a highly-tuned Radix Sort algorithm [2] which is considerably faster than alternative comparison-based sorting algorithms such as Merge Sort [3]. It is important to realize that this dispatch process incurs no performance or storage overhead: metadata encoded by iterators exists only at compile time, and dispatch strategies based on it are selected *statically*. In general, Thrust's static dispatch strategies may capitalize on any information that is derivable from the type of an iterator.

26.2.2 Interoperability

Thrust is implemented entirely within CUDA C/C++ and maintains interoperability with the rest of the CUDA ecosystem. Interoperability is an important feature because no single language or library is the best tool for every problem. For example, although Thrust algorithms use CUDA features like __shared__ memory internally, there is no mechanism for users to exploit __shared__ memory directly through Thrust. Therefore, it is sometimes necessary for applications to access CUDA C directly to implement a certain class of specialized algorithms, as illustrated in the software stack of Figure 26.1.

Interfacing Thrust to CUDA C is straightforward and analogous to the use of the C++ STL with standard C code. Data that resides in a Thrust container can be accessed by external libraries by

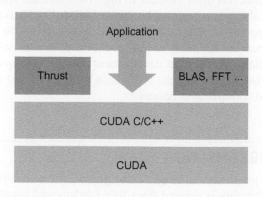

FIGURE 26.1

Thrust is an abstraction layer on top of CUDA C/C++ (see color insert).

```
size_t N = 1024;

// allocate Thrust container
device_vector<int> d_vec(N);

// extract raw pointer from container
int * raw_ptr = raw_pointer_cast(&d_vec[0]);

// use raw_ptr in non-Thrust functions
cudaMemset(raw_ptr, 0, N * sizeof(int));

// pass raw_ptr to a kernel
my_kernel<<<N / 128, 128>>>(N, raw_ptr);

// memory is automatically freed
```

```
size_t N = 1024;

// raw pointer to device memory
int * raw_ptr;
cudaMalloc(&raw_ptr, N * sizeof(int));

// wrap raw pointer with a device_ptr
device_ptr<int> dev_ptr = device_pointer_cast(raw_ptr);

// use device_ptr in Thrust algorithms
sort(dev_ptr, dev_ptr + N);

// access device memory through device_ptr
dev_ptr[0] = 1;

// free memory
cudaFree(raw_ptr);
```

(a) Interfacing Thrust to CUDA   (b) Interfacing CUDA to Thrust

Listing 26.2. Thrust interoperates smoothly with CUDA C/C++.

extracing a "raw" pointer from the vector. The code sample in Listing 26.2 illustrates the use of raw_pointer_cast to obtain an int pointer to the contents of a device_vector.

Applying Thrust algorithms to raw pointers is also straightforward. Once the raw pointer has been wrapped by a device_ptr it can be used like an ordinary Thrust iterator. The wrapped pointer provides the memory space information Thrust needs to invoke the appropriate algorithm implementation and also allows a convenient mechanism for accessing device memory from the host.

Thrust's native CUDA C interoperability is a powerful feature. Interoperability ensures that Thrust always *complements* CUDA C and that a Thrust plus CUDA C combination is never worse than either Thrust or CUDA C alone. Indeed, while it may be possible to write whole parallel applications entirely with Thrust functions, it is often valuable to implement domain-specific functionality directly in CUDA C. The level of abstraction targeted by native CUDA C affords programmers fine-grained control over the precise mapping of computational resources to a particular problem. Programming at this level provides developers the flexibility to implement exotic or otherwise specialized algorithms. Interoperability also facilitates an iterative development strategy: (1) quickly prototype a parallel application entirely in Thrust, (2) identify the application's hot spots, and (3) write more specialized algorithms in CUDA C and optimize as necessary.

26.3 GENERIC PROGRAMMING

Thrust presents a style of programming emphasizing genericity and composability. Indeed, the vast majority of Thrust's functionality is derived from four fundamental parallel algorithms: for_each, reduce, scan, and sort. For example, the transform algorithm is a derivative of for_each while inner_product is implemented with reduce.

Thrust algorithms are generic in both the type of the data to be processed and the operations to be applied to the data. For instance, the `reduce` algorithm may be employed to compute the sum of a range of integers (a `plus` reduction applied to `int` data) or the maximum of a range of floating point values (a `max` reduction applied to `float` data). This generality is implemented via C++ templates, which allows user-defined types and functions to be used in addition to built-in types such as `int` or `float` or Thrust operators such as `plus`.

Generic algorithms are extremely valuable because it is impractical to anticipate precisely which particular types and operators users will require. Indeed, while the computational structure of an algorithm is fixed, the number of *instantiations* of the algorithm is truly limitless. However, it is worth remarking that while Thrust's interface is general, the abstraction affords implementors the opportunity to specialize for specific types and operations known to be important use cases. As with inferences from memory space, these opportunities may be exploited statically.

In Thrust, user-defined operations take the form of C++ function objects, or *functors*. Functors allow the programmer to adapt a generic algorithm to implement a specific user-defined operation. For example, the code samples in Listing 26.3 implement SAXPY, the well-known BLAS operation, using CUDA C and Thrust respectively. Here, the generic `transform` algorithm is called with the user-defined `saxpy_functor`.

26.4 BENEFITS OF ABSTRACTION

In this section we'll describe the benefits of Thrust's abstraction layer with respect to programmer productivity, robustness, and real-world performance.

26.4.1 Programmer Productivity

Thrust's high-level algorithms enhance programmer productivity by automating the mapping of computational tasks onto the GPU. Recall the two implementations of SAXPY shown in Listing 26.3. In the CUDA C implementation of SAXPY the programmer has described a specific decomposition of the parallel vector operation into a grid of blocks with 256 threads per block. In contrast, the Thrust implementation does not prescribe a launch configuration. Instead, the only specifications are the input and output ranges and a functor to apply to them. Otherwise, the two codes are roughly the same in terms of length and code complexity.

Delegating the launch configuration to Thrust has a subtle yet profound implication: the launch parameters can be automatically chosen based on a model of machine performance. Currently, Thrust targets *maximal occupancy* and will compare the resource usage of the kernel (e.g., number of registers, amount of shared memory) with the resources of the target GPU to determine a launch configuration with highest occupancy. While the maximal occupancy heuristic is not necessarily optimal, it is straightforward to compute and effective in practice. Furthermore, there is nothing to preclude the use of more sophisticated performance models. For instance, a run-time tuning system that examined hardware performance counters could be introduced behind this abstraction without altering client code.

Thrust also boosts programmer productivity by providing a rich set of algorithms for common patterns. For instance, the map-reduce pattern is conveniently implemented with Thrust's `sort_by_key` and `reduce_by_key` algorithms, which implement key-value sorting and reduction respectively.

```
__global__
void saxpy_kernel(int n, float a, float * x, float * y)
{
    const int i = blockDim.x * blockIdx.x + threadIdx.x;

    if (i < n)
        y[i] = a * x[i] + y[i];
}

void saxpy(int n, float a, float * x, float * y)
{
  // set launch configuration parameters
  int block_size = 256;
  int grid_size = (n + block_size - 1) / block_size;

  // launch saxpy kernel
  saxpy_kernel<<< grid_size, block_size >>>(n, a, x, y);
}
```

(a) CUDA C

```
struct saxpy_functor
{
    const float a;

    saxpy_functor(float _a) : a(_a) {}

    __host__ __device__
    float operator()(float x, float y)
    {
        return a * x + y;
    }
};

void saxpy(float a, device_vector<float>& x, device_vector<float>& y)
{
  // setup functor
  saxpy_functor func(a);

  // call transform
  transform(x.begin(), x.end(), y.begin(), y.begin(), func);
}
```

(b) Thrust

Listing 26.3. SAXPY implementations in CUDA C and Thrust.

26.4.2 Robustness

Thrust's abstraction layer also enhances the robustness of CUDA applications. In the previous section we noted that by delegating the launch configuration details to Thrust we could automatically obtain maximum occupancy during execution. In addition to maximizing occupancy, the abstraction layer also ensures that algorithms "just work," even in uncommon or pathological use cases. For instance, Thrust automatically handles limits on grid dimensions (no more than 64K), works around limitations on the size of __global__ function arguments, and accommodates large user-defined types in most algorithms. To the degree possible, Thrust circumvents such factors and ensures correct program execution across the full spectrum of CUDA-capable GPUs.

26.4.3 Real-World Performance

In addition to enhancing programmer productivity and improving robustness, the high-level abstractions provided by Thrust improve performance in real-world use cases. In this section we examine two instances where the discretion afforded by Thrust's high-level interface is exploited for meaningful performance gains.

To begin, consider the operation of filling an array with a particular value. In Thrust, this is implemented with the fill algorithm. Unfortunately, a straightforward implementation of this seemingly simple operation is subject to severe performance hazards. Recall that processors based on the G80 architecture (i.e., Compute Capability 1.0 and 1.1) impose strict conditions on which memory access patterns may benefit from memory coalescing [4]. In particular, memory accesses of sub-word granularity (i.e., less than four bytes) are not coalesced by these processors. This artifact is detrimental to performance when initializing arrays of char or short types.

Fortunately, the iterators passed to fill implicitly encode all the information necessary to intercept this case and substitute an optimized implementation. Specifically, when fill is dispatched for smaller types, Thrust selects a "wide" version of the algorithm that issues word-sized accesses per thread. While this optimization is straightforward to implement, users are unlikely to invest the effort of making this optimization themselves. Nevertheless, the benefit, shown in Table 26.1, is worthwhile, particularly on earlier architectures.

Like fill, Thrust's sorting functionality exploits the discretion afforded by the abstract sort and stable_sort functions. As long as the algorithm achieves the promised result, we are free to utilize

Table 26.1 Memory Bandwidth of Two fill Kernels

GPU	data type	naive fill	thrust::fill	Speedup
GeForce 8800 GTS	char	1.2 GB/s	41.2 GB/s	34.15x
	short	2.4 GB/s	41.2 GB/s	17.35x
	int	41.2 GB/s	41.2 GB/s	1.00x
	long	40.7 GB/s	40.7 GB/s	1.00x
GeForce GTX 280	char	33.9 GB/s	75.0 GB/s	2.21x
	short	51.6 GB/s	75.0 GB/s	1.45x
	int	75.0 GB/s	75.0 GB/s	1.00x
	long	69.2 GB/s	69.2 GB/s	1.00x
GeForce GTX 480	char	74.1 GB/s	156.9 GB/s	2.12x
	short	136.6 GB/s	156.9 GB/s	1.15x
	int	146.1 GB/s	156.9 GB/s	1.07x
	long	156.9 GB/s	156.9 GB/s	1.00x

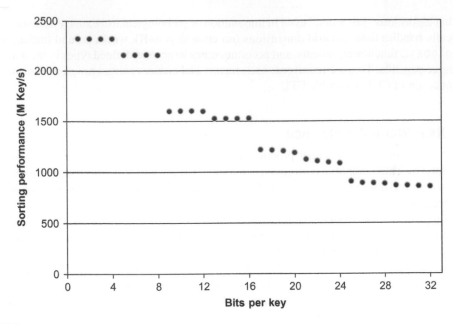

FIGURE 26.2

Sorting 32-bit integers on the GeForce GTX 480: Thrust's dynamic sorting optimizations improve performance by a considerable margin in common use cases.

sophisticated static (compile-time) and dynamic (run-time) optimizations to implement the sorting operation in the most efficient manner.

As mentioned in Section 26.2.1, Thrust statically selects a highly-optimized Radix Sort algorithm [2] for sorting primitive types (e.g., char, int, float, and double) with the standard less and greater comparison operators. For all other types (e.g., user-defined data types) and comparison operators, Thrust uses a general Merge Sort algorithm. Because sorting primitives with Radix Sort is considerably faster than Merge Sort, this static optimization has significant value.

Thrust also applies dynamic optimizations to improve sorting performance. Since the cost of Radix Sort is proportional to the number of significant key bits, we can exploit unused key bits to reduce the cost of sorting. For instance, when all integer keys are in the range [0, 16), only four bits must be sorted, and we observe a 2.71× speedup versus a full 32-bit sort. The relationship between key bits and radix sort performance is plotted in Figure 26.2.

26.5 BEST PRACTICES

In this section we highlight three high-level optimization techniques that programmers may employ to yield significant performance speedups when using Thrust.

26.5.1 Fusion

The balance of computational resources on modern GPUs implies that algorithms are often *bandwidth limited*. Specifically, computations with low *arithmetic intensity*, the ratio of calculations per memory access, are constrained by the available memory bandwidth and do not fully utilize the computational resources of the GPU. One technique for increasing the computational intensity of an algorithm is to *fuse* multiple pipeline stages together into a single operation. In this section we demonstrate how Thrust enables developers to exploit opportunities for kernel fusion and better utilize GPU memory bandwidth.

The simplest form of kernel fusion is scalar function composition. For example, suppose we have the functions $f(x) \rightarrow y$ and $g(y) \rightarrow z$ and would like to compute $g(f(x)) \rightarrow z$ for a range of scalar values. The most straightforward approach is to read x from memory, compute the value $y = f(x)$, and then write y to memory, and then do the same to compute $z = g(y)$. In Thrust this approach would be implemented with two separate calls to the `transform` algorithm, one for f and one for g. While this approach is straightforward to understand and implement, it needlessly wastes memory bandwidth, which is a scarce resource.

A better approach is to fuse the functions into a single operation $g(f(x))$ and halve the number of memory transactions. Unless f and g are computationally expensive operations, the fused implementation will run approximately twice as fast as the first approach. In general, scalar function composition is a profitable optimization and should be applied liberally.

Thrust enables developers to exploit other, less-obvious opportunities for fusion. For example, consider the following two Thrust implementations of the BLAS function SNRM2 shown in Listing 26.4, which computes the Euclidean norm of a `float` vector.

Note that SNRM2 has low arithmetic intensity: each element of the vector participates in only two floating point operations, one multiply (to square the value) and one addition (to sum values together). Therefore, an implementation of SNRM2 using the `transform_reduce` algorithm, which fuses the `square` transformation with a `plus` reduction, should be considerably faster. Indeed this is true and `snrm2_fast` is fully 3.8 times faster than `snrm2_slow` for a 16M element vector on a Tesla C1060.

While the previous examples represent some of the more common opportunities for fusion, we have only scratched the surface. As we have seen, fusing a transformation with other algorithms is a worthwhile optimization. However, Thrust would become unwieldy if all algorithms came with a `transform_` variant. For this reason Thrust provides `transform_iterator`, which allows transformations to be fused with any algorithm. Indeed, `transform_reduce` is simply a convenience wrapper for the appropriate combination of `transform_iterator` and `reduce`. Similarly, Thrust provides `permutation_iterator`, which enables `gather` and `scatter` operations to be fused with other algorithms.

26.5.2 Structure of Arrays

In the previous section we examined how fusion minimizes the number of off-chip memory transactions and conserves bandwidth. Another way to improve memory efficiency is to ensure that all memory accesses benefit from *coalescing*, since coalesced memory access patterns are considerably faster than non-coalesced transactions.

```
struct square
{
  _host_ _device_
  float operator()(float x) const
  {
    return x * x;
  }
};


float snrm2_slow(const thrust::device_vector<float>& x)
{
  // without fusion
  device_vector<float> temp(x.size());
  transform(x.begin(), x.end(), temp.begin(), square());

  return sqrt( reduce(temp.begin(), temp.end()) );
}

float snrm2_fast(const thrust::device_vector<float>& x)
{
  // with fusion
  return sqrt( transform_reduce(x.begin(), x.end(), square(), 0.0f, plus<float>());
}
```

Listing 26.4. SNRM2 has low arithmetic intensity and therefore benefits greatly from fusion.

```
struct float3                        struct float3_soa
{                                    {
  float x;                             float * x;
  float y;                             float * y;
  float z:                             float * z;
};                                   };

float3 * aos;                        float3_soa soa;
...                                  ...

aos[0].x = 1.0f;                     soa.x[0] = 1.0f;
```

(a) Array of Structures   (b) Structure of Arrays

Listing 26.5. Data layouts for three-dimensional `float` vectors.

Perhaps the most common violation of the memory coalescing rules arises when using a so-called Array of Structures (AoS) data layout. Generally speaking, access to the elements of an array filled with C `struct` or C++ `class` variables will be uncoalesced. Only explicitly aligned structures such as the `uint2` or `float4` vector types satisfy the memory coalescing rules.

An alternative to the AoS layout is the Structure of Arrays (SoA) approach, where the components of each struct are stored in separate arrays. Listing 26.5 illustrates the AoS and SoA methods of representing a range of three-dimensional `float` vectors. The advantage of the SoA method is that regular

```
struct rotate_tuple
{
  __host__ __device__
  tuple<float,float,float> operator()(tuple<float,float,float>& t)
  {
    float x = get<0>(t);
    float y = get<1>(t);
    float z = get<2>(t);

    float rx = 0.36f * x + 0.48f * y + -0.80f * z;
    float ry =-0.80f * x + 0.60f * y + 0.00f * z;
    float rz = 0.48f * x + 0.64f * y + 0.60f * z;

    return make_tuple(rx, ry, rz);
  }
};

...

device_vector<float> x(N), y(N), z(N);

transform(make_zip_iterator(make_tuple(x.begin(), y.begin(), z.begin())),
          make_zip_iterator(make_tuple(x.end(), y.end(), z.end())),
          make_zip_iterator(make_tuple(x.begin(), y.begin(), z.begin())),
          rotate_tuple());
```

Listing 26.6. The zip_iterator facilitates processing of data in structure of arrays format.

access to the x, y, and z components of a given vector is coalesceable (because float satisfies the coalescing rules), while regular access to the float3 structures in the AoS approach is not.

The problem with SoA is that there is nothing to logically encapsulate the members of each element into a single entity. Whereas we could immediately apply Thrust algorithms to AoS containers like device_vector<float3>, we have no direct means of doing the same with three separate device_vector<float> containers. Fortunately Thrust provides zip_iterator, which provides encapsulation of SoA ranges.

The zip_iterator [5] takes a number of iterators and *zips* them together into a virtual range of tuples. For instance, binding three device_vector<float> iterators together yields a range of type tuple<float,float,float>, which is analogous to the float3 structure.

Consider the code sample in Listing 26.6 which uses zip_iterator to construct a range of three-dimensional float vectors stored in SoA format. Each vector is transformed by a rotation matrix in the rotate_tuple functor before being written out again. Note that zip_iterator is used for both input and output ranges, transparently packing the underlying scalar ranges into tuples and then unpacking the tuples into the scalar ranges. On a Tesla C1060, this SoA implementation is $2.85\times$ faster than the analogous AoS implementation (not shown).

26.5.3 Implicit Ranges

In the previous sections we considered ways to efficiently transform ranges of values and ways to construct ad hoc tuples of values from separate ranges. In either case, there was some underlying data stored *explicitly* in memory. In this section we illustrate the use of *implicit* ranges, i.e., ranges whose values are defined programmatically and not stored anywhere in memory.

For instance, consider the problem of finding the index of the element with the smallest value in a given range. We could implement a special reduction kernel for this algorithm, which we'll call min_index, but that would be time-consuming and unnecessary. A better approach is to implement min_index in terms of existing functionality, such as a specialized reduction over (value, index) tuples, to achieve the desired result. Specifically, we can zip the range of values v[0], v[1], v[2], ... together with a range of integer indices 0, 1, 2, ... to form a range of tuples (v[0], 0), (v[1], 1), (v[2],2) ... and then implement min_index with the standard reduce algorithm. Unfortunately, this scheme will be much slower than a customized reduction kernel, since the index range must be created and stored explicitly in memory.

To resolve this issue Thrust provides counting_iterator [5], which acts just like the explicit range of values we need to implement min_index, but does not carry any overhead. Specifically, when counting_iterator is dereferenced it generates the appropriate value "on the fly" and yields that value to the caller. An efficient implementation of min_index using counting_iterator is shown in Listing 26.7.

```
struct smaller_tuple
{
  tuple<float,int> operator()(tuple<float,int> a, tuple<float,int> b)
  {
    // return the tuple with the smaller float value
    if (get<0>(a) < get<0>(b))
      return a;
    else
      return b;
  }
};

int min_index(device_vector<float>& values)
{
  // [begin,end) form the implicit sequence [0,1,2, ... value.size())
  counting_iterator<int> begin(0);
  counting_iterator<int> end(values.size());

  // initial value of the reduction
  tuple<float,int> init(values[0], 0);

  // compute the smallest tuple
  tuple<float,int> smallest = reduce(make_zip_iterator(make_tuple(values.begin(), begin)),
                                     make_zip_iterator(make_tuple(values.end(), end)),
                                     init,
                                     smaller_tuple());
  // return the index
  return get<1>(smallest);
}
```

Listing 26.7. Implicit ranges improve performance by conserving memory bandwidth.

Here `counting_iterator` has allowed us to efficiently implement a special-purpose reduction algorithm without the need to write a new, special-purpose kernel. In addition to `counting_iterator` Thrust provides `constant_iterator`, which defines an implicit range of constant value. Note that these implicitly-defined iterators can be combined with the other iterators to create more complex implicit ranges. For instance, `counting_iterator` can be used in combination with `transform_iterator` to produce a range of indices with nonunit stride.

In practice there is no need to implement `min_index` since Thrust's `min_element` algorithm provides the equivalent functionality. Nevertheless the `min_index` example is instructive of best practices. Indeed, Thrust algorithms such as `min_element`, `max_element`, and `find_if` apply the exact same strategy internally.

References

[1] J. Hoberock, N. Bell, Thrust: A parallel template library, 2011. Version 1.4.0.

[2] D. Merrill, A. Grimshaw, Revisiting sorting for gpgpu stream architectures, Technical Report CS2010-03, University of Virginia, Department of Computer Science, Charlottesville, VA, 2010.

[3] N. Satish, M. Harris, M. Garland, Designing efficient sorting algorithms for manycore GPUs, in Proceedings 23rd IEEE Int'l Parallel & Distributed Processing Symposium, IEEE Computer Society, Washington, DC, 2009.

[4] NVIDIA Corporation, CUDA C Best Practices Guide v3.2, NVIDIA Corporation, Santa Clara, CA, 2010 (Section 3.2.1).

[5] Boost Iterator Library. www.boost.org/doc/libs/release/libs/iterator/.

GPU Scripting and Code Generation with PyCUDA

Andreas Klöckner, Nicolas Pinto, Bryan Catanzaro, Yunsup Lee, Paul Ivanov, and Ahmed Fasih

High-level scripting languages are in many ways polar opposites to GPUs. GPUs are highly parallel, subject to hardware subtleties, and designed for maximum throughput, and they offer a tremendous advance in the performance achievable for a significant number of computational problems. On the other hand, scripting languages such as Python favor ease of use over computational speed and do not generally emphasize parallelism. PyCUDA is a package that attempts to join the two together. This chapter argues that in doing so, a programming environment is created that is greater than just the sum of its two parts.

We would like to note that nearly all of this chapter applies in unmodified form to PyOpenCL, a sister project of PyCUDA, whose goal it is to realize the same concepts as PyCUDA for OpenCL.

27.1 INTRODUCTION, PROBLEM STATEMENT, AND CONTEXT

How are computational codes created? Their life cycle often begins with a quick proof of concept in a high-level language such as MATLAB or Python that aims to examine the suitability of the proposed method for the application problem at hand. Once this is established, the problem size is scaled up, and with it, the demands for execution speed grow. In principle, it is not desirable that the working proof-of-concept code would need to be changed merely to squeeze out better computational performance. Unfortunately, at present, very few workloads can be scaled in this fashion, so eventually the need arises to employ a language that produces efficient machine code.

The desire to make this transition as seamless as possible quite naturally leads to hybrid code, in which only those pieces requiring improved performance are changed, and the remainder is kept as is. These approaches are not new (cf., e.g., MATLAB's Mex or Python's F2Py). Unfortunately, they are not as widespread as they could be because they come with a significant complexity burden. GPU computing adds a new facet to this issue, as GPU programs are always hybrids, even though NVIDIA's CUDA Runtime programming interface goes to considerable lengths to paper over this fact. GPU programs are thus very naturally split between performance-hungry and performance-indifferent parts, usually along the same lines as the CPU-GPU boundary. This is fortunate, as one may easily substitute the performance-indifferent part of the hybrid, taking advantage of the already well-defined interface between the two. PyCUDA fits exactly into this niche and allows codes written in this high-level language to obtain GPU performance from within existing Python programs with a minimum of effort.

But in addition to a practical route to high performance for existing codes, PyCUDA also has much to offer to the seasoned GPU programmer creating full-scale production codes. Many of these advanced benefits are described in detail in a recent manuscript [1], which focuses on the capability of generating GPU code at runtime and represents a more academic discussion of the software engineering aspects of GPU programming and what PyCUDA does to address them. This chapter on the other hand provides a hands-on perspective of the things one can do with PyCUDA, and how.

27.2 CORE METHOD

A common lament in the field of scientific computing concerns the ever-widening gap between hypothetical machine capabilities and the effort an individual programmer is able to spend to move a computational application towards exploiting a machine to the full extent of its capability. GPUs obviously influence this balance, by increasing the maximum capability, by increasing the performance that is obtained with an "average" amount of effort, and by requiring a different set of skills to achieve genuinely high performance.

More sophisticated tools, compilers, and libraries are generally hoped to level this field, enabling users to achieve good results even with modest investment. PyCUDA is a contribution to this discussion of tools for GPU computing. PyCUDA (and likewise its sister project PyOpenCL) has a two-fold aim. First, it aims to simplify the usage of *existing* basic concepts of CUDA C. Importantly, it does *not* attempt to change or reinvent the basic notions of GPU programming, but instead, as a foundation for further tools, just exposes them as is through a carefully engineered interface. Key features of this interface include generous use of sensible defaults (all of which can be overridden), automatic error checking, and automatic resource management. Second, and strictly *on top* of the first, basic layer, PyCUDA provides abstractions that support a number of very common usage patterns involving a GPU equivalent of NumPy [2] arrays.

As a particular consequence of the design choice to leave as much of the underlying concepts in place, device kernels occur in PyCUDA programs and PyOpenCL as simple strings. This is practical because Python allows so-called triple-quoted strings which may extend across line boundaries, thus appearing as contiguous code blocks without intervening string terminators or other traces of the host-level language. A different approach is pursued by the Clyther project[1] and similar efforts, which let the user write kernels in the host language and then translate them to the device language (C/C++) in some manner. Each approach represents one end of a trade-off. It is obviously appealing to let the user program in one single language (the host language) rather than forcing her to master two separate ones. PyCUDA and PyOpenCL sacrifice this advantage in favor of passing on the concepts of the underlying programming system in as unmodified a manner as possible in order to provide direct applicability of existing CUDA/OpenCL documentation and to decrease the maintenance burden as the underlying system evolves. One additional factor entering the trade-off is the ease with which kernel code can be automatically generated (see Section 27.3.3).

Programming in scripting languages (like Python) tends to be quite satisfying to the programmer because of near-immediate response during development, the possibility of interactive exploration, and

---

[1]http://clyther.sourceforge.net/

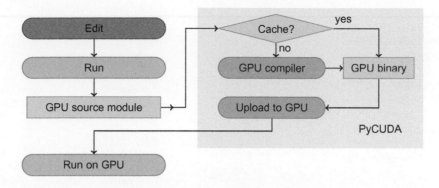

FIGURE 27.1

Workflow of PyCUDA GPU program compilation. PyCUDA aims to maintain a scripting-like "edit-run-repeat" style of working for the user. The compilation and caching operations in the gray box are performed without user involvement.

good error reporting. Although PyCUDA gives the user access to a compiled language (CUDA C), it attempts to avoid the development iteration penalty commonly associated with compiled languages, instead retaining the satisfaction and immediacy of scripting. First of all, it makes invocations to the CUDA C compiler fast and transparent. To this end, it employs a compiler caching mechanism that is pictured in Figure 27.1. As it is likely that only one GPU kernel is being changed in each development iteration, the user only needs to wait for compilation of this one kernel. The loading of all other kernels in the code will be near-instantaneous thanks to PyCUDA's caching mechanism.

We have thus completed an initial description of PyCUDA's goals and usage patterns. The next section will, by means of a number of concrete examples of increasing complexity, show how common tasks can be accomplished in PyCUDA. Section 27.4 will then briefly reflect on what was shown, and we close in Section 27.6 with a few remarks and ideas for future work.

27.3 ALGORITHMS, IMPLEMENTATIONS, AND EVALUATIONS

In this section, we will take the reader on a brief journey through different aspects of programming GPUs using PyCUDA, starting with a basic hello-world example in Section 27.3.1, through more advanced aspects in the following sections.

27.3.1 The Basics of GPU Programming with PyCUDA

Perhaps the simplest useful program that can be written using PyCUDA is shown in Listing 27.1, which we will discuss here step by step.

PyCUDA's interface to the "nuts and bolts" of the CUDA programming system can be found in `pycuda.driver` and is imported here under the alias `cuda`. The module is called `driver` because it exposes the so-called "driver-level" programming interface of CUDA, which is more flexible than the more commonly used CUDA C "runtime-level" programming interface, and it has a few features that

```
import pycuda.driver as cuda
import pycuda.autoinit
import numpy

a = numpy.random.randn(4,4) \
      .astype(numpy.float32)
a_gpu = cuda.mem_alloc(a.nbytes)
cuda.memcpy_htod(a_gpu, a)

mod = cuda.SourceModule("""
  _global_ void multiply2(float *a)
  {
    int i = threadIdx.x + threadIdx.y*4;     Compute Kernel
    a[i] *= 2;
  }
  """)

func = mod.get_function("multiply2")
func(a_gpu, block=(4,4,1))

a_doubled = numpy.empty_like(a)
cuda.memcpy_dtoh(a_doubled, a_gpu)
print a_doubled
print a
```

Listing 27.1. An example of the use of PyCUDA, showing the use of the `SourceModule` facility. This simple program uploads a 4 × 4 array of single-precision floating point numbers, multiplies them by two on the GPU, and retrieves the result.

are not present in the runtime. (If a program uses the triple-angle-bracket syntax for kernel invocation, it is using the runtime interface.)

The next imported module, `pycuda.autoinit`, automatically picks a GPU to run on, based on availability and the number, if any, to which the `CUDA_DEVICE` environment variable is set. It also creates a GPU context for subsequent code to run in. Both the chosen device and the created context are available from `pycuda.autoinit` as importable symbols, if needed. The use of `pycuda.autoinit` is not compulsory — if needed, users can construct their own device-choice and context-creation methods using the facilities available in `pycuda.driver`.

The last import in this simple example is `numpy`, the Python array package. Since most GPU computations involve large arrays of data, PyCUDA integrates tightly with `numpy`.

After creating a 4 × 4 array of random single-precision floating point numbers on the CPU in the `numpy` array identified by the variable a, memory for a is allocated on the GPU as a_gpu. The object returned here is a `DeviceAllocation` object, whose lifetime is coupled to that of the GPU memory allocation, i.e., once the last reference to the `DeviceAllocation` disappears, the object becomes eligible for garbage collection, and once that happens, the GPU allocation also disappears.

DeviceAllocation objects can also be cast to integer for pointer arithmetic. Once memory is allocated, the contents of a are copied from the host to the device (hence "htod"). Observe that no explicit error checking occurs at any stage of this program. If an error is encountered, a subclass of pycuda.driver.Error is raised as an exception.

Now that the data is prepared, the most interesting part of the program begins, in which the source code for the GPU kernel is passed to the constructor of SourceModule. At this point, the NVIDIA compiler is invoked, coupled with the caching mechanism as described in Section 27.2, at the end of which the user obtains a handle to a driver.SourceModule representing the binary code uploaded to the GPU. From this module handle, the user may then obtain a Kernel handle by means of the get_function method. Observe that C++ name mangling[2] would generally make the symbol names passed to get_function complicated and non-human-readable. For this reason, PyCUDA automatically wraps the code passed to SourceModule in an extern "C" declaration. If the use of C++ features is desired, the keyword argument no_extern_c may be passed to Source-Module to avoid this. In this case, any __global__ entry points should be declared extern "C" by hand.

The Kernel handle, once it has been obtained, can then be called like any other function. Keyword arguments grid and block determine the size of the computational grid and the thread block size. DeviceAllocation instances may be passed directly to kernels, but other arguments incur the problem that PyCUDA knows nothing about their required type. There are two ways to address this: First, pass all such arguments as numpy sized scalars, such as numpy.float32(5.7) for single-precision floating point, or numpy.intp(p) for pointer-sized integers. Alternatively, one may use *prepared kernel invocation*, in which the user informs PyCUDA explicitly about the kernel's argument types. In this case, the invocation line would need to be changed as follows:

```
func.prepare("P", block=(4,4,1))
func.prepared_call((1, 1), a_gpu)
```

Note that the prepare method only needs to be called once. Its first argument represents the kernel's arguments as a type string as accepted by the struct module in Python standard library, e.g., "P" in the example specifies a single pointer argument. The prepared call styles also differ in that the thread block size is set at prepare time (but can be changed), and the grid dimension may be set with each call. Prepared kernel invocation is also slightly faster than the explicitly-sized invocation style.

In this example, the function of the GPU code itself is trivial — for a 4 × 4 block size and a single-element grid, each entry of the corresponding array on the GPU is multiplied by two. As the kernel is invoked, the kernel call enters the queue on the GPU, but, like in the CUDA "runtime" interface, the invocation returns immediately and does not wait for completion on the GPU. An argument stream may be passed in either calling style to specify a Stream in which execution is to take place.

At the end of this simple example, memory is allocated on the CPU and results are transferred back, to be printed alongside the original array. Again, like in the CUDA runtime interface, all

---

[2]"Name mangling" facilitates function overloading in C++ and represents the encoding of signature information in the symbol name used for a function. Mangling methods vary by compiler and operating system ABI.

```
import pycuda.autoinit
import pycuda.gpuarray as gpuarray
import numpy

a_gpu = gpuarray.to_gpu(
    numpy.random.randn(4,4)
        .astype(numpy.float32))
a_doubled = (2*a_gpu).get()
print a_doubled
print a_gpu
```

Listing 27.2. An example performing the same function as Listing 27.1, but using GPUArrays.

memcpy_* functions enqueue the transfer and wait until it completes. If this is not desired, separate memcpy_*_async functions exist.

27.3.2 What Comes in the Box

After the introduction to the basic method of programming GPUs with PyCUDA, this section seeks to make the reader aware of further built-in facilities aimed at making GPU programming easier.

27.3.2.1 *GPU Arrays*

The example presented above, as an element-wise vector operation, represents not only an easy introduction, but also a common use case of GPU computations, perhaps in the form of an auxiliary step between other calculations. For this reason, PyCUDA supplies an array object, pycuda.gpuarray.GPUArray, that shrinks the code of the example of Listing 27.1 to that of Listing 27.2. Just like numpy arrays, but unlike memory allocated using DeviceAllocation, GPUArrays know about their shapes and data types. They support all arithmetic operators and a number of methods and functions, all patterned after the corresponding functionality in numpy. In addition, many special functions are available in pycuda.cumath. Arrays of approximately uniformly distributed random numbers may be generated using functionality in pycuda.curandom.

27.3.2.2 *Complex Numbers on the GPU*

In addition to CUDA's built-in support for real numbers, PyCUDA adds seamless support for complex numbers. To enable this support, add the line "#include <pycuda-complex.hpp>" to your kernel and declare complex numbers as pycuda::complex<type>, where type may be, e.g., double or float. PyCUDA's GPUArrays also natively support operations on complex data types.

27.3.2.3 *Double Precision Textures*

Another area where PyCUDA improves on native CUDA is support for double precision in texture fetches. This is easiest to achieve when binding a GPUArray to a texture reference using the GPUArray's bind_to_texref_ext method, while specifying the allow_double_hack keyword argument as true. Within kernel code, one may then use the following pattern for texture access:

```
#include <pycuda-helpers.hpp>
texture<fp_tex_double, 1, cudaReadModeElementType> my_tex;
_global_ void f()
{
  double x = fp_tex1Dfetch(my_tex, threadIdx.x);
}
```

Observe in particular that the texture type was prefixed with `fp_tex_` and the fetching function was prefixed with `fp_`.

27.3.2.4 *Efficient Evaluation of Element-Wise Expressions*

Evaluating deeply nested expressions on `GPUArray` instances can be inefficient, because a new temporary expression is created for each intermediate result. Many programming languages offering user-definable abstract vector types have this problem, for example C++. C++ also offers a way of dealing with this particular issue in the form of expression templates [3]. While we acknowledge that this is certainly a matter of taste, we strongly prefer the striking simplicity of both use and implementation of PyCUDA's facility, portrayed in Listing 27.3(a), over the significant complexity of expression templates.

The functionality in the module `pycuda.elementwise` contains tools to help generate and invoke kernels that evaluate complicated expressions on one or several operands in a single pass. The instrumental part of the example is the invocation of the `ElementwiseKernel` constructor, in which the

```
import pycuda.gpuarray as gpuarray
import pycuda.autoinit
from pycuda.curandom import rand \
      as curand

a_gpu = curand((50,))
b_gpu = curand((50,))

from pycuda.elementwise import \
      ElementwiseKernel
lin_comb = ElementwiseKernel(
      "float a, float *x, "
      "float b, float *y, float *z",
      "z[i] = a*x[i] + b*y[i]",
      "linear_combination")

c_gpu = gpuarray.empty_like(a_gpu)
lin_comb(5, a_gpu, 6, b_gpu, c_gpu)
```

(a) An example of the use of the generic facility for element-wise operations.

```
import pycuda.gpuarray as gpuarray
import pycuda.autoinit
import numpy

a = gpuarray.arange(
      400, dtype=numpy.float32)
b = gpuarray.arange(
      400, dtype=numpy.float32)

from pycuda.reduction import \
      ReductionKernel

krnl = ReductionKernel(
      numpy.float32,
      arguments="float *x, float *y"
      map_expr="x[i]*y[i]",
      reduce_expr="a+b", neutral="0")

my_dot_prod = krnl(a, b).get()
```

(b) An example of the use of the generic facility for reductive ("folding") operations.

Listing 27.3. Examples of high-level primitives for working with `GPUArrays`.

user provides both a C-style argument list and a statement (or semicolon-separated list of statements) to be executed for each value of i, which is used as a formal index variable running across each element of GPUArray instances passed to the ElementwiseKernel. All these instances are required to have the same length.

27.3.2.5 *Map-Reduce*

In a similar spirit as the support for element-wise operations, PyCUDA has built-in functionality for tree-based reductions on the GPU. To make this even more useful, evaluating an element-wise expression ahead of reduction is also supported. The facility thereby becomes a simple implementation of the MapReduce procedure [4].

Listing 27.3(b) shows the implementation of a dot product through an instantiation of the Reduc-tionKernel class. The constructor signature starts with the specification of the result dtype, in this case numpy.float32. It then proceeds as the ElementwiseKernel above by allowing a C argument signature and an arbitrary C expression on whose results the final reduction will be performed. As above, the formal variable i represents the index from which the input element should be read.

The reduction step is then specified by two further arguments, a reduction expression of two formal arguments a and b and an expression resulting in a neutral element with respect to the reduction expression.[3] Once all of this information is specified, the resulting ReductionKernel may be called as above to perform the reduction.

Observe that the end result of calling the ReductionKernel instance is a GPUArray scalar still residing on the GPU. It can be brought to the CPU by a call to its get method, or used in place on the GPU.

27.3.2.6 *Further Facilities*

In addition to element-wise operations and reductions, versions 2011.1 and newer of PyCUDA and PyOpenCL are able to assist the user with the implementation of GPU-based parallel prefix sums (also known as "parallel scan"). Further, they provide a number of tools to the GPU implementer which we will mention here, but for whose detailed description we refer to the reference documentation.

The first of those is a key optimization for programs that allocate and deallocate GPU memory at a rapid rate. Since CUDA's memory allocation functions are relatively expensive operations, it becomes expedient to retain already allocated memory in a GPU computing process instead of freeing it. These retained blocks of memory may then be reused once a similarly-sized block is requested afterwards. PyCUDA supports this through the use of *memory pools*. These pools integrate with GPUArrays, whose arithmetic operators are a good example of the need for repeatedly freed and allocated memory of recurring sizes. In addition, a memory pool implementation also exists for page-locked host memory.

Lastly, PyCUDA comes with a conjugate-gradient-based Krylov solver for large, sparse linear systems and an implementation of sparse matrices on the GPU, following [5]. These GPU-based sparse matrices integrate directly with sparse matrix support in the SciPy package [6] and provide computational performance similar to that of NVIDIA's Cusp [7] library.

---

[3]"Neutral element" is mathematical terminology for an element that turns a binary operator into an identity map. For example, zero is the neutral element of addition, and one is the neutral element of multiplication.

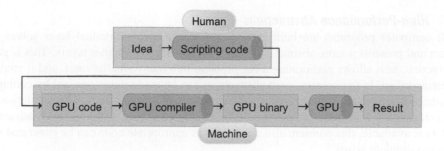

FIGURE 27.2

Operating principle of GPU code generation.

27.3.3 Code Generation: Benefits and Usage

As early as 30 years ago, the Lisp community observed that *code is data*, and that using code itself as the object of computation can be greatly beneficial. One key benefit of PyCUDA and PyOpenCL is that they make runtime code generation ("RTCG") almost trivial. Figure 27.2 clarifies the workflow used in RTCG.

This section is devoted to describing a number of issues that are commonly faced when programming a GPU. In each case, we point out how a GPU RTCG strategy can be used to address these issues.

27.3.3.1 *Automated Tuning*

During the creation of a GPU program, it is natural for the programmer to come up with a number of variants of a given code, each of which will be observed to have certain properties regarding data layout and computation speed. The conventional approach to code tuning then calls for the fastest variant to survive, while the others will be discarded. This is not necessarily a desirable course of action, as information is lost. Instead, it seems more appropriate to retain as many of these variants as is practical, assuming that they hold at least some promise. Further, each variant may have a number of tunable parameters, such as loop lengths, block sizes, etc. Retaining variant information permits choosing the best one from a reasonably-sized pool of candidates in an automated fashion, guided by some metric such as execution speed. This is the basic premise of automated tuning, which is trivially enabled by GPU RTCG. Further, automated tuning is not just enabled by RTCG, it is enabled *at the right time* — namely at runtime — when complete information is available. If desired, the reader may find a few illustrative examples of the use of automated tuning in [1].

27.3.3.2 *The Cost of Flexibility*

Flexibility is commonly seen as a desirable feature of a computer code. It should then be realized that flexibility comes at a cost: Constants get replaced by variables, formerly fixed loop trip counts become variable, and quite generally a compiler has less knowledge available, making its optimizer less effective. The process of removing this sort of flexibility by hard-coding such information into the program, therefore, is generally frowned upon. However, with the availability of runtime code generation, information can be inserted into the source of the program just in time, leading to an optimal combination of flexibility and execution speed.

27.3.3.3 *High-Performance Abstractions*

Nearly all computer programs are built in "layers," where each individual layer solves a certain subproblem and presents a more abstract, "higher-level" interface to higher layers. This is good engineering practice, as it allows partitioning a big problem into many smaller ones, and it enables reuse of engineering effort. In some cases, such abstractions can be made uneconomical by coding circumstance, namely when customization applies to the contents of an inner loop. Many solutions exist to this problem, ranging from function pointers to C++ templates, each with unique disadvantages [1]. Once RTCG is available, this problem also disappears as appropriate code can be generated whenever a different requirement arises.

27.3.3.4 *Generating Code*

We now turn to how a user might go about exploiting runtime code generation with PyCUDA. Since PyCUDA can natively process CUDA C code, the objective is the generation of such code. PyCUDA makes no assumptions about the origins of the code it processes, which allows the logic involved in the generation to be designed to match the needs of the application. There are, however, a few suggested ways of generating code that we have found to cover a variety of needs.

Code generation can (and in many cases should) be seen as a text processing task. Since one is not limited in the choice of tools with which to perform this sort of generation, code generation typically makes use of existing text processing tools. Generation logic itself can thus be simple and generally responds favorably to complexity growth.

> **Textual keyword replacement** This simple technique performs the equivalent of search-and-replace on source code. It suffices for a surprisingly large range of use cases, such as the substitution of types and constants into source code at runtime. Its technological reach is increased by combining it with C preprocessor macros. Further contributing to its attractiveness, Python's standard library can perform keyword substitution without relying on external software.
>
> **Textual keyword replacement** For code generation applications where control flow and conditionals are required, but where all code variants are textually related, the use of a so-called templating engine, commonly used for the generation of web pages, offers a natural escalation of the capabilities of keyword substitution. Many templating engines (and correspondingly, templating languages) exist. Listing 27.4 demonstrates the use of the Mako [8] engine for the generation of a simple, partially unrolled vector addition code.

In addition to these methods, the authors' cgen package also supports code generation from abstract syntax trees (ASTs); however this use is somewhat cumbersome and discouraged in all but the most demanding cases.

27.4 EVALUATION

While it is difficult to obtain quantifiable data on GPU programmer productivity and how the use of the PyCUDA and PyOpenCL packages affects it, one of the main measures of the success of any open-source package is the size and vitality of the community that uses and develops it.

As such, we believe that the wide existing user base of PyCUDA and PyOpenCL represents compelling evidence that this programming model as well as its concrete implementations are a significant

```
from mako.template import Template

tpl = Template("""
  __global__ void add(
        ${ type_name } *tgt,
        ${ type_name } *op1,
        ${ type_name } *op2)
  {
    int idx = threadIdx.x +
      ${ thread_block_size } * ${block_size}
      * blockIdx.x;

    % for i in range(block_size):
      <% offset = i*thread_block_size %>
      tgt[idx + ${ offset }] =
        op1[idx + ${ offset }]
        + op2[idx + ${ offset }];
    % endfor
  }""")

rendered_tpl = tpl.render(
  type_name="float", block_size=block_size,
  thread_block_size=thread_block_size)

smod = SourceModule(rendered_tpl)
```

Listing 27.4. Run-Time Code Generation (RTCG) with PyCUDA using a templating engine. The example generates a piece of CUDA C from a textual template implementing an unrolled version of vector addition, using the Mako engine in this instance. Full context for the example can be found in the PyCUDA source tree as `examples/demo_meta_template.py`.

improvement in the way programmers interact with GPUs, thereby serving as an important step toward bringing GPU computing to the mainstream.

One central point for user collaboration is each package's wiki at `http://wiki.tiker.net/PyCuda` and `http://wiki.tiker.net/PyOpenCL`. In a user-editable fashion, each functions as a central collection point for installation instructions on a variety of operating systems, frequently asked questions, and code examples.

In addition, a number of packages have been released by community members that build on top of PyCUDA and PyOpenCL, including

PyFFT (by Bogdan Opanchuk) An FFT package for both PyCUDA and PyOpenCL. Also a nice example of cross-CUDA/OpenCL code generation. `http://pypi.python.org/pypi/pyfft`.

Scikits.CUDA (by Lev Givon and collaborators) Offers wrappers of the CUBLAS, CUFFT and CULA packages for numerical computation on CUDA. `http://pypi.python.org/pypi/scikits.cuda`.

Atomic Hedgehog (by Cyrus Omar) Offers a higher-level programming interface for PyOpenCL. http://ahh.bitbucket.org/.

For a listing of projects that use PyCUDA or PyOpenCL in production, see [1] and http://wiki.tiker.net/PyCuda/ShowCase.

27.5 AVAILABILITY

PyCUDA is available from http://mathema.tician.de/software/pycuda, and PyOpenCL is available from http://mathema.tician.de/software/pyopencl. Both are distributed under the liberal MIT open-source software license.

Full documentation is available online at http://documen.tician.de/pycuda and http://documen.tician.de/pyopencl, respectively, and both packages include numerous examples and automated tests. The packages support all platforms on which Python and CUDA and/or OpenCL are available.

27.6 FUTURE DIRECTIONS

PyCUDA and PyOpenCL, as open-source projects, thrive on user feedback, particularly feedback regarding limitations, bugs, or missing features that users encounter. For example, much of PyCUDA's initial feature set emerged in support of an effort to bring discontinuous Galerkin methods onto the GPU, as discussed elsewhere in this volume.

As part of this continuing improvement process, we have identified a number of core areas in which we see potential for future work. Much work has recently been done to make PyCUDA easier to install. Part of this effort was the elimination of the Boost C++ library as an explicit dependency, which was released as part of PyCUDA version 0.94 and PyOpenCL 0.92 in September of 2010. We are also working on easing integration with existing CUDA tools such as CUBLAS, CUFFT, and Thrust [9]. Integration and ease of migration between PyCUDA and PyOpenCL is another key feature that we would like to facilitate. We are further planning to improve GPUArray's capability of dealing with slices of multi dimensional arrays. Finally, we are planning on improving support for automated tuning in PyCUDA and PyOpenCL by providing search algorithms on top of user-supplied search space descriptions and speeding up exploration of compilation-bound searches by exploiting all available CPU cores.

We hope that this chapter has managed to encourage you, the reader, to try what we believe is a very productive, full-featured GPU programming environment. We look forward to your questions and comments on our mailing lists.

Acknowledgment

AK's research was partially funded by AFOSR under contract number FA9550-07-1-0422, through the R/NSSEFF Program Award FA9550-10-1-0180 and also under contract DEFG0288ER25053 by the Department of Energy. NP's research was partially funded by the Rowland Institute of Harvard, the NVIDIA Graduate Fellowship, and the National Science Foundation (IIS 0963668). The opinions expressed are the views of the authors. They do not necessarily reflect the official position of the funding agencies.

References

[1] A. Klöckner, N. Pinto, Y. Lee, B.C. Catanzaro, P. Ivanov, A. Fasih, PyCUDA and PyOpenCL: a scripting-based approach to GPU run-time code generation, Brown University, Providence, RI, 2009. Submitted, http://arxiv.org/abs/0911.3456.

[2] T. Oliphant, Guide to NumPy, Trelgol Publishing, Spanish Fork, UT, 2006.

[3] T.L. Veldhuizen, M.E. Jernigan, Will C++ be faster than Fortran? in: Y. Ishikawa, R.R. Odehoeft, J.V.W. Reynders, M. Tholburn (Eds.), Proceedings of the 1st International Scientific Computing in Object-Oriented Parallel Environments (ISCOPE'97), Lecture Notes in Computer Science, Springer-Verlag, Heidelberg, 1997.

[4] J. Dean, S. Ghemawat, MapReduce: simplified data processing on large clusters, Commun. ACM 51 (1) (2008) 107–113.

[5] N. Bell, M. Garland, Implementing sparse matrix-vector multiplication on throughput-oriented processors, in: SC '09: Proceedings of the 2009 ACM/IEEE Conference on Supercomputing, ACM, New York, NY, 2009.

[6] E. Jones, T. Oliphant, P. Peterson, et al., SciPy: Open source scientific tools for Python, http://scipy.org, 2001.

[7] N. Bell, M. Garland, Cusp: generic parallel algorithms for sparse matrix and graph computations. http://cusp-library.googlecode.com, Version 0.1.0, 2010.

[8] M. Bayer, Mako: a super-fast templating language. http://makotemplates.org, Version 0.3.6, 2010.

[9] J. Hoberock, N. Bell, Thrust: a parallel template library. http://www.meganewtons.com/, Version 1.3.0, 2010.

Jacket: GPU Powered MATLAB Acceleration

28

Torben Larsen, Gallagher Pryor, and James Malcolm

This chapter describes Jacket, which is a software platform for offloading MATLAB computation onto NVIDIA CUDA-capable GPUs. The objective of Jacket is to combine the productivity and simplicity of the MATLAB environment and M-language with the raw computational power of GPUs. We describe the ideas behind Jacket and its basic use, and we provide a simple example that compares MATLAB, CUDA C, and Jacket with respect to code and computational performance. Further, we include a performance evaluation of various Jacket features including CPU-GPU memory transfer, floating point performance, etc.

28.1 INTRODUCTION

Jacket is a software platform developed at AccelerEyes [1], which allows users to execute MATLAB M-code on CUDA-capable GPUs. MATLAB (MATrix LABoratory) by The MathWorks [2] has become the standard platform for technical computing and graphics in science, engineering, and finance due to its ease of use and powerful functional capabilities. The combination of a simple matrix language, interactive prompt, automatic memory management, and on-the-fly compilation make MATLAB well suited to rapid prototyping of algorithms and exploring data. MATLAB's one drawback is performance, and Jacket alleviates this by seamless offloading of computations to the GPU. Jacket provides users access to a set of libraries, functions, and tools that facilitate numerical computation on the GPU [3] including multi-GPU support built on MATLAB's Parallel Computing Toolbox and Distributed Computing Server [4].

Over the last decade, GPUs have proliferated among both consumer and developer computers. Despite the growing mass of success stories, GPU software development appears to still be considered the realm of niche applications. The consensus is that this is due to the difficulty in programming such devices. While the hardware continues to improve and the software ecosystem continues to grow, there is still a steep learning curve for the average programmer to reach success. Jacket is one of many software tools that attempts to bridge this gap by mapping high-level languages onto the underlying hardware. Other projects have attempted to bridge the gap. Cg, GLSL, HLSL, and Brook marked the beginning of stream programming, a precursor to general purpose GPU programming, where computation is mapped onto the graphics pipeline and consequently subject to various constraints. Following on the heels of these technologies, CUDA introduced a more generally programmable software architecture.

Several companies set out to extend the capabilities of these early tools. One of the first such companies, PeakStream (now at Google) built a C/C++ runtime and library of functions providing a richer tool set to GPU development. RapidMind (now at Intel) set out to build a flexible middle-layer supporting various front-end languages and back-end hardware targets. All of these projects have sought the same thing: to bridge the gap between the hardware and developers. One of the newest platforms for GPU development, Jacket, allows programmers to use the high-level MATLAB M-language and abstracts away the low-level details of GPU programming. The result is increased productivity and performance.

28.2 JACKET

Jacket has been designed for programmers who have large data-parallel tasks but who are not low-level programmers accustomed to dealing with GPU-specific constructs. To allow them to avoid having to learn new language features, Jacket introduces only a handful of new functions to the MATLAB experience. Once data is marked as "GPU" data using these functions, Jacket provides native GPU implementations of a large set of the standard MATLAB functions to operate on that data.

28.2.1 Basics

Jacket achieves transparency by defining a new set of classes dubbed "g" objects, where each element of this set corresponds to a base class of the MATLAB standard interface: single, uint16, ones, etc. map to gsingle, guint16, gones, etc. — see [5]. These new classes function exactly as their CPU-based counterparts. In order to facilitate this functionality, each standard method currently present on the standard classes is made available on the "g" objects via GPU-enabled mex-code, the architecture of which is described below. The set of standard MATLAB language constructs from displaying the object as text to assigning values to the variables are supported, but the core of Jacket involves GPU equivalents to element-wise arithmetic, Fast Fourier Transform, matrix multiplication, singular value decomposition, etc. Large portions of already existing MATLAB programs can therefore be run on the GPU simply by changing the data types from their base class such as single to the GPU base class equivalent gsingle. Data can be copied to or from the GPU by way of a typecast between the base class and its "g" equivalent, or data can be generated directly on the GPU (either as random or constant data or as the output of some earlier GPU operation).

As a small example, suppose we want to add two random matrices Agpu and Bgpu by use of Jacket — the key to do this is the following:

```
>> Agpu = grand(3,3);   % grand() is the GPU equivalent of rand()
>> Bgpu = grand(3,3);
>> Rgpu = Agpu + Bgpu

Rgpu =
     0.5100    0.8279    0.2301
     0.4642    0.8148    0.8196
     0.5814    1.1443    1.0804
```

The call to the Jacket function grand(3,3) produces a random matrix of size 3×3 directly on the GPU, and Rgpu=Agpu+Bgpu produces the result. Since the the matrices Agpu and Bgpu are both GPU matrices so is the result matrix Rgpu, and all matrices reside in GPU memory. The above example takes advantage of the Jacket function grand to keep all computations on the GPU, but it is also possible to use the MATLAB function rand and push that result to the GPU and use the GPU for only the matrix addition:

```
>> Acpu = rand(3,3);
>> Bcpu = rand(3,3);
>> Rgpu = gsingle(Acpu) + gsingle(Bcpu)

Rgpu =
    1.2004    1.4460    0.7559
    1.5045    1.6116    0.8960
    1.0673    0.9352    0.9360
```

To pull back the result to the CPU we simply cast the result to a single:

```
>> Rcpu = single(Rgpu);
```

To make computationally efficient code, this move of data back and forth between CPU and GPU should be avoided when possible. More on this issue later.

28.2.2 Functions and Architecture

As with programming the GPU in C or C++, care must be taken by the programmer to ensure minimum memory transfer to the GPU and maximum data-parallelism — i.e., the maximum number of homogeneous operations are performed on the maximum number of data elements at a time. It is critical that MATLAB code be written in vectorized form in which large parts of data are operated upon by only a few operations in parallel. This vectorized paradigm of programming is exactly the style of programming necessary to meet the data-parallel requirement of GPU programming for maximum performance.

Unfortunately, a major feature of the M-language is M's standard convention of utilizing pass-by-value semantics: copies of objects are passed to functions instead of references. Thus, in many instances, multiple copies of objects are made throughout the execution of a MATLAB program. This convention in the M-language thus makes it impossible to effectively utilize standard MATLAB classes with completely exposed data-stores for use with the GPU. Many copies of objects on the GPU would be created, inefficiently utilizing bus bandwidth and GPU memory. Additionally, as copies of objects are made, there is no way within the MATLAB environment to intercept these events, making it impossible to achieve coherence between MATLAB and GPU memory state.

To bypass M's pass-by-value calling convention, the Jacket architecture uses object-oriented programming to handle references to data (reference counting to determine variable liveness). Such objects retain information about the location, size, and type of underlying data in memory, as well as any computations that have been performed on this data.

28.2.3 **Comparing** Jacket **to** CUDA C

To get an idea of the low-level details that Jacket hides, we construct an example of summing a vector of length n. Starting from a vector of random data, in MATLAB and Jacket this is rather straightforward:

```
% MATLAB
Acpu = rand(n,1,'single');
sum(Acpu)

% Jacket
Agpu = gsingle(Acpu);
sum(Agpu)
```

Programming just the sum function alone in CUDA C for maximum performance requires more care [6]. To achieve peak throughput, the final kernel looks something like the following and involves carefully exploiting parallelism at the level of thread warps:

```
__global__
static void kernel(unsigned n, float *d_dst, float *d_src)
{
  const unsigned tid = threadIdx.x;
  const unsigned grid = THREADS * gridDim.x;
  unsigned i = THREADS * blockIdx.x + tid;
  float sum = 0;
  while (i < n) { sum += d_src[i]; i += grid; }

  __shared__ float smem[THREADS];
  float *s = smem + tid;
  *s = sum;
  __syncthreads();

  if (tid < 64) { *s = sum = sum + s[64]; }
  __syncthreads();

  if (tid < 32) {
    volatile float *vs = s;
    *vs = sum = sum + vs[32]; *vs = sum = sum + vs[16];
    *vs = sum = sum + vs[ 8]; *vs = sum = sum + vs[ 4];
    *vs = sum = sum + vs[ 2]; *vs = sum = sum + vs[ 1];
  }

  if (tid == 0) d_dst[blockIdx.x] = *s;
}
```

To provide an idea of the relative performance of CUDA C vs. MATLAB vs. Jacket we have tested this small example on an Intel Core 2 Quad Q9400 (2.66 GHz) with an NVIDIA GeForce GTX480. The original MATLAB vector sum for 5 million elements runs in 4.80 ms while Jacket ran in 0.252 ms. Pushing everything into CUDA C (no MATLAB overhead) shaves this timing down to 0.236 ms.

This means a speed-up for `Jacket` of 19 and `CUDA C` achieved a speed-up of 20 relative to the `MATLAB` execution. The speed-up by this tuned device code compared with a naïve implementation can easily be 30 [6]. Compared to manually developing such routines on the GPU, examples such as this underscore both the productivity and performance gains achieved when moving to a high-level platform such as `Jacket`. All of the low-level tuning details are handled automatically for the user.

28.2.4 Lazy Evaluation

There are several major considerations `Jacket` must account for when compiling M-code into GPU instructions. First, M is an untyped language, meaning that types must be inferred, and since code can be loaded on the fly, much of this inference is delayed until execution. Second, GPU instructions must be grouped into a "kernel" that reads from GPU memory, performs computations, and finally writes to GPU memory. Therefore, instruction sequences cannot be prepared and issued at the same fine granularity as they can be for x86 processors. `Jacket` performs a high-order analysis of the M-code to determine appropriate segmentation of computation into independent kernels. This analysis considers the arithmetic intensity of the program, the amount of GPU memory it references, and thread block configurations for various phases of the computation. Next, data parallel algorithms might have a number of possible implementations, and the selection of the best one to use can vary substantially depending on the size of the input data, thus leading to a need for runtime optimizations such as on-the-fly compilation. Furthermore, there is a measurable overhead involved in preparing and emitting instructions for the GPU. In practice, long running computations typically contain loops and other repeated segments of code. `Jacket` maintains a cache of commonly used expressions and the code generated from those expressions for later reuse. Before beginning compilation, the `Jacket` runtime compares a candidate expression against the cache. Communication between CPU and GPU over the PCI bus introduces latency. To minimize communication, `Jacket` takes a lazy approach to evaluating computations and batches these sequences. In addition, seeing more of the computation sequence, `Jacket` has more opportunity for optimizations. The functions `geval` and `gsync` are available to provide the user with more control over this process if desired.

28.2.5 Graphics

`Jacket` includes a graphics toolbox that provides a simple method of displaying computational results on the GPU without bringing those results back to the host. Thus, the same dedicated hardware that computes results may be utilized to present those results, culminating in tightly integrated code-compute-visualize loop suitable for data mining, rapid prototyping, or production of real-time graphical applications. To balance the resources involved in computation, `Jacket` delays the dispatch of OpenGL instructions until a render pass is requested. At that point, the OpenGL pipeline is filled for the next display loop.

The `Jacket` Graphics Toolbox is exposed to the end user at varying levels and the user has a choice of interacting with any of these depending on their requirements. At the core of the API is a set of primitives that mirror `MATLAB` functionality. For example, `gsurf` mimics `surf` to draw a surface plot but adds surface texturing and lighting effects. The function `gplot` mimics `plot` to produce standard 2-D line plots, and `gscatter3` mimics `scatter3` to produce a scatterplot.

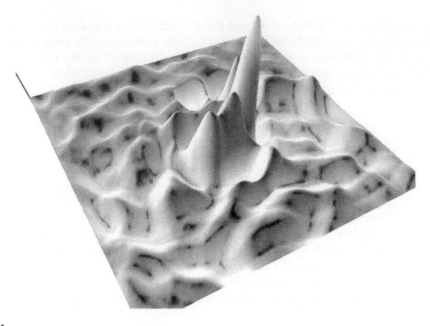

FIGURE 28.1

A droplet hitting a viscous surface utilizing the gsurf drawing primitive (see color insert).

Figure 28.1 simulates the effect of a droplet hitting a viscous surface by use of gsurf. It begins with one droplet placed in the center. Each iteration diffuses the surface outward and computes the spring pull on the surface. At the end of the loop iteration, the surface is rendered (gsurf).

28.3 BENCHMARKING PROCEDURES

Benchmarking usually involves performing some specific MATLAB function where a certain parameter is swept (typically an array size) while timing the computation for both MATLAB (CPU) and Jacket (GPU). When performing benchmarks there are several issues to consider to reach reliable and reproducible results:

1. It is essential to choose a power setting for "high performance" to ensure the CPU is running at full speed, etc.
2. The MATLAB process should be given highest possible priority by the operating system.
3. Most modern CPUs allow some kind of multithreading, which may affect results significantly. By default, MATLAB uses the maximum number of threads available, and this is also what usually should be chosen when performing benchmarks.
4. A repetition loop should be put around the benchmark computations to achieve peak throughput and amortize any timer overhead.

5. Initialize pseudo-random number generators identically across runs that are to be compared, as the timing can depend on the actual values being processed.
6. Run the test code once to warm up both MATLAB (the CPU) and Jacket (the GPU). This allows instruction and data caching.
7. Use geval and gsync to ensure computations are completed. gsync should be used immediately before the timing functions tic and toc to ensure CPU-GPU synchronization, and geval is used to force evaluation prior to setting the stop timer.

Unless these issues are addressed, it can be virtually impossible to reproduce results.

28.4 EXPERIMENTAL RESULTS

The experimental results fall into three categories: (1) CPU/GPU memory transfer, (2) floating point performance, and (3) a selection of MATLAB functions. The results are described after an overview of the hardware platforms used for the benchmarking.

28.4.1 Hardware Platforms

The computer platforms used were two identical Colfax CXT2000i's based on an Asus Supercomputer P6T7 motherboard with an Intel Core i7–975 CPU (12 GB DDR3 memory). The computers were equipped with the NVIDIA GPUs shown in Table 28.1: one computer had one Quadro 4000 and three Quadro FX3800's, and the other had one Quadro FX3800 and a Tesla C1060, Tesla C2050 or GeForce GTX580. Both computers used the Microsoft Windows 7 x64 Enterprise operating system (ver. 6.1 build 7400), NVIDIA driver 263.06, MATLAB 7.11.0.584 (R2010b), Jacket 1.6.0 (build 9686), and CUDA Toolkit 3.1. Both computers have a change in the Windows Registry to set the "TDR Delay" to

Table 28.1 Estimated Theoretical Performance of the Used NVIDIA GPUs. Data Based on GPUReview.com and NVIDIA.com. "C. Cap." Denotes "Compute Capability"

GPU type	Single pr.[†] [GFlops]	Double pr. [GFlops]	Cores [—]	RAM [MB]	C. Cap.
Core i7–975	110.8	55.4	4	—	—
FX3800	462.3	57.8	192	1024	1.3
GTX580	1572.9	393.2	512	1534	2.0
Q4000	486.4	243.2	256	2048	2.0
C1060	622.1	77.8	240	4096	1.3
C2050	1030.4	515.2	448	3072	2.0

[†]As the floating point performance is measured from matrix multiplications only two floating point operations per cycle have been used for calculation of theoretical single precision performance.

30 seconds.[1] For all results, MATLAB was running with the maximum number of available host threads (8), and the MATLAB process was running with High Priority set in the Windows Task Manager. For the Tesla C2050, ECC was enabled unless otherwise noted. All results shown in the following were fully reproducible.

28.4.2 Memory Access

Since MATLAB is hosted on the CPU and Jacket works on the GPU, minimizing the transfer of data the between the CPU's and the GPU's memories is critical for the performance of Jacket. On the test platforms the overhead in both transfer directions was measured to about 85 μs with a linear relation between transfer time and array size. Once data has been moved to GPU memory, Jacket generally has much faster access to GPU memory than MATLAB has access to CPU memory. For all tested GPUs the transfer rate from host (computer) to device (GPU) was around 3.8 GB/s, and from device to host the transfer rate was around 2.6 GB/s when the array size was larger than approximately 5 MB. Due to this, data should be transferred in large chunks whenever possible in order to minimize the total transfer time.

28.4.3 Floating Point Operations

The purpose of the floating point benchmark is to see what Jacket can achieve in terms of floating point arithmetic operations per second with respect to the size of the matrices involved. Jacket includes a highly tuned version of generalized matrix multiply (not NVIDIA CUBLAS's GEMM, at present) that provides a good candidate for measuring performance. The following high-arithmetic intensity operation is performed at the core of matrix multiplication:

$$\mathbf{R} := \alpha \mathbf{A}\mathbf{B} + \delta \mathbf{R}, \qquad \alpha, \delta \in \mathbb{R}; \quad \mathbf{A}, \mathbf{B}, \mathbf{R} \in \mathbb{R}^{N \times N} \tag{1}$$

where the number of floating point operations is $2N^3 + N^2$; see [7]. The GPUs listed in Table 28.1 perform as shown in Figures 28.2 and 28.3. The performance of an Intel Core i7–975 CPU is shown for comparison.

As seen from Figure 28.2 for single precision performance, there is the expected clear progression toward better performance for the more powerful GPUs. The GeForce GTX580 clearly outperforms everything else with a peak performance of 849 GFlops. The Tesla C2050 follows as the next with a peak performance of 550 GFlops, and more than 350 GFlops for matrix sizes above approximately 1200×1200. In single precision, all measured GPUs deliver 53–58% of theoretical peak performance. Disabling ECC on the Tesla C2050 increased the peak performance by 0.4 %.

As seen for the double precision results in Figure 28.3, the C2050 has the highest peak performance of 249 GFlops where the GTX580 delivers 193 GFlops. For double precision, the GeForce GTX580, Tesla C2050, and Quadro 4000 deliver 48–52% of theoretical peak performance where the older Quadro FX3800 and Tesla C1060 deliver 94–96% of theoretical peak performance. Disabling ECC on the Tesla C2050 increased the peak performance by 4.6%.

---

[1]See http://www.microsoft.com/whdc/device/display/wddm_timeout.mspx for more information on the WDDM Timeout Detection and Recovery mechanism.

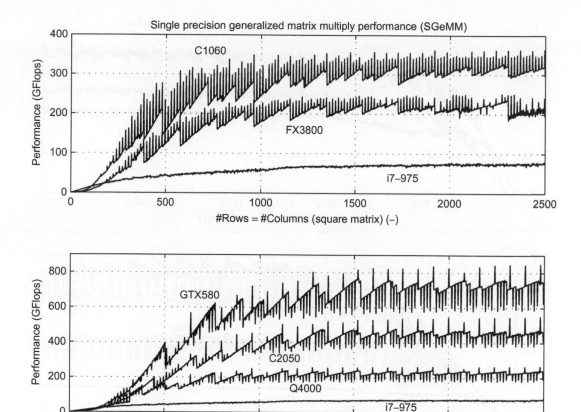

FIGURE 28.2

Measured single precision floating point performance versus square matrix size for different GPUs and an Intel Core i7–975 CPU.

28.4.4 Functions

The performance of `Jacket` has also been measured for a number of different functions for vector/matrix input and single/double precision; see Table 28.2. The reference used in all the benchmarks is again an Intel Core i7–975 CPU. When observing the results for a number of different functions some general observations can be made. Some functions are extremely fast on the GPU (e.g., `power`, `interp2`, and trigonometric functions) whereas others we refer to as "glue" functions (such as `subsasgn`). These are functions that are not ideally suited to GPU execution, but for which it can be advantageous to run them on the GPU anyway in conjunction with other GPU operations to avoid transferring data back and forth between CPU memory and GPU memory.

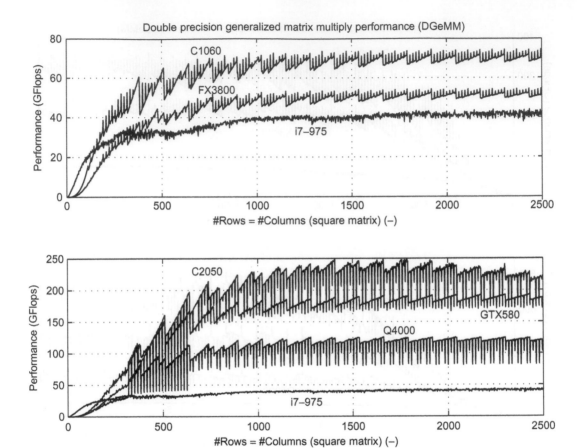

FIGURE 28.3

Measured double precision floating point performance versus square matrix size for different GPUs and an Intel Core i7–975 CPU.

Benchmarks are published regularly [8], and functions are generally improved when necessary. Other functions that work well on the GPU are `grand` and `grandn`, which generate random numbers directly on the GPU. These are important functions as they are used in virtually all scientific areas.

28.5 FUTURE DIRECTIONS

`Jacket` efficiently and transparently brings GPU computing to the popular `MATLAB` tool for computations, programming, and visualizations, delivering performance near to that of native `CUDA C` programs while maintaining the ease of programming provided by `MATLAB`'s M-language.

Table 28.2 Measured `Jacket` Performance as GPU Speed-Up Relative to a CPU. Matrix Size was 2048 × 2048, and Vector Size was $2^{22} \times 1$

Function	Measured Speed-up for Tesla C2050 vs. Core i7–975			
	Matrix		Vector	
	Single	Double	Single	Double
all	4.64	5.04	7.26	6.68
any[†]	4.62	5.15	7.37	6.85
asinh	44.34	12.72	44.12	12.60
atan2	296.95	93.49	297.38	93.71
atan	35.81	8.05	35.83	7.91
chol	29.30	1.73	—	—
conv2	2.49	—	—	—
cos	25.10	11.30	24.88	11.38
det	2.06	1.76	—	—
exp	41.95	15.58	41.54	15.68
fft	17.87	8.90	37.56	24.84
find	17.73	16.92	17.77	16.94
ifft	10.79	5.47	29.37	16.22
interp1	—	—	169.11	138.44
interp2	426.19	—	—	—
inv	—	1.56	—	—
log	31.09	13.37	31.15	13.44
lu	2.44	2.01	0.38	0.40
max	1.43	2.58	1.80	2.59
min	1.43	2.58	1.80	2.53
minus	17.53	9.31	17.55	9.62
mldivide	3.12	2.16	—	—
norm	0.64	0.92	2.44	25.60
plus	17.43	9.25	17.45	9.35
power	40.74	13.48	40.69	13.57
rand	32.21	32.75	32.16	32.72
randn	24.20	25.15	24.22	25.14
rdivide	10.50	5.96	10.61	5.98
sort	5.96	4.73	7.95	2.26
subsasgn	0.08	0.08	0.02	0.01
sum	1.42	2.60	1.85	2.57
times	21.36	9.40	21.35	9.37
trapz	2.34	20.13	0.74	0.84

[†]*The speed-up of the any function depends significantly on the density of the vector/matrix. The result shown is for the most typical case of a sparse vector/matrix.*

The near future of Jacket is focused on adding support for sparse arrays and different optimization techniques. Furthermore, the Jacket core is being segregated and repackaged as libJacket, which facilitates MATLAB–independent Jacket computing directly from the users' own C/C++ programs.

References

[1] AccelerEyes, Addr.: 800 W Peachtree St NW, Atlanta, GA 30308, USA. URL: http://www.accelereyes .com.

[2] The MathWorks, Inc., MATLAB. Addr.: The MathWorks, Inc., 3 Apple Hill Drive, Natick, MA 01760-2098, USA. URL: http://www.mathworks.com.

[3] A. Webb, MATLABs racing jacket, Autom. Trader 16 (1) (2010) 54–61.

[4] G. Sharma, J. Martin, MATLAB: a language for parallel computing, Springer Int. J. Parallel Program. 37 (1) (2008) 3–36.

[5] AccelerEyes, Jacket v1.5: Getting Started Guide: URL: http://www.accelereyes.com/services/ documentation.

[6] M. Harris, Optimizing CUDA, SuperComputing 2007 Tutorial, Reno, NV, 2007.

[7] V. Volkov, J.W. Demmel, Benchmarking GPUs to Tune Dense Linear Algebra, in: SC '08: Proceedings of the 2008 ACM/IEEE Conference on Supercomputing, Austin, Texas, 2008, pp. 1–11.

[8] Torben's Corner, Available from the Wiki of AccelerEyes at: URL: http://www.accelereyes .com/wiki/index.php?title=Torben's_Corner.

Accelerating Development and Execution Speed with Just-in-Time GPU Code Generation

29

Peter Eastman and Vijay Pande

In this chapter we describe a method for automatically generating OpenCL kernels to perform a calculation. The user supplies a set of mathematical expressions describing the calculation to be done. We analyze the expressions, transform them into optimized OpenCL code, and generate kernels to perform the calculation using an appropriate algorithm. This process allows us to simultaneously satisfy the requirements for speed, flexibility, and ease of use.

29.1 INTRODUCTION, PROBLEM STATEMENT, AND CONTEXT

The design of numerical software involves trade-offs between speed, flexibility, and ease of use. At one extreme, the developer implements only a fixed set of calculations, optimizing each one by hand, yielding excellent speed, but very little flexibility. At the opposite extreme, the developer creates a flexible environment that can perform a wide range of computations, but typically with much worse performance. A third option is to create a framework in which users implement their own computations in a language such as OpenCL or OpenGL Shading Language (GLSL). This option provides both flexibility and speed, but requires much effort and programming expertise from the users.

In this chapter we describe a different approach that achieves both speed and flexibility without sacrificing ease of use. We allow the user to provide a mathematical description of the calculation to perform in the form of one or more algebraic expressions. We parse and analyze the expressions, then generate OpenCL code to perform the calculation using an appropriate algorithm.

29.2 CORE METHODS

The need for flexibility is a common problem in numerical software. We encountered it while developing OpenMM, a library for running molecular simulations on GPUs and other high-performance computer architectures [1]. At the heart of every molecular simulation is the "force field" that describes how atoms should interact with each other. This set of equations defines the energy of the system as a function of the positions of all the atoms involved. The gradient of the energy then gives the force on each atom. For example, covalently bonded atoms should be kept at a fixed distance from each other.

This fixed distance is usually implemented with a harmonic energy term:

$$E_{bond}(r) = \frac{1}{2}k(r - r_0)^2$$

where r_0 is the equilibrium distance and k is the spring constant. Similar terms are used to restrict the angles between sets of three atoms, and the torsional angles formed by sets of four atoms. To represent the interactions between atoms that are not bonded to each other, force fields typically combine a Coulomb force to represent electrostatics and a Lennard-Jones force to represent van der Waals interactions:

$$E_{Coulomb}(r) = \frac{1}{4\pi\varepsilon_0}\frac{q_1 q_2}{r}$$

$$E_{Lennard\text{-}Jones}(r) = 4\varepsilon\left(\left(\frac{\sigma}{r}\right)^{12} - \left(\frac{\sigma}{r}\right)^6\right)$$

where q_1 and q_2 are the charges of the two atoms, and ε and σ are parameters that depend on the properties of the two atoms.

The details of these formulas are not important. They are just examples, and there are many variations of these equations that are of interest to practitioners in the field. For example, some force fields use an anharmonic potential to represent bonds. Lennard-Jones is the most common representation of van der Waals interactions, but several others have been proposed. Even among force fields that use Lennard-Jones, there are multiple ways of determining ε and σ based on the properties of the interacting atoms. Furthermore, molecular force fields are an active field of research and new interaction forms are constantly being developed. The range of force fields our users might require is effectively unlimited, yet we want to support as many of them as possible.

Our first attempt at solving this problem was to create a plug-in architecture by which users could implement new forces themselves. Unfortunately, however, we quickly realized this was not a sufficient solution. Writing a plug-in to implement a new interaction takes a lot of work and requires knowledge of GPU programming, something that few of our users have any experience with. Most of them are scientists, not software engineers, and they think in terms of equations, not algorithms. What they need is an efficient way to translate mathematics into code for this particular domain of problems: a domain-specific language [5] for molecular force fields.

We therefore created a new solution that allows users to define new forces simply by providing a mathematical expression for the energy in the form of a text string. For example, a Lennard-Jones force is implemented with the following line of code:

```
CustomNonbondedForce force("4*eps*((sigma/r)^12-(sigma/r)^6);
sigma=0.5*(sigma1+sigma2); eps=sqrt(eps1*eps2)");
```

This code specifies the energy of each interaction as a function of the distance r between the two atoms. It also specifies that ε and σ should be calculated based on the corresponding parameters of the interacting atoms using the Lorentz-Bertelot combining rules: $\sigma = (\sigma_1 + \sigma_2)/2$ and $\varepsilon = \text{sqrt}(\varepsilon_1\varepsilon_2)$. We will return to this example later in this chapter to see how it is processed.

We now have the task of processing the mathematical expression and efficiently calculating the force and energy as part of a molecular simulation. We complete this process with the following steps:

1. The expression is parsed to generate an abstract syntax tree. Expression parsing is an established technology [3], so we will not discuss this step further.

2. The expression is analytically differentiated to obtain an expression for the force. We could, of course, ask the user to provide separate expressions for the force and energy, but this would create extra work for our users while giving them more opportunities to make mistakes. Asking them to supply only the energy greatly improves ease of use. Symbolic differentiation is also a well-established technology [4], so we will not discuss it further.

3. A variety of algebraic simplifications are applied to both expressions (energy and force) to allow them to be computed more efficiently. This simplification turns out to be a critical step to get good performance. We discuss it in some detail in the next section.

4. OpenCL code is generated to evaluate both expressions. A number of optimizations are applied at this point, such as eliminating common subexpressions and efficiently computing integral powers. This also is discussed in detail later in this chapter.

5. The code is inserted into a kernel that implements the larger algorithm. Different versions of the kernel may be chosen automatically based on the hardware. For example, some kernels have different versions for NVIDIA GPUs than for AMD GPUs.

6. The kernel is passed to the OpenCL runtime for compilation and execution.

29.3 ALGORITHMS, IMPLEMENTATIONS, AND EVALUATIONS

Once we parse and differentiate the expression, the first step is to optimize both the force and energy expressions so that they can be evaluated more efficiently. This step turns out to be essential to get good performance. We have implemented more than 50 different rules for transforming expressions into equivalent ones that are faster to calculate. These rules fall into three categories:

1. Precomputing constant subexpressions. For example, in the expression sqrt(2)·x, we do not need to compute the square root of 2 every time the expression is evaluated. It can be computed once, and the constant value is inserted into the expression.

2. Basic algebraic simplifications. These simplifications are the rules that every student learns when studying algebra, like $1 \cdot x = x, 0 \cdot x = 0, -(-x) = x$, and so on.

3. Replacing subexpressions with equivalent ones that can be computed more efficiently. For example, $x^{0.5}$ is replaced by sqrt(x), and $x/2$ is replaced by $0.5*x$.

Optimization is especially important when calculating derivatives. For example, what is d(x^2)/dx? A human who has studied calculus will immediately answer $2x$, but many steps are involved in reaching that answer. To the computer, x^2 is a special case of a^b, where a and b may each depend on x. Its derivative is given by the somewhat complicated expression

$$\frac{d\left(a^b\right)}{dx} = ba^{b-1}\frac{da}{dx} + a^b \log(a)\frac{db}{dx}$$

It is only after you calculate $da/dx = 1$ and $db/dx = 0$, substitute those into the expression, and remove all unnecessary calculations that you are left with the simple result:

$$\frac{d\left(x^2\right)}{dx} = 2x^{2-1} \cdot 1 + x^2\log(2) \cdot 0 = 2x^1 + 0 = 2x$$

We now have the task of transforming the energy and force expressions into OpenCL code. Consider the Lennard-Jones force introduced earlier in this chapter. After parsing, differentiation, and optimization, we are left with the following formulas:

$$E(r) = 4\sqrt{\varepsilon_1 \varepsilon_2} \left(\left(\frac{0.5\,(\sigma_1 + \sigma_2)}{r} \right)^{12} - \left(\frac{0.5\,(\sigma_1 + \sigma_2)}{r} \right)^{6} \right)$$

$$\frac{dE(r)}{dr} = 4\sqrt{\varepsilon_1 \varepsilon_2} \left(-12 \left(\frac{0.5\,(\sigma_1 + \sigma_2)}{r} \right)^{11} \left(\frac{0.5\,(\sigma_1 + \sigma_2)}{r^2} \right) - (-6) \left(\frac{0.5\,(\sigma_1 + \sigma_2)}{r} \right)^{5} \left(\frac{0.5\,(\sigma_1 + \sigma_2)}{r^2} \right) \right)$$

You would probably write the derivative in a simpler form if you were deriving it by hand. Nonetheless, these equations are what our optimizer produces after applying all of its transformation rules, so it is the starting point for code generation.

The simplest approach to generating code is to directly translate each mathematical operation into the equivalent OpenCL function or operator. The result is given in Listing 29.1.

This code includes a total of 18 multiplies, 6 divides, 6 adds, 2 subtracts, 2 calls to the sqrt() function, and 4 calls to the pow() function. We can see immediately that it is far from optimal. It contains a large amount of redundant computation. For example, the expression `4*sqrt(eps1*eps2)` appears twice, while the expression `0.5*(sigma1+sigma2)` appears four times.

We might hope the OpenCL compiler would optimize away common subexpressions for us. To test this assumption, we created two versions of our kernel: one using the code from Listing 29.1, and one in which common subexpressions were extracted and computed only once. Using NVIDIA's OpenCL compiler from CUDA 3.1, the two kernels had identical performance, indicating that the compiler was already doing this optimization. Using Apple's version of OpenCL found in Mac OS X 10.6.4, on the other hand, the version in which common subexpressions had been optimized was measurably faster. We therefore concluded that, at least with the currently available compilers, we cannot rely on the compiler to do it for us. To ensure optimal performance on all platforms, we need to do common subexpression elimination ourselves.

We could, of course, carefully analyze the expressions, look for repeated subexpressions, and assign them to temporary variables. In practice, however, we found it was simplest to just create a temporary variable for *every* subexpression, no matter how trivial. As we process the expression tree, we keep a record of every node that has already been processed. For each new node, we check to see if an identical node has already been processed. If not, we compute it and assign the result to a temporary variable. Otherwise, we simply insert a reference to the existing temporary variable. The result is

```
energy = 4*sqrt(eps1*eps2)*(pow(0.5*(sigma1+sigma2)/r, 12)-
pow(0.5*(sigma1+sigma2)/r, 6));
force = 4*sqrt(eps1*eps2)*(-12*pow(0.5*(sigma1+sigma2)/r,
11)*(0.5*(sigma1+sigma2)/(r*r))-(-
6*pow(0.5*(sigma1+sigma2)/r,
5)*(0.5*(sigma1+sigma2)/(r*r))));
```

Listing 29.1. A straightforward transformation of the energy and force expressions into OpenCL code.

```
float temp0 = eps1;
float temp1 = eps2;
float temp2 = temp0*temp1;
float temp3 = sqrt(temp2);
float temp4 = 4.0f*temp3;
float temp5 = sigma1;
float temp6 = sigma2;
float temp7 = temp5+temp6;
float temp8 = 0.5f*temp7;
float temp9 = r;
float temp10 = temp8/temp9;
float temp11 = pow(temp10, 12);
float temp12 = pow(temp10, 6);
float temp13 = temp11-temp12;
float temp14 = temp4*temp13;
energy = temp14;
float temp15 = pow(temp10, 11);
float temp16 = -12.0f*temp15;
float temp17 = temp9*temp9;
float temp18 = temp8/temp17;
float temp19 = temp16*temp18;
float temp20 = pow(temp10, 5);
float temp21 = -6.0f*temp20;
float temp22 = temp21*temp18;
float temp23 = temp19-temp22;
float temp24 = temp4*temp23;
force = temp24;
```

Listing 29.2. The energy and force computations after eliminating common subexpressions.

shown in Listing 29.2. It certainly will not win any awards for readability, but that is irrelevant. It is generated at runtime to be processed by a compiler, so no human ever needs to look at it. The operation counts are now much lower: 10 multiplies, 2 divides, 1 add, 2 subtracts, 1 call to sqrt(), and 4 calls to pow().

The next problem we see is the use of the pow() function, which is a very slow way to compute small integer powers. Fortunately, there is an easy way to compute arbitrary integer powers through repeated multiplication. The trick is to repeatedly square a multiplier. To calculate x^n, first set $m = x$. Next, square m to give x^2, then square it again to give x^4, and so on. Now we simply need to decompose x^n into a product of values taken on by m. For example, $x^{12} = x^4 \cdot x^8$, so the line from Listing 29.2

```
float temp11 = pow(temp10, 12);
```

can be replaced by

```
float temp11;
float multiplier = temp10;
multiplier *= multiplier;
```

```
multiplier *= multiplier;
temp11 = multiplier;
multiplier *= multiplier;
temp11 *= multiplier;
```

This involves four multiplies, which is much faster than calling the pow() function.

We can do even better by computing multiple powers of the same base at the same time. In our case, we need to calculate four different powers of temp10 (5th, 6th, 11th, and 12th). If we calculate them all together, we need to generate the sequence of multiplier values only once:

```
float temp11, temp12, temp13, temp14;
float multiplier = temp10;
temp12 = multiplier;
temp14 = multiplier;
multiplier *= multiplier;
temp13 = multiplier;
temp14 *= multiplier;
multiplier *= multiplier;
temp11 = multiplier;
temp12 *= multiplier;
temp13 *= multiplier;
multiplier *= multiplier;
temp11 *= multiplier;
temp14 *= multiplier;
```

With this version, we have replaced all four calls to pow() with a total of only eight multiplies. The final version of the generated code is shown in Listing 29.3. The operation count for it is 18 multiplies, 2 divides, 1 add, 2 subtracts, and 1 call to sqrt().

We have now generated OpenCL code to compute the force and energy expressions, but that is only a small piece of the full kernel. We now need to insert it into a "shell kernel" that implements the rest of the algorithm. The methods used to efficiently compute nonbonded forces on a GPU are quite complicated. For example, they compute interactions in groups to minimize global memory access, and they use a variety of techniques to avoid computing interactions between atoms that are too far apart to affect each other [1]. The details of these techniques may vary depending on what device they are intended to run on.

This highlights one of the major advantages of this approach: because the code written by end users specifies only equations, not algorithms, it can run efficiently on a variety of hardware architectures with no modification at all, even if those architectures require fundamentally different algorithms for optimal performance. In the case of OpenMM's CustomNonbondedForce, for example, we have different versions of the kernel for ATI and NVIDIA GPUs. In the future we plan to write a third version targeted at multicore CPUs, and that version will likely use completely different algorithms than the GPU versions.

A few other optimizations are also worth mentioning. Although they do not strictly count as "code generation," they are enabled by the fact that kernels are not compiled until the program is actually run.

The first is to turn runtime constants into compile time constants. In our case, for example, the number of atoms being simulated does not change over the course of a simulation, so we can directly

```
float temp0 = eps1;
float temp1 = eps2;
float temp2 = temp0*temp1;
float temp3 = sqrt(temp2);
float temp4 = 4.0f*temp3;
float temp5 = sigma1;
float temp6 = sigma2;
float temp7 = temp5+temp6;
float temp8 = 0.5f*temp7;
float temp9 = r;
float temp10 = temp8/temp9;
float temp11, temp12, temp13, temp14;
float multiplier = temp10;
temp12 = multiplier;
temp14 = multiplier;
multiplier *= multiplier;
temp13 = multiplier;
temp14 *= multiplier;
multiplier *= multiplier;
temp11 = multiplier;
temp12 *= multiplier;
temp13 *= multiplier;
multiplier *= multiplier;
temp11 *= multiplier;
temp14 *= multiplier;
float temp15 = temp11-temp13;
float temp16 = temp4*temp15;
energy = temp16;
float temp17 = -12.0f*temp14;
float temp18 = temp9*temp9;
float temp19 = temp8/temp18;
float temp20 = temp17*temp19;
float temp21 = -6.0f*temp12;
float temp22 = temp21*temp19;
float temp23 = temp20-temp22;
float temp24 = temp4*temp23;
force = temp24;
```

Listing 29.3. The final version of the energy and force computations after applying all optimizations.

embed it in the kernel source code. This technique can save registers and can allow the compiler to do more precomputation than would otherwise be possible. In practice, we simply use symbolic constants in the source for all values that will be specified at compile time and then provide definitions for them by passing -D options to the OpenCL compiler.

A related optimization is to use high-performance "native" functions whenever possible. OpenCL includes a number of these functions such as native_sqrt(), native_rsqrt(), native_recip(), and so on.

These functions can be much faster than the standard functions they are equivalent to because they often are implemented with specialized hardware, but they also are permitted to be much less accurate.

When OpenMM starts up, it immediately executes a kernel to calculate these optimized functions for a wide range of input values, allowing it to estimate their true accuracy on the current hardware. Based on that, it selects which version of each function to use in all other kernels. This step, too, is done by simply defining preprocessor macros. For example, we pass to the compiler either -DSQRT=sqrt or -DSQRT=native_sqrt. All kernels can then simply use SQRT(x) to calculate square roots, knowing this will correspond to native_sqrt(x) if that is sufficiently accurate or sqrt(x) if it is not.

29.4 FINAL EVALUATION

The most direct way to evaluate the performance of this approach is to compare the generated code to a hand-optimized implementation of the same force. Before we developed custom forces, we had already written an implementation of the Lennard-Jones force. It uses a total of 11 multiplies, 1 divide, 1 add, and 2 subtracts, significantly better than the machine-generated version. This experience led us to analyze the differences between the two to see whether additional optimizations could be added to our code generator.

The first important difference is that the handwritten implementation does not store the per-atom parameters ε and σ on the GPU. Instead, it precomputes sqrt(ε) and $\sigma/2$ and stores those, allowing it to save one multiply and one call to sqrt(). Although the custom force does not perform this optimization automatically, a user can easily perform it by hand. CustomNonbondedForce supports an arbitrary set of user defined per-atom parameters, so one can define a parameter equal to $\sigma/2$ just as easily as one equal to σ.

The remaining differences come from algebraic simplification of the force expression. For example,

$$\left(\frac{0.5\,(\sigma_1 + \sigma_2)}{r}\right)^{11} \left(\frac{0.5\,(\sigma_1 + \sigma_2)}{r^2}\right) = \left(\frac{0.5\,(\sigma_1 + \sigma_2)}{r}\right)^{12} \frac{1}{r}$$

This is important because $\left(\frac{0.5(\sigma_1 + \sigma_2)}{r}\right)^{12}$ already appears as part of the expression for the energy. Thus, we need to compute only two powers instead of four.

The other way to evaluate performance is by execution time. In the case of the Lennard-Jones force, we find very little difference between the two versions: the machine-generated version is only about 4% slower than the hand-optimized one. This is because the generated code is only one small piece of a much larger algorithm. Even though that one piece requires significantly more operations, it has very little impact on the performance of the full calculation.

29.5 FUTURE DIRECTIONS

All of the code described here is available as part of the OpenMM open source project at https://simtk.org/home/openmm. In addition, we have separated the routines for parsing, differentiating, and optimizing mathematical expressions into a stand-alone library called Lepton, which is available at https://simtk.org/home/lepton. The OpenCL code generation facility is found in OpenMM's OpenCLExpressionUtilities class. All of this code is generically applicable to a wide range of fields, and we invite others to make use of it in their own projects.

Now that we have this capability in place, we are exploring the many ways it can be used through a growing collection of custom force types. Many of them are simple ones like CustomNonbondedForce that represent the energy with a single expression, but they can also be quite complicated. For example, we have a class called CustomGBForce that can implement a wide range of Generalized Born implicit solvent models. It represents the energy with a collection of expressions computed in different ways, which in turn may depend on intermediate values computed based on their own expressions in various ways. Implicit solvent models are an active field of research, and they can be challenging to implement correctly. Using CustomGBForce, a scientist can implement a novel solvent model in a dozen lines of code that otherwise would take a thousand lines of complex numerical calculations. This makes it a powerful tool for research and prototyping.

Another important future direction is to continue optimizing the code-generation process. Any significant further improvements will likely require more complex algebraic manipulations and higher level analyses of the computation. We have some ideas for possible approaches and hope to investigate them in our future work.

References

[1] P. Eastman, V.S. Pande, Efficient nonbonded interactions for molecular dynamics on a graphics processing unit, J. Comput. Chem. 31 (6) (2010) 1268–1272.

[2] M.S. Friedrichs, P. Eastman, et al., Accelerating molecular dynamic simulation on graphics processing units, J. Comput. Chem. 30 (6) (2009) 864–872.

[3] D. Grune, C. Jacobs, Parsing Techniques: A Practical Guide, Ellis Horwood Limited, Chichester, 1990.

[4] J.W. Hanson, J.S. Caviness, et al., Analytic differentiation by computer, Commun. ACM 5 (6) (1962) 349–355.

[5] D. Spinellis, Notable design patterns for domain-specific languages, J. Syst. Softw. 56 (1) (2001) 91–99.

30

GPU Application Development, Debugging, and Performance Tuning with GPU Ocelot

Andrew Kerr, Gregory Diamos,
and Sudhakar Yalamanchili

This chapter will discuss some implementation details of GPU Ocelot, particularly the implementation of the PTX emulator, and how GPU Ocelot may be used to prototype, debug, and tune CUDA applications for efficient execution on GPUs. This gem will explain how users may benefit from the rich application profiling and correctness tools built into Ocelot as well as how to extend Ocelot's trace generator interface to perform custom workload characterization and profiling. Additionally, we will discuss GPU Ocelot's role as a dynamic compilation framework for heterogeneous many-core compute systems that leverage GPUs and multicore CPUs.

30.1 INTRODUCTION

Graphics Processing Units (GPUs) offer considerable gains in performance for applications written to take advantage of data parallelism and of aspects of the underlying hardware such as banked memory, caches, and single-instruction multiple-thread (SIMT) execution. Efficient kernels executing on GPUs typically hide latency and maintain high throughput when hundreds or thousands of threads are launched. Consequently, complexities of the execution model, sensitivity to underlying architectural features, and the need for high concurrency present numerous challenges for developing correct and efficient GPU applications.

To address these challenges, we have implemented GPU Ocelot [1], a dynamic compilation framework for NVIDIA's CUDA programming language and API that links with unmodified CUDA applications, analyzes data-parallel GPU kernels, and launches them on available processors. GPU Ocelot consists of (1) an implementation of the CUDA Runtime API, (2) a complete internal representation of PTX kernels coupled to control- and data-flow analysis procedures, (3) a functional emulator for PTX, (4) a translator to multicore x86-based CPUs for efficient execution, (5) and a backend to NVIDIA GPUs via the CUDA Driver API. Ocelot supports an extensible trace generation framework in which application behavior such as control-flow uniformity, memory access patterns, and data sharing may be observed at instruction-level granularity.

30.2 CORE TECHNOLOGY

Ocelot's three backend execution targets — PTX emulator, multicore translator, and NVIDIA GPU — present a heterogeneous compute platform for data-parallel workloads implementd in CUDA [2]. To use Ocelot, a developer links their compiled CUDA application against Ocelot's static library instead of NVIDIA's `libcudart` making integration with existing compiled applications seamless. GPU Ocelot is tested for correctness against all of the CUDA SDK [4], Parboil benchmark suite [5], and Thrust [6] unit tests and is currently part of the development toolchains of several GPU-computing related projects. Ocelot's support for efficient execution on multicore CPUs has enabled research in heterogeneous computing such as predictive performance modeling [7] and research in optimization techniques for data-parallel workloads [8].

Depicted in Figure 30.1, GPU Ocelot is characterized by its front-end interface to existing CUDA applications, its capacity to analyze and transform PTX kernels using its IR, its complete representation of CUDA kernels and memory resources, and its support of three backend execution targets. Ocelot is implemented in C++ with source code available under BSD license and distributed both through static releases as well as anonymous SVN checkout from the Ocelot Project Site [1] available at `http://code.google.com/p/gpuocelot/`.

Compiled CUDA source files store modules as static blocks of text represented as PTX [3], NVIDIA's virtual instruction set architecture for GPUs, that are explicitly registered when the application is initialized. Ocelot implements NVIDIA's CUDA Runtime API and is invoked when applications are intialized and attempt to register PTX modules. Ocelot parses the PTX representation of registered

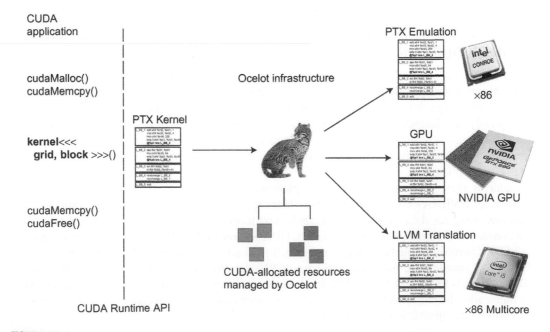

FIGURE 30.1

GPU Ocelot Dynamic Compilation Framework (see color insert).

modules and lazily translates contained kernels to the selected device backend when they are executed. By implementing NVIDIA's CUDA Runtime API, CUDA applications do not need to be modified to run with GPU Ocelot.

CUDA Runtime API functions perform resource management procedures such as allocation of memory on devices, binding of textures and arrays, and copying memory between address spaces. Ocelot implements these functions and constructs a data structure representing each resource in addition to allocating the block of memory in the selected device's address space. This enables memory checking for memcpy functions by ensuring destination regions are contained in existing allocations. The PTX emulator and multicore translator backends include support for more fine-grain memory checking by testing each address used by a load or store against the set of valid memory allocations.

GPU Ocelot supports three backend execution targets: a functional PTX simulator which will be described in greater detail in the following sections, a translator to multicore x86 CPUs, and a backend to NVIDIA GPUs via the CUDA Driver API. The multicore translator is implemented as a set of PTX-to-PTX transformations and classical compiler analyses including conversion to static single-assignment form followed by a translation from PTX to the instruction set of Low-Level Virtual Machine (LLVM) [8]. Most PTX instructions have a one-to-one correspondence with LLVM instructions, and more complex instructions that typically have hardware support on GPUs, such as trigonometric functions and texture sampling, are implemented in software. When a kernel is executed on the LLVM target, the Ocelot runtime statically maps blocks of the kernel grid onto hardware worker threads which execute each Cooperative Thread Array (CTA), serializing CUDA threads within the CTA and respecting barrier synchronizations.

The NVIDIA GPU backend is implemented by emitting PTX modules as text and compiling them to the selected GPU via the CUDA Driver API. Memory resources managed by Ocelot are allocated by calls to the CUDA Driver API, and global variables are made consistent before and after each kernel invocation. By using Ocelot as the implementation of the CUDA Runtime API, applications can benefit from memory bounds checking during copy operations. Moreover, they may register PTX-to-PTX transformations and modify the kernel before it is loaded by the GPU driver. Though we have not fully explored the possibilities of instrumenting kernels for execution on GPUs, Ocelot offers the unique capability to modify every kernel launched by a CUDA application and insert additional correctness checks, watches on global variables, and instrumentation to monitor application behavior.

30.2.1 PTX Functional Simulation

Ocelot's PTX emulator models a virtual architecture illustrated in Figure 30.2. This backend implements the NVIDIA PTX execution model and emulates the execution of a kernel on a GPU by interpreting instructions for each active thread of a warp before fetching the next instruction. This corresponds to execution by an arbitrarily wide single-instruction multiple-data (SIMD) processor and is similar to how hardware implementations such as NVIDIA's GeForce 400 series GPUs execute CUDA kernels. Blocks of memory store values for the virtual register file as well as the addressable memory spaces. The emulator interprets each instruction according to opcode, data type, and modifiers such as rounding or clamping modes, updating the architectural state of the processor with computed results.

Kernels executed on the PTX emulator present the entire observable state of a virtual GPU to user-extensible instruction trace generators. These are objects implementing an interface that receives the complete internal representation of a PTX kernel at the time it is launched for initial analysis. Then, as the kernel is executed, a trace event object is dispatched to the collection of active trace generators after

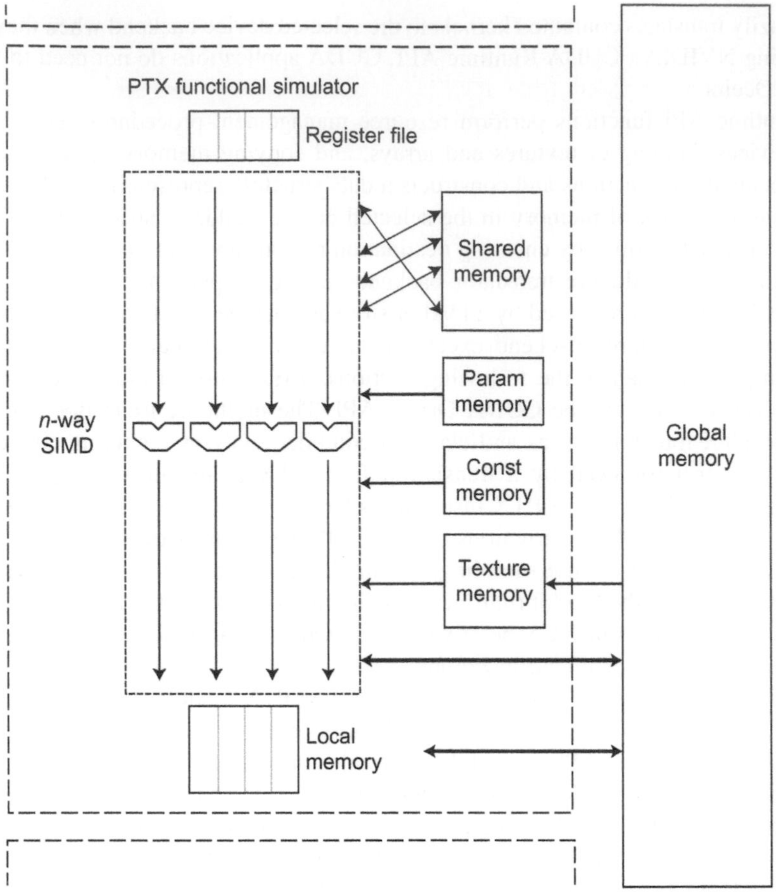

FIGURE 30.2

PTX emulator virtual architecture.

each instruction completes. This trace event object includes the instruction's internal representation and PC, set of memory addresses referenced, and thread ID. At this point, the instruction trace generator has the opportunity to inspect the register file and memory spaces accessible by the GPU such as shared and local memory. Practically any observable behavior may be measured using this approach. In the next section, we will discuss Ocelot's interfaces for user-extended trace generators that compute custom metrics.

30.2.2 Extensible Trace Generation Framework

GPU Ocelot's trace generation and analysis framework presents a clear and concise interface to user-extensible trace generators which are the preferred method to instrument and profile GPU applications.

In this section, we will explain how trace generators are invoked by the PTX emulator and discuss the scope of information that is available.

Trace generators are derived from the C++ class in Listing 30.1. Instances may be added and removed at runtime by CUDA applications using the Ocelot API function `ocelot::addTraceGenerator()` to monitor specific kernels. Alternatively and less intrusively, they may be added to Ocelot's `trace-generators` subproject which constructs and adds them when Ocelot initializes. This method does not require modifications to CUDA application source code and is the approach taken with each of the trace generators discussed in Section 30.3.1.

Figure 30.3 illustrates the sequence in which TraceGenerator event handlers are called during the execution of a PTX kernel.

Execution can be partitioned into three phases: launch configuration, computation, and finalization. Trace generators implement event handlers corresponding to each of the three phases. At *launch configuration*, the values of kernel parameters and grid dimensions are known. These are presented to

```
//! \file ocelot/trace/interface/TraceGenerator.h
namespace trace {

  //! Base class for trace generators
  class TraceGenerator {

  public:
    std::string database; //! name of the database file

  public:
    TraceGenerator();
    virtual ~TraceGenerator();

    //! called when a traced kernel is launched
    virtual void initialize(const
        executive::ExecutableKernel& kernel);

    //! called whenever an event takes place before
    //        results are committed
    virtual void event(const TraceEvent & event);

    //! called after an event commits
    virtual void postEvent(const TraceEvent & event);

    //! Called when a kernel is finished executing
    virtual void finish();
  };
}
```

Listing 30.1. TraceGenerator class declaration.

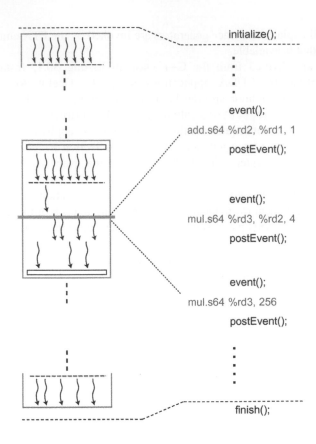

FIGURE 30.3

Sequence of TraceGenerator events in execution of PTX kernel.

each trace generator by calling its `initialize()` method and passing the internal representation of the PTX kernel to be executed as well as constant references to the entire structure of loaded modules and CUDA-managed resources. The entire state of the application is observable, and static analysis of the kernel may be completed at this point. Trace generators may, for instance, count the number of static floating-point arithmetic instructions versus memory instructions or examine the sizes of global memory allocations. As another example, the number of live registers may be counted as well as the number of synchronization points. Trace generators may update their own private data members to store the results of this analysis but should not modify the kernel or the application.

During *computation*, each instruction is fetched, and a `TraceEvent` instance is dispatched to attached TraceGenerator instances by calling their `TraceGenerator::event()` methods. The `TraceEvent` instance includes the PTX instruction's internal representation, a bit vector identifying active threads that will execute it, block ID, and a vector of memory addresses referenced by the instruction if it is a load, store, or texture sampler. `TraceEvent` is defined in Listing 30.2. `Trace-Generator::event()` is called before the instruction commits but after addresses into memory have

```
//! \file ocelot/trace/interface/TraceEvent.h
namespace trace {

  //! Models a dynamic event during the execution of PTX kernels
  class TraceEvent : hydrazine::Stringable {
  public:

    TraceEvent();

    TraceEvent(
      ir::Dim3 blockId,
      ir::PTXU64 PC,
      const ir::PTXInstruction* instruction,
      const boost::dynamic_bitset<> & active,
      const U64Vector & memory_addresses,
      ir::PTXU32 memory_size,
      ir::PTXU32 ctxStackSize = 1);

    //! ID of the block that generated the event
    ir::Dim3 blockId;

    //! PC index into EmulatedKernel's packed instruction
        sequence */
    ir::PTXU64 PC;

    //! Depth of call stack
    ir::PTXU32 contextStackSize;

    //! current instruction
    const ir::PTXInstruction* instruction;

    //! bit mask of active threads that executed this instruction
    BitMask active;

    //! Mask of threads that have taken this branch
    BitMask taken;

    //! Mask of threads that did not take this branch
    BitMask fallthrough;

    //! dense vector of addresses generated by memory operations
    U64Vector memory_addresses;

    //! size of each memory access
    ir::PTXU32 memory_size;
```

Listing 30.2. TraceEvent class declaration.

```
    //! kernel grid dimensions
    ir::Dim3 gridDim;

    //! kernel block dimensions
    ir::Dim3 blockDim;

  public:

    //! Convert to string representation
    std::string toString() const;
  };
}
```

Listing 30.2. (Continued)

been computed, so trace generators such as `MemoryChecker` may ensure subsequent memory accesses are valid. After the instruction commits, the PTX emulator calls each trace generator's `TraceGenerator::postEvent()` method, passing the same `TraceEvent` instance. This gives trace generators the opportunity to observe the result of an instruction and react accordingly.

Trace generators are notified when the kernel's execution finishes by calling their `finalize()` method, thereby presenting an opportunity to process instruction traces and insert results into a database or some other output mechanism. Each of the existing trace generators distributed with GPU Ocelot uses the Boost serialization library [10] to compile a database of all kernel invocations over all runs of an application. These may be post-processed by a collection of external analysis applications that load the serialized data issued by the trace generators, compute the metric or metrics of interest, and output results in a form suitable for visualization. Developers of custom trace generation tools are free to implement alternative I/O methods including interacation with an actual RDMS or output to a custom trace format to drive other simulation and analysis tools.

30.3 ALGORITHM, IMPLEMENTATION, AND BENEFITS

GPU Ocelot is a powerful tool for debugging GPU computing applications to ensure correctness, identify opportunities to improve performance, and characterize the behaviors of applications. Ocelot's functional PTX emulator in particular enables detailed observation of CUDA applications as they are executing and presents an opportunity to identify program errors such as memory faults, race detections, and deadlocks. Additionally, correct applications may be improved by identifying hot paths to focus optimization efforts as well as detect and avoid performance pitfalls such as bank conflicts and poor memory efficiency. In this section, we will discuss several of the facilities within Ocelot to perform this kind of correctness checking and profiling.

30.3.1 Trace Generation

GPU Ocelot is distributed with a selection of instruction trace generators intended to observe several important characteristics of program behavior. The list of trace generators is summarized in Table 30.1.

Table 30.1 Trace Generators Distributed with GPU Ocelot

Trace Generator	Summary of Functionality
Branch	Measures control-flow uniformity and branch divergence
Instruction	Measures number of static and dynamic instructions
IntegratedDebugger	Integrated debugger with GDB-like interface
KernelDimension	Measures kernel grid and block dimensions
MachineAttributes	Observes and records machine characteristics
Memory	Measures working set size, memory intensity, and memory efficiency
MemoryChecker	Instruments memory accesses and ensures they map to allocated regions
MemoryRaceDetector	Identifies race conditions on shared memory
Parallelism	Measures limits of MIMD and SIMD parallelism
PerformanceBound	Measures compute and memory throughput
SharedComputation	Measures extent of data-flow among threads
WarpSynchronous	Measures hot paths and regions suitable for warp-synchronous execution

These were implemented to ensure program correctness, detect faults at runtime, and compute several application metrics. A complete list of metrics with precise definitions appear in [11], which also contains results gathered from the CUDA SDK examples and Parboil.

30.3.2 Correctness

MemoryChecker compares the address of every load, store, and texture sampling instruction against the set of valid CUDA memory allocations. Addresses that are out of range result in throwing a runtime exception describing the thread ID, address, and program counter of the offending instruction. The following CUDA example illustrates Ocelot's PTX emulator detecting a bad memory reference and throwing a runtime exception identifying the faulting store instruction, the invalid address, the block and thread ID on which the instruction was executed, and a line number in the original CUDA source file producing the PTX store instruction. Note, the runtime exception also prints the existing allocations that constitute valid memory regions.

Cooperative Thread Arrays (CTAs) in CUDA consist of a collection of threads that may share data and synchronize at thread barriers. Threads may be executed serially or concurrently provided they all reach barrier instructions before any thread moves on to the next instruction. CTAs exchanging data among threads through shared memory necessarily must synchronize with barriers to ensure all threads have finished writing to their particular location before a dependant thread reads the value. Failure to include synchronizations is a common source of transient correctness errors in applications, and the consequences are frequently subtle enough to avoid detection. To avoid such race conditions, Ocelot's MemoryRaceDetector optionally annotates each byte of shared memory with the ID of the last thread to write to it. Subsequent loads and stores check to determine whether multiple threads have shared data without an intervening barrier synchronization. If no barrier has been excuted, a runtime

```
// file: memoryCheck.cu
__global__ void badMemoryReference(int *A) {
  A[threadIdx.x] = 0;            // line 3 - faulting store
}
int main() {
  int *invalidPtr = 0x0234;    // pointer arbitrarily chosen,
                               // not allocated via cudaMalloc()

  int *validPtr = 0;
  cudaMalloc((void **)&validPtr, sizeof(int)*64);
  badMemoryReference<<< dim3(1,1), dim3(64, 1) >>>(invalidPtr);
  return 0;
}
```

Listing 30.3. Kernel with obvious memory error.

```
===== Ocelot Runtime Exception =============
[PC 6] [thread 0] [cta 0] st.global.s32 [%r5 + 0], %r0 -
  Global memory access 0x234 is not within any allocated or
  mapped range.

All allocations On device Ocelot PTX Emulator:
===== Ocelot global memory allocations =====
=== allocation ===
= 0x1740230 - 0x174032f
= pointer: 0x1740230
= 256 bytes
= device address space: 0
= linear structure, 1D
= pitch: 256
= width: 256
= height: 1
==============================================
Near memoryCheck.cu:3:0
==============================================
```

Listing 30.4. Exception thrown when memoryCheck.cu is executed.

exception is thrown indicating a race condition. The following listing demonstrates a CUDA kernel with an obvious race condition likely to result in undefined behavior on actual hardware. A barrier is needed to synchronize all threads of the CTA before they attemp to exchange data. Ocelot throws a runtime exception identifying the source file and kernel as well as the line number of the faulting instruction.

Deadlocks in CUDA occur when two threads reach different thread barriers and both necessarily block waiting for the other to resume. Because the PTX emulator attempts to reconverge threads as early as possible, detecting whether a particular barrier synchronization instruction will result in a

```
// file: raceCondition.cu
__global__ void raceCondition(int *A) {
  __shared__ int SharedMem[64];
  SharedMem[threadIdx.x] = A[threadIdx.x];
  // no synchronization barrier!
  A[threadIdx.x] = SharedMem[64 - threadIdx.x]; // line 9 - faulting load
}
...
raceCondition<<< grid, block >>>(A);
...

==Ocelot== Ocelot PTX Emulator failed to run kernel "_Z13raceConditionPi" with
exception:
==Ocelot== [PC 15] [thread 0] [cta 0] ld.shared.s32 %r14, [%r13 + 252]
- Shared memory race condition, address 0xfc was previously written by thread 63
without a memory barrier in between.
==Ocelot== Near raceCondition.cu:9:0
```

Listing 30.5. Race detection in shared memory.

deadlock is as straightforward as ensuring all threads have reconverged and are active. GPU Ocelot's detailed runtime exception identifies the particular synchronization on which threads have deadlocked and could be used to identify the control paths taken by the diverged threads.

30.3.3 Integrated PTX Debugger

As an illustration of the power and flexibility of the trace generation inteface, we have implemented an integrated debugger with similar look and feel to GDB. The Ocelot Integrated Debugger is implemented as a trace generator like the correctness verifiers discussed in the previous sections. It responds to TraceEvents and optionally enters a loop waiting for commands on std::cin. This interactive command prompt provides a selection of commands that inspect the state of the PTX emulator and the application. Table 30.2 contains a list of the available commands currently implemented with a brief description.

The debugger may be attached to a specific kernel by specifying the kernel by name in the configure.ocelot configuration document, or it may be configured to attach to all executed kernels. Regardless, any kernel resulting in an exception by the above correctness checkers automatically invokes the debugger to enable developers to inspect the state of the offending kernel, step through subsequent instructions, and possibly resume execution.

Single-step execution enables the user to execute each PTX instruction then immediately return to the debugger rather than resume normal execution. Users may print the values of the register table, obtain a hexadecimal representation of a region of memory, or print the value of a defined region of memory.

Breakpoints are flags assigned to particular instructions that halt an executing kernel when those instructions are reached. Halting is accomplished by entering the command loop. The user sets a breakpoint with the break command and specifies the program counter of the instruction to break on.

Table 30.2 Ocelot Integrated Debugger Commands

Debugger Command	Description
jump	jump to the specified PC
break	set a breakpoint at the specified PC
remove	remove a breakpoint
watch global	set a watchpoint at a memory region
list	list watchpoints and breakpoints
print	print the value of a memory resource
print asm	print instructions near a PC
print reg	print the values of a register
print mem	print the values near an address
print warp	print the current warp status
print pc	print the PC of the current warp
print loc	print the nearest CUDA source line
step	execute the next instruction and break
continue	resume execution to next breakpoint
quit	detach the debugger and continue

The command parser adds this PC to a data structure, and the PCs of subsequent instructions are checked against the list of breakpoints.

Watchpoints are special breakpoints the debugger triggers when a kernel accesses a specified region of memory. The programmer may desire to know which threads are writing to a particular memory region, what values were previously in that region, and what values the threads are attempting to write. The programmer specifies a watchpoint in the debugger according to the base address of the region of interest, the data type of each element, and the number of elements. The debugger maintains a data structure with all such watchpoints that is tested against the elements of TraceEvent:: memory_addresses when the PTX emulator dispatches the next instruction to active trace generators. A store to the region of interest triggers the watchpoint which prints the values of the accessed memory and the new values to be written; these values are formatted according to the datatype of the watchpoint. Execution breaks before the write takes place, and the debugger prints the ID of the writing threads and CTAs.

The following sample illustrates the debugger in action, setting a watchpoint, and continuing until execution breaks when the kernel attempts to write to the watchpoint.

30.3.4 Performance Tuning

The PTX emulation and trace generation framework presents an opportunity for developers to inspect their kernels and experiment with optimizations to improve performance. Developers may identify sources of inefficiency, critical paths through their code, and verify the impacts their optimizations have on runtime behavior. This section describes several trace generators intended to capture performance-related behavior of PTX kernels.

```
$ ./TestCudaSequence
A_gpu = 0x16dcbe0
(ocelot-dbg) Attaching debugger to kernel 'sequence'
(ocelot-dbg)
(ocelot-dbg) watch global address 0x16dcbe0 s32[4]
set #1: watch global address 0x16dcbe0 s32[4] — 16 bytes
(ocelot-dbg)
(ocelot-dbg) continue
st.global.s32 [%r11 + 0], %r7
watchpoint #1 —   CTA (0, 0)
  thread (0, 0, 0) — store to 0x16dcbe0 4 bytes
  old value = -1
  new value = 0
  thread (1, 0, 0) — store to 0x16dcbe4 4 bytes
  old value = -1
  new value = 2
  thread (2, 0, 0) — store to 0x16dcbe8 4 bytes
  old value = -1
  new value = 4
  thread (3, 0, 0) — store to 0x16dcbec 4 bytes
  old value = -1
  new value = 6
break on watchpoint
(ocelot-dbg)
```

Listing 30.6. Setting watchpoints in ocelot-dbg.

30.3.4.1 *Performance Analysis*

The first challenge of optimizing an application is to identify the most significant performance bottle-necks. These are typically found in regions of code where the processor executes the most instructions and even small improvements in efficiency will result in a great reduction in runtime. To assist in identifying the most frequently executed blocks in a CUDA application, we implemented the trace generator `PerformanceBoundGenerator` to accumulate the total number of dynamic instructions executed by each basic block in addition to the number of floating-point operations executed and number of bytes transferred to and from shared, global, and texture memory.

This trace generator provides a graphical output of the kernel's control flow graph and color-codes each block with color intensity corresponding to number of instructions executed, on a logarithmic scale. Additionally, the ratios of instruction throughput to memory demand for each block and the entire kernel are presented. These may be compared to known theoretical floating-point throughput and device memory bandwidth of target GPUs to estimate whether the kernel is compute- or memory-bound. Where possible, blocks are also annotated with line numbers and file name of the CUDA source file in which the kernel is defined. Together, this information enables developers to quickly zoom in on the hottest paths of a kernel, estimate whether these are bound by memory bandwidth or computation throughput, and identify the corresponding regions of CUDA source code.

To examine Ocelot's capacity to direct performance optimization decisions, we worked with the developer of an application that accelerates synthetic aperture sonar via back propagation on GPU [12]. We ran this application on Ocelot's PTX functional emulator and used `PerformanceBound` to profile the dominant kernel. Ocelot identified compute-bound basic blocks as well as blocks with the highest number of dynamic instructions. Ocelot revealed bank conflicts to shared memory in the most compute intensive blocks as well as opportunities to relocate some statements out of the hottest path thereby eliminating partially redundant expressions. After tuning the application with this information in hand, the developer reported that application runtime decreased from 20 seconds to 14.7 seconds for large data sets when run on a GeForce GTX480.

As a simple example, Figure 30.4 illustrates performance measurements of the naive scan kernel from the CUDA SDK. Aggregate results over the entire kernel appear in the white block and present global memory demand, shared memory demand, number of bank conflicts to shared memory, number of dynamic instructions, number of FLOPs, and ratios of floating-point operations to global memory.

30.3.4.2 *Memory Efficiency*

The largest factors affecting performance of GPU applications are related to memory access and control flow uniformity. Memory behavior is impacted by spatial locality and the efficiency in which off-chip bandwidth is utilized. Ocelot measures efficiency by implementing the memory coalescing protocol defined in the CUDA Programming Guide and determining the number of cycles needed to satisfy each memory request. Figure 30.5 illustrates the average efficiency of loads and stores to global memory relative to peak memory bandwidth. This data was recorded by `MemoryTraceGenerator` over a selection of CUDA applications and offers feedback to developers by identifying which kernels are the most memory intensive and which memory instructions are the least efficient.

30.3.4.3 *Control Flow and Thread Reconvergence*

Control flow uniformity refers to the fraction of threads that take the same control paths between synchronizations. If all threads of a warp execute the same path, the single-instruction multiple-data (SIMD) datapaths in each multiprocessor execute them concurrently. If threads of the same warp take different branch targets, the warp is said to diverge, they must be serialized. Later in the program, diverged warp contexts at the same point in the program may be reconverged. In previous work [11], we define activity factor as the average number of threads that would be executed concurrently on an infinitely wide SIMD machine and provide a trace generator to measure this in actual applications. Figure 30.6 illustrates activity factor gathered from a selection of CUDA applications by `Branch-TraceGenerator` using the two different warp reconvergence mechanisms implemented by Ocelot: immediate post-dominator (IPDOM) [13] reconvergence and barrier reconvergence.

As data-parallel execution models become more widespread, efficient methods to reconverge multiple warp contexts have become an important research topic. Both a compilation framework and functional simulator, Ocelot is uniquely leveraged to evaluate novel reconvergence policies that may depend on static program analysis and transformations as well as hardware support. To simulate abstract models of current GPUs, Ocelot currently implements two widely-used warp reconvergence mechanisms: immediate post-dominator (IPDOM) [13] reconvergence and barrier reconvergence.

The IPDOM reconvergence method identifies each potentially divergent branch and computes the nearest basic block on which all control paths from the divergent branch must ultimately converge — the immediate post-dominator. This has the advantage of converging warps at locations where they

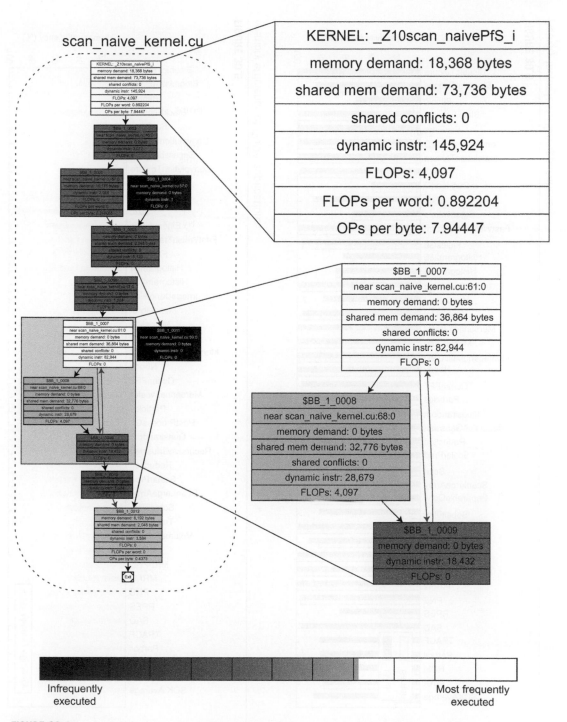

FIGURE 30.4

Performance analysis of naive scan kernel from CUDA SDK.

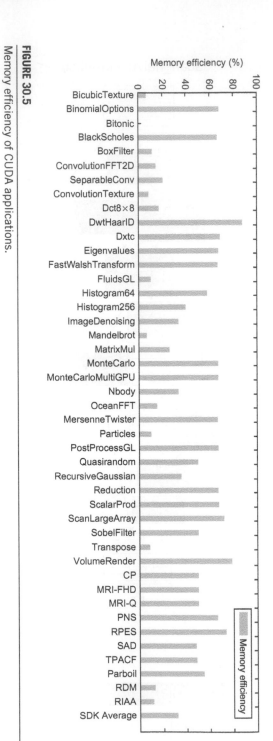

FIGURE 30.5

Memory efficiency of CUDA applications.

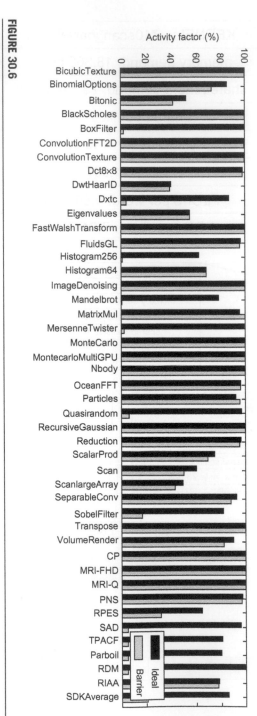

FIGURE 30.6

Activity factor for CUDA applications.

are guaranteed to come together, possibly in locations within the control flow graph where CTA-wide barriers could not be placed without deadlocking. In contrast, barrier reconvergence requires that all threads reach a CTA-wide barrier, even if reconvergence of at least some warps at an earlier point during the execution might have been possible.

One may observe the impact of these two reconvergence mechanisms by examining activity factors of selected applications as in Figure 30.6. Several applications exhibit no branch divergence, so both mechanisms achieve 100% activity. Applications such as Eigenvalues, Histogram256, and DwtHaar1D achieve nearly identical activity factors for both mechanisms which suggests the presence of barriers very near reconverge points. In other applications such as BoxFilter, Dxtc, and Mandelbrot, activity factor is very high for IPDOM reconvergence but quite low for barrier reconvergence implying few barriers and many missed reconvergence opportunities.

30.3.5 Custom Trace Generation

GPU Ocelot's trace generation framework provides a concise interface in which custom trace generators can be implemented and inserted into CUDA programs to measure application- or research-specific behaviors. `TraceEvent` objects encapsulate all structural information needed to interpret a PTX instruction, and trace generators can inspect the complete state of all CUDA-managed resources as well as control- and data-flow graphs of the kernel being executed. We have used this infrastructure to support our own research efforts [7, 11]. Additionally, Ocelot's trace generation framework has been used to construct instruction traces as inputs to timing models for GPU architecture simulation in [14, 15]. Finally, we are aware of several additional projects using GPU Ocelot to understand memory behavior of CUDA applications and to model the effects of warp formation.

30.3.6 Device Switching

Ocelot may be used to manage execution in a system with several different types of processors. To enable optimizations such as running each kernel on the device where it will execute the fastest, Ocelot supports the ability to migrate state to different execution targets as the application is executing on kernel boundaries. We envision this also being useful to expedite profiling, as all kernels will execute on their fastest processor except a particular kernel of interest which executes on the PTX emulator to gather detailed results.

To complete a device switch, all state located in the source device's address space must be replicated in the destination device's address space, and pointers must be updated to reference new locations. When the source and destination devices share an address space as in the case of the PTX emulator and the multicore backend, no replication is needed. When at least one device is a GPU, state is replicated by examining Ocelot's CUDA resource data structures which contain enough information to construct identical allocations in the destination address space via the CUDA Driver API. Then, data is copied to complete the state initialization.

After the device switch, all pointers to data in the source address space must be mapped to new pointers in the destination address space. Consequently, GPU Ocelot provides a map of source and destination addresses for copied allocations, and the application may update its own pointers with this map. This is straightforward unless device data includes data structures which themselves contain pointers. For example, a linked list meant to be traversed by PTX kernels may contain a set of nodes, each with pointers to the next node. For this to function correctly on the destination GPU, each node will have to be updated and pointers mapped. In general, Ocelot does not provide an automated solution to this problem beyond providing to the application the mapping of pointers in the old address space to the new address space. One work-around is to use indices rather than pointers when referencing other nodes within data structures. This approach requires only a single re-mapping of the base address which is likely to be a parameter to the kernel.

30.4 FUTURE DIRECTIONS

Ocelot is conceived as an infrastructure for enabling programs to run on heterogeneous compute systems. NVIDIA's CUDA language and runtime API present a convenient and productive programming model for expressing parallel computations suitable for processors such as GPUs. As a dynamic compiler, Ocelot is uniquely positioned to manage resources and execute programs composed of data-parallel kernels on each type of processor that may be available in a system. In the future, this is likely to consist of GPU-like processors from various vendors, multicore CPUs, and other types of accelerators.

In the near future, Ocelot will be released with support for AMD GPUs developed by Rodrigo Dominguez and David Kaeli from Northeastern University. Translation from PTX to AMD's GPU Intermediate Language (IL) requires the replacement of branching control flow with classical control structures such as loops and if-else blocks. Completion of this backend will enable CUDA programs to run unmodified on AMD hardware. Intel's GEN integrated GPU architecture is another possible target with similar constraints on control flow, though support is only proposed at the time of this writing.

OpenCL presents a similar kernel-oriented programming model, and vendors such as NVIDIA and AMD have been quick in releasing development tools for programming GPUs with OpenCL. To expand support for languages and tools, an implementation from OpenCL to LLVM via Apple's open-source CLANG front-end would enable OpenCL kernels to execute on Ocelot's multicore backend. Adding a PTX code generator from LLVM would enable Ocelot to run OpenCL and CUDA programs on any of the current and future Ocelot execution targets as well as enable optimizations and improvements to the LLVM project to benefit GPU computing.

Acknowledgements

GPU Ocelot has been available to the public for over one year as of the time of this writing and has benefitted from feedback and intellectual contributions from an active set of core users.

This research was supported by NSF under grant CCF-0905459, IBM through an OCR Innovation award, LogicBlox Corporation, and an NVIDIA Graduate Fellowship.

References

[1] G. Diamos, A. Kerr, S. Yalamanchili, GPU Ocelot: a Binary Translation Framework for PTX, http://code.google.com/p/gpuocelot/.

[2] NVIDIA, NVIDIA CUDA: Compute Unified Device Architecture, second ed., NVIDIA Corporation, Santa Clara, California, 2008.

[3] NVIDIA, NVIDIA Compute PTX: Parallel Thread Execution, first ed., NVIDIA Corporation, Santa Clara, California, 2008.

[4] NVIDIA, NVIDIA CUDA SDK 2.1, second ed., NVIDIA Corporation, Santa Clara, California, 2008.

[5] IMPACT, The PARBOIL Benchmark Suite, http://www.crhc.uiuc.edu/IMPACT/parboil.php, 2007.

[6] Thrust: C++ Template Library for CUDA, http://code.google.com/p/thrust/.

[7] G. Diamos, A. Kerr, S. Yalamanchili, Modeling GPU-CPU workloads and systems, in: Third Workshop on General-Purpose Computation on Graphics Processing Units (GPGPU-3), Pittsburgh, PA, ACM, New York, 2010, pp. 31–42.

[8] G. Diamos, A. Kerr, S. Yalamanchili, N. Clark, Ocelot: a dynamic compiler for bulk-synchronous applications in heterogeneous systems, in: Proceedings of the 19th International Conference on Parallel Architectures and Compilation Techniques, ACM, Vienna, Austria, 2010, pp. 353–364.

[9] C. Lattner, V. Adve, LLVM: a compilation framework for lifelong program analysis and transformation, in: Proceedings of the 2004 International Symposium on Code Generation and Optimization (CGO'04), IEEE Computer Society, Palo Alto, California, 2004, p. 75.

[10] Boost C++ Libraries. http://www.boost.org/.

[11] G. Diamos, A. Kerr, S. Yalamanchili, A characterization and analysis of PTX kernels, in: International Symposium on Workload Characterization (IISWC'09), IEEE Computer Society, Austin, TX, 2009, pp. 3–12.

[12] D. Campbell, D. Cook, Using graphics processors to accelerate synthetic aperture sonar imaging via back-propagation, in: High Performance Embedded Computing Workshop (HPEC'10), Lincoln Laboratory, MIT, Lexington, MA, Boston, 2010.

[13] W. Fung, I. Sham, G. Yuan, T. Aamodt, Dynamic warp formation and scheduling for efficient GPU control flow, in: MICRO 07: Proceedings of the 40th Annual IEEE/ACM International Symposium on Microarchitecture, IEEE Computer Society, Washington, DC, 2007, pp. 407–420.

[14] N. Lakshminarayana, H, Kim, Effect of instruction fetch and memory scheduling on GPU performance, in: Workshop on Language, Compiler, and Architecture Support for GPGPU, Bangalore, India, 2010.

[15] S. Hong, H. Kim, An integrated GPU power and performance model, in: International Symposium on Computer Architecture (ISCA-37), ACM, New York, Saint-Malo, France, 2010.

Abstraction for AoS and SoA Layout in C++

31

Robert Strzodka

Memory access patterns are critical for performance, especially on parallel architectures such as GPUs. Because of this, the choice between an *array-of-structures (AoS)* data layout and a *structure-of-arrays (SoA)* layout has a large impact on overall program performance. However, it is not always obvious which layout will better serve a particular application, and testing both of them by hand in C++ is tedious because their syntax greatly differs. Not only is the syntax for defining the container different, but worse, the syntax for accessing the data within the container is different, leading to anywhere from tens to thousands of source code changes needed to switch any given container from the AoS to the SoA layout or vice versa.

This chapter presents an abstraction layer that allows switching between the AoS and SoA layouts in C++ without having to change the data access syntax. A few changes to the structure and container definitions allow for easy performance comparison of AoS vs. SoA on existing AoS code. This abstraction retains the more intuitive AoS syntax (`container[index].component`) for data access yet allows switching between the AoS and SoA layouts with a single template parameter in the container type definition on the CPU and GPU. In this way, code development becomes independent of the data layout and performance is improved by choosing the correct layout for the application's usage pattern.

A library called ASX (Array of Structs eXtended) that implements this abstraction layer, together with code examples that execute on both the CPU and the GPU, can be downloaded from the author's homepage [8].

31.1 INTRODUCTION, PROBLEM STATEMENT, AND CONTEXT

Often our data is not scalar but rather comprises multiple components, such as the x, y, and z coordinates of a 3-D position or velocity vector, the principal components of a feature vector, or the red, green, and blue color channels of a pixel. When operating on such multivalued data, we have two major choices for the data layout: AoS or SoA. For the AoS layout, we define the multivalued structure and assemble many copies of it one after another in memory. In the case of SoA, we begin with all instances of the first component, then follow it with all instances of the second component, etc.

Collections of C++ class instances fall naturally into the AoS pattern, though this may not necessarily represent the best choice for performance for a given application (see Section 31.5.1). Consider the following examples of these two layouts. The same data is represented in both cases, but because of the different layout, the memory access patterns during computation are significantly different.

```
// Array of Structures (AoS)
struct Element {
  Type1 comp1;
  Type2 comp2;
  Type3 comp3;
};
typedef Element AoS_Container[CONT_SIZE];

// Structure of Arrays (SoA)
struct SoA_Container {
  Type1 comp1[CONT_SIZE];
  Type2 comp2[CONT_SIZE];
  Type3 comp3[CONT_SIZE];
};
```

Switching between these two layouts is labor-intensive, as the access syntax for the two forms differs, as seen below. Alternatively, a third possible access syntax could be used, which is the standard C++ solution to this problem: a class hides the data layout from the programmer by turning every structure component access into a call to a member function, thereby allowing the class implementation to switch between AoS and SoA layouts without having to change the access syntax.

```
value= container[index].component; // AoS access
value= container.component[index]; // SoA access
value= container.component(index); // C++ access
```

With the C++ member function access syntax, however, the definition of every structure (even simple structures with only a few components each) requires many additional lines of code, especially since the proper treatment of constness requires two access functions for every data member (or, alternatively, a getter and a setter function for each member):

```
const Type& component(int index) const; // read access
      Type& component(int index);       // write access
```

Besides the code bloat when defining accessor functions, the standard C++ solution has another problem: the AoS layout allows performing *in-place* updates on the container element at a certain index position with the *same* functions that are used on singleton elements:

```
Element single;                   // single element
AoS_Container container;          // AoS container
void update( Element& elm ) { elm.comp1= elm.comp2; }

update( single );                 // OK
update( container[5] );           // OK
```

With the SoA layout or the standard C++ solution, this is not possible because the component must be selected first and the index afterwards. Consequently, in that case two different functions are necessary to perform the same operation as above:

```
Element single;              // single element
Cpp_Container container;      // C++ container
void update( Element& elm ) { elm.comp1= elm.comp2; }
void update( Cpp_Container& con, int i ) { con.comp1[i]= con.comp2[i]; }

update( single );            // the same operation ...
update( container, 5 );      // ... but different syntax
```

Of course, this problem can also be solved with more C++ machinery by defining iterators and passing `Cpp_Container::iterator(single)` and `Cpp_Container::iterator(container,5)` as arguments to functions; however, this only adds to the code bloat and hardly anyone is willing to implement so many classes for every small data structure. Moreover, many changes would have to be applied to an existing AoS code before it could work with this type of C++ solution.

31.2 CORE METHOD

Our goal is to introduce SoA functionality with minimal changes to the element and container definitions and without abandoning the more intuitive AoS syntax `container[index].component`. In this way it will be easy for programmers to transition from existing AoS code to a flexible code that supports both AoS and SoA. As the data access syntax remains the same, the main additional work required from the programmer is a more flexible structure definition based on the *ASA (array of structs of arrays)* coding pattern.

```
// AoS pattern: concise but restricted to AoS layout
struct Element {
  Type1 comp1;
  Type2 comp2;
  Type3 comp3;
};
typedef Element Container[CONT_SIZE];

// ASA pattern: a bit longer but handles both AoS and SoA
template <ASX::ID t_id= ASX::ID_value>
struct FlexibleElement {
  typedef ASX::ASAGroup<Type1,t_id> ASX_ASA;
  union{ Type1 comp1;  ASX_ASA dummy1; };
  union{ Type2 comp2;  ASX_ASA dummy2; };
  union{ Type3 comp3;  ASX_ASA dummy3; };
};
typedef FlexibleElement<> Element;
```

```
// specify ASX::SOA instead for an SoA container
typedef ASX::Array<FlexibleElement, CONT_SIZE, ASX::AOS> Container;

// common access syntax: normal AoS code continues to function
Element single= {1, 2, 3};        // OK, no change
Container container;              // OK, no change
single.comp2= single.comp3;      // OK, no change
container[5].comp3= 2;           // OK, no change
```

The layout and behavior of the types `Element` and `Container` are exactly the same no matter whether the AoS pattern or the ASA pattern with AoS layout (parameter `ASX::AOS`) is used. However, the ASA pattern allows changing the in-memory data layout to SoA (corresponding to `SoA_Container` in Section 31.1) simply by replacing `ASX::AOS` with `ASX::SOA`. The normal AoS access syntax works in either case without any changes as shown above.

For some code, the above change to the container definition is everything that is required from the programmer. However, sometimes additional code adjustments are needed. First, references to ASA elements have necessarily different types depending on whether they refer to a single element, a container element, or possibly both. It is still possible to write a single function for handling of single element and container element references similar to the standard AoS solution, but the syntax of references must be adjusted; see Section 31.4.1. Second, the above ASA container definition assumes that `Type1`, which is used in `ASX::ASAGroup<...>`, is greater than or equal to `Type2` and `Type3` in size. The handling of differently-sized components, array-valued components, and nesting of structures are discussed in Sections 31.4.2 through 31.4.4.

In this article, we focus on the ASA (array of structs of arrays) coding pattern. The first three examples included in the ASX library (`simpleAoS`, `simpleSoA`, and `simpleASA`) deal with the simple three-valued structure from above and allow an easy comparison of a standard AoS solution, a standard SoA solution and the ASA solution that supports both layouts. In particular, the transition from the standard AoS solution to the ASA solution requires only few changes, while the transition from the standard AoS solution to the standard SoA solution is far more time-consuming even for this simple structure.

The code above uses the `ASX::Array` class, which provides static allocation based on a size that is known at compile-time, i.e., the equivalent of a normal array in C. All examples using `ASX::Array` are located in the directory `examples/staticCUDA` of the ASX library.

For cases requiring dynamic allocation, the ASX library also provides the class `ASX::Vector`, which uses a constructor to allocate memory in a manner similar to STL vectors. The corresponding examples are located in the directory `examples/dynamicCUDA`. Section 31.3.2 discusses the few differences between `ASX::Array` and `ASX::Vector`.

31.3 IMPLEMENTATION

31.3.1 Statically Sized Containers

The technical goal of the implementation is to enable the use of the intuitive AoS syntax `container[index].component` for both data layouts. Clearly, using AoS syntax for an AoS layout is simple; the challenge lies in defining an `operator[]` such that the AoS syntax can access an SoA container. The following code explains why this is possible under certain conditions:

```
struct SoA_Container {
  Type1 comp1[CONT_SIZE];
  Type2 comp2[CONT_SIZE];
  Type3 comp3[CONT_SIZE];
};
SoA_Container container;            // SoA container

Type3& soa= container.comp3[5];     // normal SoA syntax
Type3& aos= reinterpret_cast<SoA_Container&>
            (container.comp1[5]).comp3[0]; // AoS-like
```

The main insight is that `soa` and `aos` reference the same value if `Type1`, `Type2`, and `Type3` all have the same size in memory, because then it does not matter in which order the index offset and the structure member offset are applied. This solves the problem of swapping the order of `operator[]` and `operator.` for the data access on the SoA layout. Now we only need to hide the ugly typecast in the `operator[]` function and eliminate the trailing `[0]` by giving `comp3[0]` a fixed name with the help of an anonymous union:

```
struct SoA_Container {
SoA_Container& operator[](int index) {
  return reinterpret_cast<SoA_Container&>(comp1[index]);
};
  union{ Type1 comp1val, comp1[CONT_SIZE]; };
  union{ Type2 comp2val, comp2[CONT_SIZE]; };
  union{ Type3 comp3val, comp3[CONT_SIZE]; };
};
SoA_Container container;            // SoA container

Type3& soa= container.comp3[5];     // normal SoA syntax
Type3& aos= container[5].comp3val;  // normal AoS syntax
```

The last line here does exactly the same as the last line in the previous listing, except it is much cleaner using normal AoS syntax. Clearly, we can also access an AoS layout with AoS syntax, so we have achieved our goal of showing that the syntax can stay the same even though the layout changes. Only the `operator[]` function must be defined differently depending on the layout, and this can be achieved with a template specialization. Although no further technical tricks are involved in the implementation, the actual code of `ASX::Array` is much longer because of the template specialization and the partial compatibility of the interface with the containers of the STL library, i.e., many types and query functions are defined.

`ASX::Array` behaves like a normal array in C and therefore shares its disadvantage that the container size `CONT_SIZE` must be a compile-time constant as well as its advantages that it can be used to allocate on-chip shared memory in CUDA and that it contains nothing but the user data, so to copy a ASX::Array to the GPU, we simply invoke cudaMemcpy:

```
typedef ASX::Array<Flex,CONT_SIZE,ASX::AOS> Container;
Container host_A, *device_pA;
cudaMalloc(&device_pA, sizeof(host_A));
cudaMemcpy(device_pA, &host_A, sizeof(host_A), cudaMemcpyHostToDevice);
```

31.3.2 Dynamically Sized Containers

When dynamic container sizing is required, ASX::Vector can be used in place of ASX::Array. It circumvents the static size limitation by defining an ASX::Array of fixed size (granularity) and then allocating a dynamically defined number of them. The indexing in the operator[] function becomes slightly more complicated, but otherwise little changes. This is similar to the way an STL vector works.

Consequently, as with an STL vector, ASX::Vector itself contains only control logic and metadata, while the user data is stored at a different address. Therefore, moving the container between the host and device requires two copies: one for the metadata and one for the user data, and an adjustment of the pointer to the user data. The library provides the convenience function ASX::deepCopyVector for these actions:

```
typedef ASX::Vector<Flex,GRANULARITY,ASX::AOS> Container;
Container host_A(CONT_SIZE), *device_pA, *device_pAdata;
cudaMalloc(&device_pA, sizeof(host_A));
cudaMalloc(&device_pAdata, host_A.memory_size())
ASX::deepCopyVector(device_pA, device_pAdata, &host_A, cudaMemcpyHostToDevice);
```

Note that the container size CONT_SIZE in this example can be dynamically defined. The constant GRANULARITY controls the granularity of the allocation, or it can be set to zero to use the default setting.

Apart from the above differences, the containers defined by ASX::Array and ASX::Vector utilize exactly the same syntax as described in the other sections. Code examples with ASX::Array are located in examples/staticCUDA and with ASX::Vector in examples/dynamicCUDA.

31.4 ASA IN PRACTICE

In the following sections, we discuss some caveats to be aware of when switching to the ASA pattern as well as support for more complex data layouts as they appear in practice.

31.4.1 References to Elements

In standard AoS code, a reference to a singleton element or to an indexed element in a container always has the type Element&. For the ASA pattern, these two have different types when an SoA layout is selected: a single element has its components laid out consecutively in memory, hence the reference is of type Element&, whereas an element within a container has its components spread out in memory, requiring the reference to be of type Container::reference. If an argument to a function could be either a singleton element or an indexed container element, then a templated type for that argument is required.

```
template <ASX::ID t_id>
void update( FlexibleElement<t_id>& elm )
{ elm.comp1= elm.comp2; }                    // OK, no change

Element single= {1, 2, 3};
Container container;

Element& refSE= single;                      // OK, no change
Container::reference refSE= single;          // Type error

Element& refCE= container[5];                // Type error
Container::reference refCE= container[5];    // OK, changed

update( single );                            // OK, no change
update( container[5] );                      // OK, no change
```

Therefore, when transitioning from AoS code to ASA code, we need to replace Element& by Container::reference wherever it refers to a container element, and element references in function parameters must become template types if both single and container elements may be passed. The function calls themselves do not need to be changed, because the compiler deduces the corresponding template instantiation automatically from the passed parameter.

Besides the new container definition, the different treatments of references are the only changes that are necessary to turn the original AoS code simpleAoS into the flexible ASA code simpleASA in the example folder of the ASX library.

31.4.2 Components of Different Sizes

If the structure components have different sizes, they should be grouped such that the component groups have the same or at least similar sizes. While this sort of grouping is not strictly necessary, it is advisable, as it benefits performance and minimizes the memory footprint.

```
// AoS pattern: concise but restricted to AoS layout
struct Element {
  float  c1;
  short  c2[2];
  double c3;
};
typedef Element Container[CONT_SIZE];

// ASA pattern: a bit longer but handles both AoS and SoA
```

```
template <ASX::ID t_id= ASX::ID_value>
struct FlexibleElement {
  typedef ASX::ASAGroup<double,t_id> ASX_ASA;
  union{struct{float c1; short c2[2];}; ASX_ASA dummy1;};
  union{double c3;                      ASX_ASA dummy3;};
};
typedef FlexibleElement<> Element;
// ASX::SOA for an SoA container
typedef ASX::Array<FlexibleElement, CONT_SIZE, ASX::AOS> Container;

Container container;
container[5].c3= 2;           // OK, no change
```

The above code shows the two critical code features that must be present in every flexible structure definition.

- The structure must contain a typedef ASX::ASAGroup<GroupType,t_id> ASX_ASA, where the user chosen type GroupType defines the *grouping size*. The size of each component group must be smaller or equal than the grouping size.
- All components must be a member of a component group. Each component group must be embedded in an *anonymous union*, which includes a dummy component of type ASX_ASA. Memory is wasted if the component groups have different sizes.

Grouping of components within a union should be performed with an *anonymous struct*; otherwise, the grouped components (c1 and c2 in the example above) would occupy the same memory and could not be used simultaneously. Most compilers support this use of an anonymous structure, although it is not part of the C++ standard. If this is not supported, a normal named structure can be used instead; however, then this name has also to appear in the access syntax.

Note that in the example above, had we required just one element of type short (i.e., if float c1 were grouped with short c2 rather than short c2[2]), then both the AoS and the ASA code would still execute correctly, even though the elements in the group would have different sizes. Moreover, the overall size of the container would not change in either case: for the AoS pattern, this is because of data alignment by the compiler; for the ASA pattern, it is because of the explicit alignment according to the grouping size. The grouping of differently-sized components is demonstrated in more detail in the example groupingASA in the ASX library.

31.4.3 Array-Valued Container

In the previous example, we have already used an array of components (shorts); however, the array components were located in the same group, so they are not separated in memory if we switch to the SoA layout. If we want to put the array components into different groups then we must use a different syntax. In the simplest case we want a large array-valued container with flexible layout. This is achieved with the provided class ASX::FlexibleArray, which interacts with the container class ASX::Array in almost the same way as the user defined structures FlexibleElement in the examples before; here we merely need an additional ::TTypeASA because that is how C++ supports template typedefs.

```
// AoS pattern: concise but restricted to AoS layout
typedef float Element[ARR_SIZE];
typedef Element Container[CONT_SIZE];

// ASA pattern: a bit longer but handles both AoS and SoA
typedef ASX::FlexibleArray<float, ARR_SIZE> FlexElement;
typedef FlexElement::TTypeASA<> Element;
// ASX::SOA for an SoA container
typedef ASX::Array<FlexElement::TTypeASA, CONT_SIZE, ASX::AOS> Container;

Container container;
container[5][1]= 2;            // OK, no change
```

The full example code is available in the folder arrayASA in the ASX library.

31.4.4 Nesting of Composite Types

The flexible structure definitions can be nested to form a larger flexible structure. For this purpose, we use the FlexibleElement defined in Section 31.2 and the FlexElement defined in Section 31.4.3 and add one more component.

```
// AoS pattern: concise but restricted to AoS layout
struct Element {
    struct{ Type1 c1; Type2 c2; Type3 c3; } comp1;
    float comp2[ARR_SIZE];
    int comp3;
};
typedef Element Container[CONT_SIZE];

// ASA pattern: a bit longer but handles both AoS and SoA
template <ASX::ID t_id= ASX::ID_value>
struct LargeFlex {
    typedef ASX::ASAGroup<int,t_id> ASX_ASA;
    FlexibleElement<t_id>      comp1;
    FlexElement::TTypeASA<t_id> comp2;
    union{ int          comp3;   ASX_ASA dummy3; };
};
typedef LargeFlex<> Element;
// ASX::SOA for an SoA container
typedef ASX::Array<LargeFlex, CONT_SIZE, ASX::AOS> Container;

Container container;
container[5].comp1.comp3= 2; // OK, no change
```

Since the flexible structures already consist of component groups internally, they are not embedded in a union; only the last component of native type requires one.

Because the grouping size inside a flexible structure is hard-coded into the `ASX::ASAGroup<...>` typedef, the nesting of flexible structures is only possible if all their grouping sizes are the same. In the above example, `sizeof(Type1)` is the grouping size of `FlexibleElement` from Section 31.2 and `sizeof(float)` is the grouping size of `FlexElement` from Section 31.4.3 so for the above code to function correctly these sizes must be equal. This restriction could be removed by making the grouping size a template parameter of every flexible structure definition. But this would create considerable additional code complexity for all cases in order to resolve few exceptional cases of mismatched nested grouping sizes and therefore has not been implemented.

The corresponding example in the ASX library is named `nestingASA`.

31.5 FINAL EVALUATION

31.5.1 Performance

Memory access patterns are critical for performance, especially on the GPU where caches are smaller. The data layout greatly influences the memory access patterns and therefore the choice of AoS or SoA layout has a large impact on overall program performance. This section discusses how to make the correct decision and reports on the resulting speedups.

For testing, we choose a kernel that performs a *saxpy*-type (scalar alpha X plus Y) operation; however, alpha and the components of the containers X and Y are not scalars but structures or short arrays themselves; therefore, *gaxpy* (general axpy) is a more appropriate name. This is a good candidate to test the effective global memory performance for multi-valued containers because it has no on-chip data reuse. The tests cover the full spectrum of index access patterns from linear indexing to a random permutation. From the linear index list $0, 1, \ldots$ we create a permuted list by replacing index i with a random j that fullfills $|i - j| < d/2$ for a chosen sampling diameter d. By varying d we obtain access patterns of different irregularity and Figure 31.1 shows the results on a NVIDIA GeForce GTX 480 card in a 64-bit Linux system running the `g++-4.3.2` and `nvcc-3.1` compilers.

A SoA layout is almost always parallelized vertically, i.e., multiple instances of the same structure component are processed in parallel, whereas an AoS layout is almost always parallelized horizontally, i.e., multiple components of the same structure instance are processed in parallel. Figure 31.1 gives quantitative support for these choices, because the less typical combinations, shown as dashed lines, are clearly worse.

The comparison of the usual combinations, shown as solid lines, is dramatic. The SoA layout is $3.7\times$ faster on the regular patterns as they typically appear in structured numerical simulations, but it loses by a similar factor of $3.3\times$ on the irregular patterns that are typical of statistical and database processing. This clearly shows that one cannot rely on the same data layout for all purposes. A tool is required that can quickly switch from one layout to the other to find out which setting is best, and the ASX library provides exactly this functionality.

In practice, the situation is even more complex, because different application containers might require different data layouts. Up to now, finding the best data layout for each container was infeasible, because changing the syntax for even a single container from one layout to the other is very time consuming and error-prone. With the ASX library, each container can be easily configured to a

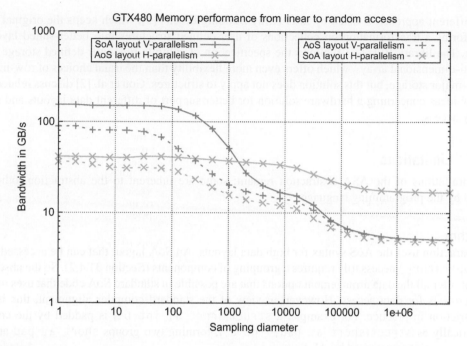

FIGURE 31.1

Memory performance on two large containers in which each element consists of four floats. Access patterns vary from linear element indexing on the left, over increasingly irregular access in the middle, to a completely random permutation on the right. All four combinations of two data layouts (AoS and SoA) and two parallelization strategies (horizontal and vertical) are presented. The mismatched combinations (dashed lines) perform clearly worse. The matching combinations (solid lines) differ by 3.7× on the left and 3.3× on the right, which demonstrates the large speedups that can be gained by choosing the correct data layout (see color insert).

different layout by setting a template parameter in the class definition. This ensures that the best possible memory performance can be obtained.

31.5.2 Related Work

AoS and SoA layouts are discussed in tutorials about SIMD processing for various architectures, e.g., CPU [4], GPU [6] or the Cell processor [3]. They advocate the use of SoA and vertical parallelism because this gives the fastest processing in case of large, linearly indexed data sets. Hybrid formats that adapt the data layout to the memory access granularity of the hardware by grouping of instances or components result in arrays of structures of arrays [1] or structures of arrays of structures [7] constructions, respectively. Such application-specific data layout optimizations appear in many high performance codes, often leading to machine-specific code paths for the most critical parts of a program. The contribution in this paper is an abstraction that allows the selection of different data layouts within the same code. The data layout can be changed at compile-time for each container.

A different approach is taken by Intel Array Building Blocks [5], which keeps the original layout but performs a transformation on collections of user-defined structures into better-suited layouts at runtime. The library Blitz++ [9] allows the specification of compile-time user-defined storage orders for multi-dimensional arrays, which offers even more flexibility than the usual choices of row-major or column-major storage, but this solution does not apply to structures. Gou et al. [2] discuss related work and new ideas concerning a hardware solution for better support of different data layouts and strided memory access.

31.5.3 Limitations

Some limitations of the ASA abstraction remain; some are inherent to the abstraction, others are induced by the programming language.

Algorithm

The abstraction uses the AoS syntax for both data layouts. An SoA layout that can be accessed with a single `operator[]` necessarily requires a grouping of components (Section 31.4.2). So the abstraction does not offer all the data arrangement options that are possible in standard SoA code that uses multiple `operator[]`s for data access. However, in view of the standard compiler alignment, this is not a big restriction in practice. For example, a `struct{short a; int b;}` is padded by the compiler automatically as `struct{short a, pad; int b;}`, forming two groups `short a, pad` and `int b` of the same size as required by ASA.

An abstraction integrated into the programming language would have a smoother syntax and better checks on correctness; therefore, a certain awareness about data type sizes and their alignment is required from the programmer as can be seen in the examples of Sections 31.4.2 to 31.4.4.

Coding

The abstraction aims at leaving the AoS code unchanged and enabling the flexible layout by simply changing the container definition. However, references to container elements must also be changed as discussed in Section 31.4.1. Nonetheless, this is still much less effort (see, e.g., the differences between the examples simpleAoS and simpleASA in the ASX library) than changing a standard AoS code to a standard SoA code (see, e.g., the differences between the examples simpleAoS and simpleSoA).

There are some restrictions with respect to dynamic memory allocation on the GPU. The statically sized ASX::Array can be used to allocate on-chip shared memory in CUDA. The dynamically sized ASX::Vector can also be stored in a previously statically allocated part of shared memory, but it cannot be used for its allocation. Concerning global memory, CUDA Toolkit 3.2 supports dynamic allocation of global memory on NVIDIA Fermi-based GPUs.

Performance

The user-chosen grouping of components is hard-coded by the placement of the unions. Optimization of the grouping size requires code changes in the container definition. Luckily, the granularity of memory access is given by the hardware manufacturers, so often it is not difficult to choose the most efficient grouping size, e.g., selecting a size that avoids bank conflicts in on-chip shared memory.

31.5.4 Benefits

Section 31.5.1 showed the performance benefits of choosing the correct data layout. In theory, one could obtain these benefits manually, if one is willing to write an exponential number of code variants that correspond to the different assignments of data layouts to the containers: two choices for each container, 2^N code variants for N containers. Clearly, this is infeasible, and the flexible ASA code improves the situation on all levels: algorithm development, coding, and performance:

Algorithm
- Algorithm development is independent of the data layout.
- Externally defined data layouts can be quickly integrated with new algorithms.

Coding
- The more intuitive AoS syntax can be used throughout the code.
- The same template function can be used to update single elements and indexed elements within a container.

Performance
- Performance of AoS vs. SoA for individual containers, groups of containers, or the entire project can be evaluated rapidly by changing a few template parameters.
- AoS vs. SoA comparison and optimization can be integrated into an auto-tuning framework without the need for source code manipulation.

Acknowledgment

A big thank you goes to Cliff Woolley from NVIDIA for helping with the organization of the paper.

References

[1] J. Abel, K. Balasubramanian, M. Bargeron, T. Craver, M. Phlipot, Applications tuning for streaming SIMD extensions, Technical report, Intel, 1999.

[2] C. Gou, G. Kuzmanov, G.N. Gaydadjiev, SAMS multi-layout memory: providing multiple views of data to boost SIMD performance, in: T. Boku, H. Nakashima, A. Mendelson (Eds.), ICS'10: Proceedings of the 24th ACM International Conference on Supercomputing, ACM, Tsukuba, Ibaraki, Japan, 2010, pp. 49–59.

[3] IBM, Developing code for Cell – SIMD. http://publib.boulder.ibm.com/infocenter/ieduasst/stgv1r0/topic/com.ibm.iea.cbe/cbe/1.0/Programming/L3T2H1_37_DevelopingCodeForCellSIMD.pdf, 2006.

[4] Intel, A Guide to Vectorization with Intel C++ Compilers. http://software.intel.com/file/31848, 2010.

[5] Intel, Intel array building blocks. http://software.intel.com/en-us/articles/intel-array-building-blocks/, 2011.

[6] B. Oster, Advanced CUDA tutorial. http://www.nvidia.com/content/cudazone/download/Advanced_CUDA_Training_NVISION08.pdf, 2008.

[7] J. Siegel, J. Ributzka, X. Li, CUDA memory optimizations for large data-structures in the gravit simulator, in: L. Barolli, W.-C. Feng (Eds.), Proc. Workshop on Simulation and Modelling in Emergent Computational Systems (SMECS) at ICPP 2009, IEEE Computer Society, Vienna, Austria, 2009, pp. 174–181.

[8] R. Strzodka, ASX (Array of Structs eXtended). http://www.mpi-inf.mpg.de/%7Estrzodka/software/ASX/, 2010.

[9] T. Veldhuizen, Blitz++ library. http://www.oonumerics.org/blitz/, 2006.

Processing Device Arrays with C++ Metaprogramming

32

Jonathan M. Cohen

In this chapter, I will explain how C++ metaprogramming techniques can be used to simplify the development of CUDA-based libraries. The chapter will walk through the design of a high-level library to process arrays in CUDA. For illustrative purposes, I will describe this library in the context of numerical solutions of partial differential equations. The basic technique can be useful in a wide variety of application domains such as image processing, agent modeling, particle systems, or other data-parallel routines. Source code for this chapter can be found online at http://code.google.com/p/cuda-metaprog.

32.1 INTRODUCTION, PROBLEM STATEMENT, AND CONTEXT

Say we have a device array class like this:

```
struct DeviceArray1D {
  int _size;
  float *_ptr; // device pointer

  DeviceArray1D(int size) : _size(size), _ptr(0) { cudaMalloc(...); ...}
  ~DeviceArray1D() { if (_ptr) { cudaFree(_ptr); } }
};
```

We wish to provide an application program interface (API) for adding two of these arrays together. For efficiency, we want the addition to be performed inside a CUDA kernel with one thread per element, so we add a CUDA routine and a host wrapper function:

```
__global__ void addition_kernel(
    int n, float *result, float *a, float *b)
{
  int i = threadIdx.x + blockIdx.x * blockDim.x;
  if (i < n)
    result[i] = a[i] + b[i];
}
```

```
void addition(DeviceArray1D &result, DeviceArray1D &a, DeviceArray1D &b)
{
  int n = result._size;
  addition_kernel<<(n+255)/256, 256>>>(n, result._ptr, b._ptr, b._ptr);
}
```

Later we need a routine for adding three arrays, so we add the following function to our API:

```
void addition(
  DeviceArray1D &result,
  DeviceArray1D &a,
  DeviceArray1D &b,
  DeviceArray1D &c);
```

We may also need a routine that adds three arrays, where each of them may have their indices shifted by a different amount (e.g., to implement a finite-difference stencil). Another useful routine would be one that scales each input array by a different constant before adding them all together. Maybe we also want one that combines scaling with shifting or pointwise multiplication.

In fact, the list of all useful permutations of these routines could be quite long for a generic API. In order to have intermediate results stored in registers rather than written out to global memory between operations, all of these shifting, adding, and scaling operations should execute inside a single CUDA kernel rather than as a sequence of separate kernels. On the other hand, fusing all operations into a single kernel would require adding a separate routine for all possible combinations of scaling, shifting, and arithmetic we wish to support. The combinatorial explosion that ensues quickly leads to an unwieldy code base that is hard to use, painful to implement, and difficult to maintain.

The techniques described in this chapter allow a programmer to create an API in which a sequence of operations over an array can be automatically fused into a single CUDA kernel at compile time. Rather than provide one API call for all possible combinations, a single functor is built using metaprogramming techniques and then applied to each element of the result array. This style of programming a graphical processing unit (GPU) has been demonstrated before in the context of Python generating CUDA [1], but it is often useful to embed the metaprogram directly in the same source file as the actual program. Because CUDA has a fully compliant C++ template preprocessor, this is possible using C++ metaprogramming techniques [2]. Although the examples in this chapter use the DeviceArray1D class described earlier in this chapter, they could also be applied to other data structures such as thrust::device_vector using Thrust's "fancy iterator" pattern [4].

32.2 **CORE METHOD**

I would like to allow a client program to write array-wide expressions using natural C++ syntax and somehow get operator overloading to "do the right thing." For example, it would be convenient to write an expression involving shifting, scaling, and adding multiple arrays using standard operators, with operator[] indicating a shifted read:

```
DeviceArray1D A,B,C;
...
A = C[0] * (B[-1] - constant(2.0f) * B[0] + B[1]);
```

Rather than to stitch together the different computations at runtime via function calls, the approach taken in this chapter is to automatically generate a custom CUDA kernel using a variant of an advanced C++ technique called Expression Templates [6]. In Expression Templates, a complex C++ expression is converted into an abstract syntax tree (AST), which is represented as a templated C++ type. In the original Expression Templates technique, the AST was evaluated statically to produce a single value. In our version, the template preprocessor walks the AST to produce a CUDA kernel. The AST is then bound to a set of input parameters to form a closure, which is encapsulated inside a C++ functor. In essence, Expression Templates is used to build a code generator, which the compiler then triggers during template instantiation. One thing that makes this technique so powerful is that, in addition to generating a CUDA kernel, the compiler can generate other routines from the same AST, such as automatic parameter validation or a version of the kernel that runs on the host. Similar techniques have been used to generate fast linear algebra kernels [3] and scientific computing routines [5].

In the preceding code example, the compiler automatically generates a single CUDA kernel to execute the specified operation. If we examine the intermediate results from the C++ template preprocessor, the kernel looks something like this:

```
__global__ void auto_generated(int n, float *A, float *B, float *C)
{
    int i = threadIdx.x + blockIdx.x * blockDim.x;
    if (i < n)
        A[i] = C[i] * (B[i-1] - 2.0f * B[i] + B[i+1]);
}
```

Using this technique, we can build simple, flexible, and clean APIs capable of achieving high performance. All of the techniques in this chapter could apply equally well to higher dimensional arrays or even to other data structures over which some set of operations is to be performed in parallel.

32.3 IMPLEMENTATION

32.3.1 Building an AST in C++

To use C++ templates to represent an AST, we need a scheme for expressing a tree as a C++ type. The basic idea is to represent a tree node (corresponding to a single operation in a C++ expression tree) as a class, which I will call an Op. All Op classes must adhere to a protocol that they implement a static function exec(int i, PARM p) that returns a value for each result array position i based on some associated parameter p. The PARM type is template parameter to the Op class, and it refers to whatever additional state may be needed to implement exec. For example, if the Op represents reading from an input array, PARM would contain the array's base pointer. A generic Op will look like this:

```
template<class PARM>
struct SomeGenericOp {
    __device__ static float exec(int i, const PARM &p) {
        /* return some function evaluated at i with input parameter p */
    }
};
```

The combination of an Op with a specific instance of its input PARM state is called an OpWithParm:

```
template<class OP, class PARM>
struct OpWithParm {
  OpWithParm(const PARM &p) : parm(p) { }
  PARM parm;
  __device__ float exec(int i) const { return OP::exec(i, parm); }
};
```

The device function OpWithParm::exec() calls the Op's exec routine, passing it the index i and the bound PARM state. Note that the contents of the state, represented by the parm member variable, is bound at runtime, while the function to be called, represented by the OP template parameter, is bound at compile time.

The OpWithParm functor represents some device routine that will be applied to every element in an output array to generate a value. To implement our flexible array processing API, we want to implement arbitrary C++ expressions as instantiations of the OpWithParm template. This step is accomplished using a variant of Expression Templates, where C++ template type calculus can be used to trigger arbitrary code generation by the template preprocessor.

For example, say we want to trigger evaluation of the expression (i + 5) for each index i. The expression tree for this function is shown in Figure 32.1.

This tree consists of two types of nodes: leaves and internal nodes. Leaf nodes, colored light gray, compute some value directly as a function of a PARM instance and an index. Internal nodes, the top circle with the + inside, aggregate result from one or more children Op nodes. The implementation of a leaf node's exec routine directly delegates to its contained PARM instance to calculate a return value. PARM classes must implement a const member function value(int i) that computes a value directly from the index and optionally from its own state. Unlike Op::exec, this value will depend on the runtime contents of the PARM structure; therefore, it is a member function.

```
template<class PARM>
struct LeafOp {
  __device__ static float exec(int i, const PARM &p) {
    return p.value(i);
  }
};
```

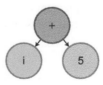

FIGURE 32.1

Tree representing the value i + 5.

The PARM class determines how to calculate the actual value. For example, consider these three basic types:

```
struct IdentityParm {
  IdentityParm(){ }
  __device__ float value(int i) const {
    return (float)i;
  }
};

struct ConstantParm {
  float _value;
  ConstantParm(float f) : _value(f) { }
  __device__ float value(int i) const {
    return _value;
  }
};

struct ArrayLookupParm {
  const float *_ptr;
  int _shift;

  ArrayLookupParm(const DeviceArray1D &array, int shift):
    _ptr(array._ptr), _shift(shift) { }

  __device__ float value(int i) const {
    return _ptr[(i+_shift)];
  }
};
```

IdentityParm returns i and does not require any internal state. ConstantParm returns a fixed constant, which is determined at runtime. ArrayLookupParm provides a way to access a DeviceArray1D by returning the associated value, optionally shifting the lookup index by a given amount (shift). A LeafOp can be bound to any of these PARM types and then bound to a particular PARM instance via an OpWithParm to create a self-contained functor.

Expression Templates can be used to build functors without requiring any of the types to be declared by the user of the API. For example, to create a functor that wraps up the ConstantParm as a functor, the API provides a host routine constant(float) that converts from a float value to a functor. Similarly with identity():

```
OpWithParm<LeafOp<ConstantParm>, ConstantParm>
constant(float value) {
  return OpWithParm<LeafOp<ConstantParm>, ConstantParm >(
    ConstantParm (value));
}

OpWithParm<LeafOp<IdentityParm>, IdentityParm>
identity() {
```

```
    return OpWithParm<LeafOp<IdentityParm>, IdentityParm>();
}
```

To expose the ArrayLookupParm via a functor, we provide an overloaded version of the DeviceArray1D::operator[] where the parameter represents the shift amount.

```
OpWithParm<LeafOp<ArrayLookupParm>, ArrayLookupParm>
DeviceArray1D::operator[](int shift) {
    return OpWithParm<LeafOp<ArrayLookupParm>,ArrayLookupParm>(
      ArrayLookupParm(g, shift));
}
```

In all of these cases so far, the functor consists of a single LeafOp. This allows expression trees consisting of only a single leaf node, which in conjunction with a way to invoke the functor for each output entry is enough to express simple assignment and copy operations.

```
template <typename T>
__global__ void kernel_assign(T functor, float *result, int size)
{
    int i = blockIdx.x * blockDim.x + threadIdx.x;

    if (i < size) {
        result[i] = functor.exec(i);
    }
}

template<typename OP, typename PARM>
DeviceArray1D &
DeviceArray1D::operator=(const OpWithParm<OP,PARM> &func)
{
    kernel_assign<<<(_size+255)/256, 256>>>(func, _ptr, _size);
    return *this;
}
```

DeviceArray1D::operator= is overloaded to take an OpWithParm functor as the right-hand side. The assignment operator calls kernel_assign, which fills the array with the results of the functor invoked at each index. Because the assignment operator is templated on the OP and PARM types, neither the API nor the user code needs to explicitly specify the functor types. The following assignment examples demonstrate the power of this technique — complex type calculus and template expansion can be invoked by the template preprocessor, but the expanded types remain entirely hidden from the API user by further templating the assignment routines:

```
DeviceArray1D A(100), B(100);
B = constant(5.0f); // assign 5.0f to all entries in B
A = B[0];           // copy B to A, with no offset
```

In order to create arbitrary expressions, we need a way to aggregate leaf nodes via internal nodes to create complex expressions trees. Each internal node will represent a single C++ operation, which can be a unary, binary, ternary, or general n-ary function. We will illustrate how binary functions can be expressed in our system for pairwise addition of input vectors; other cases are similar.

```
template<typename LPARM, typename RPARM>
struct ParmPair {
  LPARM left;
  RPARM right;
  ParmPair(const LPARM &l, const RPARM &r) :
    left(l), right(r) { }
};

template<class LOP, class ROP, class LPARM, class RPARM>
struct PlusOp {
  __device__ static float exec(
      int i, const ParmPair<LPARM, RPARM> &p) {
    return LOP::exec(i,p.left) + ROP::exec(i,p.right);
  }
};
```

`ParmPair` aggregates two `PARM` objects into a single struct that can be passed around as a single entity, while the `PlusOp::exec` adds the results of two child `Op::exec` calls together. Using the expression templates technique for building types automatically via template functions, `operator+` is overridden to emit the appropriately instantiated `PlusOp` template:

```
template<class LOP, class LPARM, class ROP, class RPARM>
OpWithParm<PlusOp<LOP, LPARM, ROP, RPARM>, ParmPair<LPARM, RPARM> >
operator+(
  const OpWithParm<LOP, LPARM> &left,
  const OpWithParm<ROP, RPARM> &right)
{
  return OpWithParm<PlusOp<LOP, ROP, LPARM, RPARM>,
          ParmPair<LPARM, RPARM> >(
            ParmPair<LPARM, RPARM>(left.parm, right.parm))
}
```

All C++ operators can be wrapped this way, which allows ASTs to be constructed to represent arbitrary C++ expressions. Because operator precedence is unaffected by operator overloading, the C++ parser will properly apply grouping to build an AST following standard order of operations. For example, the following listing produces the expression tree shown in Figure 32.2 and evaluates it for each entry A[i]. Leaf nodes are the three circles with the 0.5, B[i], and C[i] inside them, and internal nodes are the two circles with the * and + inside them.

```
DeviceArray1D A(100), B(100), C(100);
A = constant(0.5f) * (B[0] + C[0]);
```

When you compile with the "nvcc -keep" option, the output of the C++ preprocessor is written to a file that can be examined. The generated code for this expression is shown at the end of this section; it has been slightly edited for clarity. Notice that the code specifies how to walk the expression tree with sequences of .left and .right to select values from the PARM structure. Because structures are laid out at compile time, these expressions are evaluated statically and compiled into a hard-coded offset from the base of the generated_OpWithParm structure.

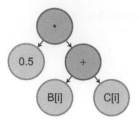

FIGURE 32.2

Abstract syntax tree for the expression: A = constant(0.5f) * (B[0] + C[0]).

```
__global__ void generated_kernel_assign(
  generated_OpWithParm ftor,
  float *dst,
  int nx)
{
  int i = blockIdx.x * blockDim.x + threadIdx.x;
  if (i < nx) {
    dst[i] = ftor.parm.left._value *
      (
        ftor.parm.right.left._ptr[i+functor.parm.right.left._shift] +
        ftor.parm.right.right._ptr[i+functor.parm.right.right._shift]
      );
  }
}
```

32.3.2 Handling Boundary Conditions

Finite-difference stencils require some way of handling the case when the stencil overhangs the edge of the array, known as a boundary condition. Because our framework allows for shifted reads, we need to handle what happens when we read from out-of-bounds values. Periodic boundary conditions are a simple example, in which case out-of-bounds reads "wrap around." For example, a read from the location -1 actually returns the value stored in location _size-1.

The simplest strategy for handling out-of-bounds reads is to check all accesses in the Array LookupParm. For this, we can write a separate version called ArrayLookupPeriodicParm:

```
struct ArrayLookupPeriodicParm {
  const float *_ptr;
  int _shift;
  int _size;

  ArrayLookupPeriodicParm(const DeviceArray1D &array, int shift) :
    _ptr(array._ptr), _shift(shift), _size(array._size) { }

  __device__ float value(int i) const {
    return _ptr[((i+_shift)+_size)%_size];
  }
};
```

Different versions of `ArrayLookupParm` can each implement a different policy for how to handle boundary conditions. Rather than overloading `operator[]`, the API can provide member functions that instantiate different boundary condition handling routines such as `read_periodic`, `read_neumann`, `read_dirichelet`, and so on.

A downside to explicitly handling out-of-bounds accesses is that it inserts boundary handling logic before every read, even though most reads will be in-bounds. An alternate approach is to use so-called ghost cells (sometimes referred to as boundary cells, apron cells, or halos). Ghost cells are suitable for situations where out-of-bounds accesses are known to be only slightly outside the allocated range. The array is padded in both directions by a small amount, and these padded "ghost" cells can be filled in with values to achieve the desired boundary conditions. No special handling is needed for out-of-bounds reads, although an extra routine is required to fill in the ghost values appropriately.

32.3.3 **Automatic Bounds Checking**

Using ghost cells, we can read past the end of an array by shifting beyond the extent of the ghost cells, resulting in undefined values or memory errors. However, because we have an explicit representation for the memory access patterns, we can automatically generate a routine to validate all accesses using range calculus before the kernel is launched.

First, define a basic range class:

```
struct Range {
  int _min_i, _max_i;
  Range(int min_i, int max_i) : _min_i(min_i), _max_i(max_i) { }
  bool contains(const Range &r) const {
    return r._min_i >= _min_i && r._max_i <= _max_i;
  }
  Range shift(int shift) const {
    return Range(_min_i + shift, _max_i + shift);
  }
};
```

We also need to extend the `DeviceArray1D` class to support ghost cells:

```
struct DeviceArray1D {
  int _padding;
  float *_base_ptr;
  ...

  DeviceArray1D(int size, int padding) : ... {
    // allocate size + 2 * padding entries
    cudaMalloc((void **)&_base_ptr, ...);
    _ptr = _base_ptr + _padding;
    ...
  }
  ~DeviceArray1D() { if (_ptr) { cudaFree(_base_ptr); } }
};
```

Given an instance of `DeviceArray1D`, we can obtain its range as `Range(-_padding, _size+_padding-1)`. We also add a routine to `OpWithParm` that checks whether the output range is entirely inside the valid region of this functor. Note that this routine will be called from the host.

```
template<class OP, class PARM>
struct OpWithParm {
    ...
    bool validate(const Range &rng) const {
      return OP::validate(rng, parm);
    }
};
```

Before the CUDA kernel gets launched, we check that the functor is valid over the desired output range.

```
DeviceArray1D::operator=(const OpWithParm<OP,PARM> &func)
{
  if (!func.validate(range())) {
      // run—time error
  }
  ...
}
```

All Op classes must follow the protocol that `OP::validate(Range)` returns true if calls to that instance's `exec` method will produce valid results inside the given range, and false otherwise. Each `PARM` class implements the same protocol, and `LeafOp::validate` delegates to its `PARM` instance. For example, the `ConstantParm::validate` will always return true, while `ReadArrayParm::validate` will check the range against its input:

```
struct ArrayLookupParm {
    ...
    Range _rng;
    ArrayLookupParm(const DeviceArray1D &grid, int shift) :
      _rng(grid.range()), ... { }

    bool validate(const Range &rng) const {
        return _rng.contains(rng.shift(_shift));
    }
};
```

Validation of a range by child nodes is recursively aggregated up the tree to the root by internal nodes. For example, `PlusOp::validate` checks whether both its left and right children are valid over the given range:

```
template<class LOP, class ROP, class LPARM, class RPARM>
struct PlusOp {
    ...
```

```
static bool validate(
    const Range &rng, const ParmPair<LPARM, RPARM> &p) {

    return LOP::validate(rng, p.left) && ROP::validate(rng, p.right);
    }
};
```

A call to `validate` on the top-level Op will walk the entire AST, aggregating results up from the leaves and returning true if the entire tree is valid at the root and false otherwise. Note that this mechanism for delegating work down to the leaves and then aggregating results back up to the top is basically the same scheme we previously used to generate the CUDA kernel. In both cases, the C++ template preprocessor is used to write a function on the fly based on a traversal of the AST, dispatching to specific code-generation snippets by type. This technique could be used in a number of other ways as well, such as to generate a multicore version of the CUDA routines or to count how many floating-point operations will be executed by the CUDA kernel.

32.4 EVALUATION

The goal of using the technique described in this chapter is not necessarily to produce the highest-performing code, but to make it easy for API users to access the power of the GPU with minimal effort. Here, we will look at two example applications demonstrating reasonable performance with highly readable code.

32.4.1 One-Dimensional Heat Equation

In this example, I will describe a program that solves the one-dimensional heat equation,

$$\frac{\partial \varphi(x,t)}{\partial t} = \alpha \frac{\partial^2 \varphi(x,t)}{\partial x^2} + s(x)$$

where φ is the unknown function describing temperature in a medium, α is the coefficient of thermal diffusion, and s is a nonvarying source term.

In a Forward-Time, Centered-Space (FTCS) discretization, the φ function is advanced forward in time using an explicit Euler update, and the spatial derivative is discretized via a centered scheme. In the following version of the program, called METAPROG, the per-step update happens in two automatically generated CUDA kernels, and spatial boundary conditions are enforced directly inside the array lookup as described in Section 32.3.2.

```
int n = ...;
float dt = 0.1f; // time step size
float dx = 0.5f; // grid spacing
float alpha = .1f; // coefficient

// no padding, since boundary conditions enforced in array read
DeviceArray1D phi(n,0), dphidt(n,0), source(n,0);

... // initialize source and phi to something
```

```
for (int step=0; step < 100; step++) {
  // update dphidt in one kernel
  dphidt = source[0] + constant(alpha/(dx*dx)) *
           (phi[-1] - constant(2) * phi[0] + phi[1]);
  // forward time step in another kernel
  phi = phi[0] + constant(dt) * dphidt[0];
}
```

I have implemented three other versions of this program: SERIAL is a serial implementation running on a single CPU thread, HAND is a hand-coded CUDA implementation, and HAND-OPT is an optimized CUDA implementation that uses shared memory to reduce the number of global memory loads. These program versions were run on both low- and high-end systems: a Lenovo T61P laptop with an NVIDIA Quadro FX 570M and a mobile dual-core Intel T7300 Centrino running at 2 GHz, and a high-end HPC workstation with an NVIDIA Tesla C2050 with ECC enabled and a quad-core Intel Core i7 running at 3.07 GHz.

Implementation	Lines of Code	Time (speed-up) — Laptop	Time (speed-up) — HPC Workstation
SERIAL	28	5760.5 ms (1x)	3068.3 ms (1x)
METAPROG	18	543.3 ms (11x)	36.5 ms (84x)
HAND	20 host + 34 device	523.2 ms (11x)	29.5 ms (104x)
HAND-OPT	20 host + 54 device	217.8 ms (26x)	30.2 ms (101x)

The METAPROG version is on par with the performance of both handwritten CUDA versions, but requires significantly fewer lines of code, with no device code written at all. Compared with the SERIAL version, METAPROG yields one order of magnitude improvement on the laptop and two orders of magnitude on the workstation, yet requires less coding effort. The SERIAL implementation could be made significantly faster by using multithreading and SSE optimizations, but then the programmer effort would increase by several factors. Given a programmer who seeks minimal effort, multiple orders of magnitude of performance are indeed achievable via the API presented here.

Note that on the workstation, HAND-OPT is actually slightly slower than the unoptimized HAND version. This demonstrates a common problem with performance programming — incremental performance improvements may take an enormous amount of programmer effort owing to complex and unpredictable performance effects. Typically, the largest return on investment is achieved by simply getting the code running on a GPU at all. Therefore, lowering the amount of effort required to port simple codes to CUDA C can be highly beneficial to a wide variety of application developers.

32.4.2 Multigrid Solver

By modifying the way array entries are accessed for reading and writing, we can add support for array slicing, where some subset of an array is treated as a new "virtual" array. For example, an array with n values can be treated as an array with $n/2$ entries by accessing only every other value. A simple use-case for this functionality is to downsample an array of n values to an array of $n/2$ values by taking the average of every adjacent pair of values. By combining array slicing with the other techniques described in this chapter, I implemented a GPU-accelerated multigrid solver for a one-dimensional Poisson equation. I also implemented an identical solver using serial C running on a CPU. The GPU version that uses the aforementioned metagprogramming API requires 119 lines of code versus 129 for the serial C version, and it also runs faster: 5 times faster on the laptop and 27 times faster on the HPC workstation. The code for this example can be found in the online googlecode repository mentioned at the beginning of the article.

32.5 FUTURE DIRECTIONS

In this chapter, I have sketched the implementation of an API for modifying 1-D arrays. The techniques presented here, however, are not specific to any particular data structure or set of operations. They could be applied for manipulation of 2-D images, 3-D arrays, collections of agents, or any other data-parallel processing system.

This style of API design provides the compiler with access to the entire AST for an expression, which allows API routines to be generated at per-expression granularity. Given an AST, a variety of routines, types, or values can be generated at compile time using the techniques presented in this chapter. One interesting use-case of this functionality is to create multiple backends for the same expression. For example, one backend could generate a function that emits an OpenCL kernel string, which can be executed via an OpenCL context. Another backend could provide a multicore CPU implementation or even a multi-GPU implementation that automatically copies data between the multiple GPUs based on declared data access patterns.

References

[1] A. Klöckner, N. Pinto, Y. Lee, B. Catanzaro, P. Ivanov, A. Fasih, PyCUDA: GPU run-time code generation for high-performance computing. http://arxiv.org/abs/0911.3456, 2009.

[2] A. Alexandrescu, Modern C++ Design: Generic Programming and Design Patterns Applied, Addison-Wesley, New York, 2001.

[3] J. Siek, A. Lumsdaine, Scientific computing in object-oriented parallel environments, in: Y. Ishikawa, R.R. Oldehoeft, J.V.W. Reynders (Eds.), First International Conference (ISCOPE'97), Springer, New York, 1998.

[4] Thrust. http://code.google.com/p/thrust/.

[5] T. Veldhuizen, Arrays in Blitz++, in: D. Caromel, R.R. Oldehoeft, M. Tholburn (Eds.), Scientific Computing in Object Oriented Parallel Environments (ISCOPE'98), Springer, New York, 1998.

[6] T. Veldhuizen, Expression Templates, C++ Report, 26–31 June 1995.

GPU Metaprogramming: A Case Study in Biologically Inspired Machine Vision

33

Nicolas Pinto and David D. Cox

In this chapter, we present a tutorial on ways that metaprogramming techniques — dynamically generating specialized code at runtime and compiling it just-in-time — can be used to greatly accelerate an application. We use filter-bank convolution, a key component of the biologically inspired machine vision systems that form the core of our research program, as a case study to illustrate these techniques. We present an overview of several key themes in template metaprogramming and culminate in a full example of GPU auto-tuning in which an instrumented GPU kernel template is built and the space of all possible instantiations of this kernel is automatically grid-searched to find the best implementation on various hardware/software platforms. We show that this method can, in concert with traditional hand-tuning techniques, achieve significant speedups, particularly when a kernel will be run on a variety of hardware platforms.

33.1 INTRODUCTION, PROBLEM STATEMENT, AND CONTEXT

In recent years, digital cameras have become increasingly inexpensive and ubiquitous, and cameras are now embedded in a wide array of devices, from cellphones to cars. This explosion in imaging technology has led to enormous opportunity in the field of computer vision, as the need grows for algorithms that can automatically analyze, organize, and react to the new torrent of digital imagery.

While traditional machine vision algorithms achieve modest success in certain tasks (e.g., detecting the presence of a face in an image), many other visual tasks that are easily achieved by humans remain extremely challenging for computers (e.g., recognizing the identity of a particular face).

Inspired by the ease with which the human brain is able to solve visual tasks, many so-called biologically inspired vision approaches have emerged [1–6]. The basic architecture of the brain-inspired vision systems that we work with is shown in schematic form in Figure 33.1. Briefly, this architecture consists of a cascade of multiple layers of linear filtering operations and static nonlinearities. Learning algorithms adjust the parameters of these operations and adapt the network to a given kind of input. Models from this class have been shown to achieve state-of-the-art performance in a variety of object and face recognition domains [4, 5, 7–9].

However, there are two major challenges associated with the construction of biologically inspired vision systems. First, the brain is a massively parallel computer, with millions of processing elements; mimicking this level of computational power is not a trivial undertaking. Second, while biology has given us some hints about how a visual system can be organized, neuroscience experiments have

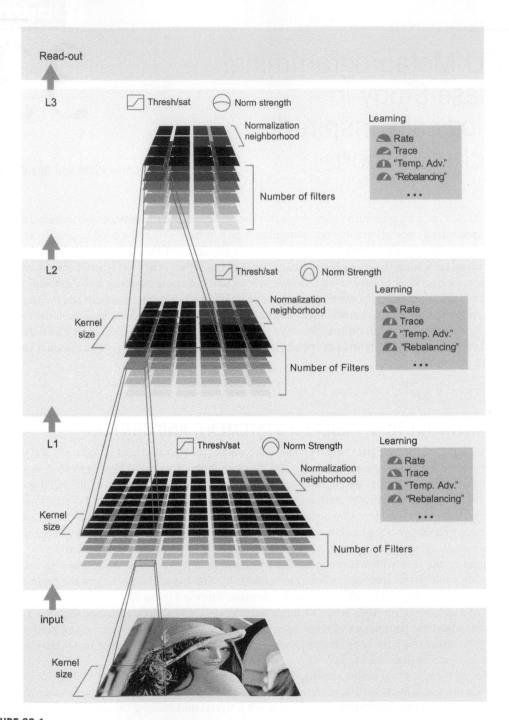

FIGURE 33.1

A schematic diagram of a multilayer biologically inspired vision system.

provided us to date with relatively few constraints on the details and parameters to be used. As a result, we are often left exploring the *space* of possible models, rather than evaluating any one model, *per se*.

The combination of these two challenges raises a unique problem in high-performance computing. The scale of the models to be studied demands enormous compute power. Properly utilized, GPUs begin to provide the level of power needed to undertake serious large-scale visual system modeling. However, the second challenge — the need to explore a wide range of different kinds of biologically inspired models — poses a serious challenge. In the process of optimization, an algorithm is typically carefully matched to a set of hardware/software resources, exploiting as much regularity in the underlying problem and inputs as possible. For instance, if an input image is always known to be small, or of a power-of-two in width and height, such information can be exploited to craft an optimal implementation. However, for our problem, we must build algorithms that can tolerate widely varying inputs, since a major drive of our work is to find model parameters that can provide high levels of face and object recognition performance.

Here, we focus on one key suboperation of our models: filter-bank convolution (i.e., the application of a number of filters to an incoming image, in parallel). We show how this operation can be performed efficiently, in spite of widely varying conditions (e.g., different sizes and number of filters) using a dynamically specialized template metaprogramming approach.

33.2 **CORE METHOD**

Optimization is often an exercise in specialization — increasing the performance of a given algorithm on a given piece of hardware requires taking advantage of specific details of the algorithm, the kinds of inputs it will see, and the resources available in the hardware (and software stack) on which the algorithm will run. In many contexts, however, we must operate within an indeterminate, broadly-defined, or changing parameter space, where we cannot be guaranteed that all inputs will look similar. In our own research, a key computational bottleneck is a compute-intensive filter-bank 3-D convolution operation (which mimics one part of the processing that is thought to be done by biological neurons). However, while optimizing such operations is straightforward using standard techniques when all of the relevant dimensions of the input and filters are known, in our research, we must search a wide range of possible neural network architectures to find those that are best at specific tasks. Thus, we need high-performance solutions not just to one particular problem but to a family of possible instantiations of that problem.

We employ a metaprogramming approach in which the high-level language Python is used to generate parameterized CUDA kernel code using a string template engine.[1] These generated kernels are then just-in-time compiled and run with the "behind-the-scenes" help of the PyCUDA toolkit [10, 11]. Meta-kernels such as these allow the developer to achieve a high degree of flexibility in exploring many different optimization strategies while avoiding unnecessary hand-coding or combinatoric issues when multiple strategic decisions interact. Finally, we show how meta-parameter selection can be turned over to an automated process, allowing for auto-tuning of kernels across different inputs (where resource requirements vary wildly) and different hardware generations (where resource availability varies).

---

[1] We note that our use of the term "template metaprograming" here is distinct from its use in the context of C++, where it often refers to the specific case of metaprogramming with C++'s built-in templating system.

While Python's strength in string processing (e.g., Cheetah, Mako, Jinja), general scientific computing (e.g., Numpy, Scipy, Matplotlib), and GPU programming (e.g., PyCUDA, PyOpenCL) provides a particularly convenient platform for metaprogramming, the techniques described here could just as well be applied in any programming language. Indeed, the only language facilities one needs to apply metaprogramming are a means of transforming a template string (available in one form or another in virtually every language) and a means to compile and run a kernel (which is readily available in both CUDA and OpenCL).

In this case study, we describe several basic regimes where metaprogramming can lead to cleaner code, improved understanding, and ultimately better performance. We discuss how a metaprogramming philosophy can lower the cost of trying out new ideas, since these ideas can be merged into an existing common code base, and how some relatively simple template-driven features (such as full/partial loop unrolling) can produce significant speedups without cluttering code. Finally, we show how meta-parameter auto-tuning can yield significant speedups, by generating many dynamically specialized kernels from a single, understandable kernel template. A sample of our approach to this problem is presented below.

33.3 ALGORITHMS, IMPLEMENTATIONS, AND EVALUATIONS
33.3.1 Towards General, Optimized Code

Figure 33.2 shows the basic components of a GPU metaprogramming approach. The central insight is that rather than writing GPU kernels, one can write kernel *templates*, with multiple optimization strategies and optional paths embedded in a single piece of code. With an appropriate template

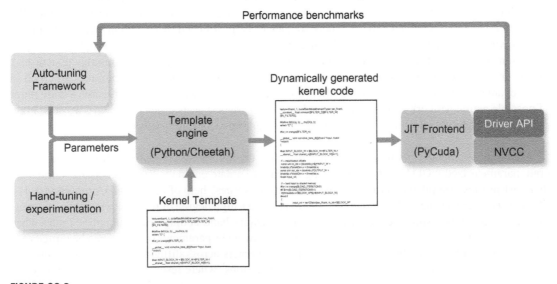

FIGURE 33.2

A schematic diagram of a basic GPU metaprogramming system (see color insert).

transformation module, a dynamically specialized kernel is generated based on a given set of parameters, and this code is compiled just in time. The choice of parameters can be done manually, or it can be turned over to an auto-tuning algorithm. We will begin by discussing general strategies for template metaprogramming and will close with a complete auto-tuning example.

In the following examples, we use Python, a high-level language, in combination with PyCUDA [10, 11], a package that seamlessly wraps the CUDA Driver API. While the use of an interpreted language might initially seem at odds with the goals of high-performance computing, the fraction of time spent in the "outer loop" of an HPC application is typically small relative to that spent in a handful of critical sections.

A key advantage of just-in-time compilation of a kernel from a string is that new kernels can easily be generated on the fly. Below, using a standard Python string templating package, Cheetah [12], we can substitute values into a kernel, evaluate conditionals, and generate iterated structures using loops. As an example (the details of which are not important, for the moment):

```
...

#for nk in xrange($N_KERNELS)

  __global__
  void cudafilter_kernel_${nk}
  (
    float4 *input
#for o in xrange($N_OUTPUT4S)
  , float4 *output$o
#end for
  )
  {

    // — Shared—memory buffer for the input tiles
    __shared__ float shared_in          \
      [$BLOCK_H]                         \
      [$N_FILTER_ROWS]                   \
      [$INPUT_D]                         \
      [$INPUT_BLOCK_W + ${int($PAD_SHARED)}];

...
```

At runtime, instances of variables such as $N_KERNELS are replaced with a value passed into the template engine, and conditionals (#if) and loops (#for) are evaluated and expanded. Note that the template allows for the manipulation of structures that are not normally accessible in C code, including variable length argument lists, and runtime generation of new functions and variable names. The resulting kernel code is then compiled and called entirely from Python. Such dynamic code generation opens up a wide range of possibilities, some of which are described below.

33.3.2 **Syntax-Level Code Control**

One major advantage of a template metaprogramming approach is that it makes it easy to produce CUDA kernels that would otherwise be tedious or error-prone to produce by hand. As a simple illustration of how templates can work, we next show how they can be used to gain fine-grained control over loop unrolling, in analogy to the "unroll" pragma provided in CUDA. Since branching is relatively expensive on the GPU architecture, large performance gains can often be achieved by avoiding for loops and unrolling a loop manually. In a template metaprogramming context, this is easy. For example, in the inner loop of our filtering operation, we could write:

```
// Loop unrolling example
#for d in xrange($FILTER_D)
    #for i in xrange($FILTER_W)
        v = shared_in[threadIdx.x+$i][$d];
        #for n in xrange($N_FILTERS)
            w = constant[$d][$i][$n];
            sum$n += v*w;
        #end for
    #end for
#end for
```

which at runtime would generate the following code, dependent on the values of FILTER_D, FILTER_W, and N_FILTERS:

```
...
v = shared_in[threadIdx.x+0][0];
w = constant[0][0][0];
sum0 += v*w;
w = constant[0][0][1];
sum1 += v*w;
w = constant[0][0][2];
sum2 += v*w;
w = constant[0][0][3];
sum3 += v*w;
v = shared_in[threadIdx.x+1][0];
w = constant[0][1][0];
sum0 += v*w;
w = constant[0][1][1];
...
```

One consequence of the above template-based approach is that we can generate distinct, specialized versions of kernels with very fine control for, say, a $N\times4\times4\times8$ filter-bank and for a $N\times8\times8\times4$ filter-bank. Creating such specialized versions by hand would be tedious and error-prone.

Of course, loop unrolling isn't universally beneficial; unrolling a loop consumes a larger number of registers, which, depending on the register usage in the rest of the kernel, can lead to dramatic decreases in performance if the number of available registers is exceeded. In addition to allowing a straightforward framework for turning on and off unrolling, it is easy to imagine how the above example could be updated to support *partial* loop unrolling, balancing register usage against branching costs. More sophisticated variants are possible as well. For instance, the unrolled portion of a partially unrolled loop needn't be implemented using the same code as the "rolled" portion. Such flexibility is valuable, for instance, when one uses shared memory resources as if they were registers (a technique known as "register spilling"), allowing potentially much deeper unrolling of loops.

More generally, control of a kernel's code at a syntactic level also enables one to have a much more fluid relationship with memory resources. Since templates operate at the level of syntax, it is, for instance, possible to use registers as an "indexable" resource (e.g., register_masquerading_as_array$index) without overly complicating the code. Conversely, as mentioned above, if one is register-limited, one can instead use shared memory resources as if they were registers.

In addition, metaprogramming can be valuable in cases where portions of an algorithm may be optionally "turned off" at runtime. In a traditional kernel, such modularity might be implemented with branching; in a metaprogram, the code for the disabled portions would simply not be generated. Likewise, any time when kernel-wide constants cannot be known when a kernel is written, but can be known at runtime (e.g., because they are user-settable), metaprogramming provides a coherent framework for "baking" these constants directly into the kernel.

33.3.3 Exploring Design Decision Space More Freely

Another important area where metaprogramming can be highly valuable is in exploring a space of design decisions. A GPU developer is typically confronted with a multitude of decisions when developing a CUDA implementation: what kind of memory to use and how to access it (e.g., linear memory, tex1D, tex2D, etc.), how to lay out data in memory, etc.

In some cases, subtle decisions can produce large differences in performance. Below we illustrate one such design decision, wherein a given filter weight is stored in constant memory (organized as filter × height × width), and the kernel is either configured to index the filter to be computed by thread index, or by a constant (with multiple filter responses being computed through multiple kernel executions). A templated example is shown below, wherein the inner loop is conditioned (at template-time) by the variable USE_THREAD_PER_FILTER:

```
# — Constant memory usage example

#for i in xrange($FILTER_W)
    #for k in xrange($FILTER_D)
        v = shared_in[(threadIdx.x+$i)][$k];

        #if $USE_THREAD_PER_FILTER
            w = constant[threadIdx.y][$i][$k];
        #else
            w = constant[$FILTER_ID][$i][$k];
```

```
        #end if

            sum += v*w;
        #end for
#end for
```

Benchmarking the code, we find that our performance is cut in half when USE_THREAD_PER_FILTER is true. Here, inspection of the disassembled cubin (using the *decuda* disassembler [13]) is instructive. A snippet from the disassembled cubin when USE_THREAD_PER_FILTER is false is shown below:

```
...
mad.rn.f32 $r0, s[$ofs2+0x0000], c0[$ofs2+0x0000], $r0
mad.rn.f32 $r0, s[$ofs2+0x0008], c0[$ofs2+0x0008], $r0
mad.rn.f32 $r0, s[$ofs2+0x000c], c0[$ofs2+0x000c], $r0
mad.rn.f32 $r0, s[$ofs2+0x0010], c0[$ofs2+0x0010], $r0
...
```

Here, each mad is a multiply-add instruction, and the cubin is dominated by a long, back-to-back stream of arithmetic. If, on the other hand, USE_THREAD_PER_FILTER is true, we see a very different pattern of instructions:

```
...
mad.rn.f32 $r4, s[$ofs3+0x0000], $r4, $r1
mov.b32 $r1, c0[$ofs2+0x0008]
mad.rn.f32 $r4, s[$ofs3+0x0008], $r1, $r4
mov.b32 $r1, c0[$ofs2+0x000c]
...
```

Here, multiply-adds are interleaved with "move" instructions, resulting in a computation that is vastly less efficient.

It should be noted that this issue is now properly documented in the CUDA C Programming Guide — indexing constant memory by a threadIdx can lead to sub-optimal constant memory access patterns. However, the issues here are subtle and easy to miss. Metaprogramming provides a mechanism for flexibly exploring multiple optimization paths at the same time, which provides a powerful tool for understanding the hardware at a deeper level. Importantly, not all aspects of the hardware contributing to performance are (or reasonably can be, e.g., for proprietary/competitive reasons) documented. In such cases, template metaprogramming lowers the cost of trying different strategies, allowing one to exploit the hardware much more fully.

There is also no guarantee that the many design choices that one must make are independent. That is, at any given stage of optimization, a particular path may legitimately represent the best one, given the current context of the rest of the program. However, as other aspects of the design are tweaked and iterated, there is no guarantee that these earlier insights still hold, especially as different approaches differently tax the scarce resources of the hardware (e.g., registers, shared memory, memory bandwidth). Metaprogramming yields the significant advantage that intermediate design decisions can be made explicit and both "forks" in the path can be kept in place, without incurring actual, performance-eroding if/then branches in the kernel itself. This approach frees up the developer to revisit past choices, without incurring a combinatoric explosion of separate pieces of code. Retesting sets of assumptions can be done frequently and programmatically from the "outer" framework of code.

33.3.4 Auto-Tuning

Above, we have shown how metaprogramming can assist in the manual optimization of an implementation in a regime where the parameters of the input (e.g., input size, filter size, number of filters, etc.) are fixed. Our optimization process also implicitly assumes a given hardware context, unless we explicitly tweak our designs on different generations and grades of GPUs. In reality, our particular problem of interest (like many problems) demands that our implementation must work over a wide range of input parameters, and on a variety of different kinds of hardware. Ideally, we'd like to have the best possible implementation in each context, without having to undertake a massive effort in hand-tuning. A powerful extension of template metaprogramming is *auto-tuning*: allowing software to choose the best set of meta-parameters for a given set of inputs and hardware/software stack.

Here, we take the simplest possible approach to auto-tuning, performing a coarse grid search across a range of possible meta-parameter values.

The meta-parameters to be tuned include:

1. Degree of Loop Unrolling
2. Amount of Register Spilling
3. Memory structure type — linear memory, tex1D, tex2D, etc.
4. Execution Configuration (i.e., Block and Grid dimensions)
5. Number of filters to compute per kernel invocation (i.e., thread work size)
6. Shared-memory padding
7. etc.

Pseudo-code demonstrating a basic auto-tuning algorithm is shown below; code for a complete auto-tuned implementation of filter-bank convolution can be found online [14].

```
"""
=======================================================
Auto-Tuning Pseudo-Code (Filter-bank Convolution)
=======================================================

Parameters
-----------
  arr:    input array (height x width x depth)
  fb:     filter-bank (nfilters x fsize x fsize x depth)
"""

# — Get the set of metaprogramming / templating parameters
```

```
# to explore during auto-tuning
mp_set = get_metaprog_parameter_set()

# -- Get information about the hardware
# (may include GPU architecture, host CPU, memory, etc.)
hw = get_hardware_specs()

# -- Get information about the software stack
# (may include CUDA Runtime version, CUDA Driver version, etc.)
sw = get_software_specs()

db = autotuning_db() # the auto-tuning database

# -- Has this combination of input array, filter-bank,
# hardware and software already been tuned ?
if (arr, fb, hw, sw) not in db:

    # -- If not, we'll loop over each element in the
    # metaprogramming parameter set, gather timing
    # information and select the fastest code
    n_warmups, n_runs = get_n_trials()
    best_func, best_time = None, inf
    for mp in mp_set:

        tmpl = get_gpu_src_template(arr, fb)

        # Render the code template (using, e.g., Cheetah).
        # Note that only a subset of 'mp' will be used here
        # (e.g., unrolling factor, register spilling, etc.)
        gpu_src = render_gpu_src_template(tmpl, mp)

        # Compile the source code or retrieve it from a cache
        # (using NVCC through, e.g., PyCUDA)
        # Note that only a subset of 'mp' will be used here
        # (e.g., using fast math, constraining the number
        # of registers through the compiler, etc.)
        gpu_bin = compile_and_cache_gpu_src(hw, sw, gpu_src, mp)

        # Load the GPU binary code and prepare the device
        # for execution (using the Driver API through, e.g., PyCUDA)
        func = load_and_prepare_gpu_execution(gpu_bin, mp)

        # Warm up the GPU
        for _ in n_warmups: func()

        # Collect timings
        timings = list()
```

```
        for _ in n_runs:
            start = time()
            func()
            end = time()
            timings.append(end-start)

        # Is this version of the code faster?
        if median(timings) < best_time:
            best_time = median(timings)
            best_func = func

        # — Add the result to the database
        db.add(arr, fb, hw, sw, best_func)

else:

    best_func = db.get(arr, fb, hw, sw)

# — Return the best performing code
return best_func
```

33.4 FINAL EVALUATION

For the purposes of demonstration, we chose a set of 73 meta-parameter configurations (i.e., 73 unique combinations of values of the above meta-parameters) and auto-tuned for four different input parameter sets, which roughly bracket the range of possible input shapes and sizes that are encountered in our experiments. The results of auto-tuning, on four NVIDIA GPUs spanning multiple generations of graphics hardware, multiple end-user markets (gaming versus professional), and a wide range of variation in hardware-level resources available, are shown in Table 33.1.

Table 33.1 Performance of Default and Auto-Tuned Implementations Across a Range of Hardware/Software Platforms and Input Problem Sizes

GPU/SDK	Input	Filter-Bank	Default (gflops)	Auto-Tuned (gflops)	Boost
8600GT	256x256x8	64x9x9x8	5.493 ± 0.019	33.881 ± 0.068	516.8%
CUDA2.3-i7-2.66-	512x512x4	32x13x13x4	11.619 ± 0.007	33.456 ± 0.045	187.9%
Ubuntu-9.10	1024x1024x8	16x5x5x8	19.056 ± 0.017	33.109 ± 0.632	73.7%
	2048x2048x4	4x8x8x4	23.824 ± 0.055	38.867 ± 0.118	63.1%
9400M CUDA3.1-	256x256x8	64x9x9x8	2.177 ± 0.013	15.796 ± 0.049	625.6%
Core2Duo-3.06-	512x512x4	32x13x13x4	5.562 ± 0.001	15.331 ± 0.004	175.6%
MacOSX-10.6	1024x1024x8	16x5x5x8	2.309 ± 0.022	4.571 ± 0.015	98.0%

(Continued)

Table 33.1 *(Continued)*

GPU/SDK	Input	Filter-Bank	Default (gflops)	Auto-Tuned (gflops)	Boost
9600M GT CUDA3.1- Core2Duo-3.06- MacOSX-10.6	256x256x8 512x512x4 1024x1024x8 2048x2048x4	64x9x9x8 32x13x13x4 16x5x5x8 4x8x8x4	6.710 ± 0.005 13.606 ± 0.002 20.034 ± 0.113 25.781 ± 0.044	36.584 ± 0.023 35.582 ± 0.003 26.084 ± 6.243 46.945 ± 0.100	445.2% 161.5% 30.2% 82.1%
C1060 CUDA2.3-i7- 2.66-Ubuntu-9.10	256x256x8 512x512x4 1024x1024x8 2048x2048x4	64x9x9x8 32x13x13x4 16x5x5x8 4x8x8x4	104.188 ± 0.051 125.739 ± 0.109 144.279 ± 0.764 180.060 ± 0.018	168.083 ± 0.372 234.053 ± 0.266 243.697 ± 0.346 322.328 ± 0.348	61.3% 86.1% 68.9% 79.0%
GTX295 CUDA2.3- i7-2.66- Ubuntu-9.10	256x256x8 512x512x4 1024x1024x8 2048x2048x4	64x9x9x8 32x13x13x4 16x5x5x8 4x8x8x4	126.563 ± 0.590 172.701 ± 0.014 104.972 ± 0.011 120.693 ± 0.020	262.848 ± 0.176 317.108 ± 0.056 168.298 ± 0.174 226.534 ± 0.195	107.7% 83.6% 60.3% 87.7%
GTX285 CUDA2.3- i7-2.66- Ubuntu-9.10	256x256x8 512x512x4 1024x1024x8 2048x2048x4	64x9x9x8 32x13x13x4 16x5x5x8 4x8x8x4	123.396 ± 0.016 143.277 ± 0.044 148.841 ± 0.465 205.152 ± 0.015	197.006 ± 0.219 270.206 ± 0.209 310.276 ± 0.538 376.685 ± 0.070	59.7% 88.6% 108.5% 83.6%
C2050 CUDA3.2- i7-3.2-Gentoo	256x256x8 512x512x4 1024x1024x8 2048x2048x4	64x9x9x8 32x13x13x4 16x5x5x8 4x8x8x4	382.169 ± 3.875 660.839 ± 2.308 435.771 ± 0.485 292.918 ± 0.427	459.263 ± 8.971 766.553 ± 2.403 457.606 ± 1.255 618.854 ± 0.079	20.2% 16.0% 5.0% 111.3%
C2050 CUDA3.2- i7-2.66- Ubuntu-10.4	256x256x8 512x512x4 1024x1024x8 2048x2048x4	64x9x9x8 32x13x13x4 16x5x5x8 4x8x8x4	358.723 ± 0.355 596.186 ± 0.972 427.330 ± 0.149 290.290 ± 0.128	361.714 ± 0.406 646.275 ± 1.809 446.557 ± 0.115 532.097 ± 0.382	0.8% 8.4% 4.5% 83.3%
GTX480 CUDA3.1-i7- 3.2-Gentoo	256x256x8 512x512x4 1024x1024x8 2048x2048x4	64x9x9x8 32x13x13x4 16x5x5x8 4x8x8x4	467.631 ± 19.100 834.838 ± 8.275 542.808 ± 1.135 378.165 ± 0.537	471.902 ± 11.419 974.266 ± 3.809 614.019 ± 0.904 806.628 ± 0.168	0.9% 16.7% 13.1% 113.3%
GTX480 CUDA3.2-i7- 3.2-Gentoo	256x256x8 512x512x4 1024x1024x8 2048x2048x4	64x9x9x8 32x13x13x4 16x5x5x8 4x8x8x4	523.316 ± 8.677 872.353 ± 12.375 634.110 ± 0.411 387.524 ± 0.176	623.759 ± 13.754 1002.976 ± 7.685 667.912 ± 0.364 811.660 ± 0.212	19.2% 15.0% 5.3% 109.4%
GTX480 CUDA3.2- i7-2.66- Ubuntu-10.10	256x256x8 512x512x4 1024x1024x8 2048x2048x4	64x9x9x8 32x13x13x4 16x5x5x8 4x8x8x4	500.089 ± 2.173 791.829 ± 3.111 618.739 ± 2.311 386.885 ± 0.180	503.348 ± 1.526 857.970 ± 2.337 666.090 ± 2.404 733.318 ± 0.449	0.7% 8.4% 7.7% 89.5%

(Continued)

Table 33.1 *(Continued)*

GPU/SDK	Input	Filter-Bank	Default (gflops)	Auto-Tuned (gflops)	Boost
GTX580	256x256x8	64x9x9x8	617.446 ± 1.340	669.465 ± 0.856	8.4%
CUDA3.2-i7-	512x512x4	32x13x13x4	979.426 ± 3.037	1074.493 ± 0.660	9.7%
3.2-Gentoo	1024x1024x8	16x5x5x8	745.302 ± 0.111	763.134 ± 0.278	2.4%
	2048x2048x4	4x8x8x4	479.679 ± 0.071	903.934 ± 0.714	88.4%
GTX580	256x256x8	64x9x9x8	585.959 ± 1.240	585.959 ± 1.240	0.0%
CUDA3.2-i7-	512x512x4	32x13x13x4	947.092 ± 2.903	1035.999 ± 0.849	9.4%
2.66-Ubuntu-10.4	1024x1024x8	16x5x5x8	726.412 ± 0.398	744.973 ± 0.571	2.6%
	2048x2048x4	4x8x8x4	474.681 ± 0.160	887.974 ± 1.017	87.1%

Table 33.2 Performance of Auto-Tuned Implementations on Two Hardware Platforms, Including Performance Tuned on One Platform and Run on the Other

	Optimized for:		
Run on:	9400M	GTX480	Tuning Speedup
9400M	0.32s	2.52s	675%
GTX480	0.016s	0.011s	52%

Large performance gains are observed for the auto-tuned meta-kernels as compared to the "default" parameter set, which was hand-picked to allow correct execution of all input ranges on all GPUs, without running up against hardware limitations.

Interestingly, we note that a different peak-performing meta-parameter set was chosen for each input size for each hardware platform. Given the many demands on system resources that trade off against each other, a different "sweet-spot" implementation exists for different incoming inputs and for different combinations of hardware resources. To illustrate this point, in Table 33.2 we show the performance with the best auto-tuned parameters for two different hardware platforms (a 9400M laptop-grade GPU, and a GTX480 desktop GPU), as well as the performance for each if the parameter sets were swapped (i.e., if we tuned on the 9400M and ran on the GTX480, and vice versa). In all cases, best parameter sets were chosen using half of the time trials, and the median performances shown in the table were computed using the remaining trials. We see large differences in performance (in some cases over 100%) when a custom hardware auto-tuned kernel is used, as compared to when an optimal kernel for a different platform is used. Such performance differences are particularly important when development is done on a different machine (e.g., a laptop) than where the code will be run in production mode. Similarly, for applications that are widely deployed on a variety of user hardware, optimal performance can be achieved by either optimizing *in situ* or shipping with a database of parameter sets for different platforms.

Table 33.3 Performance of Auto-Tuned Implementations on Two Input Configurations, Including Performance Tuned for One Configuration and Run with the Other

| Run on: | Optimized for: | | Tuning Speedup |
	Config1	Config2	
config1	11.1ms	15.7ms	41%
config2	fails	10.8ms	not comparable

Similarly, in Table 33.3 we show the effect of tuning on one input configuration and running on another. Again, significant speedups are obtained using kernels tailored to a specific input configuration, as opposed to generic kernels optimized under different conditions. Without metaprogramming, hand-tuning for each of the many hardware configurations in existence and for many different input configurations would be a tedious and error-prone process. By contrast, template metaprogramming in combination with a simple auto-tuning scheme allows optimal implementations to be chosen for any platform and input size.

33.5 FUTURE DIRECTIONS

Above, we have demonstrated how writing kernel *templates*, rather than complete kernels *per se*, can result in cleaner, more readable code and can provide a coherent framework for exploring the interactions of many implementation decisions. In our auto-tuning example code, we show a straightforward implementation of a brute-force auto-tuning approach, in which we grid search a large number of combinations and permutations of template parameters and auto-benchmark. While this brute-force search procedure leads to surprisingly good results despite its simplicity, it clearly becomes suboptimal as the number of template parameters increases. Thus, an important future direction is the application of more intelligent optimization algorithms — e.g., decision trees, simplex search, simulated annealing, genetic algorithms, or other derivative-free de-randomized methods (such as Covariance Matrix Adaptation) — to more efficiently search the space of possible implementations.

Acknowledgments

This work was funded by the Rowland Institute of Harvard, the NVIDIA Graduate Fellowship, and the National Science Foundation (IIS 0963668). Hardware support was generously provided by the NVIDIA Corporation. The authors would also like to thank Andreas Kloeckner for providing and supporting the PyCuda package and Cliff Woolley for helpful comments on earlier versions of this chapter.

References

[1] K. Fukushima, Neocognitron: a self-organizing neural network model for a mechanism of pattern recognition unaffected by shift in position, Biol. Cybern. 36 (4) (1980) 93–202.

[2] T. Serre, L. Wolf, S. Bileschi, M. Riesenhuber, T. Poggio, Robust object recognition with cortex-like mechanisms, TPAMI 29 (3) (2007) 411–426.

[3] J. Mutch, D.G. Lowe, Object class recognition and localization using sparse features with limited receptive fields, IJCV 80 (1) (2008) 45–57.

[4] N. Pinto, D. Doukhan, J.J. DiCarlo, D.D. Cox, A high-throughput screening approach to discovering good forms of biologically inspired visual representation, PLoS Comput. Biol. 5 (11) (2009) e1000579, doi: 10.1371/journal.pcbi.1000579.

[5] N. Pinto, J.J. DiCarlo, D.D. Cox, Establishing good benchmarks and baselines for face recognition, in: ECCV Workshop on Faces in Real-Life Images, 2008.

[6] K. Jarrett, K. Kavukcuoglu, M. Ranzato, Y. LeCun, What is the best multi-stage architecture for object recognition? ICCV, 2009.

[7] N. Pinto, D.D. Cox, J.J. DiCarlo, Why is real-world visual object recognition hard? PLoS Comput. Biol. 4 (1) (2008) e27.

[8] N. Pinto, J.J. DiCarlo, D.D. Cox, How far can you get with a modern face recognition test set using only simple features? CVPR, 2009.

[9] N. Pinto, D.D. Cox, Beyond simple features: a large-scale feature search approach to unconstrained face recognition, IEEE Autom. Face Gesture Recognit, 2011.

[10] A. Klöckner, N. Pinto, Y. Lee, B.C. Catanzaro, P. Ivanov, A. Fasih, Pycuda: Gpu run-time code generation for high-performance computing, Parallel Computing, Elsevier, CoRR, abs/0911.3456, 2009.

[11] PyCUDA. http://mathema.tician.de/software/pycuda, 2011 (accessed 26.02.11).

[12] Cheetah. http://www.cheetahtemplate.org/, 2011 (accessed 26.02.11).

[13] Decuda. https://github.com/laanwj/decuda/wiki, 2011 (accessed 26.02.11).

[14] Example code repository. http://www.github.com/gcg-metaprog-chapter/gcg.

A Hybridization Methodology for High-Performance Linear Algebra Software for GPUs

34

Emmanuel Agullo, Cédric Augonnet, Jack Dongarra, Hatem Ltaief, Raymond Namyst,
Samuel Thibault, and Stanimire Tomov

In this chapter, we present a *hybridization methodology* for the development of high-performance linear algebra software for GPUs. The methodology has been successfully used in MAGMA — a new generation of linear algebra libraries, similar in functionality to LAPACK, but extended for hybrid, GPU-based systems. Algorithms of interest are split into computational tasks. The tasks' execution is scheduled over the computational components of a hybrid system of multicore CPUs with GPU accelerators using StarPU — a runtime system for accelerator-based multicore architectures. StarPU enables the expression of parallelism through sequential-like code and schedules the different tasks over the hybrid processing units.

Using the StarPU framework, development is faster and cheaper than the development of algorithms exclusively for GPUs. Moreover, this framework allows the exploration of the unique strengths of the various hardware components in a hybrid system, resulting in hybrid algorithms that are better performance-wise than corresponding homogeneous algorithms designed exclusively for either GPUs or multicore CPUs.

34.1 INTRODUCTION, PROBLEM STATEMENT, AND CONTEXT

The large scale enabling of GPU-based architectures for high performance computational science depends on the successful development of fundamental numerical libraries. Major issues in terms of developing new algorithms, programmability, reliability, and user productivity must be addressed on these systems. At the same time, it becomes paramount to efficiently schedule algorithms over heterogeneous platforms to take advantage to the fullest extent of the computational power of their hybrid components. This chapter describes a methodology for developing these algorithms and libraries in the area of linear algebra (LA). The impact of developing and making LA libraries available is far-reaching because many science and engineering applications depend on them; these applications will not perform well unless the linear algebra libraries perform well.

The hybridization methodology is twofold. First, we design highly efficient algorithms optimized to run on a single GPU and its CPU host. This approach has been successfully used in the Matrix

Algebra on GPU and Multicore Architectures (MAGMA) project [1] and the libraries stemming from it. MAGMA is designed to be similar to the popular LAPACK library in functionality, data storage, and interface, to allow scientists to effortlessly port any LAPACK-relying software components to take advantage of new hybrid architectures. Second, we use the hybrid algorithms and kernels from the first approach as building blocks of higher-level algorithms designed for hybrid systems of multicore CPUs with multi-GPU accelerators. We use the StarPU [2] runtime system to schedule those tasks on the computational units. StarPU enables us to express parallelism through sequential-like code and schedules the different tasks over the hybrid processing units. We illustrate this approach with the Cholesky factorization, a fundamental and representative LA algorithm.

34.2 CORE METHOD

Our goal is to run numerical algorithms as fast as possible on complex architectures composed of multicore CPUs with GPU accelerators in a portable way. The proposed method is in three steps. The first step consists of writing the numerical algorithm at a high level of abstraction as a sequence of multiple tasks of fine granularity; a task can be executed on a CPU core, on a GPU, or on both resources simultaneously (hybrid task). The second step consists of providing high performance kernels with two interfaces, CPU and GPU, implementing each task. These kernels may already be available (such as vendor kernels) or may need to be designed (when highly optimized vendor kernels are not available). The final step requires integration of the high-level algorithm along with the kernel in a runtime system. The runtime system is then in charge of scheduling the different tasks onto the processing units without violating the dependences of the high-level algorithm while ensuring data availability and coherency.

We illustrate our method with the Cholesky factorization of dense matrices. This algorithm can be decomposed into fine granularity BLAS calls. We use CPU BLAS kernels from Intel MKL [3] and GPU BLAS kernels from the MAGMA library. We schedule the operations using the StarPU runtime system that exploits all computational CPU and GPU resources in a portable way on complex heterogeneous machines, hiding the low-level complexity.

34.3 ALGORITHMS, IMPLEMENTATIONS, AND EVALUATIONS
34.3.1 Cholesky Factorization

The Cholesky factorization (or Cholesky decomposition) of an $n \times n$ real symmetric positive definite matrix A has the form $A = LL^T$, where L is an $n \times n$ real lower triangular matrix with positive diagonal elements [4]. This factorization is mainly used as a first step for the numerical solution of linear equations $Ax = b$, where A is a symmetric positive definite matrix. Such systems arise often in physics applications, where A is positive definite due to the nature of the modeled physical phenomenon. The reference implementation of the Cholesky factorization for machines with hierarchical levels of memory is part of the LAPACK library. It consists of a succession of panel (or block column) factorizations followed by updates of the trailing submatrix. The algorithm can easily be parallelized using a fork-join approach since each update — consisting of a matrix-matrix multiplication — can be performed

```
1  for (k = 0;   k < Nt; k++)
2    A[k][k] = potrf(A[k][k])
3    for (m = k+1;   m < Nt; m++)
4      A[m][k] = trsm(A[k][k],A[m][k])
5    for (m = k+1;   m < Nt; m++)
6      for (n = k+1;   n < m; n++)
7        A[m][n] = gemm(A[m][k],A[n][k],A[m][n])
8      A[m][m] = syrk(A[m][k],A[m][m])
```

Listing 34.1. Tile Cholesky decomposition of a matrix A composed of Nt × Nt tiles.

in parallel (fork) but that a synchronization is needed before performing the next panel factorization (join). A variant of this algorithm is well suited for execution on a single GPU; we will present it in Section 34.3.2. In the multi-GPU case, the number of synchronizations of this algorithm would be a prohibitive bottleneck for performance. Instead, the panel factorization and the update of the trailing submatrix are broken into smaller tasks that operate on square submatrices of fine granularity, so-called *tiles*. The corresponding algorithm, initially developed for multicore architectures [5, 6], is called *tile Cholesky factorization*. It consists of the three nested loops of Listing 34.1 relying on four BLAS and LAPACK kernels. Since the single-GPU hybrid algorithms we present can be used as kernels for the tasks of multi-GPU algorithms, hybridization is twofold: at the task level and between tasks.

34.3.2 Kernels for Single CPU Cores and Single GPUs

Once the algorithm has been split into smaller tasks, high performance CPU or GPU kernels implementing each task need to be provided. If both the CPU and GPU implementations of a kernel are provided, the runtime will furthermore have the opportunity to schedule the task on either hardware. These kernels may already be available (such as vendor kernels) or may need to be designed (when highly optimized vendor kernels are not available). In the case of the tile Cholesky factorization, the four kernels needed are the LAPACK and BLAS routines: *spotrf*, *sgemm*, *strsm*, and *ssyrk*. Since the corresponding highly tuned implementations are already provided by the CPU vendor within the Intel MKL 10.1 library, we directly use the corresponding sequential routines from that library. For GPUs, NVIDIA provides high performance implementations of the *sgemm*, *strsm*, and *ssyrk* routines within the CUBLAS library. In different cases, depending on hardware and problem sizes, we use these kernels either from CUBLAS or MAGMA BLAS. The LAPACK *spotrf* routine is not provided by NVIDIA. We use the highly tuned version that we developed and made freely available in the MAGMA [1] library. In the rest of this section, we present the underlying algorithm as a roadmap to design high performance hybrid algorithms for a single CPU core enhanced by a GPU.

Hybrid Cholesky Factorization for a Single GPU. Listing 34.2 gives the hybrid Cholesky factorization implementation for a single GPU. Here da points to the input matrix that is on the GPU memory, work is a work-space array on the CPU memory, and nb is the blocking size. This algorithm assumes the input matrix is stored in the leading *n*-by-*n* lower triangular part of da, which is overwritten on exit by the result. The rest of the matrix is not referenced. Compared to the LAPACK reference algorithm, the only difference is that the hybrid one has three extra lines — 4, 9, and 13. These extra lines implement

```
1   for (j = 0;  j < *n; j += nb) {
2     jb = min(nb, *n-j);
3     cublasSsyrk('l','n', jb, j, -1, da(j,0),*lda, 1, da(j,j),*lda);
4     cudaMemcpy2DAsync(work, jb*sizeof(float), da(j,j), *lda*sizeof(float),
5                       sizeof(float)*jb, jb, cudaMemcpyDeviceToHost, stream[1]);
6     if (j + jb < *n)
7       cublasSgemm('n','t', *n-j-jb, jb, j, -1, da(j+jb,0), *lda, da(j,0),
8                      *lda, 1, da(j+jb,j), *lda);
9     cudaStreamSynchronize(stream[1]);
10    spotrf_("Lower", &jb, work, &jb, info);
11    if (*info != 0)
12      *info = *info + j, break;
13    cudaMemcpy2DAsync(da(j,j), *lda*sizeof(float), work, jb*sizeof(float),
14                      sizeof(float)*jb, jb, cudaMemcpyHostToDevice, stream[0]);
15    if (j + jb < *n)
16      cublasStrsm('r','l','t','n', *n-j-jb, jb, 1, da(j,j), *lda,
17                     da(j+jb,j), *lda);
18  }
```

Listing 34.2. Hybrid Cholesky factorization for single CPU-GPU pair (*spotrf*).

our intent in the hybrid code to have the *jb*-by-*jb* diagonal block starting at da(j,j) factored on the CPU, instead of on the GPU. Therefore, at line 4 we send the block to the CPU, at line 9 we synchronize to insure that the data has arrived, factor it next on the CPU using a call to LAPACK at line 10, and send the result back to the GPU at line 13. Note that the computation at line 7 is independent of the factorization of the diagonal block, allowing us to do these two tasks in parallel on the CPU and on the GPU. This is implemented by "scheduling" first the *sgemm* (line 7) on the GPU; this is an asynchronous call, hence the CPU continues immediately with the *spotrf* (line 10) while the GPU is running the *sgemm*.

To summarize, the following is achieved with this algorithm:

- The LAPACK Cholesky factorization is split into tasks;
- Large, highly data parallel tasks, suitable for efficient GPU computing, are statically "scheduled" for execution on the GPU;
- Small, inherently sequential *spotrf* tasks (line 10), not suitable for efficient GPU computing, are executed on the CPU using LAPACK;
- Small CPU tasks (line 10) are overlapped by large GPU tasks (line 7);
- Communications are asynchronous to overlap them with computation;
- Communications are in a surface-to-volume ratio with computations: sending nb^2 elements at iteration j is tied to $O(nb \times j^2)$ flops, $j \geq nb$.

34.3.3 Hybrid Algorithm Design Using StarPU

Accelerator-based platforms, such as multicore architectures enhanced by GPU accelerators, are complex to program. Not only does an algorithm need to be split into smaller tasks to enable the concurrent use of all the computational resources, but the data coherency must be ensured between the memories of the different units.

We delegate this complexity to the StarPU runtime system. This allows the programmer to focus on *what* to do (e.g., choosing a scheduling strategy) while the runtime system takes care of *how* to do it efficiently (e.g., ensuring data transfers and coherency). The monitoring of the system by the runtime furthermore allows the design of efficient, adaptive strategies. Because low-level technical issues no longer preoccupy the programmer, productivity is increased.

Once the algorithm has been subdivided into tasks, the program may be written as a succession of task insertions. As a task is a function that operates on data, those two notions are central to StarPU. First, data is registered into StarPU. Once data is registered, the application no longer accesses it directly through its memory address, but rather through a StarPU abstraction called a *handle*. The handle does not change during the program's execution. If the runtime decides to schedule a task onto a unit that does not have a valid copy of a data, the runtime will take care of the data movement. The pointer to the data will be internally updated, but the handle exposed to the application will remain unchanged. StarPU transparently guarantees that when a task needs to access a piece of data, it will be given a pointer to a valid data replica. Second, assuming that an implementation of the computational kernels is provided for each device (CPU core and GPU), a multi-version kernel called a *codelet* is defined on top of them.

In the end, a task can be defined independently of the device as a codelet working on handles. The tasks are then executed according to a scheduling strategy that can be either selected from a set of pre-existing policies or specifically designed for the task.

We now show in detail how to program the tile Cholesky factorization on top of StarPU:

Initialization. When initializing StarPU with `starpu_init`, StarPU automatically detects the topology of the machine and launches one thread per processing unit to execute the tasks.

Data registration. Each tile is registered into StarPU to be associated with a handle. As shown in Listing 34.3, the `tile_handle[m][n]` StarPU abstraction is obtained from each actual memory pointer, `tile[m][n]`. Several data types are pre-defined for the handles. Here, tiles are registered as matrices since a submatrix is itself a matrix.

Codelets definition. As shown at lines 38–42 for the `sgemm_codelet` in Listing 34.4, a codelet is a structure that describes a multi-versioned kernel (*sgemm* here). It contains pointers to the functions that implement the kernel on the different types of units: lines 1–14 for the CPU and 16–30 for the GPU. The prototype of these functions is fixed: an array of pointers to the data interfaces that describe the local data replicas, followed by a pointer to some user-provided argument for the codelet. The `STARPU_MATRIX_GET_PTR` is a helper function that takes a data interface in the matrix format and returns the address of the local copy. Function `starpu_unpack_cl_args` is

```
1  float *tile[mt][nt];                    // Actual memory pointers
2  starpu_data_handle tile_handle[mt][nt]; // StarPU abstraction
3
4  for (n = 0; n < nt; n++) //loop on cols
5      for (m = 0; m < mt; m++) //loop on rows
6          starpu_matrix_data_register(&tile_handle[m][n], 0,
7                                   &tile[m][n], M, M, N, sizeof(float));
```

Listing 34.3. Registration of the tiles as handles of matrix data type.

```
1   void sgemm_cpu_func(void *descr[], void *cl_arg) {
2       int transA, transB, M, N, K, LDA, LDB, LDC;
3       float alpha, beta, *A, *B, *C;
4
5       A = STARPU_MATRIX_GET_PTR(descr[0]);
6       B = STARPU_MATRIX_GET_PTR(descr[1]);
7       C = STARPU_MATRIX_GET_PTR(descr[2]);
8
9       starpu_unpack_cl_args(cl_arg, &transA, &transB, &M,
10                          &N, &K, &alpha, &LDA, &LDB, &beta, &LDC);
11
12      sgemm(CblasColMajor, transA, transB, M, N, K,
13            alpha, A, LDA, B, LDB, beta, C, LDC);
14  }
15
16  void sgemm_cuda_func(void *descr[], void *cl_arg) {
17      int transA, transB, M, N, K, LDA, LDB, LDC;
18      float alpha, beta, *A, *B, *C;
19
20      A = STARPU_MATRIX_GET_PTR(descr[0]);
21      B = STARPU_MATRIX_GET_PTR(descr[1]);
22      C = STARPU_MATRIX_GET_PTR(descr[2]);
23
24      starpu_unpack_cl_args(cl_arg, &transA, &transB, &M,
25                          &N, &K, &alpha, &LDA, &LDB, &beta, &LDC);
26
27      cublasSgemm(magma_const[transA][0], magma_const[transB][0],
28              M, N, K, alpha, A, LDA, B, LDB, beta, C, LDC);
29      cudaThreadSynchronize();
30  }
31
32  struct starpu_perfmodel_t cl_sgemm_model = {
33      .type   = STARPU_HISTORY_BASED,
34      .symbol = "sgemm"
35  };
36
37  starpu_codelet sgemm_codelet = {
38      .where     = STARPU_CPU|STARPU_CUDA, // who may execute?
39      .cpu_func  = sgemm_cpu_func, // CPU implementation
40      .cuda_func = sgemm_cuda_func, // CUDA implementation
41      .nbuffers  = 3, // number of handles accessed by the task
42      .model     = &cl_sgemm_model // performance model (optional)
43  };
```

Listing 34.4. A codelet implementing *sgemm* kernel.

also a helper function that retrieves the arguments stacked in the `cl_arg` pointer by the application. Those arguments are passed when the tasks are inserted.

Tasks insertion. In StarPU, a task consists of a codelet working on a list of handles. The access mode (e.g., read-write) of each handle is also required so that the runtime can compute the dependences between tasks. A task may also take values as arguments (passed through pointers). A task is inserted with the `starpu_insert_Task` function.[1] Lines 33–41 in Listing 34.5 shows how the *sgemm* task is inserted. The first argument is the codelet, `sgemm_codelet`. The following arguments are either values (key-word VALUE) or handles (when an access mode is specified). For instance, a value is specified at line 34, corresponding to the content of the `notrans` variable. On the right of line 40, the handle of the tile (m,n) is passed in read-write mode (key-word INOUT). Listing 34.5 is a complete implementation of the tile Cholesky algorithm from Listing 34.1, showing the ease of programmability.

Finalization. Once all tasks have been submitted, the application can perform a barrier using the `starpu_task_wait_for_all()` function (line 53 in Listing 34.5). When it returns, we can stop maintaining data coherency and put the tiles back into main memory by unregistering the different data handles. Calling `starpu_shutdown()` releases all the resources.

Choice or design of a scheduling strategy. Once the above steps have been completed, the application is fully defined and can be executed as it is. However, the choice of scheduling strategy may be critical for performance. StarPU provides several built-in, pre-defined strategies the user can select during initialization, depending on the specific requirements of the application. When the performance of the kernels is stable enough to be predictable directly from the previous executions (as is the case with Tile Cholesky factorization), one may associate an auto-tuned history-based performance model to a codelet as shown on lines 32–35 and 42 in Listing 34.4. If all codelets are associated with a performance model, it is then possible to

```
1  void hybrid_cholesky(starpu_data_handle **Ahandles,
2                       int M, int N, int Mt, int Nt, int Mb)
3  {
4   int lower = Lower;      int upper = Upper; int right = Right;
5   int notrans = NoTrans; int conjtrans = ConjTrans;
6   int nonunit = NonUnit; float one = 1.0f; float mone = -1.0f;
7
8   int k, m, n, temp;
9   for (k = 0; k < Nt; k++)
10  {
11    temp = k == Mt-1 ? M-k*Mb : Mb ;
12    starpu_Insert_Task(spotrf_codelet,
13      VALUE, &lower, sizeof(int), VALUE, &temp, sizeof(int),
14      INOUT, Ahandles[k][k],        VALUE, &Mb, sizeof(int), 0);
```

Listing 34.5. Actual implementation of the tile Cholesky hybrid algorithm with StarPU   *(continued)*

---

[1] Other interfaces not discussed here are also available.

```
15
16    for (m = k+1; m < Nt; m++)
17    {
18     temp = m == Mt-1 ? M-m*Mb : Mb ;
19     starpu_Insert_Task(strsm_codelet,
20       VALUE, &right, sizeof(int),    VALUE, &lower, sizeof(int),
21       VALUE, &conjtrans,sizeof(int), VALUE, &nonunit, sizeof(int),
22       VALUE, &temp, sizeof(int),     VALUE, &Mb, sizeof(int),
23       VALUE, &one, sizeof(float),    INPUT, Ahandles[k][k],
24       VALUE, &Mb, sizeof(int),       INOUT, Ahandles[m][k],
25       VALUE, &Mb, sizeof(int),       0);
26    }
27
28    for (m = k+1; m < Nt; m++)
29    {
30     temp = m == Mt-1 ? M-m*Mb : Mb;
31     for (n = k+1; n < m; n++)
32     {
33      starpu_Insert_Task(sgemm_codelet,
34        VALUE, &notrans, sizeof(notrans),
35        VALUE, &conjtrans, sizeof(conjtrans),
36        VALUE, &temp, sizeof(int),     VALUE, &Mb, sizeof(int),
37        VALUE, &Mb, sizeof(int),       VALUE, &mone, sizeof(float),
38        INPUT, Ahandles[m][k],         VALUE, &Mb, sizeof(int),
39        INPUT, Ahandles[n][k],         VALUE, &Mb, sizeof(int),
40        VALUE, &one, sizeof(one),      INOUT, Ahandles[m][n],
41        VALUE, &Mb, sizeof(int),       0);
42     }
43
44     starpu_Insert_Task(ssyrk_codelet,
45       VALUE, &lower, sizeof(int),    VALUE, &notrans, sizeof(int),
46       VALUE, &temp,  sizeof(int),    VALUE, &Mb, sizeof(int),
47       VALUE, &mone, sizeof(float),   INPUT, Ahandles[m][k],
48       VALUE, &Mb, sizeof(int),       VALUE, &one, sizeof(float),
49       INOUT, Ahandles[m][m],         VALUE, &Mb, sizeof(int), 0);
50    }
51    }
52
53    starpu_task_wait_for_all();
54    }
```

Listing 34.5. (Continued)

schedule the tasks according to their expected termination time. The most efficient scheduling strategy (among those available in StarPU) for the Cholesky factorization is based on the standard Heterogeneous Earliest Finish Time (HEFT) [7] scheduling heuristic which aims at minimizing the termination time of the tasks on heterogeneous platforms. Given the impact of data transfers, especially when it comes to multiple accelerators, we extended this policy to take data transfer into account and keep it as low as possible. StarPU also provides a framework to develop *ad hoc* scheduling strategies in a high-level way, but the methodology to write a scheduler in StarPU is outside the scope of this chapter.

34.4 FINAL EVALUATION
34.4.1 Performance Results Using Single GPU

The performance of the hybrid Cholesky factorization from Listing 34.2 simultaneously running on a NVIDIA GeForce GTX 280 GPU and on one core of a dual socket quad-core Intel Xeon running at 2.33 GHz is given in Figure 34.1. The factorization runs asymptotically at 300 Gflop/s in single and almost 70 Gflop/s in double precision arithmetic. The performance has been evaluated on a number of NVIDIA GPUs, including the Fermi-based Tesla C2050. For example, for matrix size of 9984, the hybrid algorithm runs at 631 Gflop/s on the GTX 480 and 507 Gflop/s on the C2050. The double precision performance on the C2050 is 240 Gflop/s for the same matrix size.

34.4.2 Multi-GPU Overall Performance

We now present performance results for a hybrid system of eight Intel Nehalem X5550 CPU cores running at 2.67 GHz enhanced with three NVIDIA Quadro FX 5800 GPUs running at 1.30 GHz. The overall performance of the method depends on the choice of the tile size which trades off parallelism and kernel performance. For the sake of simplicity, we chose a constant tile size. We empirically chose it equal to 960, which is well-suited for large matrices. The performance of matrix-matrix multiplication (*sgemm*) for this tile size is 20 Gflop/s per CPU core (obtained with the Intel MKL 10.1 library) and 333 Gflop/s per GPU (obtained with the MAGMA 0.2 library), respectively. A GPU kernel needs a dedicated CPU core to be executed. Therefore, the node can be viewed as three GPU/CPU pairs and five supplementary available CPUs. If the supplementary CPUs are not used, a performance upper bound of the node is equal to 1000 Gflop/s; if they are used, the upper bound becomes equal to 1100 Gflop/s.

Using the three GPUs, the Cholesky factorization achieves 780 Gflop/s (Figure 34.2). This corresponds to a perfect speedup equal to 3. The use of the five additional cores allows us to achieve a total of 900 Gflop/s. Note that this 120 Gflop/s improvement in the hybrid system is greater than the aggregate potential of those five CPU cores alone, since their cumulative *sgemm* peak is 100 Gflop/s. Although this result is non-intuitive, it can be explained as follows: GPUs are very efficient on regular level-3 BLAS computations such as *sgemm* (333 Gflop/s) but not as efficient for irregular level-2 BLAS kernels such as *spotrf* (56 Gflop/s). When both CPUs and GPUs are available, the CPUs can run most of the *spotrf* instances so that GPUs execute *sgemm* operations almost exclusively. StarPU, being able to detect that property on the fly, schedules 80% of the *spotrf* on CPUs and dedicates GPUs for running *sgemm* whenever it can.

Furthermore, this method transparently handles cases where the whole matrix does not fit in the memory of a GPU (when the matrix is larger than 4 GB; see Figure 34.2). Indeed, the runtime system

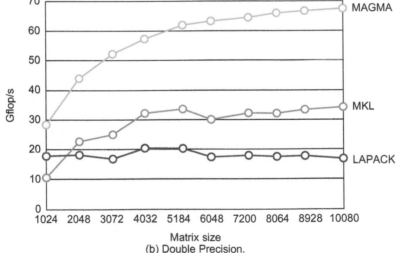

FIGURE 34.1

Parallel performance of MAGMA's hybrid Cholesky on GTX 280 *vs* MKL 10.1 and LAPACK (with multi-threaded BLAS) on Intel Xeon dual socket quad-core 2.33 GHz.

simply moves back and forth parts of the data from the GPU memory to the CPU main memory, taking care of its coherency as it would do it between two different GPUs. Having a strong impact on the overall performance, the amount of data movement is automatically kept as low as possible according to the data-aware algorithm mentioned in Section 34.3.3. Figure 34.3 shows the impact of

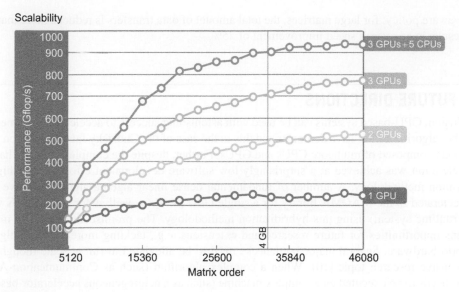

FIGURE 34.2

Performance scalability of the single precision Cholesky factorization.

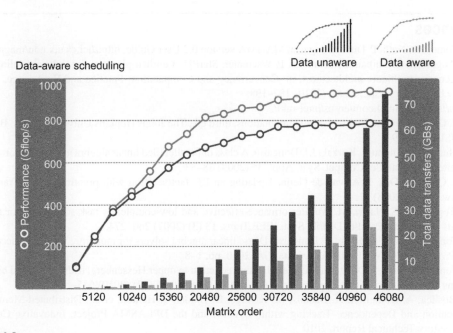

FIGURE 34.3

Impact of the data-aware policy on the amount of data transfers and on performance for the single precision Cholesky factorization.

the data-aware policy: for large matrices, the total amount of data transfers is reduced more than twice, which results in an overall speed improvement of 25%.

34.5 FUTURE DIRECTIONS

In conclusion, GPU-based systems can be used with astonishing success to accelerate fundamental linear algebra algorithms. We have demonstrated this in the case of the Cholesky factorization on a single hybrid node composed of multicore CPUs and GPUs. Further, despite the complexity of the hardware, this acceleration was achieved at a surprisingly low software development effort using a high-level hybridization methodology. A number of fundamental dense linear algebra algorithms have already been accelerated in the MAGMA library for a single GPU [8, 9] (as well as for multi-GPUs with the StarPU runtime system) using this hybridization methodology. The promise shown so far motivates and opens opportunities for future research and extensions, e.g., tackling more complex algorithms and hybrid hardware. Several major bottlenecks need to be alleviated to run at scale though, which is an intensive research topic [10]. When a complex algorithm (such as Communication-Avoiding QR [11]) needs to be executed on a complex machine (such as a heterogeneous accelerator-based cluster), scheduling decisions have a dramatic impact on performance. Therefore, new scheduling strategies must be designed to fully benefit from the potential of future large-scale machines.

References

[1] S. Tomov, R. Nath, P. Du, J. Dongarra, MAGMA version 0.2 User Guide. http://icl.cs.utk.edu/magma, 2009.

[2] C. Augonnet, S. Thibault, R. Namyst, P. Wacrenier, StarPU: a unified platform for task scheduling on heterogeneous multicore architectures, in: Concurrency and Computation: Practice and Experience, Euro-Par 2009 best papers issue, 23 (2) (2010) 187–198.

[3] http://software.intel.com/en-us/intel-mkl/.

[4] G.H. Golub, C.F. van Loan, Matrix Computations, third ed., The Johns Hopkins University Press, Baltimore, MD, 1996, p. 694.

[5] A. Buttari, J. Langou, J. Kurzak, J.J. Dongarra, A class of parallel tiled linear algebra algorithms for multicore architectures, Parallel Comput. Syst. Appl. 35 (2009) 38–53.

[6] E.S. Quintana-Ortí, R.A. van de Geijn, Updating an LU factorization with pivoting, ACM Trans. Math. Softw. 35 (2) (2008) 11.

[7] H. Topcuoglu, S. Hariri, M. Wu, Performance-effective and low-complexity task scheduling for heterogeneous computing, Parallel Distrib. Syst. IEEE Trans. 13 (3) (2002) 260–274.

[8] S. Tomov, R. Nath, H. Ltaief, J. Dongarra, Dense linear algebra solvers for multicore with GPU accelerators, in: Proc. of IPDPSW '10, IEEE, Atlanta, GA, 2010, pp. 1–8.

[9] S. Tomov, R. Nath, J. Dongarra, Accelerating the reduction to upper Hessenberg, tridiagonal, and bidiagonal forms through hybrid GPU-based computing, Parallel Comput. 36 (12) (2010) 645–654.

[10] G. Bosilca, A. Bouteiller, A. Danalis, M. Faverge, H. Haidar, T. Herault, et al., Distributed-Memory Task Execution and Dependence Tracking within DAGuE and the DPLASMA Project, Innovative Computing Laboratory Technical Report, 2010.

[11] B. Hadri, H. Ltaief, E. Agullo, J. Dongarra, Tile QR factorization with parallel panel processing for multicore architectures 2010, in: Proceedings of IPDPS' 2010, pp. 1–10.

Dynamic Load Balancing Using Work-Stealing

Daniel Cederman and Philippas Tsigas

In this chapter, we present a methodology for efficient load balancing of computational problems that can be easily decomposed into multiple tasks, but where it is hard to predict the computation cost of each task, and where new tasks are created dynamically during runtime. We present this methodology and its exploitation and feasibility in the context of graphics processors. Work-stealing allows an idle core to acquire tasks from a core that is overloaded, causing the total work to be distributed evenly among cores, while minimizing the communication costs, as tasks are only redistributed when required. This will often lead to higher throughput than using static partitioning.

35.1 INTRODUCTION

To achieve good performance on graphics processors, with their many-core architecture, it is important that the work to be done can be distributed evenly to all available cores. It is also vital that the solution can scale well when newer graphics processors arrive with an increased number of cores.

Many problems can be decomposed relatively easily into multiple tasks that all have the same computation cost. These tasks can then be distributed evenly to all cores. Depending on the number of cores, the work can be decomposed into a varying number of tasks, allowing the solution to scale. There is, however, a large category of problems where (i) it is difficult to predict how long a task will take to complete and (ii) new tasks are created dynamically during runtime. For these irregular problems, it becomes difficult to achieve a uniform utilization of the cores using a static assignment of the work to the cores. Instead, the need arises for a more dynamic solution that can adapt to changes in the workload at runtime.

In popular GPU computing environments such as CUDA and OpenCL, one can achieve load balancing by decomposing the work into more tasks than can be scheduled concurrently, allowing cores that finish early to acquire new unfinished tasks. This eases the problem of scheduling tasks with unknown computation cost. However, it requires that all the tasks are available prior to the invocation of the kernel. To perform the subtasks created during runtime requires waiting for the kernel as a whole to finish, and then to perform these new tasks in a new kernel invocation or for each core to perform all of its own subtasks. Either way tends to lead to uneven workloads, as can be seen in Figure 35.1(a).

A solution to this problem is to have a dynamic work-pool of tasks, from which each core can receive tasks to perform, and to which it can announce new subtasks. This will allow cores to acquire

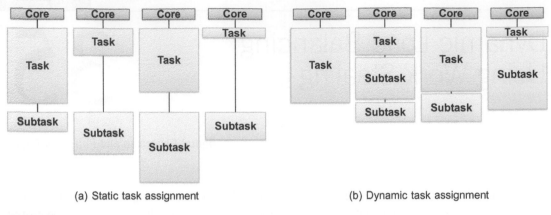

(a) Static task assignment   (b) Dynamic task assignment

FIGURE 35.1

Comparison between static and dynamic task assignments.

new tasks as soon as they become available, instead of having to wait for a new kernel invocation. In this chapter we will investigate how to implement such a work-pool in CUDA using two different approaches, one dynamic, using work-stealing, and one static approach.

35.2 CORE METHOD

There are many different ways to implement a dynamic work-pool. Most of them, however, require the use of atomic primitives to handle synchronization, which was a problem earlier when few graphics processors supported them. Some of the atomic primitives could be emulated using the graphics processors memory access semantics [1], but today most newer graphics processors supports advanced atomic operations natively. These primitives, such as Compare-And-Swap and Fetch-And-Add, have made it possible to implement some of the more advanced data-structures used in several well known dynamic load balancing schemes.

A popular technique used in some of these schemes is *work-stealing* [2], which is used extensively in the Cilk programming language and has been a part of its success [3]. In a work-stealing scheme, each thread has its own pool of tasks. When a thread has finished a task, it acquires a new one from its own work-pool, and, when a new subtask is created, the new task is added to the same work-pool. If a thread discovers that it has no more tasks in its own work-pool, it can try to *steal* a task from the work-pool of another thread. This will allow a thread to always have tasks to perform, while minimizing communication among threads.

One such scheme is the popular lock-free work-stealing algorithm by Arora et al. [4]. A paper comparing different load balancing schemes have shown that it works well on graphics processors and can achieve better performance than other schemes [5]. In the following sections we will describe the components of this design and how it can be used to implement dynamic load balancing in CUDA that can outperform other static load balancing techniques.

35.3 ALGORITHMS AND IMPLEMENTATIONS

The basic idea behind work-stealing is to assign to each thread its own work-pool, which is then used primarily by that thread. This allows for newly spawned subtasks to be handled by the same thread that handled their parent task. As subtasks often access the same data as their parent, this will usually lead to better cache utilization. When a thread no longer has any tasks to perform, it will try to steal one from another thread's work-pool. For a thread to know if there are any tasks left to steal, one needs to create a condition that can be checked to see if the total work has been completed or not. This condition is often trivial to create, so if the problem faced can be easily decomposed into multiple tasks, work-stealing is an efficient scheme to achieve an even load balance.

In the following sections we will give an overview of the work-stealing scheme followed by a detailed explanation and motivation of the design of a well known algorithm for work-stealing. But before we do that, we will describe an alternative to work-stealing, which we will later use as a baseline for our experiments.

35.3.1 Static Assignment

To evaluate the performance of the work-stealing scheme, we have implemented a load balancing scheme using a static assignment of the tasks to each thread block. The reason that we talk about thread blocks here instead of threads is that for some applications (e.g., where control flow across tasks can diverge heavily) it can be more efficient to have multiple threads within a block collaborate on a single task rather than to have each thread work on its own task.

The work-pool in this scheme is implemented using two arrays (Figure 35.2). The first array holds all the tasks to be performed and the other array holds subtasks created at runtime. In the first iteration, the input array holds all initial tasks. The array is then partitioned so that each thread block gets an equal number of tasks. Since no writing is allowed to the input array, there is no need for any synchronization.

When new tasks are created during runtime, they are written to the output array with the help of the atomic primitive Fetch-And-Add (FAA). This primitive atomically increments the value of a variable and can thus be used to find a unique position in the array. When all tasks have been completed, the two arrays switch roles and the kernel is invoked again. This is repeated until no more new tasks are created.

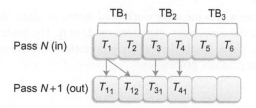

FIGURE 35.2

The two arrays used for static assignment.

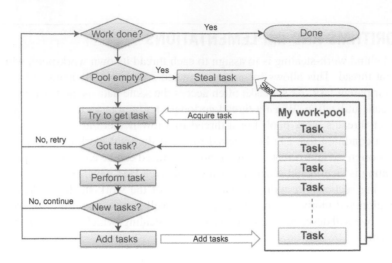

FIGURE 35.3

Task sharing using work-pools and work-stealing.

35.3.2 Work-Stealing

A general overview of the work-stealing scheme can be seen in Figure 35.3. Every thread block is assigned its own work-pool with, potentially, some initially allotted tasks in it. Each thread block tries to repeatedly acquire new tasks to perform from its work-pool. If a new task is created during execution, it is added to the thread block's own work-pool. If a thread block fails to get a task, it checks a condition to see if all work is done. If it is not, the thread block tries to *steal* tasks from the other thread block's work-pools.

There are several ways to implement work-pools for work-stealing. We have decided to use the algorithm by Arora et al. [4], which is a popular method on conventional systems and has two interesting features. The first one is that it is lock-free and the second one that it avoids expensive atomic operations in the most common cases. We will try to motivate the importance of these two features for graphics processors in the two following sections.

35.3.2.1 Lock-Freedom

As multiple thread blocks can access the same work-pool during stealing, the underlying data structure must be able to synchronize the concurrent operations made to it. The basic way to synchronize operations is the use of spinlocks. Using spinlocks for synchronization is, however, very expensive and does not scale well, especially on graphics processors.[1]

---

[1]GPUs prior to the NVIDIA Fermi architecture do not have writable caches, so for those GPUs, repeated checks to see if a lock is available or not require expensive repeated accesses to the GPU's main memory. While Fermi GPUs do support writable caches, the use of locks is still not recommended, as there is no guarantee that the thread scheduler will be fair, which can make it difficult to write deadlock-free locking code. OpenCL explicitly disallows locks for these and other reasons.

A better way, then, is to take advantage of lock-free techniques [6, 7]. Lock-freedom is a progress guarantee for algorithms that states that at any given time, at least one thread block will always make computational progress, regardless of the progress or status of any other thread block. This means that a thread block never has to wait for a lock to be released, so no matter the scheduling, at least one thread block will always be able to finish its operation in a bounded amount of time. One common design method to make an algorithm lock-free is to take all the changes that need to be performed in mutual exclusion and rewrite them so that they can be performed with just one atomic instruction.

35.3.2.2 *Atomic Primitives*

Atomic primitives were an important addition to the instruction set of the graphics processors, as using only read and write operations is not enough for nonblocking synchronization. In the set of atomic primitives, the Compare-And-Swap (CAS) operation is among the most powerful. The CAS operation is used to atomically change the value of a variable, if and only if it currently has the value given as a parameter to the operation. The CAS operation can be seen as a word level transaction supported by the hardware. However, for the hardware to be able to perform the CAS operation atomically, the memory bus needs to be locked to guarantee that no other thread block is concurrently writing to the same memory location. This is expensive, and an atomic operation will be many times slower than a normal read or write operation. Because of this, it is recommended to avoid using atomic operations when possible. In the Fermi architecture the performance of the atomic operations has been increased, but a normal read or write will always be faster.

The algorithm by Arora et al. only uses atomic operations during stealing and when there is just one element left in the work-pool, cases that are not common.

35.3.3 **The Work-Stealing Algorithm**

The work-stealing algorithm uses double-ended queues (deques) for work-pools and each thread block is assigned its own unique deque. A deque is a queue where it is possible to enqueue and dequeue from both sides, in contrast to a normal queue where you enqueue on one side and dequeue on the other.

Tasks are added and removed from the *tail* of the deque in a Last-In-First-Out (LIFO) manner. When the deque is empty, the thread block tries to steal from the *head* of another thread blocks deque. Since only the owner of the deque is accessing the tail of the deque, there is no need for expensive synchronization when the deque contains more than one element. Several thread blocks might however try to steal at the same time, and for this case synchronization is required, but stealing is expected to occur less often than a normal local access.

A double-ended queue is depicted in Figure 35.4. We base our implementation on an array that holds the tasks and have a head and a tail pointer that points to the first and last task in the deque. The head pointer is divided into two fields due to the ABA-problem (described in Section 35.3.3.4) that can occur if the head pointer is written to by two different thread blocks. These data structures are defined in Listing 35.1.

As each thread block needs to have its own deque, we have to allocate memory for as many deques as we have thread blocks. We cannot use the shared memory to store the deques, as other thread blocks need to be able to access them to steal tasks. The maximum number of tasks to make room for in the deque will have to be decided for the specific application and must be decided on beforehand. The tasks can be of any size. If they are larger than a single word, one should try to make sure that multiple threads read them in a coalesced manner.

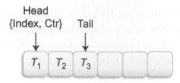

FIGURE 35.4

Double-ended queues used to represent work-pools.

```
struct Head {
    unsigned short index;
    unsigned short ctr;
}

struct Deque {
    Head head;
    unsigned int tail;
    Task tasks[MAX_TASKS];
}

Deque deques[MAX_THREAD_BLOCKS];
```

Listing 35.1. Data structures needed for the work-pools.

```
push(task)
    tasks[tail] = task;
    tail++;
```

Listing 35.2. Code for the **push** operation.

35.3.3.1 *Push*

The push operation (Listing 35.2) is used by the owner thread block to add new tasks to the tail end of the deque. As tail is only written to by the owner thread block, there is no need for any synchronization. The task is simply written to where tail is pointing to and then tail is incremented to point to the next empty slot.

35.3.3.2 *Steal*

The steal operation (Listing 35.3) tries to take a task from the head of the deque. It first checks if the deque is empty or not by comparing tail to head (step ①). If tail is equal to or lower than head, the deque is empty or became empty while performing the comparison. In this case, the steal operation returns null, and the caller will have to try to steal from another deque.

If the deque is not empty, the steal operation will read the task that head is pointing to (step ②) and try to move head to point to the next element in the array (step ③). Multiple thread blocks might try to

```
Task steal()
   Head oldHead, newHead;
   Task task;

   oldHead = head;  ①
   if(tail ≤ oldHead.index )
      return null;

   task = tasks[oldHead.index];  ②

   newHead = oldHead;  ③
   newHead.index++;
   if( CAS(&head, oldHead, newHead) )
      return task;

   return abort;
```

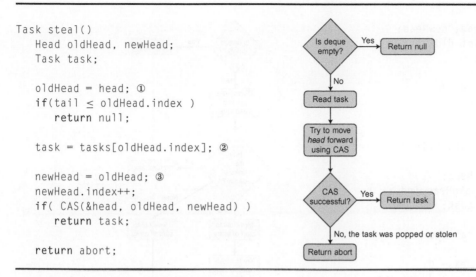

Listing 35.3. Code for the **steal** operation.

steal the task at the same time and the owner might try to pop it, so we need to use a synchronization primitive to make sure that only one thread block is successful in acquiring the task. Using CAS to update head gives us this guarantee.

If the CAS is successful, it means that the steal operation as a whole was successful and it can return the stolen task. If the CAS failed, it means that some other thread block stole or popped the task, and the calling thread block will have to try to steal again, perhaps this time from another dequeue.

35.3.3.3 *Pop*

The pop operation (Listing 35.4) tries to take a task from the tail end of the deque. It first tries to find out if the deque is empty by checking whether tail points to the first element of the array or not (step ①). If it does, the deque is empty and the pop operation simply returns null. The calling thread block will now have to decide if it wants to steal a task from another deque.

If tail is not pointing to the first element, then the pop operation decrements tail by one and reads the task that it is now pointing at (step ②). As it is only the owner of the deque that can change tail, there is no need for any synchronization. It then makes a local copy of head and compares it to tail (step ③). There are now three different possible scenarios:

1. tail is strictly *larger* than the local copy of head. Any new steal operation that is invoked will see that the tail has been moved in step ②, so it will not try to steal the task. However, a concurrent steal might have already performed the comparison at step ① in the steal operation (Listing 35.3)- and not noticed that the tail has changed. This is no problem, as no matter how many concurrent steals are in progress, they can only move head one step forward in total before they have to look at tail again. And when they do, they will find that the task is no longer in the deque. There is

```
Task pop()
    Head oldHead, newHead;
    unsigned int oldTail;
    Task task;

    if(tail == 0) ①
        return null;

    tail--; ②
    task = tasks[tail];

    oldHead = head;
    if(tail > oldHead.index) ③
        return task;

    oldTail = tail; ④
    tail = 0;
    newHead.index = 0;
    newHead.ctr = oldHead.ctr + 1;

    if( oldTail == oldHead.index ) ⑤
        if( CAS(&head, oldHead, newHead) )
            return task;

    head = newHead; ⑥
    return null;
```

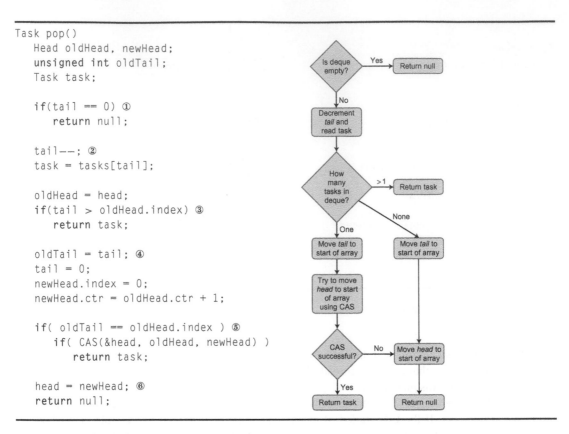

Listing 35.4. Code for the **pop** operation.

thus no possibility for a conflict with another thread block and the task is successfully popped and can be returned by the operation.

2. `tail` is strictly *smaller* than the local copy of `head`. This scenario happens when a steal operation took the last element in the deque before the call to the pop operation was made. In this case, `tail` and `head` are changed to both point to the beginning of the array (steps ④ and ⑥), so as not to waste space when new tasks are pushed to the deque. As the deque is empty, the operation returns `null`.

3. `tail` is *equal* to the local copy of `head`. This means that we read the last available task in the deque. This task might be concurrently stolen by another thread block, so to make sure that only one thread block will be able to acquire the task, we use the CAS primitive to move `head` to the beginning of the deque (step ⑤). This is done, as mentioned before, to not waste space when new tasks are pushed to deque, but has the additional benefit that it will prevent other thread blocks from stealing the task if it is successful. If it fails, it means that the task was stolen. In this case the deque is empty and we can move `head` to the beginning of the array without using CAS (step ⑥). If it was successful, we can return the popped task.

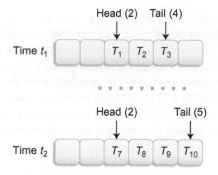

FIGURE 35.5

The CAS operation cannot differentiate between the head pointer at time t_1 and at time t_2, opening up for the possibility that a task can be stolen twice.

35.3.3.4 *ABA-problem*

One downside of the CAS operation is that it is susceptible to the ABA-problem. In most lock-free algorithms, the CAS operation is used to make sure that a write to a variable will only succeed if no other thread block has changed the value of the variable in the meantime. But if the value has changed from A to B and then back to A again, there is no way for the CAS operation to discover this. The ABA-problem is thus something that needs to be considered whenever using CAS.

In the context of work-stealing, the ABA-problem can occur when the pop operation moves head to point to the beginning of the array while another thread block is concurrently trying to steal a task. As an example, in the scenario in Figure 35.5, thread block X is trying to steal task T_1 at time t_1. It reads head and learns that it should try to steal from position 2. But just as it is about to change head using the CAS operation, it gets swapped out by the scheduler. In the meantime, the deque experiences an arbitrary number of push, pop, and steal operations, leaving the deque at a completely different state at time t_2, which is when thread block X is swapped in again. Unfortunately, head is still pointing to position 2 in the array, so thread block X will believe that it successfully stole task T_1, when in fact task T_1 has already been performed by another thread block.

This problem is avoided by adding a counter to head, which is incremented every time that head is moved to the beginning of the deque. This guarantees that a task can never be stolen more than once, as head will always be unique. A problem with this approach is that eventually the counter will wrap around and start counting from zero again, but the probability of this occurring can be made very small by setting a good counter size. Note that tail is only written to by the owner thread block, so it is not susceptible to the ABA-problem the way head is.

35.3.3.5 *Parameters*

There is very little parallelism in the code for the queue management work done *within* the individual thread blocks. Most of the work is performed by thread 0 and does not take advantage of the SIMD instructions to any larger degree. The number of threads in a thread block should therefore be decided mainly by the need of the application that uses the dynamic load balancing. When it comes to selecting the number of thread blocks, one should try to run at least as many thread blocks as can run concurrently. If one starts more thread blocks than can run concurrently, the excess thread blocks will immediately see that the work has been completed when they start and exit right away.

The main things to consider when using the dynamic load balancing scheme presented in this chapter is how to divide the problem into tasks, what information the tasks should contain and how large they should be. Too small tasks will create extra overhead, while too large will cause imbalance in the load. It is also required to have a condition to check, to see if the total work has been done or not. In the following section, we present two example applications to show how this can be done.

35.4 CASE STUDIES AND EVALUATION

To evaluate the dynamic load balancing scheme, we implemented two applications that fulfill the criteria that they should dynamically create new tasks that can be hard to predict the total computation cost for. The first is an implementation of a computer opponent for a four-in-a-row game and the second is an octree partitioner that divides a set of particles in 3-D space into a hierarchical data structure. In the first application, each task has about the same computation time, but the number of sub-tasks that each task will spawn is unknown. In the second application, the computation time for each task is also unknown.

For comparison we also performed the experiments using the static assignment scheme presented in Section 35.3.1. We performed measurements using different numbers of thread blocks on a NVIDIA GTX280 graphics processor with 30 multiprocessors. The measurements taken were the total amount of tasks per millisecond that were performed, as well as the memory consumption for the two different load balancing schemes.

35.4.1 Four-in-a-Row

Four-in-a-row is played by two players, where in each turn a player drops a token in one of seven slots in a 6×7 grid. The first player to get four of his own tokens in a row wins the game. Figure 35.6 shows a possible game scenario.

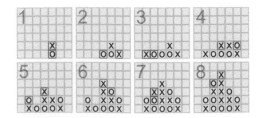

FIGURE 35.6

A possible game scenario for four-in-a-row.

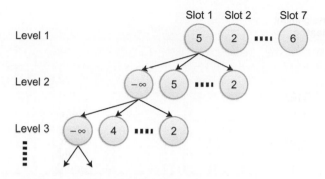

FIGURE 35.7

A minimax decision tree for four-in-a-row. Each node is a task.

35.4.1.1 *Design*

To help the computer pick the optimal move, we look ahead *n* moves and use a minimax algorithm to pick the move that gives the best worst case scenario. In Figure 35.7 we see the decision tree used in the algorithm. The nodes at the first level represent the possible moves that the computer can make. The children of these nodes represent the moves that the human opponent can take in the next turn, given the computers move. The children of these nodes in turn represent the move that the computer can make and so on, until we have looked *n* moves ahead.

When a leaf node is reached, either due to one of the players winning or because we have looked *n* moves ahead, a heuristic function is used to give each leaf node a value depending on how good that outcome is. The computer winning is infinitely positive and the player winning is infinitely negative. The other scenarios are valued by the difference in how many two or three token sequences each of the players have. The nodes at even levels, which represent the human player, take the value of the child node with the *lowest* value, as this represents the player's optimal move. On the other hand, the nodes at odd levels, which represent the computer player, take the value of the child with the *highest* value. In the end, the node on the first level with the highest value represents the best next move for the computer opponent.

It is hard to predict how much time will be spent in each branch. By making each node in the minimax decision tree a task, we can use dynamic load balancing to achieve an even load. We set each task to hold information on what level the node is on, its parent node, its value and the moves taken by its ancestor nodes. We save memory by only storing the moves taken and not the entire board state, as the new board state can be generated quickly from the current board state and the moves taken. To know when the problem has been solved, we keep a counter at each node that keeps track of the number of child nodes it has received a value from. When the root nodes have received values from all of their children, the work is complete.

35.4.1.2 *Evaluation*

We evaluated the performance of the computer player by playing the game scenario shown in Figure 35.6 with different number of lookahead moves.

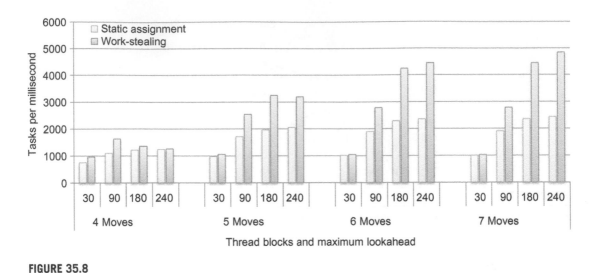

FIGURE 35.8

Four-in-a-row: Tasks performed per millisecond for different number of lookahead moves and thread blocks.

The graph in Figure 35.8 shows the performance for different numbers of lookahead moves (4 to 7) as well as different numbers of thread blocks (30 to 240). The maximum number of thread blocks that can run concurrently is 240, as each multiprocessor can support up to 8 thread blocks (given enough register and shared memory resources) and there are 30 multiprocessors available on the graphics processor we used. We use 64 threads per block, as the work in each task is not sufficient to take advantage of more than this, due to the small size of the game board. More threads would just add overhead.

We can see that using only 30 thread blocks gives poor performance for all four cases. With only four lookahead moves we have few tasks to distribute between thread blocks, something which hurts performance for the work-stealing when using too many thread blocks. When the number of tasks increases, we benefit from having many thread blocks and the best result for lookahead higher than four is when have 240 thread blocks.

Figure 35.9 shows the number of tasks per millisecond performed by the two different load balancing schemes using 240 thread blocks. We see that the dynamic load balancing scales much better, when faced with a higher load, than the static load balancing. At 7 lookahead moves it is twice as fast as the static scheme.

The figure also shows the number of tasks that we have to allocate space for. Note that the scale is logarithmic. For the static load balancing, this is the maximum number of tasks that can be created in a kernel invocation. The dynamic load balancing has a deque for every thread block, so here we need to multiply the maximum number of elements used in a deque with the number of thread blocks. The graph shows the memory requirement for 240 thread blocks. For 7 lookahead moves, the static load balancing requires around ≈800,000 tasks to be stored, while the dynamic only requires around 50 times the number of thread blocks, ≈12,000 tasks.

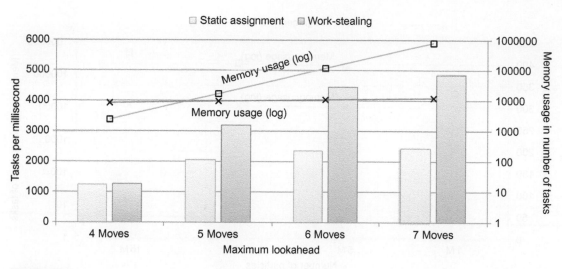

FIGURE 35.9

Four-in-a-row: Tasks performed per millisecond and memory usage in number of tasks for 240 thread blocks.

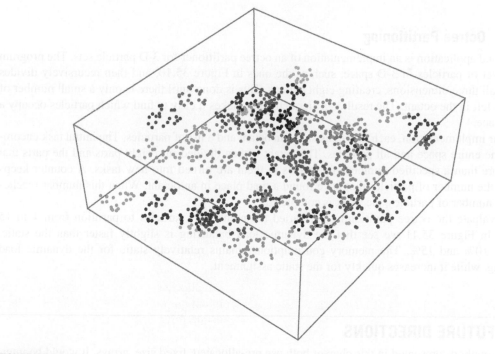

FIGURE 35.10

A set of 3-D particles to be placed inside an octree.

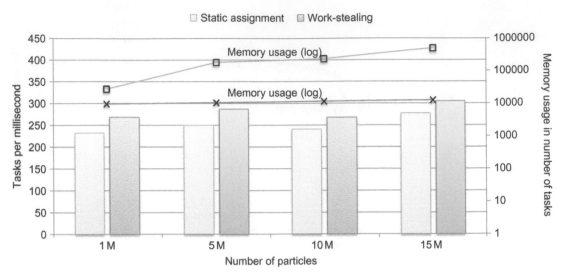

FIGURE 35.11

Octree partitioning: Tasks performed per millisecond and memory usage in number of tasks for 240 thread blocks.

35.4.2 Octree Partitioning

Our second application is an implementation of an octree partitioner for 3-D particle sets. The program takes a set of particles in 3-D space, such as the ones in Figure 35.10, and then recursively divides them in all three dimensions, creating eight octants. This is done until there is only a small number of particles left in the octant. The result is a hierarchy that makes it easy to find which particles occupy a given space.

In our implementation, each task consists of an octant and a list of particles. The initial task encompasses the entire space and all particles. The octant is then divided into eight parts and the parts that have more than a specified number of particles in them are turned into new tasks. A counter keeps track of the number of particles that have found a final place in an octant. When this number reaches the total number of particles, the work is completed.

To evaluate the octree partitioning we varied the number of particles to partition from 1 to 15 million. In Figure 35.11 we see that the dynamic load balancing is slightly faster than the static, between 10% and 15%. The memory consumption remains relatively static for the dynamic load balancing, while it increases quickly for the static assignment.

35.5 FUTURE DIRECTIONS

The two methods presented in this chapter both use pre-allocated, fixed size, arrays. It would be interesting to investigate if there is a lock-free way to dynamically resize these arrays, so that the maximum memory consumption does not need to be known in advance.

Another important area to look into is task dependencies. The two applications we have presented in this chapter both spawn tasks that can be performed immediately, but in other scenarios there might be cases where a task cannot be performed until some other tasks have been finished. Finding a lock-free method to deal with task dependencies efficiently on graphics processors would be useful.

Acknowledgments

This work was partially supported by the EU as part of FP7 Project PEPPHER (www.peppher.eu) under grant 248481 and the Swedish Research Council under grant number 37252706.

References

[1] P. Hoai Ha, P. Tsigas, O.J. Anshus, The synchronization power of coalesced memory accesses, IEEE Trans. Parallel Distrib. Syst. 21 (2010) 939–953.

[2] R.D. Blumofe, C.E. Leiserson, Scheduling multithreaded computations by work stealing, in: Proceedings of the 35th Annual Symposium on Foundations of Computer Science, IEEE Computer Society, Santa Fe, NM, 1994, pp. 356–368.

[3] R.D. Blumofe, C.F. Joerg, B.C. Kuszmaul, C.E. Leiserson, K.H. Randall, Y. Zhou, Cilk: an efficient multithreaded runtime system, in: R.L. Wexelblat (Ed.), Proceedings of the Fifth ACM SIGPLAN Symposium on Principles and Practice of Parallel Programming (PPoPP), ACM, Santa Barbara, CA, 1995, pp. 207–216.

[4] N.S. Arora, R.D. Blumofe, C. Greg Plaxton, Thread scheduling for multiprogrammed multiprocessors, in: Proceedings of the ACM Symposium on Parallel Algorithms and Architectures, ACM, Puerto Vallarta, Mexico, 1998, pp. 119–129.

[5] D. Cederman, P. Tsigas, On dynamic load balancing on graphics processors, in: Proceedings of the 23rd ACM SIGGRAPH/EUROGRAPHICS symposium on Graphics Hardware, Eurographics Association, Sarajevo, Bosnia, 2008, pp. 57–64.

[6] M. Herlihy, N. Shavit, The Art of Multiprocessor Programming, Morgan Kaufmann, Boston, 2008.

[7] D. Cederman, A. Gidenstam, P. Ha, H. Sundell, M. Papatriantafilou, P. Tsigas, Lock-free concurrent data structures, in: S. Pllana, F. Xhafa (Eds.), Programming Multi-Core and Many-Core Computing Systems, Wiley-Blackwell, 2011.

Applying Software-Managed Caching and CPU/GPU Task Scheduling for Accelerating Dynamic Workloads

Mark Silberstein, Assaf Schuster, and John D. Owens

In this chapter we cover two difficult problems frequently encountered by GPU developers: optimizing memory access for kernels with complex input-dependent access patterns, and mapping the computations to a GPU or a CPU in composite applications with multiple dependent kernels. Both pose a formidable challenge as they require *dynamic adaptation and tuning of execution policies* to allow high performance for a wide range of inputs. Not meeting these requirements leads to substantial performance penalty.

We first describe our methodology for solving the memory optimization problem via *software-managed caching* by efficiently exploiting the fast scratchpad memory. This technique outperforms the cache-less and the texture memory-based approaches on pre-Fermi GPU architectures as well as on the one that uses the Fermi hardware cache alone.

We then present the algorithm for minimizing the total running time of a complete application comprising multiple interdependent kernels. Both a GPU and a CPU can be used to execute the kernels, but the performance varies greatly for different inputs, calling for dynamic assignment of the computations to a GPU or a CPU at runtime. The communication overhead due to the data dependencies between the kernels makes per-kernel greedy selection of the best performing device suboptimal. The algorithm optimizes the runtime of the complete application by evaluating the performance of all the assignments jointly, including the overhead of the data transfers between the devices.

We demonstrate these techniques by applying them to a real application for computing probability of evidence in probabilistic networks. The combination of memory optimization and dynamic assignment results in up to threefold runtime reduction over the non-optimized version on real inputs, and up to fivefold over a highly optimized parallel version running on Intel's latest dual quad-core 16-thread Nehalem machine.

36.1 INTRODUCTION, PROBLEM STATEMENT, AND CONTEXT

This chapter endeavors to assist developers in overcoming two major bottlenecks of the high-end GPU platforms: memory bandwidth to the main (global) memory of the GPU, and the CPU-GPU communications. We faced both these problems when developing an application for computing the probability of evidence in probabilistic networks, and only by solving both did we achieve the desired performance improvement. Yet we believe that our techniques are applicable in a general context, and can be employed together and separately. In the chapter we describe the solution for each problem and demonstrate their combined effect on a real application as a whole.

Memory access optimization is among the main tools for improving application performance in CPUs and GPUs. It is of added importance if the algorithm has a low compute-to-memory access ratio. Often the same data are reused many times, and reorganizing the computations to exploit small but fast on-die caches might thus reduce the main memory bandwidth pressure and improve performance.

Hardware caches employ input-independent replacement algorithms, such as Least Recently Used (LRU). Maximizing cache performance to exploit data reuse requires restructuring the code so that the actual access pattern matches the cache replacement algorithm. Unfortunately, high performance is difficult and sometimes even impossible to achieve without the ability to control the replacement decisions.

Modern NVIDIA GPUs expose fast scratchpad memory shared by multiple streaming processors on a multiprocessor. By design, the scratchpad memory lacks hardware caching support;[1] hence, it is the responsibility of the kernel to implement a *software-managed cache*, which implies determining which data to stage from the main memory and when to stage it. For cases where this determination is data-dependent, the decision must be made at runtime. The main challenge, then, is to minimize the overhead of the cache management code, which resides on the critical path of every memory access. In Section 36.3.1 we introduce techniques for analyzing the data access patterns and designing a read-only low-overhead software-managed cache for NVIDIA GPUs.

Kernel performance optimization, however, is only one component in making the complete application run faster. Often, despite optimizations, the kernel performance may vary substantially for different inputs. In some cases executing the kernel on a GPU may actually decrease the performance, such as when not enough parallelism is available. Furthermore, the overhead of the CPU-GPU communications over the PCI Express bus may reduce or completely cancel out the advantages of using a GPU. In Section 36.3.3 we focus on optimizing the choice of the processor for the kernel execution in applications with multiple inter-dependent kernels.

A simple approach is to greedily assign the device providing the best overall performance for a given input. It will work well for isolated kernels, where both the kernel input and output must reside on a CPU. For such cases, the data will always be transferred from the CPU to the GPU and back, thus allowing for a *local* decision that considers only the performance of a given kernel on each device.

However, for applications composed of multiple kernels with data dependencies, whereby the subsequent kernels use the results of the previous ones, different assignments or *schedules* of the

---

[1] The on-die memory in the Fermi architecture is partitioned into a hardware cache and a scratchpad; in this chapter we focus on the efficient use of the latter.

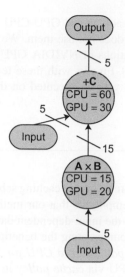

FIGURE 36.1

An illustration of the program task dependency graph for computing $A \times B + C$ of matrices A, B, C.

computations on a CPU or a GPU may decisively influence the application running time. The schedule, which optimizes the performance of each kernel separately, is no longer sufficient for obtaining the best performance of the application as a whole.

Figure 36.1 shows a *task dependency graph* of a program for computing $A \times B + C$ for three matrices A, B, C. The nodes and edges of the graph denote kernels and their data dependencies, respectively. Computations are performed by traversing the graph according to the directionality of the edges. The computations of a node can be started only if all its predecessors in the graph are complete. In this example the first kernel computes $A \times B$ and the second one adds C to the result. The respective graph node labels denote the expected running time (the lower the better) of the kernel on a CPU or a GPU. Edge labels denote the data transfer times given that the adjacent nodes are executed on different devices. Input data nodes represent the original input data residing in CPU memory.

Were the schedule to consider the performance of each kernel alone, it would assign the product kernel to a CPU and the summation kernel to a GPU, yielding an execution time of 65 time units. (We assume that input transfer of matrix C for the summation kernel can be overlapped with the execution of the product kernel on matrices A and B.) However, the best schedule requires only 60 time units to complete, assigning both kernels to a GPU. Note that the higher cost of the data transfer between two kernels would increase the performance gap between the greedy and the optimal schedules.

We show a simple and fast algorithm which solves this scheduling problem for task dependency trees (task graphs without undirected cycles). Although the algorithm does not produce an optimal schedule (finding the optimal schedule is known to be computationally hard), it has been shown to improve the performance in real-life computations. Its main advantage is that it does not require changing the original sequential program flow, complementing other optimizations such as overlapping the data transfers with the kernel execution.

Combining the software-managed caching and GPU-CPU scheduling yields marked performance improvements over the version which does not use them. We compared the performance on random and real-life inputs using three generations of NVIDIA GPUs: GeForce 8800 GTX, GeForce GTX 285, and the Fermi-based Tesla C2050. Finally, with these techniques we obtained up to a factor of 5 speedup over the CPU-only parallel version executed on the latest dual quad-core Intel Nehalem E5540 CPUs.

36.2 CORE METHOD

We first demonstrate an efficient software-managed caching scheme that provides a structured approach to using the scratchpad memory. We emphasize that our method is applicable to applications where static prefetching is not possible due to the input-dependent data access pattern. Cache management at runtime would incur high overhead, counteracting the benefits of using the scratchpad memory. Our key idea is to *precompute the access pattern on a CPU for each input* before the kernel execution and make the results available to a GPU via *cache policy* in the form of lookup tables used by the kernel at runtime. Not only does such a structured approach yield substantial speedups even over the implementation that uses the hardware cache alone, it also facilitates the development process by allowing a separation of concerns between data management and computation.

We then apply a graph-theoretical approach to optimizing the execution of multi-kernel composite applications with inter-kernel data dependencies and input-dependent performance of each kernel on CPU-GPU platforms. We show a fast algorithm which assigns the kernels for execution on a CPU or a GPU at runtime, while taking into account the joint impact of the assignments of all kernels on the entire application performance rather than just the impact of assigning each separately.

We conclude by showing the application of these techniques to the computation of probability of evidence in large probabilistic networks.

36.3 ALGORITHMS, IMPLEMENTATIONS, AND EVALUATIONS

We now present a "recipe" for designing a kernel with a scratchpad-based software-managed cache. We then apply this recipe to build a software-managed cache for the sum-product kernel.

36.3.1 Software-Manged Cache Recipe

Optimize for Locality

As in a CPU implementation, the GPU implementation also requires optimization for spatial locality (for coalesced memory accesses when fetching data to the cache), and temporal locality (for the working set reduction) of memory accesses.

Divide into Thread Blocks with Regular Memory Accesses and High Reuse

The number of threads in the thread block may be dictated by the need to minimize the size of metadata tables used by the caching mechanisms. For example, if every third thread reuses the data of the first one, the number of threads in a thread block should be a multiple of three. Then, the access pattern would be the same for all thread blocks and can be computed only once. Internal reuse is important since the cache is private to a single thread block. For example, in the matrix product kernel, assigning threads of the same thread block to compute the entire output row (instead of a block) is suboptimal since the data in the columns are not reused within the thread block.

Note that the first two "ingredients" above are also important for making optimal use of a hardware cache.

Define Cache Page, Determine the Cache Replacement Policy and Granularity

Input blocks used concurrently by all the threads in a thread block must reside in the cache *at the same time*. We will call such a resident set a *cache page*. The policy determines when to switch to a new cache page, which part of the cache page is to be replaced, and which part of the reused data should remain in the main memory without being cached at all. The granularity of the replacement decisions is critical to cache performance. A fine-grained replacement policy might improve the cache hit rate, but would incur higher overheads at runtime.

We emphasize that organizing the computations so that the accesses are localized in a cache page is also useful when using a hardware cache. However the size of the cache page as well as the specific access pattern within the page must be adjusted to the hardware replacement policy in order to avoid cache thrashing. Furthermore, the same L1 cache is shared by multiple concurrently running thread blocks, as opposed to the disjoint spaces per thread block for the software-managed cache. This makes the hardware cache performance dependent on the interplay between the access patterns of different thread blocks and the cache policy, whereas the software-managed cache is immune to this problem.

Determine the Cache Address Scheme

Obviously, the data replica in the software-managed cache cannot be accessed by using its original global memory addresses. Mapping between the old global memory and the new cache memory addresses is required. Computing that mapping may be quite expensive as the address depends on the offset of the data in the cache and the cache policy, thus necessitating access to multiple cache policy lookup tables. Hence it may be beneficial to precompute it on a CPU as well. Fortunately, once constructed for a single thread block, the same mapping may be valid for all other thread blocks, thanks to access regularity.

36.3.2 Software-Managed Caching for Sum-Product

Here we demonstrate the application of this "cache recipe" to the sum-product kernel, which forms the core of the inference computations in probabilistic networks. In general, sum-product computations arise in a wide variety of scientific applications, such as artificial intelligence, bioinformatics, statistics, image processing and digital communications. (See, e.g., Pakzad and Anantharam [4] for a comprehensive overview of sum-product.)

Consider the following expression:

$$\psi(x) = \sum_{y,z,w} f(x,y,z) \otimes g(x,w) \otimes h(y,z,w). \tag{1}$$

This equation describes a function $\psi(x)$, which is computed by performing a series of tensor products followed by a summation. We skip the formal explanation here and focus on the access pattern of these computations as shown in the example below.

Understanding the Access Pattern

The individual functions $f(x,y,z)$, $g(x,w)$, and $h(y,z,w)$ can be thought of as similar to multidimensional arrays in C. For example, in the function $f(x,y,z)$ (with $x \in X, y \in Y, z \in Z$), the value $f_{x,y,z}$ is located in the memory at the offset $z + |Z| \times y + |Y| \times |Z| \times x$.

Figure 36.2(a) illustrates the memory accesses for computing $k_{000}, k_{001}, k_{010}, k_{011}$ in $k(x,y,w) = \sum_z f(x,y,z) \otimes g(w,z)$ for the case where X, Y, Z, and W are all of size 2. Observe that $g(w,z)$ is accessed in exactly the same manner when computing $k(x=0, \mathbf{y}=\mathbf{0}, w=0)$ and $k(x=0, \mathbf{y}=\mathbf{1}, w=0)$, whereas different locations of f are accessed for the same output, exhibiting no reuse at all.

As Figure 36.2(a) shows, the input data are reused and the access pattern is periodic. Furthermore, the data are accessed in segments since the summation variables are always grouped and iterated together (this is, in fact, a result of optimizing the locality of accesses as described in our previous work [5]). However we also see that the reuse pattern differs for each input function and depends on the specific variables in the function's scope.

Dividing into Thread Blocks

Each output location can be computed independently in a separate thread, but each thread is assigned multiple output locations to improve data reuse, as will be explained later.

The size of the thread block cannot be chosen arbitrarily. In the example in Figure 36.2(a), we see that the access pattern is correlated with the domain size of the function variables: for any group of power-of-two outputs, the data used have the same offsets, but different base addresses. Here, computing the pairs of outputs k_{000}, k_{001} and k_{010}, k_{011} requires accessing two adjacent entries in f, starting

xyz	f (x,y,z)	wz	g(w,z)	xyw	k (x,y,w)
000	■▲	00	■★	000	■
001	■▲	01	■★	001	▲
010	★•	10	▲•	010	★
011	★•	11	▲•	011	•

(a)

f (x,y,z)		g(w,z)				Output k(x,y,w)
000	001	00	01	10	11	000 001
010	011	00	01	10	11	010 011
100	101	00	01	10	11	100 101
110	111	00	01	10	11	110 111

(b)

SegmentSizes

f	g
2	4

SegmentOffsets

f	g
0	2

PageOffsets

page	f	g
0	0	0
1	2	0

PageInvalid

page	f	g
0	0	0
1	0	1

(c)

FIGURE 36.2

Access pattern and cache structures for computing $k(x,y,w) = \sum_z f(x,y,z) \otimes g(w,z)$. (a) Input and output accesses for computing $k_{000}, k_{001}, k_{010}, k_{011}$. The symbols in the diagram represent which locations in the tables are accessed when computing the outputs with the same symbol. For example: to obtain the output k_{000} one computes $f_{000} \times g_{000} + f_{001} \times g_{001}$. In the diagram the respective inputs and the output are marked by ■. Note that computations of different outputs reuse the same inputs. For example: f_{000} is accessed when computing both k_{000} and k_{001}. (b) Layout of the cache pages, one cache page per row. The data in the memory locations in the same page reside in the cache at the same time. (c) Content of the cache policy tables assuming two cache pages accessed by a thread block, two threads per thread block.

from offset 0 for the first pair and offset 2 for the second one. So for the access pattern in different thread blocks to be the same, the set of outputs for every block should be aligned to a multiple of power-of-two. Hence, if we let one thread compute one output, the thread block size can be 2, 4, or 8. For the case of 4, the first thread block would compute k_{000}, k_{001}, k_{010}, and k_{011}.[2]

Cache Page

Each cache page is split into multiple *segments*, one per input function. The size of each segment depends on the amount of data accessed in each function by all the threads of one thread block. For example, each row in the table in Figure 36.2(b) represents one cache page (assuming one output per thread, two threads per block). The sizes of the segments as well as the total cache size are computed on a CPU for each set of input functions, as will be explained below. The results are stored as arrays in the GPU constant memory[3] (*SegmentSizes* and *SegmentOffsets* arrays in Figure 36.2(c)).

Cache Replacement Policy

The amount of data accessed concurrently by all the threads, or, in other words, the size of one cache page, may exceed the available scratchpad memory size. Reducing this size by decreasing the number of threads per thread block may reduce the hardware utilization. Partial caching of the data, whereby one part of the function data can remain uncached, would require that an additional policy table be checked upon *every memory access* in order to determine whether the specific location is cached.

Our solution balances cache management overhead and cache hit rate. We mark some functions as not cached. These functions are accessed directly from the global memory, bypassing the cache. The choice of which functions to cache is precomputed on a CPU as follows: we add the functions in the order of the sizes of their cache segments, starting from the smallest and continuing for as long as cache space permits. Alternative replacement algorithms may of course be better suited for other computations.

Which data to fetch when switching to another cache page is also determined by the replacement policy. As mentioned above, multiple cache pages are accessed by the same thread block to exploit data reuse between the pages. (In Figure 36.2(b), the same data of function g is used in all four cache pages, which can be leveraged if all four pages are processed by the same thread block.) Upon switching to the next page, only the data of the functions which differ from the previous cache page are fetched. In the example above, if all four cache pages are processed by the same thread block, only the data of f would be replaced when moving to the next page.

A CPU is used to determine which functions are to be replaced when moving from one page to another; this information is used by the kernel each time the cache page is switched.

Examples of all the cache policy tables are presented in Figure 36.2(c). These policy tables correspond to the setup with two threads per thread block, two outputs per thread (hence, two pages per thread block). *SegmentSizes* and *SegmentOffsets* are used to determine how much data to fetch per cache page and where each function is placed in the cache. *PageOffsets* is used to determine the offset to the respective input function for each cache page. The *PageInvalid* table determines which function should be replaced when the page is switched. In this example both functions are to be

---

[2]These sizes are used only for the purpose of this example; but in practice much larger thread blocks should be used.
[3]See the CUDA C Programming Guide for more details on the constant memory.

fetched when the first cache page is accessed, but only f has to be fetched again. The data corresponding to the second page of this thread block is to be read from the global memory starting from offset 2.

Cache Address Scheme

Each thread determines the data to be accessed by computing the offset using the local thread index and the cache segment offset for the function being accessed. For example, in Figure 36.2(b), the thread with index 1, which computes k_{001}, will access two values from each input function (for $z = 0$ and $z = 1$), with offsets 0 and 2, respectively. Since all the summation values are accessed sequentially, computing the offset is necessary only once per summation loop (provided proper loop unrolling).

36.3.2.1 *Kernel for Computing Sum-Product*

The kernel that computes sum-product is presented in Listing 36.1. The identifiers starting with capital letters denote the data structures precomputed on the CPU, and the underlined names denote the cache policy tables in the constant memory. The remaining precomputed data are placed in the texture memory.[4]

The kernel can be logically split into four parts: determining the input blocks to be processed by a given thread block (lines 3–8), cache prefetching via the *cachePrefetchPage* procedure (lines 26–41), computation loop (10–23), and writing back the result (23).

A few important points should be emphasized. First, despite the many conditional statements in the kernel, all the threads in a warp follow exactly the same execution path, i.e., there is no *divergence*. This is because the outcome of the statement is independent of the thread identity and thus is the same for all threads in the warp. Second, all the threads in a warp always access the same location in the cache policy tables, which is ideal for the constant memory cache. Similarly, the data structures residing in the texture memory (e.g., *PageOffsets*) are small and fit the small texture cache well. Finally, this procedure can be heavily unrolled, which allows the overhead of accesses to the policy tables to be amortized over several iterations, reducing it even further.

The full GPU kernel code together with the CPU preparation procedures are available for download [1].

36.3.3 **Algorithm for Task Tree Scheduling**

Here we present a fast algorithm for scheduling task dependency trees by assigning the tasks for execution to a CPU or a GPU.

The problem of task dependency graph scheduling on heterogeneous architectures has drawn a lot of attention (see, for example, an overview of the DAG scheduling [3]). All these algorithms try to decrease the running time by keeping all the processors busy, scheduling different graph nodes to different processors in parallel. Finding an optimal schedule that accounts for bandwidth constraints and processor heterogeneity is hard even for task trees (graphs without undirected cycles).

Our approach is different. We target an *acceleration schedule*, for the programming model where a GPU is considered *a co-processor*. In such an asymmetric setup, a GPU cannot operate on its own;

---

[4] See the CUDA C Programming Guide for more details on the texture memory.

```
 1:  Function SumProductKernel
 2:  Input: Input functions
 3:  outputPtr ← call computeOutputPtr(blockIdx)
 4:  for all  input functions f do
 5:      inputPtrs[f] ← call computeInputPtrs(blockIdx,f)
 6:  end for
 7:  for all  cache pages page do
 8:      call cachePrefetchPage(page,inputPtrs)
 9:      sum ← 0, counter ← 0
10:      for all summation values do
11:          product ← 1
12:          for all input functions f do
13:              if SegmentSizes[f] > 0 then
14:                  value ← call cacheFetch(ThreadOffsets[threadIdx][f] + counter)
15:              else
16:                  offset ← inputPtrs[f] + PageOffsets[page][f] + ThreadOffsets[threadIdx][f] + counter
17:                  value ← call memoryFetch(offset)
18:              end if
19:              product ← product × value
20:          end for
21:          sum ← sum + product, counter ← counter + 1
22:      end for
23:      outputPtr[page × ThreadBlockSize + threadIdx] ← sum
24:  end for
25:
26:  Function cachePrefetchPage
27:  Input: page number to fetch page, pointers to the the thread block inputs inputPtrs
28:  for all  input functions f do
29:      if PageValid[page][f] is false AND SegmentSizes[f] > 0 then
30:          call __syncthreads()
31:          call parallelCopy(SegmentOffsets[f], inputPtrs[f]+ PageOffsets[page][f], SegmentSizes[f])
32:          call __syncthreads()
33:      end if
34:  end for
35:
36:  Function parallelCopy
37:  Input: cache offset cOffset, global memory pointer gMem, words to copy size
38:  for i = threadIdx to size  do
39:      CACHE[cOffset + i] ← gMem[i]
40:      i ← i + ThreadBlockSize
41:  end for
```

Listings 36.1. GPU kernel pseudo-code.

the CPU must dedicate some of its time to GPU management. Hence the algorithm optimizes the runtime for the case where the CPU or GPU do not concurrently execute tasks. Indeed, an acceleration schedule may not be an optimal parallel schedule in cases other than the chain dependency graph. That is because the algorithm does not exploit the parallelism available in the graph itself: while one branch is processed on a CPU, another could be processed on a GPU. Yet the acceleration model is very popular among GPU developers: it allows for a simple and easily implementable algorithm, while still enabling performance improvement over only-CPU or only-GPU implementations, and over the greedy algorithm combining both.

Because the assignment of a task in one tree branch does not influence the assignment of a task in another branch, we can apply a dynamic programming approach.

The input to the algorithm is a task dependency tree $T(V,E)$ with the nodes V and edges E. Every node $v \in V$ has the following attributes:

1. Kernel performance vector P_v with two entries for the expected kernel execution time for the respective task v on a CPU or a GPU, respectively.
2. Transfer time matrix D_v with four entries for the time required to transfer the kernel input for all the combinations of source and destination: GPU$\rightarrow$ CPU, CPU$\rightarrow$GPU, GPU$\rightarrow$GPU, CPU$\rightarrow$CPU. Clearly, $D_v[CPU \rightarrow CPU] = D_v[GPU \rightarrow GPU] = 0$, as long as the source and destination are the same GPU.

For every node $v \in V$, the algorithm maintains the following variables:

1. Subtree processing time vector S_v of the subtree rooted at v, with two entries $S_v[CPU]$ and $S_v[GPU]$, each for the best processing time of that subtree assuming v is executed on a CPU or a GPU, respectively.
2. Subtree scheduling decision vector O_v, containing the task assignment $O_v^d[CPU]$ and $O_v^d[GPU]$ for every immediate descendant (child) d of v corresponding to $S_v[CPU]$ and $S_v[GPU]$. This variable stores the assignments of d which resulted in the best total elapsed time including the memory transfer from d to v, and accounts for both the case when d is assigned to a CPU and when it is assigned to a GPU. It is used in the backtracking step.
3. Scheduling decision A_v regarding where to execute the node.

The acceleration schedule algorithm presented in Listing 36.2 runs in two steps: in the forward traversal it traverses the tree from the leaves to the root. For each node v it computes the cost for all possible assignments of node v given the cost of computing its child nodes on a CPU and a GPU and the respective data transfer times (lines 11–21). When this step completes, every node holds the best costs of computing its subtree for both its schedules on a CPU or a GPU. The backtracking step then traverses the tree in the prefix DFS order from the root and determines the assignment for all the nodes, using the optimal scheduling decision for their respective parents and generating an optimal acceleration schedule.

36.3.3.1 *Transfer and Execution Time Predictions*

The algorithm requires knowledge of the expected running time of a given task on a CPU and a GPU, and the times of the input data transfers. The latter is easy to estimate using the hardware bandwidth and the input data size known before the run.

1: **Input:** $T(V,E)$ - Task dependency tree, R - postfix DFS traversal order of T
2: **Output:** Scheduling decisions A_v for all the nodes $v \in V$.
Forward traversal

3: **while** R is not empty **do**
4:     //get next tree node
5:     $v \leftarrow \textbf{pop}(R)$
6:     **push** $v \rightarrow \widehat{R}$ {maintain prefix DFS order}
7:     **for all** $device \in CPU, GPU$ **do**
8:         // set the cost of v on $device$
9:         $S_v[device] \leftarrow P_v[device]$
10:        // compute the costs assuming d is executed on a CPU (GPU) and v on $device$
11:        **for all** $d \in$ child nodes of v **do**
12:            $CPUCOST \leftarrow S_d[CPU] + D_v[CPU \rightarrow device]$
13:            $GPUCOST \leftarrow S_d[GPU] + D_v[GPU \rightarrow device]$
14:            // choose the best schedule for d assuming v is executed on $device$
15:            **if** $CPUCOST > GPUCOST$ **then**
16:                $O_v^d[device] \leftarrow$ GPU
17:                $S_v[device] \leftarrow S_v[device] + GPUCOST$
18:            **else**
19:                $O_v^d[device] \leftarrow$ CPU
20:                $S_v[device] \leftarrow S_v[device] + CPUCOST$
21:            **end if**
22:        **end for**
23:    **end for**
24: **end while**
Backtrack

25: $v \leftarrow \textbf{pop}(\widehat{R})$
    {choose the device to compute the root node}
26: **if** $S_v[CPU] > S_v[GPU]$ **then**
27:    $A_v \leftarrow$ GPU
28: **else**
29:    $A_v \leftarrow$ CPU
30: **end if**
31: // traverse in prefix DFS order
32: **while** $\widehat{R}$ is not empty **do**
33:    **for all** $d \in$ child nodes of v **do**
34:        // schedule d on the device which led to the best cost for v
35:        $A_d \leftarrow O_v^d[A_v]$
36:    **end for**
37:    $v \leftarrow \textbf{pop}(\widehat{R})$
38: **end while**

Listings 36.2. Acceleration scheduling algorithm pseudo-code.

The kernel time prediction is more complicated, and several approaches exist. The first approximation is to assume a constant device capacity and derive the running time from the total number of computations to be performed. More precise methods apply various machine learning techniques to predict the performance by using the profiles of the previous kernel invocations. In our work we applied a regression tree classifier, which allowed runtime predictions to be derived from the traces of the kernel microbenchmarks.

36.3.4 Application to Inference in Probabilistic Networks

The general problem is:

$$\sum_{\mathbf{M}} \bigotimes_i f^i(\mathbf{X}^i), \quad \mathbf{M} \subseteq \bigcup_i \mathbf{X}^i, f^i \in \mathbf{F}, \tag{2}$$

where $\mathbf{M}$ is the set of summation variables, and $\mathbf{F}$ is the set of all input functions. One method for computing this expression is to split the set of all functions into groups, called buckets, and process each bucket separately using the sum-product kernel described in Section 36.3.2.1. The algorithm for creating the buckets is outside of the scope of this chapter and can be found elsewhere [2].

For a given set of buckets, computation can be represented as a task dependency tree traversal from the leaves to the root, where each bucket is a tree node and the edges between the nodes represent the data dependencies.

We use the scheduling algorithm in Section 36.3.3 to assign the computations to a CPU or a GPU, and then employ the GPU kernel described in Section 36.3.2.1 to compute the results of the GPU-assigned nodes.

We partially relax the assumption of no concurrency between CPU and GPU execution by implementing CPU execution and GPU management in two different CPU threads. All the nodes scheduled on a CPU are computed by an OpenMP-based parallel CPU kernel that uses multiple CPU cores. The CPU execution thread keeps processing the nodes assigned to a CPU until the node for a GPU is found. When that happens, the CPU execution thread analyzes the input to tune the kernel invocation parameters and then passes this information to the GPU management thread, which is responsible for transferring the data and invoking the GPU kernel. Meanwhile, the CPU thread continues processing the tasks in another task tree branch, until it runs out of CPU-assigned nodes because of data dependency, or there are no GPU-assigned nodes left to be prepared for execution.

36.4 FINAL EVALUATION

We conducted our experiments on both synthetic benchmarks and real probabilistic networks used for analyzing genetic data [6]. We performed three sets of experiments: (1) single kernel performance comparison on random inputs in order to test the software-managed caching on different GPU architectures; (2) the impact of CPU-GPU scheduling on the application performance; (3) complete application speedups over CPU-only execution.

36.4.1 Software-Managed Caching Performance

Figure 36.3(a) and (b) present the kernel performance on two different NVIDIA GPUs (GeForce GTX 285 and Tesla C2050) and the Intel E5540 hyper-threaded dual quad-core machine on 5000 random inputs. The inputs were generated by randomly selecting various input parameters: the number of

Table 36.1 Peak Double-Precision Performance in GFLOPs/s Achieved on Different Processors

E5540 1 Core	2xE5540 Quad-Core, 16 HW Threads	GTX 285	C2050
1.8	15.5	34	84

variables per function, number of functions per input, variable domain size, data reuse per input, output size and number of summation variables per input. Each dot in the graph represents the performance of one run. Here and in the rest of the experiments in this subsection, the running times represent only the actual computing times without the data transfer. The input complexity FLOPs were computed by counting only the theoretical number of double-precision multiplications and summations required to compute the results. The CPU OpenMP implementation used up to 16 threads.

Table 36.1 summarizes the peak performance results for double-precision execution. Note that the peak speedup may reach **up to a factor of 50** for some inputs: for these inputs, a CPU performs poorly, but a GPU achieves the highest performance.

Observe the performance variability which characterizes the kernel: it is due to the internal properties of the computations. Some of the inputs have more parallelism available and require less cache space, thereby enabling higher performance gains on a GPU and on a CPU alike. That is why the dynamic selection of execution policies is imperative — some inputs clearly perform better on a CPU than on a GPU.

36.4.1.1 *Cache Performance Comparison*

Figure 36.3(c) presents the relative speedup of the software-managed cache over the version that uses only global memory and the version that uses texture memory for the input on NVIDIA GeForce GTX 285. We see that the hardware texture cache improves the kernel performance but falls short of the performance achieved by the software-managed caching techniques. Overall, the lack of proper hardware cache on this and earlier architectures made software-caching *the only way* to achieve high performance.

Figure 36.3(d) shows the hardware/software cache comparison on a Tesla C2050 GPU featuring a hardware cache. The experiments with the software-managed cache were performed using a 48K/16K scratchpad/L1 partition; thus, the figure reflects the combined performance of the hardware and software-managed caches.

To test the hardware cache performance, we modified the original kernel by removing all the cache-related logic, including the thread synchronizations, and configured a 16K/48K scratchpad/L1 partition. We see that the software-managed cache performance is not stable and can be both worse and better than the hardware-only cache, with the speedup being about 25% on average. Despite the low average-case speedup, there are two important observations that justify application of software caching. First, the software cache enables much higher peak performance. Only 0.4% of the hardware cache-based runs exceeded the 60 GFLOPs/s performance threshold, and none reached 70 GFLOPs/s, versus 5.5% and 2% of the software-managed cache kernel runs, respectively. Second, for a given input, the best of both worlds can be achieved by analyzing the input properties and selecting the expected-to-be-optimal kernel configuration on the fly. We observed that the hardware cache usually performs better for inputs with fewer summation variables, where the software-managed cache access overhead cannot be amortized over multiple memory accesses. Thus, we dynamically select the best

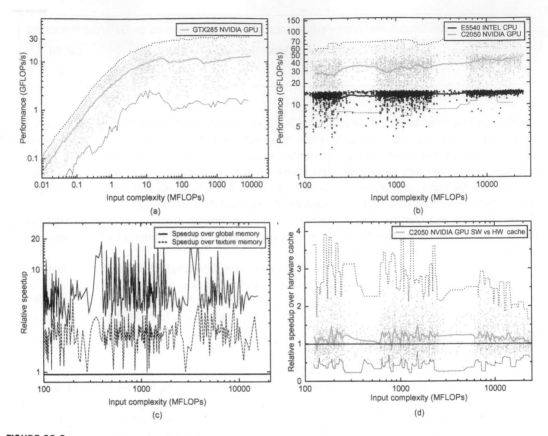

FIGURE 36.3

Random-input performance of the double-precision kernel execution. Each dot represents the performance of one run. The dotted lines represent the peak and the lowest performance measured. The continuous line is the average performance. (a) NVIDIA GeForce GTX 285 GPU. (b) NVIDIA Tesla C2050 GPU and OpenMP parallel execution on dual 4-core 8-thread Intel E5540 2.53 GHz CPU. (c) Relative speedup of the software-manged cache over pure global memory and texture memory runs in GeForce GTX 285. (d) Relative speedup of the hardware and software-managed cache combined over hardware-only cache in Tesla C2050.

expected kernel configuration as a part of the complete application. As we will show in the following sections, the use of software caching was critical for attaining high performance exceeding that of the CPU implementation.

36.4.2 **Influence of CPU-GPU Scheduling**

Another set of experiments examined the impact of the CPU-GPU schedule on the performance of the entire multi-kernel application. The experiments used task dependency trees from probabilistic networks for genetic linkage analysis, and were invoked on a 4-core Intel Core 2, 2.33 GHz CPU with

Table 36.2 Comparative Performance Analysis of the Dynamic Schedule for Several Real Genetic Analysis Inputs. The Optimal Acceleration Schedule is the One Produced by the Algorithm Described Here. The Hybrid-Greedy Schedule Considers Only Single Kernel Performance

	Runtime (Seconds)				Nodes Mapped to GPU	
Tasks in Tree	Hybrid Communication-Aware	Hybrid-Greedy	CPU-only	GPU-only	Hybrid Communication-Aware	Hybrid-Greedy
390	**110**	126	213	211	25	14
529	**86**	86	119	174	41	28
268	**55**	55	408	67	86	62
595	**21**	25	174	33	139	111
1194	**35**	44	364	60	301	230
505	**126**	140	494	250	46	21

FIGURE 36.4

Part of the 268-node task tree with the hybrid-greedy and hybrid communication-aware schedule. Nodes marked with diamonds denote the tasks assigned to a GPU by both schedules. Circles denote only the tasks assigned to a GPU according to the communication-aware schedule. All unmarked nodes are assigned to a CPU (see color insert).

the NVIDIA GeForce GTX 285 GPU. The performance results for a few representative inputs are shown in Table 36.2.

We observe that the best CPU-only multi-threaded version or GPU-only version can be each up to a factor of two slower than the combined CPU-GPU execution using the hybrid communication-aware schedule produced by our algorithm. Observe that this schedule (the column marked in bold) usually results in more nodes being mapped to a GPU. Figure 36.4 shows a part of the task tree, with the diamonds denoting the nodes scheduled on a GPU by both the hybrid-greedy and hybrid communication-aware schedules and the circles denoting those scheduled by the communication-aware schedule only. Observe that the latter effectively reschedules the "islands" of CPU-scheduled nodes to a GPU.

We found, however, that for the task trees having a set of dominating complex tasks for which GPU performance substantially exceeds CPU performance and the I/O to CPU ratio is low, mapping kernels with larger input sizes is sufficient for achieving the best performance. Still, even then, the dynamic schedule that combines CPU and GPU execution remains superior to the static schedules that use only one or the other.

Table 36.3 Complete Application Performance on Large Inputs. The First Column Shows the Absolute Runtime in Seconds, while the Rest Show the Relative Speedup over the Quad-Core Execution. Some Inputs could not be Computed on GeForce GTX 285 Due to Insufficient Memory

Network	E5540 4 Core	E5540 1 Core	2xE5540 8 Cores	GTX 285	C2050 (h/w Cache)	C2050 (s/w Cache)
BN1	97s	0.26	1.9	2.3	1.1	3.8
BN2	27s	0.29	2.0	–	1.9	2.28
BN3	3s	0.37	1.8	1.3	1.4	1.3
BN4	21s	0.25	2.0	0.5	1.4	1.8
BN5	844s	0.25	1.5	–	1.7	3.3
BN6	66s	0.26	1.3	–	3.1	6.0
BN7	316s	0.31	2.1	–	1.7	5.4
BN8	74s	0.25	1.9	2.9	2.4	5.4
BN9	17s	0.25	1.8	–	1.6	3.3
BN10	72s	0.25	2.1	–	3.9	6.5
BN11	91s	0.25	2.1	–	1.9	4.3

36.4.3 **Performance on Large Probabilistic Networks**

The last set of experiments evaluated the speedups of the entire application with all the optimizations. The experiments were carried out on real-life probabilistic networks used for the analysis of genetic diseases. Table 36.3 summarizes the results of execution on 11 different networks. The table shows speedup over the quad-core only execution on a single chip E5540 CPU. Using the single-chip performance as the baseline allows for a chip-to-chip comparison with GPUs. We also provided the results of the dual-CPU performance with 16 concurrent hardware threads; hence the speedup may exceed 2.

The kernel that uses the software-managed cache outperforms the parallel single CPU version by up to a factor of 6.5. Furthermore, using the hardware-only cache results in an up to threefold performance drop, often yielding slower execution than the eight-core parallel CPU version. Observe that the software-managed cache is faster than the hardware cache in all but one case. This is the result of the automatic selection of the purely-hardware and combined hardware-software cache configurations, depending on the specific input, as described above.

References

[1] Sum-product GPU kernel. http://sites.google.com/site/silbersteinmark/Home.
[2] M. Fishelson, D. Geiger, Exact genetic linkage computations for general pedigrees, Bioinformatics 18 (Suppl. 1) (2002) S189–S198.
[3] Y.K. Kwok, I. Ahmad, Benchmarking and comparison of the task graph scheduling algorithms, J. Parallel Distrib. Comput. 59 (3) (1999) 381–422.
[4] P. Pakzad, V. Anantharam, A new look at the generalized distributive law, IEEE Trans. Inf. Theory 50 (6) (2004) 1132–1155.

[5] M. Silberstein, A. Schuster, D. Geiger, A. Patney, J.D. Owens, Efficient computation of sum-products on GPUs through software-managed cache, in: 22nd ACM International Conference on Supercomputing, Island of Kos, Greece, 2008, pp. 309–318.

[6] M. Silberstein, A. Tzemach, N. Dovgolevskiy, M. Fishelson, A. Schuster, D. Geiger, On-line system for faster linkage analysis via parallel execution on thousands of personal computers, Am. J. Human Genet. 78 (6) (2006) 922–935.

Index